MW01087861

College Sports

COLLEGE SPORTS

A HISTORY

ERIC A. MOYEN AND JOHN R. THELIN

JOHNS HOPKINS UNIVERSITY PRESS   BALTIMORE

© 2024 Johns Hopkins University Press
All rights reserved. Published 2024
Printed in the United States of America on acid-free paper

9 8 7 6 5 4 3 2 1

Johns Hopkins University Press
2715 North Charles Street
Baltimore, Maryland 21218
www.press.jhu.edu

Library of Congress Cataloging-in-Publication Data

Names: Moyen, Eric Anthony, 1974– author. | Thelin, John R., 1947– author.
Title: College sports : a history / Eric A. Moyen and John R. Thelin.
Description: Baltimore : Johns Hopkins University Press, 2024. | Includes
    bibliographical references and index.
Identifiers: LCCN 2024010342 | ISBN 9781421450094 (hardcover ; acid-free paper) |
    ISBN 9781421450100 (ebook)
Subjects: LCSH: College sports—United States—History. | College sports—
    Economic aspects—United States. | College sports—United States—Management. |
    College sports—Political aspects—United States. | National Collegiate
    Athletic Association.
Classification: LCC GV351 .M69 2024 | DDC 796.04/30973—dc23/eng/20240627
LC record available at https://lccn.loc.gov/2024010342

A catalog record for this book is available from the British Library.

*Special discounts are available for bulk purchases of this book. For more information, please
contact Special Sales at specialsales@jh.edu.*

For Missy, Anna Grace, and Emmy
  My all-star team

For Sharon
  Writer, editor, muse, and teammate

Contents

Preface

Surveying the Legacies and Landscape of College Sports

The year 2024 was a good time for us as coauthors to write about college sports past and present. Celebrations, confrontations, collisions, and collusions characterized the events and issues that took place on intercollegiate playing fields, *sometimes on the court and in court, as well as in locker rooms and boardrooms.* All have captured the imagination and attention of the American public. The year was especially dramatic as a result of changing configurations and geographies of such major conferences as the Big Ten, the Pac-12, the Southeastern Conference, the Big Twelve, and the Atlantic Coast Conference. Equally conspicuous were changes in the rights and profile of college student-athletes.

We were not prescient nor was our timing original or calculated. That's because we as historians of higher education could have found comparable drama and documents had we been writing a century earlier, in 1924. The same holds true for just about any selected year in that hundred-year span. American college sports then and now are a topic that has become both timely and timeless for our national culture and institutions.

The American saga of college sports has been powerful, but its course has not always been inevitable, nor has it been predictable. The popular momentum sponsoring intercollegiate athletics provided by students and alumni might have been derailed by resistance from academic leaders about 150 years ago. In 1873, for example, thirty students from the University of Michigan challenged a group of students at Cornell University to meet in Cleveland to play a game of football. Cornell's president, Andrew Dickson White, telegraphed to the University of Michigan continent of student-athletes, "I will not permit a group of thirty men to travel four hundred miles merely to agitate a bag of wind."[1] President White's strong stand won that battle but lost the war.

Since 1873, college football and an accompanying array of varsity sports gained a strong hold on the American campus and culture that is still thriving today. One indicator of the enlarged scale and scope of college sports since 1873 is that in 2024, the prospect of a team road trip of 400 miles raises no presidential eyebrows. Rather, a big-time university's football team usually has a chartered air flight directly to and from games away from its home campus.

Long-distance air travel also has become the norm for the so-called Olympic sports. Current conference alliances and scheduling mean that "As part of the Big Ten Conference, a Rutgers volleyball player might fly more than 2,800 miles to compete in a game at the University of Washington on a Tuesday, before returning for a Wednesday morning exam."[2]

The contrasts in intercollegiate game travel between the end point years of 1873 and 2024 were hardly the whole story about changes in college sports. Consider the midpoint year of 1952, when the president of the University of Oklahoma addressed the state legislature with the earnest plea and proposition for added state funding for educational programs, "I hope to build a university of which our football team can be proud."[3] The appeal of intercollegiate competition in football—and other sports—captured the imagination of American college students nationwide. It also attracted alumni and local townspeople to create an enduring, distinctive embrace of what we call "college sports."

The irony of the university president's plea and pitch is that they did not work as he had hoped. His logic was that a national championship football team at the University of Oklahoma provided the requisite favorable publicity, state pride, and good feeling that would persuade state legislators to use football success as the base for greater academic and educational success. Evidently, in his case he was wrong. The consensus of the state legislature was that they were delighted with the championship state university football team—but felt little enthusiasm or inclination to increase state funding for academic programs. To the contrary, many state legislators resented the president's opportunism.

The University of Oklahoma president was off the mark on another related attempt to bring football metaphors into academic leadership. He titled his memoir *Presidents Can't Punt*. A more accurate observation would have been the resolution, "presidents shouldn't punt." Unfortunately, as our historical research shows over nine chapters and 150 years, when it comes to leadership and sound values in governance of college football, university presidents can—and do—punt time and time again. To continue the football metaphors for academic leadership, our historical research indicates that with college sports policies, university presidents often fumble. One of the fundamental questions this book attempts to answer is why that has been the case.

Higher education in the United States is unique among nations in having colleges and universities indelibly linked with sports contests that pit the students of one institution against those of another. And beyond that micro-level observation, individual games are not isolated. They coagulate and converge into conferences and competitions that are regional and national in character and composition. All this may seem obvious to Americans today. In fact, the historical story is no less than an American saga—a fascinating mix of real and embellished figures and events, all of which often result in a larger-than-life story in which past and present are continually connected, renewed, and revisited.

American college sports are an enigma in that although they are central to higher education and to American popular culture, there is little indication that universities have formally acknowledged intercollegiate athletics as part of their respective institutional missions. We know of no college or university charter that mentions colleges and universities as essential commitments or charges. Our resolution is to look within and beyond institutional structures to exhume and explain the culture of college sports as part of the campus, community, and country. Students who play varsity athletics are no less than "all-Americans" in their popularity and in honors and awards. An irony is that their actions and activities in the classroom and on the playing field continually compete for attention with the games colleges play in the governance, control, and promotion of elaborate seasons, conferences, and national championship events.

Higher education in the United States today is a sprawling enterprise with more than three thousand colleges and universities and a typical annual enrollment of about twenty million students per year. Yet most media attention focuses on a relatively small number of big-time programs at large universities and on a handful of sports, such as football and basketball. Our perspectives and priorities as historians, professors, and former students lead us to know and appreciate a wide range of intercollegiate sports, student-athletes, coaches, and programs. We hope this tone and perspective are evident throughout our history of college sports.

For one of us as coauthors, the frame of reference and experience has been primarily with the large universities of the Southeast Conference. For the other, it has included the Ivy League, the Pac-12 Conference and California, as well as the College of William and Mary and the Big Ten experience of the large midwestern universities. We have been fans and participants in a wide range of college sports—including wrestling, water polo, swimming, cross-country, track and field, as well as the ubiquitous football and basketball. We are participant-observers in our own academic lives to the transformation of expanded inclusion in matters of race, gender, and family income for students as athletes. Our history of college sports reflects our tone as dissenting loyalists.

Our involvement and analyses go beyond the immediate campus experience of student-athletes playing games while pursuing their studies. It extends to layers of administration within a campus and with connections to policy analysis and determination, including membership on research advisory committees at the National Collegiate Athletic Association (NCAA), faculty representation in the Southeastern Conference, and presentations for such national groups as the Knight Commission on the Future of College Sports. All these accumulated experiences and assignments remain isolated and transient unless they are thoughtfully connected with historical research that relies on archival materials, oral histories, and appreciative reading of secondary sources. Above all, we think that the history of college sports is essential both to the study of American colleges and universities and to American social history writ large.

In analyzing intercollegiate athletics over 150 years, we have discerned recurrent concerns that resurface from one era to another. Problems and abuses such as cheating, excessive spending, recruitment violations, and misuses of funds are seldom solved once and for all. To the contrary, we find organizational and administrative "reforms" often to be bittersweet and ironic in that frequently the solution is to change regulations so that they henceforth accommodate some practice once considered excessive or wrong to now be acceptable. In other words, reforms by conference commissioners and the NCAA in concert with athletics directors and coaches' associations often tend to ratify and legitimize conduct and practices that previously had been considered to be improper.

If the melodrama of scandal and outrage has been a source of continuity in college sports for more than a century, what have been the examples and characteristics of *change*? The general answer is that major changes in college sports, especially since 1900, have been both quantitative and qualitative in nature. They represent at the very least *growing pains* in which external groups prompted established practices and programs to expand and extend opportunities and inclusion for participation in college sports at all levels and places.

A good starting point to chart historical change is the geographical and regional spread of college sports, as the spread of colleges and rise of college enrollments in the Midwest soon led to the establishment of powerful football teams in what we know as the Big Ten Conference. By 1920, these teams were a source of great state pride and gained large crowds and national attention. The Pacific Coast universities such as Stanford, the University of California, Berkeley, the University of Southern California, and the University of Washington were also in the mix for success, popularity, and prestige, not only in football but also in track and field, baseball, swimming, tennis, rugby, and crew.[4] An important extension to that regional trend has been the legacy of track and field and cross-country fostered and maintained by the University of Oregon for over a half century. No doubt the original, historic powers such as Harvard, Princeton, and Yale resented sharing the stage with, for example, the University of Michigan or Ohio State University.

In some cases, the spread of strong teams was neither gradual nor even. College sports innovation and excellence often spread from the West and South to the Midwest and East. Texas high school football, for example, caught the rest of the nation by surprise for its speed, power, reliance on passing, and lack of deference to established programs and coaches in the East. In comparable fashion, high school basketball in such midwestern states as Kansas and Indiana meant literally a "whole new ball game" that provided the model and momentum to popularize college basketball nationwide. For wrestling, high schools and colleges in Oklahoma and Iowa gained power and prominence by 1930 and fostered the full national development of this intercollegiate sport.[5] By the 1930s, crew at the University of California, Berkeley, and the University of Washington gained prominence collegiate competition and in the Olympics.[6]

Demographic change of rising population combined with increased local and state funding for public high schools were the foundation of state and regional changes in academics and athletics nationwide. In the twenty-first century, the success and power of football in the South, as demonstrated in the national championships and bowl game victories by teams from the Southeastern Conference and the Atlantic Coast Conference, are fixtures. But the historical record shows the surprising fact that the colleges and the universities of the South were latecomers to national recognition and championships. That transformation included changes in civil rights and commitments to social justice that slowly but persistently led to some increased opportunities for underrepresented groups.

Race—and related issues of exclusion and disparities—was central to the creative tension but was not the entire story. Often overlooked today is the bigotry and exclusion that Catholics, especially Catholic immigrants, faced in admission to and participation in activities of American public schools and state universities. The irony was that exclusion led to an American model in which outsiders established their own institutions—and varsity teams. An obvious, important example in both mascot and team records was Notre Dame and its "Fighting Irish."[7] But Notre Dame was hardly alone, as one finds a flourishing of Catholic universities, especially in urban areas nationwide, that were of national caliber in talent and achievements: Boston College, Fordham University, Georgetown University, Loyola University, Providence College, St. John's

University, and the University of San Francisco. St. Louis University set the pace as a longtime NCAA soccer champion, drawing its players and coaches from local Catholic high schools whose Jesuit priest teachers and coaches had emigrated from Germany—and brought soccer as part of the package.

An important, often overlooked historical legacy for all higher education was that our contemporary model of the large, comprehensive, and diverse flagship state university evolved slowly. For most of our national history, the model for college-building was that of "separate and unequal," with special interest groups tending to build their own colleges. The model held for gender, as many colleges remained either "all men" or "all women" into the 1960s before a surge toward coeducation. A comparable pattern held for religious groups and for religious, racial, and ethnic groups. College sports reflected this pattern in their alumni and fan base and in their choice of mascots—and in heated rivalries—in what was for the most part an "unlevel playing field."

An example that concentrates these various levels of change by region, religion, race, gender, and class along with expanded educational opportunity was the case of the women's varsity swim team at the University of Georgia. It illustrated regional change in that competitive scholastic and collegiate swimming had been slow to come to the South. It also showcased changes in gender equity and Title IX. These combinations eventually included high-level national achievement. The University of Georgia's women's swimming team, started in 1974, won seven NCAA team championships between 1999 and 2016. If Rip Van Winkle had been a college sports fan who fell asleep in 1980 and awakened twenty years later, he would have been surprised at such changes in the character, composition, diversity, and achievements of intercollegiate athletics nationwide.

The thread that binds these assorted changes over time is that they have not been inevitable, nor have they been achieved easily. The result is a paradox of sorts. For women as college student-athletes, coaches, and athletics directors, the gains since passage of Title IX in 1972 have been relatively great. Yet despite such gains, as of 2024, the disparities between men's and women's intercollegiate athletics programs in terms of funding, facilities, donations, and media coverage remain substantial. A comparable syndrome holds for other matters of social justice, such as race. In a similar vein, although many—perhaps most—intercollegiate athletics programs at colleges and universities nationwide have gained in support and offerings, there persists a relatively small circle of institutions, conferences, and sports with disproportionate power and prestige. And within many universities, disproportionate attention and resources continue to go to the traditional big-time sports of football and basketball. Some colleges have added favorites, often with a regional emphasis, such as ice hockey in the upper Midwest and New England.

Likewise, expansion and extended opportunities have not proceeded on a smooth trajectory. One of the biggest changes in American collegiate football was the number of Catholic universities, mostly in urban areas, that dropped their football teams between 1950 and 1970. Looking at all sports and conferences nationwide, the historical trend is that imbalances often have remained the rule as an undercurrent in the larger trend that college sports grew as a popular, powerful activity.

The Historians' Workshop: Our Approach to Writing and Research on College Sports

This book developed from conversations between us coauthors in December 2019 and January 2020. After discussing the idea for a historical survey of higher education and athletics with Editorial Director Greg Britton at Johns Hopkins University Press, our collective worlds were jolted by a global pandemic. COVID-19 upended plans for extensive archival research. Instead, we were forced to focus on existing literature regarding the history of college sports and its administration. This unfortunate circumstance, however, possessed a silver lining. It confirmed what we believed—namely, unlike earlier decades in the twentieth century, a wealth of historical scholarship on the history of higher education and athletics existed. What did not exist was a study to try to place the historical record of intercollegiate athletics into an integrated whole. This is our earnest effort to do so.

Any comprehensive history faces the difficult task of omission. For the sake of brevity and usefulness, there are many stories, characters, and policies that are either addressed briefly or not addressed at all. This account will not satisfy readers looking for tales of bowl victories, basketball championships, or profiles of larger-than-life coaches. Instead, it seeks to provide an account of how (and why) big-time sports managed to become such an infused enterprise among various institutions within the academy. As we sought answers to these questions, recurring themes developed that will add to the historiography of athletics, higher education, and their intersection.

We identify two prominent themes that have rarely been explored in detail. First, big-time intercollegiate athletics found room to flourish in the modern American university. Although often considered an anomaly by academics, this history will elaborate upon the fact that the new structure of the university, and the aims of many "modern" university presidents, actually encouraged big-time athletics. In some cases, stadiums still bear their names (Sanford Stadium in Athens, Georgia, or Bryant-Denny Stadium in Tuscaloosa, Alabama). Second, the generations of athletic reformers who have lamented the abuses in college sports generally failed to notice that their "reforms" involved polices to return to a previous state of athletic affairs that never fully existed in the US sporting world. In terms of athletics, the policy changes were what political scientists generally referred to as "reactionary" policy: again, an attempt to return to the past. In contrast, many traditional liberal arts colleges managed to retain the characteristics that many critics (often academics) sought to achieve.

Along these same lines, most universities moved slowly on matters of social justice and athletics, especially when dealing with women and minorities and their place on the field or court. When reform arrived in the form of slow and incremental change, the leading national organization for intercollegiate athletics, the NCAA, used the opportunity to exert its own power over the associations that had previously administered intercollegiate sport.

In an attempt to provide a more comprehensive picture of the world of intercollegiate athletics, we have devoted space to address many groups often neglected in the history of college sports: small schools, "minor" (or Olympic sports), women's teams, and historically Black colleges and universities. Some may view these sections as too brief, and in many ways, they are correct. Yet the historical record reveals that big-time sports at big-time universities in big-time conferences drive the policy that affects all of the aforementioned groups—and others. We believe that is a story worth telling.

Some scholarly critics of big-time athletics may note that sports scandals at the college level are addressed but do not become the major focal point of this history. The reasons for this are many. First, coauthor John Thelin has written a text on scandal and reform in intercollegiate athletics. Second, if there is an area in the history of college sports that has been well documented, it is the exposure of many disgraces in athletics. Finally, we have taken time and space to address some of the more recent atrocities that have occurred in athletics programs to highlight the difference in severity. While many programs have been found guilty of breaking NCAA violations for at least a century, more recent events have highlighted criminal activity that has occurred on campus under the umbrella of athletics. Without minimizing previous transgressions, the more recent developments are simply ones in which "business as usual" is unacceptable.

Readers may note a conspicuous omission in our account of the characters and cast in the college sports drama. Namely, we make little mention of collective faculty involvement in policies and programs. That omission is deliberate, because we think that past and present decision-making and organizational structures have largely precluded substantive participation and leadership by such bodies as faculty senates. Rather, the faculty role as suggested by our story and bibliography has been as concerned, astute scholars who have provided analyses of the character and conduct of intercollegiate athletics programs.

It is reasonable to predict that some fans, alumni, promoters, and administrators (both current and future) will have hoped for a greater emphasis on the thousands of athletes' lives that have been positively influenced by the opportunity to participate in college sports. It is equally reasonable to assume that other former college athletes and current scholars might find this work less critical than they hoped it would be, wishing that more attention be paid to the decades-long exclusion and exploitation of college athletes. We find value in both perspectives, and it is this tension that makes the history of college sports valuable. We invite you to engage in this history. We know it will become more valuable as scholars add their voices to the discourse.

Acknowledgments

Writing about college sports, as with playing college sports, calls for teamwork. We are indebted to colleagues and friends who have generously provided commentary and resources for our historical research over many years.

Foremost is the late Michael A. Olivas, whose untimely death in April 2022 leaves us sad and at the same time grateful for his longtime encouragement of our work and for our being able to draw on his knowledge about intercollegiate athletics and the law. We also mourn the loss of some other prominent colleagues—James Axtell of the College of William and Mary; Winton Solberg of the University of Illinois; John Sayle Watterson of James Madison University; Judith Schiff, archivist for Yale University; Thomas Dyer of the University of Georgia, Terry Birdwhistell of the University of Kentucky; J. Douglas Toma of the University of Georgia; and Myles Brand, president of the NCAA. These dear colleagues endure as genuine great scholars and good sports.

We have read and relied on numerous books and articles by Professor Emeritus Ronald Smith of Pennsylvania State University, spanning publications from 1983 to 2023. The added dimension is that he takes time to correspond and has the patience and insight to be both analytic and inspiring in our mutual fascinations with the issues associated with the history of college sports. Nowhere was his leadership more evident than in the team of six historians he assembled to write an influential amicus brief for the US Supreme Court case *NCAA v. Alston* (2021).

To extend from Ronald Smith's role and award in the *Alston* case, we are grateful for the scholarship and contributions on the history of college sports provided by members of Ronald Smith's team of historians—Taylor Branch, Professor Dick Crepeau of the University of Central Florida, Professor Sarah Fields at the University of Colorado Denver, and Professor Jay Smith of the University of North Carolina at Chapel Hill. For this book's coauthor John Thelin, it was an honor to be part of his Supreme Court amicus brief team.

Jeffrey Orleans, president emeritus of the Ivy League, has led by example for many years in combining national leadership in policy deliberations along with his own writing and scholarship. He personifies the Ivy League ideal of excellence and integrity both in academics and athletics. Donna Lopiano, now president of the Drake Group, has been a pioneer in college sports as a leader, player, coach, and athletics director. Professors Robert and Pam Baker of George Mason University have been trusted colleagues and discussants in the research, teaching, and leadership associated with intercollegiate athletics.

Marybeth Gasman of Rutgers University has read and shared our books and articles for many years. She has taken time to do so in her multiple roles—as the Samuel DeWitt Proctor Endowed Chair in Education, as a distinguished professor, and as the associate dean for research in the Graduate School of Education at Rutgers University. She also serves as the executive director of the Samuel DeWitt Proctor Institute for Leadership, Equity, and Justice and the executive director of the Rutgers Center for Minority Serving Institutions.

At the University of Kentucky, our colleagues Professors Kelly Bradley, Eric Weber Joseph Fink, Joe Waddington, Neal Hutchens, Steve Parker, and Justin Nichols have contributed courses and conversations over many years, bringing various disciplines ranging from philosophy and law to statistics and sports leadership to bear on serious consideration of intercollegiate athletics. Rasheed Flowers and Eric Snyder, in their work as doctoral students and research assistants, combined commitment and insights to our own book project. Amy E. Wells-Dolan, professor and associate dean at the University of Mississippi, has continued the contributions to the topic of higher education and athletics in the South that first started in her PhD studies at the University of Kentucky. Richard Trollinger, vice president emeritus of Centre College, has been a coauthor on articles and books on philanthropy and has provided insights about academic and athletic excellence at a liberal arts college that plays in NCAA Division III.

Professor Scott Kretchmar of Pennsylvania State University contributed invaluable insights on the history of college sports in his own writings, as a fellow member of the NCAA's initial Research Advisory Board, and in his editorial work with the *Journal of Intercollegiate Sport*. Professor Margaret (Peg) B. Weiser of the University of Arizona provided philosophical perspective for our research, including her editorial role for the 2021 issue of the *Journal of Intercollegiate Sport* that focused on the legacy of her late husband, former president of the NCAA Myles Brand.

Professor Eddie Comeaux of the University of California, Riverside, has been a longtime colleague and friend whose work as both a researcher and editor has been influential in reshaping the focus and findings of analyses of college student-athletes and social justice.

Stanley Katz, professor emeritus at Princeton University's Woodrow Wilson School, has made certain over several decades that issues of ethics and education be combined with public policy and law in the consideration of college sports as an important topic. He always finds time to read our queries and articles.

Three colleagues at the University of South Carolina have shaped the course and character of social justice and college sports in recent years. We thank Professors Christian Anderson, Katherine Chaddock, and Amber Fallucca for their scholarship and their projects in public history.

Two colleagues at the College of William and Mary in Virginia have been longtime supporters of our college sports research. We are indebted to the late Professor Emeritus James Axtell for his articles and commentaries. Jay Gaidmore, director of special collections at the College of William and Mary, has provided both primary documents about college sports episodes and an archival home for John Thelin's research files and manuscripts about the history of intercollegiate athletics.

Michael Oriard, professor of English emeritus at Oregon State University, has been a perceptive and pioneering scholar in the historical study of college sports from the perspectives of popular media and public policy. He is one of our heroes, as he has quietly yet effectively parlayed his achievements as both an honors student and all-American football player at Notre Dame along with his successful career as a National Football League player for the Kansas City Chiefs. What can be more inspiring and admirable than an outstanding NFL and collegiate football player who opted to use his success as a means to pursue a PhD in English at Stanford University, going on to an exemplary calling as a professor at Oregon State University? His scholarship has shaped the study of media and college sports.

Our research debt extends nationwide. Charles C. Clotfelter, professor and provost at Duke University, has brought the perspectives of economics and public policy to bear on the serious issues of college sports as part of the larger domain of American higher education.

Former doctoral students from Indiana University, David Campaigne and Gerald St. Amand, have kept us posted on provocative articles and books about higher education and athletics.

Lawrence Wiseman, professor emeritus of biology and John Thelin's colleague at the College of William and Mary, combined faculty leadership with advanced research on the economics and ethics of athletics policies. In 1989,

Wiseman and Thelin were invited to Washington, DC, to present a major address about the financial problems of big-time college sports at the first gathering of the Knight Commission on the Future of College Sports. Our collaborations led to publication of a major study, *The Old College Try: Balancing Academics and Athletics,* and a research monograph, *Fiscal Fitness? The Peculiar Economics of Intercollegiate Athletics,* as well as an invited editorial in the *Washington Post.*

For more than a half century, the History of Education Society and its journal, the *History of Education Quarterly,* have provided a forum for essay reviews and articles that connect the social history of American education to intercollegiate athletics. Longtime colleagues and authors and editors to whom we are beholden include Professors Linda Eisenmann of Wheaton College in Massachusetts, Luther Spoehr of Brown University, and Kimberly Tolle of Notre Dame de Namur University.

At the University of Southern California, Professor Emeritus William Tierney fused national scholarship on higher education and athletics with a leadership role in campus governance as president of the university senate to discuss and dissect the complexities of athletics policy and university leadership with the board of trustees and national groups. His work has shown that scholarship can be analytic and principled as an effective entrée into influential policymaking. In short, his scholarship has made a difference.

John Thelin's classmates at Brown University—Alan W. Blazar, Fred Berk, and Bobby Wayne Clark—bring their respective perspectives as student-athletes and journalists to long-term thoughtful discussions. Thelin's Brown University wrestling teammates—including Bob Christin '69, Serge Brunner '71, Stephen Gluckman '67, the late Rich Whipple '67, Louis Schepp '71, Barry Nathan '70, Peter Gottert '70, Steve Morrow '70, Rob Davidson '70, and Jim Mitchem '70—have combined their experience as student-athletes with their later professional perspectives from such fields as law, medicine, business, philanthropy, teaching, computer science, linguistics, and banking to add depth to the ideals and realities of college students as athletes past and present.

Jonathan Imber, professor of sociology and longtime editor of the journal *Society,* encouraged analyses of the Varsity Blues admissions athletic scandal and other college sports issues in our articles about the history of higher education. Higher education as a field of study is fortunate to have editors and writers at outstanding periodicals, magazines, and newspapers who have been pioneers in serious coverage of college sports. Michael Nietzel, himself a former university president and provost, has made higher education an important feature in *Forbes* magazine with his flow of outstanding essay reviews and articles about colleges and universities, including college sports. We owe thanks to *Inside Higher Ed* editors Sarah Bray, Scott Jaschik, Doug Lederman, and Elizabeth Redden for their coverage and for publishing our periodic essays. At the *Chronicle of Higher Education,* reporters Scott Carlson, Karen Fischer, and Lee Gardner have included our commentaries in their own excellent feature stories.

Sharon Thelin-Blackburn read, edited, and critiqued several chapter drafts and the book proposal. Once again, over many years and book projects, she has been John's editor, muse, and fellow researcher and writer. For Eric, the opportunity to engage in discussion on college sports and many other topics has been a welcomed addition and a pleasure both personally and professionally.

In the summer of 2000, a young doctoral student at the University of Kentucky walked into Professor (and "Coach") John Thelin's History of Higher Education and Athletics class. This course, along with John's continued teaching and mentorship, changed that student's life. Now as a coauthor, Eric is humbled to have been the beneficiary of his intellect, wisdom, guidance, kindness, and patience for nearly a quarter century. Beyond exemplary research and writing, he has imparted the lesson that investment in students as individuals is a noble and fulfilling calling.

Johns Hopkins University Press has been a leader in publishing books about the history of American higher education for decades. We owe special thanks to Editorial Director Greg Britton for his support once again by encouraging and endorsing our book proposal. Editorial Assistant Adriahna Conway has been outstanding in guide our manuscript through various stages of publication and production. Production Editor Kyle Kretzer, Copy Editor Ashleigh Elliott McKown, and Indexer Devon Thomas were excellent and essential in assuring our book would come to fruition—and publication! In short, as coauthors we are in debt to Johns Hopkins University Press.

College Sports

Introduction

Higher Education and Athletics

Legacies and Legislation in American College Sports

The president of the National Collegiate Athletic Association (NCAA), Mark Emmert, appeared before a US Senate subcommittee on February 11, 2020. The subcommittee questioned Emmert on the topic of player compensation for the use of their name, image, and likeness (NIL). Thrust upon college athletics when the California State Legislature passed Senate Bill 206 the previous fall, many other states followed with similar legislation allowing college athletes to profit financially from endorsements and other commercial ventures. Emmert sought cooperation from Congress to oppose such compensation but instead faced stinging criticism from senators regarding the NCAA's lack of transparency and unwillingness to address proactively these issues raised by NIL. In return, Emmert informed the subcommittee that help in the form of federal legislation might be required to create national uniformity regarding player remuneration.[1]

Emmert's visit to Washington, DC, was not unprecedented. Many times during the preceding century, university officials had been called to address challenges with college sports. Probably the most famous example came in the fall of 1905 when President Theodore Roosevelt invited the coaches and chairs of the alumni athletics committees (not the presidents) from the nation's leading football programs at Harvard, Princeton, and Yale to the White House. Roosevelt loved football and hoped to save it from the violence and brutality that marred the game and led to calls for its dissolution. In the short run, his efforts failed as nineteen football players died that season, most from the prep school ranks. But the death of college student Harold Moore during a Union College–New York University game late that fall galvanized the reform movement and led to the creation of what would become known as the NCAA.[2]

After altering the rules of football to make it a safer game (relatively speaking), the NCAA slowly but surely became the primary governing body over a wildly successful collegiate enterprise. By 2020, Mark Emmert now represented this organization, which had seen college athletics revenue skyrocket but had done little to remedy the ongoing criticisms surrounding seemingly endless scandals. The very organization created to solve the problems associated with college sports had become so successful that it was either unable or unwilling to address any criticism that might harm its revenue-generating sports. As one senator noted, the NCAA's responses to modern issues were "as antiquated as leather helmets." Senator Richard Blumenthal (D-Connecticut) also lectured Emmert, "The NCAA has a role to play, but only if it gets into the game, which, right now, it is failing to do."[3] In short, those in control of intercollegiate athletics had once again been slow to promote change.

To be fair, few politicians, professors, or spectators understood the amazingly complex challenges facing universities if forced to provide a free market for the services of student-athletes. At the same time, college sports had been generating billions of dollars in annual revenue, but the vast majority of it came from approximately seventy to eighty institutions engaged in big-time athletics. It is worth noting that the hearing regarding player compensation had been organized by a Senate Commerce Subcommittee on Manufacturing, Trade, and Consumer Protection—not the Department of Education. This fact, as well as the committee's interest in money, student compensation, and the administration of college athletics, spoke to the resounding commercial success of college athletics, particularly football.

Despite its popular appeal and the national attention it attracted, college athletics had been a long-neglected area of study by academics, including historians. As scholar Charles Clotfelter noted, the role of athletics on many university campuses, along with the lack of research on the topic, "is jarring, if not shocking." He added, "In the popular perception, it is an important part of universities. But in the world of institutional pronouncements and scholarship, big-time sports is seldom more than a footnote."[4] In that void, sports journalists and other fans wrote books detailing the glories of star players and national championships. The popular texts were written to appeal to fans desiring to identify with a winner—their winner.

Clotfelter's critical concern may have been tempered by a promising groundswell of scholarly research on college sports—including, for example, our own books and articles. Although relatively late to the game, academics (and some journalists) began applying their craft to college sports, showing some traction in the 1970s and 1980s. An abundance of excellent research has been published during the past thirty years.[5] Much of that literature has been extremely critical of universities and their athletics, highlighting a system plagued by abuse. The historical and current scholarly narrative often focuses on cultural themes driven by greed and fraught with cheating and corruption. Scandal remains a primary focus in such studies, as it should. To the dismay of many scholars, somehow college sports have survived and still grow despite multiple attempts at deemphasis.

Both the celebratory writing outside of the academy and the more sobering scholarly tomes contain a great deal of truth. While not factually incorrect, their perspectives diverge wildly. Former college athletes have gone on to lead Fortune 500 companies and to become university presidents, war heroes, governors, and members of Congress. Six former collegiate athletes—Theodore Roosevelt, Dwight D. Eisenhower, John F. Kennedy, Richard Nixon, Gerald Ford, and George H. W. Bush—even became presidents of the United States. A seventh president, George W. Bush, had been a varsity cheerleader at Yale. Hundreds of thousands of young people who might not have otherwise had the chance to attend college were provided the opportunity thanks to college sports, and many of them speak to these virtues. At the same time, other student-athletes have been injured, abused, manipulated, and exploited. While many coaches and administrators have been recognized as inspirational leaders and lifelong mentors to their athletes, other coaches have been guilty of cheating, abuse, and player mistreatment.

Such a story of monumental success and shocking scandal sounds both innately human and, in many ways, distinctly American in nature. After all, a system of big-time college athletics is uniquely American. Nearly a half million students participate in intercollegiate athletics each year. Select sports at the NCAA Division I level remain part of an "affinity" enterprise: people love their teams and feel passionately about the outcome of contests and the future of the games. That fact has created unprecedented revenue for a relatively small group of universities. It has also led to emotional and often polarizing writing about the topic. Celebration and controversy have followed intercollegiate athletics from its inception to the present day.

Despite an ever-expanding body of literature on college athletics, new areas for scholarly inquiry exist and familiar topics warrant reconsideration. Many scholarly studies have emphasized "what is wrong" in college sport. Conversely, academics have not highlighted "what is right" in intercollegiate athletics. Why has this been the case? The helpful clue may come from cultural critic John Jay Chapman, who wrote in 1898: "We must never expect to find in a dogma [in this case the predominance of college athletics] the explanation of the system which props it up. That explanation must be sought in history. The dogma records but does not explain a supremacy."[6]

Chapman's observation generally describes the scholarship addressing college athletics. The supremacy and scandal of college sports have been well documented, but few have addressed why this is the case. Perhaps it is difficult for professors to explain a problem that is intertwined with the very system that provides their academic security and income.[7] Maybe or maybe not. Regardless, with Chapman's advice, we attempt to examine and address the key foundational questions historically: *How* did college sports evolve into such a massive commercial enterprise? Moreover, *why* does it matter?[8] This story will address these questions and provide new perspectives on some old themes that have characterized the academy's own take on its most popular creation: college sports.

The historical record preserved in archives, newspapers, articles, and books provides evidence of a much closer relationship between the modern American university and its athletic programs. Nevertheless, scholars have been steadfast in their analysis that the relationship between the two is somehow a mismatch or an anomaly. After more than a century of failed "reform" efforts, it is time to consider the possibility that big-time athletic programs and modern American universities are linked to the same foundation. After all, one produced the other. Perhaps big-time athletics, without the scandals, accomplish exactly what the leaders of modern universities desire. This relationship is not without conflict, but little in higher education is. Rather, the growth of big-time athletics, despite nearly continuous efforts at reform, indicates a symbiotic relationship between higher education and athletics that few scholars have attempted to adequately explain.

Consequently, this study seeks to provide a deep understanding of the development of intercollegiate athletics within the historical context of changes among American colleges and universities. This remains an essential theme throughout this work. Before elaborating on the history of institutions and issues, we note that in the vernacular, *college* and *university* often are used synonymously. This convention persists even though the two institutional categories have important differences in mission and scale. The same is true in this book, save the brief history below in the introduction. Here, the differences between the historical college and university are essential in understanding the development of higher education and athletics.

The Transformation of American Higher Education

First and foremost, athletics grew along with the development of the university, not the college. From the Colonial Era until the Civil War, American colleges were just that—colleges. Debates about the nature and aims in higher education existed, but the liberal arts model with a prescribed curriculum and strict rules based on the concept of in loco parentis dominated. A distinctly American character existed in these institutions, but it remains a relatively simple task to trace the British influence in American higher education through 1860. A quote widely attributed to President James Garfield summarized the American institution well: "The ideal college is Mark Hopkins on one end of a log and a student on the other."[9] College professors and administrators monitored students' academic and moral development by keeping them close. These small colleges served a minuscule percentage of the population and remained extremely small by twenty-first-century standards.[10] There were athletic contests among classmates, often taking the form of rivalries between upperclassmen and their younger peers. Despite the proximity of institutions to one another (particularly in the Northeast), they did not engage in *intercollegiate* sport until the 1850s.

Only in post–Civil War America did attempts to transform American colleges into true universities gain traction. During the war, Congress passed the Morrill Land Grant Act, which provided funding for institutions that included studies in engineering and agriculture. After the war, as the national government "reconstructed" the South, a group of visionary academic leaders in other regions of the country began remodeling higher education as well. These pioneers led a monumental shift in the structure and mission of higher education and the role of the university in American life. Although the transformation took decades, by 1910 the structure of the American university had been established.

As one historian noted, "Out of the cocoon of the old-fashioned American college . . . emerged that strange schizophrenia native to the New World, the American university."[11] It combined elements of the traditional British Ox-Bridge experience and the German research model. Structurally, blending these different approaches on a single campus involved having an undergraduate college as a central component of the university along with a graduate school as part of the same institution. Although generally overlooked, by the turn of the twentieth century, most of the leading universities in the United States also boasted the best football teams. Ambitious presidents at aspiring institutions emulated this model, and in most instances included the growth of intercollegiate sport, especially football.[12]

So, what defined a university in the United States? According to Frederick Rudolph's classic history, new universities were marked by an "appetite for expansion." This thirst for growth required increasing student enrollment, expanding campus facilities, and offering new curricular programs for both undergraduate and graduate students. New majors were inextricably linked to the universities' progressive impulse. The incredible growth in curricula sought to meet the numerous practical needs of a complex democracy. New majors in agriculture, engineering, social work, education, business, and public relations challenged the traditional bachelor of arts degree. At the same time, universities recruited specialized faculty who often focused on research more than teaching undergraduates. Some faculty were hired to conduct utilitarian research that directly benefited states, such as training farmers, construction workers, and teachers. As Rudolph summarized, the new landscape gave "all careers . . . an equal hearing and an equal opportunity within the university."[13]

This transformation in higher education required a new type of campus leader. Innovative presidents created a novel administrative model far different than that of their predecessors, who had closely monitored faculty instruction and student morality. In contrast, modern executives monitored budgets and statistics while attempting to find a competitive advantage against rival schools. Thorstein Veblen coined the term "captains of erudition" to describe these university presidents because of their similarities to the "captains of industry." Among these presidents and the wealthy philanthropists who helped fund their plans, "there was distrust, contempt, chicanery, and sabotage." This included the presidents as well as the philanthropists who helped fund the modern university. When presidents found an advantage, they were quick to promote it in press releases, so publicity bureaus became essential parts of the administrative machinery. University presidents even found it beneficial to show a certain level of hostility toward their rivals, so long as it was not done excessively or distastefully. Successful presidents became politically savvy in an effort to keep dissimilar groups and stakeholders happy. This included faculty members, donors, politicians, alumni, and, most of all, boards of trustees.[14]

For students, the new university model meant unprecedented access to higher education. Although homogeneous and limited by later standards, universities began opening their doors to an expanding middle class with a more diverse group of matriculates. Presidents equated growth with success, and more students were the solution. With regard to admissions officers, even at "elite" institutions, "scarcely anyone would demand that the university limit itself to the few who fervently cared for science and letters." For the throngs of new students, college provided an opportunity for a successful career rather than an experience to "liberate their souls." Indeed, by 1910, nearly two-thirds of students majored in vocational or professional subjects, with one-third still earning a traditional bachelor of arts degree that would have been mandatory less than a half century earlier.[15]

Along with this new curricular focus, students used their growing freedom to create what historian Roger Geiger termed the "collegiate revolution" within the university structure. It provided what Yale undergraduate Henry Seidel Canby called "a little space of time . . . where the young made a world to suit themselves." Students created or further developed singing clubs, debating societies, religious groups, fraternities and sororities, literary societies, secret clubs, newspapers, magazines, *and* intercollegiate sporting contests. Through the extracurriculum, undergraduates found ways to distinguish themselves from their peers. Wealthier students maintained the fashionable ability to keep such activities at the heart of their collegiate experience but still needed a degree to retain their social status. First-generation matriculates, sometimes called "grinders," often studied long hours each day in the belief that academics marked by a university degree provided a ticket to a better life, even if they spent little time reflecting on the life of the mind. Nevertheless, for most undergraduates across the socioeconomic spectrum, college meant good times, pleasant friendships, and the expectation of lifelong prestige resulting from a degree. A popular slogan among students of the era stressed, "Don't Let Your Studies Interfere with Your Education."[16]

As undergraduate enrollments swelled and students found their social place in campus life, professors began shifting attention from students' moral development and conduct to the development of academic skill sets. This was a natural transition as more classes were offered in majors from engineering, agriculture, and business to home economics and social work. Other talented faculty retreated into their academic life that emphasized research, writing, and graduate-level teaching. Professors created national professional associations in their respective disciplines to promote the creation of knowledge in their fields of study. In turn, these scholarly associations provided an academic community for faculty members that existed beyond the walls of any individual campus. It also provided a means for a select few to become "stars" in their discipline. As university administrators sought prestige, the wealthier institutions engaged in recruiting the most prolific scholars away from competing institutions.

Even those professors who were not recruited by other universities still gained unprecedented independence and autonomy in their professional work. Although slow in developing, the influential shift away from small denominational colleges to large research universities also fostered the growth of academic freedom. The ability for a faculty member to publish and teach as she or he saw fit had always faced challenges, but the modern university certainly offered most professors a freedom from interference unknown during most of the eighteenth and nineteenth centuries. Academic freedom initially developed less as a high-minded ideal and more from an outgrowth of the modern university structure. Growing independence (and isolation) within the larger university bureaucracy created a natural buffer for faculty. As long as professors evaded "sensationalism," their teaching and research were "relatively free from intrusion."[17] This freedom came with a price, however. The university system, without any official statement, began making a trade-off. As faculty gained more control over the curriculum and their academic work, they slowly began losing their voice in many administrative decisions, including those dealing with extracurricular activities such as intercollegiate athletics.[18]

Laurence Veysey's time-tested historical analysis in *The Emergence of the American University* offered a compelling interpretation of how these changes for presidents, faculty, and students were operationalized in the university's organizational structure. As campus reforms isolated various university constituencies, "the university could mean no one thing" to everyone. It had become impossible "to define—or to control." Growing student numbers, departments, and divisions all led to a multifarious governing systems and fragmentation. Veysey described the new "incoherence" in this way: "The university throve on the patterned isolation of its component parts, and this isolation required that people continually talk past each other, failing to listen to what others were actually saying." Disparate parts of the institution could go in different directions at the same time. Hence "The marchers of the autumn [football] Saturday brushed almost unknowingly against the scattered individuals bent for the laboratory or the stacks." Both had become very real parts of the university.[19]

Professionalization, specialization, growth, and bureaucracy kept administrators, professors, students, and athletes all at arm's length from each other. Veysey called this "the price of structure." The modern university protected all kinds of individuals and enterprises through isolation. Veysey concluded, "Factions of whatever sort were almost never purged. Athletics and intellect alike could usually be pointed to as evidence of affirmative institutional service. The university, already diverse in so many ways, thus grew also to include its own severest critics." Veysey rightly believed that the ability to absorb the voices of unhappy faculty "malcontents" without making any substantive changes was a defining characteristic of the modern university.[20]

Having described the structure of the American university, Veysey attempted to capture the ethos or feeling of change in academia by quoting George Santayana. A Harvard philosophy professor and cultural critic, Santayana noted in the 1890s that the intellectual values of "polite America," consisting of Eastern Seaboard aristocrats drawing their ideological lineage from English Puritans, had been challenged by a "crude but vital" American strand that consisted of the "prodigal children of the old colonial families as well as the new immigrants from across Europe." These individuals, many of whom found themselves at universities, were less concerned with the "godly commonwealth" and more interested in the benefits of a new American life. They also shunned the old attributes of the upper class and brought a newfound vitality to American higher education. It was this same attitude that had permeated the modern American university, including athletics.[21]

The crude but vital element that Santayana had identified as central to the university's new spirit also embodied collegiate athletic programs. As historian Ronald Smith noted, in England, "There was an upper-class understanding in rugby, as in other sports, that the spirit of the rules was as important as the rules themselves. In America, the letter of the rules might be observed, but the spirit of the rules was much undervalued."[22] This dichotomy was distinctly American. Except for those brought through the insidious slave trade, the United States consisted primarily of people from the lower economic classes who had fled Europe for a better life.[23] These parts of the immigration story continued and brought with it more diversity and vitality. Many newcomers to the academy were lower- and middle-class students utilizing college, and often college athletics, to better their lives. This altered American culture, the modern university, and it certainly influenced athletics. Success—in this case winning—remained critically important.

This attitude so prevalent in the larger culture and athletics also flourished in modern American universities. Even so, the relationship between the burgeoning American university and the growth of athletics has largely been ignored. Sports were nourished in the modern university environment as institutions provided an apparatus for publicity that helped make it a successful public spectacle. Athletic victories generally led to increased gate receipts (ticket sales) and free advertising in the press.[24]

In short, general transformations in American culture and specific changes engendered in the creation of the American university are key to understanding the unrivaled commercial success as well as the many shortcomings of intercollegiate athletics. General themes in higher education find their way into athletics and vice versa. As one of the authors noted in an earlier publication, "A university's athletic policy is ultimately important for defining its educational philosophy." After years of study, this remains true, but it should include an essential corollary. Namely, an institution's educational philosophy plays an essential role in defining its athletic policy. Intercollegiate athletics is not on the historical periphery of many institutions but is an essential component of the larger story.[25]

The Key Players

As this work examines the past to recount the nature of the relationships between universities and their sports teams, it will consider the historical ties among many important "players" in order to better understand the totality of intercollegiate athletics. There have been several key players in the story of college sports whose interactions have created a complex and compelling story. Most but not all of these participants had an identity *within* the university structure. They include athletic conferences and their officials, alumni boosters, presidents, athletics departments and their directors, coaches, athletes, critics, campus outsiders, and members of the media. These disparate groups, sometimes complementary and sometimes competing, played a significant role in college athletics since the nineteenth century and have influenced college sports in indelible ways.

The NCAA: A familiar topic of study, the National Collegiate Athletic Association developed out of a need to reform the excessive brutality and violence in college football. After doing so, the organization then served largely as a "faculty debating society" for the next four decades. With no official oversight or power, presidents and professors met annually to discuss the progress they were making in improving college athletics. During the 1950s, at the same time television opened the door for more revenue, the NCAA took on formal regulating control, which it has held ever since.[26]

Athletic Conferences: Originally formed for faculty oversight in college sport, conferences have evolved into something much different. Unlike individual institutions or the NCAA, athletic conferences remain an understudied part of the college athletic enterprise, even though they have transformed into powerful regional promoters of big-time athletics. They have also developed rivalries of their own. Historically, their interaction with each other and within the NCAA has been one of cooperation and conflict. While some conferences have faded, others have grown in influence, especially the "power conferences." This has been especially true since the 1980s.

Alumni Boosters: Alumni are an essential asset to a university. Because so many enjoyed their undergraduate experience, they have proven to be an excellent source for fundraising. Alumni fund scholarships, buildings, arts programs, and more, but at universities with big-time athletic programs, large sums flow to athletics departments. Although rarely a topic for academic study, universities' "athletic associations" raise the money, and they are separately incorporated and operate under their own guidelines. In addition, some of the most prominent boosters become members of the boards of trustees at their respective institutions. These boards remain the ultimate authority for universities, and they wield a great deal of influence, usually in promoting big-time athletics.

Athletics Departments: The administration of an institution's athletic program has evolved over time as well. For years, football coaches often served as athletics directors (ADs) as well, but the complexity of the business operation has made such arrangements a thing of the past. These departments also possess oft neglected but essential relationships with the athletics associations mentioned above. ADs, coaches, sports information directors (SIDs), and players are all employed (or enrolled) by universities, and they often include the popular personalities on campus. That is one reason why athletics have been called the "front porch" of the university, and these departments witness both celebration and scrutiny. In more recent decades, athletics departments have given more control to companies who purchase a school's media rights and then run the advertising and sponsorship sides of college sports. This activity has been "under the radar" to most scholars, but its impact on revenue and operations has been substantial.

Coaches and Players: These individuals, for nearly the entire history of intercollegiate athletics, have been front and center in the story of college athletics. The power position of each has been radically different, however. Coaches are "professional" in every sense of the word, and the most popular ones make substantially more money than anyone else at their institution. The most successful coaches often have larger-than-life personas and carry an incredible amount of power, influence, and celebrity. The coach's players (also students) have had an important role as well. Historically, the best players have won a certain amount of celebrity on campus and in their respective states. Despite their celebrated status, they have held virtually no power regarding athletic policy. In recent history, players have begun to wield more influence. Either way, players remain central to the story of college sports because they are almost always part of the successes or scandals of university athletic programs.

University Presidents: As this study will detail, despite history's clear lesson that presidents have been unwilling or unable to change the trajectory of commercialized sports, they have been heralded as the key to any substantive change in college athletics. Understandably, these executives are primarily concerned with keeping various stakeholders on their campuses contented. Because this has often included the need for athletic success, collectively presidents have failed to support colleagues pushing for a deemphasis on college sport. Successful leaders have understood that the vast majority of a college's constituents want winning teams, and challenging the athletics system poses a risk to their own job security. Hence "booster" presidents who have pushed for athletic success while avoiding rule violations have been the most successful in their positions.

Big-Time Programs and Sports: This story will often elaborate upon the sports and programs that have had the most revenue, power, and control in athletics. Generally, these have been referred to as universities who engage in "big-time" sports. As this study will reveal, this group has changed over time. Today, most of these programs and sports hold membership in a power conference, along with a few institutions desperately trying to break into the leading group. Hundreds of aspiring institutions desire to compete with these schools, but it does not mean that they are big-time in the truest sense of the term. In addition, there are only a handful of big-time sports. Football remains the undisputed champion, and men's basketball is the clear runner-up. Some programs in women's basketball, men's baseball, and women's softball, however, have come to fit the profile of a big-time sport on specific campuses.

The Marginalized: While we will focus on big-time athletic programs, any comprehensive examination of college sports must address important associations and entities that have shaped the landscape of intercollegiate athletics. These include the Amateur Athletic Union (AAU), the National Association of Intercollegiate Athletics (NAIA), the Association for Intercollegiate Athletics for Women (AIAW), the National Invitation Tournament (NIT), and sports at historically Black colleges and universities (HBCUs). The schools often labeled "mid-majors" as well as institutions participating at the Division II and III levels of the NCAA are also part of the story. For the most part, glimpses into the past of these institutions and associations provide a poignant counternarrative to most writing on the subject.

The Media: An essential component to the popularity and growth of inter-collegiate athletics, the media, probably more than any other agency or influence, has successfully adapted its operations over time. Newspaper reporters were the first to popularize college sports in the nineteenth century. Coverage expanded with radio transmission, television broadcasts, cable stations, conference networks, sports talk shows, and live-streaming content. The media promotes college athletics and benefits financially from it at the same time. Unlike other "players," however, the media does not have a role on a campus or among institutions. Still, the media has become the primary force in big-time college sports because of the revenue it generates. Much like other industries in America, the media's local flavor has given way to centralized corporate operations. For those schools and conferences with enough fans to lure big contracts, it offers universities unprecedented exposure and revenue. In return, it has assumed a level of control that has created problems for the "amateur" model espoused by the NCAA.

The Critics: From the nineteenth century forward, intercollegiate athletics has faced a host of critics, yet the enterprise continues to grow. In the early twentieth century, Princeton's Woodrow Wilson asked, "What Is a College For?" In his essay, Wilson lamented that "the sideshows . . . have swallowed up the circus. Those who perform in the main tent [professors] must often whistle for their audiences, discouraged and humiliated."[27] Critics remained throughout the twentieth century and into the present. Nearly a century after Wilson's complaints, Professor Murray Sperber wrote a book titled *Beer and Circus: How Big-time College Sports Is Crippling Undergraduate Education*.[28] But these scholars have been unsuccessful at curbing the excesses of college sports. More than anything, the critiques of college athletics have revealed how little substantive influence faculty and academic administrators have had in the regulation of college athletics. Money and perceived prestige still win, and they are essential elements driving both higher education and its athletic programs.

The Themes

By examining the interaction of these various groups over time, several important themes emerge. They reinforce the notion that the university structure allows for big-time sports and big-time critics to coexist in the university sphere, so long as nothing substantive changes. Additionally, the actions of these interested parties reveal a number of other elements that have remained consistent over time.

First, the general lack of historical awareness or understanding causes an exaggeration of the intensity of issues and controversies of the day while dismissing the past as diminutive. A simple online search retrieves dozens of recent articles characterizing college athletics as being "out of control" or "broken." More than a century ago, famed historian Frederick Jackson Turner at the University of Wisconsin bemoaned that intercollegiate athletics had "become a business, carried on too often by professionals, supported by levies on the public, bringing in vast gate receipts, demoralizing student ethics, and confusing the ideals of sport, manliness, and decency."[29] Without minimizing the importance or severity of current concerns, critics lacking historical understanding have usually lent themselves to ahistorical solutions, which simply have not solved the challenges in college athletics.

A related theme addresses the lack of understanding regarding the popularity and power of college sports. The current view that college athletics today has an unprecedented number of fans and excessive media coverage ignores the historical record. A quick look at photographs from University of Michigan–Ohio State football games from the 1920s reveals that the fervor for college sport has been long-standing. The interest today remains impressive but far from unique. Before mergers of local newspapers, college sports news filled the pages of multiple newspapers in major cities. Before universities consolidated their radio broadcasts to one official radio network, it was not uncommon for college teams to have four or five "originations"—different announcers broadcasting games on multiple radio channels across a state. Radio stations would have only engaged in such a practice if it were profitable. Regardless of the type of media, college sports has always met the demand for news. What has changed is the technology and the ability of individual institutions and conferences to harness this fan support and revenue through centralized media mechanisms.

Why has the history of big-time college athletics been so consistent in its themes over the past century? Why have so many attempted to change the "circus" but failed so miserably? One of the key arguments we offer is that many of these problems have emerged from a century of misunderstanding or misuse of the term "reform" when applied to college athletics. In his 1910 study *Great American Universities,* Edwin Slosson wrote, "The essential difference between a college and a university is how they look. A university looks forward and a college looks backward. The aim of one is discovery; the aim of the other is conservation."[30] Here we find a contradiction within the university and in Slosson's definition. Virtually all university reforms have "looked forward," except those in athletics. Reforms in athletics have almost always "looked backward," with a desire to return to a bygone (and mythical) era of purity in sport. Progressive reform in the American tradition, by definition, generally meant some policy or structural change to improve conditions for individuals. Yet reform has meant something altogether different when applied to intercollegiate athletics.[31]

Much of the confusion regarding reform stems from the notion that college sports must perpetually mean an attempt to return athletics to an "amateur" model. The perceived purity of amateurism has been held closely by the NCAA from its earliest years.[32] But this model for sports competition came from the British aristocracy in order to solidify its social position and avoid losing to competitors from lower classes. It was adopted by American colleges as an ideal, but it never fully existed in intercollegiate athletics in the United States. While American universities "professionalized" virtually every other part of higher education, it sought to keep its most popular and lucrative product— athletics—amateur.[33] In fact, amateur athletics is alive and well among millions of college students. Tens of thousands of amateur athletes compete in non-revenue-generating sports each year. An even larger group of undergraduates play intramural sports on their respective campuses. In many respects, the amateur nature of the contests is exactly why they do not draw similar concern or publicity.

This conservative, or even reactionary, approach to intercollegiate athletics administration has led to another historical trend: reform of college sports has rarely originated from within universities, their conferences, or the NCAA. There are important exceptions to this rule, but generally reform in athletics has come from the government. Court rulings and legislation supported by popular opinion have been the primary agents of change in big-time athletics. From the civil rights movement calling for desegregation to the push for equal opportunities for women, change has generally been imposed on college sports by the law. NCAA president Mark Emmert's visit to Congress in 2020 offers a case in point. By April of the same year, in the midst of the COVID-19 pandemic, the NCAA released a vague report that signaled it would move forward with player compensation. California had passed SB 206 into law in 2019, and other states followed suit. Two years later, the US Supreme Court, in *NCAA v. Alston*, ruled that the organization's policies prohibiting compensation for using a player's NIL violated the Sherman Antitrust Act. Once again, laws and lawsuits spurred action within the NCAA, which would have done nothing otherwise.[34]

Finally, if universities desire true reform, those engaged in big-time athletics may consider the historical reality that sport has played a central—even missional—role at many institutions. This idea, proposed as a possibility by renowned scholar and university administrator Charles Clotfelter, has been echoed by others.[35] While some would oppose this "fit" in the American higher education, it is worth noting that American universities now boast more than three hundred academic degree programs in sports management and administration. The North American Society for Sport Management provides an academic association for professors and students in this field. There is nothing morally wrong with sporting contests with the highest level of talent. There is also nothing inherently evil with the generation of revenue and the positive economic impact college sports has on its host communities. Nor is there anything morally superior about big-time athletics. Virtue might be found in the acknowledgment of a reality that most interested American sports enthusiasts have long since accepted: the important role of big-time athletics at American universities. Such a move may produce other positive results for intercollegiate athletics. For instance, hundreds of colleges and universities that simply cannot compete financially may decide to pursue a truly amateur model of intercollege sport.

This history explains how and why intercollegiate athletics has developed into a multi-billion-dollar industry, without casting aspersion or claiming victory. Some may find that troubling. But it provides an analysis regarding the challenges universities face when leaders remain unwilling to be truthful about the system of athletics in which they engage. All is not well, but all is not lost. Regardless of the perspective readers bring to this study, we hope that it will accomplish what the best histories are capable of: challenging assumptions, promoting critical thinking, and developing deeper understanding of complex issues. These are desperately needed attributes in higher education and the sports they play.

1

The Creation of Sports in American Higher Education, 1852 to 1900

From Extracurricular Activity to Organized Intercollegiate Contests

The Advent of Organized College Sports

In the twenty-first century, organized intercollegiate athletics remains a ubiquitous part of college life at large research universities and small liberal arts colleges alike. For many in the American public, big-time college sports are synonymous with higher education. This was not always the case; there was no "manifest destiny" vision of an overarching organization dedicated to the operations of college sport. From humble beginnings when students looked to develop on-campus activities for their own entertainment, college athletics has landed on the front page, the television, in Congress, and the Supreme Court. The origin and early history of college sports reveal a great deal about current successes and struggles.

Long before intercollegiate sports became a national pastime, students created games as entertainment for themselves at their host institutions. For decades during the nineteenth century, the beginning of the fall semester at Harvard College included a long-standing student tradition. The "Sophs" and the "Fresh" would meet on a field of the Cambridge, Massachusetts, campus and usher in the new academic year with a class battle. New matriculates would face the group of second-year students in a football battle. Although the rules included getting a leather-bound animal bladder (or an otherwise stuffed leather casing) across a goal line, few other guidelines existed.

This lack of rules appeared to be exactly what the students wanted. Although scoring goals in those early nineteenth-century football games mattered, students also proved their mettle by kicking the shins and bloodying the noses of members from other class. The ability to take a beating and deliver one as well proved to be a sign of valor and strength. After all, the football ritual had evolved from eighteenth-century wrestling matches between incoming first-year students and their sophomore superiors. At some point, a ball had been added to the traditional brawl, and a game of some sort had been added to the extracurriculum of the American college.

In 1827, a Harvard student wrote a poem describing the ritual. Titled "The Battle of the Delta," it offered a setting for the game in the following lines:

> The college clock struck twelve—that awful hour
> When the Sophs met Fresh, power met opposing power:
> To brave the dangers of approaching fight,
> Each army stood of literary might;
> With warlike ardor for a deathless fame
> Impatient stood–until the football came;

Describing the battle's hero, the poem continued:

> The well-blown ball he casts upon the ground;
> How stern the hero looked, how high the ball did bound!
> "Let none," he says, "my valour tried impeach,
> Should I delay the fight—to make a speech"—
> "Let it be warned," a youthful Stentor cries,
> "No speeches here,—but let the football rise."
> Through warlike crowds a devious way it wins,
> And shins advancing meet advancing shins;

After discussing the ensuing battle at great length, the student-poet concluded:

> He said, and furious rushed upon his foe;
> As when two cows to deadly combat go;
> Fate interfered, and stopped the impending blow;
> For hark! the summons of the Commons-bell,
> That music every hero knows so well;
> All sympathetic started at the sound,
> And ran for dinner from the battle ground.[1]

Harvard was not alone in its intramural football events. A Yale student wrote his own brief poem to describe football at Yale:

> There were yellings and shouting and wiping of noses,
> Where the hue of the lily has changed to the rose's,
> There were tearing of shirts, and ripping of stiches,
> And breaches of peace, and pieces of britches.[2]

The football phenomenon spread among colleges in the Northeast between 1820 and 1850. But it was not the first attempt by students to engage in athletics. During the 1700s, student-imposed rules at Harvard required freshmen to furnish upperclassmen with "bats, balls and foot-balls."[3] Faculty at colonial colleges were far less enthused by such extracurricular activities. Yale prohibited students from playing "Hand-ball, or Foot-ball, or bowl[ing]" on the college yard with a six-pence punishment for offenders.[4] In the early nineteenth century, Princeton declared athletics "low and unbecoming gentlemen and students."[5]

By the 1820s, the growth in literature regarding the value of exercise helped loosen the stranglehold of institutional rules prohibiting athletic activity. The notion that sport subverted students' spiritual growth dissipated to an extent. In turn, underclassmen engaged in various forms of athletic contests. On pleasant days, students engaged in handball, baseball, football, bowling, and other recreational activities. For much of the nineteenth century, baseball remained a favorite game. Yet the "football rush" between classes at the beginning of the fall term proved to be the event during which class heroes were made by exhibiting athletic prowess and brute strength.[6]

The growth in student activities during the first half of the nineteenth century provided a key component of social life and community development at a time when collegiate life remained unbelievably strict by modern standards. Daily chapel attendance early in the morning, class recitations, and strict rules forbidding things like card playing or traveling to a nearby city led to students creating their own social lives on campus. This growth loosely paralleled the development of fraternities in higher education. These opportunities allowed students to build a social world outside the watchful eyes of college faculty and administrators.

John Langdon Sibley, Harvard graduate of 1825 and longtime librarian at his alma mater, provided an account of the football game that kicked off the semester on August 31, 1846, in his journal: "College lessons began. After evening commons the Sophomores and Freshmen met, as has been the custom for many years . . . to try themselves with football." He continued, "The different classes came together. The football is thrown down among them and the object of each class is to kick the other and 'bark the shins' as much as possible." As students developed relationships, they continued to play fall football games until the weather turned colder. Sibley then noted that students turned to "bat-and-ball" and cricket for sporting in the spring. Nearly a decade later, Sibley wrote another journal entry in which he added that there were examples of "violence and brutality," but at the end of the game, all the classes joined in a circle and sang "Auld Lang Syne." This roughhousing occasionally led to broken noses and torn clothes, but it provided a sense of ownership for students in an otherwise rigid environment.[7]

This newly developed freedom had its limits. As the popularity of the football rush spread, so too did the violent elements of the game. During the 1850s, Harvard's football rush became known as "Bloody Monday," and interested onlookers as well as reporters traveled to watch the spectacle. As news of the violent games spread, the annual game came under scrutiny. In 1857 the Yale administration banned the annual "rush." The following year, the town of New Haven prohibited Yale students from using the town green for their match, ensuring the game remained unplayed. On July 2, 1860, the Harvard faculty voted to abolish the game as well.[8] The first Monday in September following the faculty prohibition, Harvard students held a procession and funeral for football. An elegy was provided, and they buried a leather-bound pigskin bladder in a casket and sang a tune of "Auld Lang Syne" to the words:

Ah! Woe betide the luckless time
When manly sports decay,
And football, stigmatized as a crime,
Must sadly pass away.[9]

These early accounts of football highlight a few essential points regarding the origins of college sports. First, students organized the events for their own pleasure. They provided an outlet from a rather ridged curriculum, and faculty members with watchful eyes engaged in strict discipline during the era of in loco parentis. The students used athletics as a part of the extracurriculum to bring diversity to their own collegiate experience. A student's class (as in the class of 1856) team provided a solidarity, and on-campus athletics engendered a level of pride and community in one's cohort.

Crew and the Creation of Intercollegiate Competition in the United States

The football rush may have been banned at Harvard, but the game continued to be played among undergraduates on other college campuses. As it did, other sports began to flourish. Students played cricket, baseball, handball, and other sports. Boat races were the first to feature intercollegiate competition. After all, the earliest American colleges had been British colonial institutions and in many ways resembled the aristocratic Oxford-Cambridge (OxBridge) model.

American institutions often emulated elements and activities from the two most prominent British universities, including football, cricket, and rowing.

Crew emerged at American colleges after William Weeks and some of his classmates at Yale purchased a boat in 1843. A group of Harvard students followed suit the next year. America's two leading colleges quickly formed their student boating clubs. Like football, races were held between classes of the same institution. Unlike football's Bloody Monday, crew remained a far more appealing sport for administrators to accept. This remained true even though Charles Eliot, who attended Harvard in the late 1840s and early '50s remembered that the boats were often used to take students to and from bars and taverns in Boston. Even though students used the boats for drinking excursions, the sporting side of the enterprise was considered far more civilized than football.[10]

In May 1852, Yale junior James Whiton traveled home to New Hampshire to rest at his parents' home after a grueling term in New Haven. Whiton's father was a successful businessman who served as a director of the new Boston, Concord, and Montreal Railroad. While aboard the BC&M train skirting Lake Winnipesauke, James talked with James Elkins, a conductor and agent for the railroad. Whiton, a member of a Yale boat club, commented on a stretch of the waterway that would be ideal for a regatta. Elkins replied with a proposal, "If you will get up a regatta on the lake between Yale and Harvard, I will pay the bills." Elkins hoped to use the race as an opportunity to promote the railroad. Whiton agreed to make it happen.[11]

Whiton's classmates welcomed the opportunity for a "a jolly lark."[12] The three participating teams from Yale along with the one crew from Harvard met in Concord, New Hampshire, and traveled on the BC&M to Lake Winnipesaukee, where they stayed at the Center House. After a dinner on Saturday, the students rested on the Sabbath and practiced on Monday. August 3, 1852, provided nearly perfect weather for the students and onlookers alike. The BC&M had promoted the event, and the railroad hired a brass band to add to the excitement. "The shore was lined with a numerous and excited throng," which included Josiah Abbott, a prominent politician from Massachusetts, along with Democratic presidential candidate Franklin Pierce. Harvard's Oneida won a preliminary (or practice) meet. As the crowd waited for the 4:00 p.m. start of the official race, spectators bet on the contest. Harvard's lone crew won the main event. Franklin Pierce presented the victors with two silver-tipped black walnut oars. A race the following day was rained out, but the teams rowed on Wednesday for the onlookers' amusement. The students then received tickets and travel expenses, compliments of the railroad, to return to their respective campuses.[13]

As students returned from their free vacation, the first intercollegiate sporting event in the United States came an end, but it began a precedent that those in 1852 could not have imagined. As one newspaper reporter wrote, collegiate games were predicted to "make little stir in a busy world."[14] Yale's loss to Harvard prompted students to form the "Yale Navy," to organize more inter-class races, and to improve the crew program in New Haven. No doubt, Yale hoped to beat their counterparts in Cambridge. In 1855 the Yale club challenged Harvard to a rowing match on July 22 at any location. The crews agreed to a re-gatta on the Connecticut River in Springfield, Massachusetts. In front of a five-hundred-seat grandstand and "thousands" of spectators lining the river, Harvard once again beat their rival. Historian Thomas Mendenhall noted the growing interest among students and the general public.[15]

An 1858 regatta slated to include Brown and Trinity was cancelled when a Yale crew member drowned a week before the event. The following year, Brown did join Harvard and Yale on Lake Quinsigamond on the outskirts of Worcester, Massachusetts. Harvard won again, but Yale finally secured its first victory over their rivals the next day when Worcester put up prize money for an unofficial race between the two. Only six years after the first intercollegiate competition, the Boston and Worcester Railroad ran special trains to a town with fully booked hotels. Another band entertained the crowd of approximately fifteen to twenty thousand people. Additional activities were added for the event, which took on a carnival-like atmosphere. The press offered front-page coverage of the meet.[16]

As the Civil War raged, America's two historic elite universities once again agreed to compete against each other in 1864. This time, Yale's crew members hired a professional coach, William Wood, to help lead them to victory. Under his tutelage, Yale beat Harvard by more than forty seconds. After Yale repeated the next year, the *New York Post* managed to capture the feelings of some American's newfound love of competitive college sports: "By some process of soul chemistry, the stains of the world have been expunged, years are rubbed out of the calendar, and there is nothing left but youth and hope and joy." Yale's star rower, W. R. Bacon, gained celebrity status on campus, and some attributed Yale's bump in enrollment during the next couple of years to its rowing success.[17]

Not to be outdone, Harvard crew captain William Blaikie traveled to England to study British rowing technique. Harvard secured a win at the 1866 race, which had evolved into a three-day spectacle that included baseball games and collegiate glee club performances, among other activities. Harvard's dominance continued through the rest of the decade as William Blaikie became a star on campus. As another alumnus reminiscing on his undergraduate years said, "My reverence lay in the fact that he was the typical strong man of the college. . . . Bill Blaikie was (to my mind) the central fact of the university."[18]

Confident in its abilities, Harvard challenged Oxford to a regatta on the River Thames in 1869. That same year, Harvard's second team still managed to beat Yale. In England, more than half a million spectators showed up to witness the race between the two countries. Fifteen American reporters traveled across the Atlantic to watch Harvard pull out to an early lead, only to give it back to the Oxford team. Interestingly, Harvard had an opportunity to take Oxford's lane of water "and also to 'wash' their boat." Harvard chose not to do either, and according to the *Harvard Advocate*, Oxford did both once in the lead. The Americans lost to Oxford by a length and a half, but the showing revealed that the United States had embraced college athletics in a way that had not existed twenty-five years earlier.[19]

In the United States, the 1870 regatta and its aftermath had an incredible impact on the growth and nature of intercollegiate athletics. Yale finished first in the 1870 boat race, but a foul by Yale gave the victory to Harvard. Yale protested to the race judge, and according to the Harvard faithful, "throughout the hearing the Yale men acted in a manner which we sincerely hope no Harvard man will ever be guilty of. . . . Casting severe reflections on the integrity of that gentleman." Yale challenged Harvard to a rematch, but Harvard refused without an acknowledgment of the original foul. In the first of many rowing disputes between the two, Yale later announced they would only row against Harvard on a straight course. Harvard wanted to invite other institutions, but Yale remained interested only in beating Harvard. The back-and-forth continued with no resolution as inflated egos and an emphasis on winning resulted in a break of Harvard-Yale athletic relations.[20]

In the spring of 1871, Harvard instead decided to help organize the Rowing Association of American Colleges with a small group of schools. The new association agreed to a regatta on the Connecticut River near Springfield, Massachusetts, on July 21. Multiple crews ended up withdrawing before the race, leaving only Brown, Harvard, and tiny Massachusetts Agricultural College. The school had welcomed its first thirty-four students in 1867, and the farmers' college remained an afterthought to most press reporters and fans. But the "aggies" had employed the services of coach Josh Ward, and their brute strength combined with his training led to a stunning victory, with Harvard trailing by more than a half minute and Brown even farther behind the up-start crew. The press reported the news, showcasing the agricultural college and giving less prestigious colleges hope that they, too, could earn the notoriety that came with such a victory.[21]

The first association regatta transformed the value of a win in the boat race. It also exposed the difference between higher education and athletics in England as opposed to the United States. The OxBridge model operated on the ideal of "gentlemen" engaging each other in amateur sports for recreation. Historians have often interpreted such competition as being between aristocrats who were unwilling to admit defeat to working-class "professionals" who made money while winning contests. The less rigid US class structure allowed for fascinating "David versus Goliath" stories between upper- and lower-class citizens. Harvard and Yale may have wanted to act like Oxford and Cambridge, but American culture would not extend that same level of privilege—especially in college sports.

The next year, Amherst and its professional coach managed to beat the field, including Harvard and Yale. Clearly frustrated by the loss, the association's newly elected president, Bob Cook of Yale, successfully fought to ban professional trainers in collegiate rowing. Harvard still relied on the expertise of alum William Blaikie, who was not considered a professional even though he had traveled to England to study rowing and would later write a popular treatise on physical fitness. As a student at Yale, Cook was not considered a professional even though he took a leave of absence for a semester to study rowing technique in England. Upon his return, Cook's Yale team managed to win the 1873 race in a controversial finish, as Harvard thought it had crossed the finish line (which had apparently been incorrectly set up diagonally) and stopped rowing.[22]

In 1874 the race moved to Saratoga, where a new champion was crowned: Columbia. Returning home in a luxury train car, the rowers were honored with a parade in New York City. Columbia president Frederick A. P. Barnard congratulated the team, stating that "In one day you have done more to make Columbia College known than all your predecessors have done since the foundation of the college, by this your great triumph." In foreshadowing collegiate sport financing in the future, he also informed the young men that their monetary requests for training and operations would likely be provided. The 1875 race witnessed a victory by another land grant institution, as Cornell was victorious. The crew received treatment similar to that provided to Columbia the previous year. Cornell's president, Andrew Dickson White, noted the jubilation on campus. He and campus founder Ezra Cornell had helped financially support the young crew team just years earlier. The investment had proven to be a good one.[23]

Unable to stomach losses to less distinguished institutions, Harvard and Yale dropped out of the league and raced against each other, revealing the vestiges of England's class-conscious culture in American higher education. Without the two most venerable institutions, interest in the annual regatta waned, but not before less prestigious institutions witnessed firsthand the enthusiasm and esprit de corps created for multiple constituencies of a university with an athletic victory. Before a decline in popular appeal, crew had provided much of the foundation for intercollegiate athletics. Led by students, the races became popular spectacles. Newspapers both reported and promoted the contests. Tens of thousands of fans flocked to regattas. Professional trainers had been banned, but training and study of the sport continued to grow. The carnival-like atmosphere surrounding the annual races actually led to the first intercollegiate track meet as well as numerous baseball games being hosted during the regatta weekend.

Crew continued into the twentieth century and beyond. Yale and Harvard's rivalry on the water continues to this day, as do boating teams at many other institutions. A critical examination of the history, however, reveals that early intercollegiate crew included many of the more controversial issues surrounding college sports into the twentieth century and beyond. Commercial interests led to the first athletic contest between two schools in America. College students received a free paid vacation in order to entertain spectators and promote a railroad. In the decades ahead, communities would lobby to host the event.

Many other challenges to the British concept of amateurism developed in the first decades of rowing. Boat races evolved quickly from an academic diversion among students to a scientifically studied sport where individuals looked for advantages in technique in order to win races. Rudimentary as they were (and sometimes harmful), crew captains implemented training regimens and strict diet restrictions. Professional coaches were hired, won races, banned from competition, and then hired again.

Looking at the historical record, the greatest threat to amateurism was not the press attention, the monetary perks, the large crowds, or the coaches. These developments were merely a symptom of a larger issue: the quest to win instead of a desire for healthy recreation. The amateurism espoused by university leaders remained an upper-class British ideal, and it was far less of a reality in America than in the England.

In the United States, even aristocratic-minded students wanted to prove they were the best, or at least better than their closest peer institutions. Yale desperately desired to beat Harvard but could not handle losing to the likes of Massachusetts Agricultural College, Amherst, or Cornell. Although the most elite institution, Harvard exhibited aloofness as well. *The Crimson* followed Yale in leaving the regatta after being beaten by lesser colleges. Their departure fatally wounded the regatta and its popularity, revealing the public's respect for America's two leading institutions. When Harvard and Yale chose to race each other exclusively, most Americans also lost interested in that event. Clearly, public interest in Harvard and Yale's boating exploits did not translate into an allegiance to a caste system in higher education, as it did in England. As such, athletic interest in the United States highlighted an important difference between British and American cultures.

Despite these nuances, rowing remained an important part of college sports in the nineteenth century, but leading teams remained regional in character, as they all came from schools in the Northeast. Without a regular schedule for fans to follow in the papers, crew took a backseat to other intercollegiate sports by the 1880ss. Yet the annual regattas in the 1870s fostered the growth of other college sports and experienced the same problems that would plague intercollegiate athletics in the future.

Track and Field

One of the great legacies of early intercollegiate regattas proved to be its unintended role in popularizing what would become known in the twentieth century as track and field. Foot-racing existed for essentially the entirety of human history, but it was slow to become an organized intercollegiate sport in America. According to oarsman William Blaikie, Thomas Hughes's book *Tom Brown's School Days* played an integral role in popularizing running races at England's elite public schools. Students read the book as American universities began organizing intramural races, sometimes for prize money.[24]

Many future track and field events traced their origins to Scotland, so it was not surprising that Presbyterian Princeton played a role in the popularization of such games. In 1869, Princeton hired George Goldie to serve as an instructor of physical education and director of the gymnasium. Goldie was an accomplished gymnast and "Caledonian" athlete. Caledonian games (occasionally referred to as Highland games because of their Scottish roots) included races as well as events such as the hammer throw, the hop-skip-and-jump, swords, high jump, and hurdles. Goldie's interest in such events helped popularize these contests at Princeton, just as a few other northeastern schools began organizing what would become known as track or cross-country races.[25]

The lack of organization regarding any intercollegiate track events changed when the flamboyant and eccentric owner/publisher of the *New York Herald*, James Gordon Bennett Jr., announced a prize for a race to be held during the Association Regatta in 1873. As historian Ronald Smith noted, the prize was valued at five hundred dollars and attracted the attention of athletic college students. A Canadian student from McGill University, Duncan Bowie, won the race. His eligibility had been unsuccessfully challenged by another competitor because Bowie had won money in the 1872 New York City Caledonian Games.[26]

The event highlighted another fundamental principle found early in American collegiate sport. Although amateur in name, the money, prizes, and newspaper coverage allured students from all classes. Capitalism and corporate support proved instrumental in the development of college sports, despite the twentieth-century narratives of college sports' amateur roots. Although most faculty promoted the amateur ideal, the popular press, money, and professionalism existed in track as well.

By 1875, ten colleges were represented at the regatta track races held in Saratoga. Harvard and Yale claimed victories in multiple track events, but their continued embarrassment in the boat races led to Yale's withdrawal from the association. Harvard followed suit a year later. Although the two decided to boat race against only each other, student representatives from Harvard and Yale still invited other institutions to join a new track and field association. Without the ready-made fan base provided by the annual regatta, Bennett ended his sponsorship of the track races. Students once again controlled their own sports when they created the Intercollegiate Association of Amateur Athletics of America, or what later became known as the IC4A. The new league sponsored track and field meets into the twentieth century. Since Harvard and Yale continued to dominate many of the events, they remained in the new association.[27]

The IC4A did not draw the same popular press as other intercollegiate sports, but the growing system of intercollegiate track played an increasingly important role in other ways. First, track and field motivated American college students to challenge British supremacy in the sport. For example, Yale managed to defeat Oxford in 1875. Second, leaders in the track and field movement played an important role in the Olympic movement in the United States. Baron de Coubertine, a French aristocrat, spent years in the late 1800s attempting to organize the modern Olympic Games. He recruited Princeton professor William Sloane to help promote the games in America. Sloane eventually chaired the US Olympic Committee and helped organize the US Olympic team that traveled to Greece in 1896.[28]

Because track and field events dominated early American Olympic events, the IC4A played an important role in promoting the international games. The role of amateur college track and field in promoting the Olympic Games became an important and lasting cultural legacy in the United States. In the future, it would also create challenges regarding the administration and control of amateur sport in America.

College Baseball in the Late Nineteenth Century

The official definition of amateurism was also difficult to determine in baseball. The first college baseball games were played in 1859, but the sport did not become a fixture in American higher education nationwide for several decades. A reasonable, documented assessment is that college baseball came of age when numerous intercollegiate teams engaged in regular seasonal competitions in the early 1890s. Although college baseball was older than college football, its players and proponents neither sought to challenge nor resented football's primacy in publicity or popularity. To the contrary, the two sports were complementary because they were markedly different in character, constituency, conduct, and calendar. Football, which was played in the autumn before large, noisy crowds of paying spectators, was dramatic and often violent. Baseball, in contrast, was a highly ritualized, rhythmic game that brought the academic year to a graceful end in summer. It was marked by sportsmanship on the field and relaxed applause by knowledgeable spectators in the bleachers or grandstand. In short, by the end of the nineteenth century, baseball, which was established as "America's pastime," had also found a happy home on the American campus.

How did college baseball become so enduring and endearing? The start of college baseball in 1859 featured two landmark games: first was Amherst College versus Williams College on July 1st in Pittsfield, Massachusetts. Four months later in the boroughs of New York City, the Fordham Rose Hills Baseball Club of St. John's College played against the College of St. Francis Xavier. The summary data for these two pioneering games provide some important clues to the nature and conduct of the early collegiate sport.

Most evident was that college baseball was provincial. Its rules and regional sites were local, with no pretense of a national association. Travel was limited, so college games had to be played close by, usually against familiar opponents. Amherst and Williams, for example, were intrastate institutional rivals and played according to what was known as "Massachusetts Rules." Innings were known as frames. Instead of a baseball diamond, the field was laid out as a square, with no designated foul ball area. This along with other allowances resulted in a game that spectators outside Massachusetts would have considered curious. The rules were certainly different than what spectators consider standard practice today. For example, a batter who had hit a ball and was running toward first base could be declared out if a fielder seized the ball, then threw and hit the runner. Its partial resemblance to cricket resulted in high scoring, as Amherst won by a score of 73 to 32. In contrast, the first game, played in New York, abided by the local "Knickerbocker rules," which eventually prevailed as the national standard—and closely resembles contemporary American baseball.

In both the Massachusetts and New York games of 1859 the contests involved negotiation by student players about site and protocols. The Amherst versus Williams baseball game was part of a two-day social athletic gathering of students from both colleges that included a competitive chess match as well as a banquet. The *Amherst Express*, a campus newspaper by and for Amherst College students, ran a special edition with headlines proclaiming:

Williams and Amherst

Baseball and Chess

Muscle and Mind

At the closing banquet following the game and other activities, the losing Williams College baseball team graciously presented the victorious Amherst squad with a championship trophy of game balls. These mementos are still on display in a sports showcase at Amherst College today. Furthermore, the two competing colleges have continued their academic and athletic rivalries well into the twenty-first century.[29]

In New York, the lines between secondary school and college teams were blurred. The College of St. Francis was really a preparatory school, eventually becoming Xavier High School. The Fordham Rose Hills Baseball Club of St. John's College was a spin-off team from what would be known formally as Fordham University.

The 1859 games in Massachusetts and New York were exceptional in that there was a hiatus before many other colleges adopted baseball as an organized, recurring activity. By 1865, Harvard, Wesleyan, and Yale joined Williams and

Amherst in fielding varsity teams. In 1869, Harvard and Yale played in Brooklyn, marking the first time these two historic colleges played one another in baseball. One sign that the appeal of the college game was extending across regions occurred in 1869 when the University of North Carolina baseball team played the nearby Raleigh All-Stars.

Many college baseball teams had both a fall and a spring season but eventually compressed them into a single season that started in April and extended into June. Also, most teams in the formative years relied on students who were players and team captains to act as managers or coaches. Colleges within each region had a critical mass of varsity teams in geographic proximity to create conferences and keep records and championship standings. A pioneering example was the Intercollegiate Baseball Association, which was founded in 1879 and operated through 1886. It was essentially a New England federation, featuring Amherst, Brown, Dartmouth, Harvard, and Yale. A few years later, its successor, the College Baseball Association, extended the map and membership to include Columbia and Princeton and other mid-Atlantic teams.

A good snapshot of this extended map could be found in the Northeast in 1888. At that time, varsity teams existed at Amherst, Brown, Columbia, Dartmouth, Harvard, Penn, Princeton, and Yale, among others. Harvard started its program in 1865. Yale assembled a team in 1869 with the express purpose of meeting Harvard and leading them to travel to the neutral site of Brooklyn for the launching of the Harvard versus Yale baseball rivalry, still going strong today.

The University of Chicago, which opened for classes in 1892, wasted no time in fielding a baseball team. Moreover, its coach from 1892 through 1912 was the legendary Amos Alonzo Stagg, coach of the University of Chicago Maroons football team and athletics director for what was ostensibly the most sophisticated, well-funded intercollegiate athletics program in the nation. The University of Chicago was a charter member of the Western Conference. By 1896, this newly formed conference of universities in the Midwest (later renamed the "Big Ten") announced a conference schedule and championship standings for varsity baseball. Illustrative of participation was the University of Illinois, which had started its baseball team with a short schedule in 1879 and became established by 1893. To show the popularity and pervasiveness of the sport, at least among college players, in 1891, Illinois followed the pattern of offering a fall and spring schedule—and touched all bases by including an indoor season during the winter. No blueprints of such an ambitious construction project for an indoor baseball facility were readily found in our research.

There is no comprehensive, verified census of all college baseball programs in the nineteenth century. But core samples across regions and campuses nationwide document the spread and growing popularity of the sport even at a time when the vast majority of the American population was east of the Mississippi, with particular density along the mid-Atlantic coastal urban centers. On the Pacific Coast, many young colleges and universities founded after the Civil War included baseball as part of their formal extracurricular activities. In the Pacific Northwest, the University of Oregon fielded a team in 1877 and established a formal baseball program in 1881. The University of Washington's first team played in 1901. In California, the University of California in Berkeley started its varsity team in 1892, with its inaugural game against the squad from nearby Stanford University. In Los Angeles, records show that the University of Southern California sponsored a team in 1881.

Intercollegiate baseball gained momentum in the South. For example, in addition to the 1867 University of North Carolina team mentioned above, several varsity programs were in place elsewhere during the 1890s. These included teams at Vanderbilt in 1886 and the University of Tennessee in 1897. One of the oldest, most intense rivalries was that between University of Mississippi (Ole Miss) and Mississippi Agricultural and Mechanical College (now Mississippi State University), starting in 1893. Jumping ahead into the early twentieth century, to illustrate the talent that was germinating, the legendary New York Yankees manager Casey Stengel was the head baseball coach at Ole Miss in 1913. Other luminaries from the South included Grantland Rice, the famous sportswriter who coined the term "Four Horsemen" for Notre Dame, who coached the Vanderbilt baseball team in 1908. The University of Virginia and Richmond College vied for the Old Dominion championship with their initial game in 1889. In the Southwest, one pioneer school was the University of Texas, starting in 1894 and establishing a presence as champion of the Southern Intercollegiate Athletic Association.

Beyond this nationwide summary of vital statistics, one can gain a sense of the collegiate baseball character by looking closely at selected data. Consider, for example, the schedule for Columbia University baseball between 1888 and 1894. Located in a metropolitan area with a heavy concentration of colleges, Columbia was able to play a full slate of about twenty games per season, all within reasonable commuting distance for away games. On one level, it confirms an important fact about prestige and power in higher education—namely, a tendency for prestigious colleges to associate and play within their own ranks.

On closer inspection, one also finds fluidity and some unexpected alliances in the early years of college baseball. In addition to those traditional games and prestigious rivalries of Harvard versus Yale or Amherst versus Williams, and other forerunners of what would later be called the Ivy League, what about other games and opponents? Every college team, including the oldest universities, scheduled several games against local athletic clubs (known as ACs) as well as against nearby semiprofessional teams and squads from what would be called "sand lot leagues." A review of Columbia's baseball schedule in 1894 shows games against the US Military Academy at West Point, the University of Virginia, Lehigh College of Pennsylvania, and a spirited contest with the team from the General Theological Seminary. So, in addition to a schedule including Brown, Harvard, and Princeton, examples of teams playing against Columbia University included Bergen (New Jersey) AC, the Staten Island AC, and municipal teams from Jersey City, Murray Hills, and Newark. Opponents sometimes included top-tier professional squads. For example, Columbia even played against the major league team, the New York Giants, at the Polo Grounds, perhaps sounding like an unlikely venue for a baseball game. As such it hinted at the confusing, unsystematic character of American sports given that that polo was about the only sport never played at the Polo Grounds. The motley mix of teams, sports, and sites illustrated the incoherent, diverse nature of a growing sports enterprise, including college baseball, in modern American society of the late nineteenth and early twentieth centuries.

These early college baseball contests provide evidence of an exception to the notion of scholar-gentlemen only playing against real amateurs. It also suggested that contemporary standards of student athletic academic eligibility had little clear definition or enforcement in the late nineteenth century. Furthermore, by the early twentieth century, many top college baseball players spent their summers getting paid to play for semiprofessional teams, often using pseudonyms to protect amateur standing. Evidently no one told star student-athlete and all-American football player Jim Thorpe of the Carlisle School for Indians in Pennsylvania about this widespread ploy. It demonstrated a key feature of American sportsmanship—namely, that it was all right to break laws so long as one abided by customs. Hence amateurism remained vague and uneven in its definition and enforcement. Thorpe's naivete and unfamiliarity with the practices meant he played semiprofessional games using his real name. Later, such actions would force Thorpe to forfeit the Olympic gold medals he won in the 1912 Stockholm games on the grounds that he had violated Olympic requirements for amateur standing. Ironically, there was no congruence or conformity of collegiate regulations for eligibility. Thorpe, of course, was exceptional in his achievements in college football, baseball, and track and field. Tragically, he was neglected and exploited in his extended athletic endeavors.

The norm by 1890 was that American farms, small towns, boroughs, and cities were fertile sources of enthusiastic young baseball players. This spilled over to the college teams in which eager students sought a place on the college "nine," without athletic scholarships or other special privileges. In contrast to "King Football," college baseball was pragmatic and resilient—and a genuine student sport. The student-run character of college baseball remained strong well into the 1890s. Few if any teams had a hired coach until the 1890s. By 1900, however, this practice would change. Expenses for equipment and facilities were minimal. Players provided their own fielder's gloves, and uniforms were inexpensive flannels. Bats and balls were the major expense. Every neighborhood or community had its accessible baseball diamond and playing field.

College baseball game crowds were not large, seldom surpassing two thousand spectators. The side benefit of that relatively small scale was that it also meant that little to no capital investment in an expensive stadium was required. It was this low-key style that wove baseball into the fabric of American campus life in the late nineteenth century. The institutionalization of college baseball was reinforced when it became a welcomed, accepted part of the annual elaborate commencement week events held in June or early July. Degree recipients and their families, as well as alumni gathering for class reunions, had an opportunity to enjoy a baseball game. Long before college football hosted its October homecoming weekends, college baseball was a fixture at "Class Day," with a big game taking place the day before graduation exercises. By 1900, college baseball was here to stay.

Soccer, Rugby, and "American" Football

While baseball experienced a gradual growth in popularity, another collegiate sport had a meteoric rise in interest across the nation. Football was not new to American colleges. Even though the annual freshman-sophomore battles to inaugurate the fall semester had been banned at places like Harvard and Yale, football games had remained popular as an informally organized sport on campus during the 1850s and 1860s.

Soccer-style football entered the intercollegiate sporting ranks on November 6, 1869, with Rutgers challenging Princeton to a game in New Brunswick, New Jersey. Princeton's baseball club captain and future New Jersey Supreme Court Justice William Gummere agreed to the challenge. The day of the game,

Gummere and Rutgers captain William Leggett (future Dutch Reformed cler-gyman) agreed upon the rules for the game that afternoon. Generally follow-ing association soccer rules with a few differing regulations between the two, Princeton agreed to follow the host's preferences in New Brunswick. Players could kick or hit a ball between two goals posts on a field measuring 360 feet long by 225 feet wide. The players (twenty-five to a side) could catch the ball, but they could not throw or run with it. Players generally advanced the ball by dropping and kicking it. The game continued until a team scored six points, which Rutgers accomplished first, winning 6–4.[30]

The following week, the Rutgers team made the twenty-mile trek to Prince-ton, where the home team once again prevailed. In 1870, Princeton defeated Rutgers, while Rutgers earned a victory over Columbia in the only other inter-collegiate game that fall. Nothing like a football season existed. But the growth of football clubs on college campuses revealed the popularity of the game among college students and the latent enthusiasm that would become evident in the decades to follow.

As the number of games grew slowly, the players struggled with differing rules on each campus. To remedy the situation, students arranged a meeting on October 19, 1873, to establish uniform rules for the game. Harvard chose not to attend because its football rules deviated further from those governing the other institutions, and the young men from Cambridge preferred their version of the game. As they stated, "We consider the game here to admit much more science." Despite Harvard's absence, Princeton, Rutgers, and Yale created the Intercollegiate Football Association (IFA) and devised rules for the association games that more closely resembled soccer's guidelines.[31]

Without a league in which to participate, Harvard agreed to play two games with McGill University of Montreal. The McGill students traveled to Cambridge in May and played two games on the 14th and 15th—the first with Harvard's "Boston" rules and the second with the rugby-style rules that were used at the Canadian institution. Harvard won the first game and then tied McGill in the rugby-style match. Most importantly, the Harvard students so enjoyed McGill's game that they adopted it for themselves as well. In an ironic historical detail, the "American" game of football so popular in the United States had been in-troduced by a Canadian team. This decision provided a monumental shift in what modern Americans would continue to call football. As one Harvard stu-dent noted, "The rugby game is in much better favor than the somewhat sleepy game played by our men."[32]

Convinced of rugby football's superiority, Harvard searched for a college in the United States to agree to play a game of rugby-style football. Yale initially refused, so Harvard agreed to play a game against neighboring Tufts College in May 1875. Yale finally conceded and played a game in New Haven on November 13, 1875. A crowd of two thousand spectators paid fifty cents each to watch the matchup. Harvard won, and the game proved to be more popular than soccer-style football. In 1876, students from the "Big Three" (Harvard, Princeton, and Yale) along with Columbia met in Springfield, Massachusetts, to set rules for the new game. The association also created a Thanksgiving Day game to be held for the two best teams in the association, beginning what would become an American holiday tradition. Approximately one-third of the IFA's original rules are still used in modern football. Although not recognized by the NCAA, the true origin of American college football began with Harvard's contest against a Canadian team in 1874, and the first matches between US colleges occurred in 1875.[33]

Football evolved during the next few decades, slowly beginning to resemble the twenty-first-century version of the game. Nobody was more influential in early rules changes than Yale's Walter Camp. The "father of American football," Camp played at Yale for six years beginning in 1876. This was allowed at the time since he enrolled in medical school after finishing his bachelor's degree. As a player at Yale, Camp lost only one game. More important for the sport, Camp joined the Intercollegiate Football Association's Rules Committee in 1878 and dominated that group for decades. Many of Camp's rules improved the game, while others led to violence. With each change in rules, however, Camp kept his Yale Bulldogs at the forefront of the game. Since he had a full-time job, he was not considered a professional coach. Camp's wife Alice Graham Sumner essentially served as his assistant coach for three decades. When Camp missed practice due to work, Alice watched and provided him with detailed reports, which Camp would then discuss with the team. If Camp was indeed the father of college football, Alice Graham Summer was certainly the sport's mother.[34]

In 1880, Camp successfully convinced the committee to do away with the rugby "scrummage." When a ball carrier was downed or placed the ball to the ground, the team now retained possession of the ball and started a new play on the scrimmage. Coach Alonzo Stagg praised this reform, claiming the scrummage was "weird and unscientific." In a scrummage, players from both teams huddled around the ball and fought to kick it out to a teammate. The new line of scrimmage helped create an offensive and defensive side of the ball. It also led to new problems. A team could literally retain possession of the ball for an entire half without making progress toward a score. Princeton did just that in two championship games in 1880 and 1881.[35]

Camp's solution to the problem he helped create was the idea of "downs." A Canadian innovation to the game, teams were given three tries to move the ball five yards. Failure to gain the distance gave the ball to the opponents. The five-yard rule required the field to be marked off by yards, creating a "gridiron" for football games. These innovations, along with the adoption of Camp's rule to allow tackles below the waist, led to the development of mass momentum plays. The flying wedge became the most infamous mass momentum play, during which a team would form a wedge shape (much like the one migrating geese make) and protect the ball carrier by pinpointing a weak link in the defensive line. Harvard first used the play against Yale, and the *New York Times* reported, "What a grand play! A half ton of bone and muscle coming into collision with a man weighing 160 to 170 pounds."[36]

This and other mass momentum plays increased the violence of the game and were eventually banned. While some practices were outlawed, other elements of the game were ignored and then approved. For example, the practice of "interference" (what we know today as blocking) was considered ungentlemanly conduct in England and in early American football. When the American teams began playing rugby-style football, they started engaging in interference, and the referees generally ignored it. In the late 1880s, the rules committee then officially allowed blocking, adding an integral part of the American game. It also highlighted the difference between aristocratic England and egalitarian America. In England, the elite had already won in the "game of life," and sport remained an important part of recreation. In America, sport became a way to prove one's superiority, and in a nation of immigrants seeking a better life, sports—football in particular—became a cultural phenomenon where superiority was determined. Winning mattered more than anything else.[37]

Outside Influences and Expansion of the Game

In addition to creating a rules committee, in 1876 the Intercollegiate Football Association established a Thanksgiving Day football game to determine the champion of the IC4A. The Thanksgiving football game became the primary championship for intercollegiate athletics. The small group of schools in the league ensured that only the most elite universities in the Northeast would win the championship. Yale prevailed over Princeton in the first Thanksgiving game, which was held in Hoboken, New Jersey, without much fanfare. When the IFA moved the game to the New York City's Polo Grounds, however, it became a much larger social event during the 1880s and 1890s. With the game played on a holiday, students, alumni, New York's social elite, and average fans were able to converge on the scene.

Spectators witnessed the evolution of the game as rule changes made their way onto the gridiron. Crowds exceeding twenty thousand became commonplace during the 1880s. After years without experiencing success, Harvard withdrew from the association, but unlike the annual regatta, Yale was developing into a football powerhouse, and the popularity of football continued its momentum. By the 1890s, the holiday crowds regularly exceeded thirty thousand fans, and for some games even forty thousand spectators attended. Parades were introduced before the games, and expensive box seats were reserved for the social elite. The biggest games had become what critics termed a public "spectacle."

In a matter of a decade, the game had transitioned from a soccer-style game into the beginnings of modern American football. The student-led IFA took the annual football championship to New York City, and the game expanded its reach beyond campus into popular culture. In 1891, *Harper's Weekly* offered the following summary:

> It used to be that Thanksgiving Day in New York was, like the day all over the Eastern part of the country, a holiday which centred around a dinner. . . . A great and powerful and fascinating rival has come to take the place of the Thanksgiving day dinner . . . the Thanksgiving Day Game. And now everybody goes out to see Princeton and Yale decide the football championship, and instead of boring each other around a dinner table, grow hoarse and exhausted in shouting for their favorite son or the college of their son. . . . You must all agree that the fresh air and the excitement and the wonderful movement of the great crowd and color of the whole scene are better even than turkey and pumpkin pie.[38]

This transformation of Thanksgiving in New York developed from a combination of factors during the late eighteenth century. As the city's socialites desired to be seen, many attended the championship games. The popularity of the game brought out the press, but over time it became apparent that the press played a much larger role in bringing the game to the people of the city. During the 1870s, newspapers began to play an integral role in the growth of college football's popularity. Initially, the reporting of football game results remained relatively minimal, but by the end of the century, newspapers revolutionized football reporting and helped promote the game in the process.

The revolution began in 1883 when Joseph Pulitzer acquired the *New York World*. Pulitzer continued perfecting the paper industry's move toward generating news rather than simply reporting it. He created a separate sports division with its own editor. Big games, including the Thanksgiving Day championship, began receiving front-page attention. Pulitzer employed the use of game illustrations along with the reporter's narrative. Coverage soon expanded to the second and third pages as well. The innovations at the *New York World* were not designed to increase the popularity of college football. Rather, Pulitzer wanted to increase circulation of the paper he owned. He managed to do both. College football played an important role in newspaper reporting. When Pulitzer purchased the *New York World*, the paper's circulation hovered around fifteen thousand. By 1892, it boasted a more than two million readers. With Saturday football games, the lager Sunday readership was introduced to college sports, and its popularity continued to grow.[39]

When William Randolph Hearst purchased the *New York Journal* in 1895, he largely imitated Pulitzer's business model, including attempts to entertain readers along with reporting the news. This, along with the development of print syndication, rapidly increased the popularity of college football not only in the Northeast but also across the nation. As college football scholar Michael Oriard noted, the expansion of football's popularity paralleled the growth in press coverage. He surmised that newspaper coverage "created college football to an even greater degree, transforming an extracurricular activity into a national spectacle."[40]

Football remained a northeastern intercollegiate sport during most of the 1870s, but it began spreading slowly across the country in the 1880s before booming in the last decade of the nineteenth century. The University of Michigan led the way in the Midwest, defeating Racine College of Wisconsin at a game in Chicago on May 30, 1879. Michigan had rejected Racine's challenge to play in the fall but agreed to a game in the spring. As the Michigan student newspaper *The Chronicle* noted, "One very important point must not be overlooked. It is essential that we win the first game," adding, "Defeat would put an end to all our fond expectations, while success alone can make them possible."[41]

In fall 1881, Michigan became the first midwestern team to play the Big Three. During a five-day span, Michigan lost to Harvard, Princeton, and Yale, but they did prove that competitive football had spread beyond the Northeast. As Michigan waited for larger universities in their region to form teams, they generally played club teams from midwestern cities and Canada. While a few intercollegiate games between schools had occurred across the country, most football activity remained intramural until the late 1880s and early 1890s. By the late nineteenth century, intercollegiate football had spread to every region of the country.

While the press popularized the sport, the key to fielding a successful football team usually involved hiring a northeastern college graduate with football experience. As historian Winston Solberg noted, by 1890 the dominant Yale football teams had produced forty-five young men to coach teams across the country. Thirty-five additional alumni from Princeton and twenty-four from Harvard also accepted coaching positions across the country. While critics were condemning professional coaches, they remained in high demand because winning remained a chief priority among students, alumni, local boosters, and many college administrators.[42]

Further evidence that football had rapidly become more than a simple extracurricular activity controlled by students involved two nascent and well-endowed institutions, both with ambitious young presidents. Shortly after President David Starr Jordan spoke at the opening ceremony of Stanford University in Palo Alto, California, students from the University of California challenged Stanford's new matriculates to a game on Thanksgiving Day. Stanford's captain John Whittemore knew his team was unprepared, so he denied the initial invitation but challenged Berkeley to a spring game. Played in front of more than six thousand fans (a crowd larger than had attended the opening ceremony of the institution), Stanford's student manager, future US president Herbert Hoover, and his counterpart at Berkeley counted the thirty thousand dollars from ticket sales. The upstart Stanford team won the game. The victory brought celebrations, press coverage, and immediate attention. As historian Brian Ingrassia noted, the immediate impact of the football game "was perhaps even bigger" than the institution's inauguration the previous fall. In preparation for a rematch, Whittemore wrote Yale's Walter Camp, requesting a suggestion for a coach. Camp responded that he would coach the team after Yale completed its season. California countered with a common practice—hiring one of Camp's former players to coach its team.[43]

The father of American football coached Stanford for three seasons, winning twelve games and losing only three. One of Camp's losses came at the hands of a coach from a new university being subsidized by John D. Rockefeller. The University of Chicago opened its doors in 1892, with its newly appointed prodigy president William Rainey Harper. Dean Albion Small, who served as close advisor to university president William Rainey Harper, was effective in persuading the president and the board of trustees to be energetic in deliberate efforts to recruit students and to gain public support. Dean Small was on the Pacific Coast to recruit students and took time to send a firm message to President Harper: "We must obey the first and last law of advertising—Keep ever lastingly at it."[44]

Dean Small's lessons were not lost on President William Rainey Harper. Although he was legendary as a precocious scholar who spoke numerous ancient languages, graduated from college at age 16, and completed his PhD at Yale by 21, Harper was most remarkable as an enterprising president. He took the pulse of Chicago as a brash, energetic city—and fused the new University of Chicago with this metropolitan momentum. The grand Gothic Revival campus, which opened in 1892, coincided in time and space with Chicago's hosting the Columbian Exposition and World's Fair. Indeed, the Great White City of the exposition was adjacent to the Great Gray City of the university's heroic campus.[45] To this day, the 1892 World's Fair boasts one of the largest attendance records in the United States. While there, hundreds of thousands of visitors also took time to visit—and marvel at—the University of Chicago.

President Harper realized early on in his academic administration that college sports provided an ideal forum for promoting his university. He hired a young Yale alumnus, Amos Alonzo Stagg, who had been an all-American football player on the national championship Yale teams. Harper wanted Stagg to coach teams that "we can send around country and knock out all the colleges." He added, "we will give them a palace car and a vacation too."[46] The happy, successful result was that the University of Chicago enjoyed decades of athletic success and university publicity. Even though Harper was among the most charismatic and successful of university presidents nationwide, his chosen football coach was so successful in both winning and promoting that the University of Chicago eventually came to be called "Stagg's University."[47]

Today, the University of Chicago does not bring to mind powerful football programs. Often overlooked is that it was a charter member of the Big Ten and for many years won the title of conference champion. Most important for the character of college sports nationwide, Amos Alonzo Stagg was the coach who created the structural prototype of the intercollegiate athletics program. Eventually Stagg was featured on the cover of *Time* magazine. The Amos Alonzo Stagg Society honors outstanding academic and athletic achievement—an ironic award given that Stagg as coach at the University of Chicago stretched admissions requirements and semester grade transcripts to make certain that star players were academically eligible to play on Saturday afternoon.

In addition to serving for forty years as head football coach at the University of Chicago, Stagg held an appointment as a tenured professor and negotiated with the president to serve simultaneously as athletics director. Furthermore, his budget proposals for the athletics department were exempted from the typical process of deliberations among academic deans and department chairs. Stagg was allowed to present his budget directly to the board of trustees. This was especially fortuitous because Chicago meatpacking czars such as Henry Swift along with department store moguls such as Marshall Fields liked Stagg and loved University of Chicago football.

One result of this support was the construction of a football stadium on campus that seated about thirty-five thousand. Its construction was architecturally magnificent, with castle towers and stonework that blended perfectly with the Gothic Revival style of the university's residential quadrangles and ornate libraries and laboratories. And its funding and construction were only possible because of the generous donations of local industrialists and commercial entrepreneurs who were persuaded to be part of this university sports enterprise and large-scale philanthropy that had no precedent in American life. No one was more pleased than President Harper, who cultivated the city's mercantile princes—such as Marshall Field and Cyrus McCormick—to be his guests in special box seats to watch the championship Chicago Maroons defeats such conference opponents as Indiana, Iowa, Michigan, Ohio State, and crosstown rival Northwestern. Philanthropy and football truly were joined at the hip, as the University of Chicago stadium became known as Marshall Field, in honor of this donor and guest and civic leader.

The collegiate football frenzy traveled south as well. Just how far behind the region remained in football became apparent when Princeton defeated Virginia 115–0 in 1890. Despite the drubbing, the sport's popularity in Virginia and across the South grew in the ensuing years. Vanderbilt first played Sewanee in 1891, starting a rivalry that lasted decades. The University of Georgia and Georgia Technological Institute began their intercollegiate football programs in 1892 with games against Mercer University in Macon, Georgia. The Deep South's "oldest rivalry" began that same year with a contest between Alabama Polytechnic Institute (Auburn) and Georgia. Serious about improving its football fortunes, Auburn hired John Heisman, who had played football at both Brown and the University of Pennsylvania, as a trainer. In turn, the University of Georgia hired Glenn "Pop" Warner, who coached the team in Athens for two seasons. The University of Alabama and Louisiana State University both began intercollegiate football in 1893. Baseball remained the most popular sport in the South during the early 1890s. But football rapidly grew in popularity during an era when the "lost cause" of the Civil War weighed heavily on the psyche of the white South.[48]

Football Problems and Attempts at Control

As football spread across the country, so did athletic problems. Most of the abuses identified by critics of intercollegiate athletics included athletes missing class, encroaching professionalism and commercialism, and player eligibility. All of these issues had been identified in baseball and crew as well as football, but the gridiron also produced one important and distasteful addition: violence. Finding solutions to these problems led to an important transition in college sports: students lost control of the intercollegiate games they helped create as faculty moved in to regulate athletic affairs.

Problems existed years before the massive expansion of football in the 1890s, and the leading institutions in the East had attempted to solve them, but they failed to do so. Two challenges plagued virtually all early competitive intercollegiate sports: the rapid erosion (if it had ever truly existed in America) of pure amateurism in athletics and player eligibility. Such concerns had been raised even before the first intercollegiate football game, but the popularity of football exacerbated those tensions. Princeton led efforts at faculty control by creating a faculty athletic committee in 1881. Harvard followed the next year, and before long most successful programs formed some sort of faculty committee to provide guidance or oversight of student athletics. Even so, numerous examples of students failing to tend to their studies while focusing on athletics continued to plague some universities. Eventually some called for an interinstitutional agency to assist with the regulation of college sports.[49]

The first instance of attempted intercollegiate cooperation occurred when Harvard called for a meeting of colleges and universities in New York City after the 1883 football season. Eight institutions attended the meeting, although Yale left before the committee reported its resolutions. In short, the committee recommended that schools not employ professional coaches, prohibit games with sports clubs, limit eligibility to four years, and create faculty committees to regulate college sports. The resolutions were sent to more than twenty institutions, but only Harvard and Princeton voted in favor of the proposal. Regardless of platitudes issued in public, many faculty and administrators revealed that they desired "home rule," and the prospects of beating a powerhouse offered more allure than an intercollegiate contest of pure amateurism without regard for winning or losing.[50]

As soccer evolved into rugby and then gridiron football, violence became a serious problem. The new football rules ushered in by Camp led to mass momentum plays that often led to serious injury. Broken bones, chipped teeth, and head injuries became more common. Unfortunately, intentional brutality or unsportsmanlike play warranted two warnings before an official could eject a player from the game. As Princeton's student newspaper noted after a loss to Yale in 1882, "The methods of our sister college [involved] as many fouls as possible without being warned three times. In other words, Yale would have us understand that it is fair to do what is prohibited by the rules, if by any means, the referee can be deceived and the play escape the penalty of a foul. . . . Here then is a Yaleism—an underhanded and constant evasion of the rules." Substantive change to remedy the violence of the game would not come for more than twenty years.[51]

During the 1880s, player eligibility became a bigger problem as schools believed they had lost contests to ineligible competitors on the opposing team. With no specific rules guiding eligibility, graduate students and those in professional schools often played. Teams charged each other with playing ineligible students. In protest, Harvard once again resigned from the Intercollegiate Football Association. Then, Harvard football player H. O. Stickney produced a letter from Princeton's football captain, who attempting to recruit Stickney told him, "I can get your board, tuition, etc. free. The athletic men at Princeton get by all odds the best treatment in any of the colleges." Stickney himself had inquired about playing at Yale, and Yale's Pat Corbin wrote Camp to find out what they could offer the athlete. Apparently, the star player was pleased with his current financial arrangement as he decided to stay in Cambridge. These deals, all supposedly illegal, came from the institutions. It was even harder to regulate the avid alumni boosters' offerings to a promising young athlete. Once again, the Big Three could not come to a consensus on ruling against players who had received scholarships for their athletic services.[52]

Nascent football programs across the country soon experienced similar problems. University of Oregon football players reported playing against the same opponent who appeared on three separate teams. The legendary Fielding Yost, when coaching at Kansas, played a nonstudent to help beat the University of Missouri. Years earlier, Yost had played for Lafayette in their historic win against Penn, even though he was a student at West Virginia before and after that game. Georgia Tech recruited Captain Leonard Wood, a 33-year-old army surgeon who would later serve as colonel of Teddy Roosevelt's Rough Riders, to help beat Georgia in 1893. Such practices were common enough to elicit their own terminology. "Tramp" athletes were those who traveled from team to team. "Ringers," in contrast, were players who were not students at any institution.[53]

Into the 1890s, attempts at curbing such practices had been futile. But the events of 1894 were serious enough to have faculty take their first successful steps toward controlling college sports. In that year, the rivalry between Harvard and Yale helped spur the process. Twenty-five thousand fans ascended on Springfield, Massachusetts, for the game. The city brought in additional police to monitor the crowd, but the violence occurred on the field. The *New York Times* reported, "An ordinary rebellion in the South American or Central American States is as child's play compared with the destructiveness of a day's game." The author added, "Prize fighting seems a tame and perfectly harmless game in comparison with the sort of thing that people saw on the field here today." One Yale player who suffered a concussion was rumored to have died after the game, but that proved false. Harvard's players suffered a broken leg, a broken collar bone, and a broken nose. The "foul and ugly play . . . disgusted the army of spectators to-day."[54] Harvard president Charles Eliot became one of the fiercest critics, arguing, "The game of football grows worse and worse as regards foul and violent play, and the number and gravity of injuries the players suffer."[55]

That same season, the University of Michigan football team captain decided to utilize the services of nonstudents, as seven members of the starting lineup were not enrolled at the institution. According to the *Michigan Alumnus*, the incident "aroused faculty to the necessity of participation in the management of the athletes." The university's athletic board forced the resignation of the captain and "published that fact at once" in an attempt to deflect any criticism. The alumni report noted, however, that "newspaper notoriety of the event was harmful to the good name" of Michigan. The institution immediately created the new Board of Control for the Regulation of Athletics, which dealt with issues like player eligibility. But the financing of athletics remained with the athletics association that had been created three years earlier.[56]

Cognizant of Michigan's scandal and other problems plaguing football in the Midwest, regional presidents began considering reform. Henry Rogers, president of Northwestern, sent a letter to some fellow executives to discuss opinions on the abolition of football. While those discussions came to naught, Purdue president James Smart successfully organized a meeting in

January 1895 to discuss regulating athletics, football in particular. The presidents took their plans back to faculty, who then organized the Intercollegiate Conference of Faculty Representatives. Composed of Chicago, Illinois, Michigan, Minnesota, Northwestern, Purdue, and Wisconsin, the conference was soon called the Western Conference and eventually the Big Ten. The organization focused on rooting out professionalism and ensuring the integrity of the eligibility of players.[57]

While the Big Ten has often been cited as the original regional conference regulated by faculty, the South actually beat the Midwest to the punch. At the end of the 1894 football season, Vanderbilt's dean of the medical school, Dr. William Dudley, called for a meeting of southern universities in Atlanta. Held on December 22, 1894, the meeting yielded a faculty organization that was chartered for "the development and purification of athletics."[58] The Southern Intercollegiate Athletic Association was initially more concerned with eligibility in baseball, as tramp athletes and ringers were finding their way onto teams. Football, however, soon received primary attention from conference officials. Until the advent of conferences, students had been the creators and organizers of intercollegiate sport.

Although the development of what would evolve into "power" conferences began years later, during their formative years, many conferences remained rather fluid. Communication remained poor by modern standards, and general regulations that had been approved were regularly ignored by member institutions. During the next decades, more universities created regional associations, but university membership in individual conference often changed. Institutional home rule, as championed by Yale, remained a fixture well into the twentieth century.

One of the key roles of the conferences, although rarely discussed, involved expansion of the organization of college athletics. Schedules became more routine, and fans knew when their teams were playing. Conferences also crowned "champions." In short, an important early legacy of intercollegiate conferences proved to be their promotion of athletics, all the while claiming to promote amateurism—sport played by the students for their own enjoyment. Intercollegiate conferences did not possess the same influence wielded by newspapers. They did provide an apparatus for continued growth, however. By the middle of the twentieth century, a conference's promotional role was largely accepted by the public, even if faculty members remained opposed.

After the creation of a conference designed to promote the "purification" of the game, events in the South and elsewhere revealed both the brutality and popularity of college football. In October of 1897, Georgia hosted Virginia in Athens. With Governor William Atkinson in attendance, Richard "Von" Gammon suffered a head injury trying to make a tackle. The young athlete from a prominent family in Rome, Georgia, died the next day at Grady Hospital in Atlanta. The press along with many evangelical ministers called for football's abolition. One of the few defenders of football immediately following the tragedy, University of Georgia chemist Charles Herty called for reform rather than abolition. In spite of this recommendation, the Georgia Legislature overwhelmingly passed legislation to ban the game. Papers predicted the governor would sign the bill, as the *Atlanta Journal* proclaimed, "Football will never become a great American game."[59]

Then, Gammon's mother Rosalind wrote a letter to her state representative. She pleaded, "It would be the greatest favor to the family of Von Gammon if your influence could prevent his death from being used as an argument detrimental to the athletic cause and its advancement at the university." After noting Professor Herty's editorial, she stated, "Grant me the right to request that my boy's death should not be used to defeat the most cherished object of his life." Published in the *Atlanta Constitution*, her letter gave the governor support in his decision to veto the bill, leading Rosalind to be called the "woman who saved football" in Georgia and beyond.[60]

In the wake of that season, Brown University professor Wilfred Munro held a conference to discuss reform of intercollegiate athletics. Representatives from all future Ivy League schools, save Yale, attended the conference. Yale's unparalleled success in intercollegiate athletics made Walter Camp and university president Arthur Hadley hesitant to support change in athletic governance. Despite Yale's absence, the Brown Conference submitted a report regarding an overemphasis on college athletics and issues with student-run sports that harmed the academic mission of universities. The report recommended twenty policies to bolster academic standards and curb sports' overemphasis, professionalism, commercialism, and playing of ineligible players. In short, the report recommended a "return" to amateur athletics under faculty oversight. Not a single institution adopted the reforms, and college sports continued unabated.[61]

Southern football became one of the few things that prospered in the nineteenth century. One institution's success revealed the allure of athletic success for university presidents, alumni, and students. Sewanee: The University of the South, an Episcopalian school on the Cumberland Plateau in Tennessee, made history and brought acclaim to the institution in 1899. In order to fund the football team's season, team manager Luke Lea scheduled a trip of more than two thousand miles to play five football games in six days. The gate receipts shared by these larger institutions would help subsidize the remainder of Sewanee's season. The Iron Men of Sewanee played Louisiana State, Texas A&M, Tulane, the University of Mississippi, and the University of Texas. Not only did they win every game, but they also held their opponents scoreless. The team returned to Tennessee and finished out the season with seven more games. John Heisman's Auburn squad was the only team to score against Sewanee the entire season as they finished 12–0. The university's vice chancellor (president) Benjamin Lawton Wiggins was one of the team's biggest promoters. As historian Woody Register noted, this accomplishment "formed part of the university's heritage."[62]

Higher Education's Relationship with Intercollegiate Athletics

Sewanee's fabled football season provided a fitting bookend to college sports in the nineteenth century. Their success, along with the growth in other sports, signified an important development in American higher education: less than fifty years after the first intercollegiate contest, college sports had spread from the most elite universities in the country to some of the most rural outposts across the land. Some criticized the attention provided to sports, and others—primarily faculty—lamented growing scandals. Alumni, students, most university presidents, and many local fans did not share the professoriate's concerns outside of brutal and violent play. Regardless, athletics had assumed an important place in the life of American higher education. And like Sewanee, victorious teams had become part of universities' heritage and an easily identified point of institutional pride and promotion.

To understand exactly how and why this happened, one must examine the transformation taking place at the institutions that fielded the most successful athletic teams. The history of college sports has been well documented, and the same is true for the history of American higher education. What scholars have paid less attention to is the historic interplay between the two as both experienced eras of unprecedented change.

American colleges founded during the Colonial Era and into the nineteenth century were, in many ways, patterned partially and superficially after some elements associated with Oxford and Cambridge. Most were religious, and professors taught the liberal arts to instill wisdom and theology to guard the soul. A set of courses dominated the curriculum, and professors and presidents enforced strict behavioral codes of conduct. These standards developed out of the in loco parentis model designed to guard students' well-being in and outside of class. In the early years, college rules often prohibited engaging in competitive sports, presumably for the welfare of students. The older and more prestigious institutions generally educated sons of the wealthiest families. Newer colleges tended to be much smaller and often served young men from middle-class (and sometimes lower-class) families. America's future physicians, attorneys, and clergy received an education to prepare them as "gentlemen." Although most schools shared a similar curriculum, colleges honored their own provincial customs and cultures. Above all, governance of American colleges remained intensely local.

As the nineteenth century progressed, more professional and practical courses began entering the curriculum at select colleges. *The Yale Report of 1828* provided a staunch defense against the threat of a modernized collegiate curriculum. Over time, however, American popular opinion favored a more useful curriculum that would prepare students for professional careers. After all, the new nation boasted few aristocrats but possessed many eager citizens looking to improve their lot in life. Agriculture science and mechanical arts received a huge boost with the passage of the Morrill Land Grant Act of 1862, which provided federal funds for colleges offering degrees in agriculture and engineering.

As the curriculum evolved and incorporated new subjects, the leading (i.e., wealthy) American colleges began emulating German universities and their emphasis on research. Most institutions in the United States incorporated these ideals by adding scientific schools, professional programs, and graduate schools to already existing undergraduate colleges—making themselves modern universities. A few new schools such as Clark, Johns Hopkins, and the University of Chicago were founded with a research model as a part of their foundational mission. Institutions like Harvard, Princeton, and Yale established a more common pattern by turning their attention from religious training and moral discipline of young men to a new discipline: an academic field of study.

In short, the evolution of the American college into the American university had begun. Although few institutions boasted the resources and large student bodies necessary to succeed in the university endeavor, the model of the modern university became a standard to emulate at wealthy private schools as well as state "flagship" and agricultural and mechanical schools. When the landscape of American higher education consisted of colleges, undergraduates first played games on campus against classmates. Students then created intercollegiate contests and their own rules committees. But the growth of intercollegiate sport occurred as many of these same institutions evolved into a very different type of higher education enterprise.

How were universities different than the colleges that preceded them? Although individual universities possessed a diverse set of characteristics, historians of education have identified many common themes. The developments mentioned below, which have been highlighted in the introduction, were all in place before the beginning of the twentieth century. Each of these traits, either expressly or tacitly, played a role in creating an environment ripe for the growth of big-time college athletics.

1. *A New Curriculum*

    The complexity of the modern university, along with the diversity of institutions that did develop, made defining a university more difficult, but the schools did share certain characteristics, especially the desire for growth. They reformed the curriculum to include new majors in agriculture, engineering, social work, education, business, and public relations, to name a few. Scientific study, which had been considered a curriculum for second-class students at the nation's oldest and most prestigious institutions, suddenly gained more prominence. Research, graduate programs, and specialized training were becoming hallmarks of the new university. While college sports did not offer a degree program, physical education had become a course of study as well.

2. *New Executive Leaders*

    The university transformation in higher education was ushered in by (and required) a new type of campus leader. Innovative university presidents created a new administrative model far different than their predecessors. "Old-time" presidents had focused effort and energy on student conduct, classroom teaching, and preservation of the traditional curriculum. Modern presidents turned their attention toward recruitment, fundraising, and competitive advantage among rivals. Nobody exemplified Thorstein Veblen's "captains of erudition" moniker more than William Rainey Harper at the University of Chicago. Harper's understanding of the ways in which football could bring popularity and prestige to the new University of Chicago provided a model for other eager leaders across the country. For these presidents, success in academics and success on the football field all fell under the umbrella of the modern university. Both activities had different stakeholders, and keeping such disparate interest groups enthusiastic about the institution provided evidence of successful leadership.[63]

3. *A New Model of Undergraduate Culture*

College sports had been the creation of undergraduate students, just like Greek organizations, student clubs, and myriad other extracurricular activities. Even when athletic events remained intramural, the enthusiasm (and violence) among students led to various levels of administrative regulation. The advent of intercollegiate sport, however, rapidly developed a passionate following from individuals beyond the boundaries of campus. The immediate overemphasis and time spent away from the classroom led to further attempts at regulation by faculty and presidents. Nevertheless, in terms of the world students had made for themselves in the modern university, athletics remained an important and exalted part of the undergraduate campus culture.

As an aspiring middle class moved through the collegiate ranks, the social status afforded to athletes may have been a frustration to many faculty (and some students). Yet most undergraduates still rewarded their peers with popularity and privilege based on their athletic exploits. Just as fewer students were engaged in studying for a traditional bachelor of arts in favor of professional subjects, many athletes viewed athletics as a way to climb the social ladder.[64]

Furthermore, as big-time athletics expanded during the decades spanning the second half of the nineteenth century, it also meant that undergraduates in growing numbers became alums of their alma mater. If interest in university athletics was any indicator, it appeared that the slogan "Don't let your studies interfere with your education" held sway beyond the college years as well. This connection between past and current students further solidified athletics as part of the undergraduate culture.[65]

4. *A Changing Role for Faculty*

With the growth of students and majors at universities across the country, the very definition of "discipline" shifted. Some faculty at small denominational colleges still focused on discipline as the formation of good habits. For professors at universities, however, the term emphasized specialization in one's own field of study. This shift in emphasis from student conduct to the development of academic specialization was a natural transition for faculty at universities who focused on research, the generation of new knowledge, and graduate-level teaching.

Becoming a specialist or leading scholar in one's field also led to greater independence and academic freedom for professors. Yet during this era, faculty members' failed attempts to influence intercollegiate athletics provided one of the best examples that academic freedom in one's discipline also meant a limited voice in other university affairs.[66]

5. *The Structure of the Modern University*

The structure of the modern university, when compared to traditional liberal arts colleges, could be described in one word: big. The growth of majors, professional schools, new courses of study, and rapidly growing student populations required a new organizational structure. Universities developed silos and worked on specialized subjects or initiatives rather than working as an integrated whole. As mentioned previously, Laurence Veysey observed that modern universities not only survived but also "throve" with this new division of labor. It allowed various departments, programs, and colleges to grow in isolation. In fact, isolation spurred growth rather than hindered it. Within this structure, critics from one branch of a university may have exercised their freedom to criticize another department (such as athletics), but this often resulted in little change as universities incorporated critics into its new structure.[67]

The convergence of this new professionalized university, along with an emphasis on specialization and growth, became part of the university bureaucracy. In short, college sports grew with the assistance of the modern university structure not in spite of it. While administrators, faculty, and the curriculum specialized and professionalized in nearly every sense of the word, somehow students and their athletics programs were supposed to remain amateur. University faculty desired to be governed by the new spirit of higher education, focused on freedom from interference of outside influence. Sports, however, were to be governed by collegiate ideals that had been adopted from the British aristocracy and molded by the religious ethos of an earlier era. As the Brown Conference of 1898 surmised, "We should not seek perfection in our games, but rather, good sport."[68] While universities moved away from the "gentleman's C" in the classroom in favor of scientific research by professionals, faculty wanted to ensure amateurism remained on the ballfield. In short, reformers of college sports were to identify with the collegiate past while the rest of the university apparatus was to move into the modern era. This grand irony escaped most, making efforts at change exceedingly frustrating.

This faculty view was not monolithic. Many of the early coaches across the country were alumni of elite northeastern institutions who had accepted faculty positions at university across the country. Historian Ronald Smith noted that renowned Harvard philosopher George Santayana argued that athletics possessed, like other art forms, "the value of talent, the beauty and dignity of positive achievements depend on the height reached, and not on the number who reach it."[69] Santayana further argued that college sports were not "Children's games." Instead, "young men, carefully trained and disciplined, contend with one another in feats of strength, skill, and courage. Spectators are indispensable, since without them the victory, which should be the only reward, would lose half its power."[70] The philosopher also utilized the analogy between war and sporting contests. Sport mirrored the "dire struggle" of armed conflict, but he praised athletics because, unlike combat, victory served not to subordinate people or usher in a new regime. Rather, in sport there was "nothing to conquer or defend except the honor of success."[71]

Santayana's "Philosophy on the Bleachers" touched on two important themes popular during the rise of college athletics and into the twentieth century. First, historians have documented the many quotes by professors, presidents, and coaches alluding to the masculine attributes of American culture in the late nineteenth century as a reason for the expansion of football. Such defenses of football continued into the early twentieth century during Teddy Roosevelt's presidency and his emphasis on the "strenuous life" and "muscular Christianity." While these themes are not to be downplayed, such quotes often came in defense of football while it was under attack for its violence. When Walter Camp cited a professor who worried about effeminate "dudes" from urban areas enrolling in college and banning football, Harvard was preparing to ban the game from campus. Camp's own belief was that "If there is one virtue more to be desired in a manly character . . . that virtue is courage."[72] For Camp, football provided the perfect opportunity to build character, noting that the best teams at Yale had "contained the most moral and religious men."[73] Likewise, a wave of presidential comments lauding the manly virtues came as faculty members looked to assert control in athletics. Likewise, reforms often were heralded for their "scientific" approach to games.[74]

While distinguishing between manliness as a defense of football rather than its raison d'être may seem like minutiae, scholars may be wise to consider its direct relation to the Santayana's second point. Namely, athletes and fans of the game found sport exhilarating "for the sake of victory" and success. While difficult to document, the ethos of the era (and in present day) suggests that

Americans attended games, purchased newspapers, and supported college athletics for the feeling of victory, rather than to develop a strenuous life or a sense of manliness. Teams did not recruit ringers or tramp athletes to ensure that their urban background had not made them soft but to beat their rival. Similarly, players hired coaches, studied technique, kept strict diets, and engaged in conditioning not to instill Walter Camp's version of courage, but to claim victory, especially over those who were considered superior.

It is likely not a coincidence that the era's greatest presidential critic of college sports in general and football in particular was Charles Eliot, president of the nation's preeminent institution, Harvard. Harvard could already claim victory, even with loses in athletics. Nor is it likely that the nation's leading collegiate athletics program across most team sports in the nineteenth century was Yale, keenly aware of its status as the second-place institution in terms of prestige and desperate to beat its rival in Cambridge. When Harvard and Yale dropped out of the intercollegiate regatta, they did so because they could not win. Losing to Massachusetts Agricultural College or Cornell in a boat race threatened the elites' sense of superiority more than their masculinity. As a nation of immigrants, athletics provided an avenue for social mobility. Similarly, athletic victories provided recognition to up-and-coming universities.

What was taking place among the college students was a jockeying for position and distinction—a forerunner to "branding," even though that term was alien in 1900. For a college to "find its place" in the public eye took thoughtful effort. As Canby elaborated, "Furthermore, the younger colleges, whether they were 'state' or 'privately endowed' institutions, modeled their life and aspirations upon the older colleges, which were usually in the East, and which drew heavily from the best schools, and the wealthiest or most cultivated classes. Fashions began there and spread, so that a new twist to a hat brim or a new method of teaching traveled in a few years from ocean to ocean and gave a unity to college life."[75]

Taken as a whole, the athletic enterprise that developed in higher education during the second half of the nineteenth century became unique to the world. In no other country did a system of college sports consume the calendar as it did in the United States. It was an unplanned creation resulting from a convergence of the many developments. Trains were required to provide transportation as a railroad became a corporate sponsor of the first intercollegiate athletic contest in America. Undergraduates seeking freedom to develop their own extracurricular culture created intercollegiate sport, and students discovered a way to distinguish themselves among their peers outside of the classroom.

Alumni and a growing percentage of the public found the contests entertaining. Media outlets identified subject matter that sold newspapers. Modern presidents understood the value of free publicity and the role victory played in promoting school pride.

Many professors understood athletic scandals and the threat that sports posed to the primacy of the academic enterprise. They also learned that as they gained greater freedom in research and teaching, they lost influence in university affairs occurring outside of the classroom or their academic discipline. Games were often played off campus for their monetary and commercial appeal. The long-held tradition of local campus control prevented intercollegiate cooperation in the development of uniform rules of governance. Home rule remained paramount, even as governance began transitioning from students to faculty. The ideal of amateurism often succumbed to professionalism. All of this occurred in American college athletics before the twentieth century.

Intercollegiate sport began as a student-run enterprise in the context of small liberal arts colleges. But the mechanism that protected (and often promoted) the growth of college sports could be found in the structure of the modern American university. The perennial powerhouse athletic teams in the nineteenth century generally represented the institutions evolving into universities. Yet occasional successes by small or upstart colleges provided hope for victory across the nation. These tensions continued to define the successes and scandals of *college* sports in the American *university*.

2

Building Local, Regional, and National Programs, 1900 to 1929

College Sports and Campus Life

By 1900, college students had succeeded in making intercollegiate athletics a fixture on American campuses. Whether college presidents liked this or not, they eventually recognized that henceforth they would have to live and work with this distinctively American academic enterprise. The student sports movement had invaluable allies in the major donors who between 1890 and 1910 had been responsible for the unprecedented resources to construct and expand of colleges and universities. On balance, the American tradition of philanthropy in higher education was that the "captains of industry" often supported the "captains of erudition."

Creating the new and expanded extracurricular programs of the early 1900s was not only exciting and expensive; it also was colorful. College sports were the driving force in connecting the institutional name with a color—or combination of colors. In the case of Brown University, the choice was obvious—Brown! Elsewhere, there were debates and discussions as to how the students and alumni of a college wanted to connect their alma mater to distinctive colors. Harvard had set the practice into motion with its crew team in the 1860s—setting aside the original head scarves of magenta for the enduring Harvard Crimson. In Hanover, New Hampshire, student editors proudly proclaimed in 1880, "Dartmouth chooses green!" The University of Virginia set out to honor shed Confederate blood by picking gray and red for the athletic teams. But a problem with dyes at the manufacturing plant meant a delay in delivering the jerseys. The Virginia players agreed to use navy blue and orange temporarily—a move that proved to be permanent, as those colors still define their team uniforms and banners today.

College athletic teams also pioneered the practice of distinctive nicknames and mascots. Virginia invoked its colonial roots with the Cavaliers. Other colleges made American higher education look like a zoo—as lions, tigers, wild-cats, and bears roamed the playing fields. Some state universities staked out icons of state heritage—the Oklahoma Sooners, the Indiana Hoosiers, and the Pennsylvania Quakers. Purdue projected its land grant identity for educating future engineers by calling its team the Boilermakers. Native American heri-tage, whether inspired or real, led to the Illini, the Indians, the Chippewa, the Seminoles, and the Huron. Classical heroism led some universities to call their athletic teams the Spartans. Journalists marveled at the tenacious University of Southern California team who "played like Trojans!" The Trojans became the permanent symbol, which was more attractive than the original Methodists. Nearby Whittier College stuck with its namesake roots as the Whittier Poets. In the 1970s, college officials took the bold step of transforming this into The Fightin' Poets—perhaps to show that the pen was mightier than the sword, even on the gridiron as well as in the classroom. Each college had a special tale about its mascots and colors, which led one writer to compile the stories for 293 college sports teams.[1]

College sports brought these elements of icons and identity together by 1900 with the nationwide trend of student-athletes wearing varsity letter sweaters. The Harvard crew team originated the practice as the team captain designated those stalwart rowers and allowed them to keep their white jerseys with the crimson H after the season ended. Yale University remained foremost in the public imagination—with the block letter Y on a white wool sweater—featuring team captains seated on the "Yale Fence."

Although football's popularity had surpassed that of other sports, na-tional magazines also capitalized on the continued popularity of other col-lege sports, especially crew. The *Saturday Evening Post*—the largest weekly circulation magazine in the United States—periodically highlighted college sports on its covers. The June 7, 1902, issue featured rowers from Harvard and Yale alongside the Charles River racecourse, noting that this was "The College Man's Number"—that is, the entire issue was devoted to articles about college life.

The American public became involved as fans and spectators. By the start of the twentieth century, newspaper accounts of New York City events noted that the buildings were festooned with large pennants and draperies broadcast-ing the black-and-orange P or the blue-and-white Y as the football teams for Princeton and Yale got ready to play in the sold-out Polo Grounds for what sportswriters considered the national championship game.

Augustus "Gus" Silliman Blagden, captain of Yale's 1901 crew team, posing in a standard crew sweater, 1901. Yale University Manuscripts and Archives

The Graphics Revolution and College Sports Marketing

In the twenty-first century, one frequently reads obituaries and eulogies for the "death of books," the "demise of print culture," and the absorption of traditional magazines and books into digital Internet publication format. Often left out is that in order for a print culture to expire, first it had to be born and nurtured to maturity. Nowhere was this story more apt than in an account of the print journalism that covered college sports starting around 1880 and ascended for

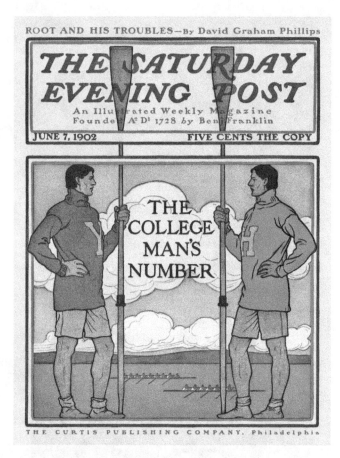

The crew jersey became a fashionable status symbol on and off campus in the early 1900s, as evidenced by this 1902 *Saturday Evening Post* cover image. Curtis Publishing / *Saturday Evening Post*

more than a century. The expansion and diffusion of the popular press as part of mass culture arose from what historian Daniel J. Boorstin called a "Graphics Revolution."[2]

This meant that the technology of large-scale, rapid printing converged with some expansion of popular literacy. Furthermore, the quality of mass publications improved dramatically, with the ability to reproduce photographs as well as etchings. Most fortuitous was that tens of thousands of copies could be produced, marketed, and read within a day or so. The combination of breadth and speed meant that by the early 1900s, most major American cities were home to numerous daily newspapers. Boston, New York, and Philadelphia

The "College Girls" series of postcards by F. Earl Christy became popular during the first decade of the 1900s, revealing that the varsity letter sweater was a feature of women's fashion as well. Courtesy of the Princetoniana Committee of the Princeton Alumni Association

typically had at least six daily newspapers—three morning editions and three afternoon or evening editions. They were highly partisan, unregulated, and competitive. In addition to the standard morning and afternoon releases, editors and publishers pushed their reporters and photographers to file copy for special editions, a practice associated with the Hearst empire's "yellow journalism." It was a deliberate journalistic style that emphasized bold headlines and graphic illustrations to present sensationalized stories of scandal and intrigue, including such topics as politics and sports, to mass audiences.

College sports fit into this picture, as enterprising publishers realized the campus games originally played and watched by students and alumni were a fertile source of popular interest. In other words, stories about college sports found a mass audience, of whom few had ever set foot on a college campus, let alone enrolled in college. Indeed, it was the vicarious thrill of being a follower that enhanced the newspaper frenzy. Editors fed this popular appetite by means of deliberate strategies over weeks, even months, to provide coverage of a college team's football practices, profiles of coaches and players, and above all create a dramatic buildup to a "big game" against a traditional rival.

James Michener and Michael Oriard have documented that fans were not born—they were made. Even if one had learned the rudiments of reading at home or in elementary school, following college sports in daily journalism was an acquired skill. As Oriard emphasized, newspapers and magazines taught Americans to be fans by teaching them to "read football."[3] It required a new lexicon of sports terminology about uniforms, rules, skills, and techniques. Even these were relatively straightforward when compared to the advanced lessons in following the rhetoric and prose that dramatized coaches and players.[4]

If metropolitan newspapers were the pillars of college sports coverage, they were buoyed by a flourishing market for new kinds of weekly and monthly publications. "Dime novels"—weekly and monthly magazines and pulp fiction, a hybrid of a comic book and a paperback novel—included college sports as a staple. And here the focus was on the heroic college athlete. Foremost was "Frank Merriwell of Yale." Author Gilbert Patton (also known as Burt Standish) cranked out weekly serials for over twenty years, with a weekly circulation and sales of more than 150,000 readers over three decades. The magazine proclaimed itself to be "An Ideal Publication for the American Youth." This meant that adolescent boys were the primary audience, and they were loyal and immersed. Not only did they subscribe to *Tip Top Weekly*, but they also bought from the same publisher—Street & Smith—a succession of spin-off novels about Frank Merriwell and his Yale teammates.

Frank Merriwell excelled in many pursuits, ranging from varsity sports to automobile racing. He was talented yet at the same time stood out from the crowd owing to his serious training and dedicated efforts. As depicted on one cover of *Tip Top Weekly*, Frank Merriwell's "Great Victory" in cross-country (over the Harvard runner, of course) was no less than "The Effort of His Life," elevated to high drama by cheering crowds of fellow students.

Frank Merriwell's adventures at Yale were so popular with readers that his undergraduate career distorted reality, stretching the traditional four college years to two decades. For both readers and writers, images of courageous competition and collegiate sportsmanship were in far greater demand than accuracy.

By 1900, Street & Smith executives discovered that juvenile readers mixed the collegiate fiction and adventure stories easily with the factual accounts of the newspaper sports pages. In fact, the line between college sports fiction and fact were blurred for two reciprocal reasons: the juvenile fiction was based on real-life colleges and their rivalries, such as Yale versus Princeton. Second, the allegedly "real" newspaper sports stories were written in a highly embellished style in which actions (and decisions) on the field—or on the sidelines—were connected to allegorical images of Greek gods and Roman emperors. Nothing in either genre was tepid or subdued. Reading the newspaper sports pages did require one to be disciplined in the vocabulary and symbolism, let alone the clichés, of emerging sports journalism. On the one hand, a demanding insider's knowledge was necessary: rules of the game, elaborate diagrams of play-by-play action up and down the field, with extended postscripts for days after a game explaining how—and why—a coach and his players happened to win (or lose). As college sports, especially football, became an all-American game and pastime, they provided a refuge from mundane daily life. Crucial for sports media and coverage over the next half century was that Street & Smith eventually expanded into successful sports publications, including the *Sporting News* weekly magazine as well as annual preview magazines for major league baseball, college football, and other high-profile sports.

For years, college football was a highly regional game that enjoyed a nationwide coverage. This meant that a combination of media headquarters and powerful college teams were concentrated in the major cities of the Northeast. Harvard, Princeton, and Yale reigned as the Big Three largely because of their winning records. But their prestige was enhanced by a virtual monopoly on media coverage, as suggested by the monumental figure of Walter Camp, an alumnus and former player known as the "father of American football." Camp perfected multiple kinds of nationwide publications to advance collegiate football as an all-American pastime—and as a stage for him to select and praise the all-American football squads he selected each year. It was both partisan and effective.

Football's Role in the Creation of a National Sports Association

Despite football's development as the most popular college sport and cultural phenomenon, the true ascendency of football's dominance would not be achieved until the Roaring Twenties. By then, a growing number of fans possessed time and money to spend on leisure activities like attending football games. The contest became an obsession among many, but in higher education it also remained a game of emulation.

Interestingly, an academic named Charles Frederick Holder played a key role in creating one of college sports' greatest spectacles. Holder had served as curator of the Museum of Natural History in New York City before moving to Pasadena, California, for health reasons. A naturalist and professor at Throop College (California Institute of Technology), Holder and other members of the Valley Hunt Club decided to show off Southern California in January while much of the Northeast and Midwest suffered through bitter cold winter weather. As Holder stated, "In New York, people are buried in snow. . . . Here our flowers are blooming and our oranges are about to bear. Let's hold a festival to tell the world about our paradise."[5]

The first parade, then called the Battle of the Flowers, occurred on January 1, 1890. By the end of the decade, the event became known as the Tournament of Roses. Looking for additional entertainment to boost popularity and draw visitors, the Tournament of Roses Association invited Michigan and Stanford to play a New Year's Day bowl game following the parade and agreed to pay all the teams' expenses. Grandstands were built to accommodate fans who purchased tickets, the sales of which likewise subsidized the cost of the game. Meeting on the first day of 1902, Feilding Yost's Michigan team had won ten games by a total score of 550–0, and they demoralized Stanford during the first-ever Rose Bowl football game.[6]

The expenses outweighed the profits, and the lopsided score resulted in the cancelation of the football festivities for more than a decade. Without a collegiate spectacle, the tournament turned to races for entertainment. Jockeys rode ostriches, camels competed against elephants, and for more than a decade, chariot races attracted thousands of spectators. Football returned to the Pasadena stage in 1916. By that time, the game had been transformed. Boosters finally found the profitability and popularity they desired.

Many colleges and universities at the turn of the century experienced similar challenges to those at the first Rose Bowl. The expenses of football did not always match the income, so peculiar funding and financing models were often developed. Although historians have generally focused on the most popular games in the Northeast that drew tens of thousands of fans, most schools had far different experiences. Rivalry games on Thanksgiving Day often helped subsidize the rest of football season. As revenue increased, so did expenses.

Paying for college sports programs at the start of the twentieth century was haphazard and varied across the collegiate landscape. Yale University, followed by Princeton and Harvard, had the advantages of successful teams and generous alumni to give their programs exceptional strength. Elsewhere, ambitious colleges scrambled to sell tickets to paying customers and look for other sources of support. Brown University provided a good example: football lagged baseball in popularity because Brown did not have its own football stadium. In 1891, "it took the combined efforts of the players, the manager, and President Andrews himself to raise the $750 needed to take the team through a ten-game schedule."[7] At most colleges and universities between 1900 and 1930, funding and control of intercollegiate athletics usually were outside the central administrative structure. One result was the emergence of student athletic associations, self-supporting campus organizations that typically relied on student fees or subscriptions. Prior to World War I, the most successful example was the Yale Athletic Association, more familiar as the YAA. In 1907–8, its annual operating budget was $110,000. At some major universities, the structure and tradition of the autonomous student association persisted as the unit responsible for funding college sports—including paying salaries of coaches.[8]

In addition, critics of football began calling for the game to be banned. Some were reporters, others were university presidents and faculty members. Although historians often highlight the tens of thousands of fans attending games of the most prestigious institutions, such crowds were rare in the early 1900s. But a pattern had been established at Yale and other leading universities, and leaders at schools across the country sought to implement the blueprint on their campus.

During the first few years of the twentieth century, football continued to grow in both controversy and popularity. The changes in football between the first Rose Bowl game in 1902 and the second in 1916 were the result of athletic policies developed by university presidents and supported by many faculty. Even the president of the United States played a role.

Newspapers played a vital role in this transformation, highlighting glorious triumphs while condemning stories of brutality and rule violations. Both types of stories sold papers. In turn, a dichotomy of sorts developed between the critics and supporters of football. On one hand, faculty and university administrators lamented professionalism and violence in intercollegiate sports. They longed for the day when athletics provided healthy leisure and a reasonable break from academic responsibilities. On the other hand, many students, alumni, and spectators were enthralled with the game. Much of the American public ignored faculty concerns because they did not care if a student's tuition had been paid by a booster or if a college had hired a professional coach. Football injuries and fatalities, however, found critics both within and outside the campus. Hence football violence became the issue in which reform took root.

Harvard's Charles Eliot became one of the few leading university presidents who remained steadfast in his criticism of football for more than two decades. His earliest efforts at interinstitutional cooperation centered on professionalism and its role in diminishing the mission of higher education. His attempts were futile. Most other university presidents were willing to lament the problems in college sport, but few were interested in any substantive reform to change these problems.

After years of futility, Eliot changed his focus to the brutality of football, a topic on which both the academy as well as boosters and alumni could agree. His report to the Harvard Board of Overseers that year lambasted football's violence and warlike tactics. The strong preyed on the weak. Those eager to break the rules triumphed because "disabling opponents by kneeing and kicking and by heavy blows on the head and particularly about eyes, nose, and jaw are unquestionably profitable toward victory." Eliot argued this immoral behavior led to distrust among institutions that otherwise remained friendly. Touching briefly on the academic side, Eliot resorted to conjecture by asserting that the "mental qualities" of "brawny athletes" were "inferior to slighter quick-witted men."[9]

Harvard's president was prepared to ban football, but many others still hoped to reform the game. President Theodore Roosevelt remained one of them. Frustrated with Eliot's stance, Roosevelt believed changes to the game could solve its challenges. He used his speech at Harvard in June 1905 to make that point. Celebrating the twenty-fifth anniversary of his graduating class of 1880, President Roosevelt highlighted the value of the physical game but warned against continued brutality. The president believed intentional injury not only caused physical harm but also damaged the character of young men. It was clear to Roosevelt that reforming the game rather than ending it was the wise path.

That same summer, Henry Beach Needham published a two-part series in *McClure's Magazine* on "The College Athlete." Both articles focused on the shift from amateurism to professionalism, which had been fueled by commercialism in college sport. Professional coaches needed "material" to win, so they recruited players. Boosters helped with the process. For example, Yale's James Hogan had been recruited to Yale. A star player who eventually became captain, Hogan had a sales agreement with the American Tobacco Company, giving him a percentage of sales at a local store along with the smokes he sold individually. Clearly, name and image could be profitable in the early 1900s. The American Tobacco Company employee who made the deal with Hogan said that it was an experiment, but it had proven so successful they would look to replicate it at other schools. Hogan and two of his teammates also had exclusive permission from the YAA to sell scorecards before Yale baseball games and keep the proceeds. Finally, at the conclusion of the 1903 football season, the association paid for Hogan and a Yale trainer to take a ten-day vacation to Cuba. Needham wrote about similar arrangements at other institutions.[10]

A key booster recruited athletes from leading prep schools Exeter and Andover to Princeton, even if they were academically unprepared. A cribbing scandal broke when seventeen of thirty-one students taking an exam were caught cheating. One prep school player wrote his weight, 205 pounds, across the top of his exam, insisting that the booster promised him he would be able to enroll at Princeton. Needham took Harvard to task for its "unmistakable air of self-satisfaction or smug self-righteousness—a 'holier than thou' contentment." At the same time, he noted that Harvard did not provide scholarships to their athletes, instead offering them well-paying jobs to cover their college costs. In fact, Harvard employed the same tactic in hiring their "amateur" coach Bill Reid, who did not take a salary from Harvard for coaching but accepted funds for his lost salary and expenses, totaling seven thousand dollars annually.[11]

Giving additional attention to baseball, Needham noted that players tainted their amateur status by playing at summer resorts and in semiprofessional leagues, often earning money as well as room and board. Needham naively claimed that such pay-for-play arrangements existed because the issue "was not clearly understood." He proceeded to report that attempts to enforce bans on summer baseball led to disingenuous modifications. Players were no longer paid to play. Instead, they took on menial jobs for a salary and played baseball for fun.[12]

Only one small section of the two-part series dealt with "unnecessary roughness" in football, but it garnered the most attention. Once again it revealed that outside of a small circle of faculty, administrators, and a minority of college alums, most were not concerned about a player making money playing summer baseball or football players earning income from other jobs on campus. The greatest challenges to professionalism in college sports usually came from college teams who challenged player eligibility on opposing teams shortly before a game. It seemed to escape Needham that the problem was not a lack of understanding, but a key example of another problem: the desire to "win at any cost."[13]

Needham's section on violence and football highlighted the story of Matthew Bullock, a Black athlete at Dartmouth who had his collarbone broken by Princeton players on the first play from scrimmage in 1903. The injury ended Bullock's senior season. When another Black athlete at Harvard, William Matthews, confronted one of his friends on Princeton's team about injuring Bullock because of his race, the Princeton quarterback replied, "We didn't put him out because he was a black man. . . . We're coached to pick out the most dangerous man on the opposing team and put him out in the first five minutes of play." Regardless of intent regarding this one play, violence—and racism—existed in intercollegiate sport.[14]

It was the violence that concerned football fans, including President Roosevelt. To that end, Roosevelt called the coaches of the Big Three (Harvard, Princeton, and Yale) to the White House to discuss ways to end wanton brutality in football. On October 9, 1905, Roosevelt met for lunch with the coaches and a second athletic representative from each school. He told them "football is on trial." Roosevelt also shared that he was a fan of the game and wanted to see it improved. He told stories of violence and foul play, but the coaches pleaded ignorance to such charges. The president excused himself to tend to other matters, and when he returned, he asked the three coaches to sign a joint statement agreeing to improve the climate of college football. Walter Camp of Yale penned the letter, agreeing to "carry out in letter and in spirit the rules of the game of football relating to roughness, holding, and foul play." Roosevelt approved of the resolution.[15]

The presidential pact was as effective as virtually all other agreements made among intercollegiate football teams. It did little to stop violence on the gridiron. In fact, three deaths and more than eighty serious injuries occurred during the 1905 college season. One infamous injury came on Thanksgiving Day in front of forty-three thousand spectators at Harvard Stadium. Harvard's all-American guard Francis Burr had called for a fair catch on a punt, but two Yale players collided with Burr, and Yale's Jim Quill punched Burr in the face, breaking his nose. Despite the clear unnecessary roughness, official Paul Dashiell refused to make a call. The livid crowd jeered at the official. Yale won 6–0, concluding an undefeated season.[16]

After the game, Harvard coach Bill Reid found Dashiell and informed him he would never officiate another Harvard game. Attempting to get to the facts of the case, Roosevelt asked Reid to return to the White House. Dashiell was a member of the Camp's Football Rules Committee as well as an instructor at the US Naval Academy who was up for a promotion. Since President Roosevelt had direct control over the academy, Dashiell's fate hung in the balance. He pleaded with Reid not to destroy his career. Reid remained understandably unsympathetic. He questioned Dashiell's fitness to serve as a professor at Annapolis.[17]

Although out of the football spotlight in December, President Roosevelt used Dashiell to bring about needed changes in college football. Dashiell had written the president, apologizing for his failure and regretting criticism it had brought to the game. Roosevelt, in turn, held up Dashiell's appointment for months and used his role on the rules committee to bring change to the game.[18]

The Burr-Quill incident was not the most powerful example of football brutality that Thanksgiving Day in 1905. In New York, New York University hosted Union College. During the game, Union's Harold Moore was tackling a runner when he was crushed by a throng of players who piled on top of him at the end of the play. Once the defense was removed, Moore lay face-down on the field, unconscious. He was taken to the hospital but never regained consciousness, dying of a cerebral hemorrhage that night. The story made the front page of the *New York Times* the following morning, as did a story of a prep school player who died during a game when a broken rib bone punctured his heart. Football was immediately under attack.[19]

NYU president Henry MacCraken asked Harvard's Charles Eliot to convene a conference for the reform of football. Eliot's cynicism (or maybe realism) led him to decline. He stated, "Death and injuries are not the strongest argument against football. . . . That cheating and brutality are profitable is the main evil."[20] He also added that university presidents "certainly cannot reform football, and I doubt if by themselves they can abolish it."[21] Still stunned by the players death during a game with NYU, MacCraken decided to take the lead in either reforming football or abolishing the sport.

Representatives from thirteen of the nineteen institutions MacCraken invited showed up for a meeting in New York on December 8. Columbia presented a resolution to ban football. Of the thirteen institutions present, five voted in favor of abolition, but a group led by West Point voted against the proposal, and reform of the current game became the chief agenda for the conference.[22] Unfortunately for MacCraken, not a single member of the Big Three attended the conference. Clearly, power in the administration of football rather than the development of a clean game was of most importance. The thirteen institutions in attendance decided to move forward without the nation's most prestigious colleges.

Interestingly, the day after the first MacCraken conference, Camp's Intercollegiate Football Rules Committee, including Paul Dashiell, met in Philadelphia and proposed more rule changes to the game. Camp was set on making ten yards, rather than five, the required distance for a first down. But he was adamantly opposed to legalizing the forward pass. Harvard's Coach Reid told the committee that he could not vote on any new rules until his institution's recently formed committee informed him of the direction Harvard desired to take regarding football reform.[23]

In the meantime, the fate of intercollegiate football hung in the balance. Publications such as *The Nation* and the *Chicago Tribune* called for the sport's abolition. Blame and finger-pointing intensified. Harvard's Bill Reid continued to stall the old rules committee by not meeting in December. President Roosevelt also encouraged Dashiell to support a change. This delay allowed MacCraken's group to further organize. Meeting again on December 28, sixty-eight institutions sent representatives to address reforming football. Harvard, Princeton, and Yale remained absent. With numbers on their side, the new group offered to merge the rules committee of the new organization with the old. Camp's group wanted to retain all of their leadership roles on a merged committee, so MacCraken's alliance rejected the offer. Coach Reid then resigned from the organization and joined the new group. Forcing Camp's hand, the old committee had no other option but to join the new rules committee.

In January, the merged rules committee elected Haverford professor James Babbitt as secretary. Babbitt, in turn, resigned from the post, and Harvard's Reid was appointed as his successor. The reform group finally had the upper hand. Camp's role had been minimized, and the new committee was positioned to bring fundamental change to the game. Camp may have been the father of American football, but in reality this coup in leadership allowed the game's modernization in the name of safety.[24]

The new association, calling themselves the Intercollegiate Athletics Association of the United States (IAAUS), developed a new organization that would bring more popularity to intercollegiate athletics. In five short years the organization would change its name to the National Collegiate Athletics Association, and its reform of football would make the sport more popular than ever. At the same time, a new element had been added during this revolution. Small colleges, for the first time, had a say that was somewhat equal to the most prestigious universities in the country. This egalitarian approach helped save football, but it also created a lasting tension with big-time athletics programs as burgeoning universities sought a place among the nation's elite athletic institutions.

In the short term, rule changes slightly minimized the number of deaths and serious injuries, but when the casualties spiked again in 1909, more turmoil ensued. Of the many important effects of the NCAA, two stood out as particularly important at the end of the first decade of the twentieth century. First, as football rules changed to make the game safer, the popularity of the sport soared—a trend some in higher education found disheartening. Second, the creation of a national body to deliberate issues of college sports provided a mechanism for the continued growth of sports such as track, baseball, and crew. It also provided an administrative apparatus to foster the growth of additional sports.

Basketball as an Intercollegiate Sport

Just as school faculty and administrators succeeded in organizing a national association to address issues of intercollegiate athletics, another sport began developing rather quickly across the country. American football had its origins in a rugby-style game introduced by McGill University students. Basketball also had ties to the Canadian institution. James Naismith graduated from McGill University in 1887. After completing a theology degree at Presbyterian College in Montreal, he accepted a post as an instructor of physical culture at the Young Men's Christian Association (YMCA) Training School in Springfield, Massachusetts. The institution eventually became Springfield College.

Outdoor sports were not feasible in the harsh New England winter climate. In December 1891, his boss, Professor Luther Gulick, assigned the new instructor to what Naismith called "the class of incorrigibles" and tasked him with devising an indoor game to capture their attention and channel their energies in a positive direction while stuck indoors. After nearly two weeks of frustration, Naismith wrote down thirteen rules and in so doing devised the game of basketball. His goal remained the development of a game that would build character, discipline, and healthy teamwork.[25]

In an attempt to avoid the violence of football, players could only advance the ball by passing it. They were prohibited from moving with the ball (originally a soccer ball), negating the need to tackle the carrier. In order to minimize the aggressive throwing of the ball, Naismith placed peach baskets ten feet above the ground on either end of the gym, requiring a gentle shot with arch in order to score. Since his class had eighteen students, the first basketball games were played with nine boys on each side.

Naismith's students enjoyed the game, and they were quick to spread it across the country (and world) as they took jobs at YMCA centers, attended college, or served as missionaries. By 1893, basketball was being played at YMCAs from coast to coast. Colleges quickly picked up the sport as well. Vanderbilt played a Nashville YMCA team in February 1893, and Geneva College played against the Brighton YMCA that same April. The first recorded intercollegiate game took place in 1895 when Hamline College faced the Minnesota School of Agriculture. As sport historian Chad Carlson noted, Naismith invented the game "to be a part of a *college* physical education curriculum. From its birth, basketball was a college game created by a college instructor for college students to play." Naismith had no interest in benefitting from financially from basketball; he simply hoped the game would improve physical education instruction.[26]

The game evolved rapidly. Peach baskets were replaced with metal rims, backboards, and nets. An official basketball, rather than a soccer ball, was created specifically for the game. College players in different parts of the country began adopting their own versions of basketball, and some of them varied significantly. In some instances, the courts were enclosed within cages, so there was no out-of-bounds. Other teams instituted the dribble, a way for a player who was stuck to relinquish control of the ball and quickly regain possession. In effect, it allowed players to advance the ball without passing. Other teams continued to focus on passing rather than dribbling. To Naismith's frustration, the game also witnessed a good bit of violence.

By the turn of the century, dozens of colleges were playing intercollegiate basketball while leaving games against YMCA teams or local athletic clubs on the schedule. During the first decade of the twentieth century, the relative isolation faced by many teams led to different types of games being played in different regions or cities across America. Some regions allowed more physical contact, others relied on dribbling, and some teams remained focused on the passing part of the game. Officials often refereed games based on their own region's norms regarding physicality and finesse.

Some interesting cultural changes and transportation advances have occurred since the mid-nineteenth century. Early football and baseball games varied wildly from city to city, even those that were less than two hundred miles apart. By the time basketball became a common intercollegiate sport, transportation had improved to the point that regional variations rather than institutional differences of the game had emerged. Games in the South or in the West (including the Midwest) varied from the way basketball was being played on the East Coast. For those who paid attention, universities in the East played a much more violent game that generated some criticism. Basketball remained a minor sport, however, so calls for reform and standardization were largely voiced among basketball coaches themselves and did not involve substantive media coverage.[27]

In a move to assist with standardized rules, Naismith spoke to the NCAA annual meeting in 1913 to explain the evolution of the game and the informal rule changes that had taken place. At the same meeting, the NCAA created a rules committee that consisted of members from the NCAA and the YMCA. Not wanting to lose any control as the leading amateur association in the United

States, the Amateur Athletic Union (AAU) asked to join the rules committee, and the other two organizations accepted the request.

During the following years, attempts at some form of national championships emerged, but they never took root. Such championships were almost always won by local favorites, and it took time for basketball to become a "standardized" sport because the game's founder was not interested in controlling the game. After earning an MD in Colorado, Naismith became the basketball coach of the University of Kansas (KU) basketball team. To the game's inventor, the value of basketball lay in its ability to teach moral principles, instill work ethic, and build character. Emphasizing the educational aspects of basketball rather than victories, Naismith ended up being the only coach in the storied history of KU basketball with a losing record.[28]

After Naismith retired from coaching, the first generation of professional basketball coaches who were focused on winning emerged. As these coaches' teams played around the country, the regional differences in the style of play continued. Although not controversial, the most hotly contested question concerned the use of the dribble. Basketball's original rules did not allow a player with the ball to move, but dribbling became common practice for many, but not all, basketball teams in the 1920s. In 1927, some coaches moved to ban the dribble from basketball. The joint rules committee, in a split decision, voted to allow only one dribble in a single possession.[29]

This move pleased coaches who had developed traditional approaches to the game, including Wisconsin coach Walter Meanwell. But up-and-coming coaches like Forrest "Phog" Allen at Kansas relied on the dribble in elaborate offensive schemes. In 1927, Coach Allen called a meeting among coaches to discuss the matter, leading to the creation of the National Association of Basketball Coaches, which remains in existence to this day. Influenced by its founder, basketball coaches across the country managed to successfully keep the dribble a part of the game.

The dribble remained part of basketball, and the new the intercollegiate sport would eventually become the second most popular college game. Basketball played another important role in college athletics. With only five players on the court, it afforded an opportunity for smaller colleges to compete with more prestigious universities. Once a gym had been built, the sport was far less costly to operate than football, helping teams with fewer resources remain competitive.

Peculiar today is that basketball was slow to catch on as a commercially viable spectator sport. When Edwin Slosson, influential editor of *The Independent*, visited Stanford University in 1909 as part of his fact-finding study of great American universities, he observed a bleak campus landscape in which several large buildings, including the gymnasium, were in rubble after the San Francisco earthquake of 1906. Slosson thought that there was little need for Stanford to rebuild its basketball gymnasium, arguing that he felt such dark, crowded indoor sports facilities would hold little appeal either for student-athletes or for spectators. He predicted instead that Stanford and other colleges on the Pacific Coast would opt for open-air festivals committed to celebration of healthy living. College basketball eventually did persist—thanks in part to its popularity in high schools throughout the Midwest. It would not, however, enjoy the popular appeal of football in part because seating capacity at even the largest university gymnasiums usually did not exceed one to two thousand spectators until after World War II.

College Sports and Women

The growth of basketball also altered the discussion of women and college athletics. The most popular intercollegiate sports were overwhelmingly masculine in character, for obvious reasons. Many colleges and universities, especially the historic private academic institutions, enrolled only men as students. At coeducational institutions public and private, women in the early twentieth century often were excluded from campus groups as leaders or as members.[30] Despite their exclusion, there were signs of gains by women as student-athletes at numerous colleges and universities, especially at women's colleges. Pioneers included the "Seven Sisters" colleges of the Northeast. At Wellesley and Smith Colleges, the college curriculum included a comprehensive array of sports, teams, activities, and competitions—often intramural, yet in some cases with intercollegiate field days. In 1906, Brown University constructed Sayles Gymnasium, which was dedicated to women's sports and physical education. It included a running track, a basketball court, a reading room and reference library, classrooms, a locker room, and a recreation and resting room for tea breaks.

At a time when American mores were still influenced by Victorian England, Dr. Naismith's emphasis on a less violent game that would serve as recreational education provided a perfect opportunity for college women to make their mark on college athletics. Senda Berenson, a new gymnastics instructor at Smith College, read about Naismith's game and decided to modify the rules for women. At a time when women were not allowed to engage in masculine sports, Berenson divided the court into thirds, and players needed to stay within their assigned zone during the game. A player with the ball could not dribble more than three times and then had to pass the ball within three seconds. This encouraged movement in the game, while at the same time providing rules that would ensure less violence. "Basket ball" proved wildly popular at Smith College, but the game was not utilized for intercollegiate contests.[31]

As with men's hoops, women's basketball quickly spread across the country, and games exhibited regional differences. Down south, Clara Gregory Baer created a set of rules for women's basketball at Newcomb College in New Orleans. The professor of physical education introduced the game to her students in 1893. Two years later, the first game played in front of fans occurred when Baer's students showcased basketball to more than five hundred women in New Orleans. Baer's game involved seven zones on the court in which one offensive and one defensive player remained for the game. Different point totals could be earned for shots taken from greater distances from the basket. Baer published the rules of her game in what was sometimes referred to as the "Newcomb Basquette" that same year.[32]

On the West Coast, Stanford boasted a women's basketball team before the men. The team played its first intercollegiate game against University of California, Berkeley, on April 4, 1896. Stanford hoped to host the game, but Berkeley was unwilling to play the game in front of male spectators. Boasting approximately seven hundred female spectators, Stanford won the game, 2–1. When the victors returned to campus, they were met with the band playing and young college men celebrating their victory.[33]

Although contests between institutions were few and far between for women, basketball spread rapidly as a college game for women. With few intercollegiate contests, rules could vary from school to school. In 1901, Senda Berenson served as the editor of a Spaulding publication titled *Basket Ball for Women*. The book laid out a series of uniform rules. In these rules the court maintained three zones, but teams could consist of between five and ten women per side. While most followed Berenson's rules, some still chose to play by the "Basquette" rules, while others simply utilized the rules from the men's game.

The speed at which professors of physical education for women adopted the game of basketball, usually before men on most campuses, suggests the desperate need women had for a team sport that encouraged physical activity and teamwork within the context of an educational mission to train the whole person. This paradigm proved to be entirely different than that of men's college sports, which focused primarily on winning.

The trajectory of women's basketball at Oberlin provided an example that generally held true at many colleges and universities. Women's basketball arrived on campus years before the men played. It was instituted by the physical education department, under the progressive ideals of professionally trained experts who would coach young women to use scientific principles in the game. As Marc Horger noted, basketball "fit perfectly the educational prerogatives of professional physical education philosophy, for the simple reason that it was invented specifically to do so."[34] It offered institutional control administered through the faculty. Annual games between dorms or different classes were key elements to the spring intramural championships. Football success in the 1890s brought attention to Oberlin, and men's sports could remain outwardly focused on the goal of beating rivals in Ohio and beyond. Physical educators, however, never envisioned women's basketball as an intercollegiate activity in which young women would compete for institutional prestige or popularity. Educators attempted to improve women's health and social values by keeping the game within the institution itself.[35]

The history of women's athletics at the University of Kentucky offered a different perspective on basketball and competitive sports for women. The first intercollegiate game occurred between the University of Kentucky and crosstown rival Transylvania University. More than five hundred spectators filled the gym, and they "kept the air ringing with their songs and yells." The newspaper account compared the women's basketball game to that of a Thanksgiving football game. The 1904 annual reported that for two years the women's basketball team attracted packed gyms with "an appreciative crowd of fellows—mad, riotously mad, over contests abounding in snappy spectacular plays." When men were banned from attending women's games, a student dressed in women's clothing in order to attend the game with nearby Georgetown College. Once discovered, the young man was ejected.[36]

All of these events disturbed Women's Physical Education Director Florence Offut Stout, who slowly clamped down on intercollegiate competition. By 1909 the women's basketball team along with seventy-three other coeds sent a petition to the faculty senate, requesting that the athletic association assume administration of the women's basketball team. Incensed, Stout protested but without success. In response, she kept her position as physical educator but resigned as dean of women. During the next years, the teams continued to play intercollegiate contests with a succession of illustrious coaches. University of Kentucky Professor John Tigert, future president of the University of Florida and US commissioner of education, coached women's teams in the 1910s. Sarah Blanding (later president of Vassar) served as a student player-coach before future Kentucky governor and commissioner of Major League Baseball A. B. Happy Chandler took over the team.[37]

When Sarah Blanding returned to the University of Kentucky as the dean of women, she and Stout petitioned President Frank McVey to ban intercollegiate sporting contests for women. They argued that interinstitutional games were too strenuous for young women and created health problems for coeds. McVey agreed, and despite further petitions from students, UK ended intercollegiate basketball (or other sports) for women. Taken at face value, these events appear perplexing. Leading women educators were parroting Victorian Era views about the fragility of women and the nervous problems caused by strenuous competitive sport. For some women, such arguments did resonate. There were much larger contextual issues involved, however. The women's teams frequently had greater success than the men's teams. In 1924, despite a perfect 10–0 season, the university senate passed a bill to abolish women's basketball in part because, according to the university administration, "basketball had proven to be a strenuous sport for boys and therefore was, therefore, too strenuous for girls."[38]

For progressive educators like Sarah Blanding, women's basketball across the country was in the midst of a power struggle that those in Lexington might not have understood. The American Athletic Union, which had been formed in the nineteenth century and claimed control of amateur athletics in the United States, including those at the college level, posed a serious threat. In 1922 the AAU sponsored a women's team to participate in the Paris Women's International Athletic Games. Fearing a move by the male-dominated AAU to control all women's amateur athletics, physical educators across the country withdrew from their positions in the organization. In turn, they joined the National Amateur Athletic Federation (NAAF) and created a women's committee in that organization. The NAAF took exception with many of the AAU's policies and actions. If the AAU could claim jurisdiction over all amateur athletic contests, women would no longer be in control of their athletics programs. For this reason, physical education instructors, through their national organization, the American Physical Education Association, pursued a policy of intramural athletics and annual "Play Days" sponsoring women's sporting contests among three or four colleges.[39]

The story of women's basketball at the University of Kentucky exposed the philosophical differences and policy implications revolving around women's athletics. On the one hand, arguments regarding the characteristics of a "weaker sex" played to the mindset of many administrators. But a reading of the platform of the NAAF's Women's Division revealed a clear, concerted effort to protect women's athletics from the common abuses of big-time college sports. Across the country, women educators like Sarah Blanding wanted "a game for every girl, and every girl playing a game." Blanch Trilling, a key member of the Women's Division of the NAAF put it this way: "Unless a very definite stand is taken . . . we will find ourselves fighting the same vicious system that men are doing, and that our women will be having commercially sponsored athletics."[40]

Scholar Welch Suggs framed the distinction in the following terms. Some women's coaches wanted to keep the games under their control and away from public spectacles in order to "preserve young women's modesty and accommodate their perceived daintiness." As key leaders in women's physical education proclaimed, girls and boys needed different athletics programs. At the same time, leading educators were protecting college women from the "win-at-all-cost" attitude prevalent in men's intercollegiate sport. In this way physical educators would keep athletics in its proper place in the educational mission: teaching lessons of teamwork, sportsmanship, and healthy activity. In the midst of all of this was a power struggle with athletic associations and the AAU, both of which were dominated by men. Victory for the women's control of athletics on the national level generally meant removal of women's intercollegiate competition, with little activity for decades. Almost all games would be played as intramural sports until after World War II.[41]

A paradox of college sports between 1900 and 1930 was that American women who were college student-athletes won championships and medals in national and international competitions, including the Olympics, when given the opportunities to play. But their intense training usually was incidental to their college activities and opportunities. Two students who were members of the swimming team at Pembroke College of Brown University, for example, won gold medals at the 1928 and 1932 Olympics. Helen Wills of Berkeley, California, won the Olympic gold medal in 1924, but she did so without any college sports affiliation.

The Foundation for the Golden Age of Football: The 1910s

Although the 1920s have been labeled the "golden age" of college sports, the foundation for the massive expansion of football's popularity had been established during the previous decades. Some general trends in athletics administration and governance combined with a few key events set the stage for college football to become a cultural phenomenon. By the end of the 1920s the number of universities with large stadiums and even larger fanbases had boomed across the country. In short, football's golden age was in many ways simply the replication of the big-time model established in the East at colleges and universities across the country.

One of the key developments leading to a more exciting game involved the evolution of the forward pass. The NCAA initially introduced the forward pass in 1906, but an untouched incomplete pass resulted in a turnover, limiting the passing game for most teams. Initially, the rules appeared to limit the number of serious injuries and deaths in college football. But a detailed analysis revealed that the numbers had changed little. Instead, the popular press had turned its attention to other issues. That changed in 1909 when ten college football players died.[42]

Intense pressure to reform the game again occurred in 1909–10. Over the next three years, the IAAUS changed its name to the National Collegiate Athletic Association, the old rules committee merged to form a single body with the new committee, and the regulations governing the forward pass were liberalized, so an incomplete pass only resulted in the loss of a down rather than a turnover. In essence, the game became the "modern" game of football, which would be totally recognizable by fans in the twenty-first century. Deaths and serious injuries in the college game did, in fact, diminish after this second round of reforms, setting the stage for increased popularity without the same criticisms. The faculty-led NCAA's greatest accomplishment of the era remained its ability to alter the game of football to both minimize casualties and make the game more interesting for spectators.

Although the forward pass had been legal in some form since the 1906 season, few schools had made it an important part of their offense. Once an incomplete pass no longer resulted in a turnover, it took only one game for the football coaches and fans alike to realize its potential. That game involved a relatively small and unknown Catholic institution in Indiana that had little football tradition. In 1913, Notre Dame scheduled a game against Army, one of the strongest programs in the country.

Knowing his team was outmatched, Notre Dame coach Jesse Harper used his two best players—Knute Rockne and Gus Dorias—to unleash a passing attack in West Point that would embarrass Army. The press took note, and coaches began emulating Notre Dame's passing attack. History tells us that Glen "Pop" Warner and the Carlisle Indians should be credited with utilizing the forward pass as an integral part of the offense scheme in 1907. That year, the football team from the Native American boarding school beat the otherwise undefeated University of Pennsylvania before more than twenty thousand fans in Philadelphia by completing eight of sixteen passes and racking up more than four hundred yards of offense to Penn's seventy-six. The game was not a fluke. Carlisle went on to beat Harvard and Chicago that same season, losing only one game to Princeton.[43]

With the game modernized and popular appeal of college football growing across the country, the Tournament of Roses in Pasadena once again hosted a football game on January 1, 1916, pitting a Pacific Coast team against an eastern powerhouse. Washington State beat Brown University 14–0, and the following year, Oregon shut out Penn by the same score. The return of the Rose Bowl game highlighted a number of important developments in college athletics.

First, the marketing of college sports directed to American popular culture received a big boost from civic groups who sought to attract tourists, especially during the winter months. Starting in 1916, the commercial appeal of a college football game could not be denied by university and civic leaders, and the game's popularity only continued to grow. The Rose Bowl game eventually found a permanent home in 1922 with the construction of a stadium with seating for fifty-seven thousand spectators—a capacity that would be expanded periodically over several decades, eventually reaching more than one hundred thousand.

Another reform instituted a year before the resumption of the Rose Bowl signaled an understanding of the importance of spectators (as well as individual players) at football games. One of the truisms in American sports culture is, "You can't tell the players without a program." Interestingly, coaches and athletics directors failed to see this. Looking at photographs of college football games from the 1890s and early 1900s, one sees anonymous players, with both teams wearing almost identical dark jerseys. All this changed in 1915 when the University of Pittsburgh introduced a new feature that revolutionized college sports marketing and fan identification with the game. Each Pitt football player was assigned a unique number on his jersey.[44] These numbers in turn were listed on the rosters published in the program sold to each ticketholder. The university athletics department gained revenues from increased program sales, and ticket-buying fans gained greater interest and information that helped them be part of the team—and the game on the field. The innovation spread rapidly to all college teams nationwide.

By 1917, college football seemed poised to grow by leaps and bounds. World War I soon disrupted college sports activities, however. While the "War to End

All Wars" did limit athletic operations for the 1917 and 1918 seasons, an often neglected part of the history of college athletics at this time was the role of the 1918 influenza pandemic. Not only had college teams been hampered by a decreased number of students on campus, but the public health crisis also led to the cancelation of games across the country. The suspension of football was not uniform, and many successful teams continued to play. One photo of Georgia Tech football under legendary coach John Heisman captured the extent of football's appeal. In the midst of a life-threatening pandemic, fans still wanted to cheer the Golden Tornadoes on to victory.

One of the biggest controversies developing from World War I was the use of freshmen on varsity teams during the war. Many schools suspended the first-year ban on athletes during the war, but after the signing of the Armistice in November 1918, many small colleges hoped to continue the use of first-year students on varsity teams. The debate was controversial enough to cause a conference split. Larger universities wanted to retain the rule prohibiting first-year students from playing varsity sports. The smaller schools, hoping to remain competitive, wanted first-year students eligible to play football. When the smaller institutions narrowly outvoted the larger schools and voted for first-year eligibility, many larger universities resigned the conference in protest and formed the new Southern Conference in 1921.[45]

These events in southern athletics offer a glimpse at both the complexity and irony of faculty control and reform in college athletics. The schools that would end up becoming "big time" formed a new conference because the smaller schools—the ones generally viewed as putting less emphasis on athletics—had determined they needed to do away with the freshman rule in order to remain competitive. The larger universities, forming a new conference to preserve a policy aimed at minimizing recruiting and helping students acclimate to academic life in college, actually boosted the popularity of southern football. During the 1920s, Alabama and Georgia Tech both represented the conference in Rose Bowl games. The victories helped raise the visibility of football in the South and bring greater attention to the region.

Successes and Shortcomings of Conference Control in Sports

The move toward "faculty control" of athletics has always been a bit of a misnomer. Certainly, faculty did assert greater authority over the administration of extracurricular athletic activities, but they rarely (if ever) controlled the entire enterprise of college athletics on campus the way students did in the nineteenth century, or the way athletics departments would in the decades to follow. In most cases, faculty gained little authority or influence over controversial elements of sports, either within the campus or in governance of conferences. The response to this marginalization was either to absent themselves from the scene because of their objections to the administration and board, or simply to have been evaded and shut out.[46] The combination of the loosely coupled organization of sports within the campus governance structure and the prospects for markets and marketing with external groups created a force faculty dissenters could not stop. The affinity and available resources of spectators and fans set the stage for intercollegiate athletics to be enterprising, continually poised to take advantage of outside opportunities and constituencies. This meant that football was followed by facilities, fans, funding, festivals, and philanthropy.

Professors, coaches, and university administrators created athletics committees on their campuses to curb abuses and excesses by students. Regional associations like the Southern Conference grew in power as the NCAA remained primarily a body to debate issues and create specific game rules. With the NCAA interfering little in operational affairs, the conferences slowly gained some regulatory authority while still providing deference to home rule on each campus.

Despite the Southern Intercollegiate Athletics Association's distinction as the first college athletic association, the Western Conference (or Big Ten), formed in 1895, remained the clear leader among regional conferences during the first decades of the of the twentieth century. In the early years of the 1900s, their member institutions were the only schools with the resources to compete athletically with long-established elite schools in the Northeast. As more conferences developed, they patterned their constitutions and bylaws off the precedent set by the Western Conference. The Missouri Valley Intercollegiate Athletic Association (later named the Big Eight) formed in 1907, and the Southwest Conference held its organizational meeting in 1914. The Pacific Coast Conference began formal operations in 1916.

These nascent conferences were formed to protect amateurism, utilize sport as an educational tool or a healthy extracurricular activity, and promote clean play through conference regulations. In reality, these associations provided an organizational apparatus for planning season schedules, promoting athletic events, and holding tournaments. The prospect of becoming a conference champion would provide a huge public relations boost for the winner, increasing the intensity of competition and creating new conference rivalries. In an interesting twist of fate, the very individuals and conference organizations that claimed to uphold amateurism actually played a key role in further eroding amateurism by promoting popular spectacles that brought money and publicity to winning institutions.

The success of college sports also created a power struggle outside of the NCAA and its regional conferences. The growing popularity of amateur college athletics posed a threat to the AAU, which had successfully claimed to be the national governing body of amateur sport since its formation in 1888. The two associations held overlapping interests that created conflict during the 1920s and beyond.

The NCAA might have been able to ignore the regulatory role of the AAU, except for the fact that colleges and universities were deeply concerned about negative publicity stemming from violations of amateurism, an area in which the AAU claimed authority. As early as 1913 the NCAA reported: "There has been and will continue to be much friction between local authorities of the AAU and college athletics until the authority of the Union is more definitely defined."[47] The AAU had determined that every amateur event required official approval by their organization. If not officially sanctioned, all participating athletes in the contest would lose their amateur standing, even if the event avoided all elements of professionalism. This meant that if a college team played a local sports club in basketball without certification from the AAU, those collegiate athletes could lose their amateur status even if they had not violated any rules. The AAU did not claim authority over college football, but it did claim governance over most other NCAA sports. The NCAA agreed to seek sanctioning of its events by the AAU because this officially certified them as amateur contests. The final authority on such decisions remained unclear, however.[48]

This theoretical problem became a reality during the 1920 Olympics held in Antwerp, Belgium. American athletes roundly criticized the conditions on their ship to Europe as well as their accommodations in Antwerp. The American Olympic Committee, which organized the travel and accommodations, was largely controlled by members of the AAU. The NCAA requested that an American Olympic Association with more representation from other amateur athletic associations be developed.

Feeling threatened, the AAU decided to "flex its muscle" when it banned any international athletic participation ahead of the 1924 Olympics. The International YMCA hosted a sporting event in Paris in 1923, and Charles Paddock, a track and field athlete from the University of Southern California, decided to participate. He had been cleared for the event by the Southern Pacific Association of the AAU, but when the national body learned of his plans, they denied his request. Paddock traveled by train from California to New York on his way to France. While in New York, Paddock appealed the decision, but the AAU denied his request. The college athlete went to Paris anyway and won multiple events at the games.[49]

The AAU then ruled that Paddock had disqualified himself as an amateur. Having broken no amateur rules, the NCAA protested the ruling as nothing more than a power play that was not designed to protect amateur athletics but the AAU's control of such sports in the United States. The NCAA asserted its right to determine the eligibility of its own students and their participation in such events, and the NCAA also voiced its view that the American Olympic Committee, not the AAU, held the right to determine eligibility for Olympic participation. Paddock applied to have his status reinstated by the AAU, at which time the AAU asserted its own authority by granting a reinstatement.[50]

The resolution of Paddock's case did not solve questions of authority regarding Olympic participation by NCAA athletes. In 1926, members of the AAU who were also members of the American Olympic Association (AOA) successfully passed a rule lowering the required two-thirds vote for the election of successors to a simple majority. The AAU and other members sympathetic to their cause controlled more than half of the votes, and they proceeded to elect officials who would give responsibility of choosing Olympic athletes to the AAU. In protest, AOA representatives from the US Navy, the Marine Corps, the NCAA, the NAAF, the YMCA, and the Big Ten all withdrew from the AOA. Shortly after their resignation, the AOA's president William C. Prout died unexpectedly, and Brigadier General Douglas MacArthur was selected as his successor. MacArthur invited representatives from the withdrawn organizations to return, and they obliged.[51]

The reentry of college representatives to the AAU-dominated American Olympic Association did not end the battle. In April 1928 the commissioner of the Western Conference, Major John Griffith, called for a new Olympic association to "end the domination of the Amateur Athletic Union over American amateur athletics." Griffith claimed that the AAU was composed of "cheap politicians" and that the Olympic managers, officials, and committee members were "henchmen of the A.A.U." MacArthur had no comment, as his position with the AOA was temporary, and he had simply tried to keep the AOA from imploding during his short tenure.[52]

After MacArthur's departure, however, the AAU proceeded to disqualify the Northwestern swimmers who had competed against the Chicago Athletic Association in a meet not approved by the AAU. In response, Griffith said, "No longer will the Western Conference bend under the yoke of the AAU. . . . We are tired of its continual demands and its general attempts to dominate our affairs. Henceforth we will conduct athletic meets with clubs and teams that we choose, and will not pay the regular $10 tribute to obtain heretofore required sanction."[53]

In short, the Northwestern swimmers had not violated any rules of amateurism. Their crime had been participating in an athletic event not sanctioned by the AAU. The head of the most powerful collegiate conference had called out the AAU on their decision. The AAU had no option but to back off or be relegated to obscurity. The AAU agreed to allow colleges and universities to certify their athletes as amateurs, and the AAU would accept these certifications from NCAA institutions. The AAU now retained "nominal supervision," but it no longer held the undisputed right to disqualify athletes for Olympic competition. This arrangement kept the peace between the two organizations for decades.[54]

College Sports and the Limits of Social Justice: Attacks, Exclusion, and Separation

The complexity of intercollegiate sports and its governance was even more challenging for African American athletes and academics as they faced systemic racism both north and south of the Mason-Dixon Line. Black players on white college teams in the South remained out of the question. As sports were developing in the South, so were Jim Crow laws codifying segregation and second-class citizenship for African Americans. In the North, integration developed at a glacial pace, so during the first decades of the twentieth century, few Black students found their way onto rosters of white teams. The majority of Black athletes played for historically Black colleges and universities (HBCUs) in the South whose budgets were intentionally strangled by racist state legislatures set on keeping Black Americans "in their place." Despite all of these struggles, Black collegians, professors, and administrators carried on and developed thriving athletics programs that had a deeper missional sense than many of their white counterparts.

Moses Fleetwood Walker and his brother were possibly the first players known to break the color barrier in intercollegiate sport when they played baseball for Oberlin College in Ohio. Their talent did not go unnoticed, as Michigan recruited Moses away from Oberlin in 1881, and his brother followed the next year. The brothers left Michigan to play professional baseball, and slowly other Black students followed their lead, integrating baseball, football, and other sports.

William Henry Lewis and teammate William Tecumseh Sherman Jackson integrated football at Amherst College in 1889. Lewis went on to be named team captain his senior year, and he was chosen by his classmates to give the class oration, in which he spoke of the "Amherst Idea" of equality for all. Attending Harvard Law School, Lewis played two more seasons and became the first Black player to receive all-American honors. He went on to an illustrious carrier in civil service and was eventually named assistant attorney general of the United States by President William Howard Taft.[55]

Few college sports stories involving race were as positive as the experience Lewis had at Amherst. The road was not easy for the pioneers of integration in college sports. When Michigan's first Black football player, George Jewett, traveled to play Albion College in 1890, fans and opposing teammates tried to goad Jewett into getting ejected from the game—even shouting, "Kill the N——." Jewett kept his cool and helped his team win the game. On campus, Jewett dealt with a professor and dean who did not believe he could study medicine and play football at the same time. So, Jewett transferred to Northwestern, becoming their first Black football player and earning a degree in medicine two years later.[56]

When Black Harvard student and star baseball player William Clarence Matthews first played in 1902, he made an immediate impact. Matthews was then benched during the next two games against the University of Virginia and the US Naval Academy. After returning to the lineup, he missed more games as teams refused to play against an integrated team. During his next two years, Matthews stayed on campus when Harvard made its annual trek to warmer weather and played teams in the South.[57]

When Paul Robeson integrated the Rutgers football team in 1915, he was the lone African American student on campus. When he showed up for a scrimmage with his teammates, someone punched him in the face and smashed his nose. When he fell to the ground, another player used his knee to fall on Robeson and dislocate his shoulder. After spending ten days recovering, the young man returned, only to have another teammate use his cleats in an attempt to break the bones in Robeson's hand. As Robeson recalled, "That's when I knew rage." The six-foot-three-inch Robeson picked the white student up and lifted the teammate over his head and was ready to harm him when his coach interceded. This story illustrates just the resistance he faced from his own team. It is little wonder that when Robeson became an accomplished singer and actor, his radical socialist leanings brought him more trouble during the Cold War.[58]

When Fritz Pollard joined Brown University in 1915, he did not face the attacks from teammates like Robeson. The slights and exclusion he faced remained palpable, however. When Pollard helped lead his team to the 1916 Rose

Bowl, the team arrived at Hotel Raymond, and Pollard was initially denied a room. His teammates then threatened to all leave the hotel, and Pollard was eventually given lodging. The story is interesting considering the fact that he was allowed to live in an on-campus university dormitory at Brown—but he ended up living alone, as no white classmate or other student at Brown would agree to be his roommate. His grandchildren recall his telling stories about playing at Yale and the fans would sing "Bye, Bye Blackbird" when he entered the game. He occasionally needed a police escort on and off the field. Pollard left Brown after two seasons and joined the army during World War I. He went on to have an illustrious career as a player and served as the first African American coach in professional football.[59]

The first Black athlete at Iowa State College was football player Jack Trice. He was not allowed to live in a dorm, so he found lodging off campus. His mother took out a mortgage on her house to help pay tuition, while Trice also worked as a custodian. The University of Missouri athletics director sent a letter to reaffirm the agreement that his team would not play against Iowa State if a Black man participated. As it turned out, such a "gentleman's agreement" would not be a concern that year. During Trice's second varsity game, the team traveled north to play the University of Minnesota. He wrote a note before the game and stuck it in his coat pocket:

> To Whom It May Concern:
> My thought just before the first real college game of my life: The honor of my race, family + self are at stake. Everyone is expecting me to do big things. I will! My whole body + soul are to be thrown recklessly about the field tomorrow. Every time the ball is snapped, I will be trying to do more than my part. On all defensive plays I must break thru the opponents line and stop the play in their territory. Beware of mass interference, fight low with your eyes open and toward the play. Roll block the interference. Watch out for cross buck and reverse end runs. Be on your toes every minute if you expect to make good.[60]

The next day, Trice did throw his body recklessly about the field. Most accounts recounted a defensive play in the second half where Trice lay defenseless on his back after throwing himself at the Gopher blockers. He was then trampled by an onslaught of players. Trice was helped off the field as the crowd chanted, "We're sorry Ames." After being taken to the hospital, the young sophomore was released to travel home with the team, but his condition worsened. He was immediately taken to the hospital where he died two days later, likely from internal bleeding and an infection. Although the intentionality of Trice's injury and death remain a mystery, critics have noted that the Ku Klux Klan's popularity in Minnesota had risen to a level that included having a float in the homecoming parade that fall. More than seventy years later, the Iowa State University named the stadium in honor of Jack Trice.[61]

These incidents of racism and violence of football in the North led many Black athletes during the Jim Crow Era to play in the segregated South among fellow Black teammates and opponents. The first documented intercollegiate baseball game occurred in 1888 between Morehouse College and Atlanta University. Two years later, Biddle College (Johnson C. Smith University) beat Livingstone College in Salisbury, North Carolina, in the first intercollegiate football game between HBCUs.[62] In 1894, Howard College hosted Lincoln University (of Pennsylvania) in what historian David Wiggins characterized as a "vicious and bloody affair," a description characteristic of late-nineteenth-century football. After another harrowing game the next year, the two teams stopped playing football against each other until 1904.[63]

Such challenges, along with the enforcement of Jim Crow laws that gripped the South and hampered the opportunity for Black institutions and individuals alike, kept intercollegiate matchups somewhat sporadic outside of regional centers like Atlanta. By the first decade of the twentieth century, athletic activity gained momentum. More college professors and administrators began calling for an association to direct and govern HBCU athletics. In 1912, Howard College professor and football coach Ernest J. Marshall organized a meeting for representatives from a number of HBCUs on the East Coast. Representatives from Hampton Institute, Howard, Lincoln University, Shaw, and Virginia Union became the founding members of the Colored Intercollegiate Athletic Association (CIAA). With a constitution and bylaws, the group sought to organize athletic events and serve as the national association for intercollegiate athletics for HBCUs. But the creation of rival conferences such as the Southeastern Intercollegiate Athletic Conference (SIAC) and the Southwestern Athletic Conference (SWAC) precluded a national governing association for HBCUs. Despite the lack of a national governing body, the CIAA boasted membership of some of the most prestigious HBCUs in the country.[64]

Two of these institutions, Howard and Lincoln, created a football rivalry that garnered the attention of the Black press across the country. In 1919 these colleges popularized and promoted the game as a "Thanksgiving Classic," with a celebratory atmosphere that included socials, additional student productions, and alumni parties culminating with the football game. The event showcased both universities, successfully commercialized football, and created an opportunity for Black social elite to celebrate their alma mater and develop a unique experience highlighting African American culture.[65]

The annual Thanksgiving Classic attracted ten thousand or more spectators and greatly increased the publicity offered to the two institutions. As billed, it was the most popular sporting event for HBCUs across the country. Unfortunately for the CIAA, in 1924, Howard played an ineligible student, a transfer who did not sit out the required season before participating in intercollegiate events. When approached by the CIAA regarding the rules violation, Howard withdrew from the conference. When Lincoln chose to play Howard in the annual classic that year, the CIAA chose to stick by its guns and revoke Lincoln's membership as well, something rarely seen among conferences consisting of primarily white institutions. By the time both colleges returned to the conference, the nation was entering into the Great Depression, and the game no longer held the same broad appeal that it did during the 1920s.[66]

With the CIAA no longer claiming what was viewed as the national classic, other conferences and schools filled the void. That same year, Tuskegee and Alabama State Normal School (Alabama State University) met for the first edition of its classic between members of the SIAC. Played at the Cramton Bowl in Montgomery, the two institutions emulated the festivities of the Howard-Lincoln rivalry with "golf tournaments, step shows, beauty pageants, parades, battle of the bands performances, concerts, and tailgating." More classics developed throughout the South, providing publicity, prestige, and a reason to celebrate an HBCU with pride.[67]

Another notable development in the SWAC was the creation of the Prairie View Bowl by Prairie View A&M College. Knowing they would not receive an invitation to the Rose Bowl, Prairie View decided to showcase its own talent during a New Year's Day bowl in Texas. The second-oldest bowl in the United States behind the Rose Bowl, the event increased public relations for PVAM and played an important role in helping the institution become a perennial football powerhouse.[68]

Experiences of Black players during this era at primarily white institutions remained one of isolation. Young men paid a deep price to become the pioneers of integration on northern teams. In the segregated South, HBCUs managed to follow the pattern of other big-time programs in creating publicity and prestige through athletics. At the same time, HBCUs, through the establishment of classic games, added to the character and pageantry of college sport.

The Golden Age in College Football: The 1920s

By the time the 1920s arrived, a number of forces outside of the university helped grow the sport into a spectacle unlike any other. Foremost among them remained newspapers. Unlike the muckraking journalists at the turn of the century, most sports writers of the 1920s were uncritically enthusiastic about big-time college football. They provided readers with hyperbole and melodrama purporting to be news. One of the best examples was a publicity stunt in which the Notre Dame backfield posed on horseback as the "Four Horsemen"—even though there is little evidence any had ever been on a horse before. The horses looked more like candidates for the slaughterhouse than the Kentucky Derby. None of this mattered, as sportswriter Grantland Rice of the *New York Herald Tribune* wrote on October 18, 1924, in a syndicated column that captured the American public's imagination:

> Outlined against a blue-gray October sky, the Four Horsemen rode again. In dramatic lore they are known as Famine, Pestilence, Destruction and Death. These are only aliases. Their real names are Stuhldreher, Miller, Crowley and Layden. They formed the crest of the South Bend cyclone before which another fighting Army football team was swept over the precipice at the Polo Grounds yesterday afternoon as 55,000 spectators peered down on the bewildering panorama spread on the green plain below.
>
> A cyclone can't be snared. It may be surrounded, but somewhere it breaks through to keep on going. When the cyclone starts from South Bend, where the candle lights still gleam through the Indiana sycamores, those in the way must take to storm cellars at top speed.
>
> Yesterday the cyclone struck again as Notre Dame beat the Army, 13 to 7, with a set of backfield stars that ripped and crashed through a strong Army defense with more speed and power than the warring cadets could meet.
>
> Notre Dame won its ninth game in twelve Army starts through the driving power of one of the greatest backfields that ever churned up the turf of any gridiron in any football age. Brilliant backfields may come and go, but in Stuhldreher, Miller, Crowley and Layden, covered by a fast and charging line, Notre Dame can take its place in front of the field.[69]

A football and baseball player at Vanderbilt while earning a degree in the classics, understatement and lean prose were alien to Grantland Rice and his fellow sportswriters. A game was magnified to heroic proportions with adjectives and adverbs that invoked classical themes and historic motifs. When Rice typed out his story at the New York Polo Grounds, he was in good company—as more than 240 fellow journalists were in the press box—after all, one had to assure that the game got total coverage. The publicity associated with college sports was illustrative of a spirited popular interest in college rivalries and reputation. It was a friendly battleground of competition among peers for respect and fame—ironically played out in ritualized forms and images before a mass American audience of whom most had not even graduated from high school—and among whom only a minuscule number and percentage had gone to college. It was in large measure the vicarious thrill of a glimpse at the elite collegiate life and activities, including sports, within the American campus that fascinated and thrilled a new generation of readers.

As Michael Oriard asserted in *Reading Football*, the newspaper media continued to play an important role in the 1920s. Newspaper coverage began to change after World War I, however. "As the mass media have grown collectively more powerful, the power of a specific media has declined." This was true of newspapers. Oriard also noted that as local and regional papers across the country expanded their own coverage, they began measuring teams against a region such as "southern" or "midwestern" football. No longer was the popular press focused on a few teams in the Northeast. This, in many respects, propelled the popularity of the sport in new ways, even as traditional elite teams lost sway in newspapers across the country.[70]

While printed coverage continued to hold an important position with regard to media and college athletics, a new medium gained traction during the decade and spread the glories of college football beyond the boundaries of print pages in the cities' dailies. At the beginning of the decade, radio had developed into a commercially viable product. On October 8, 1921, KDKA out of Pittsburg broadcast the first college football game on the radio, featuring the rivalry between Pittsburgh and West Virginia University. To underscore the commercial value of college football, the first professional baseball game to hit the airwaves had occurred only months earlier on the same station. In addition, the same Grantland Rice who so eloquently wrote descriptions of college football games served as an early broadcaster of professional baseball.[71]

When Pop Warner's Stanford team faced Knute Rockne's undefeated Four Horsemen from Notre Dame in the 1925 Rose Bowl, WGN out of Chicago had a direct wire to the game and broadcast results as soon as they received them. They also relayed the details to WCBS in New York. For the large number of Catholics in America, the game offered an opportunity to engage as equals with Protestant schools.[72] The following year, Charlie Paddock (who had created the controversy between the NCAA and the AAU) called the game between

Washington and Alabama on local radio stations. Alabama's victory had been dubbed "the game that changed the South," and radio had been part of that transformation. The success of the radio broadcasts led to NBC's coast-to-coast broadcast of the 1927 Rose Bowl, when Alabama and Stanford finished in a 7–7 tie.[73] The commercial success of radio broadcasts in the 1920s revealed the extent to which the American public had bought into college football as a spectacle and an entertaining sport to be followed by individuals who had never dreamed of attending college.

Along with newspaper and magazine coverage, radio broadcasts helped create football stars because it also led to increased ratings. Those ratings played both roles of cause and effect in creating the first national football celebrities in history. Before this era, there were players who became the "big man on campus," but the print and radio media allowed college football players and coaches to become larger celebrities in their own right.

No player symbolized the convergence of amateurism, athletic heroics on the field, and media coverage like Harold "Red" Grange. Newspaper reporters called him the "Illini Flash" or "Galloping Ghost" during football season and the "Wheaton Ice Man" during the summer because he worked a job delivering ice in the Chicago suburb since he did not have an athletic scholarship. The press felt compelled to discuss the fact that he held a job during the summer, suggesting that it was an oddity for all-American football players to have to work to pay for school, even though subsidies were a violation of NCAA and Big Ten rules.[74]

Grange was named an all-American during his sophomore season, which was rare at the time. But true fame took hold in 1924 when the junior scored four touchdowns in the first quarter with runs of 95, 66, 55, and 40 yards. WGN's Quin Ryan called the play-by-play over the airwaves that day, and his exploits garnered national attention. It began a press frenzy that continued through his senior year. After one especially impressive performance, Damon Runyon called the undergraduate "Three or four men rolled into one. He is Jack Dempsey, Babe Ruth, Al Jolson, Paavo Nurmi, and Man o' War." The press created a celebrity based on his athletic performance, and that in turn drew throngs to watch him play. Everywhere Grange stepped on the field, crowds followed.[75]

Noting his celebrity while at the same time adding to it, *Time* magazine put the senior from Illinois on the cover of its magazine. The following month, on November 21, 1925, Grange played his final college game at Ohio Stadium against the Ohio State Buckeyes. The stadium, built three years earlier, boasted a seating capacity of 66,210. When Grange showed up, more than 82,000 attended the game. The next day the *New York Times* reported, "A proposal has been made to nominate him for Congress in spite of his age ineligibility. They are considering naming a town after him. Thousands would recognize him anywhere, having seen his photograph so many times. Hundreds of thousands have watched him play; millions have followed his career."[76] The same article also reported that Grange was leaving the University of Illinois effective immediately, dropping out before earning his degree. He signed with an agent and joined the Chicago Bears of the nascent and struggling National Football League. In a postseason tour of games, Grange made a hundred thousand dollars in the next four months and brought the NFL desperately needed publicity.[77] Grange had set a precedent hundreds of athletes would later follow: forgoing college to turn pro.

Condemnation from colleges was swift and unrelenting. His coach chastised the move; the Big Ten banned professional football players from coaching or officiating. Other conferences followed suit. The NCAA recommended that no coach be hired who had ever played or "connected in any capacity" with professional football. No coach or conference seemed to lament the large crowds Grange drew to stadiums, raising the question as to whether coaches and university officials were fighting amateurism or competition from professional football.[78]

The NCAA lamented professional football while also heralding the professional football coach—at the college level. During the first decades of the twentieth century, universities recruited and paid excessive salaries to find winning coaches. The biggest names included John Heisman, Amos Alonzo Stagg, Pop Warner, and Fielding Yost. All but Stagg held multiple coaching positions, being wooed by universities with greater resources and liberal contracts. If Grange had a counterpart in the coaching ranks to be both coach and celebrity during the 1920s, however, it was Knute Rockne of Notre Dame. Having a successful career as a college football player, Rockne played professional football, returning to his alma mater as an assistant coach and then assuming the head coaching position in 1918.

During the next thirteen years, Rockne's prowess made him a coaching legend. A common theme in the myriad popular books detailing his life was that Rockne, Notre Dame football, and American values were inseparable. Providing a twentieth-century version of a Horatio Alger novel, the son of Norwegian immigrants grew up in the melting pot of Chicago. The gifted athlete and student attended Notre Dame, excelling at sports and science. Having to choose between a career in football or chemistry, Rockne chose the former. As a coach,

Rockne was not just a winning coach; he was also a teacher, student, disciplinarian, motivator, and family man. Despite some reservations (and exaggerations), historical records indicate that Rockne was an impressive man and a worthy sports hero.[79]

More critical scholarly works have pointed out Rockne's shrewd acumen in developing publicity for his teams. He wooed sportswriters by giving them free tickets and offering speaking engagements. He used student assistants in what could be described as early sports information and publicity directors. One of these students later helped popularize the Fighting Irish, while Grantland Rice drew on biblical apocalyptic imagery dubbing Notre Dame's backfield as the Four Horsemen. When Notre Dame's Four Horsemen faced Pop Warner's Stanford team in the Rose Bowl in 1925, more than fifty thousand fans filled the stadium while others observed from the hillsides outside the stadium. Sigmund Spaeth announced the game on WGBS, which was carried by wire to New York City. Media also employed a telepix to send photos "On Wings of Lighting."[80]

Rockne masterfully utilized the media to bring national fame to his football team and his own coaching. In turn, Rockne devoted time and effort in lucrative endorsements and promotions. The coach sponsored products and went on speaking tours. He was a sales promotion director for the Studebaker Corporation. Interestingly, Rockne almost left Notre Dame shortly before his Rose Bowl victory when Iowa offered him a ten-thousand-dollar salary. Notre Dame matched the salary, but after more success on the gridiron, he was planning to leave the Fighting Irish for Columbia when they offered him a whopping twenty-five thousand dollars a year. With contractual obligations to Notre Dame, the coach turned down the Columbia offer when it became public before a resolution had been made.[81]

Rockne's life ended tragically in a plane crash on March 31, 1931. Still at the height of his coaching career, his fame became immortal. The 1940 movie *Knute Rockne, All American* further solidified his iconic status. Ronald Reagan starred as late college football player George Gipp, whose death at a young age inspired Rockne's motivational "Win One for the Gipper" speech. Rockne's life and career embodied the contradictions in college sports, as he mixed character-building with commercialism. The conference and the NCAA publicly denounced his high salary and lucrative endorsements while fans lauded him as a coach and educator of young men. Whatever the verdict, Rockne's life and legend exposed growing tensions in college athletics. Clearly, big-time coaches had drifted far from the company of professors, even as some faculty claimed control over athletics.

Massive stadium construction during the 1920s also signified the ascendency of college football into sporting spectacles for the general public. Harvard had led the way near the turn of the century with the inaugural game in 1903 at its Soldiers' Field, which originally seated more than twenty-eight thousand fans and over time expanded to accommodate crowds of more than fifty thousand.[82] Not to be outdone, Yale followed suit, opening the Yale Bowl with a seating capacity of seventy thousand. Princeton's more modest stadium, opening the next year, accommodated forty thousand fans.

Once again, aspiring American universities followed the Big Three's lead. The floodgates opened nationwide after World War I, as many universities constructed a "Memorial Field" in tribute to citizens and alumni who had been killed in military service during the war.[83] Historian Winton Solberg detailed the construction and expansion of stadiums across the Big Ten during the era, noting that good roads and automobiles made travel to such entertaining events feasible.

The stadiums in the Midwest began to supplant academic buildings on postcards, which were immensely popular during the era. Postcards depicting the campus stadium were unique in college scenes because they were the only ones that featured thousands of cheering fans. Other, more staid postcards displayed campus dormitories and libraries photographed early in the morning before students and professors were on-site. Picture postcards provided the crucial print medium that visitors could send to the folks back home, showcasing the architectural grandeur they had seen as tourists.[84]

Stadium construction was not confined to the Midwest. Both Stanford and the University of California, Berkeley, constructed stadiums that seated more than sixty thousand. Although more modest in size, stadiums were also built at southern universities. The University of Georgia inaugurated its Sanford Stadium with a victory over mighty Yale. Alabama built a new stadium, and Tulane led the way in the South with a stadium seating more than thirty-five thousand that would host the Sugar Bowl for decades to come.

Large stadiums signaled the ascendancy of college sport—football in particular. Such building projects also necessitated that advertising and publicity continue. The University of Chicago's football coach and athletics director Amos Alonzo Stagg proved to be a master of publicity, using Chicago's stadium to extend the university's athletics empire. He arranged for the University of Chicago to host numerous state high school championships, including track and field, both to attract paying spectators and news reporters as well as to recruit high school stars to his own University of Chicago teams. Stagg was an

An aerial view of Ohio Stadium in 1928, commonly referred to as "The Horse-shoe." Like many college football stadiums, it was constructed with an open end, emulating the first college football stadium built by Harvard in 1903. The Ohio State University Archives

organizational genius who understood the importance of maximizing revenues and diversifying activities and sponsorship. Since all university athletic facilities, including tennis courts, were under his jurisdiction, he charged admission fees for university faculty and staff who wished to play recreational tennis.

Promotion and branding of college sports made a "great leap forward" when Stagg as athletics director and coach persuaded President Harper to use modern media to publicize University of Chicago football games. In 1928, Stagg spent five hundred dollars per month for two and a half months to rent prominent billboard space downtown that broadcast, "THE UNIVERSITY OF CHICAGO Announces Its Football Schedule for 1928." Drivers and pedestrians were enticed by the university's marketing emphases as they read the bold letters proclaiming, "Season tickets and single game tickets may be obtained from FOOTBALL TICKETS COMMITTEE, 5625 ELLIS AVENUE." By utilizing the new technology of telephones, viewers were informed, "For information, telephone Fairfax 4405."[85]

In the late 1920s, Harvard added steel bleachers to enclose the open endzone, expanding capacity to more than fifty-seven thousand. Author's collection

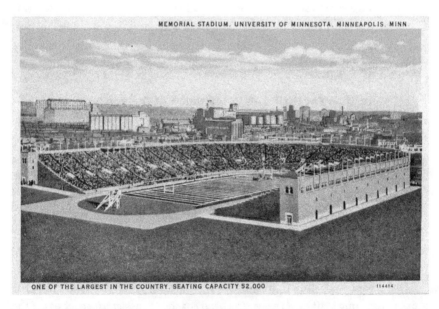

The University of Minnesota Memorial Stadium, like others across the country, was constructed during the 1920s and dedicated to those at the university who had served in World War I. Author's collection

This billboard advertising University of Chicago football was posted at two key intersections in the city for the upcoming 1928 season. Courtesy of the Wellcome Collection

College and university presidents nationwide took notice of the marketing and public relations innovations by Athletics Director Stagg and President Harper at the University of Chicago. Most of them eventually applied the lessons of college sports success to their own initiatives. The general lesson was that college and university publicity was good and necessary. In addition, promotion and publicity involving intercollegiate sports was particularly effective in attracting student applicants, community support, or major donors.

More Than Football: The Proliferation of College Sports

Packed stadiums led to exorbitant salaries for many big-time football coaches. On many campuses, the popularity of college football also fostered an expansion of numerous other new varsity teams. By the 1920s, several established colleges and universities offered as many as twenty varsity squads for men. The 1926 edition of the US Military Academy's yearbook, *The Howitzer*, illustrated a strong commitment to excellence and competition in sixteen varsity sports, including football, boxing, wrestling, swimming, crew, track and field, cross-country, soccer, lacrosse, baseball, basketball, gymnastics, polo, rifle, and pistol. Harvard and Yale offered a comparable slate.[86]

One reason such growth in teams was affordable was that members of the football coaching staff often served as head coaches or assistant coaches for the so-called minor or Olympic sports. Indeed, one national benefit of the growth of American intercollegiate sports was the reliance of the US Olympic squads on college student-athletes or recent alumni to fill teams. Although this recruitment created controversy with the Amateur Athletic Union, men's American college athletes usually had spectacular results in international competitions and the Olympic Games.

Educational Lessons on Athletic Expansion: 1900 to 1930

As had been the case in the nineteenth century, the athletic emphasis at American universities appeared to conflict with the academic aspirations of the same institutions. A closer look at the tends and themes in higher education provides an interesting counternarrative.

University officials established what would become the National Collegiate Athletics Association in 1906. This paralleled the establishment of professional academic associations by professors across the country. Professionals in academic fields became highly prized during the first three decades of the twentieth century. The American Psychological Association formed in 1892. The American Sociological Association was created in 1905, at nearly the same time as the NCAA. Approximately one decade later, the American Educational Research Association developed from a group of research specialists in the National Education Association. A year after the formation of the NCAA, the Organization of American Historians created an association for their field. In short, a national organization devoted to the study of problems of athletics fit within the larger framework of American academic life. Leading universities competed over the best and brightest faculty members as well, just at lower salaries. They sought out specialists in specific fields of study to lead increasingly diverse and insular fields of study.

In the early nineteenth century, American colleges hired intelligent generalists who could teach young students the classics to help them live a life guided by the wisdom of the ages. These professors slowly gave way to professional academics who held doctoral degrees in specific disciplines. Newly trained professors focused on meticulous research in their field of study. As one study noted, "Harvard, founded for the training of preachers, turns out electrical engineers and Masters of Business Administration."[87] Professionalism had taken hold of the best universities in the country. Similarly, athletics afforded professional coaches the opportunity to focus on their specialized field—generally football—and become the very best in their discipline. These similarities were contrasted only by the salaries paid to winning coaches. Of course, few if any professors could command an audience of seventy thousand devoted adherents on any given Saturday. Hence general popularity and profits provided the distinction between professors and coaches.

Despite the degree of difference, capitalism, competition, publication, and celebrity all existed in academics. As one example, John Dewey, the famous philosopher of education, left the University of Chicago in 1904, became the president of the American Philosophical Association, and then accepted a position at Columbia.[88] Almost a decade before that, Columbia hired away history professor William Sloane from Princeton. Sloane had been a key figure in the development of the Olympic movement in the United States. At Yale, a fifteen-million-dollar gift from the will of John William Sterling in 1918 led to the creation of multiple endowed Sterling professorships, designed to recruit or retain the very best faculty.[89] When Yale appointed its first Sterling Professor in 1920, the *Harvard Crimson* ran an article boasting that Harvard had recruited two faculty members away from both Wisconsin and Yale, along with another professor from Oxford.[90] Big donations from devout capitalists, competition among elite universities, and the quest to be the best existed in academia. But the public simply did not offer the same enthusiastic interest that exhibited in athletic contests. Why? Simply put, the competitive games in academics did not offer an entertaining aspect like athletic events. No space existed for the spectator.

The solution to this dilemma, according to Harvard's president Lowell and some of his fellow college presidents, was to seek "the introduction of the competitive motive into the field of scholarship." Editor Edwin Slosson of *The Independent* magazine and author of *Great American Universities* concluded, "The professors, it appears, are to take lessons from the coaches," and academics were to seek "an inducement to exertion with the greater glory of banners and bands and newspaper headlines." Slosson posed the rhetorical question, "If we are to have intercollegiate contests in intellectualism, what form will they take? Will there be public disputations, in the style of the schoolmen? Will the two sides alternately propound to each other mathematical puzzles and logical subtleties? Will the Association of American Universities prescribe the rules and the Carnegie Foundation and General Education Board offer the prizes? And will the public take the same interest in the contest that they now take in baseball?"

For academics to match the appeal of athletics, Editor Slosson proposed the following scenario:

Let us suppose that the new *regime* of intellectual is in effect now and Columbia and Cornell are matching their dissertations. In New York City, Park Row is packed with upturned faces watching the bulletin boards. Clerks and their employers hurrying home have stopped to get the returns Bootblacks and messenger boys, sitting in a row on the fences, have staked their last nickels. The stockbroker nudges the man with a dinner pail and asks him for the score. On the blackboard in front of the newspaper office appears the announcement that Dr. Kropff, of Columbia, has prepared some new derivatives of diaminoisophthalic acid. Cornell counters with Dr. Ray's triazo-compounds of resorcin. Then Columbia scores with Dr. Tripp's dissertation on "Groups of order p3 q2," followed by Dr Mead's. . . . That part of the crowd which has its money on Cornell looks gloomy, but recovers when markers chalk down. . . . A shout from a thousand throats is heard when the street sees that Dr. Haas of Columbia has translated the Dasarupa of Dhanamajaa, until the applause is checked by the announcement of Dr. McKelvey's study. . . . So the contest goes on hour by hour, while the popular excitement grows more intense, and extras of the yellow journals, with portraits of the wining men and explanatory diagrams of their theses, spread the news to the suburbs. The real heroes of the university thus receive the honor that is their due, and the athletic student must get his gratification from the mere joy of exercise.[91]

Slosson's projection, along with Lowell's comment, revealed the appeal of collegiate sports as part of American values. It also revealed the recurrent ways in which university presidents and academic leaders tried to harness and align the entertaining aspect of athletics with some equivalent activity on the academic side of the campus. As historian Brian M. Ingrassia has argued, many college presidents did not ignore or resist the appeal of college football. Rather, their quest was to reconcile the popularity of college football and its lessons of character-building and competition with some counterparts in the formal curriculum.[92]

The attempts to tie the appeal of athletics with professionalized academics failed to popularize academic research, but it did reveal how modern university leaders were philosophically attuned to compartmentalize athletics in order to use it for popular appeal and fundraising. As David Levine convincingly wrote about the higher education in the early twentieth century, "the major innovations in higher education ended with the professionalization of the elite university."[93] Once again, the professional academic had become the center of the modern university. But critics expected the professional coach and player to be excluded from the professionalized university. This was simply an untenable proposition considering the publicity and funding gained from success on the gridiron.

So, why did the 1920s become the golden age of football? The professionalized university, the expansion of daily newspapers across the country, and the creation of radio broadcasts to millions of listeners all played essential roles. A neglected piece of the puzzle, however, was that the modern university, previously existing in the Northeast and a few other outposts, expanded across the country. State flagship universities, land grant universities, and well-endowed private institutions all sought the attention and prestige given to "Great American Universities." This term was the title of Edwin Slosson's 1910 study on higher education in America. According to Slosson, fourteen universities in the United States deserved to be called a great American university. Of these fourteen, thirteen engaged in big-time athletics. Only the young Johns Hopkins University, modeled on the German research university, had a football team, but it remained truly "amateur."[94]

Athletics in general and football in particular played an important role in the ability of "standard" American universities to climb the ladder of prestige. Modeled on the great American universities but lacking the resources of elite universities, standard American university presidents utilized the publicity of athletics to promote their institutions. These universities sought newspaper coverage in an attempt to climb the competitive ladder of elite universities, and football played an important role in this pursuit. In his study, Slosson regretted his inability to include athletics programs. As he noted, "Among my omissions are two conspicuous tendencies in American University life to which I have merely referred in the proceeding articles; that is, the growth of ritualism and of athleticism."[95]

Slosson made a poignant observation in 1910: "University presidents, with few exceptions, express approval of intercollegiate contests, alumni give enthusiastic support, students vent their displeasure upon any who presume to question their values, and the outside world encourages and applauds." Slosson noted that faculty disapproved of big-time athletics, but he pointed out that many professors would complain about the practices of rival institutions. Then, as he visited those rival institutions, individuals would claim that the real scandals existed at the institutions from which Slosson had already visited.[96] In short, everybody wanted the best possible football team they could field, and those who challenged the supremacy of a rival school were engaged in unethical practice. Even among critics, athletics played a central and ubiquitous role in the spread of the popularity of football and other intercollegiate sport.

In this way, the growth of sports emulated structural and curricular developments in the modern university. If a particular reform or program proved successful at one institution, other institutions emulated the practice (such as the development of business programs). As Laurence Veysey noted in *The Emergence of the American University*, by 1910, the blueprint for the American university had been established. An architect was no longer needed to build an American university, only a contractor who understood the key elements needed to bring publicity for a university. These contractors viewed competitive athletics, especially football, as helping to make the standard American university a great one.

Athletics played an important role in the promotion of university life, and by the end of the 1920s, most university presidents understood the importance of athletic prowess. In 1924, Kentucky's Centre College beat Harvard in their football game played before a large crowd at Harvard's home field in Cambridge, Massachusetts. The publicity for Centre was worth the hiring of a professional coach and vaulted the small Presbyterian college into national fame.

By 1929, higher education and college sports were wed in such a way that it would be impossible to root sports out of college life. The American university, despite its complaints about big-time athletics, built athletics programs across the country. On the field, players and coaches wanted victories. For presidents, football proved to be an important activity in promoting young universities. In sum, presidents and universities welcomed big-time athletics. They were part of the modern university structure, and they helped aspiring institutions to follow the same model. In sum, intercollegiate athletics played an important role in the growth of universities and vice versa.

3

Big-Time Football and Backlash,

1929 to 1941

The Paradox of Popularity and Problems

in College Sports

By 1929 the character of college sports was that of success and excess. The former had led to the latter, leaving intercollegiate athletics as a fixture in American life whose box office appeal combined with publicity and prestige provided a powerful momentum. It was difficult, if not impossible, for colleges and their conferences to control the conduct of athletic contests so that they would align with their institutions' educational mission. College presidents were either unable or unwilling to rein in the juggernaut of big-time football. Indeed, when sportswriters and even historians hailed the "Golden Age of Sports" of the 1920s, college football remained indelibly linked with the professional pursuits of Major League Baseball, championship prizefighting, and Triple Crown horse racing.

Even though the federal government had ventured into regulation in the form of antitrust laws to curb the incessant growth of railroads and oil refining, no such oversight extended to the highly commercialized activities of big-time college sports. The United States was one of the few industrialized nations that did not have a central ministry of education to regulate schools and colleges. In the early twentieth century, any initiative at reform and restraint in higher education came from foundations, which followed a mission of "Private Power for the Public Good." Foremost were the Carnegie Foundation for the Advancement of Teaching (CFAT) and the Rockefeller Foundation and its General Education Board, both based in New York City. The strong-willed president of the CFAT, Henry Pritchett, had been president of the Massachusetts Institute of Technology. As such, his agenda was to bring the order and principles of engineering to bear on educational problems. Standards and standardization were the solutions the CFAT brought to the public forum as antidotes to the sprawling, incoherent practices in American colleges and universities.[1]

Pritchett's approach with the CFAT was to promote social engineering of American institutions. This meant reliance on the systematic data and analysis of a detailed research report to lead to reasonable observations and, ultimately, the moral imperative to set things aright. Under Pritchett, CFAT's major initiatives included analyzing problems and investigating malpractices—and then providing incentives for colleges to standardize their admissions requirements by adhering to the "Carnegie Unit" of high school courses and transcripts. The carrot was to provide compliant colleges with the faculty pension plan—the legacy of which is still familiar today as TIAA-CREF. One of its most publicized projects was to compile systematic information on the proliferation of medical schools, documenting that most of these had little if any academic rigor or professional accountability.

Eventually the CFAT turned its attention to the distinctive, visible phenomenon of big-time, competitive, and commercialized sports hosted by American colleges. It was an obvious topic that had been ignored but not unnoticed. Colleges pushed back against this investigation, both unabashed and unapologetic about their programs that had expanded and extended within the campus and across the nation. For the CFAT the rationale for serious study and reform was that sports, especially college football, had sprawled without accountability, producing chaos. This was the context for the well-funded CFAT to undertake an unprecedented project. Properly aligned with academic offerings and educational mission, the role of the CFAT and other major private foundations was to use their resources to bring coherence to chaos in educational practices. This included intercollegiate athletics.

The Carnegie Report: American College Athletics

In October 1929 the Carnegie Foundation for the Advancement of Teaching released Bulletin No. 23, *American College Athletics*. The NCAA had requested a study of college sports, and in January 1926 the foundation accepted the invitation, naming Howard J. Savage as the lead investigator for research and reporting. Savage, a Harvard PhD who had served as a faculty member at Bryn Mawr before accepting a post at CFAT, had already completed a short study of college sports in America and had researched the same topic in England. He and his team of researchers made campus visits to 112 institutions across the United States and Canada to gather more information. Researchers visited large and small schools alike. After more than three years of fact-finding research and writing, Bulletin No. 23 went public.

The 349-page narrative on the administration of college sports across North America offered a detailed account of data addressing a wide array of facets in college sports. The first four chapters of Bulletin No. 23 provided context for the state of college athletics in the 1920s. Savage covered the history of college sports in America, the evolution of amateurism, and the state of sports and physical education at the high school level. The remainder of the report (chapters 5–12) addressed multiple components of the college sports enterprise, including the administrative structure of Intercollegiate athletics, welfare and medical care (or lack thereof) for student-athletes, the role of the professional coach, external influences, the recruiting and subsidizing of athletes, and the influence of the press in the commercialization of college athletics.[2]

The report's detail and narrative style made the document something few individuals would ever take the time to read in its entirety. Instead, most of the public (as well as college leaders) received their information about the report from newspapers. Unlike the general tone of the report, headlines across the country emphasized sensationalist elements. The front-and-center headline of the *New York Times* read, "College Sports Tainted by Bounties, Carnegie Fund Finds in Wide Study." The *Chicago Daily Tribune* front page declared, "Carnegie Report Hits Big Ten Athletics: Three Year Probe Indicts American College System." Closer to the home of the Michigan campus, page 1 of the Detroit Daily exclaimed, "U. of M. Accused."[3]

Virtually all these headlines and stories addressed chapter 10 of the report, "The Recruiting and Subsidizing of Athletes." Savage and his team reported that the overwhelming majority of football programs engaged in the recruitment of players subsidized the cost of college for the most outstanding athletes. Both activities violated the NCAA's amateur code. Football recruitment frequently occurred through athletics departments, but about thirty percent of the institutions utilized alumni to "proselytize" the best talent, and almost ten percent of colleges' senior-level administrators assisted in the endeavor.[4]

Recruiting promises by alumni, coaches, or administrators remained directly linked to subsidizing athletes. Subsidies for college players varied widely in both methods of payment and amounts. The essentially unregulated funding could come through various means. An interested alum could provide cash directly to a family to cover tuition, room, and board. Other boosters might donate money to a university scholarship fund earmarked for qualified athletes. Athletics departments regularly connected athletes with jobs on campus or around town. Employment regularly became "phantom" work without any responsibilities. Other institutions offered loans, and repayment often remained optional. The most onerous forms of payment remained the most difficult to document, such as slush funds of cash distributed by someone in the athletics department from a "black box" or desk drawer.[5]

Savage's chapter on recruiting and paying players addressed topics that the NCAA and regional conferences had grappled with for years. The difference between previous debates and Bulletin No. 23 lay in the fact that conferences and the NCAA attempted to address the problem without identifying abuses at specific universities. *American College Athletics*, in contrast, detailed these practices and listed the offending institutions. Nearly all elite northeastern schools (the Ivy League had not yet been formed) engaged in recruitment and subsidies, as did universities in the Big Ten, the Southern Conference, and the Pacific Coast Conference. In short, disregard for the rules of amateurism permeated college athletics.

Publishing these details in headlines across the country led to immediate denials and criticism of Savage's work by coaches, athletics directors, and others. These replies, taken as a whole, provide evidence of what has been termed the "Ritual of Rhetoric" in the modern university. Vanderbilt's chancellor denied knowledge of unethical practices, while Alabama's President Denny explained that many students were employed by the university but positions were not held for star players.[6] The Brown University Athletic Council claimed the report "in part false" and "so misleading" that they were surprised the Carnegie Foundation supported it. After Brown conducted its own on-campus investigation of practices, the institution could not refute Savage's findings.[7]

The Big Ten, generally viewed as a leading conference at the time, offered some of the strongest denials and denunciations. Savage had listed eight of the ten conference institutions as violators. Michigan's celebrated football coach turned athletics director Fielding Yost denied that the university subsidized athletes. Regarding recruiting he stated, "I know of no such system of agents in operation." Big Ten commissioner John L. Griffith told the *New York Times* he had not had a chance to read the entire report, but he believed that it failed to provide "a fair picture" of his conference. Griffith asserted that the Big Ten had "nothing to be ashamed of" and questioned the study's research and reporting, noting that relying "upon facts uncovered by an agent in a twenty-four hour visit to a university" was unfair.[8] These were interesting assertions considering that Griffith had been apprised of the preliminary findings of the report months earlier and told the conference's athletics directors, "You can well appreciate that there will be considerable excitement when this report is made public."[9] Griffith understood the modern university, the press, and the value of rhetoric.

Despite the sensationalized headlines newspapers printed to report on *American College Athletics*, in reality the report understated problems of recruiting and subsidizing athletes. As historian Ronald Smith noted, Savage's team incorrectly stated that six big-time programs had no subsidies: Chicago, Cornell, Illinois, Virginia, West Point, and Yale. Of these, Smith stated, "only Virginia might have been clean."[10] The Big Ten had suspended relations with the University of Iowa over blatant disregard for the recruiting and payment of players. Yet Savage avoided any sensational account of Iowa's troubles. Rather, the report focused only on documented evidence and testimony.[11]

These problems were not new. In the mid-twenties, the University of Southern California began challenging the football dominance of Stanford and the University of California, Berkeley, on the West Coast. In turn, the two universities then protested the eligibility of USC's star players, later announcing during the season that Stanford and Berkeley would sever athletic ties with USC. The schools resumed playing when they realized how much money they were losing from games played in the new Rose Bowl, but USC used the snub to highlight the "superior and elitist attitudes"[12] of Stanford and Berkeley. When Navy went winless against Army between 1922 and 1927, the Annapolis university announced it would only play institutions with a strict three-year eligibility rule, ending the rivalry with Army, which allowed four years of eligibility. President Herbert Hoover encouraged resumption of the rivalry, but not until the US War Department ordered the two to play a charity game in December 1930 did the two schools meet on the gridiron. After Princeton beat Harvard five out of six years in a row in the twenties, Harvard responded by dropping Princeton from the schedule in favor of a game with Michigan. The *Harvard Crimson* argued that Princeton was an inferior institution and prestige came "from the fact that she has long been included in the Big Three" (along with Harvard and Yale).[13]

Newspapers generally ignored the other concerns raised in the Savage report. Unsurprisingly, reporters did not emphasize Savage's chapter addressing the deleterious impact of press coverage on college sports. Conference relationships, professional coaches, undue press attention, as well as the health and well-being of athletes all played important roles in the growth of big-time athletics but made for less intriguing headlines. Savage noted that college sports provided print material and "augmented profits and salaries."[14] As historian

John Watterson noted, the press gave little attention to Bulletin No. 23's discussion of "The Hygiene of Athletic Training." The chapter revealed the ways in which training had improved from the nineteenth century, when players starved or dehydrated themselves. Scientific knowledge discouraged such activities, but football coaches often ignored players' physical health and safety in order to win. Some coaches offered players strychnine as a performance enhancer. Milder drugs such as caffeine tablets were provided before games. One coach "offered to inject cocaine" into a player's injured leg to dull the pain so he could continue in the game. Another coach overrode the team physician's orders and had a plaster cast cut off an injured player's leg to put him in the game.[15]

American College Athletics clearly explained the various abuses and challenges facing intercollegiate sports. Savage asserted that big-time athletics existed at institutions where "the primary emphasis has been transferred from the things of the spirit or the mind to the material."[16] Unfortunately, it offered little in the way of policies that would solve this dilemma. In order to remedy the current state of affairs, material and commercial (i.e., monetary) interests needed to be "diminished." Savage's second charge offered even fewer specific policy suggestions: "The American college must renew within itself the force that will challenge the best intellectual capabilities of the undergraduates." Savage added, "Happily this task is now engaging the attention of numerous college officers and teachers."[17]

Longtime CFAT president Henry Pritchett wrote an incendiary preface to Savage's study. Unlike Savage's sober analysis, Pritchett offered a blistering critique of higher education and college athletics. He offered solutions far more to the point:

> The paid coach, the gate receipts, the special training tables, the costly sweaters and extensive journeys in special Pullman cars, the recruiting from the high school, the demoralizing publicity showered on the players, the devotion of an undue proportion of time to training, the devices for putting a desirable athlete, but a weak scholar, across the hurdles of the examination—these ought to stop . . . and the intercollege and intramural sports be brought back to a stage in which they can be enjoyed by large numbers of students and where they do not involve an expenditure of time and money.[18]

Savage spoke in generalities about solution, while Pritchett offered specific activities needing eradication. On matters of intellectual growth and academic rigor, Pritchett stated that the president and the faculty were responsible.

Regarding the key issues of commercialism, recruiting, and subsidies to players, however, the report clearly opined: "Experience has shown that, of all who are involved in these evils—administrative officers, teachers, directors of athletics, coaches, alumni, undergraduates, and townsmen—the man who is the most likely to succeed in uprooting the evils of recruiting and subsidizing is the college president."[19] Yet the report did not offer any examples of presidents successfully curbing such abuses.

While relatively easy for Bulletin No. 23 to argue that presidents were the key to ending commercialism and all the "evils" that it produced in college sports, such claims crashed headlong into reality. Presidents seeking reform were confronted with several problems. First, in traditional American fashion, colleges and universities remained autonomous, including each institution's athletic policy. Although none openly claimed to do so, any institution retained the freedom to pay athletes and to recruit the best players. The result might have been expulsion from a conference or refusal of other institutions to play such a school, but the NCAA remained a debating society without the authority to enforce its ideals or punish institutions guilty of violations. Second, multiple constituencies—including the public, alumni, students, and donors—saw nothing wrong with helping pay a college student's tuition if it resulted in wins on the football field. Why shouldn't a wealthy alum of a university be allowed to fund a student's education if they so desired? In fact, civic groups and boosters were welcome to do so, as long as the student was not an athlete.

Also interesting to note was that faculty opinion may have not aligned with students or alumni. In the wake of the Carnegie Foundation's report, the American Association of University Professors (AAUP) offered its position in a review of *American College Athletics*. The review first noted that Savage's findings had "long been known as fact to every individual who has come in contact with college sport in this country."[20] The reviewer lamented a change in attitude among college athletes. In decades past the abuses already existed, but in the 1920s athletes believed they were doing the "common sense, practical thing" by accepting funds. These athletes offered no moral or ethical reason "why they should not exploit their college for personal gain." The article expressed equal distress with the typical undergraduate attitude: "Why shouldn't so-and-so earn a little easy money on the side if he can? Think of the money he brings in to the institution. It is simple justice he ought to have his share and the rules that prevent it should be done away with." Such opinions provided evidence of "the moral blind spot" that had grown and "obscured if not obliterated normal vision."[21]

The AAUP review also noted that regulations and legislation would not prevent an alumnus from helping a "promising" schoolboy financially. Rather, the one way to stop this "evil" was the education of the athlete "to the point where he will refrain" from such unethical practices. In Bulletin No. 23 the AAUP provided a primer that, if followed, would "in due course of time stamp out the abuses which constitute so dark a stain on the cleanliness of American college athletics." In retrospect, the AAUP had not noticed its own blind spots regarding ethics and exploitation of college athletes.[22]

Faced with the moral platitudes of the AAUP and the Carnegie report, along with the growing sense among other constituencies that paying an athlete's tuition was not a moral violation, presidents found themselves in a nearly impossible situation. It remained far easier to state who needed to bring pure amateurism back to college sports than to execute such a plan. Hinting at the difficulty of attempting to reform athletics, the Carnegie report noted, "If neighboring presidents are like-minded, his task is a little lightened. . . . Such are the position and powers of the American college president that, once having informed himself of the facts, and being possessed of the requisite ability and courage, he will succeed."[23]

Conferences Attempt Change

The Southeastern Conference

The first substantive efforts to create systematic change in athletic policy and governance occurred in the South. Future Ivy League institutions along with leading universities in the Big Ten generally believed in their own superiority and exercised greater autonomy despite the Carnegie report's findings. Hence efforts to curb abuses were intermingled with defenses of current practices. In contrast, recruiting and subsidizing athletes in the South, along with lax academic standards, allowed southern colleges to begin competing and occasionally beating the superior and far wealthier universities across the country. In the era of the modern university, football victories against the nation's leading institutions created pride at state universities, led to extensive regional and national press coverage, and galvanized support for higher education institutions in a way that the South had never seen.

The sense of pride engendered by big-time football in the South ran deeper than scores printed in a newspaper. At a time when the region lagged the rest of the nation in nearly every economic, health, and educational demographic, football provided an arena in which southern states could compete and beat the nation's leading institutions. Some historians have claimed this fervor was tied to the lost cause of the Civil War, which was partially true. Archival evidence does include references to southern football as an extension of Confederate generals fighting against Yankee challengers. But big-time football also served as an attempt by southern universities to join the rest of the nation and embrace the "New South" and its progress in modern America.[24]

Amid this cultural battle, many southern university presidents expressed unease with the abuses in athletics that Howard Savage detailed in his report. At the 1930 meeting of the Southern Conference, a small group of university leaders met to discuss the possibility of leaving the twenty-three-member organization in order to form a more compact group that could better enforce uniform academic standards as well as address recruiting and subsidizing abuses. The following year, eight institutions pledged to bring about needed changes to the Southern Conference or form a new group of their own. When news of the "inner group" leaked to the press, other institutions bitterly complained that their individual universities enforced standards as strongly as the inner group and resented the implication that they were somehow inferior to or more lax than the eight schools pledging to improve the administration of college athletics.[25]

The heated debates in the Southern Conference provided glimpses into the importance of image and prestige in the modern American university, both in academics and athletics. The formation of a conference to hold athletic governance to a higher standard immediately suggested lower standards among other institutions. These insinuations precluded any attempt to pick the purest institutions and maintain positive relationships with the uninvited members. In such an environment, the only amicable solution was a geographical split among the members of the sprawling Southern Conference. In 1932 the institutions west of the Appalachian Mountains formed a new athletic association ironically named the Southeastern Conference (SEC). The universities east of the mountains remained in the Southern Conference.[26]

The thirteen members of the new Southeastern Conference elected President Frank McVey of the University of Kentucky as its president. As a sober-minded progressive president, McVey opposed big-time athletics in the Bluegrass State. His willingness to investigate athletic abuses at his own institution earned him respect among his peers while also ensuring that Kentucky's football team remained relatively insignificant among other southern powers. McVey's efforts hampered athletic boosters' attempts to compete against conference foes, and not until he retired did his successor embrace big-time football and hire a promising young coach away from the University of Maryland: Paul "Bear" Bryant.[27]

McVey was also familiar with the Carnegie report and believed in its suggestions for reining in big-time athletics. In his words, he believed the newly formed conference provided "a golden opportunity to put athletics in the University organization and take it out of the hands of the coach and the news writers." Savage had highlighted both culprits. To remedy the problem, McVey hoped to institute Bulletin No. 23's suggestion to place presidents in control of athletic conferences.

In late 1932, McVey called a meeting of all the presidents in the newly formed SEC, and they agreed to accept administrative control of the conference. When the SEC voted on its constitution and bylaws in March of 1933, it became the first major conference to place presidents in control of the league's policies and procedures. The SEC charged each executive with enforcement of conference rules and regulations at the individual institutions. In addition, only the president or a single person appointed as the president's delegate would be recognized as the official voting member on policy matters. Coaches and faculty representatives still met to discuss matters of common concern, but the authority rested with the presidents.[28]

While some histories have suggested that the SEC was formed to embrace big-time football, a reading of the SEC's original constitution and bylaws paints a much different picture. The purpose of the conference was stated in the following manner:

> The Southeastern Conference is organized to form a more compact group of institutions with similar educational ideals and regulations in order that they may by joint action increase their ability to render the services for which they were found and for which they are maintained, by making athletics part of the educational plan and by making them subservient to the great aims and objects of education and placing them under the same administrative control. The Conference proposes to accomplish this end by promoting mutual trust and friendly relations between members; by controlling athletic competition and keeping such competition within the bounds of an educational activity; by promoting clean sportsmanship; and by developing public appreciation of the educational, rather than commercial, values in intercollegiate athletics.[29]

To accomplish the lofty aims of deemphasizing commercialism in college athletics, the presidents agreed to strict rules banning recruiting of athletes and any financial inducements offered to the prospective students. Players receiving a gift of any kind or remuneration for athletic participation would be ineligible. Each institution agreed to document any scholarships or loans athletes received. They limited scouting of other teams and prohibited "training tables," where only athletes were allowed to eat. The conference emphasized the importance of academic eligibility, while allowing institutions to maintain their own entrance requirements. In short, the SEC provided a primary example of a conference formed to take the Carnegie report seriously and implement its suggested reforms.[30]

This intercollegiate agreement to enforce amateurism and reduce commercialism failed abysmally. President McVey struggled to keep up with accusations of ineligibility among players on opposing teams. As he noted in his diary, "I have the distinct impression that I am not getting anywhere in the direction of the affairs of this Conference. I feel that all that is happening now is merely holding it together." He added, "Everybody is going about as they want." After one year as president of the SEC, McVey spoke to his colleagues at the annual meeting and asked, "Has the time come when the members of the Southeastern Conference can disarm?" He believed it was possible to do away with recruiting and subsidizing of athletes, but presidents needed to learn what abuses existed on campus and have the courage to address them. McVey was elected to a second term as SEC president, but his efforts failed to create substantive change. He noted that the "hiring" of players had "reached the point of repealing all restrictions or being continued as liars."[31]

John Tigert of the University of Florida succeeded McVey as SEC president. As Tigert took office, he sent a survey to fellow presidents in the conference. Tigert asked his colleagues if they wanted to continue in the same manner, move toward extreme enforcement of the rules, or create "Some change whereby the present practice of surreptitious subsidizing might be openly recognized and the conditions upon which students can be aided, definitely stated." After months of debate, the SEC became the first conference to openly finance college athletes by allowing "athletic ability" to play a factor in the awarding of scholarships. The conference said such scholarships should not be "granted primarily" for athletic skill, but as a University of Tennessee faculty athletic representative noted, "Everybody in athletics in the United States knew what the Conference was trying to do." The move away from pure amateurism changed American college athletics permanently, but the reform did not occur without a major battle.[32]

The Southern Conference

As the SEC came to terms with supporting athletes by awarding grants-in-aid, the Southern Conference chose the opposite path. It resembled the SEC's original attempt to curb athletic abuses two years earlier. Frank Graham, president of the University of North Carolina, presented a plan to improve intercollegiate athletics to the Committee on Student Life at the National Association of State Universities (NASU). The committee endorsed his proposal, and it then received approval from the larger organization. With the NASU's support, Graham decided to take his proposal to the Southern Conference without seeking the approval of UNC's stakeholders first.

Like McVey at the University of Kentucky, Frank Graham was a progressive president. Unlike McVey, Graham was at the helm of an "elite" university. UNC was one of only two southern universities in the prestigious American Association of Universities, and his proposals had been endorsed by the NASU. So many assumed that Graham's proposal would ban recruiting and financial assistance provided to students for their athletic prowess, and that postseason contests would be supported among members of the Southern Conference, beginning a national trend toward deemphasizing college sports.

These assumptions proved untrue. The Southern Conference voted Graham's plan into policy for 1936, but it was a split vote of 6–4. The general opinion at UNC was actually much less positive than the sixty percent majority in the conference. North Carolina's Athletic Council, with representatives from faculty, students, and alumni, unanimously opposed their president's plan for the Southern Conference. A survey of alumni confirmed that they did not want athletic authority transferred to the president, hoping to keep authority broadly based.[33] Students in Chapel Hill overwhelmingly favored financial aid for athletes administered by alumni and the university. Undergraduates expressed fear that UNC's football team would become a conference doormat like the University of Virginia, an institution that took its honor code seriously and therefore followed the principles of amateurism far more strictly than other institutions.[34] Despite objections at UNC, the Southern Conference adopted the Graham Plan. K. P. Lewis, UNC trustee and supporter of Graham, told the president his plan was noble, but its success was "just about as likely to be effective as the famous charge of Don Quixote on the windmill."[35]

The Southern Conference's move to enforce stricter standards clearly aligned with the sentiment of most institutions in the NCAA. After news of the SEC's acceptance of athletic scholarships in December, the NCAA resolved "its unalterable adherence to the principles and practice of strict amateurism." The SEC's move was viewed as an "emergency" and "a serious threat to the very life of amateur sport." The NCAA created a committee to study "all of the influences that are in any way inimical to the best interests of intercollegiate sport and threaten its very existence." The committee would present its finding at NCAA's annual convention in December 1936.[36]

During the ensuing year, the Graham Plan fell apart within the Southern Conference. Complaints concerning enforcement started almost immediately. As historian Richard Stone noted, the new plan "was doomed only four months after it was implemented, and it was laid to rest just a year later."[37] As had been the case since the beginning of college football, few institutions were enforcing the rules on their own campus while making complaints about other institutions in the conference. By the end of the year, the University of Virginia announced its resignation from the conference, because its members were not following the Graham Plan. As an independent, UVA allowed athletic scholarships to be funded by alumni.

UNC's own subsidized football team lost only one Southern Conference football game during 1936 when they fell to Duke University. William Few, Duke University's president, presided over Duke's transformation from Trinity College into a leading American university when Ben Duke donated twenty-four million dollars to the institution in the 1920s. Few emulated the University of Chicago's plan to use football as a promotional tool and hired Wallace Wade away from the University of Alabama in 1931. The institution became an instant competitor in the Southern Conference and opposed the Graham Plan, which had been introduced by the president of Duke's rival eight miles down the road.

At the December 1936 NCAA Conference, Tulane's Wilbur Smith penned the annual report for the NCAA Third District (representing the South). He noted the SEC's decision to offer aid for athletic ability produced a "wholesome improvement over the idealistic prattle" that previously existed with institutions claiming purity while evading conference rules. Smith also noted the Southern Conference's "high motives" with the adoption of the Graham Plan while adding that the Southern Conference planned to repeal the plan because virtually everyone skirted the rules, but no violations had been reported. The NCAA still condemned the move by the SEC. But the NCAA's special committee "On Influences Inimical to the Best Interests of Intercollegiate Sport"[38] condemned schools offering grants-in-aid for athletes and proclaimed that any school taking its educational mission seriously would "drop a sport rather than submit to its professionalization."[39]

A professor from the University of Michigan representing the NCAA's Fourth District (Midwest) was less kind in his attack on the SEC. As he noted in his official report, "Ruthless and unethical tactics of a small number of institutions create a situation that drives most of the others" to engage in unethical practices. Then defending the Big Ten, Ralph Aigler stated that his report should not be viewed as a "confession" that institutions in his region were engaged in such practices. Of course, Bulletin No. 23 had clearly delineated the abuses of the Big Ten, negating claims that Michigan or other Big Ten conference institutions remained "pure" with regard to recruiting and financial support.

The Big Ten

From the release of the Carnegie Report, the Big Ten defended its athletic practices despite Savage's findings. The Big Ten was the oldest enduring major intercollegiate athletics conference. Founded in 1895, it came to be known as the Western Conference and was formally incorporated in 1905 as the Intercollegiate Conference of Faculty Representatives. Its collective organization and strength signaled the spread of intercollegiate athletic victories and power to the Midwest. By 1930, it was nationally known as the Big Ten, reflecting a stable, full membership of two private universities—Northwestern and the University of Chicago—and eight midwestern state universities: Indiana University, Ohio State University, Purdue University, University of Illinois, University of Iowa, University of Michigan, University of Minnesota, and University of Wisconsin. It employed a full-time commissioner whose headquarters were in Chicago. As a conspicuous and powerful conference, the Big Ten illustrated a conundrum of college sports. It was an activity that required cooperation yet also was characterized by competition and conflict, even within—especially within—the ranks of conference members.

The Big Ten was a leader in the orchestration and sponsorship of a wide range of varsity sport competitions and annual championships. Although football was its dominant and most successful sport in terms of national coverage and ticket sales revenues, the conference nurtured a comprehensive varsity sports program. By 1940, for example, the conference had sponsored championship tournaments and standings in basketball, swimming, track and field, cross-country, wrestling, baseball, golf, and gymnastics.

The Big Ten originally was a well-intentioned initiative by faculty from member universities to ensure that principles of academics and amateurism shaped conference practices and policies. These ideals probably were never completely fulfilled, but the standard of having faculty representatives from each member institution persisted for a quarter of a century at least. This mission would change drastically following World War I. By 1920 the Big Ten Conference embraced all the components we associate with big-time college sports today, including large stadiums, media coverage, high salaries for popular head coaches, and giving in to the temptation to pay star college athletes. Even though Big Ten football was considered the strongest in the nation, the conference delegates and presidents held fast to their prohibition of postseason bowl games. This would change in the 1940s, leading to the pact between the Big Ten and the Pacific Coast Conference for their respective champions to meet on New Year's Day in the Rose Bowl game.

The Big Ten often used its structure and influence to defy its founding principles. The conference became adept at legitimizing the practices in college sports it was supposed to suppress. As noted by a prominent professor at the University of Illinois, Winton Solberg, the saga of the Big Ten by 1940 was characterized by an interesting mix of "courage, corruption, and commercialization." Central to this development was the emergence of the conference commissioner as a powerful figure in higher education. The most interesting episodes took place in the 1930s. First, the conference suspended Iowa for recruiting and subsidizing athletes and readmitted them a month later. Second, the Big Ten Conference commissioner became a paid consultant to the University of Pittsburgh in a strange relationship that raised eyebrows while it raised expectations that the university would be invited to join the conference (a false hope).[40] Meanwhile, John Hanna, the ambitious president of Michigan State College, began lobbying to gain conference membership, which eventually was granted in 1946.

The Big Ten led the NCAA's condemnation of the SEC's move to fund athletes. It continued its staunch public opposition to athletic grants-in-aid, but its member institutions continued a system of minimal (or no-work) jobs for players. Alumni continued assisting with tuition through gifts and loans, while fraternities often provided room and board to athletes. Despite the prohibition of recruiting, the practice continued at Big Ten schools.[41]

As the 1930s came to a close, the conference most active in attempting to hold the line on activities considered antithetical to amateurism could not control the practices it had claimed to have curbed. During the decade, the Big Ten had suspended Iowa from the conference. But an investigation revealed similar activities existed at Indiana, Northwestern, and Purdue. The conference eventually overturned its prohibition on training tables (special dining accommodations for athletes only). When Commissioner Griffith requested information regarding aid to freshman athletes in 1937, the responses confirmed that subsidizing was widespread. The following year, the Big Ten disbanded its committee on infractions, diminishing its own policing power.[42]

In short, the Big Ten preferred to carry on as elite northeastern institutions had done in the late nineteenth and early twentieth centuries and as the NCAA had done for the past three decades. Regular denunciations of professionalism, recruiting, and funding of athletes were combined with elaborate systems to skirt the rules. An examination of the practices revealed that the Big Ten had the most to gain from maintaining the prevailing system of big-time athletics.

A more critical view of the Big Ten's attempts to hold the line on college athletics could be found in economics. As the traditional elite northeastern universities lost preeminence in sports, the Midwest and South competed to fill the vacuum. Midwestern cities located within the boundaries of the Big Ten Conference had the population and workforce base to raise sufficient revenue to support leading universities, yet corporately they desired to be the best—a claim future Ivy League members held to even as they became less competitive. As a conference, the Big Ten found itself in Yale's position during the nineteenth century—in second place. In the South, the population and productivity were lacking. State flagship universities in the South were a fraction of the size of their midwestern counterparts, universities were poorly funded, and their alumni bases remained minuscule in comparison to those at Big Ten universities. Most of the South's institutions understood their laggard place in the race for prestige in higher education, and football provided virtually the only opportunity to compete with leading universities across the country. Without a wealthy alumni base, southern universities required institutional grants-in-aid.

The population and budgetary differences between the two regions were stark. Contrast, for example, Ohio and Georgia in 1930. Ohio boasted a population of 6.6 million with a net income tax revenue of nearly $1 billion. Georgia, even with its "New South" city of Atlanta, had a population of 2.9 million and income tax revenues amounting to $128 million.[43] Ohio State had an enrollment of 10,000, and the University of Georgia had 1,869 students. Southern institutions needed to offer grants-in-aid to athletes to compete against the well-financed alumni associations in major midwestern cities. The Big Ten needed to hold the amateur line (without strict enforcement) to maintain its dominance among conferences.[44]

The Pacific Coast Conference

While the SEC and Southern Conference struggled with reform efforts, the Big Ten did its best to maintain the status quo. In 1938, in contrast, the Pacific Coast Conference (PCC) paid former Federal Bureau of Investigation agent and private investigator Edwin N. Atherton forty thousand dollars to investigate recruiting and funding of athletes at its member institutions. Unlike *American College Athletics*, Atherton submitted his report privately to conference officials, who then redacted university names attached to abuses.[45]

Released to the public in January 1940, Atherton noted rampant "high-pressure" recruiting and "financial inducements" offered to athletes to attend a specific school. Alumni assisted with payments and tuition at prep schools to get athletes eligible. Universities offered jobs to promising athletes (some of which required no work). Many schools offered tuition grants that were funded by alumni donations or ticket sales. Fraternities offered cheap living expenses, loans, and other perks for its star players. Essentially, Atherton's report revealed that the PCC operated with a business-as-usual approach to assisting promising athletes.[46]

Other Developments Affecting College Sports in the 1930s

The Athletic Association

Historians have generally interpreted the Carnegie Foundation's Bulletin No. 23 and the ensuing decade as a missed opportunity to "reform" college athletics. In reality, the standard American university model that had spread across the United States in the early twentieth century would not allow it. The system in which universities had been placed may have offered false hope of purely amateur sports, but the importance of alumni, booster donations, the press, and popular culture all proved too much for ambitious universities and their leaders to stop big-time sports. Many university professors and presidents wanted big-time athletics and the benefits they afforded their institutions. Other executives and faculty truly believed in positive change and its inevitability. Their noble naiveté often became a hindrance, looking at events as an isolated incident rather than outgrowths of much larger phenomenon.

Take, for example, the Graham Plan in the Southern Conference. By the end of its first year in operation, the conference scrapped the plan in 1937. That same year, the Southern Conference attempted to reconcile athletic aid in an honorable manner, keeping subsidies for athletes separated from ticket sales, which resembled professionalism—payment for winning. At the same time, the Southern Conference avoided the ire faced by the SEC for offering institutional scholarships. In 1938, a group of UNC alumni then organized the tax-exempt Educational Foundation to raise money to fund athletic scholarships. Soon, others replicated UNC's move, and the Graham Plan managed to spur the opposite of what it was created to do.[47]

UNC was not the first to incorporate an athletic association. Informal associations to promote athletics had existed in the nineteenth century. The University of Georgia Athletic Association, incorporated in 1929, borrowed the money to build Sanford Stadium, keeping the liability away from the university. The University of Florida followed suit the same year in constructing its new football field. The incorporation of athletic associations across the country did not make the headlines, but they would fundamentally transform the financing and governance of athletics in higher education. Georgia and Florida used them to fund construction. North Carolina's innovation was to name such associations as educational, raising funds specifically to subsidize athletes—all while the NCAA continued to debate a path forward to preserve an amateurism that did not exist.[48]

The creation of such associations did not happen in a vacuum. Probably more than any academic activity, college sports transformed "town and gown" from conflict to cooperation. The loyalty and affiliation extended beyond alumni and students because the American campus was a source of state, local, and civic pride and the heart of community relations. In addition, universities often remained the largest landowner and employer in the city or county. College sports fans were drawn from the ranks of local merchants, citizens, schoolchildren, and college donors. The expanding popularity was both stimulated and then fulfilled by an extended surge of stadium construction that had started around 1920 and continued up to the eve of World War II. Between 1930 and 1940 these "popular palaces" drew crowds ranging from fifty thousand to a hundred thousand. In places like Chapel Hill, North Carolina, and Athens, Georgia, as well as Champaign, Illinois, and State College, Pennsylvania (and many other locations across the country), game attendance far surpassed the town population.

In the 1930s, campus and community were joined at the hip. The popularity of college football as a spectator sport had the added benefit of boosting the local economy with patronage and purchases at concession booths, souvenir stands, restaurants, hotels, clothiers, and other local stores. The merchants who owned these stores usually were donors and members of the "Downtown Boosters" clubs, which met each week and hosted local college coaches as guest speakers and recipients of Citizen of the Year awards. Construction or expansions of football stadiums typically represented a packaging partnership of private donations from alumni and fans combined with state bonds and local tax exemptions.[49]

The New Medium: Radio

This expansion of a fan base and boosters along with radio broadcasts and newsreels meant that universities were able to accommodate statewide and regional audiences as well as local ones. Radio broadcasts of college sports existed in the 1920s but exploded during the 1930s. As President Franklin D. Roosevelt sent his fireside chats across America's airwaves, university officials grappled with the use of the new medium and how to manage it. These debates occurred at the same time that NCAA institutions were attempting to address the findings of Carnegie's *American College Athletics* report.

Disagreements on broadcasting college sports contests, football in particular, were numerous and varied. Virtually all decisions led to financial concerns and publicity, however. Early in the decade, as the nation sank into the Great Depression, administrators generally opposed radio transmission of college football. These views had little to do with the preservation of amateurism and maintaining sport as an educational activity. Rather, institutions and conferences that voted to prohibit radio broadcasts did so because they feared games announced on the airwaves would harm attendance and further diminish ticket sales, which had plummeted in many places during the first two years of the Depression.

The Pacific Coast Conference rejected conventional wisdom and instead opted for commercial radio broadcasts negotiated at the conference level. Within a couple of years, the PCC broadcasts generated a hundred thousand dollars annually for the conference. The PCC agreement remained unique during the 1930s, as most radio deals were negotiated by individual universities. In 1934, a Detroit radio station paid Michigan twenty thousand dollars for its football broadcasts, with Chevrolet serving as the sponsor. Two years later, Yale sold rights to its radio broadcasts for the same amount, while the University of Pennsylvania commanded ten thousand dollars for a similar deal.[50]

Not all universities engaged in sponsored radio deals. Some institutions favored "sustaining" radio broadcasts, for which no rights fees were collected and no commercials aired during the contest. Ironically named, sustaining broadcasts proved to be unsustainable in competition versus the profit motive. In one rare instance, the presidents of Harvard and Princeton fought to retain sustained broadcasts. Being two of the wealthiest and most prestigious institutions, such a move was possible, yet they still succumbed to commercialized radio.

Notre Dame became the most prominent university to operate sustained radio during the decade. The reasons for rejecting commercial offers had little to do with the preservation of amateur sport, however. Rather, Notre Dame used fee-free radio to attract local and national broadcasts of its football games. Winning teams and coast-to-coast coverage helped solidify Notre Dame's position as America's flagship Catholic university. The publicity helped propel the small college in South Bend, Indiana, into the national spotlight. As historian Ronald Smith noted, Notre Dame's original plan set aside profits to "maximize publicity" and "bring it greater renown as an educational institution."[51]

Notre Dame's strategy worked. Fighting Irish football literally helped build a nationally recognized university, and the free national broadcasts created an appetite for football that would generate impressive revenue and interest in the university for decades. The radio played an important role in the expansion of Notre Dame's Subway Alumni, a group named after New York's subways filled with Notre Dame fans when the Irish played in the Big Apple. The Subway Alumni spread across the country as a large group of boosters who supported Notre Dame football even though most had not set foot on the campus. With such a large national following, Notre Dame would in future decades cash in on media deals after building a national following.[52]

Radio also cultivated an audience interested in listening to bowl games. During the Great Depression, enterprising business professionals and local civic boosters looking for opportunities to generate revenue replicated the Rose Bowl in cities with mild winter weather. On January 2, 1933, organizers established a game between Manhattan College and Miami in the first-ever Palm Festival game. A second game the following year between Miami and Duquesne proved to be the last Palm Festival because organizers opted to create an official bowl by inviting two different teams each year. On January 1, 1935, Miami hosted the first-ever Orange Bowl. On the exact same day, Tulane faced Temple in New Orleans for the inaugural Sugar Bowl. The New Year's Day spectacles proved to be a hit, generating money and bringing publicity to their host communities. Radio provided publicity for the cities, and it did not deter attendance. Broadcasts of football and other college sports added to the print press coverage already provided. Newspapers had created a relationship between college sports and the media. Radio built on that foundation and expanded the base of fans who might not otherwise attend a game or read about it in the paper.

Political Football

By the 1930s, numerous governors hailed their respective state university as an enduring source of state pride. When the University of Minnesota's Golden Gophers were selected by a national poll of sportswriters as the top football team in the nation in 1934, the governor of Minnesota declared a state holiday and joined in the motorcade seated with the university president in a parade through downtown Minneapolis.

Earl Warren, governor of California in the 1930s, embraced a tradition of the annual November "Big Game" pitting the University of California against Stanford University by sitting on the Stanford side for one half and on the Berkeley side for the other half. When the game ended, Governor Warren presented the Axe Trophy to the captain of the victorious team. As an undergraduate at UC Berkeley, Warren played clarinet in the Golden Bears marching band, following behind the drum major, classmate Robert Sproul, who would serve as president of the University of California System from 1930 to 1952. Elsewhere, especially in the Midwest, each football season was marked with traditional rivalries, some intrastate, such as Purdue playing against Indiana University for the Old Oaken Bucket, or the University of Michigan playing against the University of Minnesota for the Little Brown Jug. This pattern of boosterism played out nationwide.

No governor in the country promoted "his" university football team like Louisiana governor (1928–32) turned senator (1932–35) Huey Long. Like other booster presidents and politicians, Long sought to build Louisiana State University both academically and athletically. He did it with unmatched flare, however. Promoting big-time football became an important piece of his promotional efforts on behalf of LSU. From 1928 to 1935, he secured more than nine million dollars for campus projects, many of which did not involve athletic facilities. The Huey P. Long Fieldhouse and adjoining pool benefited athletics and student affairs in general. Long also pushed the novel idea to build dormitories into the side of Tiger Stadium, which increased seating capacity from 10,000 to 22,000 while also providing housing for 1,500 matriculates.[53] In addition, the renovation provided office space for the football, track, and baseball teams. Before Long's assassination in 1935, he began plans to utilize the New Deal's Works Progress Administration grant program to add additional dormitory rooms and seating capacity by again combining two construction projects into one. Completed after his passing, Tiger Stadium expanded its capacity to 46,000 while an additional 250 rooms housed more than 1,000 new students.[54]

Long's penchant for demagoguery led him into the locker rooms to offer halftime speeches to the football team. He used the band to promote the football team, the university, and himself. Long often led the band in paradelike fashion in host towns on the way to the football stadium. The most notable event occurred in Nashville on a Saturday in October 1934 when thousands of LSU students and fans descended upon Vanderbilt. When the Illinois Central Railroad rejected Long's request to lower the nineteen-dollar round-trip fare, he threatened to drastically increase the rail taxes in Louisiana, leading the railroad to drop the cost to six dollars. Long then handed out seven-dollar loans to students for a rail ticket and lunch. Parading the streets of Nashville, Long met the mayor and other dignitaries. After LSU beat the Commodores, the *Nashville Banner* stated that the "Louisiana Kingfish" had a "tremendous talent for showmanship [and] made this city his debtor." Despite Long's multiple and deep flaws, he showed how the efforts to promote football and a university were not mutually exclusive.[55]

Big-Time Defectors: Sewanee and Chicago

Political showmanship, incorporated athletic associations, radio broadcasts, and bowl games all grew after the publication of *American College Athletics* and amid the greatest economic crisis in the nation's history. Faced with indisputable evidence of professionalism, athletic subsidies, and commercialism, most institutions blinked briefly with an eye toward deemphasis but continued down the same commercialized path. For many, the late 1940s and 1950s seemed like the crucial decade in which the battle for amateurism was lost. In reality, the decisions had been determined much earlier. The 1930s revealed that the overwhelming number of university officials chose the commercialized path that they shunned publicly. For example, at the NCAA's 1935 convention, the Radio Broadcast Committee affirmed the right of institutions to sell commercial broadcasts of athletic contests. At the same NCAA convention, university representatives also spoke out against the evils of commercialism in college sports and the ability of college athletes to earn a scholarship for their participation in athletics.

Near the close of the 1930s, two institutions understood the landscape of college sports—football in particular—and finally chose to quit big-time football. Sewanee: The University of the South in Tennessee quit competing in Southeastern Conference football in 1938. The University of Chicago announced its intention to drop big-time football a year later, in 1939. The decisions made

Governor Huey Long leading the Louisiana State University marching band in a parade before a football game, promoting both LSU and himself. Louisiana State University Special Collections

by these two very different institutions provide insight into the relationship of American higher education and athletics.

Sewanee, an Episcopalian liberal arts institution located on the rural Cumberland Plateau in Tennessee, possessed a storied football tradition. In 1899, Sewanee's famous Iron Men boasted a 12–0 record, outscoring its opponents 322–10. The extraordinary season included victories over LSU, Ole Miss, Texas, Texas A&M, and Tulane—all in a one-week road trip. Sewanee continued as a Southern Conference power in the early twentieth century, and the institution became a founding member of the SEC in 1933.[56]

In 1938, Sewanee's new vice chancellor Alexander Guerry announced that the institution would drop big-time football, noting Sewanee's prestige was not

Governor Huey Long posing with cheerleaders before a Louisiana State football game. His support for the university was matched by his meddling, which almost lost LSU its accreditation. Louisiana State University Special Collections

predicated upon gridiron glory but on the academic and spiritual ideals. Guerry's task had been made somewhat easier by Sewanee's more recent football history. By the 1920s, Sewanee became less competitive as growing universities across the South adopted big-time football. The school's losing records at the hands of the larger state universities incensed some alumni, who called for the firing of the football coach and vice chancellor. After five seasons of football in the SEC, Sewanee remained winless in football. When Vice Chancellor Finney retired, Guerry agreed to succeed him on the condition that Sewanee would end big-time football. He did so, heralding the traditional academic and spiritual virtues of a liberal education for undergraduates based upon the traditional higher education model.[57]

Farther north, the University of Chicago possessed a storied football program as well. Stagg's Maroons found gridiron glory in the late nineteenth and twentieth centuries, bringing recognition to Rockefeller's nascent but ambitious university. A founding member of the Big Ten, Chicago's football team accomplished exactly what its founding president, William Rainey Harper, had hoped. Harper's life was cut short by cancer, however, and he passed away in 1906. Stagg continued his influential role as a tenured faculty member of physical culture and football coach. That changed when Chicago selected Robert Maynard Hutchins as its new president in 1929.

Hutchins's presidency meant marginalization for Stagg and his desire to field a competitive football team. Hutchins denied Stagg's request to continue as coach when he reached the mandatory retirement age of 70, instead offering Stagg a job in public relations. Stagg retired after the 1932 season. New coach Clark Shaughnessy worked for an administration set on maintaining college football on an amateur basis. Despite public expressions by the Big Ten's commissioner and coaches that strict amateurism had been maintained, the conference clearly engaged in recruiting and subsidizing of athletes. The Chicago Maroons' record as a truly amateur squad made this clear. By 1938 the football team lost all its conference games and won only one game—a victory over DePauw of Indiana.[58]

Faced with such a humiliating record, the Executive Committee of Chicago's Alumni Foundation still rejected the possibility of dropping football or leaving the conference it helped found decades earlier. Alumni then began devising plans to recruit better players to their alma mater. Before implementing a strategy, the Maroons played the 1939 season. Boasting only two wins (against Oberlin and Wabash), Chicago failed to score a single point against any other opponent, losing to Beloit 0–6, Harvard 0–61, Illinois 0–46, Michigan 0–85, Ohio State 0–61, and Virginia 0–47.[59] The drubbing by Virginia was telling. Three years earlier, UVA abided by a strict amateur athletic code and beat only Hampden-Sydney and the College of William and Mary. That year the Cavaliers lost to Harvard 65–0 and 59–14 to UNC. Virginia then left the Southern Conference, not because they wanted out of big-time football, but because they wanted to be both competitive and honest about their fundraising. They immediately began allowing alumni subsidies to help pay tuition for athletes, and they were back on the winning track. Hutchins was unwilling to adopt such a model at Chicago, and the differences on the gridiron were evident.

President Hutchins had exactly what he needed to abolish football: a team embarrassed by semiprofessionals and a university constituency unwilling to play truly amateur liberal arts colleges. Hutchins had long argued that academic prestige and football prowess were unrelated, yet he agreed with the Alumni Foundation that Chicago's image could be tarnished by losing to Oberlin or Beloit. Learning that alumni were ready to raise funds for recruiting and subsidizing players, Hutchins moved quickly, and the University of Chicago dropped football.[60]

In 1938, Hutchins wrote an article for the *Saturday Evening Post* titled "Gate Receipts and Glory." In it, he criticized university administrators for being overly concerned with money and publicity. This, of course, was an easier position to take as Hutchins presided over a university that had received nearly thirty-five million dollars from John D. Rockefeller and during the previous half century had cultivated donations from wealthy and prominent alumni. Still, Hutchins weathered serious backlash from alumni for his position. As Sewanee had done a year earlier, Hutchins argued that Chicago had taken the high road toward academic integrity rather than chasing football revenue and glory.[61]

For years, administrators had asserted that if a president at a leading university agreed to "disarm," other institutions would follow. The fact that virtually no other institutions did so explains just how entrenched big-time football had become at American universities.[62] Asked later why other presidents maintained big-time football, Hutchins responded, "They could not stand the pressure."[63] Although conjecture, it is interesting to ponder whether Hutchins could have handled the pressure with a winning team and a tighter university budget. It was continuous losing that brought important alumni and board members to Hutchins's side of the argument.

Higher Education and Athletics in the 1930s: The Carnegie Report Reconsidered

Carnegie's *American College Athletics* report failed in its attempts to reform college sports. Growing publicity efforts by universities, expansion of commercial radio broadcasting, and acceptance of more postseason bowl games occurred while most members of the NCAA claimed to desire a deemphasis of college sports—especially football. When Sewanee and the University of Chicago finally gave up on big-time athletics, no other universities followed suit. How could this be explained? Most historians have presented college sports as an anomaly that did not belong in the modern American university, yet most institutions not only maintained intercollegiate sports but also promoted them whenever possible. An understanding of the nature of the typical "State U" along with a close study of historical sources provide pieces of the puzzle that have generally not been placed together to offer a new historical interpretation of higher education's relationship with college sports.

The first important clues exist in CFAT president Henry Pritchett's preface to *American College Athletics*. Most histories, including this one, quote Pritchett's famous recommendations for improving the abuses in intercollegiate sport. They involved getting rid of highly paid professional coaches, ticket sales, fancy train rides to games, excessive publicity, and ending the subsidization of athletes' college tuition and expenses. Implementing these recommendations certainly would have curtailed many of the abuses, but the decade of the Great Depression actually witnessed the opposite.

The reality was that these elements were not going to be eradicated without first altering the mission or organizational structure of the modern American university. Pritchett explained the problem in his preface. Only fifty years prior to the publication of *American College Athletics*, higher education still possessed its traditional liberal arts curriculum and in loco parentis model. Their collective purpose was to teach young men to think deeply and therefore to lead better lives. But German universities had taken the lead in research, and American institutions desired to elevate their status. They did so by calling themselves universities and by superimposing "a graduate school on the old college. Two disparate educational agencies were merged into one."[64]

As Pritchett explained, this merger "had a profound effect upon the ideals and methods of the college." Professors focused on research while undergraduates gained freedom offered previously only to graduate students. Curricular changes and the quest for larger enrollments allowed students to study "the elementary technique of business, banking, accounting, transportation, salesmanship, journalism, and, in effect, all the vocations practiced in a modern industrial state." All of these options could be had without ever teaching "students to think hard and clearly." Higher education institutions then emulated each other in "competition rather than scholarship." While lauding the democratic impulse of American higher education, which made it far more accessible than in Europe, Pritchett lamented the admission of students who would be better suited in trade or vocational school, but the "mere sweep of the tide" led them into universities. The result was that "intellectual quality" suffered.[65]

Pritchett noted, "In this situation the athletic competition has played a minor part." The same university presidents who oversaw stadium construction and excessive salaries for professional coaches also sought to expand "scholarship and research" at their institutions. This apparent contradiction led Pritchett to ask a number of important questions, not all of which involved athletics. "Can a university teach equally well philosophy and salesmanship? / Can it sponsor genuine education and at the same time train raw recruits for minor vocations?" The remainder of Pritchett's preface suggested he may have offered these questions rhetorically, but history proved that they were much more complex.[66]

In one of the first issues of the *Journal of Higher Education*, editor W. H. Cowley lamented Pritchett's "obvious prejudice not only against athletics but, indeed, against the entire organization of modern education."[67] In the same issue, Commissioner Griffith noted that Pritchett did not believe that universities teaching professional courses of study could train students to "think clearly" unless they offered the classes of colleges from a different era. Griffith insightfully noted that Pritchett judged American universities "by German educational concepts and our athletics by British standards of sport." Pritchett also lamented that American higher education served largely as a socializing agency rather than an intellectual enterprise.[68]

The networking opportunities for students in American universities, along with multiple new majors offering career preparation for well-paying jobs, were all part of what historian David O. Levine described as "The American College and the Culture of Aspiration."[69] While opportunities to engage in the life of the mind for its own sake existed, a new emphasis had been placed on fields of study that either helped students financially or assisted states in economic development. After all, economic development for the individual and for the larger society provided an impetus for the land grant universities that now dotted the higher education landscape and played an important role in the growth of big-time athletics.

One blunt quote from a student newspaper of the era highlighted this element and its influence in higher education. Vanderbilt and Sewanee had been Thanksgiving Day rivals on the gridiron for nearly three decades, even though the Commodores dominated the series during the 1920s. This lopsided matchup led to decreased interest in the game and declining ticket sales. In 1929, Vanderbilt informed Sewanee that they would no longer play them on Thanksgiving Day. Vanderbilt decided to schedule Auburn and Alabama for their Thanksgiving showdowns. As Vanderbilt University's student paper *The Hustler* argued, "Tradition . . . must give way to materialism."[70]

Griffith's comments regarding German and British standards were insightful considering the two institutions that abandoned big-time football. In presenting Sewanee's dropping SEC football, the vice chancellor couched the decision in terms of maintaining the integrity of an institution focused on academic and spiritual ideals. In short, Sewanee harkened the old British model in which commercialized football did not fit. After all, the Episcopalian college traced its roots to British theology and the rural liberal arts college model.

Chicago, in contrast, found itself moving toward the German model of higher education. Hutchins removed an American coaching legend, Amos

Alonzo Stagg, and replaced him with a coach and a system that resulted in multiple losing seasons. At the same time, Hutchins presided over the implementation of a far more rigorous undergraduate curriculum and a steadily declining body of undergraduate students. When Hutchins assumed the presidency, Chicago boasted an undergraduate enrollment of 4,707. During the first season without football in 1940, Chicago had 3,512 undergraduates. In the next few years, graduate enrollment would surpass undergraduate matriculates and remain that way into the twenty-first century.[71]

When Chicago opened under President William Rainey Harper in the 1890s, Stagg's football team served as a publicity tool for an aspiring American university. Nearly a half century later, President Hutchins was secure in the academic status and financial resources of the university, allowing him drop football. As he did so, aspiring universities like Duke and Southern California chose to utilize football in the same way Harper had in Chicago's early years. As philosopher Mortimer Adler stated, "In 1904 the Chicago School meant one thing; in 1936 it meant another." As Harper's vision of the university gave way to Hutchins's view of Chicago's mission, football went by the wayside. In short, as an aspiring university seeking to grow and become an elite institution, football played a key role in the process. Once an established academic power with the financial resources to sustain itself, Chicago could afford to drop football in the name of academic rigor and scholarly research.[72]

Sewanee and Chicago were anomalies in the landscape of college athletics. Their histories reveal that the two institutions were also different from the standard American university model that had been replicated across the country during the first decades of the twentieth century. Sewanee retreated into the traditional undergraduate British model, while Chicago began emulating the German research model. This fact, considered in the context of Pritchett's critical preface to *American College Athletics*, provides a more nuanced explanation regarding the failure of universities to solve the problems of college sport during the previous half century (and in the future).

Pritchett argued that athletics had "played only a minor part" among many larger problems plaguing American higher education. He believed the democratic impulse in higher education created fundamental, even existential, problems for American universities.[73] In his view, the admission of marginal students who would have been better served in commercial or trade occupations, along with the creation of vocational tracks of study, diminished the academic rigor of the university. It was "under this regime" that commercialized and professionalized intercollegiate athletics spread. His inspirational vision of higher education involved "a university devoted to the pure intellectual ideal *sans* athletics, schools of business, of salesmanship, and of other commercial vocations."[74]

Pritchett, the longtime president of the Massachusetts Institute of Technology and the Carnegie Foundation for the Advancement of Teaching, desired well-financed institutions focused on the art of thinking or the activity of scientific research. He lamented the commercialized and acquisitive approach to admissions, curricula, and athletics. The vast majority of nascent American universities did not fit that profile and either could not or did not share this view of the modern university.

Could the president of the average "State U" have managed to follow Hutchins's actions at Chicago? At the University of North Carolina, the venerable Frank Graham's efforts brought editorials that he might be fired. Those rumors remained unfounded, but Graham did write that his proposals created "the hardest and hottest fight that I have ever been in in my life." His critics, he wrote, "opened up machine guns, and in some cases . . . poison gas."[75] After Frank McVey, the founding president of the SEC, failed in his efforts to curb recruiting and subsidizing at the conference level, he faced criticism from Kentucky alumni who blamed him for not putting enough emphasis on big-time sports. When Kentucky's board rejected McVey's suggestion that the institution should leave the SEC, he then turned to Vanderbilt's Chancellor Kirkland and asked him to lead the fight against commercialized sport. Kirkland, wisely, did not pick up the "reform" torch during his remaining year in office. A newspaper quote concerning the Graham Plan's failure summed up well the struggle faced by well-intentioned and earnest presidents seeking to return to pure sports. A North Carolina native writing for the *Baltimore Sun* worried for Graham because "integrity and candor" were not the attributes of successful university presidents. Rather, "pliant gentlemen, supple and slick gentlemen, who know how to lick the boots of rich alumni in an artistic manner" were more effective administrators.[76]

The trouble for university presidents may have not been their lack of honesty as much as a struggle to reduce the size, funding, interest, and professionalism of sports in the modern American university. Virtually every other reform effort in education attempted to do the exact opposite: increase the size, funding, interest, and professionalism in order to move an institution forward. In the process, universities became compartmentalized, what academics referred to as the "silos" that made up each institution. Scientific knowledge and specialization dominated almost everything: academics, public relations, fundraising, admissions, and athletics. Traditionalists still criticized these trends in academics and athletics, but their critiques were absorbed rather than adopted by the complex university and its many constituencies.

To illustrate the near impossibility of a return to games for the sake of students and their well-being, one should consider the 1937 publication of *The Student Personnel Point of View*, sponsored by the American Council on Education (ACE). In explaining the need for recognition of a new type of professional that began appearing in American universities, the report claimed that colleges and universities were responsible for a student's "intellectual capacity and achievement, his emotional make up, his physical condition, his social relationships, his vocational aptitudes and skills, his moral and religious values, his economic resources, [and] his aesthetic appreciations." The report argued that "a long and honorable history stands behind this point of view," noting that "Until the last three decades of the nineteenth century interest in the whole student dominated the thinking of the great majority of the leaders and faculty members of American colleges."[77]

Since the late nineteenth century, wealthy and modern universities began emphasizing research, leading faculty to a "preoccupation" of an academic discipline done at the "neglect of the student as an individual." The emphasis on scientific technique (which was also applied to athletics), the growth of university student populations, and the expansion of the universities' larger objectives all led to the need for (and development of) student affairs professionals. These university employees would fill the void vacated by professors and administrators as liberal arts colleges transformed into American universities. In short, faculty abdicated their previous oversight of student life outside the classroom. By dropping their in loco parentis role, faculty and administrators also lost a great deal of authority in the regulation of athletics.

Big Ten commissioner John L. Griffith understood this development as he navigated the 1930s with the savvy of a successful administrator. Griffith publicly criticized the findings of the Carnegie report and the SEC's move to offer grants-in-aid for athletes. At the same time, as historian Winton Solberg noted, Griffith privately spoke about the mutual relationship between academic and athletic goals. The commissioner also believed that those who maintained the traditional notions of higher education were "increasingly out of touch with the trend of social changes."[78]

Griffith's moderate views, which avoided both strict enforcement of amateurism or outright scholarships for athletes, could be attributed to the competitive nature of American higher education and its athletics. Nearly all Big

Ten schools offered jobs to their star players and alumni helped financially as well. During the 1930s, only the University of Chicago attempted to remain "pure," and they paid the price on the field. For the Big Ten, athletic scholarships in the SEC and elsewhere were problematic because official grants-in-aid would make the conference less competitive on the national scene. Yet they couched their opposition in terms of protecting amateurism.

Amateurism and Reform in Retrospect

This challenge emanating from the modern American university created questions regarding two of the most popular terms of the era for college athletics: amateurism and reform. Amateurism could be defined rather simply, even if scholars, students, or alumni disagreed on its role in college sports. This elitist British concept of playing a sport simply for the joy of recreation had permeated the language of American higher education, even though most universities in the United States could not claim the elitism and classism exhibited by Oxford and Cambridge. Some faculty, coaches, and administrators finally began to openly challenge antiquated role of amateurism. As Ohio State professor Delbert Oberteuffer defended the SEC's move to allow financial aid to athletes, he noted that British amateurism was "immutably bound into the social life of a people who were highly sensitive to class difference." Oberteuffer argued, "The traditional aristocracy-based idea of amateurism is incompatible with American life today."[79]

The amateur idea in America developed before the modern university structure had taken shape. It also assumed a social status to which few in the United States could relate. Elitism may have been in vogue among a couple dozen institutions in the United States, but the ethos of the vast majority of universities could be found in its "democratic" approach. Duke's football coach Wallace Wade opposed the Graham Plan and its emphasis on amateurism because it was not democratic. Wade argued that Graham's rigid rules would prohibit all but students from wealthy families to attend college. Historian Ronald Smith surmised that in England, "There was an upper-class understanding in rugby, as in other sports, that the spirit of the rules was as important as the rules themselves. In America, the letter of the rules might be observed, but the spirit of the rules was much undervalued." Interestingly, Smith's quote addressed the playing of a game and the American desire to win. This remained true not only on the field but also with many coaches, players, and presidents in the policymaking and administration of football.[80]

The question of "reform" in college athletics requires a much more nuanced explanation. The institutional and societal reforms in the United States during the Progressive Era and into the New Deal looked quite different from the initiatives being proposed for college athletics. Although a simplistic description, reform in the United States generally meant creating laws or adopting policies to aid individuals and groups in society. These attempts often claimed to promote democracy and expand benefits to working-class individuals, such as extending voting rights to women in the 1920s or establishing a minimum wage in the 1930s. During the first years of the NCAA, reform included changing the rules of football to make it a safer game. Beyond this, the NCAA offered few examples of reforming anything.

Until the SEC's adoption of an athletic scholarship model, virtually all reform proposals to curb abuses in college athletics were just the opposite—conservative or even reactionary responses to address problems in intercollegiate competition. The founding constitution of the SEC and the Graham Plan in the Southern Conference both claimed to offer attempts at reform. In reality, those seeking reform were either hoping to return to a mythical period of athletic purity from the nineteenth century, or they wanted to preserve the status quo in college sports. By strict definition, these were not reformers in the true sense of the word. At the same time, the structure of the modern American university made attempts at deemphasis nearly impossible.

At this point in history, it is important to return to Edwin Slosson's quote in *Great American Universities*: "The essential difference between a college and a university is how they look. A university looks forward and a college looks backward. The aim of one is discovery; the aim of the other is conservation."[81] This definition once again revealed the tension between higher education and athletics. In the 1930s, most administrators desired to move forward with the curriculum and backward with sports.

Even though the NCAA, in a moment of clarity, made this distinction clear, historians of college sports have largely ignored it. After the SEC recognized athletic grants-in-aid, the NCAA established a committee on "Influences Inimical to the best Interest of Intercollegiate sport." Sharing their findings with member institutions, the report declared, "Those who are studying the problem of inter-collegiate athletics and who are seeking remedies for its shortcomings are not reformers. Rather, in the opinion of your committee, they are conservationists endeavoring to preserve American college sports."[82]

The conservatives hoping to save amateur college sports attempted at the end of the decade to punish those institutions bringing recruiting and scholarships into the open. During the 1939 NCAA Convention, held in Los Angeles that December, the overwhelming majority of NCAA institutions voted to ban grants-in-aid for athletic ability. It marked an important turning point for the organization. Until then, the NCAA defended home rule and avoided policies and procedures that would (eventually) require enforcement and punishments for offenders. The bombing of Pearl Harbor and America's entry into World War II meant that the final debates on athletic scholarships would have to wait until the conclusion of the war.

The 1930s confirmed Alexis de Tocqueville's observation that Americans were "a nation of joiners." This description applied to higher education in general and to college sports in particular. Intercollegiate athletics, especially big-time football, was the magnet for voluntary associations that combined love and money for their alma mater. A good example of this enthusiastic support was the annual fall event known as "homecoming," usually held on the weekend of a home football game. Student organizations, especially fraternities and sororities, held open houses, picnics, and other special events where old grads and dear friends were welcomed back to the campus, culminating in a packed attendance for a football game against a traditional rival.

The social scene surrounding football did not preclude serious organizational strategy to bring home victories. The various booster groups' ceremonial rituals were in fact the public image of serious structural, administrative, and financial arrangements that were essential to the funding and operation of college sports. The genius of the innovation was that it gave the athletics director, who often was also the head football coach, a formal organization that was simultaneously a part of and apart from the university's administration and financial offices. It was comparable to a Trojan Horse, allowing athletics to be impervious to budgetary procedures used in the university proper, while still accepting subsidies from the university, as the Georgia Athletic Association did. The enduring legacy was that college sports had gained both formal and symbolic stature as "most favored" standing within the publicity and funding of many American colleges and universities.

University administrators, athletes, alumni, and fans would have to wait until the post—World War II era to witness how the NCAA would handle the implications of big-time football. While clashes at the NCAA in the late forties and early fifties made it appear that the future of big-time athletics was in doubt, the policies and structures put in place during the thirties guaranteed the continuation and expansion of big-time athletics.

4

The Consolidation of Control in College Sports, 1941 to 1954

Contradictions, Contraction, and Resilience during World War II and Beyond

When the United States declared war following the bombing of Pearl Harbor on December 7, 1941, college sports officials promptly halted business as usual, suspending games and tournaments. Athletics directors and coaches joined in the overall campus response of cooperation and adjustment to the new wartime demands. But there was not an immediate or total suspension of intercollegiate athletics nationwide. Rather, one finds a cumulative pattern of concern, caution, and cooperation with the national defense efforts.

One example was the decision to move the Rose Bowl game from Pasadena, California, to Durham, North Carolina, in 1942 in anticipation of possible air attacks directed at the Pacific Coast. More typical was that colleges shortened their schedules and playing seasons, and suspended some games and programs owing to overlapping reasons. First, many students (including student-athletes) enlisted in various branches of military service, which greatly reduced the pool of players. Second, rationing of gasoline and other transportation resources meant that there were fewer games, with emphasis on nearby spectator groups. For example, when the annal Army-Navy game was moved from Philadelphia to Annapolis, Maryland, the crowd size shrunk from more than a hundred thousand to ten thousand, largely because federal regulations restricted spectators from traveling more than ten miles to a sporting event.

As college sports programs were put on hold, a simultaneous development was the creation of football teams and other sports at thirty-five military bases. These were surrogate de facto college teams and included such nicknames as the Randolph Field Ramblers, the North Carolina Pre-flight Cloud Busters, the Great Lakes Navy Bluejackets, and the Georgia Pre-flight Aircrackers. These teams were often staffed by college coaches who had been enlisted for military service with team rosters of sailors and soldiers who a year earlier had been college students playing varsity sports.

College programs and athletics directors were resilient and even resourceful. College teams frequently included the military squads as opponents on their collegiate schedule. Sportswriters even included the military teams in their weekly and seasonal rankings of top college teams. One ingenuous response to the wartime constraints came from the president of the University of Maryland in 1945, when the war ended. He offered the head football coaching position to Paul Bryant, coach of the North Carolina Naval Station football squad. To sweeten the deal, he invited the new coach to bring a busload of seventeen players and guaranteed them admission to the University of Maryland. The players were discharged from the navy on September 18th, were enrolled at the University of Maryland on September 19th, and played in the opening game of the season on September 27th—even before fall semester classes had started. This partnership of a president, a new coach, and new players provided the foundation for a nationally ranked college team when regular schedules resumed a few months later.[1]

From 1942 to 1945, college students (including athletes) rallied to national defense by voluntarily dropping out of college to enlist in the military. Meanwhile, the head coach of West Point invoked an obscure clause that exempted service academy cadets and midshipmen from being drafted. The result was that the West Point coach recruited and enrolled a large number of established college players from various universities who found a new home and team at West Point. These "special status" privileges and exemptions worked well. In sportswriters' annual polls, both West Point and the US Naval Academy vied for the top ranking among all college teams.

This ploy by the West Point coach heralded a larger, continuing innovation: promoting college football as a part of national defense. The federal government, especially top military leaders, harnessed the winning teams of West Point as a public relations vehicle during the Cold War. A star West Point halfback was described in sports headlines as "The Army's New 160 lbs. Secret Weapon." Coaches socialized with generals and members of Congress. It was truly an "all-American" affair. The dysfunctional downside was that other college coaches became fed up with the West Point advantages. Notre Dame, for example, cancelled its regularly scheduled annual football games against West Point between 1948 and 1956.[2]

Seeking "Sanity": The NCAA and the Principles
for the Conduct of Intercollegiate Athletics

As World War II came to an end, big-time football returned with a vengeance. Schools broke attendance records and returned full force into the recruiting abuses that had plagued the sport for so many decades. In addition, the relatively lax rules governing football eligibility during the war proved difficult to reimpose immediately. Superior athletes who had served in the military were eligible for the GI Bill's free tuition for veterans. With this cost covered, many schools and their alumni offered additional financial inducements for coveted recruits returning from service.

As big-time football ramped back up, the NCAA picked up where it had left off in 1939 regarding subsidies to athletes. The Big Ten, through its representatives that led the NCAA, resumed its attacks against the Southeastern Conference's decision to allow grants-in-aid for athletic ability. University of Iowa's Karl Leib served as NCAA president at the time, and Kenneth "Tug" Wilson held the post of secretary-treasurer for the organization. These leaders from the Big Ten found allies in the Pacific Coast Conference as well as some northeastern colleges and universities. By the late 1940s, however, the SEC developed allies in the Southern and Southwestern Conferences, which also allowed athletic scholarships.

The NCAA supported the so-called Purity Code in January 1947 and sent it to committee for a final draft to be created for formal adoption. Despite claims that the code was "doomed to failure," the NCAA passed the "Principles for the Conduct of Intercollegiate Athletics" in January 1948. What then became known as the "Sanity Code" prohibited scholarships based primarily on athletic talent. At the same time, it allowed for need-based scholarships, academic scholarships, and campus jobs for athletes. All of these items had been addressed ad infinitum for more than a half century. The original code prohibited off-campus recruiting, but the final version allowed the practice so long as no financial offers were made to prospective players.[3]

The real difference in the Sanity Code lay in its empowering the NCAA to become an enforcement agency. To do so, the NCAA created a Compliance Committee and named the athletics director at Tufts University, Clarence Houston, as chair of the committee. The committee would accept complaints or accusations from other institutions as well as keep abreast of newspaper reports and magazine articles that implied grants-in-aid were being offered to prospective athletes. The Compliance Committee would then send correspondence to accused institutions and require a defense.[4]

Historians have mused as to why the Sanity Code passed with virtually no dissent. A closer look at historical documents offers insight into the reasoning of conference institutions that favored athletic grants-in-aid but still voted to adopt the NCAA's new restrictions. After the passage of the Sanity Code, the acting secretary of the SEC, Nathan Dougherty, sent an important letter to the conference's member institutions. In it he asked that members "read very carefully the recent bulletin issued by the NCAA's 'Compliance Committee.'" Need-based aid and academic scholarships would require documentation. Additional scholarships would receive "special scrutiny" and "created awards for athletics . . . will not be acceptable." Dougherty noted that despite the SEC's resistance to on-campus work, "ultimately it must become a real part of our athletic activity." He added that campus employment could not accommodate all the scholarships for athletes, so institutions' work programs needed to include "any job which has been approved by a responsible faculty committee."[5]

Dougherty then cautioned against athletics staff members criticizing the Sanity Code or other conferences, noting that it brought "direct attention to their own shortcomings." He concluded, "Since we have placed our hand to the plow and have adopted the new regulations, let us strengthen the hand of Commissioner Moore and with his leadership let us give the plan a real try." In short, SEC members collectively decided to move funds formerly allotted to athletic scholarships and instead adopted the Big Ten model of work programs for athletes.[6]

Such policy changes were not secretive or misunderstood. For example, after the passage of the Sanity Code, an opinion piece in Kent State's student newspaper noted that schools like Kent State voted for the code either because they disagreed with subsidies or "because they are not in a financial position to subsidize if they did wish to." For the big-time conferences already offering subsidies, they agreed to the Sanity Code because "they know how easy it'll be to arrange loopholes . . . [which] are so well-known and easily arranged that they hardly need repeating." The article concluded that the new Sanity Code should instead be named a "Football fable."[7]

Clarence Houston, chair of the NCAA's newly created Compliance Committee, was both meticulous and relentless in his requests for information and clarification regarding violations of the Sanity Code. After fielding dozens of requests for information from Houston, one SEC president wrote SEC commissioner Bernie Moore, noting his suspicion that "the NCAA may be looking for a 'southern victim' that they may make an example of one of our institutions."[8] Apparently, he was not alone. The Southern, Southeastern, and Southwest

Conferences all agreed to a meeting to be held at Georgia Tech in Atlanta during the Southern-Southeastern track meet in May 1949. During that meeting, the delegates from institutions in the three conferences wrote amendments to the Sanity Code. They also discussed the possibility of one or all of the three conferences resigning from the NCAA. Although choosing not to create an official alliance, the three conferences' collective attitude toward the Sanity Code and its enforcement was one of frustration.[9]

Although the big-time conferences in the South decided to remain members of the NCAA, their dislike of the Sanity Code provided an ominous sign for members of the NCAA leadership. These concerns had also been expressed by Notre Dame's president, Rev. John J. Cavanaugh, who had asserted, "True reform in athletics will not be accomplished by the mere publishing of noble, high-sounding codes which are often hypocritically evaded in actual practice." Cavanaugh also challenged the "so-called reformers . . . who seem to say that an indefinable something has to be done in athletics in a way nobody knows when, in places that nobody knows where, to accomplish nobody knows what."[10]

In 1949 the University of Virginia claimed that it could not comply with the Sanity Code. Virginia had been through this dilemma before, when it chose to leave the Southern Conference because its members had adopted the Graham Plan but refused to properly enforce it. As an independent institution, UVA began offering grants-in-aid to athletes. More than a decade after leaving the Southern Conference over its sham code, Virginia called the NCAA's bluff. Rather than divert funds for athletic scholarships to jobs programs, UVA's president simply stated that the institution's high academic standards precluded the possibility of being able to participate in competitive athletics, hold down a job, and meet the academic demands of the institution. Virginia was unwilling to begin "sacrificing" the academic careers of student-athletes by having them "take a bunch of assorted courses that lead nowhere." In sum, Virginia proclaimed, "We consider our honor system . . . more important than the N.C.A.A. Code."[11]

All told, six other institutions comprised what became known as the Sinful Seven, each of which faced expulsion at the 1950 NCAA Convention. Not surprisingly, the accused consisted of five southern institutions (Maryland, Virginia, Virginia Tech, and two military schools, Virginia Military Institute and the Citadel) along with two Catholic institutions in the Northeast (Villanova and Boston College). Virginia asked for an individual vote on expulsion, believing that another university "would not publicly vote to expel somebody for something it, too, practices." The NCAA denied the request, keeping the voting by secret ballot. Clarence Houston noted he had the "embarrassing job" of bringing charges against the seven members. His accusations were also combined with attacks by Michigan's Ralph Aigler, another member of the Compliance Committee. The institutions then had the opportunity to defend themselves. Virginia maintained its simple and honest stance that it would not abide by the Sanity Code. Other schools questioned the timeline for compliance. In a veiled attempt to protect his own institution, Maryland's president Harry "Curley" Byrd questioned, "Does Ohio State want to vote for the expulsion of Virginia when Ohio State has facilities to take care of four to five times as many athletes as Virginia?"[12]

After counting the secret ballots, Iowa professor and NCAA president Karl Leib eagerly announced that the institutions were expelled by a vote of 111–93. He was quickly corrected by yells from members who noted that the vote did not meet the two-thirds requirement for dismissal. As the *New York Times* reported, "After a brief pause, he smiled and said, 'You're right. The motion is not carried.'"[13]

Scholars have often characterized the failure of the NCAA to expel the Sinful Seven as a missed opportunity for reform. Although not the historian's task to project what might have been, there is little evidence that booting a handful of members from the NCAA would have accomplished anything. Many of the big-time universities in the Big Ten, Pacific Coast Conference, and the SEC had complied with the letter of the Sanity Code, and they were no closer to having purified big-time football. Deemphasis for the minority of NCAA institutions who desired big-time football was a lost cause. The Sanity Code sought to establish a "level playing field" among the commercially successful programs. Despite the rapid failure to rein in selected aspects of commercialized athletics, it would still be seven years before the NCAA would formally recognize athletic scholarships, at which time the organization determined such assistance no longer infringed upon an athlete's amateur status.

In addition, most academic accounts of the Sanity Code's failure and repeal point to the voting block of the Southern, Southeastern, and Southwest Conferences and their determination to keep athletic grants-in-aid. While this is true, it does not paint a complete picture. Of the hundreds of schools in the NCAA, most played outside the confines of a "power" conference, and contrary to the opinion of many historians at research universities, many of them found the Sanity Code fight unappealing. As historian Kurt Kemper documented, "the depth of ambivalence toward the Sanity Code within the small college group is hard to exaggerate. The code prohibited practices that small colleges did not engage in from the standpoint of either ideology or financial reality." For example, a representative from Drexel asked, "What is the place of the small college in the Sanity Code discussion? . . . What is the place of the small college in this whole program?" Another small-time athletics representative noted, "The practices mentioned in the Sanity Code in no way touch the activities of the small school. . . . That is why I don't see why we, as a small college, are particularly interested in the Sanity Code." Had the power conferences in favor of the Sanity Code been interested in the philosophical approach liberal arts colleges maintained with regard to athletics, an altogether different outcome might have been possible.[14]

The true transformational change the Sanity Code brought to intercollegiate athletics was the strategic attempt to give enforcement power to the NCAA. This provided tacit evidence to the fact that the driving force behind commercialized athletics would be the power schools operating through the NCAA—all while claiming to preserve amateurism. For scholars frustrated by decades of failed attempts to reform college sports, their inability to separate rhetoric from historical reality has left many flummoxed at the trajectory of college sports. This failure does not diminish the solid ethical ground on which arguments are made for pure amateurism. Rather, it is a misunderstanding of what the powerbrokers of the NCAA were attempting to accomplish, in spite of the soundbites and quotes offered to media. NCAA's Walter Byers, who became chief executive in 1951, clearly understood this reality. That is why he remained in his post for more than three decades. It would not be long before the NCAA exercised its new authority.

The Scandals of 1951

The defeat of the "Principles for the Conduct of Intercollegiate Athletics" did not mean the end of all amateurism in college athletics. It also did not mean that being honest about subsidies to athletes would "clean up" big-time college sports. The scandals of 1951 made that painfully evident. The uncovered improprieties gave college sports a serious public relations problem. The impact of those scandals would shape the future of governance in intercollegiate sport.

In February 1951, Frank Hogan, the district attorney for New York City, announced that multiple college basketball players had accepted bribes from gamblers to influence the outcomes of games. It initially appeared that these scandals involved games played at Madison Square Garden by universities in the New York City area. A handful of players from the City College of New York, Long Island University, Manhattan College, and New York University had admitted to accepting bribes and "shaving" points of the game. Gambling was not a new vice in college sports, but these accusations sent shockwaves through the college sports world.[15]

To contextualize the gambling controversy of 1951, one must understand the changes that occurred in the gambling world in the 1940s. Until that time, gamblers placed wagers on games based on odds. If a powerhouse faced an underdog, 50-to-1 odds were not uncommon. But the odds-on games with a powerhouse team against a noted underdog created financial risks for gamblers and bookies alike. For example, a 100-to-1 victory in favor of the underdog could destroy a sports book. At the same time, individuals with the need for quick cash were likely to gamble on such outlandish odds. This type of gambling had existed for centuries, but a new method of betting changed the landscape.

In the early 1940s, a University of Chicago alumnus and former high school math teacher, Charles K. McNeil, altered the landscape of professional and collegiate sports gambling. McNeil's gifts with statistical information made him a highly successful gambler. In fact, his ability to predict winners led sports books to limit the amount of money McNeil could wager at their establishments. As legend would have it, McNeil opened his own sports book in Chicago and changed the way gamblers bet on games. Rather than bet the odds of a favorite or underdog to win a game, McNeil created the "line," which involved setting a point spread by which the favorite was supposed to win a game. By McNeil's standards, a bet was not necessarily won if a big-time college team won the game. For gambling purposes, a team had to win a game by a projected number of points in order for gamblers to collect.[16]

McNeil called his new system an opportunity to bet on "wholesale odds," meaning that if a team was favored to win a game by six points, a wager on behalf of that team would make money only if the team won by seven or more points. Likewise, the underdog could lose the game by five points and the gambler would still double his money if he bet against the spread in favor of the underdog. The authors of Betting the Line: Sports Wagering in American Life surmised, "The most plausible explanation is that it originated with—or at least was refined and popularized by—Charles K. McNeal . . . a man blessed with a special talent for understanding complex statistical and probability problems."[17]

Manipulation of the line was a criminal offense, but players fell prey to the temptations offered by corrupt bookies and gamblers. As many historians have noted, these were not the first gambling scandals, and various athletics administrators and coaches had been warning the public about the dangers of illicit gambling. Nevertheless, when the scandal broke and continued to expand during the spring and summer of 1951, much of the sporting world looked on in dismay.

As the press continued to report on the basketball gambling scandal, another crisis went public at a relatively small liberal arts campus in Virginia. The College of William and Mary was the second-oldest college in the United States, younger than only Harvard. As many of the original colonial colleges grew into full-fledged universities, William and Mary struggled through much of the nineteenth and early twentieth century. As it found its traction in the 1900s, many members of the board of visitors desired a strong football team to promote the college. Following World War II, the board rejected President John Pomfret's request to compete against other small colleges. Instead, the board stated that William and Mary should successfully compete in "the Southern Conference to such an extent that we may reasonably expect to win more contests than we lose."[18]

In order to field winning teams, coach (and athletics director) Ruben McCray doctored high school transcripts for football and basketball players who would not have been eligible. Once in school, some athletes had their grades altered, and others received credit for phantom courses. The basketball coach illegally took money from a female administrative assistant and threatened that if she reported the indiscretion, her boyfriend on the basketball team would lose his scholarship. The new dean of the college, Nelson Marshall, pressured the president to punish the wrongdoers, but Pomfret moved slowly in an attempt to avoid any scandal. Instead, the president asked the coaches to address the issues of academic fraud or retire at the end of the season. The coaches chose to resign.[19]

When a letter discussing the academic dishonesty surfaced in the press, Pomfret had a public scandal on his hands, one he had desperately tried to avoid. The board, which stood in favor of big-time athletics, blamed the president for a lack of both control and communication. Pomfret resigned his post, and that fall, the William and Mary faculty issued a statement condemning the state of affairs in athletics and demanding more faculty oversight moving forward. While many on the board hoped to continue with big-time athletics, deemphasis occurred at William and Mary. In the process multiple administrators, faculty and staff resigned their posts.[20]

Before the William and Mary situation had been resolved, a scandal at West Point Military Academy hit the press. This was particularly troublesome for Army alumni, for two reasons. First, the exposure of a cheating ring including more than thirty football players brought the integrity of West Point into question. In addition, the scandal threatened to harm the football team, which had experienced unprecedented success during the war years. Benefitting from an influx of cadets during World War II, head coach Colonel Earl Blaik had multiple undefeated seasons and found himself at the pinnacle of college football.[21]

In the spring of 1951 there was news of a cheating scandal at West Point. The press reported that ninety cadets had been guilty of "cribbing," even though the exact term didn't fit the violation. With two rounds of tests, those taking exams in the morning shared answers with cadets taking the test later in the day. When a student admitted to this violation of the honor code, an investigation ensued, and ninety individuals were asked to "resign" rather than be dishonorably discharged. Thirty-five of the students were football players for Blaik, including his own son. This caused another media storm for college athletics, even though Blaik always claimed he knew nothing of the cheating ring. That fall, Army finished 2–7. It would take years for Army to rebuild a successful program.[22]

After newspaper reports concerning Army and William and Mary came and went, the point-shaving scandal in college basketball continued as more revelations led to a steady stream of arrests by Frank Hogan. During the summer, arrests of Bradley College players expanded the scope of the scandal well beyond New York City. Until that point, however, only smaller schools had been implicated. That changed in October with the arrests of three star players for University of Kentucky. All three were found guilty, but in testifying against gambling fixers and the university itself, they received suspended sentences. Coach Adolph Rupp's pronouncement earlier in the year that gamblers "couldn't reach my boys with a ten-foot pole" became infamous.[23]

All told, more than thirty college basketball players at seven different institutions were guilty of taking bribes from fixers and banned from college basketball if they had remaining eligibility. The Kentucky players, along with others talented enough to play professional basketball, were all barred from playing in the National Basketball Association. The toll on the guilty young men was extreme. Kentucky player Ralph Beard apparently said, "I'm guilty. Let me out of here. Let me die."[24] Years later, he remained bitter about the incident and the impact it had on his career.

General Sessions Judge Saul S. Streit felt the gravity of the situation and the weight of the consequences that the collegians received for their misdoings. As such, he wrote more than sixty pages on the state of college athletics.

As he noted, "These conditions are so closely interwoven with the crimes of these defendants that before imposing sentence I feel that I must, in the interest of crime prevention, and the restoration of high standards of scholarship and integrity in our colleges, relate some of the lurid details and state of my finds, conclusions and recommendations. . . . The exposure before me is only the lifting of the curtain for a small glimpse of intercollegiate football and basketball."[25]

Streit's commentary against commercialized athletics implicated universities across the country regarding illegal funds, cheating, and academic double standards for athletes. There was one caveat in which the judge's narrative did not directly follow a key line of reasoning: Kentucky provided the only example of a big-time program that found itself in the point-shaving scandal. City College of New York, Long Island University, and Manhattan College operated programs far smaller than those at Kentucky, Michigan, Notre Dame, and Texas. The direct correlation between commercialization and point-shaving did not exist. If it had, the list of guilty teams would have looked much different. Furthermore, Kentucky was one of a handful of schools in which big-time abuses had found their way into basketball. For most large universities, college hoops remained a secondary sport that did not yet generate excessive revenue.

Regardless of the logic utilized by Streit, he took the liberty to suggest ways in which college athletics could cleanse itself from wrongdoing. Along with the familiar calls of deemphasis, he listed specific steps to implement for righting the wrongs of commercialized athletics. The most notable reform offered by Streit called for the creation of a committee on "grievances, expulsion, and suspension," adding that the group should be "entirely independent of the colleges or of any of its officials."[26]

Eager to *not* have an independent group investigating university abuses, the SEC and the NCAA needed to deliver some sort of punishment. Understanding the precarious position in which Kentucky stood, its president Herman L. Donovan and athletics director Ab Kirwan called for an investigation of the program by its member conference and the NCAA. The SEC decided to suspend UK from conference play during the 1952–53 season, but it allowed nonconference opponents to schedule games with the Wildcats. But SEC commissioner Bernie Moore apparently worked with Walter Byers to make sure that did not happen. As Byers recalled in his memoir, "Bernie and I concluded, however, that terminating Kentucky's NCAA membership was not necessary." Instead, they "planned to enforce our 1952 death penalty by asking NCAA members to cancel games with Kentucky." UK's athletics director Ab Kirwan agreed to the cancellation of the season, so "enforcement" of the NCAA ban was unnecessary but understood.[27]

In the wake of the 1951 scandals, the American Council on Education (ACE) formed a committee of ten university presidents to study problems in college sports and offer recommendations. Although historians have characterized the ACE committee as a missed opportunity, it is more accurate to label it a public relations effort to heal the "black eye" college sports received in 1951. The committee consisted of colleges from multiple conferences, including some presidents representing smaller colleges. Reports suggested their interest in removing spring practice, eliminating bowl games, integrating athletics into academics, and improving recruiting and subsidizing procedures.[28]

The most powerful athletics programs represented on the committee were Michigan State College, Notre Dame, and the University of Washington. Michigan State's president John Hannah chaired the group. Hannah had improved Michigan State's academic status while incessantly pushing for its admittance into the Big Ten. Despite attempts from the University of Michigan to keep their "little sibling" out of the most powerful athletic conference in the country, Hannah had finally secured the support of enough institutions to earn an invitation from the Big Ten in 1948. John Cavanaugh and Notre Dame managed to avoid scandal at the time but clearly remained in the camp of big-time football. The University of Washington's president Raymond Allen would leave for the same post at the University of California, Los Angeles, in 1951. Both schools faced football scandals in the fifties, and Allen opposed enforcement by the Pacific Coast Conference. If anything, the membership and then the report of the ACE committee represented a victory for big-time sports.[29]

In the wake of the 1951 scandals, the NCAA was the real winner from a power and policing perspective. The NCAA exercised its enforcement authority against Kentucky without protest. The point-shaving scandal provided the NCAA something it did not previously have: university athletes committing crimes and violating rules that were not widespread among its member institutions. At the end of the day, the Sinful Seven were not operating much differently from other big-time football programs, the organization's members failed to revoke their membership, and the Sanity Code died. Point-shaving in basketball remained both shocking, criminal, and relatively rare when compared to the common football violations of recruiting and subsidizing players. Therefore punishing the University of Kentucky for that (along with other abuses) gave the NCAA the oversight authority it had unsuccessfully been seeking since the 1930s, after the SEC voted to allow athletic grants-in-aid. In addition, the SEC's willingness to take the lead in suspending Kentucky from conference play, followed by the NCAA shutting down nonconference games, set a precedent of conference and NCAA cooperation.

The National Association of Intercollegiate Athletics: Counternarrative to Commercialized Basketball and Unlikely Social Justice Pioneer

Not all member institutions of the NCAA were ready to move past the scandals of 1951, even after the SEC and NCAA banned Kentucky from basketball for a season. Chief among those who remained unassuaged were the liberal arts colleges who had been longtime members of the NCAA. They felt that the commercialized model that led to the scandals cast all of college sports in a negative light, even as many schools conducted their athletics ethically. As these issues came to a head in the 1950s, an alternative to the NCAA had begun to make inroads among small colleges across the country.

While football remained the dominant college sport, the post–World War II era witnessed the growth of a clear second-place sport in the world of college athletics. It also witnessed the creation of a second national athletics association. The early history of the National Association for Intercollegiate Athletics (NAIA) provides a glimpse into college sports outside of the big-time orbit. Despite its lack of national media attention, the creation of the NAIA as an alternative to the NCAA demonstrated the complexity, competition, and meaning of status in college sports.

At the beginning of World War II, there were three "national" basketball tournaments: the NCAA Tournament, the National Association of Intercollegiate Basketball (NAIB) Tournament, and the National Invitation Tournament (NIT). These nascent college basketball tournaments that developed in the late 1930s all represented competing interests in college athletics. The NAIB Tournament in Kansas City provided smaller colleges and universities an opportunity to compete for a national championship. The NIT at Madison Square Garden developed as a commercialized moneymaking event outside the NCAA's control. The NCAA, in many respects, instituted its own postseason event to curb the growth of the other two popular events.

The denominational colleges, teachers' colleges, and regional universities that comprised most institutions participating in the NAIB Tournament were less prestigious than the elite liberal arts colleges that comprised much of the small-college membership of the NCAA. At the same time, the thirty-two-team tournament continued to grow after World War II, and many small NCAA institutions found it appealing. In 1947 the US Olympic Committee (USOC) offered one of its eight spots for Olympic qualification to the NAIB champion.[30]

Hosted at the Municipal Auditorium in Kansas City, Missouri, the event was still subject to the state's segregationist policies, even if they were not always strictly enforced in the border state. The tournament's organizer, Emil Liston, had coached integrated teams at Baker College in Kansas, but he allowed segregation in the tournament, which included many white teams from the South. The first victim of this policy after World War II was Rosamond Wilson, a freshman at Morningside College in Iowa. Unaware of the tournament's Jim Crow policy, Wilson rode the bench while his teammates played. The following year, the first-year coach at Indiana State University, John Wooden, declined an invitation to the tournament rather than subject his team's one Black player to exclusion. While this bothered some tournament members and organizers, the NAIB did not change its policy until its hand was forced.[31]

In 1948, Manhattan College, a small Catholic college in New York, earned an invitation to Kansas City for the 1948 championship. It declined the offer unless the tournament publicly renounced its segregation policy before the games began. Liston then extended an invitation to two other northern schools, which also declined. When USOC member Harry Henshel learned of the segregation policy, he requested that the US Olympic Basketball Committee disallow the NAIB Tournament's winner from qualifying for the Olympic games. Faced with a crisis, Liston had his tournament committee vote by telegraph on rescinding the segregationist policy, which it did by a 6–1. With that move, Manhattan College agreed to play, and Indiana State's integrated team participated as well.[32]

The following year, Liston passed away suddenly, and Pepperdine basketball coach Al "A. O." Duer resigned his post in California to become the executive director of the NAIB Tournament. Far more committed to expansion of racial justice within the organization, Duer's actions eventually provoked backlash from the NCAA. At that time, leading Black coaches like John McClendon and Mack Greene had continually pushed the NCAA to include a Black college in the tournament, and they were continually rebuffed. Black coaches were told that no rule prohibited them from playing in the NCAA tournament, but that the NCAA could not determine the quality of Black teams. When Greene then asked the NCAA to encourage interracial scheduling, which would provide such determinations, it refused to do so.[33]

Even as the NCAA was discouraging primarily white institutions from participating in the NAIB Tournament, Big Ten commissioner and key NCAA official Tug Wilson encouraged the Black coaches to seek admission to the same event. Mack Green did just that. His Central State College became the first Black college to play in the NAIB Tournament. Duer then informed the all-Black National Athletic Steering Committee that its tournament winner would automatically qualify for the NAIB Tournament.[34]

At nearly the same time, the NAIB changed its name to the National Association of Intercollegiate Athletics, or NAIA. In 1952 the new organization held national championship events in track and field, golf, and tennis. Now the executive director of the NAIA, Al Duer created a "district at large" so that historically Black colleges and universities (HBCUs) and predominantly white institutions could avoid breaking the law in Deep South states that did not allow interracial games to be played. In 1953 the National Athletic Steering Committee held its tournament for HBCUs. Tennessee Agricultural and Industrial College (later Tennessee State University) won the event and became the first team to integrate the NAIA tournament. They won their first two games before losing in the quarterfinals to East Texas State Teachers College. This victory occurred a year before the historic *Brown v. Board of Education* (1954) case that declared segregation in public education unconstitutional.[35]

The success of the NAIA Tournament created problems for the NCAA. First, many small colleges in the NCAA correctly noted that the organization was biased toward big-time programs, and that few small schools would ever be able to play for a national championship. In 1951 the NCAA expanded its tournament field from eight to sixteen teams, but it did little to address the concerns of small colleges, which then began joining the NAIA. By the mid-fifties, the NAIA had a larger membership than the NCAA. As its membership grew, the NAIA added more national championship sporting events, and it was decidedly more progressive on racial inclusion than the NCAA had been.[36]

In an effort to slow the momentum of the NAIA, the NCAA created a committee on small-college concerns in 1953. It became evident to the NCAA's young executive director, Walter Byers, that the NCAA needed to offer a basketball tournament to keep the allegiance (and membership) of many small schools. After announcing the creation of the tournament, Byers contacted the USOC and asked them to revoke the NAIA's champion from the qualifying events for the Olympic Games. Not all were happy with the NCAA's power move. The *New York Times* predicted the death of the NAIA Tournament. A local paper in Louisiana clamed, "Bluntly, it shapes up like this: the NCAA is out to put the NAIA out of business because it has been doing its job too well." The NCAA appointed its first African American member to a committee when it placed Mack Green on the newly created College Division Basketball Tournament Committee. It was an effort to win back the loyalty of HBCUs, but it also segregated the same institutions from the big-time universities in the South that played in the university division tournament.[37]

Walter Byers succeeded in damaging the influence of the NAIA. Many colleges that had been served well by the NAIA returned to the NCAA Tournament. As historian Kurt Kemper clearly documented, much of the success in harming the NAIA came from the NCAA's elite liberal arts colleges. These small institutions had been neglected by the NCAA for decades, as members gave lip service to the principles of amateur athletics while siding with universities that sought commercialized big-time football. Even so, these wealthy liberal arts colleges sided with the larger universities rather than affiliate with the small denominational schools, HBCUs, and teachers' colleges that made up a majority of the NAIA membership.[38]

The NCAA did not destroy the NAIA, which exists to this day. But the College Division Basketball Tournament cut into the membership of the NAIA and ensured the NCAA's privileged position as the primary organization for intercollegiate athletics. By the late 1950s the NAIA could not compete with the revenue generated by big-time athletics programs and by the growing revenues from televised games. That was never the focus of the NAIA, though, and it remained true to its egalitarian roots. Although prodded into addressing racial injustice by Manhattan College and the USOC, the NAIA did take a far more progressive stance toward integration than the NCAA. For the NCAA, the creation of the small college division helped protect the big-time programs that would seek to expand the commercialized athletics in the years to come.

The Ivy League Stands Apart

In the fall of 1940, a young athlete from Lowell, Massachusetts, by the name of Jack Kerouac enrolled at Columbia on a football scholarship. The promising speedster ran a ninety-yard kickoff return during his first team game. Unfortunately, on the next play, he injured his leg. The Columbia trainer examined Kerouac and determined he had a sprain, but the freshman believed he had sustained a more severe injury. His coach, Lou Little, believed Kerouac was exaggerating the injury and forced him to practice until an X-ray proved that he had indeed suffered a broken bone.[39]

Missing the remainder of his first season affected Kerouac. As he recalled, "It was great. . . . That's when I started reading Thomas Wolfe."[40] Kerouac showed up to fall practice his sophomore season one day late and incurred his coach's wrath. Quitting the team in 1941, Kerouac joined the Merchant Marine. After a stint at sea, he returned to Columbia in the fall of 1942. After failing to perform to his coach's liking, Kerouac was demoted off the first team. One October day after being benched for the game against Army's powerhouse team, Kerouac sat in his room watching snow spit from the sky. As he revealed later, he thought to himself, "Scrimmage my ass. . . . I'm gonna sit in this room and dig Beethoven. I'm gonna write noble words." As a result, Kerouac lost his scholarship and proceeded to drop out of college and follow his own path as a writer.[41]

The founder of the Beat Generation, Jack Kerouac's existential moment of giving up big-time football created an interesting parallel for Columbia and the entire Ivy League. Although the analogy eventually breaks down in various ways, at some level the elite northeastern universities decided to let go of the pursuit of athletic victories in favor of Thomas Wolfe, Beethoven, and noble words. It took a world war and one wayward institution to galvanize the Ivy League's newfound direction.

Talks of a formal Ivy League conference had existed for years, as had feuds and misgivings among many of the rival institutions that eventually comprised the nation's most elite academic/athletic group. For example, in 1936, student newspapers at seven future Ivy League schools all called for the creation of an athletic conference. Administrators at the elite schools emphasized their desire to cooperate while maintaining institutional self-rule regarding policy matters. As one study noted, they provided "a polite way for the Big Three to imply that the University of Pennsylvania had markedly lower academic standards and that it certainly emphasized varsity football at a level beyond what Harvard, Yale, and Princeton now found appropriate." By the late thirties, however, the Big Three worked closely to formulate consistent policy regarding athletics.[42]

In 1945, Harvard, Princeton, and Yale agreed the time had come to invite eight university presidents to sign on to an "Intercollegiate Agreement" that would maintain "the value of the game while keeping it in fitting proportion to the main purposes of academic life."[43] This agreement gave life to what sportswriters had already dubbed the "Ivy League." The presidents of the Big Three had witnessed dramatic declines in football attendance during the war, and it appeared that they had an opportunity to deemphasize football. After some debate, the three presidents agreed to invite the five other institutions to discuss ways to minimize big-time football, but no formal conference had been formed.[44]

Even though the University of Pennsylvania received an invitation into the group, it still carried far more scholarship players than any of the other institutions. Not surprisingly, this benefitted the football team. The Quakers' 7-0-1 record in 1947 led to crowds of seventy thousand at Franklin Field, and the team finished the season ranked seventh in the nation. In response to Penn's continued athletic emphasis, Harvard and Yale continued refusing to schedule games against them, as they had done since the conclusion of World War II.

The following year, the University of Pennsylvania hired a popular midwestern governor, Harold E. Stassen, as its new president. Stassen had completed three terms as the chief executive of the State of Minnesota. The progressive Republican ran for president in 1948 but fell short in the Republican primary. Penn chose the charismatic leader for his promotional and fundraising abilities, as the university needed his help. In 1946, Penn started a campaign for its University of Pennsylvania Fund. It also embarked on a campus expansion plan. By the time Penn hired Stassen the campaign had raised only $2.5 million, and the university still owed $1.6 million on its football stadium while running a $200,000 deficit on "minor" sports.[45]

Stassen had earned two degrees from the University of Minnesota, and when he arrived in Philadelphia, he brought his midwestern sensibilities toward higher education with him. The attitude of an aspiring university president differed from the elite visions of institutions that had already "arrived," so to speak. A booster president from the start, Stassen began raising money and cutting university costs, but he believed mediocre football in 1948 and 1949 made that more difficult. Ticket sales had dropped, but the cost of running a large athletics program had not.[46]

To stem the tide, Stassen decided to utilize big-time football. In 1950 he replaced the well-respected Penn athletics director, H. Jamison Swarts, with former Penn football star Francis Murray. Far from an academic, Murray's career experience included serving as a sports radio personality, an event and sports promoter, and executive director of the Philadelphia Inquirer Charities. In his public introduction of Murray as the new athletics director, Stassen articulated his "Victory with Honor" program for Penn Football. The president claimed, "This date will be a milestone in Pennsylvania athletics. . . . We want victories with honor. We want to improve our schedules. We want to be able to appeal to star high-school athletes." Stassen also claimed that Penn could adhere to the "NCAA Code" (Sanity Code) and still have success.[47]

Much to the disdain of the other institutions in the Intercollegiate Agreement, Stassen and Murray did just that. Big games were scheduled, attendance increased, and even the band received an overhaul, as they played much more up-tempo songs. In 1950 he broke the unwritten rule of the elite northeastern universities to not schedule a game with Notre Dame, which they deemed too tainted with abuses, although Ivy League schools played against teams from the SEC, Southern Conference, and Western Conference. Whatever the true reason for blackballing Notre Dame, Stassen obliged Father John J. Cavanaugh's request for a matchup by scheduling a game for the 1952 season. In addition, Penn signed an exclusive deal with the DuMont Television Network for televised home games during the 1951 season for two hundred thousand dollars.[48]

With big-time football clearly taking hold at Penn, the other members let Stassen know their displeasure. Yale and Harvard already refused to play the Quakers. During the 1950–51 winter, Columbia, Dartmouth, and Princeton all refused to add Penn to their 1953 slate of games. As other institutions claimed the need for more "diversity" in their schedules, Cornell remained the only Ivy school that agreed to play Penn. As Mark Bernstein pointed out, "In keeping with another tradition, it [the boycott] remained a whispering campaign until a sportswriter finally broke the story." A *New York Times* article in January 1951 blamed the boycott on Penn's scheduling of Notre Dame. Yale athletics director Bob Hall argued that there was "no foundation" to the statement that Yale would not play Penn because of a game with Notre Dame. He did not add that Yale had not scheduled Penn in years owing to the regular beatings they took from the Quakers. Notre Dame and Penn both responded, with President Stassen claiming the Quakers would not quit playing another team because that team regularly beat Penn. This veiled shot at Harvard and Yale certainly was not the typical presidential banter Ivy schools expected from its leaders.[49]

Not surprisingly, Stassen's comments did not elicit improved cooperation from the other Ivies. Stassen's political instincts finally kicked in, and he suggested a meeting of the Ivy presidents to address the Intercollegiate Agreement moving forward. All agreed and held a meeting in April 1951. During the ensuing months, Penn embroiled itself in a debate with the NCAA regarding the right to negotiate contracts for televising football games. The NCAA had been examining the issue of television broadcasts, and a majority of member institutions believed that television threatened ticket sales for home football games. Although the evidence remained inconclusive, the NCAA voted 161–7 to ban television broadcasts for the upcoming season. Penn's Murray and Stassen were the most vocal critics of the NCAA's moratorium, arguing a national ban violated the Sherman Antitrust Act. As Penn's protests continued, the NCAA proceeded with its plan to provide one televised game a week and keep most of the profits for itself.[50]

Considering the long history of home rule by the NCAA, the overwhelming support for dictating policy for individual universities seemed puzzling. Game attendance had slipped in some places, but nobody attempted to block radio broadcasts. Alabama's athletics director Jeff Coleman, however, offered a concise explanation for the vote: "We had to act to keep Penn and Notre Dame from being on every week. . . . That would have been bad for college football."[51]

Rumors were swirling that the Ivy group might extend its ban against Quaker football to an expulsion of Penn from their association, but Stassen and Murray moved forward with their own television contract. When Murray informed the NCAA of Penn's new deal to televise its home games, the organization labeled Penn a "member not in good standing" with the organization.[52] Stassen sought the assistance of other Ivy schools to protest the NCAA's actions, but nobody followed his lead. Already refusing to schedule Penn for 1953, four of the Ivy schools said they would drop Penn from their 1952 games if they proceeded with their television plans. Facing further ostracism from its sister institutions, Stassen reneged on its contract. As AD Murray remembered, "I was just stunned by their [the Ivy Group] response. . . . It was like they were holding a gun to our head."[53]

Penn's decision not to televise its 1951 football games had not entirely assuaged the leaders of the Ivy schools. Had they joined Stassen in his fight, the Quakers would have gladly snubbed the NCAA's ruling and moved forward with the broadcasts. Instead, Stassen ended Penn's feud with the NCAA and waited to see how the Intercollegiate Agreement group responded. Stassen and the institution he led stood at a crossroads.

In the wake of the 1951 college athletic scandals, Intercollegiate Agreement members met again in December. Desiring to declare themselves separate from the scandals that had shaken college sports, the group agreed to assume policy authority in athletic governance and condemn athletic scholarships. Not all presidents were sure that Penn would follow suit. Before the meeting, Yale president Alfred Griswold wrote Harvard's James B. Conant with a wager, "I will lay you two to one that neither Pennsylvania nor Cornell will go along with us." Griswold expressed doubts about Dartmouth's commitment as well.[54]

Despite the misgivings of both the Ivy school leaders and Penn, Stassen and Murray signed on to the new agreement. Shortly thereafter, new athletic policies were introduced. One of them involved banning spring football practice. Penn, along with Princeton and Cornell, had expressed their desire to continue the practice. When put to a vote, however, Penn broke with the other two institutions and voted in favor of the ban. Stassen's decision to vote against spring practice was designed to solidify Penn's place in the Ivy League, and it worked.[55]

Stassen's decision paid dividends. In the summer of 1952 the college presidents, for the first time, officially labeled themselves the "Ivy Group" and established a "Presidents' Policy Committee" along with eight rules to guide the deemphasis of college football. Penn scored a victory when the members of the group agreed to schedule the Quakers in football. In the next years, the Ivy Group evolved into the Ivy League and adopted a round robin schedule. After Columbia president Dwight Eisenhower won the US presidency, Stassen left Penn for a position leading the US Foreign Operations Administration in the Eisenhower administration. During the 1954 and 1955 seasons, the Quaker football team failed to win a game.[56]

Harold Stassen's brief tenure at the University of Pennsylvania may have been the galvanizing factor in the formation of an Ivy League. Without his Victory with Honor strategy along with scheduling big-time games for television, the Ivy schools may have continued their path as a loose alliance. But Stassen's plan for televised and commercialized football allowed the Ivies to define what they did not want to be and gave them a specific program to rally against.

The creation of the Ivy League provides a number of historic considerations. First, the new athletics association did not symbolize an end to the importance of prestige and publicity. Rather, amid the scandals of the 1950s, a small group of institutions possessed the wealth and prestige to step away and engender a new type of publicity. Stassen's signing on to the Ivy Group agreement in 1952 embodied this different quest for positive publicity. In sum, for the University of Pennsylvania, membership in the Ivy League provided prestige that the institution viewed as more important than football publicity. Few other institutions have found themselves with the option to answer such an existential question, the most notable of which was the University of Chicago.

The creation of the Ivy League and its deemphasis on athletics signaled another important theme: its members felt academically exclusive enough to walk away from big-time sports. With growing endowments, a wave of new undergraduates to engage in selective admissions, and a general assumption that these were the most elite institutions in the country, the Ivy League gained in notoriety by publicly stepping back from commercialized athletics. In America, this privileged association of institutions now utilized the protection of *amateur* (i.e., elite) status along the lines of the British model, which they had claimed to subscribe to for the past century. The notion of the amateur did not exist apart from the existence of an elite group. After a century of intercollegiate sport, the Ivy League asserted its privileged position, which included amateurism.

There is some irony in the fact that the institutions that created big-time football in America were the first to collectively walk away from it. As historian Mark Bernstein has documented, "the Ivy League origins of an American obsession" are unmistakable.[57] For the vast majority of burgeoning research universities that attempted to model their aspirations after Ivy League institutions, football remained a key element of the promotional program— just as Stassen desired it to be. In the early years of the NCAA, the Ivy schools were slow to join the association because they feared it would weaken their power in college sports and threaten the autonomy each institution possessed. Ivy schools also feared that joining the NCAA would diminish their status, and in some ways they were correct. A half century later, the Ivy Group removed themselves from big-time athletics while remaining in the NCAA. This move made it even more difficult for aspiring universities to emulate the Ivy League institutions.

Finally, the Ivy Group's unwillingness to join Penn in fighting the NCAA on its restrictive television plan created a much stronger NCAA. This same group of institutions so valued institutional autonomy in policymaking (including athletics) that they had been unable to form their own regional association. Then, in the blink of an eye, they supported the NCAA's approach to controlling television broadcasts—a policy that would eventually be declared unconstitutional by the US Supreme Court. The group's quest to keep Penn in its place created tacit consent for the cartel-like behavior of the NCAA. As David Goldberg and Paul Lawrence surmised, the NCAA was engaging bullying tactics while claiming to protect the interests of amateur athletics. The NCAA accomplished this coup with the support of the Ivy League members.[58]

The Demise of the Pacific Coast Conference

On the other side of the country, the Pacific Coast Conference (PCC) attempted to address its own concerns regarding big-time athletics, commercialization, and abuses. In some ways the PCC's demise provided a last stand of sorts for the notion of big-time athletics operating on a purely amateur basis. The conference operated under the guidance of faculty representatives. During World War II, many of its members suspended football. At the end of the war, the PCC and the Western Conference (i.e., Big Ten) returned to their battle against the leading southern conferences to allow grants-in-aid for athletic ability. The PCC and Western Conference, being of like mind, signed an exclusive deal to each send a representative team to play in the Rose Bowl.

In the 1950s, however, the PCC suffered from scandals that included many of the elements that had existed across the country since the beginning of football rivalries. The violation of conference regulations, snobbish attitudes (both academic and athletic), jealousies, and perceived unfair treatment snowballed into the destruction of the conference. It also raised important questions about conference-level and NCAA enforcement.

The California schools of the PCC, through dramatic increases in population and wealth creation, had grown rapidly in prestige compared to other members in Idaho, Oregon, and Washington. Unable to compete, the Montana Grizzlies had already resigned from the conference in 1950. Within the California group, the University of Southern California and UCLA still dealt with opinions and attitudes suggesting that they were not quite on par with Stanford and Cal Berkeley. USC tried to overcome this in the thirties with power football teams. USC's gridiron success immediately brought accusations of recruiting and eligibility violations, so both Berkeley and Stanford threatened not to play the Trojans. UCLA, in contrast, was part of the University of California system, but UC Berkeley remained the flagship campus. While UCLA's enrollments exploded and its academic trajectory was on the rise, it remained a branch campus within the UC system. Its yearbook's title, *The Southern Campus*, bore this out. From this context, concerns regarding prestige continued, and athletics became a primary way for each campus to validate its own status.

Oregon was the first PCC institution in the 1950s to suffer scandal when its coach was caught offering illegal financial inducements to recruits. Oregon fired its coach to avoid possible expulsion but also pointed fingers at other members to the south. That did not slow the avid recruiting by eager alumni in the PCC. In 1953, UC Berkeley managed to convince Southern California high school superstar Ronnie Knox to commit to the Golden Bears despite his proximity to UCLA and USC. Knox's stepfather, Harvey Knox, had played an integral role in Knox's college choice. After one year of freshman football, the young football player decided to return to Southern California and play for UCLA.[59]

The decision to transfer raised questions and allegations about financial offerings by both California system universities. At that point, Knox's stepfather took to the pages of *Sports Illustrated* to provide his account of his stepson's recruitment. Harvey referred to the alumni boosters attempting to recruit his stepson as "Curbstone Cuties" and stated that "Ronnie got plenty of offers and promises" from multiple institutions, but he decided to attend Cal Berkeley. While there, Ronnie felt that Berkeley had not fulfilled its agreement to him. So, his stepfather called a meeting with Cal coach Pappy Waldorf. He claimed that the coach asked, "Harvey, just what do you want for Ronnie?" The stepfather responded, "Pappy, it's simple. Just what you promised him." Displeased with his situation on and off the field, Ronnie decided to transfer to UCLA.[60]

Part of Berkeley's package to bring Ronnie Knox to campus included a coaching position for Knox's high school coach, Jim Sutherland. After events unraveled for Knox at UC Berkeley, Sutherland then took a position as an assistant coach at the University of Washington. While there, numerous players signed a petition to have Washington head coach "Cowboy" Johnny Cherberg fired. Sutherland attempted to undermine the head coach and convince Huskie players that he should be their new leader. Eventually, the university administration terminated Cherberg's employment. Once fired, Cherberg revealed the underhanded dealings of the Greater Washington Advertising Fund in its attempts to build a winning Huskies football team. Washington booster Roscoe "Torchy" Torrance operated the fund in Seattle. Torchy's slush fund helped pay players, buy plane tickets, and purchase cars.[61] Cherberg's revelations led to investigations by both the Washington state government and the Pacific Coast Conference.[62]

Only a few years before the Washington scandal broke, its president, Raymond B. Allen, left Seattle to accept the newly created position of chancellor for UCLA in 1951. As scandals cascaded across the PCC, they hit Westwood in 1956. This time, former UCLA player George Stephenson, who had transferred to Cal Berkeley, exposed the underhanded financial dealings of UCLA's alumni. Stephenson claimed to share these misdeeds because the other PCC schools "abide by the rules." The Bruins Bench and the Young Men's Club of Westwood were the culprits. As PCC commissioner Vic Schmidt attempted to conduct his investigation by interviewing the players themselves, UCLA chancellor Allen prohibited the interviews for more than two months.[63]

Possibly provoked into proving Stephenson wrong, UCLA alum J. Miller Leavy proceeded to bring charges against USC and accusations against UC Berkeley. The accusations proved to be correct. Both USC and UC Berkeley had operated slush funds to assist athletes. While Berkeley's alumni had subsidized twenty-nine athletes, USC had given impermissible funds to forty-two football players and two track athletes.[64]

The PCC commissioner and the group of faculty athletic representatives that oversaw the conference's investigations and resulting punishments had an extremely busy year in 1956. Washington was fined $53,000 and banned from postseason games in all sports. In July, the PCC fined USC $63,400 and banned it from playing in any postseason sports, including the Rose Bowl. UC Berkeley, which had offered improper benefits to only twenty-nine football players and cooperated with the PCC's investigation, received a fine of $25,000. The PCC saved its harshest punishment for UCLA: a fine of $95,000 and a three-year ban from postseason play in all sports. The steep fine was due, in part, to Chancellor Allen's refusal to cooperate with Vic Schmidt's investigation. Allen denied blocking the investigation and added that he was "not surprised" by the harsh punishment, and he encouraged the conference to continue investigating other institutions in the PCC.[65]

It did not help that a few months later, Ronnie Knox, whose recruiting saga helped kickstart the conference-wide controversy, provided an interview to *Collier's* magazine in which he laid out all the inducements he received to attend UC Berkeley. His stepfather received four hundred dollars each month as a talent scout for the football team (something Harvey failed to mention in his *Sports Illustrated* article). In addition, Ronnie earned five hundred dollars annually for football tickets, another five hundred dollars in spending cash, and an additional five hundred dollars to pay for family travel to his games. Knox claimed he received inducements from twenty-seven institutions, including a car from a booster at the University of Illinois. He added that he was offered thirty-five dollars more a month above the legal amount to attend Stanford, a university that managed to stay above the fray in the PCC scandal. Then Knox also reported that a member of the athletics department at Berkeley "coached" him on how to answer questions from the PCC commissioner Victor Schmidt. Knox noted that when he had "conspire[d] to break the rules at the University of California . . . I was investigated thoroughly by the conference commissioner and cleared." While playing at UCLA, however, "I never took a penny of undercover payment." He famously added, "I found college football pro football—only the salaries were much smaller."[66]

The crisis of the Pacific Coast Conference involved illegal player subsidies, but its aftermath revealed far deeper issues. In most instances during the previous hundred years of college football, the latent condescension involved with academic and athletic prestige generally existed but remained below the fray. As scandals and penalties occurred on the West Coast, it became apparent that conference members viewed themselves differently within the higher education landscape, which influenced their respective attitudes toward the crisis. The complexity of university responses to the crisis highlighted many issues needing resolution. At the same time, it also provided room for reinterpretation of the key players and competing interests that drove athletic policy long before and long after 1956–57.

Opposition to the penalties levied against USC and UCLA focused on the severity of discipline of the southernmost members of the conference. Anger at University of Oregon faculty member Orlando Hollis, who chaired the PCC's enforcement committee, strained relations between these institutions and the California schools. Further, for years, USC and UCLA had chafed at the insinuation that they were lesser institutions than Stanford and Berkeley. Football provided an opportunity to prove their equality, and in their minds, the PCC now punished them more severely for the same actions. While complaining about the attitudes of condescension, UCLA and USC then asserted that their own athletic superiority provided a sound reason to leave the PCC. Why travel to Washington State College, the University of Idaho, or Oregon State College to engage in mediocre competition at institutions of lesser academic prestige? The acrimony traveled both ways. Reporting on the "Strife-torn" conference "from Seattle to Southern California," author Herman Hickman noted that "Pullman, Corvallis, Eugene, Palo Alto, and Moscow have not been touched [with scandal]. Truthfully, these seats of learning are in no way sympathetic to their suffering brethren, particularly those in the Los Angeles area."[67]

Questions of elitism and equity had existed from the early days of rowing, when elite universities in the Northeast did not want to compete against colleges whose students were from a different "class." The same theme carried over into football and had been commonplace, even if far less public. The attitudes of USC and UCLA had been common among universities in the Midwest (toward the northeastern schools) and the South (toward every other region). The two Southern California schools (including alumni, students, administrators, *and* faculty) felt slighted by other conference members. Attempting to illustrate this frustration, UCLA chancellor Raymond Allen and athletics director Wilbur Johns complained to Walter Byers at the NCAA. Both Allen and Johns had participated in Kentucky's NCAA hearings. They pointed out that Kentucky had been treated respectfully despite their athletic sins. The chancellor and the athletics director at UCLA noted, "In the [Pacific Coast] Conference . . . they treat us as if our words cannot be believed. It's a vendetta."[68]

In this environment, public pressure mounted in Southern California to break relations with the PCC. USC and UCLA administrators began seriously contemplating leaving the conference to protest their punishments and assert greater institutional autonomy in athletics. For UCLA, questions of secession extended to separation from the UC system. The first president of the University of California system, Robert G. Sproul, stood in the middle of the controversy both geographically and politically. Sproul, hoping to keep the system intact, eventually sided with USC and UCLA in their move to leave the organization. In 1957 the University of California system developed the Regents' Plan to improve athletic conduct. But the irony remained: two of the four schools on probation had devised a plan for cleaner play. It included a minimum grade point average (GPA), financial assistance based only on need, honest jobs, and fair wages for athletes. Most importantly, it added that each institution, rather than the conference and its commissioner, be responsible for enforcement.[69]

The PCC rejected the Regents' Plan, and UC Berkeley, UCLA, and USC announced their intentions to leave the conference. They remained in the PCC long enough, however, to support the faculty representatives' ouster of conference commissioner Vic Schmidt. In short, a majority of conference members did not want a commissioner who vigorously enforced the rules established by those same institutions. Oddly, less than a decade earlier, the Pacific Coast Conference stood with the Western Conference (Big Ten) in support of the Sanity Code and its strict regulations on recruiting and subsidizing. What the institutions stated publicly and what they actually desired remained worlds apart.[70]

The history of the PCC, which was governed by faculty, had generally been viewed as a model for cleaner athletics. But a closer look at the record reveals that faculty representatives, along with students and presidents, faced the same challenges and engaged in the same pitfalls in pursing successful big-time athletics. The faculty athletic representatives for the conference had established lofty aims, as had every other big-time athletic conference formed in the United States. Yet abuses on multiple campuses suggest that they did not monitor or control illegal activity as it occurred. In their defense, how could they? Many of these faculty members had productive and illustrious careers in academic disciplines having nothing to do with athletics administration. One wonders how they could accomplish their professional work while also enforcing conference rules and regulations. It might be fair to say that a faculty representative was not always representative of the entire professorate at an institution.

President Sproul of the UC system expressed his own frustration that faculty often sided with athletics directors rather than with the university presidents. Although his sincerity has been called into question, the Regents' Plan to improve athletic governance had been supported by the conference's university presidents, but the faculty representatives proceeded to vote down the measure. The president of the University of Idaho wrote President Sproul stating that conference regulations had been established, but "knowingly and wittingly their representatives did not comply."[71]

The attitudes of faculty athletic representatives at guilty institutions remained puzzling as well. While on probation, UCLA was looking for schools with which to schedule games. After facing multiple rejections, the UCLA athletics director had to remind his faculty representative, "We cannot issue statements that institution x, y, or z fails to meet the academic requirement of our policy." Such a move would be "courting disaster from a public relations standpoint. Our present position calls for a little more common sense." After UCLA's violations had been made public, its Faculty Senate Committee on Athletics did not condemn its athletic activity. Rather, it recommended that UCLA should ban athletic competition against Stanford.[72]

The most questionable action of the PCC's faculty representatives came in 1957. In 1956 the NCAA publicly commended Vic Schmidt for his work on behalf of college athletics. A year later the faculty representatives voted to demand Vic Schmidt's resignation as conference commissioner. As Schmidt himself lamented, "They hired me to keep it clean."[73] The president of the University of Idaho (the conference's clear outlier) noted the conference representatives from offending institutions either wanted "special consideration" because of their prestige or "they just don't intend ever to comply with any kind of regulations if they are not according to their desires."[74]

Indeed, after three California universities guilty of recruiting abuses left the conference, the remaining institutions lasted only one more year, and then the PCC dissolved in 1958 while agreeing to complete its athletic commitments through the 1959 academic year. Even as the PCC played out its final contractual obligations, a "Big Four" developed in order to provide a representative to the Rose Bowl. It consisted of the four offending members of the old PCC: UC Berkeley, UCLA, USC, and Washington. The group initially took the name Athletic Association of Western Universities (AAWU). The group hired Admiral Tom J. Hamilton as its first chief executive. Hamilton held no enforcement powers over recruiting violations, however. The AAWU adopted institutional oversight through "mutual trust and confidence" that universities would enforce regulations. As Walter Byers recalled, Hamilton had been instructed to ignore enforcement and instead promote football and avoid scandal in the press.[75]

During the first thirteen years of the Rose Bowl's exclusive contract with the PCC and the Western Conference, the West Coast teams won only one game while losing twelve. This was also the era of Vic Schmidt's enforcement of conference regulations. Considering the many recruiting abuses uncovered in the

PCC, the Western Conference's policy of allowing jobs for athletes was successful in attracting the best talent that led to nationally prominent teams.

With the creation of the AAWU and institutional enforcement, that all changed. In 1960, Washington handed the Big Ten its worst loss in the Rose Bowl, defeating heavily favored Wisconsin 44–8. During the next twenty years the West Coast teams proved to be much more competitive in games against the Big Ten. In the 1960s the AAWU added Oregon, Oregon State, and Washington State and became known as the Pacific-8, or Pac-8.

The history of the old Pacific Coast Conference offers important lessons in big-time athletics. A clear lesson emerged after faculty representatives, at the request of PCC athletics directors, forced Vic Schmidt to resign his post as PCC commissioner. Clearly, regulations were not to be enforced widely at the conference level. To do so would more than likely cost coaches, presidents, and conference commissioners their jobs, as it had in the PCC. It was easy to punish the University of Kentucky for a point-shaving scandal carried out in secret by a few basketball players. That remained a novel abuse in college athletics. It was an entirely different matter to challenge corruption among multiple institutions within the same conference.

In the end, the dissolution of the PCC did not reduce the penalties issued by the NCAA. In that way the NCAA gained some precedence over conference penalties. Even when a conference faltered, Walter Byers and the Rules Committee ensured that some form of punishment would be issued for violators of conference and NCAA rules. Once again, the NCAA found a way to strengthen its hand amid controversy.

Beyond Big-Time Football: Expansion and Excellence in All College Sports

The expansion of a wide range of varsity sports for men was at the heart of American higher education from the late 1930s through the years following World War II. If one looks beyond football, especially at the big-time programs, one finds an important success story of student-athletes and coaches that came close to fulfilling the all-American ideal of the dedicated student who also was serious about playing one or more college sports.

Expansion was neither expensive nor excessive. As late as 1960, athletics directors even at large universities offered little in scholarships or financial aid to most varsity athletes. Furthermore, it was not unusual for students to play more than one varsity sport. Head coaches outside of football often had part-time positions in which they served as assistant coaches in other sports or taught physical education classes. The operations of a comprehensive intercollegiate varsity team looked far different on campus than they did in the newspaper focus on a handful of big-time and high-profile sports geared to spectators.

Facilities such as swimming pools and practice fields were austere. Ice hockey often was played in outdoor rinks. Yet the student-athletes and coaches were excellent and dedicated. A good example was the rise of collegiate crew beyond the traditional teams of the Northeast, with "varsity eights" from state universities such as Washington and the University of California, Berkeley, winning national championships—and, later, winning gold medals in representing the United States at the Olympics.[76]

Although baseball was the most popular sport in the United States, college baseball was seldom a route to a professional sports career. Most promising baseball prospects signed minor league contracts right after high school graduation. A landmark for the formal stature of college baseball came in 1947 when the NCAA sponsored the first "College World Series." The championship series of three games pitted Yale against UC Berkeley. The captain and first baseman for the Yale team was George H. W. Bush, a decorated military veteran who later became the vice president and then president of the United States. His team lost to California's Golden Bears, who were led by Jackie Jensen. Although Jensen would later gain fame as the American League's Most Valuable Player as a slugging outfield for the Boston Red Sox, Jensen was a two-sport athlete at Cal, best known as an all-American fullback who led his team to the Rose Bowl.

Memoirs of student-athletes from this era were understated and modest in tone, usually conveying gratitude for the opportunity to have attended a college where they could play on a varsity team. Many of the sports had a strong regional grounding—such as hockey in the upper Midwest and New England. The University of Southern California won numerous NCAA championships in track and field starting in the 1930s, drawing on local talent from nearby high schools with strong scholastic programs and optimal weather conditions for year-round training. The University of Michigan staked out a commitment to swimming and diving, resulting in a succession of Big Ten and NCAA championships. Most important is that campus pride in varsity teams extended to wrestling, boxing, cross-country, gymnastics, track and field, lacrosse, and swimming.

Basketball eventually gained stature as a major sport, but on close inspection, it remained largely local in character and moderate in attendance. Few campus basketball facilities, often known as "the cage" or "the field house," seated more than two thousand fans.

When John Wooden accepted the head coaching position at UCLA in 1948, he visited the campus and was surprised to discover that the men's gym was less impressive than many high school gyms in his home state of Indiana. It was so decrepit, small, and smelly that students good naturedly called it the "B.O. Barn."[77]

The conditions of minor sports revealed that the vast majority of American college athletes competed in a way that most university professors and administrators applauded. Even at big-time universities, nearly all athletes outside of the football program participated in a noncommercialized sporting environment. But newspaper coverage, radio programs, and television shows focused primarily on football and secondarily on basketball.

An often overlooked development when examining college sports is the growth of intramural athletics. Intramural sports, by definition, fit the amateur definition espoused by college leaders since the nineteenth century. The first formal intramural operations run by universities occurred before World War I at the University of Michigan and Ohio State University. Oregon State College and the Universities of Illinois and Texas soon followed suit. Even during the Great Depression, intramurals organized by universities continued to grow. Only after World War II, however, did a national association devoted to the promotion and growth of intramurals develop.[78]

William Wasson, a professor at HBCU Dillard University, led the way in founding this association. Wasson secured a grant from the Carnegie Foundation to study intramural programs at HBCUs. At the conclusion of his study, Wasson organized a conference at his host university that included representatives from eleven HBCUs. In February 1950 the group created the National Intramural and Recreational Sports Association (NIRSA), whose subsequent growth in membership included primarily white institutions.[79]

It is not surprising that NIRSA developed through HBCUs. Systematically denied access to big-time athletics and the revenue it generated, recreation leaders at HBCUs focused on the development of their students. The success of their efforts continued into the twenty-first century as NIRSA became the leading professional association for intramurals and recreation across the nation. With millions of student participants each year, intramurals have remained a neglected topic of the success of college sports.

Women and College Sports in the 1940s and 1950s

Women remained outside the arena for varsity sports competition at coeducational colleges and universities. Typically the director of athletics dealt exclusively with the men's intercollegiate squads. One early formal development for women's intercollegiate athletics came about in 1941 when, despite protests from the Division for Girls' and Women's Sports (DGWS) of the American Association for Health, Physical Education, and Recreation, Ohio State hosted a national championship in golf. Such moments were few and far between in the 1940s. A continuing mystery of competitive athletics in the twentieth-century was that, despite the lack of interscholastic or intercollegiate teams and games, some women, especially those at HBCUs, continued to provide the United States with successful athletes in international competition such as the Olympic Games. As philosophy and policy regarding women's athletics changed, so would representation on women's US Olympic teams.

The dominant philosophy at the leading white colleges and universities led to an interesting development. Namely, some of the best intercollegiate opportunities for women existed at HBCUs, which were systematically discriminated against owing to their lack of resources and opportunities for intercollegiate competition. But PWIs generally dismissed women's athletics. HBCUs, largely dismissed altogether by PWIs, ignored the profit motive and focused on the educational opportunity sport provided for young Black women. As a result, HBCUs provided some of the best opportunities for women that existed in the United States.

Significant Minorities: African American Student-Athletes at Historically White Campuses

A profile of college student-athletes from 1935 to 1960 shows a conspicuous minority of African American student-athletes who stood out both because of their color and their excellence amidst a sea of white. At colleges and universities that had undergone desegregation by 1940, inclusion of African Americans on varsity squads was gradual and minimal. Yet African American student-athletes showed disproportionate talent and achievement on the field, in the classroom, and later as alumni, all accomplished despite numerous obstacles and exclusions.

When Jackie Robinson broke Major League Baseball's racial color line in 1947 as an infielder for the Brooklyn Dodgers, he became an enduring national hero. Often overlooked, however, was his prior role as a pioneering college student-athlete. After transferring from Pasadena City College to UCLA in 1939, Robinson was a four-sport star in football, basketball, track, and baseball. Most important was that he was part of a critical mass of Black student-athletes at UCLA, including such outstanding players as Thomas Bradley, Woody Strode, and Kenny Washington. Bradley, an all–Los Angeles City star in track and football, later served as Los Angeles chief of police and then mayor. His classmate and teammate Kenny Washington was considered by many to be the best college football player in the nation and would star in professional football, enduring avoidance and exclusion because of his race. Woody Strode encountered racial exclusion in his professional work following graduation but eventually became a highly regarded actor in Hollywood.

UCLA was exceptional in its concentration of outstanding Black student-athletes on the same teams at the same time. Elsewhere nationwide, however, Black students achieved campus and national honors for their athletic achievements. Among the most outstanding African American college football stars of the era, they demonstrated exceptional achievement as students and then as achievers and leaders in adult life. Several had interrupted their studies to serve in the military during World War II.

Black stars in the galaxy of college sports were recurrent. Levi Jackson was a New Haven, Connecticut, local whose father worked in Yale dining halls. As a high school standout on the football team in the early forties, Jackson joined the military to serve during World War II. Utilizing the GI Bill, Jackson chose to attend Yale, where he made the varsity football team. Jackson made headlines when his teammates selected him as their captain for the 1949 season. He was also the first Black student tapped for membership at a secret senior society at Yale. After graduation, Jackson took a job at Ford, eventually being promoted to a vice president position at the company. Jackson played a key role in promoting minority hiring and training practices in the late 1960s, leading to the hiring of thousands of marginalized workers in Detroit.[80]

In the Big Ten, outstanding all-conference and all-American football players in this era included University of Illinois player Claude "Buddy" Young, who was a conference and national champion in track and field, and later a World War II veteran. He also played as a professional football star and then became a successful business executive. At the University of Michigan, Lowell Perry was an all-American receiver, star player in the National Football League, recipient of a law degree, the first African American plant manager for Chrysler Motors, and the first African American to be an assistant coach and television broadcaster in the NFL.

At Indiana University, George Taliaferro starred as a multiposition player who earned all-American honors three times and led the Hoosiers to their only undefeated season as they were crowned Big Ten Champions. Although located in the Midwest, Taliaferro recalled that when he arrived at Indiana, he was barred from the dormitories, the pool, and the dining commons. The young star

Indiana University football player George Taliaferro poses for a photo during the 1948 season. Indiana University Archives

helped change the campus culture and then became the first Black player drafted by an NFL team. He would later have a distinguished academic career, returning to IU as the dean of the School of Social Work and as "special assistant to the President of Indiana University."[81]

Interestingly, the Big Ten had been slightly accepting of Black athletes on the gridiron but remained slow to fully integrate the hardwood. An unwritten agreement not to recruit or place any Black basketball players at Western Conference Institutions remained in effect through World War II. In 1944, Iowa became the first conference institution to integrate its team when Richard Culberson played varsity basketball. After passing up on multiple African Americans, Indiana coach Branch McCracken finally capitulated and recruited Bill Garrett to play for the Hoosiers in 1948. Garrett became the first Black player to see significant playing time in basketball.

The high points of pioneering achievement in athletics and academics by African American students at historically white colleges coexisted with flagrant discrimination. One conspicuous and violent incident occurred when Drake University played an away game against Oklahoma A&M in Stillwater, Oklahoma. Johnny Bright, a standout at both halfback and quarterback, was viciously attacked by Oklahoma A&M's Wilbanks Smith. Photographers John Robinson and Don Ultang caught the assault, which broke Bright's jaw, on film as they were testing new multisequence photo equipment.

Even though the images won the Pulitzer Prize for photography, the mixed response from many was telling. Incensed members from Drake University football team, student body, and administration were equally as frustrated by the lack of concern from Oklahoma A&M officials and the Missouri Valley Conference (MVC). When the MVC failed to punish Oklahoma State or its offending player, Drake University resigned from the conference in protest. Bradley University also left the conference to signify its support of Drake and Johnny Bright. As historian Lane Demas noted, the violence of the event was compounded by the marginalization of Bright, as the photographers received more notoriety for the images than the victimized player.[82]

Resistance to racial exclusion was evident in the courage of the University of San Francisco's undefeated football team in 1951. Players voted promptly and unanimously to reject a bid to play in the New Year's Day Orange Bowl Game when the bowl sponsors offered an invitation by phone along with the condition that USF had to agree not to have the two African American players on the team travel with the squad and play in the bowl game. One of those players, Ollie Matson, was an all-American halfback who would become an Olympic track medalist and later a professional football player selected for the NFL Hall of Fame. Courage to promote racial justice came with a heavy cost. Without the funds offered to play in the bowl game, USF's football program could no longer make financial ends meet, and the program was discontinued shortly thereafter.[83]

In 1946 the University of Tennessee traveled to Pennsylvania to play Duquesne. An argument ensued when UT protested that they would not play against Duquesne's center, Charles Cooper, an African American player.

The Duquesne players refused to play UT without their Black teammate, so Tennessee returned home. The case revealed the tensions surrounding integration and revealed that the long-held "gentleman's agreement" for northern schools to bench the few Black players they had when competing against a southern team. As historian Charles Martin noted, the controversy led to more southern teams traveling above the Mason-Dixon Line to play games, and it appeared gradual integration on the field and court might occur.[84]

The "Secret Game," played between Duke University's Medical School team and HBCU North Carolina Central University in 1944, highlighted both the hope and persistent prejudice that characterized the era. Legendary coach John McLendon's NCCU team finished the season 19–1. After a friendly discussion among players from both teams, the two squads decided to play against each other. McLendon's Eagles bested the team from Duke. Although the game could not be reported, it seemed that racial prejudice might soon be waning. Then, when the US Supreme Court made its ruling in the *Brown* decision, the South moved away from its slow acceptance of playing integrated teams in the North (or in secret) and instead chose "massive resistance" to preserve segregation.[85]

Even with the 1954 *Brown v. the Board of Education* decision, racial inclusion proceeded slowly in college sports at colleges in states that had heretofore prohibited coeducation of Blacks and whites. Ironically, although advocates of college sports often invoked the liturgy and language of sports as a "level playing field" where "talent counted," this goal seldom was realized. To the contrary, in at least thirteen states in the South, one finds little if any acceptance of Blacks as student-athletes at predominantly white institutions until the late 1960s. In other words, the predominant pattern was that even when Black students were allowed to enroll, they were treated as second-class citizens within campus life, excluded from dormitories, dining halls, fraternities, and sororities—and from varsity sports.

The Up-or-Out Syndrome in College Football: A Season of Reckoning and Readjustment

The University of San Francisco dropping its championship football program in 1952 was not an isolated case. The paradox of football popularity was that after World War II, it fostered an up-or-out syndrome, exerting a pressure for athletics directors to spend more each year to remain competitive in terms of teams, players, and publicity. At the same time that universities in the Big Ten were expanding stadium capacity from about forty thousand to seventy thousand, football teams elsewhere faced declining attendance. The result was that numerous colleges and universities nationwide made a deliberate decision to drop football. Following USF's lead, some Catholic colleges also discontinued football. The loss of football programs was especially pronounced in metropolitan areas where there was fierce competition for spectator dollars from a concentration of several college programs along with the relatively new, growing presence of the National Football League teams. Also ending their football programs were Fordham in New York City, Georgetown University in Washington, DC, Loyola University in Los Angeles, St. Mary's College in the San Francisco Bay Area, and Villanova in Philadelphia—even though many of these institutions had enjoyed high points of regional and national fame as well as championships.

One interesting side effect of the football cuts is that it freed up athletics department resources to focus on other sports, especially basketball. The athletics programs at Georgetown University, Loyola University of Chicago, Providence College in Rhode Island, Seattle University, St. John's in New York City, and the University of San Francisco helped to spread the reputation of basketball as a "city game," as these programs increasingly gained prominence in national tournaments such as the NCAA and the NAIA.

The up-or-out pressure also led to the creation of a new group of institutions known as "medium-time" programs. Universities located in states with small populations, teachers' colleges that were expanding their curriculum beyond educator preparation, and midsized private schools began to realize that their academic and athletic interests did not align with either big-time commercialized sport or the strictly amateur philosophy of athletics at elite liberal arts institutions. For a while, many of these institutions found a home in the NAIA, but their desire to grow in both academic and athletic prestige created a strategic dilemma that would not be resolved during this era.

There was also an impact on another key conference on the national landscape. Since splitting with the Southeastern Conference in the early 1930s, the Southern Conference maintained a membership of seventeen institutions that included both big-time and medium-time programs. In 1951, Southern Conference presidents recommended that no members play in bowl games. An undefeated Maryland team planned to play the University of Tennessee in the Sugar Bowl, but when they sought the standard exemption from the conference, Maryland's request was denied. The conference announced that participation in bowl games would result in a one-year suspension from league play. The measure had been championed by the conference's smaller schools, which wanted to deemphasize athletics.[86]

Maryland played in the Sugar Bowl anyway, and Clemson accepted an invitation to play in the Gator Bowl. The resulting suspension resulted in a group of seven institutions leaving the Southern Conference: Clemson, Duke, Maryland, North Carolina State, South Carolina, UNC, and Wake Forest. After adding the University of Virginia the next year, the new conference named itself the Atlantic Coast Conference. The new league included most of the power programs in the Southern Conference, and they wanted to maintain big-time athletics and promote stronger academics as well. The ACC members had the means and the desire to move up rather than out.[87]

The ten institutions left "out" were smaller institutions, many of which focused on the liberal arts. Of that group, only two universities would move back "up" into big-time athletics: West Virginia and Virginia Tech. Other colleges like Davidson, Furman, Richmond, and Washington and Lee (to name only a few) ended up outside of the quest for big-time athletics. The creation of the ACC provided further evidence that a particular type of institution (the "standard" American university) was the best suited type of school for big-time athletics.

Higher Education and Athletics in the Postwar Era

After World War II, America's colleges and universities experienced what one historian called an era of "prosperity, prestige, and popularity." These three themes found common ground across the various institutional types in higher education. Yet the "3 P's" also created growing divisions among institutions. While fewer than 1.5 million students attended college in 1940, by 1950, that number exceeded 2.6 million. By 1960, American collegiate enrollment stood at 3.6 million. Save for two world wars and the Great Depression, American higher education had witnessed robust growth for the first half of the twentieth century. But the post–World War II boom truly began "mass access" for higher education.[88]

The democratic impulse in higher education that had developed in the late nineteenth century had almost reached full bloom in the 1950s, but some groups remained marginalized. Unfortunately, access was often denied to racial and religious minorities. When admitted, such individuals were often token in terms of numbers, and higher education did not create an equitable playing field for minorities. White women, in contrast, found more democratic admissions but then faced relegation into specific fields of study.

It is not surprising that these same trends existed in athletics as well.[89] Aspiring universities continued seeking recognition with elite conferences and teams. At most aspiring universities, increased enrollments only further encouraged big-time athletics programs. Students, alumni, and boosters cheered on their teams in increasing numbers. But institutions in the South still banned Black players long after *Brown V. Board* (1954), while universities in other regions generally employed a token approach to Black athletes. Sporting opportunities for women, with a few notable exceptions, were generally relegated to intramural activities that culminated in "play days" with other colleges. Athletics at American universities very much resembled the universities themselves. Despite the tradition of self-congratulation about college sports and opportunity, the prospects for athletics to serve as a means for social mobility remained closed to all but a select few.

The 1950s also witnessed the growth of prestigious research universities, which expanded their budgets through private philanthropy, corporate grants, and federally funded research. As the gulf in funding between the "great" American universities and the "standard" ones widened, aspiring institutions attempted to highlight their own prestige in both academic *and* athletic competition. For private universities, like those in the Ivy League, stepping away from big-time athletics proved to be an avenue to clarifying this distinction. For public research universities, beholden to state politicians and budget appropriations, athletics remained an important piece of the promotional puzzle.

Federal interest in higher education focused on military-industrial development as well as increased access to higher education for more of the American public. This was apparent in the mammoth study created by President Harry Truman's Commission on Higher Education for Democracy. Volume I, *Higher Education for Democracy*, elaborated on the need to expand the role and opportunities in America's colleges and universities. Regarding the study, Chicago president Robert Maynard Hutchins stated, "It is big and booming. It is confused, confusing, and contradictory. It has something for everybody. . . . It has great faith in money. . . . It is anti-humanistic and anti-intellectual. It is confident that vices can be turned to virtues by making them larger." He added that the report "Skirts on the edge of illiteracy, and sometimes falls over the brink. . . . The cry is 'more'; more money, more buildings, more professors, more students, more everything."[90] A nearly identical complaint had been directed at big-time athletics programs for decades.

The postwar university faced other critics as well. Clyde Burrow has argued that the dramatic shift in federal funding after World War II was not aimed at democratizing education but accumulating wealth for capitalists. As such, uneven development across the American regions (such as the South) resulted. In addition, class struggles among universities (and their constituents) ensued. To state it more concisely, economics professor Henry Rosovsky, who taught at UCLA in the fifties and early sixties before spending his career at Harvard, wanted to know who actually held "ownership" of the American university.[91] The answer was not simple.

Clark Kerr, chancellor of the University of California, Berkeley, campus before becoming president of the University of California system, offered some thoughts on the years after World War II in his memoirs. He noted the importance of "defense-related university research" in making public universities the primary instruments in "helping build the necessary technostructure that the new age of industrialism required."[92] The best public universities, he argued, became research universities while also pursuing universal access within the system.[93] As the research emphasis took hold, so did relationships with government and industry.

The new emphasis on research and "grantsmanship" changed the dynamic of college teaching as well. In most instances, research dollars lead to placing junior faculty and graduate assistants as instructors in the undergraduate classroom. For this, Kerr noted, "celebration was in order but also consternation."[94] Closer to the 1950s, Kerr explained these changes in the following way: "The university is so many things to so many different people that it must, of necessity, be partially at war with itself."[95] It is no wonder that Kerr noted the UC system's driving goal to "go beyond being a leader among public universities and become a leader among all universities public and private."[96] What Kerr failed to answer was, "For what purpose?" How could he? He believed the purposes were varied and contradictory. The modern university had become what Kerr labeled the "multiversity." Kerr was focused on specialization that led to grants, research, and the expansion of knowledge. It was within this university context of fighting to be the best that big-time athletics began to grow as well.

Page Smith, who began his career at the College of William and Mary in 1951 and eventually became a professor at UCLA as a historian before becoming an administrator in the UC system—and provost at the new University of California campus at Santa Cruz in 1965—developed controversial thoughts of his own. Looking back on his career, he noted that "universities sold their souls . . . when they began accepting enormous federal grants to do work for the military-industrial complex." At the end of his career in 1990, he hoped to "hear no more pious pronouncements about the universities' being engaged in the 'pursuit of truth.' What they are clearly pursing with far more dedication than truth is big bucks."[97]

Smith's criticisms were directed at the structure and aims of postwar American universities, but his critique generally applied to the big-time athletics programs at many of the same institutions. Long before *U.S. News & World Report* popularized college rankings for parents and prospective students to consider, research university presidents followed rankings published by in various reports. Such reports ranked graduate programs, PhDs conferred, research dollars expended, and numbers of "distinguished" departments on a campus. They did not, however, attempt to quantify the quality and value of undergraduate instruction, which critics of big-time athletics had always prioritized. But one might argue a link existed between university rankings and the quest for football revenue and rankings. Teachers' colleges, elite liberal arts colleges, HBCUs, and Ivy League members either could not or chose not to chase the athletic prestige, but most aspiring standard American universities did.

Michigan State provides a compelling example of the relationship between academic and athletic ambition. When John A. Hannah became president of Michigan State College of Agriculture and Applied Science in 1941, he set out to transform the college into a nationally recognized university. MSC's enrollment, including students in extension and short courses, stood at just over 8,400 in 1939–40. That number dipped slightly during World War II, but by 1950, that number exceeded 17,000. In 1960, enrollment eclipsed 24,000. While seeking big numbers and big grants, the ambitious Hannah relentlessly sought entrance into the Big Ten. Utilizing opinion pieces in the sports pages and Michigan State's growing prestige, Hannah continued his letter-writing campaign to other Big Ten presidents.[98]

Based on its location, size, and mission, Michigan State appeared to be a perfect fit for the Big Ten, yet the strongest objections to their admission into the conference came from the University of Michigan. Once again, power and prestige played a role. Michigan's dominance in the state meant that the state flagship had nothing to gain from the upstart land grant college and its athletic aspirations.

Highlighting the political nature of such decisions, Michigan officials publicly supported extending an invitation to Michigan State while privately fighting against its admission. As Walter Byers noted, "Michigan could appose Hannah only at peril of jeopardizing its own state appropriations."[99] Despite Michigan's machinations and posturing, Hannah's persistence paid off as the conference officially extended an invitation to join in 1948. Upon hearing the news, thousands of students (and a good number of faculty members) celebrated in the streets of East Lansing.

Insistent that big-time athletics could operate on ethical standards, President Hannah chaired the American Council on Education panel to address athletic abuses after the scandals of 1951. During that same time, the Spartan football team claimed at least a share of the title "national champions" in 1951 and 1952. Shortly thereafter, accusations surfaced that the Spartan Foundation had improperly subsidized athletes. When asked for records, the foundation dissolved itself and destroyed its records. The Big Ten placed MSC on a one-year probation. The following year, an assistant football coach began a slush fund to help aid athletes, and Michigan State found itself in trouble with the NCAA. In 1955, Michigan State's growth, research, and prestige led the institution to change its name to Michigan State University of Agriculture and Applied Science. It was officially big time, and it also struggled with big-time athletics.

Another essential development during the fifteen years following World War II was the rapid evolution of the NCAA from a "debating society" into a centralized system that promoted big-time athletics while dictating policy and enforcing its regulations through punitive discipline of violators. Under the direction of Walter Byers, the NCAA managed to assume both control and funding in college sports. Each crisis that developed in the 1950s provided Byers with the opportunity to consolidate the organization's grip on the administration of athletics. The failure of the Sanity Code still provided tacit consent of the NCAA's enforcement authority. During the point-shaving scandals in 1951 the NCAA asserted that authority without protest. When the Ivy League bailed on big-time sports, it did so while giving the NCAA total control of television rights and revenue. When the Pacific Coast Conference dissolved in the wake of widespread scandal, the NCAA remained and enforced punishments against the offending institutions. In short, in a decade and a half, the NCAA had truly consolidated power that had once belonged to institutions and their conferences.

Television served as an integral piece of the NCAA's newfound authority. As the popularity of TV grew after World War II, so did the desire to broadcast games and generate revenue. Yet administrators also feared that telecasts might harm the bottom line if ticket sales plummeted. The NCAA, with overwhelming support of its member institutions, asserted its authority into the television debate. The organization did not do this to ensure amateurism but instead to protect profits. The NCAA's original plan to keep sixty percent of television revenue and distribute the remainder to the institutions playing on TV revealed the NCAA's true goals. As television moved forward under the NCAA's direction, the big-time sports programs with larger viewing audiences demanded more of the profit. This still left enough money for the NCAA to conduct its enforcement responsibilities while subsidizing the many championship events for nonrevenue sports.[100]

This dominant narrative, however, does not do justice to the diversity of institutions and individuals engaged in college sports. Most colleges and university could not replicate the big-time model that continued to increase in popularity. Hundreds of institutions and thousands of athletes participated in the newly developed NAIA, despite the NCAA's successful efforts to minimize the associations power. HBCUs leveraged their role in the NAIA to push for greater inclusion in the NCAA. Dozens of conferences without a chance of capitalizing on the revenues of big-time athletics still managed to organize seasons and tournaments for multiple sports.

Large universities with big-time football offered a growing list of sports for men. The competitive excellence of these programs was showcased every four years, as college athletes and alumni dominated the rosters of Olympic sports teams and individual events. While colleges and universities continued to gain a greater voice in the selection of men for Olympic sports, they generally ignored women's sports, leaving the selection of female Olympians up to the Amateur Athletic Union. The obvious sexism exhibited by colleges and universities in curricular tracking of its coeds was matched by its general disinterest in women's Olympic sports on campus. After all, "minor" sports required financial subsidies from universities, and big-time athletics programs desired to spend money in ways that would keep football (and to a lesser extent men's basketball) competitive.

Owing to their marginalization in competitive intercollegiate sports in the 1950s, women and minorities found athletic outlets in growing intramural programs across the country. Small colleges and large universities operated successful intramural programs and funded multiple initiatives with the funding that Walter Byers and the NCAA offered to participating universities. Small liberal arts institutions, teachers' colleges, and HBCUs often operated competitive and healthy sports programs—leading such schools to wonder what their place would be in this new era for both academics and athletics.

Just like universities themselves, American athletics programs developed into complex systems with various and competing interests. The administration of different sports involved different aims. As such, college athletics mirrored the diversity of the American higher education institutions. Many marginalized colleges and their athletes found themselves outside of the

NCAA's largess. If viewed as a pyramid, the most powerful athletic institutions were claiming a privileged space at the top of the higher education landscape while collecting more revenue—not only in ticket sales but also from a centralized agency wielding more control than could have been imagined before World War II: the NCAA. In the following decades, hundreds of colleges began to challenge this status quo of higher education's most powerful athletic organization.

5

Civil Rights, Racial Desegregation, and Regulations, 1954 to 1973

The NCAA and the Control of College Sports

By 1960, big-time college sports had weathered scandals involving player recruitment and had solved numerous serious financial problems that threatened the well-being of athletics departments nationwide following World War II. Television broadcasts of live games to large audiences had posed new challenges that were held in abeyance. At the same time, the increasing spectator appeal of professional sports raised the NCAA's concern about declining attendance at small college games.

How did athletics directors and their institutions address these assorted threats? First, they granted the NCAA the right to be the collective representative on policies and programs for televising all college games. Member institutions and conferences were not allowed to negotiate their own television broadcast packages. The NCAA approach was to limit football broadcasts to a total of eight per week. On a given Saturday, the nationwide television market would be divided into four regions. The NCAA then selected for each region two games: one starting at noon and a second around three in the afternoon as the NCAA Game of the Week. The NCAA signed a contract of $6.5 million with NBC in 1965 for exclusive rights to broadcast twenty-nine selected college games. Each subsequent year the contract increased substantially, to the benefit of the NCAA. By 1970, for example, the NCAA had ended ties with NBC and in its new television football contract with ABC received $12 million for a single season, almost double the amount in the agreements for 1965 and 1966.[1]

For the period 1960 to 1972, it meant that the NCAA, not a campus or a conference, controlled broadcasts, advertisements, revenues, and, above all, selection of the teams and games to be showcased. Limiting the number of television broadcasts was intended in part to halt the decline in fans buying tickets and attending games at their nearby colleges. The NCAA became, in fact, a cartel.[2]

The NCAA, having turned television into a source of revenue for itself, and to a lesser extent for its member institutions, also succeeded in defusing the threat posed by the increasing popularity of professional games, especially in the National Football League. The deal struck was that Friday night was reserved for high school games, Saturday for college games, and Sunday for professional games. The NFL and the NCAA also resolved another potential conflict when the NFL adopted its own regulations to prohibit drafting a college player until his class was scheduled to graduate. This truce allowed all segments to prosper and was mutually beneficial, since each level of sports team depended on the others for a succession of players.

Commercial broadcast contracts signed by the NCAA and NBC ensured that for college sports, football would be the goose that laid the golden egg. The NCAA oversaw a revenue-sharing program in which some broadcast monies were shared, albeit unevenly, across all member institutions. This income was crucial to most small- and medium-sized college sports programs, which had trouble balancing their budget based on the limits of their ticket sales or media broadcasts. It also caused resentment among a relatively small number of big-time programs that did not like being thwarted in their own broadcasts, with the added insult of having to share income with what they considered to be marginal spectator teams. Radio station contracts, which were not controlled by the NCAA, provided some institutional autonomy and funding. To balance the budget, most athletics departments relied on mandatory student fees as a substantial and guaranteed revenue stream.

The importance of this trend involved more than simple growth in a television market. It also included a philosophical approach to the television market and its purpose. Uses of television in the 1960s were varied and contradictory. For example, Martin Luther King Jr.'s leadership in nonviolent civil disobedience relied on television to broadcast the atrocities inflicted on Black Americans. This helped create a national political will to support civil rights legislation. Conversely, the NCAA used college sports, particularly football, to generate popularity and revenue. As such, any racial tensions on the field or court were generally ignored.

The Context for Civil Rights in Southern Sports

Continued newspaper and radio coverage, along with larger television contracts, did not negatively affect game attendance, as fan bases in the South and across the country continued to grow. Despite its popularity, there were persistent signs that intercollegiate athletics as public spectator events perpetuated rather than reduced inequities in American life. Numerous college stadiums maintained racially segregated seating. Some major college football teams in the South did not allow Blacks to buy tickets or even attend games. Rather than solving such problems through the NCAA, the US government was once again required to create real change.

The 1960s witnessed the development of many important forces and policies in college sports. None of them proved more important than federal involvement in civil rights regarding racial desegregation—which proved to be quite different than full integration. The issues of government involvement, race, and integration were related, but they also included distinct spheres with regard to implementation and impact. A recounting of the history reveals that the story of Black players at primarily white institutions (PWIs) never followed a straight line of progression. Uneven chronological progress was matched by even greater regional variation across the United States.

One enduring question the athletics revolution raised was whether college sports were a source of educational opportunity leading to upward mobility. Closely related was the "truism" that college sports represented a level playing field based on talent, not privilege. Systematic studies increasingly cast doubt on such traditional claims. One obvious dissent in the national liturgy was that at colleges and universities in numerous states, intercollegiate athletics remained racially segregated. While the issue of racial exclusion has often focused on the South, most universities in other regions that integrated in the early twentieth century usually did so with one or two token Black players. Coaches in basketball and football often monitored the racial composition of their teams. For a basketball coach to send a majority of Black players onto the court was to run the risk of angering the fans, alumni, and donors. As previously discussed, many of these individuals showcased acumen in both athletics and academics. To survive in this racial climate anywhere in any conference required exceptional talent and temperament from the young athletes.

For most Black students who wished to play college sports, especially those from the seventeen or so southern states, most opportunities were in the historically Black colleges and universities. HBCUs such as Florida A&M, Grambling State University, and Southern University played in segregated conferences. Scheduling games against PWIs in the South remained illegal, and finding PWIs north of the Mason-Dixon Line willing to schedule games was nearly impossible in the NCAA. Hence many HBCUs joined the National Association of Intercollegiate Athletics (NAIA) while continuing to put pressure on the NCAA.

Black players who made their way to integrated institutions outside the South faced the humiliation of the "gentleman's agreement," which allowed coaches of racially exclusive sports programs to extend their institutional racism to other colleges that were scheduled to be opponents. Early in the twentieth century, northern universities benched their own Black players not only when they traveled south but also when they hosted southern teams. Small challenges to this attempt to keep college sports a white-only space appeared in the 1920s. For example, Virginia's Washington and Lee traveled to Pennsylvania to play the John Heisman–coached Washington and Jefferson in football during the 1923 season. When the Virginians showed up and realized their Pennsylvania hosts had a Black player, Charles West, they demanded that he not play. Heisman and the rest of the Washington and Jefferson team refused, so Washington and Lee forfeited the game and returned south. Until the 1940s, most cross-sectional games maintained this agreement.[3]

The rise of Nazi Germany and ensuing World War II brought issues of racism to the fore in America. Fighting to make Europe democratic for all its citizens made Americans more cognizant of their own contradictions, as Jim Crow laws still dominated the South and few African Americans were given the opportunity to attend college in other regions. Those that did slowly witnessed the dismantling of the gentleman's agreement as teams refused to bench their Black players. This trend made slight progress in the South after the war as more teams recruited Black players. For example, an integrated Penn State football team played Southern Methodist in the 1948 Cotton Bowl. The Sun Bowl soon followed suit, and it appeared that gradualism slowly gained ground.[4]

Then, in 1954, the US Supreme Court ruled segregated education unconstitutional. Across the Deep South, governors and other politicians (state and federal) who had run on segregationist platforms dug in their heels and planned for "massive resistance." Long before the Little Rock Nine entered Central High School in 1957 or James Meredith enrolled at the University of Mississippi in 1962, few college sports and contests challenged the systemic racism inherent in segregated athletics. While states in the middle and upper South had not yet integrated, they had begun playing other integrated teams. The Deep South states, in contrast, opposed any single "crack" in the wall that kept people of color second-class citizens.

Massive Resistance and the Color Line
in College Sports

In 1955, a college sports story captured the media's attention in Georgia and across the nation when representatives from the Sugar Bowl offered invitations to Georgia Tech and a University of Pittsburg team with one Black player—Bobby Grier. Tech Coach Bobby Dodd celebrated the invitation and publicly stated his excitement about playing Pitt. But Georgia's governor, Marvin Griffin, telegrammed the board of regents, warning them, "The South stands at Armageddon. The battle is joined. We cannot make the slightest concession to the enemy. . . . There is no more difference in compromising the integrity of race on the playing field than in doing so in the classroom." Griffin summed up the philosophy of massive resistance by stating, "One break in the dike and the relentless seas will rush in and destroy us."[5]

When Georgia Tech students learned of the governor's plans to keep their football team from competing in the Sugar Bowl, more than two thousand students marched through Atlanta to the governor's mansion, where they burned Griffin in effigy, defaced a Confederate monument, and demanded that the Yellow Jackets play the game. Interestingly, students from Emory, Mercer, and even the University of Georgia all protested against the governor's stance. One Black paper in California described the monumental event as "the first time in the recent history of the South that any sizeable segment of white people have uttered a defiance of lily-white policies."[6]

Members of the Georgia Board of Regents held differing views on the governor's hardline segregationist stand. Some sided with the governor, other politely disagreed, and one member called the governor's stand "utterly ridiculous." The story gained national attention and ire as well. The board voted against the bowl ban, and on January 2, 1956, Bobby Grier made history by integrating the Sugar Bowl in front of more than eighty thousand spectators.[7]

Students in Georgia were not on a social justice mission, protesting the inability of Black students to attend white universities. Instead, they opposed edicts keeping their football teams from national glory. Nevertheless, newspapers across the country praised the students and the board for their stand against absolute segregation. In Georgia, some praised the move while others bemoaned the crack in the dike that Governor Griffin said could not happen. Regardless of the editorials, the fact remained that shortly after the *Brown* decision, schools in the Deep South remained segregated, but citizens from New Orleans representing the Sugar Bowl invited an integrated team to play against a lily-white institution from Georgia. Both sides of the social issue viewed this small step as a first move toward integration. An African American newspaper editor, Marion Jackson, noted the significance, correctly predicting that "in five years" Black players would be playing at UGA's and GT's stadiums "or both will be out of the football business."[8]

Mississippi had a similar situation at the end of the 1955 football season. It simply did not receive the same press coverage because it involved football at the junior college level. Mississippi's Jones Junior College boasted a 9–1 record and earned an invitation to the Junior Rose Bowl in Pasadena. Jones accepted the invitation to play against the integrated Compton Junior College in California. During the next few weeks, the decision by Jones Junior College received criticism in the press, but there were no serious threats not to participate. The Compton Tartars football team included eight Black players, and they defeated the Mississippi team in the Rose Bowl with more than fifty-eight thousand spectators watching.[9]

Shortly after the loss, a Mississippi state representative introduced legislation to ban integrated sports competition for institutions in the Magnolia State, regardless of where the game was being played. The bill, however, never made it beyond the House floor. Generally considered the most vehemently racist state in the country, Mississippi's ruling elite had developed what historian James W. Silver correctly labeled as a "Closed Society" that allowed no dissent when it came to racial justice or, more accurately, the lack thereof.[10] At first glance the stalled bill seems perplexing. But Mississippi's powerbrokers knew that such a law would eventually be overturned in federal court, so they adopted an unwritten law that could not be overturned—since it did not officially exist. Members of the legislature, the state's governor, and Mississippi's statewide board of trustees for higher education essentially determined that any college that played an integrated game would lose funding, and those responsible would be punished as well.[11]

The "law" was first put to the test in December 1956 when the Mississippi State College Maroons played in a holiday basketball tournament in Indiana against an integrated University of Denver. The victorious Maroons were slated to face the host institution, Evansville (also integrated), in the next game. When the press noted the integrated tournament, MSC's president, Ben Hilbun, ordered the Maroons to withdraw from the tournament immediately. Ole Miss then refused to play an integrated Iona team in a separate tournament. As Tad Smith, athletics director at Ole Miss, noted to the press, "There is not a written rule [against playing integrated teams], only policy."[12] The unwritten ban on integrated play applied to HBCUs as well. Jackson State Teachers' College for

Negroes turned down an invitation the NCAA small colleges basketball tournament in 1957 for the same reason.[13]

The unwritten rule came at an unfortunate time for the Mississippi State basketball team. New coach "Babe" McCarthy turned the team into a conference juggernaut in the late fifties and early sixties. The newly named Mississippi State University (MSU) and their Bulldog basketball team won the Southeastern Conference championship in 1959, 1961, and 1962, and each time the university turned down invitations to the NCAA basketball tournament. The University of Mississippi was in the midst of unparalleled football success with head coach Johnny Vaught, but the Rebels managed to participate in postseason play by accepting bowl bids in the South (usually the Sugar Bowl) against all-white teams.

In the fall of 1962, however, James Meredith challenged segregation by attempting to enroll at the University of Mississippi. Defying a federal court order, Mississippi's governor Ross Barnett opposed Meredith's integration at every possible turn and helped create a volatile situation in Oxford. Two people were killed in riots the night before Meredith registered as a student, but the federal government had enforced the law, and Meredith became the first Black student to attend the University of Mississippi—or any white institution in the state.

Although James Meredith had desegregated higher education in Mississippi, the unwritten rule remained in force. Yet with each denial of an NCAA tournament bid, MSU coach McCarthy became increasingly frustrated with Mississippi's racist policy. As others states in the SEC began playing integrated teams, Mississippi remained steadfast in maintaining its strict segregationist society. When the Bulldogs once again clinched the SEC crown in 1963, McCarthy stated, "It makes me heart sick to think that these players, who just clinched . . . their third straight SEC Championship, will have to put away their uniforms and not compete in the NCAA tournament." He added, "That is all I can say, but I think everyone knows how I feel."[14] After the Bulldogs clinched at least a share of the SEC title, hundreds of students marched in front of President Colvard's home to protest the state's policy, but Colvard remained noncommittal in his remarks to the students. The student senate requested that the university accept the NCAA's invitation, and Colvard's office was flooded with letters for and against playing in the tournament.

As it turned out, unquestioned allegiance to the unwritten law broke down in 1963. Two key events made this possible. First, MSU had hired a new president, Dean Colvard, an outsider from North Carolina State University. Colvard was the first nonnative president of Mississippi State, and he was not part of the "closed society" that had been established by the state's political power-brokers. Just as important, James Meredith integrated the University of Mississippi in the fall of 1962. As a result of Barnett's meddling in the Ole Miss integration process, all of Mississippi's public colleges and universities had been placed on probation by the Southern Association of Colleges and Schools. Further intrusion into the operations of a university may have resulted in the loss of accreditation. In short, Mississippi power brokers could not come out and publicly enforce the unwritten law.

Segregationists retained strong popular support throughout the Deep South. After the 1962 football season, the University of Florida accepted a bid to play integrated Penn State in the Gator Bowl. The Gators used the opportunity to create a North versus South atmosphere by putting confederate flag logos on their helmets, along with the band playing its regular rendition of "Dixie." Then, in 1963, Alabama's governor George Wallace stood in front of the doors at Foster Auditorium and gave his infamous "Schoolhouse Door" speech. These two incidents revealed, at some level, that universities and politicians knew desegregation was at the door, and they would yield to the US government while using it for political gain.

The intense public pressure Colvard faced was matched by lack of support from the state's board of trustees. As historian Russell Henderson noted, in the wake of the James Meredith crisis, the board announced that it did not have a policy to enforce—which had clearly not been the case. Instead, they expected MSU's new president to "dutifully accept" the unwritten law.[15] Colvard instead announced that he would allow the basketball team to participate in the tournament, opening himself up to criticism across the state.

Branded as a traitor, there were calls to remove Colvard from the presidency. Colvard pressed forward. In a last-ditch effort to prevent the game, two state politicians requested and received a temporary injunction prohibiting the president and the coach from taking the team outside of the state. When Colvard and McCarthy learned the news, they left Mississippi immediately in order to avoid being served. The basketball team, leaving the next morning, devised a plan in which the junior varsity team pretended to be the varsity squad in case the segregationists tried to stop the team from leaving. In the end, all involved parties were able to leave the state before anyone tried to stop them.[16]

The Bulldogs traveled to East Lansing, Michigan, where they faced Loyola of Chicago, which started four Black players. MSU lost the game, and Loyola went on to win the 1963 NCAA championship. In the process, the last bastion of lily-white segregation in sports incurred its first lethal blow, but segregation

Mississippi State University and Loyola of Chicago players shake hands before playing the Game of Change in 1963. Office of Public Affairs, Mississippi State University

would still die a slow death in southern college sports. It would be years before any Southeastern Conference team integrated their own rosters, but another step had been gained that would eventually open the door for a semblance of greater racial equality.

Georgia Tech's entrance in the 1956 Sugar Bowl against the University of Pittsburg created cracks in the post-*Brown* massive resistance movement, and Mississippi State's participation in what became known as the "Game of Change" in 1963 brought the last states into integrated play, at least away from home. A key detail in both cases: neither of these milestones required a federal intervention. Both events were sparked by student protests, not to challenge segregation but to let their teams join in national competition. These events were also essential because they provided two examples of university presidents who had the courage to challenge powerful politicians with the ability to exact financial retribution on their respective institutions.[17]

The South's Slow Move toward Integrating College Athletics
Mid-Major Conferences Lead the Way on Desegregation

Playing against an integrated team and actually desegregating sports at southern universities were two very different issues. No doubt, the move toward social justice was incredibly slow. For example, when Mississippi State University played an integrated basketball game outside of the South in 1963, the *Brown V. Board of Education* decision striking down segregation laws had been settled nearly a decade earlier. At that point, no Black athletes suited up for football or basketball in the three major southern conferences: the Atlantic Coast Conference, the Southeastern Conference, and the Southwest Conference.

What were called "power conferences" in the South were slower than many smaller schools in their efforts to desegregate. States in the Deep South refused to allow integration at any college, practicing massive resistance in an effort to maintain their way of life. Yet universities outside of cultural Deep South that pioneered integration generally came from small colleges and regional universities. The urban universities of Louisville and Houston also broke barriers in recruiting African American football and basketball players. One of Louisville's first Black basketball players, Wade Houston, eventually became the first Black coach of a major sport when the University of Tennessee hired him as men's head basketball coach in 1989. Historian Charles H. Martin in *Jim Crow in the Gymnasium* suggests that "coaches at major independents and small colleges, both of which suffered from lower status, opportunistically realized that integrating their teams would attract better athletes and help win more game."[18]

State schools in Texas were some of the first to integrate in the 1950s. In 1955, Texas Western College basketball coach George McCarty recruited Charles Brown to join the Miners basketball team. This eventually included an offer to Charles's nephew Cecil as well. These two junior college transfers were eligible immediately, and Charles made an immediate impact, averaging more than twenty-one points and ten rebounds a game as a sophomore.[19] The Border Conference selected Charles as the league's most valuable player in 1957, and he helped his team win conference titles in 1957 and 1959. Texas Western's football coach Ben Collins followed suit and started offering African Americans scholarships in 1959. The first two recruits left school after their freshman season, so Collins then recruited provided scholarships to four Black students, all of whom remained on the team through varsity competition. When Texas Western hired "Bum" Phillips as coach in 1962 from Amarillo High School, he immediately began expanding the number of Black scholarship players, removing any sense of tokenism from the team.[20]

At nearly the same time, two Black football players on the other side of the Lone Star State tried out for the freshman football team at North Texas State College (now University of North Texas). Abner Hayes and Leon King, both Denton natives, made the squad. North Texas had recently joined the Missouri

Valley Conference, which boasted a tougher schedule as well as multiple integrated teams. After a challenging season playing all-white institutions in Texas, King and Hayes joined the varsity squad and helped lead North Texas State to an MVC football championship berth and an invitation to the Sun Bowl.[21]

A few years later, Western Kentucky State College recruited two African American students from that region of the commonwealth as Clem Haskins and Dwight Smith joined the Hilltoppers basketball team. After their freshman campaign, the two players made a major impact in the Ohio Valley Conference, and Haskins was selected as the conference player of the year three times. In many respects, players at "mid-major" programs paved the way for Black athletes, and these institutions benefitted from their contributions.

Desegregation of the Atlantic Coast Conference and the Southwest Conference

Among the three major conferences holding out in desegregation, the ACC was the first to integrate. Within the conference, the University of Maryland led the way, when assistant football coach Lee Corso recruited Darryl Hill, who was transferring from the Naval Academy after his freshman year. When approached by Corso, Hill quipped, "You must have forgotten what conference you play in." The Corso replied, "That's the point,"[22] and Hill agreed to join the Maryland football team. After sitting out as a transfer, he became the first Black player in the ACC when he stepped on the field in the fall of 1963. When Maryland traveled to conference opponent Clemson, Hill became the first Black player to compete on the gridiron in Memorial Stadium. Two years later, Maryland's Billy Jones became the first African American to integrate the hardwood.[23]

Wake Forest followed Maryland in the slow desegregation march in the ACC. As the Game of Change controversy enveloped Mississippi in 1963, Wake Forest announced that it would "actively recruit" Black players. After playing freshman football, Butch Henry and Robert Grant played varsity football for the Demon Deacons.[24] Wake Forest also attempted to recruit Black basketball players without success in the early and mid-1960s. Duke became the second ACC institution to integrate the hardwood when C. B. Claiborne (who attended on an academic scholarship) successfully walked on to the team. Charles Scott became the first all-American to play basketball in the ACC when Dean Smith managed to convince Scott to renege on his commitment to Lefty Driesell and his Davidson squad. Scott signed with UNC in the spring of 1966 and averaged 22.1 points as well as 7.1 rebounds during his career as a Tar Heel. In the 1969

NCAA Tournament, Scott hit a buzzer beater to defeat Davidson and advance the Tar Heels to the national semifinal game.[25]

Clemson, the University of South Carolina, and the University of Virginia remained the last bastions of lily-white teams in ACC basketball and football. All three began recruiting football and basketball players in the late sixties, but none of them desegrated varsity football until the early 1970s. In the meantime, other southern conferences had begun desegregating squads as well.[26]

The Southwest Conference, consisting of both public and private universities in Texas along with the University of Arkansas, began desegregating athletic teams only after students protested on behalf of social equality. As proved to be the case across the South, undergraduate students were far more interested in integration than administrators. In 1961 the student government presidents of the SWC schools (excluding Arkansas) petitioned the conference to allow Black athletes, but conference officials ignored the request. Many of the SWC institutions, like other universities in the South, had not desegregated their undergraduate student bodies, but they began to do so after James Meredith's matriculation at the University of Mississippi. When most SWC universities finally admitted Black undergraduates in 1963, the SWC also changed its segregated athletic policy. As with most southern universities, the first students of color competed in track and field, which did not attract the same attention as football and basketball.[27]

For a brief moment in the 1950s, it had appeared that Texas and the Southwest Conference might lead the South in desegregation efforts. After the US Supreme Court handed down the *Brown* decision in the spring of 1954, seven young Black men applied to the University of Texas. Marion Ford was one of them. After rejecting the recommendation that he consider HBCU Texas Southern, Texas admitted Ford and a few other Black students. In an interview that appeared in a Houston paper, Ford mentioned that he intended to play football. A UT board member circulated the article to the other regents. The governing body determined that Ford and others should take the general education requirements at an HBCU and rescinded their admissions decision.[28]

Ford enrolled at the University of Illinois, where he played football for two years. Upon returning home to attend UT, Ford watched the Longhorns go down in defeat as an integrated University of Southern California Trojans team demolished Texas 44–20. After the game, Ford once again volunteered his services, telling Coach Ed Price, "You need me. I can help you." Texas, which finished the 1956 season 1–9, still refused to consider Ford's offer. Texas would be one of the last teams in the SWC to integrate the gridiron.[29]

Integration of the gridiron in the Southwest Conference began with its private, religiously affiliated institutions. But the University of Houston may have assisted in the process when, in 1964, it desegregated its basketball team with Elvin Hayes and Don Chaney. The rapid success of Houston basketball offered a model for the SWC. In the fall of 1966, Jerry LeVias (Southern Methodist University) and John Westbrook (Baylor) integrated the conference in football. Even though these two created a civil rights milestone in Texas, the trajectories of their athletic careers took different paths. Neither one of them had an easy road as racial pioneers.[30]

John Westbrook attended Baylor because he planned to double major in psychology and religion. Ordained as a minister at 15, Westbrook hoped to make an impact in the church. The state-supported HBCUs that recruited him did not offer the theological studies he desired, so he attended Baylor and tried out for the freshman football team. He made it as a walk-on and became one of the first two Black football players in the Southwest Conference. A knee injury cut short his sophomore season, and a serious concussion the following year continued to limit his playing time. Although he contemplated quitting the team, he continued to play through his senior season and then began a professional career in ministry.[31]

Jerry LeVias's arrival at SMU was much more intentional. New football coach Hayden Fry had originally turned down SMU's offer to coach because the institution refused to allow him to recruit African American players. As Fry told it, he had grown up with Black friends who lived on the "wrong side of the tracks," and he had lived there too. When he took the SMU head coaching job, he did so with plans to desegregate the conference. Looking for the right individual who could withstand the trials that would come with integrating the conference, Fry and his coaching staff landed on Jerry LeVias from Beaumont, Texas.[32]

LeVias planned on following his cousin Mel Farr to the University of California, Los Angeles, to play football. When Fry came to his house, however, he changed his mind. Fry was the first coach who spoke with LeVias and his family about education rather than just football. Fry also made a promise to Jerry's grandmother that the two would call her before every game so that she could pray for them—a promise Fry and LeVias kept. LeVias's athletic talent drew a spotlight on desegregation in SWC football (rather than Westbrook at Baylor). During his first season on the varsity squad, LeVias helped lead his team to their first SWC title in nearly twenty years, earning the Mustangs a trip to the Cotton Bowl. He was an all-conference player each varsity season and earned honors as both an all-American athlete and all-American student his senior season.[33]

As Westbrook and LeVias integrated the SWC on the football field, James Cash integrated Texas Christian University's basketball team. Cash joined the varsity team in 1967 and immediately became an impact player. By the time he graduated, Cash registered sixth on the Horned Frogs all-time scorers list and was the fourth all-time rebounding leader, averaging more than eleven rebounds a game. He earned academic all-American awards during his junior and senior seasons. Although most SWC conference teams had desegregated basketball by the time of Cash's graduation, the conference would not fully integrate until the early 1970s.

The Southeastern Conference: The Last Bastion of Segregation

The Southeastern Conference remained the last bastion of segregated athletics in college sports. It was home to the most ardent segregationist states in the Deep South (although the ACC remained home to both South Carolina and Clemson in the Palmetto State). The only "border" state in the conference, Kentucky, helped lead the campaign for integrated sports in the SEC. Shortly after Kentucky's Nate Northington integrated football during a home game against Ole Miss, Vanderbilt's Perry Wallace broke the color barrier by becoming the first Black basketball player in the conference.

Unlike the SWC and ACC, integration actually threatened the composition of the conference. In the wake of the Mississippi State–Loyola Game of Change, the University of Kentucky student newspaper called for UK to leave the SEC and begin recruiting Black athletes. The paper reasoned that Kentucky's southern neighbors were entrenched in segregation, and UK needed to take the moral high ground while improving its national reputation by making such a move. Kentucky's young president, Frank Dickey, had replaced his segregationist predecessor in 1956. While president, Dickey increased UK's African American enrollment, but its sports remained lily white.[34]

Dickey, who had recently announced his retirement from the presidency to lead the Southern Association of Colleges and Schools, understood the precarious position for both Kentucky and other institutions in the Deep South. He had previously called integration "inevitable" and told students that he agreed with allowing Black students to fully participate in university activities—including athletics. But he also noted that UK had just issued bonds to build a new football stadium, and departure from the SEC could be disastrous for UK's finances. After a meeting of the UK Athletics Association,

Faculty Athletic Representative W. L. Matthew publicly stated his desire to both integrate athletics and remain in the SEC. To make matters more complex, SEC membership required that each institution play at least six league football games, but the conference offered no round robin schedule. Each institution negotiated its games with other conference members. If UK could not find six SEC opponents, it would lose membership in the conference.[35]

In this context, President Dickey then wrote the other SEC presidents, asking if they would be able to play home and away games against integrated Kentucky teams. As scholar Zebulon Baker noted, Dickey tried to couch his dilemma at UK as a shared issue among conference presidents and "launched a charm offensive" in order to keep Kentucky in the SEC's good graces. In 1963, this appeared to be a long shot. Only months earlier, MSU had to sneak out of the state to violate Mississippi's unwritten prohibition on playing integrated teams. Two years earlier, the University of Tennessee (which along with Vanderbilt was one of only two SEC institutions not located in the Deep South) had cancelled a track meet in Knoxville because of an integrated visiting team. That same year, athletics director Robert Neyland verbally accosted a young Black UT student who had tried out for the Volunteer basketball team.[36]

Dickey found an unexpected ally in Edwin Harrison, president of Georgia Tech. In 1961, a cheap shot by an Alabama player against GT's Chick Graining gave the halfback a concussion while knocking out five of his teeth and breaking multiple bones in his face. When Coach Bryant failed to punish the player, GT coach Bobby Dodd refused to renew the rivalry game against the Tide. Dodd also refused to play the two members of the SEC from Mississippi, stating, "Whatever is there to go to Mississippi for? We like to take our fans to exciting places and Mississippi isn't one." With the number of schools Coach Dodd was willing to play dwindling, President Harrison wanted to ensure the Yellow Jackets had enough SEC opponents to maintain the required six-game schedule. Harrison also hoped to play "schools nearer our academic level," and he viewed Kentucky as one. So, Tech's president convinced the chair of the Georgia Board of Regents to change its policy banning segregated play in the state.[37]

SEC institutions decided to address Dickey's question at a conference meeting in May 1963. Louisiana State University had been mainstay on Kentucky's football schedule, but the Tigers' AD, Jim Corbett, planned on dropping the Wildcats from their schedule if Kentucky integrated. Believing the vast majority of conference schools would do the same, Corbett asked for a show of hands from those who supported keeping Kentucky on the schedule. Vanderbilt and Tulane voted in the affirmative, and surprisingly so did Florida, Georgia, and

Georgia Tech. Tennessee football coach Bowden Wyatt did not raise his hand in support of UT's rival, but most believed they would still play Kentucky. With that, Kentucky had six opponents it could schedule.[38]

All seemed safe for integration in SEC football until Georgia Tech announced it would leave the conference in January 1964. Coach Bobby Dodd had long requested that the SEC overturn its "140 Rule." The recruiting policy allowed conference members to recruit up to 55 football and basketball players each year, but the total number of athletic grants-in-aid could not exceed 140. Dodd's campaigning led to a reduction of annual grants-in-aid to 45; institutions could offer 180 scholarships over four years, but only 140 could be subsidized players. The rule had been designed to make room for players who dropped out of school or quit athletics. Instead, it led to coaches "weeding out" weaker players though brutal practices and abusive behavior. Dodd refused to engage in such brutal practices, which placed Georgia Tech at a competitive disadvantage. He believed that if he offered a scholarship to a football player who persisted successfully through the collegiate curriculum, the institution needed to retain the scholarship even if he did not excel on the gridiron.[39]

Dodd's high-minded ideals, however, were couched in language that offended other member institutions. The papers reported that Georgia Tech representatives noted its high admissions standards and academic focus as a reason more students persisted in college. In addition, Georgia Tech presented the issue as an ultimatum: either do things our way, or we will leave. Through the years, Dodd had also alienated and offended conference members by refusing to schedule home-and-home series, and it appeared that some of the votes against the repeal of the 140 Rule were actually attempts to curb Dodd's autocratic assertions. The SEC determined to keep the 140 Rule for the time being, and Georgia Tech withdrew from the conference.[40]

Georgia Tech's departure, along with Kentucky's announcement that all students were eligible to participate in intercollegiate athletics, led the conference to take over football scheduling. All but one of the five members on the SEC scheduling committee had indicated a year earlier that they would not play an integrated team. The scheduling committee set Georgia, Mississippi, Tennessee, and Vanderbilt as Kentucky's four permanent football opponents. While three of these universities were located in the northernmost states within conference, Ole Miss still refused to play an integrated team in Oxford. In turn, UK's new president, John W. Oswald, who had come to Kentucky from a vice presidency at the University of California, Berkeley, then went on the offensive, declaring that UK should not be required to play Ole Miss, which refused to recognize Kentucky's right to play whom it desired. Oswald strongly encouraged SEC commissioner Bernie Moore to reconsider Kentucky's schedule at its January 1965 meeting.[41]

Oswald's request might not have been successful, but only weeks earlier, Tulane announced that it would withdraw from the SEC, creating one less conference opponent. Tulane couched its argument as an elite university desiring to develop a more national, rather than regional, football schedule. The reality, however, was that Tulane believed it was not in the financial position to continue the player scholarship subsidies required to be successful in the SEC. Since the end of World War II, Tulane administrators had unsuccessfully attempted to recruit other private universities like Rice, Southern Methodist, and Vanderbilt to create an elite academic athletic conference in the South. But these self-selected peers did not have the same challenges in meeting the increased financial demands of fielding big-time athletics programs. Tulane, in contrast, had not won more than one SEC football game each season for over a decade.[42] More than just an interesting anecdote, the pressure felt by Tulane was common among many schools that prior to World War II had been far more competitive against larger state flagship and land grant universities.

Regardless of their intentions, the departures of Georgia Tech and Tulane, along with Kentucky's push to integrate, led many to believe that the Southeastern Conference would dissolve. In fact, Auburn's president Ralph Draughon, who was beginning his term as SEC president, stated that it appeared "like I am going to have to preside over the decomposition of the Southeastern Conference."[43] Instead, the conference removed Ole Miss as a permanent opponent and adopted a new schedule that included five permanent opponents with two additional conference games in which opponents would rotate. The conference voted for the plan, and nobody announced opposition to Kentucky's plan to begin integrating.

That spring, UK president John W. Oswald, along with assistance from the new progressive governor Ned Breathitt, sought to find the right players to integrate football. Football coach Charlie Bradshaw complied with the request, and UK recruited Nate Northington from Louisville. In December 1965, Governor Breathitt hosted a dinner with Northington and his family, recruiting the young man and explaining the historical significance of integrating the conference. Northington, compelled by the challenge, signed with Kentucky. One other Black player, Greg Page, from southeastern Kentucky, agreed to play for the team as well.[44]

From *left to right*: Kentucky governor Edward T. Breathitt, University of Kentucky coach Charlie Bradshaw, Thomas Jefferson High School coach Jim Gray, and UK president John W. Oswald accompanied Nate Northington when he signed to play for the Wildcats. University of Kentucky's Special Collections Research Center

Even before the two students arrived on campus, UK lost part of the campaign to situate itself as a progressive institution to the rest of the country. After defeating an all-white Duke team in the national semifinals of the NCAA Basketball Tournament, Kentucky faced the Texas Western Miners in the championship game. Texas Western, which had pioneered integration in the 1950s, had gone beyond "tokenism" and had an all-Black starting five—almost unheard of at a historically white institution. The Miners' stunning upset of Rupp's all-white Wildcats became an inspiration for minorities and progressive-minded sports fans. Many watched to see if the Southeastern Conference was prepared to join the rest of the nation in desegregating its conference.

The history of desegregation has generally ignored the first Black athlete to play in the Southeastern Conference. Just before its exit from the SEC, Tulane's Stephen Martin became the first Black varsity athlete in the conference as a member of the baseball team. Attending Tulane on an academic scholarship, Martin's desegregation efforts were incomplete, as he remained on the bench for some games that were determined to be too dangerous. As baseball was considered a minor sport, little was reported on the integrated games Martin played in his first varsity season, and that was probably best for his safety.[45]

As Tulane left the SEC, Nate Northington and Greg Page matriculated to UK and played freshman football during the fall of 1966. Facing the typical hardships encountered by racial trailblazers, the two became best of friends during their freshman year. As sophomores, they prepared to join the varsity squad and make history against the Ole Miss Rebels in the 1967 season home opener. Then, just weeks before the game, Greg Page suffered a fatal injury in practice. The freak accident occurred during a practice drill in which Page ended up on the bottom of a pile and suffered critical spinal damage.[46] Notably, Coach Bradshaw had been criticized for his brutal practices he thought created "hard-nosed" football players. *Sports Illustrated* had done a story on Bradshaw after his arrival at UK when, during spring training and summer practice, he ran off fifty-three of the eighty-eight members of the team, creating what became known as the "thin thirty."[47]

Page remained in the hospital for weeks and eventually passed away only one day before UK's first SEC game. Page's family expressed their desire to see the game played, and on September 30, 1967, Nate Northington integrated SEC football. Ironically, UK's opponent was arguably the staunchest defender of segregation in higher education—the University of Mississippi. Page sustained a dislocated shoulder in the game, hindering his play moving forward with the season. Nevertheless, Page had done what he came to Kentucky to do: desegregate the SEC.

Kentucky basketball did not follow the Wildcat football team's lead. Instead, Vanderbilt led the way. It was reported that Vandy coach Roy Skinner "had been recruiting Black players [for the basketball team] but could never convince any to play in Nashville." Perry Wallace, an exceptional local player, received recruiting calls from Iowa, Kentucky, Michigan, Northwestern, Purdue, UCLA, and the University of Tennessee, yet Skinner convinced Wallace to join his Vanderbilt Commodore basketball team for the 1966 season his freshman year. Alongside Wallace, Coach Skinner also successfully recruited Godfrey Dillard, another talented prospect from Detroit. In a later interview with Wallace, he attributed his decision to join Vanderbilt based on Skinner's willingness to meet with him and his family for a genuine conversation about the opportunities the school had to offer for him.[48]

In the fall of 1968, two more Black players, Wilbur Hackett and Houston Hogg, joined Kentucky's varsity football team, ensuring uninterrupted integration on the Kentucky football squad. Tennessee desegregated its football team that same year when Nashville native Lester McClain chose to play football in Knoxville for the Vols. Interestingly, Auburn became the second university in the conference to integrate its basketball team. Despite Auburn's location in the rural Deep South, head coach Bill Lynn actively recruited Henry Harris from his rural town of Boligee, Alabama. After integrating the freshman team in the fall of 1968, Harris became the second Black varsity basketball player in the SEC and the first varsity athlete to compete in the SEC from the Deep South. Harris's promising career was marred by a knee injury late in his junior season, but during his final year, he became a mentor of sorts for James Owens and Thom Gossom, who became the first players to integrate Auburn's football team. In Tuscaloosa, C. M. Newton told head football coach and athletics director Bear Bryant that he would only accept head coach of the basketball team if he could recruit Black players. Bryant agreed. Newton immediately recruited Wendell Hudson. He started varsity in 1970 and in 1973 was named SEC Player of the Year.

As other SEC teams in the Deep South moved toward desegregation, the Universities of Alabama and Southern California played a pivotal game in Birmingham. With an open date on the schedule, Bear Bryant invited an integrated Trojan team to open the 1970 season. USC's all-Black backfield consisted of quarterback Jimmy Jones and running backs Sam Cunningham and Clarence Davis. This crew shredded the Alabama defense on its way to a 42–21 rout of the Crimson Tide. Much of the historical lore following the game has proven to be untrue. Coach Bryant did not drag Sam Cunningham in front of his team and say, "Gentlemen, this is a football player." Nor did the game convince Bryant that he needed to recruit Black athletes. He had already attempted to recruit African American football players to Alabama, and one, Wilbur Jackson, had signed with Bryant and played on the freshman team that year.

The importance of the game was not in convincing Bear Bryant to recruit Black athletes, as many have supposed. Instead, the value was in convincing a contingent of white Alabamans that discriminating against Black players harmed their beloved Crimson Tide. As Bryant's former player and assistant coach Jerry Claiborne noted, "Sam Cunningham did more to integrate Alabama in 60 minutes than Martin Luther King did in 20 Years." The unfair comparison between a college football player and the nation's most revered civil rights leader falls short in many ways, but it did help explain that self-interest rather than social justice helped prepare southern football fans for desegregated football. The next year, when Wilbur Jackson stepped onto the field, he was joined by Mobile, Alabama, native and community college transfer John Mitchell. These two football players and their teammates led the resurgence of Alabama football in the seventies that included standouts like Ozzie Newsome and Sylvester Croom (who went on the become the first Black head football coach in the SEC when he accepted the post at Mississippi State in 2008).[49]

Bryant's Black players spoke of their coach's fairness, but the legendary coach had chosen to follow rather than lead in the area of athletic desegregation. For example, when Huntsville, Alabama, native Condredge Holloway was being recruited by programs around the South, Bryant told the high schooler that the state of Alabama was not ready for a Black quarterback. Since that was the position Holloway desired, he instead accepted coach Bill Battle's scholarship offer to attend the University of Tennessee, where he became the first Black quarterback in the SEC, just edging out Mississippi State's Melvin Barkum, who alternated the position with MSU's other sophomore quarterback Rocky Felker.[50]

Bryant's attitude and actions regarding desegregation still proved to be more forward thinking than coach Adolph Rupp at Kentucky. For example, when Bryant coached Jerry LeVias in an all-star game, the legendary coach put his arm around LeVias and told the SMU star, "Jerry, when they let me, I'm gonna get some of y'all." LeVias would later explain that Bryant's comment was not meant to be derogatory.[51] In contrast, Adolph Rupp moved slowly and seemed frustrated by the fact that in the sixties he had a governor and a university president eager for Kentucky to recruit Black basketball players. Located in a border state, UK still followed Auburn in desegregating its basketball and recruited its first Black player at the same time that former player C. M. Newton did the same at Alabama.[52]

The Toll on the Trailblazers: Three Individual Stories

Desegregating the three power conferences in the South took a brutal mental, emotional, and physical toll on the "firsts"—young Black athletes who pioneered a first step toward integration of college athletics at southern universities. With hundreds of athletes integrating different sports at myriad colleges and universities, a retelling of the first football players in the ACC, SWC, and SEC provides a glimpse of the challenges faced by Black athletes desegregating primarily white institutions across the South.

When Darryl Hill transferred to Maryland after playing freshman football at the US Naval Academy, he faced numerous challenges when he arrived in College Park. NCAA rules limited his participation to the practice team that fall.

Some teammates roughed him up in practice. Jerry Fishman, who had be-friended Hill, made a proposition. As Fishman recalled asking Hill, "Darryl . . . you get me through economics, and I'll get [you] through your year on the scout team." Fishman was the lone Jewish player on the team, and the antisemitism he faced brought the two players closer together as they called themselves "the onlys."[53]

Hill did not quite know what to expect as he suited up for his first ACC game in 1963. The home crowd was neither overly enthusiastic nor hostile when he became the first Black football player to participate in a game between two power programs in the South. Maryland lost to North Carolina State that day without any incident. Week two of the season was much different as the Ter-rapins traveled to play the University of South Carolina in Columbia. Accom-panied by the National Guard, the crowd lustily booed the Terps, with many fans chanting "Kill Hill, Kill Hill" during the game. Although he kept it quiet, head coach Tom Nugent received plenty of hate mail along with a death threat, claiming he would be shot during the game. A riot almost broke out at halftime as hundreds of angry fans stormed the field.[54]

In Durham, a store owner told Maryland players he was going to kill "that n——" on their team. Wake Forest donned Confederate flags on lampposts to welcome Hill to campus. According to Fishman, the verbal taunting and racist slurs were the worst on their visit to Winston-Salem. After one late hit that left Hill disoriented, the trainers at the game were not going to let him use an oxy-gen mask because he was Black. Hill responded with two touchdown scores and a shut-out win against the Demon Deacons.[55]

On Maryland's road trip to Clemson, Hill's mother, Palestine, ignored her husband's advice and took a train to South Carolina to watch her son play. When she showed up with her ticket, she was denied admission, as African Americans were not allowed inside the stadium. Blacks were to watch the game from a hill facing "Death Valley," as it was called. Hill learned of his mother's predicament shortly before kickoff and ran to the gate to help her. Fortunately, a few fair-minded individuals came to his aid when he needed it. As Hill greeted his mother at Clemson, the institution's president, Robert Edwards, introduced himself. Edwards invited Palestine to the president's box, and the president's wife looked at Darryl and said, "You go out and show 'em."[56]

Despite an excellent performance from Hill, Clemson prevailed. Fearing the worst, Coach Nugent ordered his players not to change out of their football uni-forms after the game and instead instructed them to go directly to the team bus. The attacks continued throughout the season. When Wake Forest's fans taunted Hill with racist epithets before the game, Wake's team captain Brian Piccolo apologized for the crowd's behavior. He then put his arm around Hill and walked toward the bleachers, temporarily silencing the crowd. Maryland's coaches removed their entire team from hotels and dining establishments that refused to accommodate Hill. Throughout the season, Jerry Fishman roomed with Hill on the road and always looked out for him, threatening to retaliate against the opponents' quarterback if anyone maliciously harmed Hill.

It would be three more years before another Black varsity scholarship football player took the field in another southern conference. That task would fall to Jerry LeVias. Choosing to attend Southern Methodist University, LeVias first spent a year on the freshman football team in 1965. During LeVias's first year, he regularly had teammates jump on him and attempt to harm him. Occasionally they succeeded. He had two ribs cracked and injured his back. The trainers on the team were reticent to help him because of his color. His assigned roommate's parents refused to let their son room with Jerry, so he lived alone and ate almost all his meals alone. He had no social life on campus. Daily walks to class on the sidewalk were dangerous as students called him racist names, spit on him, and often walked in a line across the sidewalk, forcing him out of the way in an effort to avoid trouble. The police regularly pulled him over when he drove off campus into (white) North Dallas. He considered that first semester one of the worst seasons of his life.[57]

During the spring term of his first year, the Reverend Martin Luther King spoke on campus. He and LeVias met privately, and the civil rights leader gave the young man some advice. People were going act in ways that would tempt LeVias to react in anger. King told LeVias that he needed to "always keep your emotions under control." It was wisdom LeVias took to heart and carried with him into the remainder of his time as a football player and student at SMU.[58]

During his sophomore season, LeVias faced multiple instances in which his ability to maintain control of his emotions would be tested. Like nearly all pioneers of integration in college athletics, LeVias faced cheap shots and racial slurs at away games. At the University of Texas, some brought ropes with nooses to greet LeVias. At Texas A&M, some in attendance released black cats on the field to note Jerry's presence in College Station. Even though his mail was inspected, he still received hate mail. Even with success on the gridiron, LeVias was not completely integrated on campus. Terry May, a white teammate, admired LeVias and befriended him. After agreeing to room with him, however, May came to LeVias and told him that he was being ostracized socially. May moved out. LeVias understood why he decided not to room with him, but he continued to face challenges of being a Black player at a PWI.[59]

The most serious threat came before the rivalry game against Texas Christian University in Fort Worth. An anonymous caller made a death threat against LeVias's life. Coach Fry asked Jerry to exit the bus last and had him warm up in the locker room rather than on the field. FBI agents patrolled the sideline during the game. Before kickoff, Fry let his star player know why he had been so protective and gave him the option of sitting out the game. LeVias decided to play, and he had an excellent game as SMU went on to clinch its first Southwest Conference title in eighteen years, defeating TCU 21–0 and accepting a bid to the Cotton Bowl.[60]

During his next two seasons, LeVias continued to excel even though SMU struggled to remain atop the Southwest Conference. His continued success led to honors as an all-American on the football field and in the classroom. During his senior year, however, LeVias faced the one challenge he would eventually call a failure. During his senior season in a game against TCU, an opponent called LeVias the N-word and took a cheap shot at the SMU player. LeVias returned to the sideline and threw his helmet in disgust. Coach Fry came by and calmed his star player down, asking him to reenter the game. LeVias then returned a punt for more than eighty yards, clinching the win. Coach Fry called it "the most spectacular punt return I've ever seen." In retrospect, LeVias called it the one play motivated from hatred, and in some ways it was a moment he wanted to take back. During his four-year career at SMU, he had managed to keep his emotions in check, but in that one moment, LeVias lost control.[61]

LeVias finished his degree in business in four years. After his NFL career, he became a successful businessman. Yet forty years later, Fry admitted that he still struggled emotionally because of the "living hell" that LeVias endured during his college years. During his time at SMU, he viewed Coach Fry as his saving grace. Fry kept an eye out for his player's well-being and helped him through some of his more difficult times on campus.

Darryl Hill had a coach and a white friend in his corner. LeVias did not have the same friendship with a teammate, but his coach was looking out for him. When Nate Northington desegregated the SEC, he stood alone. Before the season started, his best friend and teammate Greg Page passed away. During the University of Kentucky's loss to Ole Miss, Northington dislocated his shoulder. Kentucky then traveled to Auburn for Northington's first game on the road in the SEC, where he endured racial slurs from a hostile crowd. Police were assigned to protect him at Cliff Hare Stadium. But his guardians donned Confederate flags on their gun belts and joked with the fans that they were there "to protect Leroy," another derogatory name often used as the butt of racist jokes.[62]

As Kentucky continued to lose and Northington continued to reaggravate his shoulder in games, the young player struggled with his emotions and loneliness. In a game against Virginia Tech, Northington misjudged a punt, which resulted in poor field position for the Wildcats. After that game, he was called into the office by an assistant coach who informed Northington that his meal ticket was being cancelled for skipping classes. Feeling alone and emotionally drained, Northington quit the team. In his memoir, Northington pointed to the coaching staff's ignorance of the challenges he was facing and said that the coaching staff's ignorance played a role in his departure. They simply did not understand the burdens of desegregating the SEC while mourning the loss of his friend. Northington would go on to have a solid college career at Western Kentucky. But his brief stint at Kentucky revealed the value of having another player or coach willing to empathize with the challenges and abuse heaped on the trailblazers who desegregated sports in the South. It was a heavy price to pay that paved the way for others.[63]

Black Students and College Sports:
From Exclusion to Exploitation

The desegregation of college sports has generally been discussed within the framework of conferences. Doing so provides organization to issues that were both vast and complex. It also provides a clear historical narrative and has allowed conferences to celebrate their own social justice milestones years before the full desegregation of a particular conference was complete. Taken as a whole, however, the timeline of desegregation in college sports generally followed from institutions on the southern periphery, with universities in the Deep South proving to be the last to break down racial barriers.

The unbalanced progress in the South and across the country could be noted by the many sit-ins and protests held across the country during the late sixties. The 1968 summer Olympics in Mexico City also provided a stark contrast regarding the progress and shortcomings of social justice for Black athletes. Two San Jose State University athletes, Tommie Smith and John Carolos, medaled in the 200-meter race. As the National Anthem played, they lifted their black-gloved fists in protest against domestic and global racial injustice. The controversial Black Power salute brought vilification in many circles and praise in others. The two athletes were participants in the Olympic Project for Human Rights, a project initiated by San Jose State Professor Harry Edwards.

As student protests for more Black faculty members and curricula including Black studies engulfed some universities, other institutions in the South had yet to desegregate their own sports programs. The more militant approach and its demands also created challenges for college athletes. Some were eager to participate in such movements, while others wanted to avoid any sensationalism (or trouble) that might develop from their participation. Many athletes found themselves stuck in an uninvited conundrum. Some felt racial injustice required college athletes to use their platform for change. Others believed their participation in sport alone provided the necessary activism. While individual personalities played a role in this dilemma, so did geography.

The larger historical context of the civil rights movement and the violent responses from racists must be remembered. Only months after Mississippi State played against an integrated Loyola team in the NCAA basketball tournament, Medgar Evers was assassinated in Jackson, Mississippi, because of his civil rights activism. That same summer, Birmingham's "Bull" Connor unleased dogs and high-powered water hoses on children participating in a peaceful protest. That fall, Maryland's Darryl Hill would desegregate football in South Carolina. In 1966, as Jerry LeVias desegregated Southwest Conference football and Kentucky began recruiting football players to do the same in the SEC, James Meredith (who had earlier integrated the University of Mississippi) began his one-man "March Against Fear" from Memphis, Tennessee, to Jackson, Mississippi. In north Mississippi, Aubrey Norvell shot Meredith three times in an attempt to take his life. The last holdouts began desegregating athletics in 1968, the same year Martin Luther King Jr. was assassinated in Memphis.

An understanding of the timeline of these events makes the willingness of students to integrate various sports that much more heroic. It also makes the general acceptance of Black athletes at universities in the Deep South only a few years later an important step in the process toward racial justice. In contrast to the plight of James Meredith in attending Ole Miss or the first pioneers of desegregation in sports, the experiences of James Reed and Ben Williams, the first Black football players at the University of Mississippi, much improved.

In an honest assessment of his experience at Ole Miss, James Reed said there were times he disliked being there, but he also noted that his best memories from college consisted of traveling with the team throughout the South playing football. Reed also pointed out that when some derogatory comments were made by teammates, the coaching staff immediately addressed the entire team and made a point that they would not tolerate such comments. Again, the actions (or inactions) of coaches set the tone for teams as they desegregated.[64]

Reed's teammate Ben Williams was a stellar football player and became a popular personality on campus. Speaking publicly about his experience at Ole Miss, Williams acknowledged that many people found it hard to believe that he had such a positive experience at Ole Miss. Yet he insisted that he did not have any problems. Part of that stemmed from his personality, as students and fans alike referred to him as "Gentle Ben." During his senior year, Williams was elected as "Colonel Rebel," an honor given to the most popular male student on campus. While his election should not be embellished to suggest problems and tensions had ceased, it is worth highlighting as an example of the progress that had been made in one decade.

Progress had its limitations, and many scholars have used a picture from the Ole Miss annual to share the reality. In it, Colonel Rebel Ben Williams and his counterpart, Miss Ole Miss Barbara Biggs, are photographed together, but there is a fence between the two. The image symbolized both the progress that had been made and the racist barriers that still existed. As Barbara Biggs shared years later, she received death threats for posing with Williams in the photo.[65]

The image and the symbolic interpretation regarding the limits of desegregation raise an important theme addressed by Martin Luther King Jr. and applied to the history of race in athletics by historian Derrick White, among others. Namely, "desegregation" and "integration" had (and have—even in this chapter) been inappropriately used interchangeably. As King noted, desegregation was "negative" in that it simply removed the legality of segregation. Integration, however, involved the "positive acceptance of desegregation" as it "welcomed participation of Negroes into the total range of human activities." For King, desegregation might occur even as people remained "spiritually segregated, where elbows are together and hearts are apart."[66]

The problem with the historical narrative, as Derrick White has highlighted, is that sport historians have "described the desegregation of athletics as integration." Speaking broadly, in the minds of most white Americans, the southern battle against segregation was over and integration had been achieved. In reality, desegregation had occurred, but only the first steps toward integration had been taken. Where one group saw the end of an issue, another group understood (often through personal experience) that the process of integration had just begun.[67]

Ben Williams and Barbara Biggs

In 1976, Ben Williams and Barbara Biggs were photographed together as Colonel Rebel and Miss Ole Miss. University of Mississippi Archives and Special Collections

Although the major trends in college sports in the 1960s (especially deseg-regation) had been characterized by consolidation and confidence, the begin-nings of *actual* integration created dissatisfaction among many athletes and civil rights advocates. Standard practices and customs were called into question by some athletes and assorted student groups. Foremost was what was called the "revolt of the Black athlete."[68] Racial change—including opportunities and exploitation for (and of) Black student-athletes often took place at racially de-segregated colleges that did not have the reputation or resources of the estab-lished big-time programs of the Big Ten, the Southeastern Conference, the Southwestern Conference, the Pacific Coast Conference, and the Atlantic Coast Conference. The racial strife of 1969 was, as Michael Oriard expressed it, "col-lege football's season of discontent."[69]

The NCAA and the Student-Athlete: Controversies and Contradictions

The civil rights issues in college sports did not occur in a vacuum. A separate discussion that had inordinate influence on Black athletes involved NCAA policies regarding academics for athletes. As noted previously, the NCAA's 1956 public relations campaign to create the construct of the "student-athlete" had been effective in persuading Americans that college sports were indelibly linked with an embellished tradition of amateurism. It also was calculated and pragmatic to protect the NCAA and member colleges from liability law-suits alleging that college students playing sports were institutional em-ployees. This turned out to be unfinished business, as the student-athlete ter-minology raised fundamental questions about academics and athletics.

To understand how the NCAA's invocation of the student-athlete brought chaos rather than clarity to American intercollegiate athletics between 1960 and 1972, it's helpful to dissect the two components—the student and the athlete—separately.

Defining the "Student" in "Student-Athlete"

A central tenet of the NCAA's definition of a student-athlete was that a varsity athlete was foremost a student. By extension, this meant that he had met collegewide admissions standards for high school grades and then devoted primary attention to college classes. The college athlete was expected to be a full-time student carrying a full course load, all the while remaining in good academic standing over four years while playing one (or more varsity sports).

One traditional practice to promote and fulfill this standard was that freshman students were not eligible to play varsity sports. Hence, starting with one's sophomore year and with a satisfactory grade point average (GPA), then one could try out for the varsity squad. If college officials, including coaches and deans, required prospective athletes to comply with these regulations, the problem remained as to how one would codify and then enforce them across hundreds of colleges and universities that belonged to the NCAA. Importantly, the NAIA did not have the same requirements and allowed freshmen to compete as varsity athletes.

That difference in definition alone between the NCAA and the NAIA alerted to the relativism in making and then enforcing regulations about what constituted an academically eligible student-athlete. According to historian Ronald Smith, in 1956 the NCAA hired Arthur Bergstrom as their first enforcement agent. It signaled that the NCAA was taking on formal responsibility for regulating measures intended to protect academic integrity.[70] But at each juncture of proclamation and regulation, there were exceptions to the rule. For example, on January 16, 1961, the NCAA voted "to allow five years to complete four years of participation, thus basically recognizing the practice of redshirting younger players."[71] On January 13, 1965, the "NCAA passes the 1.600 grade point average for freshmen to receive grants-in-aid and to be eligible for athletic participation."[72]

Who could be opposed to establishing and enforcing academic eligibility standards? In this case, the answer was that many colleges and universities were not supportive. The most severe protest came from a group of institutions associated with high admissions and academic standards—the presidents of the Ivy League. Objections were twofold: first, colleges and universities, especially selective and established ones, resented being told by the NCAA which of their college students were eligible and which were not. Second, many higher education leaders pointed out the limits of a nationwide 1.6 GPA litmus. Differences across institutions in academic rigor and grade point averages meant that the NCAA was a blunt instrument. A 1.6 GPA was a low bar and a dubious indicator of good academic standing.

A new, growing concern that surfaced in the 1960s was recognizing and reconciling the role of Black male students who played varsity sports at colleges, especially predominantly white institutions. Black student-athletes constituted an important subgroup that was center stage in showing the uses and abuses of high-powered intercollegiate athletics between 1960 and 1972.

The ideal of the outstanding collegiate athlete who also was a model student and campus citizen long occupied a prominent place in the American popular imagination. It was hailed in the popular culture with cases such as Princeton's Bill Bradley, an all-American basketball player who was selected to be a Rhodes Scholar in 1965. Often overlooked is that in the early 1960s, some of the most celebrated collegiate achievements came from young Black men who excelled in both studies and sports. These men were pioneers in desegregating their athletic conferences, and they did it while enduring insults and threats. Indeed, the theme that would surface and then gain momentum was that the college sports machinery often exploited Black athletes and overlooked their exceptional talents and achievements on and off the playing field. In 1962 and 1963, for example, African Americans John Edgar Wideman, University of Pennsylvania class of '62, and J. Stanley Sanders, Whittier College class of '63, were selected as Rhodes Scholars.

Other exemplary Black student-athletes from early in the sixties include UCLA's Rafer Johnson, who was both an NCAA and Olympic decathlon champion. Arthur Ashe, UCLA class of 1966, was an honor student and a member of naval ROTC who won the NCAA tennis singles championship and led his UCLA squad to the team title. He was the first African American member of the US Davis Cup team, won the tennis championship at Wimbledon, and was top ranked tennis player in the world. Ashe had grown up in segregated Richmond, Virginia, where he was not allowed to play on the premiere tennis courts, and graduated first in his high school class. Ernie Davis excelled as a student and athlete at Syracuse University and was the first African American to be awarded football's Heisman Trophy, in 1961, his senior year.

The list of exceptional achievements continued as southern universities desegregated. In 1967, for example, Wallace Perry, an undergraduate at Vanderbilt University, was the first Black student-athlete to receive a basketball scholarship in the Southeastern Conference. Perry excelled in basketball and graduated with a degree in electrical engineering. He then received his juris doctor degree from Columbia University Law School and had a long career as professor of law at American University in Washington, DC.[73] Duke's first Black basketball player, Claudius "C. B." Claiborne, went on to earn a master's degree at Dartmouth and a PhD at Virginia Tech before having a successful career in academics. Texas Christian University's first Black basketball player, James Cash, became the first tenured Black faculty member in the Harvard Business School. An expert in applying information technology to business, he served on the boards of multiple Fortune 500 companies.

In contrast to these success stories, a common portrayal of the Black student-athlete as primarily an athlete and only marginally a student remained. The important historical fact is that Black student-athletes were the latest in a long succession of stereotypes ascribed to a passing parade of outsiders in American colleges and universities. Newcomer immigrant groups since the late nineteenth century took their turn in being recruited as college athletes—from Irish to Swedes to Slavs and Italians, with Blacks gaining the spotlight in the 1960s. The "dumb jock" image that numerous sociologists, historians, and psychologists have documented came about because athletics departments often recruited student-athletes whose high school records and preparation did not predict academic success at the college level. The devious strategy was to keep such outstanding athletes barely academically eligible for two or three seasons by providing them with help in writing term papers and in other academic areas. Then, when they completed their senior year of varsity competition, the props were withdrawn, and student-athletes were allowed to drop out or flunk out, leaving college without a bachelor's degree.[74]

Jack Olsen's 1968 series in *Sports Illustrated*, "The Black Athlete—A Shameful Story," provided evidence that some understood these exploitative practices. The articles also elicited tremendous interest. As *SI* would report at the conclusion of the five-part series, Olsen's articles had "produced a greater reader response than any other story, or group of stories, in *Sports Illustrated*'s fourteen-year publishing history." By detailing the exploitation of Black athletes and highlighting the social and educational challenges these students faced, Olsen and *SI* aimed to "open a way toward correction of some of the abuses." The editors hoped it would start with solutions from the NCAA and the universities who recruited Black students.[75]

Reconfiguring Athletic Scholarships

According to the NCAA, a college athlete was to be an amateur. In its purest form this meant, or at least connoted, that one played college sports without remuneration and for the love and glory of the game and of alma mater. Yet any historical review of intercollegiate sports at colleges and universities in the United States, shows an abundance of alterations and allowances that rendered the realities of the amateur ideal at very least to be incomplete and vacillating. That is because both by regulations and by custom, American college sports had a strong record of providing tangible benefits and financial support both in recruiting and then rewarding those who played college sports. This in turn brought recurring attention and debate about reconciling and defining what would be permissible as athletic scholarships. The NCAA also battled with the long-established Amateur Athletic Union for governance and control of intercollegiate athletics, including formal and operational definition about which athletes qualified as amateurs and which did not.

"Athletic scholarship" was a convenient but troubling term.[76] An interesting chronicle is to follow how the NCAA defined and then redefined what was permissible for college athletes as amateurs to receive in aid. On January 11, 1957, the NCAA officially defined athletic scholarships for the first time to include tuition and fees, room and board, and fifteen dollars per month for incidentals.[77] In 1967 the NCAA approved a motion "to take away an athletic scholarship if the athlete 'voluntarily renders himself ineligible for intercollegiate competition,' generally for quitting or not being cooperative." Then, in January 1973, the NCAA passed, "by a show of hands with no debate, one-year scholarships to replace four-year scholarships, granting coaches greater control over athletes."[78]

An open secret during this period of increased NCAA regulation on athletic grants-in-aid was that American intercollegiate sports had a long custom of unofficial and sometimes illegal financial support for college athletes. Beneath the major scandals, practices included such perks as summer jobs, cash payments, uncollected loans, free meals, and automobiles provided by alumni and boosters. It's hard to know how effective or pervasive enforcement of NCAA and conference regulations were. One obvious temptation is to call the rewarded athletes "shamateurs" or "professionals." In fact, they often were used and abused by the boosters and perhaps sometimes by the college athletics departments and coaches. The illicit perks and payments paled in comparison to the benefits of revenues and publicities that a winning team in a major sport brought to a university.

If the NCAA's 1.6 GPA requirement was intended to signal both academic integrity and enforcement among athletes, this message was not reinforced in subsequent NCAA regulations passed between 1968 and 1972. During that time the NCAA voted first to allow freshmen eligibility for all NCAA sports except in football and basketball, reversing decades of precedent. That momentum continued in January 1972 when the governing body allowed freshman eligibility for football and basketball. Furthermore, regulations passed in these years allowed a student to take five years to complete the maximum of four years of varsity eligibility. The long-held policy of not allowing freshmen to participate in order to acclimate to college life had been used as evidence of student-athletes being true amateurs. Its removal, along with the one-year scholarship, was hardly noticed by the public, but it revealed a great deal regarding the NCAA's own views on the balance between the student and the athlete.

Taking Stock of the Student-Athlete Model by 1973

On balance, between 1960 and 1972, the NCAA's jurisdiction over regulating what constituted a student and an athlete increased. At the same time, the standards for being an academically eligible athlete decreased and the provisions for allowable financial support via grants-in-aid had increased. Illustrative of this confluence of changing regulations was that a graduating high school senior needed only a 2.0 GPA to be eligible as a freshman for any and all varsity sports. And, once enrolled in college, that student needed to maintain no more than a 1.6 GPA. In sum, the NCAA had legitimized a new model of the American student-athlete.

One legacy was that a college or university's economic considerations often took priority over educational values and practices. Allowing freshmen to compete immediately on varsity squads meant a reduction in athletics department expenses associated with staffing and funding freshman squads in all sports. It also meant that if an athletics director awarded a student an athletic grant-in-aid, the new rules meant four years of varsity performance in contrast to the older practice of paying a four-year scholarship and receiving only three years of varsity play.

Replacing the original commitment of a four-year athletic grant-in-aid to the new practice of one-year, renewable awards increased the opportunities for exploitation. One syndrome for football players was that after completing a final year of athletic eligibility in the fall semester of their senior year, they dropped out of school without having completed the bachelor's degree. The one-year scholarship practice also allowed coaches to stockpile talent. The NCAA placed no restrictions on the number of athletic grants-in-aid a coach and athletics director could award. This led to accumulation and then severe weeding of surplus players.

Proliferation of athletic scholarships went hand in glove with other institutional practices of college sports excess. In the 1960s as part of this expanded focus on athletics, many universities approved the funding and construction of elaborate dormitories reserved exclusively for student-athletes, usually football players. The NCAA exerted no restrictions or oversight. Depending on point of view, such facilities could be described as serving student-athletes, but a chorus of critical analysts pointed out that these amenities tended to exploit student-athletes by indulging them in luxuries without giving much concern to their academic success as long as they remained eligible to play for the season. Football coaches at big-time programs created new staff positions such as the academic athletic advisor, sometimes known as the "brain coach."

In addition to providing tutors for student-athletes, the academic advisor worked as a liaison between the head football coach, academic deans, and the faculty. The culmination of these staffing measures was that toward the end of his career, Coach Bear Bryant conceded that the term "student-athlete" really was misleading; "athlete-student" was more accurate.

Commercialism and College Sports as an American Civil Religion

By 1973 the desegregation of American college sports was essentially complete. This allowed the athletics establishment of the NCAA, conference commissioners, athletics directors, and celebrity coaches to consolidate their position and increase the commercialization and spectator appeal of big-time college sports. Students, whether as athletes or as a campus constituency, lost ground in the governance of intercollegiate athletics, as accountability and revenues spiraled into autonomous departments, many of which had their own boards of directors drawn from alumni booster clubs and major donors. In other words, the threads of discontent that were intended to lead to wholesale reform in intercollegiate athletics made a dent in student awareness and had some public shock value. But they were defused by coaches and athletics directors who responded with increased public relations campaigns and promotions of championship teams and big games. Most university presidents stood outside the fray and acquiesced in this backlash. University presidents, for example, had little formal or informal influence on the policies and initiatives advanced by the executive director of the NCAA.

Desegregation also allowed big-time college sports to enjoy a halo effect of praise as their metaphors and jargon worked their way into speeches by governors, congressmen, and even the US president. Although national politics, especially issues and politicians with a conservative tilt, might have been a source of attraction to the college sports establishment, their most important consideration was on campus matters.[79] The demonstrations for racial justice and the response by the NCAA revealed an important reality. The main concern was that athletics directors and coaches considered demands for rights for student-athletes to represent a threat to administrative control.

Students who were dismayed with the conduct and condition of established varsity sports programs gained a measure of energy and justification to create their own sports clubs and teams. As college sports entered the 1970s, these innovations did little to impede the growing commercial success and spectator appeal of big-time college sports for fans who bought tickets at the stadium, for television viewers, or for sponsoring advertisers. The athletics department was part of but apart from college and university operating procedures and accountability. These allowances meant that big-time college sports enjoyed an era of consolidation and confidence with prosperity and autonomy.

6

Women's College Sports during the
Cold War Era, 1945 to 1984
Politics and Policies of Equity and Equality

Just as Black athletes faced unequal treatment in college athletics, women also faced dwindling opportunities to participate in intercollegiate competition. Ironically, the curtailment of competitive athletics often came at the hands of women professors and administrators. Although women's basketball played with different rules from the men's game, it still generated excitement and enthusiasm from spectators. This led college sports pioneer Senda Berenson to state, "Unless we guard our athletics carefully in the beginning, many objectionable elements will quickly come in . . . the great desire to win and the excitement of the game will make our women do sadly unwomanly things."[1]

The popularity of Berenson's philosophy led women physical education instructors and administrators to dismantle any system of intercollegiate athletics for coeds by the 1920s. Many of the sexist arguments against competitive athletics came from men and women alike: strenuous activity and competition were harmful to the more physically and emotionally fragile college women. In a relatively swift fashion, intercollegiate women's athletics gave way to intramural games sponsored by women's athletic associations (WAAs) on individual campuses.

Another argument that has received somewhat less historical attention stemmed from the fact that women leaders in college athletics and administration feared that coeducational athletics might fall into the same state as men's competitive sports. As Berenson also argued, "The greatest element of evil in the spirit of athletics in this country is the idea that one must win at any cost— that defeat is an unspeakable disgrace." She did not mention men or women, simply the fact that "in this country" (unlike in Europe, where forebearers clung to amateurism), winning mattered more. Hence women needed to control women's athletics so that it would not fall prey to the same evils and abuses so prevalent in men's college athletics.[2]

By ending large-scale intercollegiate competition, women physical educators and leaders adopted the "A Sport for Every Girl, and Every Girl in a Sport" platform offered by National Amateur Athletic Foundation's Women's Division. The platform relied on the traditional versions of in loco parentis and amateurism in athletics. This Victorian Era version of femininity was in part the women's corollary to the upper-class British concept of a proper gentleman and his amateur approach to athletics. As previously discussed, such arguments did not align with the professionalized, specialized, and commercialized modern American university. While university men were unsuccessful (and often unwilling) at reining in the American working-class effort to beat the privileged class, they were all too eager to join university women in demoting women's athletics because of the unseemly character some believed it engendered.[3]

Hence women's athletics managed to do what men's athletics had attempted to do for decades: place it under faculty control. This occurred first in 1899 when the American Physical Education Association (APEA) created the Women's Basketball Rules Committee. In 1917, APEA created a Committee on Women's Athletics within its own structure that included five subcommittees to regulate the most popular college women's sports. A name change in 1932 led to the National Section on Women's Athletics. During that same era, Blanche Trilling at the University of Wisconsin organized a group of midwestern physical educators and students who named themselves the Athletic Conference of American College Women. In 1933, that group changed their name to the Athletic Federation of College Women. They too opposed high-level competition. As Trilling noted, the "evils of commercialization and exploitation of outstanding girl athletes often lead to the dander of nervous breakdowns."[4]

Regardless of the name changes, these national committees worked to promote "play days" rather than competitive sports. A typical women's play day involved inviting girls from multiple colleges to one campus. Women's physical education instructors then divided the students into teams that included students from various schools, thereby removing the temptation to create a rivalry with another school. After a day of activities, the coeds would then share a meal together or even spend the night on campus before returning to their respective institutions. It was amateurism at its best, cloaked in Victorian stereotypes—viewed as fitting for upper-class girls in collegiate settings. Allen Guttmann made this point in researching the history of women's sports, noting that recreational activities in England during the eighteenth and nineteenth centuries remained "unquestionably a pastime in which social class mattered more than gender."[5]

In men's athletics, it appeared that classist notions of propriety were not enough to slow the engine of commercialized college athletics. But classism and sexism worked together to keep women's intercollegiate competition at bay during the first half of the twentieth century in America.

Women's Athletics between World Wars

As colleges moved away from competitive women's athletics, the Amateur Athletic Union (and some high schools) stepped in to fill the void in the 1920s. One of the first female stars to gain notoriety through AAU-sponsored events was Sybil Bauer. The daughter of Norwegian immigrants who settled in Chicago, Bauer attended Northwestern University. While in college, she participated in the Women's Athletic Association on campus, but Northwestern did not offer intercollegiate sports for women. Instead, Bauer turned her sights toward the AAU and Olympic gold medals. She won the 100-yeard backstroke six years in a row, and in 1922 she broke the men's world record for the 440-yard backstroke. It was one of approximately twenty records that she broke. At the 1924 Olympics in Paris, she won a gold medal. She could have accomplished much more, but in 1927 the Northwestern senor tragically died of cancer, leaving behind her family and a fiancé, the future television host and celebrity Ed Sullivan.[6]

Although Bauer gained press attention, it did not compare to the high school star and future AAU basketball champion Mildred "Babe" Didrikson. The daughter of Norwegian immigrants who settled in Beaumont, Texas, Didrikson loved competitive athletics. Her modest background precluded any social distinction, but her athletic ability brought her impressive acclaim. After dominating in high school basketball, Melvin McCombs recruited her to play for the "amateur" team sponsored by the Employers Casualty Company of Dallas. Didrikson left high school early to take a secretarial job with the company so that she could play AAU-sponsored basketball for the Golden Cyclones.[7]

During her second season with the Cyclones, Didrikson led her team to the 1931 AAU title. After reaching the women's pinnacle in basketball, she began training for the 1932 Olympics. Impressed with her athletic prowess, McCombs sent Didrikson as the lone (and entire) member of the Employers Casualty team at the Olympic qualifying meet sponsored by the AAU. Didrikson won six of eight events and singlehandedly won the team award for her employer. At the time, women were only allowed to compete in three events during the Olympics; she captured two gold medals and one silver in Los Angeles.[8]

Most newspaper reporters were unkind in their sexist remarks about Didrikson's "mannish" build and behavior. As one history detailed, a *Vanity Fair* article in 1932 described her as a "Muscle Moll" and noted that she possessed the same ethos that "keeps me lingering in front of the bearded lady" at a circus. The author surmised, "She knows she is not pretty, that she cannot compete with other girls in the very ancient and honored sport of man-trapping."[9]

While other reporters labeled her an "Amazon" or a "Viking Girl," at least one legendary reporter, Grantland Rice, gave her the proper credit. Certainly no feminist, Rice still declared: "She is an incredible human being. She is beyond all belief until you see her perform. Then you finally understand that you are looking at the most flawless section of muscle harmony, of complete mental and physical coordination the world of sport has ever known. There is only one Babe Didrikson, and there has never been another in her class—even close to her class."[10]

Didrikson had been recruited by the director of women's athletics at Employers Casualty and employed by the business in order to play competitive sports sponsored by the AAU. These actions closely resembled the common activities of competitive men's sports in the NCAA, but the AAU maintained its own purity as truly amateur. Nevertheless, the AAU stripped the gold medalist of her amateur status when she appeared in an automobile advertisement. Didrikson denied that she had given her permission for the ad, but before the AAU eventually cleared her of any wrongdoing, she resigned from her position at the Employers Casualty Company and announced her decision to turn pro. The trailblazing athlete went on to have a dominant career in golf, becoming one of the founding members of the Ladies Professional Golf Association (LPGA) tour before dying of cancer at the young age of 45 in 1956. Golf, many reporters noted, was a more proper sport for women.[11]

Didrikson's struggles exemplified the challenges faced by many women in the first half of the twentieth century. Raised in a working-class immigrant family, she shattered gender stereotypes. Facing resistance nearly her entire life, Didrikson still managed to become a sporting legend without the assistance of intercollegiate athletics. At the same time, the AAU's sponsorship of women's athletic championships helped the organization maintain its status as the leading agency responsible for competitive athletics among young women. Meanwhile, women physical educators maintained truly amateur athletics. No recruiting, scholarships, scandals, or big-time budgets. It was a system many faculty and administrators had called for in men's athletics, and it was a system that did not have a place for someone like Babe Didrikson.

Unlike Didrikson, a few women athletes managed to compete in intercollegiate sports when they were good enough to join a men's team. For example, Dorothy "Dot" Anderson hoped to join the men's tennis team at Carnegie Tech (eventually renamed Carnegie Mellon University). After the dean of women refused to allow her to join the team, she left the university and eventually found her way to Penn State in 1933. Anderson participated in play days on campus but desired to join the men's tennis team.[12]

Anderson's quest for eligibility on a men's tennis team caused quite a stir in State College, Pennsylvania, but received little attention elsewhere. Once she was finally given permission to join the team during her senior year in 1935, she exacted revenge in her first match by beating a player from Carnegie Tech. Anderson went on to win her next five matches, including a victory over the number one player for Syracuse. Only one institution refused to allow Anderson to play: the US Naval Academy.[13] Off the court, Anderson faced other challenges. The team's coach mentioned the pressure she faced, stating, "A lot of people wanted to see this weirdo," as he characterized the attitudes of many. A campus paper noted the frustration among some young men on the team who resented Anderson's playing. She did hold one advantage over Babe Didrikson, as male press members found her attractive. As syndicated columnist Henry McLemore wrote, "Dorothy Anderson, a pretty gal, is the ace player of the Penn State varsity tennis team."[14]

Anderson's perseverance paid off as she became the only female "letterman" at Penn State. Her trailblazing efforts opened doors for other women in the region. Having prohibited Anderson, Carnegie Tech in Pittsburgh added Naomi Thompson to their freshman team in 1936, and she made the varsity team the following year. Although rumors spread that Pitt would boast a woman tennis player as well, the Panthers athletics director disallowed it. Despite this setback, other small colleges in the region brought women onto their men's teams.[15] But Anderson's experience revealed that sportswriters still found it essential to discuss a woman athlete's femininity and looks. As scholar Susan Cahn determined, "The central, underlying tension in American women's sport" continued to be "The contradictory relationship between athleticism and womanhood."[16]

The female tennis players who broke the gender barrier in tennis helped create weaknesses in the anti–varsity women's sports model of intramurals and play days. The first women's physical educator at the University of Arizona, Ina E. Gittings, considered the conservative model "extremely weak and offer[ing] little or none of the joy and values of real games played skillfully . . . and eagerly by well-matched teams." She compared the young women at play days to "sheep" when instead they should be "young mustangs."[17] In her 1931 essay "Why Cramp Competition?" published in the *Journal of Health and Physical Education*, Gittings declared that "Buried in every game . . . is the thing that makes it appeal to thinking emotional beings—Competition." These views gained little traction among the leading women's PE instructors across the country at the time. She was prophetic, however, noting that "the chief value of the Play Day may be to re-introduce varsity competition (of the best kind), the thing it sets out to oppose; in fact, it will evolve into actual Varsity competition or die from pure ennui."[18]

Later in the thirties, however, Gladys Palmer (and her colleagues) at Ohio State University challenged the status quo. Palmer sought the creation of an association to govern intercollegiate contests between women. She continued to agitate for reform with her 1938 essay "Policies in Women's Athletics," arguing for competitive games for women. She also offered to organize a national golf tournament for college women. The National Section on Girl's Women's Athletics (which was part of the male-dominated American Association for Health, Physical Education, and Recreation) rejected her initiatives. Instead, Palmer took it upon herself to organize a national championship golf tournament. Held in 1941, the event attracted more than thirty golfers and was a smashing success. As historian Brad Austin has noted, Palmer did not act alone. Numerous other dedicated women across the country (and at Ohio State) worked patiently and diligently to accomplish their goals, always pushing when possible.[19]

Here the National Section on Girls' and Women's Sports (NSGWS), claiming to act differently than the NCAA, responded in a manner that mirrored the NCAA's actions for decades. After praising the success of the tournament, the group still criticized her for utilizing the words "national" and "intercollegiate." They recommended instead the use of the word "invitational." Trying desperately to disassociate from competitive men's athletics, the NSWA resorted to the same type of linguistic nuance common among leaders in the NCAA. Regardless of their opinion, Palmer set a precedent that would continue after World War II.[20]

Women's Athletics after World War II

College women participated in and often excelled at sports. But they were seldom allowed to be part of college sports. This paradox provides the plot and cast in the story about the peculiar exclusion women faced as student-athletes and

College women pose for a photograph at the first national intercollegiate championship (in any sport) for women in 1941. The Ohio State University Archives

as coaches between World War II and the late 1980s. This period included the 1972 Title IX legislation, in which official campus accommodation of women as student-athletes, coaches, and athletics directors made gains in federal regulation. But this landmark measure was limited because college and university officials and the athletics establishment were either resistant or hesitant to change standard practices and policies at most American colleges and universities.

Where did college women and recent alumnae make their mark in high-level competitive athletics? The most prominent women's sports were swimming, track and field, tennis, volleyball, figure skating, field hockey, lacrosse, equestrian, fencing, and gymnastics. Notable achievements included Olympic gold medals, national championships sponsored by the Amateur Athletic Union, wins at the Wimbledon tournament, and several other national association championship events. Taking stock of colleges, conferences, and the NCAA in the late 1980s, women in college sports were justified in celebrating their hard-fought gains. At the same time, their optimism was tempered because uncompleted work required them to be vigilant in persistent efforts to edge toward fair treatment in the governance and funding of the vast intercollegiate athletics enterprise.

What are the details that resolve the puzzle of college women as participants and champions in a variety of organized sports while having little if any official collegiate structure and sponsorship? One important strand is that competitive women's sports tournaments and conferences operated outside and beneath the radar of the NCAA and its member conferences and their colleges and universities. To understand the gulf between women and men in campus student activities, it is useful to look beneath the major legislative and policy deliberations and first reconstruct the general experiences for women's colleges teams at coeducational institutions.

The Campus Composite: A Profile of a Women's College Sports Program

Reconstructing the character and composition of women's college sports programs is not easy. Seldom did their games receive coverage in the daily student newspapers. There were no press releases from the official university news bureau or the department of intercollegiate athletics media relations office. Women's sports programs were not included in the varsity sports governance structure. A good place to start reconstructing a profile of women's college sports programs is to examine a widespread artifact of campus life: the annual yearbooks published at the end of the academic year by student editors. At coeducational colleges and universities, women's sports often received some coverage with photographs and text. But it was cursory—usually only one or two pages. In place of team pictures for each sport along with season results and game by game photographs, typically one finds a group picture featuring one woman athlete per sport and perhaps one or two action photographs from one game, usually basketball. In contrast, at major universities, men's varsity sports often received about fifty pages of coverage. The football team section included game-by-game photographs and statistics, followed by compilations of the season's record, statistics, and awards.

Women's sports were confined to a local or regional territory with tournaments scheduled within short driving distance. A customary way to save money was to hold play days and tournaments where several neighboring college teams converged on one host campus for multiple games. There were no chartered air flights or team busses. One customary practice was for team members to pile into station wagons with their equipment, driven by their coaches. Athletes and their coaches had to scrounge to assemble makeshift uniforms, often bought out of their own pockets. Athletic grants-in-aid were both unknown and alien to their model of amateur college sports.

Structurally, women's and men's intercollegiate athletics were distinct in funding and offerings from the commercial model of the dominant entity, men's varsity sports. Coaches, almost always women, usually held faculty or staff appointments, often in physical education, where they taught activity classes. Unlike the coaches of men's varsity squads, women's team coaches did not receive a full-time or half salary, but rather a modest add-on stipend. The women's gym had few if any bleachers for spectators. Coaches of the women's teams usually lined the playing fields with chalk, mopped and swept up the gymnasium floors, and gathered soiled towels to send to the laundry. One indispensable piece of equipment for a woman coach was a station wagon or a van, as players and coaches piled in with equipment to drive to nearby colleges for games and tournaments. The women's athletic activities often had their own director, a part-time appointment combined with coaching and teaching. Women students were required to pay the same mandatory athletic fee as men, even though the bulk of it provided subsidies for the men's varsity teams.

As noted in chapter 4, World War II provided a watershed moment for American culture—including the world of sports. As Black veterans returned from Europe, having liberated the continent from Nazism and Fascism, many refused to return to the Jim Crow South and endure segregation, racial slurs, and systemic racism. In a different way, World War II opened the door to greater equality for women as well. Women had entered the workforce in unprecedented numbers. Athletics were viewed as indispensable to the cooperation and discipline required of soldiers, and women filled similar roles. The All-American Girls Professional Baseball League formed in 1943 and continued well into the 1950s. The door toward equality in athletics opened slower for women than it did for minorities, but when Title IX's civil rights legislation for women in higher education finally passed, college women eventually gained more opportunity while female administrators lost control of their own programs.

Following World War II, the vast majority of higher education institutions offered no opportunities for women to play varsity intercollegiate athletics. This was intentional. The philosophy of athletics that physical educators (both male and female) implemented for women before the war ended virtually all competitive athletics for coeds. This system, or lack thereof, continued without complaint from male-dominated administrations across the country. But the geopolitical forces of the Cold War created an opportunity to challenge the narrative of college sports for women. The civil rights movement and the feminist movement eventually played a role in the transformation of women's intercollegiate athletics.

The Soviet Union first competed in the 1952 Olympics with an impressive showing by both their men and women. With increasingly hostile political rhetoric between them and the United States, the Olympics provided another front on which to fight the cultural Cold War. Both superpowers used these athletic events to seek validation of their political systems in the world court of public opinion. Athletics literally became an element of public relations and foreign policy. The Soviet Union held a distinct advantage in Olympic competition, however. While American culture rebuked competitive sports for women because they diminished "femininity," the Soviet Union sought simply to win the most medals—with men or women—to provide evidence of the empire's cultural superiority.[21]

Without a system to identify talented female athletes and provide them with competitive games or meets, women's sports in America languished behind the Soviet Union and much of the Western world. A perceived need to beat the Russians in the Olympics—not an innate desire to expand opportunities for women—led to the first attempts at creating a system of competitive women's sports. Looking to find ways to identify and develop athletic talent among young women, a longtime member of the Women's Committee of the American Athletic Union asked athletics directors at American universities to identify a representative at each institution to promote women's athletics.[22]

The response from the NSGWS was to resist attempts by the AAU to control their sports. NSGWS chair Josephine Fiske hoped the AAU would "refrain from suggesting to colleges the type of program they should offer." She stated that the AAU wanted to groom "star athletes" for the Olympics and argued that it would be a detriment to the larger female student populations across the country. It was true that the AAU hoped to be more competitive in international competitions, many of which focused on track and field events. The leading women physical educators argued that such an approach was diametrically opposed to the philosophy employed by professors who sought broad participation in athletics for enjoyment and healthy leisure while protecting their femininity.[23]

In contrast to the AAU's suggestion for promoting competitive sports, the NSGWS released an updated version of *Standards in Sports for Girls and Women: Guiding Principles in the Organization and Administration of Sports Programs.* The *Standards* sought to distinguish between men's competitive sports and the virtues of "appropriate" sports for women. By appropriate, women sports leaders meant those that promoted control over competition, femininity instead of masculinity, and white upper- and middle-class conservative sexual mores. For example, individual sports (as opposed to team ones) that had "a social and heterosexual significance" were deemed "especially desirable."[24]

Philosophically, the *Standards* argued that sports "belonged to the participants, not the audience, alumni, or business sponsors." Apparently, faculty did not see the irony in claiming that sports belonged to the participants while at the same time governing all elements of athletic events. This included controlling the types of uniforms young women wore, regulating the competitive nature of the games, and promoting their version of the "proper" sports to play. Members of the NSGWS also found it essential to dismiss the sports that diminished femininity and led to mannish traits. The maternalistic nature akin to in loco parentis of the old-time college model remained intact for women's athletics. The sports played by college women remained strictly supervised by physical educators, that is, under faculty control.[25]

Much of the thinking espoused by physical educators remained tainted by racism and sexism. When Cleve Abbott developed a dominant track and field program at the historically Black Tuskegee Institute (now Tuskegee University) in Alabama, one organization leader announced that track and field did not meet the physiological or social needs of college women. Upset by the proposition of college women filling the roster of a competitive national team in basketball, another female physical education leader bemoaned the possibility of a team filled with "Amazons" who would be "of questionable value" as representatives of women's athletics in America.[26]

In response to these claims the AAU conducted a study and published the results in their publication, *Amateur Athlete*. The AAU survey sought to determine whether athletics harmed women, whether they tended "to make a girl lose her charm and beauty," and whether sports made "childbirth difficult." Not surprisingly, the resounding response was "a big NO!" The AAU continued making its case for identifying and developing athletic women in the United States. But they needed support of colleges and universities to make their efforts productive.[27]

As the pressure mounted for the United States to train and develop competitive athletes in international/Olympic sports, two things happened. First, a small but growing group of younger physical education professors began promoting greater opportunities for women in competitive athletics. For example, at the American Association of Health, Physical Education, and

Recreation (AAHPER) annual convention, Celeste Ulrich of the North Carolina Women's College (now UNC Greensboro) presented to the Division of Girls and Women's Sports (or DGWS, what had been previously known as the NSGWS) and made "a plea for permitting women to compete in sports at their own skill level" while still calling for a "controlled, regulated, tournament-type situation." The DGWS team sports panel responded that a recent survey found that ninety-two percent of college administrators "believe there is a place for team sports in competition for women." At the same time, the women's panel asserted that "a lack of interest in team sports on the college level" from college women made such efforts futile.[28]

In sum, by the conclusion of the 1950s, control of college athletics for women was inextricably tied to what types of sports would be offered. The male-dominated AAU (as well as some AAU members who were women) desired to develop more competitive sports to showcase on the international stage. Women's physical educators, conversely, remained highly protective of their vision for athletics that remained largely social and emphasized "feminine" virtues. In the 1950s and 1960s, athletes at historically Black colleges and universities, particularly track and field athletes, posed the greatest threat to this traditional view.

Trailblazers in Women's Intercollegiate Basketball

At the intersection of these two marginalized groups—women and minority athletes—stood HBCUs and their female athletic teams. History reinforces the notion that while racism and sexism played a critical role in the sidelining of athletes, elements of the upper-class British worldview that influenced American colleges in the nineteenth century played an integral role as well in defining the proper place for women's athletics. Upper-class mores still dominated much of higher education in the United States. As scholar Welch Suggs noted, America's elite HBCUs followed the attitudes of America's physical educators at other prestigious institutions in rejecting competitive women's athletics.[29]

Following trends established by primarily white institutions, leading HBCUs such as Howard and Spelman shunned the idea of competitive sports for women. In contrast, Black institutions that focused on industrial, vocational, and agricultural education welcomed the competition. Land grant Institutions like Alcorn College, Florida A&M, Fort Valley State College, and Prairie View A&M all boasted competitive women's track and field teams and/or basketball squads. But these programs paled in comparison to the domination of Tuskegee

Institute, which had become a trailblazer in women's sports under the leader-ship of athletics director Cleveland "Cleve" Abbott. Abbott, a South Dakota native, became a varsity athlete in multiple sports as an undergraduate at South Dakota State University. As a coach and AD, Abbott utilized athletics as a way to promote civil rights during his Tuskegee career, which spanned more than three decades.[30]

Although track and field would eventually garner far more attention in the late fifties and sixties, basketball became the leading team sport for both Black and white working-class girls and women. During the first decade after World War II, Jim Crow laws remained in force throughout the South, so col-lege women's basketball teams at HBCUs were prohibited from playing against white AAU teams. Colleges played in their own conference tournaments, but they received little public attention. Yet the game continued to grow in popu-larity in specific regions across the country.

A year before *Brown v. Board* (1954), Missouri Arledge graduated from Hill-side High School in Durham, North Carolina. From twelve scholarship offers, she chose to attend Philander Smith College in Arkansas because it was the far-thest from her home and she wanted to travel. During her sophomore year, she and her team won the South Central Athletic Conference and received an invite to play in the AAU National Tournament, where they became one of the first Black teams to participate in the event. Arledge won all-American honors, but a different college team from Texas claimed the championship.[31]

In 1955, Wayland Baptist College from Plainview, Texas, won the AAU cham-pionship. Their reformist president, Bill Marshall, had already made waves by becoming the first liberal arts institution in the old Confederacy to voluntarily integrate before the *Brown* decision in 1954. In an attempt to promote his insti-tution, Marshall employed commercial and competitive basketball for women. The local Harvest Queen Mill originally donated uniforms to the squad. Presi-dent Marshall raised money for women's basketball scholarships and convinced alum Claude Hutcherson to use airplanes from his successful business to trans-port the team to away games. The Wayland Baptist "Flying Queens" personified everything the DGWS and traditional physical educators opposed.[32]

Marshall's gamble paid off. In the mid-1950s the Wayland Baptist Flying Queens went on an unprecedented 131-game win streak that included four AAU national championships. The team finally met their match during the 1958 na-tional tournament when all-American Nora White and her team from the Nashville Business College (NBC) defeated the Queens. The NBC was not a col-lege in a traditional sense but a proprietary business that taught secretarial skills to women. NBC became the new powerhouse in the AAU, as they recruited their players and provided them with jobs that had flexible work schedules to accommodate basketball games, even as they were still considered amateurs. The NBC team held one major advantage over Wayland Baptist and HBCU squads: they were not bound by four-year limits for their players. Throughout the 1960s, both Wayland Baptist and the Nashville Business College dominated their competition during the 1960s, but NBC held the upper hand. Most importantly for female physical education professors and administrators, NBC's dominance managed to keep other institutions from emulating Wayland Baptist's commercial model of athletics. The Flying Queens remained an anomaly during the fifties and sixties, as most universities avoided competitive basketball for college women and left the administration of national championships up to the AAU.[33]

With a stranglehold on the definition of "appropriate" sports for women, female athletics administrators allowed the AAU to govern national-level basketball competition in the United States. With the AAU in charge and the leaders of women's sports unwilling to offer competitive play, the United States lagged the sport that had been invented in Massachusetts less than a century earlier. In the 1967 World Championship held in Prague, the US women's team went an abysmal 1–6 and finished in last place in the field of eleven teams. Basketball had been an Olympic sport for men since the 1930s, but the women's game had not yet been approved. Without that impetus, the women's sporting establishment felt no pressure to make its game more competitive. Track and field would become the sport in which battles over competitive sports for women would be waged. That would occur in the South at historically Black colleges and universities.[34]

Ed Temple, Wilma Rudolph, and the Tennessee State Tigerbelles

While Tennessee State University developed the most prolific track and field team for women after World War II, the model had first been established by Tuskegee. Under the direction of Cleve Abbott, Tuskegee created a women's track team in the late 1920s. Abbott then began recruiting and offering scholarships (along with its work-study program) to high school athletes. Such inducements were not allowed by the NCAA, but it did not matter. They had nobody else to compete against. In the absence of intercollegiate national tournaments, Abbott instituted the Tuskegee Carnival, which became the premier track and field event for Black college and high school athletes. In a twelve-year span from

1937 to 1948, Tuskegee won eleven AAU team titles in the annual outdoor event. In 1948, Tuskegee graduate Alice Coachman became the first Black woman to win an Olympic gold medal, placing first in the high jump.[35]

Following World War II, Tennessee Agricultural and Industrial State College (later renamed Tennessee State University) began to supplant Tuskegee's dominance, using the same template Abbott utilized. They first hired Jessie Abbott, whose father had served as the legendary football coach and athletics director at Tuskegee. In the same Olympics in London in 1948, Tennessee State's Audrey Patterson was the first African American to medal, taking a bronze not long before Tuskegee's Alice Coachman won her gold medal. The two primary programs for Black women track athletes medaled in 1948, but the torch was about to pass to Tennessee State.

In 1950, Tennessee State president Walter Davis hired Ed Temple as the women's track and field coach. A recent Tennessee State graduate who ran track, Temple accepted an offer of $150 a month and dormitory housing to work on his master's degree, coach the women's track team, and work in the post office. Temple accepted the offer and began developing what would become a world-renowned team. With major college teams and the NCAA remaining inhospitable to both integrated and competitive athletics for women, Coach Temple decided to build his program with support from the integrated Amateur Athletic Union.[36]

Temple understood how to recruit in the segregated South. He became a referee and scouted athletes at all-Black high schools in Tennessee and across the region. He invited high school students to his summer AAU-sanctioned program. During his first years, Temple admitted that Tuskegee continued to "beat us like a drum," but he began to attract the attention of highly skilled athletes. Temple's success improved when he managed to recruit Olympic veteran Mae Faggs from New York. She became the team's leader, and in 1955, Tennessee State won its first AAU national outdoor team championship. They would win twelve more times in the next thirteen years.[37]

By the following year, six women whom Temple coached participated in the 1956 Olympics in Melbourne, Australia. Four Tennessee State students were joined by two high school athletes who attended Temple's summer track program. Not chosen as a coach for the Olympic team, Temple remained at home but tapped veteran runner Faggs as the unofficial captain of his runners. Faggs joined teammates Isabelle Daniels, Margaret Matthews, and high school student Wilma Rudolph to take home a bronze medal in the 4 by 100 relay. Additionally, 16-year-old Willye White won a silver medal in the long jump.

Earlier that year, White chose to attend Temple's summer program in Nashville to get out of working in the cotton fields at her home near Greenwood, Mississippi. Once in Nashville, White realized that if she made the Olympic team, she could avoid the entire cotton-picking season. That proved to be the motivation she needed. The experience, however, was life changing. As White later noted, she believed lynchings and cross burnings existed everywhere, "But after 1956 I found there were two worlds, Mississippi and the rest of the world." White became the first American woman to participate in five consecutive Olympics.[38]

During the next four years, the Tigerbelles, as Tennessee State's sports information director named the team, continued their dominance in women's college track. In 1958, eight Tigerbelles qualified for the women's track team that would travel to Moscow for the first of many USA-USSR dual track meets. The dual meets were established as a Cold War diplomacy tool, with both countries using them to tout their superiority. While the US men's track team continued with good showings internationally in the 1950s, the US women were well behind the Soviet Union and other developed nations. Exploiting this weakness, the Soviet Union demanded a combined score to determine the winner of the meet. The US men beat the Soviets, but the women suffered worse losses, and the USSR won the team challenge. The second dual meet in 1959 resulted in a similar outcome, as one report noted that without the Tigerbelles, "We [the US team] would be smarting from a great American tragedy—no women's track." This was not an understatement. Temple's Tennessee State track team largely carried the United States against the Soviet Union. This proved to be particularly frustrating for many Americans as the Cold War created an environment in which both world powers sought to prove their superiority.[39]

It was in this context that Ed Temple and his US women's track and field team competed in the 1960 Rome Olympics. During the first ever worldwide telecasts, the seven Tigerbelles (along with Tennessee State men's long-jumper Ralph Boston) shone brightly across the globe. Boston won gold in the long jump when he broke Jesse Owens's Olympic record in the event. Wilma Rudolph anchored a Tigerbelle team that won gold in the 4 by 100 relay, and she went on to win two other gold medals in Rome. In the midst of the Cold War and with the help of expanded television coverage, Rudolph instantly found herself in the national spotlight. As historian Carroll Van West noted, the *New York Times* called Rudolph the "World Speed Queen" and labeled Tennessee State as the "cathedral of Women's track . . . with Ed Temple the high priest."[40]

Rudolph's personal history and exploits in Rome made her an instant celebrity. Having overcome polio as a child, Rudolph's success story provided the type of narrative American powerbrokers promoted during the Cold War. After the 1960 Olympic Games, "Welcome Wilma Day" became the first publicly integrated event in Clarksville, Tennessee, during the twentieth century. She was summoned to the White House to meet President John F. Kennedy and Vice President Lyndon Johnson, and later represented the United States on a goodwill tour of West Africa. A 1977 made-for-TV movie, *Wilma*, told her success story (and served as an acting debut for Denzel Washington, who played Rudolph's husband).[41]

The story of Wilma Rudolph as an American heroine has undergone great scrutiny by twenty-first century scholars who have highlighted political use of Rudolph's fame to serve the sexist and racist status quo. For example, Clarksville's integrated celebration diminished the plight of Black citizens who remained marginalized by the local culture. Rudolph herself clearly understood this, and in 1963 she unsuccessfully attempted to eat at the whites-only Clarksville Shoney's, despite the city holding a celebration in her honor three years earlier.[42]

Discussions of gender surrounding Rudolph's success were equally complex. An essentially all-male press remained fixated on Rudolph's physical appearance. The attractive college student, as one writer put it, "Was probably the first negro girl athlete to be described as being 'beautiful' in the general-circulating daily press. She proved that a girl didn't require a face by Frankenstein to qualify for the world of track and field." As *Sports Illustrated* described Rudolph's final competitive meet before retiring in 1962, "[It was] the best track meet of the year, but also was the prettiest." The article then went on to note that Soviet women had historically been much prettier, but the Americans were gaining ground.[43]

The question of beauty fit within Coach Temple's strategic plan. As Temple said, "I had a motto. . . . I don't want oxes, I want foxes. I want nice looking girls." In qualifying his statement years later, "A lot of people black and white believed that if girls got muscles they could never have babies . . . black folks got funny about their daughters playing sports as maturing young women." Temple set out to prove that young women could be competitive athletically while retaining femininity. So, Wilma Rudolph specifically (and the Tigerbelles generally) tore down biased stereotypes of female athletes while also reaffirming the traditional and proper "look" for female athletes.[44]

Members of the 1955 Tennessee State Tigerbelles track team pose with coach Ed Temple. *Front*: A summer school participant with Martha Hudson. *Back*: Willye White, Ed Temple, Wilma Rudolph, and Darlene Scott. Tennessee State University Special Collections and Archives

Just as lower- and middle-class students and coaches had challenged Harvard and Yale's definition of proper intercollegiate athletics in rowing and football in the nineteenth century, Tennessee State developed a highly competitive women's track program. Ed Temple created a summerlong training program sanctioned by the AAU. He used the summer program to recruit the most talented Black women runners to Tennessee State. Without the luxury of scholarships, Temple utilized a strategy adopted by many powerhouse athletics programs before the NCAA allowed grants-in-aid for sports: campus jobs for exceptional athletes. The Tigerbelles took classes, worked on campus, and endured a rigorous training regimen. Temple essentially adopted a professionalized "big-time" model for a marginalized women's program at an HBCU.[45]

In short, Ed Temple's program shunned the pure amateur model in favor of what began to be called the "men's model" of athletics, which higher education administrators had fought unsuccessfully to stop for decades. Women collegiate sports administrators, for complex reasons that had converged, had managed to keep the competitive model at bay. In this context, Temple's teams disrupted stereotypes about Black athletes as well as women in track and field. As historian Jennifer Lansbury noted, Temple and his track stars used "the stereotype of the 1950s white middle-class femininity for their own purposes."[46]

What historians have generally ignored is that Ed Temple rejected the long-established women's college sports model and became an icon in the sport he coached. The DGWS had largely condemned track and field as too masculine for collegiate women, but Temple proved otherwise. Women physical educators also rejected the idea of men controlling or coaching women's college sports. For decades, they postulated that differences in women required oversight from highly educated women who understood the "proper" role of sports for women. The women Temple coached loved and admired him for his investment in their lives. Both the NCAA and the DGWS undoubtedly took note.

Temple's program at Tennessee State remained an anomaly in women's college sports. Standing in stark contrast to Wilma Rudolph's college and athletic career was that of Chris von Saltza. Von Saltza also won three gold medals (along with a silver medal) in the 1960 Rome Olympics, in swimming. Yet von Saltza planned on attending Stanford after finishing high school. Like almost every other university in the United States, there were no competitive sports programs for women at Stanford. Chris von Saltza and countless other young women like her would give up their sporting careers to go to college.[47]

Chris von Saltza's experience was not isolated. At the 1964 Olympic Games in Tokyo, US women's swimming star Donna de Varona won two gold medals. In 1964, she was featured on the covers of both *Time* and *Life* magazines. After the Tokyo games, she was selected as the most outstanding woman athlete of the year. Despite her talent, achievement, and youth, her competitive swimming career was over, as there were few if any options for formal training and participation in competitions in higher education or elsewhere. She soon became one of the first women sportscasters, eventually earning a degree from the University of California, Los Angeles, in the 1980s.

The highs and lows in the experiences of women athletes such as Wilma Rudolph, Chris von Saltza, and Donna de Varona demonstrate decisively that although the 1960s have been celebrated as a period of advances for equity and social justice, there is slim to no evidence that colleges showed much concern for women as student-athletes. Conventional analyses portray passage of Title IX in 1972 as ushering in a new era for women in scholastic endeavors and in college sports. As one historian of women's sports in the Ivy League observed, funding made some progress in going from "bake sales to budgets."[48]

The Cold War and the Fight to Control Women's College Sports

The experiences of Chris Von Saltza and Donna de Varona were by design. Physical education professors across the country (both women and men) devised and enforced women's athletics programs based on leisure and wide participation, while men's sports continued on a highly competitive track. Tuskegee and then Tennessee State University remained outliers, while the vast majority of higher education administrators adopted the pure "amateur" (i.e., elitist) version of athletics for women, and it was reenforced by the sexist stereotypes of the day. The two HBCUs did not fit into the upper-class white tier of universities that implemented their own version of amateur athletics that had come to define male athletics.

The dominant faculty view of women's athletics in American higher education severely hindered attempts at success (over the Soviet Union) in the Olympics and in the annual track and field dual meet that began in 1958. Only a few forward thinking women's PE instructors had voiced concern regarding the lack of competitive athletics for women, and their complaints were largely ignored. This started to change when the Soviet Union began dominating women's Olympic events. With such disparate philosophies regarding gender and athletics, it is not surprising that the US men, most of whom trained in universities across the country, often led summer Olympic competition in the medal count. American women, with few competitive college sports programs, garnered far fewer medals. As the Soviet Union trained both men and women in competitive sports, they began to defeat the United States in overall medal counts. They also overtook the men in total medal counts in the 1956 and 1960 summer Olympics.[49]

Displeased with the results of American athletes and the general administration of Olympic sport, the NCAA abandoned its "alliance" with the Amateur Athletic Union in 1960. The two organizations had a contentious relationship concerning the administration of amateur athletics, but they agreed to a détente at the end of World War II. The NCAA gained greater representation, but the AAU retained its favored status within the US Olympic Committee. Weakening international performances along with frustrations concerning the administration of the Olympic teams led the NCAA to end its partnership with the AAU.[50]

The NCAA was not alone in its frustration with the AAU. In 1961, multiple athletes announced a boycott of the dual meet between the United States and the Soviet Union. They bemoaned the grueling track schedules leading up to the meet and complained about meagre accommodations and funding. The general disregard of athletes' well-being was not an uncommon complaint, but the threat of a boycott for the meet against the USSR brought negative attention to the AAU. When the AAU appointed athletic representatives to share their concerns, they backed off of their boycott, but it did not end the tension between the two organizations. The NCAA saw an opportunity to claim greater control of amateur athletics in America.[51]

The battle for control of women's athletics has often been portrayed as a decadelong battle occurring after the passage of Title IX in 1972, until the NCAA began offering women's championships in the early 1980s. Only a few historians have taken a closer look at the historical record, which revealed that the battle for control over women's athletics had been an issue for decades. During the 1960s and 1970s, the battle over women's athletics was part of a larger war between the NCAA and the AAU.[52]

Not only did the Soviets dominate the 1960 Olympics, but more athletes also began complaining publicly about the treatment they received from the AAU. Poor travel arrangements, minimal per diem for meals, and lousy housing accommodations eventually led Olympic gold medalist Hal Connolly to organize a boycott of the AAU-organized events—including the dual meet with the Soviet Union. The athletes agreed to end their boycott if the demands for better treatment were met. The AAU, in damage-control mode, agreed to assign athletic representatives to provide a voice for athletes.[53]

In this climate, Walter Byers saw his opportunity to weaken the AAU's grip on Olympic operations and amateur athletics in America. After the 1960 Olympics, the NCAA backed out of its Articles of Alliance with the AAU. The National Collegiate Track Coaches Association (composed of primarily college coaches) broke ties with the AAU and formed the US Track and Field Federation (USTFF). Loyal to the NCAA, the USTFF harshly criticized the AAU. In 1961 the NCAA invited Thomas Hamilton of the Olympic Development Committee to speak at the organization's annual conference. The former naval officer and athletics administrator emphasized the importance of providing more opportunities for competitive sports for young women to improve the United States' standing in international competitions. To that end, he worked to assert the NCAA's authority in transforming American Olympic administration.[54]

In response, the NCAA first terminated its committee for communicating with the AAU. It also devised a plan to work with coaches' associations and promoted the "Federation Movement" because the USTFF had been successful in challenging the AAU. In early 1962 the NCAA sponsored a meeting to organize new "federations"—associations consisting largely of coaches and administrators who were sympathetic with the NCAA. By the end of the year, national federations had been established for baseball, track and field, basketball, and gymnastics. The track and basketball federations also sought to expand opportunities for women in their respective sports. In so doing, the federations challenged the authority of the AAU.[55]

Sensitive to the NCAA's newfound interest in women's athletics, the American Association of Health, Physical Education, and Recreation asked the DGWS to examine the possibilities for more competitive athletics for college women. Such a move represented a complete departure for the DGWS, which functioned as a women's organization within the AAHPER. At nearly the same time, the AAU responded to the NCAA's encroachment, courting the AAHPER by offering important positions within the AAU's governance structure. The AAHPER accepted.

By the end of 1962, tensions had flared to a point that the NCAA-supported USTFF stated publicly that it might hold a meet at the same time as the AAU's national championship. US Attorney General Robert F. Kennedy intervened, convincing the USTFF to cancel its meet and refrain from selecting a team to represent the United States in its dual meet with the Soviet Union. After the event, the power struggle continued to rage. The AAU then accused the NCAA of challenging the AAU's authority to unilaterally control Olympic qualifying and the selection of athletes. Unfortunately for the AAU, the NCAA had support from junior colleges, high school athletics associations, as well as college athletes.[56]

As the 1964 Olympics approached, the continuing AAU-NCAA feud prompted President Kennedy to tap General Douglas MacArthur to negotiate a peace between the two organizations during qualifying events. The truce lasted only through the Tokyo Olympics. In 1965 the USTFF directly challenged the AAU's governing authority by announcing that the AAU would need sanctioning from the USTFF to hold its events. The AAU had jealously guarded its own sanctioning authority for decades, so they flatly refused to seek official permission from another organization. In turn, the USTFF boycotted the AAU's 1965 qualifying event for that year's dual meet with the Soviet Union. To enforce the boycott, the USTFF threatened college athletes with the loss of their scholarship if they participated in the AAU's event. Only three college track and field athletes won events at the AAU meet. Then, for the first time, the US men lost to the Soviets in their dual meet. Walter Byers and the sports federations had made its point: the NCAA was crucial to the success of the AAU and American Olympic athletics.[57]

The NCAA and the USTFF proved a point at the expense of college athletes and the men's international track team. To be fair, they emulated a practice the AAU had exercised for decades. In response, the US Senate held an official hearing to study the men's track loss and find a solution for the NCAA-AAU power struggle. Even though it would not solve the debate, the lengthy hearing provided the NCAA with greater support with regard to assuming control of all intercollegiate activities, including women's sports. For example, a regional AAU president stated, "The most criminal and reprehensible neglect of all . . . is the NCAA's almost complete neglect of women's competitive sports." After highlighting the success of Tennessee State, the respondent claimed that the NCAA lacked interest in women's sports because of the lack of "box office appeal."[58] The AAU was correct, but they left out one important point. As Al Duer, the head of the NAIA, noted, "There are some problems in relationship to other national organizations such as the American Association of Physical Education and Recreation."[59] In short, the AAHPER did not want the NAIA and the NCAA to be involved in the governance of women's sports.

Walter Byers determined that the NCAA's lack of involvement in women's sports harmed its ability to gain greater control in national Olympic governance. He also surmised, correctly, that NCAA involvement would improve US women's performance in the Olympics and vault the NCAA into a more powerful position in all of amateur athletics. In 1963 the NCAA sponsored an Institute for Women's and Girls' Sports in conjunction with the DGWS and the US Olympic Development Committee. The NCAA also formed a committee to follow developments in intercollegiate sports for women. In 1964 the NCAA invited two leading women athletics administrators to speak at a roundtable discussion on women's athletics. As the NCAA studied women's sports, female physical educators took note.

Concerned about the NCAA's newfound interest in women's sports, the DGWS asked the NCAA to ban women from competition on men's teams, and the NCAA willingly obliged. In reality, the NCAA's membership at large remained disinterested in women's intercollegiate athletics. Most were only concerned with athletics on their own campus. Byers, in contrast, desired the leverage women's athletics would provide in claiming control of amateur sport in America.

Threatened by Byer's interest in women's sports, the DGWS created the Commission on Intercollegiate Athletics for Women (CIAW). It was the first group from the AAHPER to focus solely on intercollegiate athletics for women. As historian Ying Wushanley pointed out, the CIAW started under pressure to maintain what little control there was of intercollegiate athletics. The CIAW was charged with preserving the two national tournaments that did exist for college women in tennis and golf—tournaments that the DGWS had opposed when it was first created. Additionally, the CIAW sought to "prepare for possible growth" of women's intercollegiate athletics and govern any expansion that did take place.[60]

The NCAA responded by forming its own committee "to study the feasibility of establishing appropriate machinery to provide for control and supervision of women's intercollegiate athletics." The NCAA held multiple strategic advantages. It already possessed an organization of institutional members, an organizational apparatus for hosting national tournaments, and a well-funded organization developed by lucrative television contracts. The DGWS and the CIAW took exception with the NCAA's move. Nevertheless, the CIAW found itself in a precarious position. As Charles "Chuck" Neinas wrote to Byers, the DGWS thought "they have the right to the colleges, without having any program." Meanwhile, the NCAA had a program without the will of its presidents or athletics directors to assume responsibility for women's sports.[61]

The CIAW and its parent organization, the DGWS, had a fundamental problem: many faculty members who were part of the organization were philosophically opposed to expanding competitive sporting opportunities for college women. At the beginning of the decade, Phoebe Scott had addressed the issue with her colleagues, urging them to change their view on women and athletics. As she told her peers, "We have educated a whole generation to believe that somehow there was something slightly evil or immoral in competition for the highly skilled girl." She then stated to the DGWS, "We cannot be bound by the traditions and thinking of the past." For taking such a stand, Scott was criticized by her senior peers.[62] This attitude was captured in an opinion piece published in the AAHPER's *Journal of Health, Physical Education, and Recreation* in 1974. In it, Sandra Stutzman and Charles McCullough noted the DGWS's "steady refusal to change" frustrated young women athletes.[63]

The CIAW's conflicting views limited opportunities for growth. Created in January 1966, it would be almost two years before the CIAW announced that it would sponsor additional collegiate championships. The commission did so only after Walter Byers challenged the CIAW's self-proclaimed right to govern women's intercollegiate athletics. As he had stated to the chair of the CIAW, "The question of whether the NCAA is the organization to take on this job is a question yet to be determined."[64]

To make matters more challenging for the CIAW, the AAHPER was a professional association populated by individual faculty memberships. Institutions themselves were not members, nor did they financially support the organization. As the CIAW announced its rollout of multiple national championship events, it was still trying to determine a way to fund a full-time employee to assist with the planning. Without revenue from institutional dues, the CIAW needed subsidies from its parent organization. In 1967, Byers himself had recommended to the DGWS leadership that they move away from an academic organization and adopt an institutional membership organization.[65]

In February 1971 the NCAA's legal counsel informed its executive director that the practice of prohibiting women from participating in NCAA events, along with the lack of programs and opportunities for female athletes, placed the NCAA in a precarious legal position. The NCAA's exclusion of women probably would not stand in a legal battle if a female athlete or administrator brought a discrimination suit against the NCAA.[66] Conversely, the DGWS viewed the NCAA's legal interpretation as a threat to its control of women's sports, and late in 1971 it responded by announcing the creation of the Association for Intercollegiate Athletics for Women (AIAW) in order to combat the NCAA's potential takeover.

In June 1972, the same month as the passage of Title IX, the CIAW officially dissolved and transferred the administrative duties of women's intercollegiate athletics to the AIAW. The new membership-based organization consisted of more than 270 founding member institutions. In its bylaws, the AIAW banned athletic scholarships and off-campus recruiting in an attempt to keep athletics within the educational framework of each college, with athletes naturally matriculating from member institutions. In essence, the AIAW's model resembled earlier attempts to safeguard men's college athletics—all of which had failed earlier in the twentieth century.

Walter Byers did not oppose the creation of the AIAW. In fact, he had recommended such an association to the DGWS four years earlier. Byers had been a proponent of an institutional membership association because it provided the best opportunity to remove faculty control and usher in competitive athletics for women. Athletics controlled by universities provided a direct challenge to the AAU and opened the possibility of a merger with the NCAA.

The Unassuming Passage of Title IX

Two years before the creation of the AIAW, the move toward greater equality in higher education for women was already underway. In 1969, Bernice "Bunny" Sandler had been passed over for seven different faculty positions at the University of Maryland. Although she had been an excellent student and had completed her doctorate, she was unable to secure a position. In a moment of candor, one of her male colleagues told her, "Let's face it . . . you come on too strong for a woman."[67]

The unapologetic acknowledgment of the gender discrimination she faced led Sandler to study higher education and the prejudice women faced in academic hiring. Working with the Women's Equity Action League (WEAL), Sandler gathered evidence to document "an industry-wide pattern" of discrimination against women in academia. WEAL filed a complaint with the US Department of Labor against all higher education institutions in general and the University of Maryland in particular.

Sandler and WEAL also pushed for a legislative solution to sex discrimination, and they soon won the support of important politicians. Representatives Edith Green (Oregon), Martha Griffiths (Michigan), and Patsy Mink (Hawaii) joined to oppose sex discrimination in educational settings. Another supporter, Representative Shirley Chisholm (New York), argued that her sex had been a much greater hinderance to her success than the fact that she was an African American.[68] Senator Birch Bayh (Indiana), whose wife had been denied admission to the University of Virginia because she was a woman, also joined the cause. With the support of these and others, Title IX was added to the Educational Amendments of 1972. The section stated, "No person in the United States shall, on the basis of sex, be excluded from participation in, be denied the benefits of, or be subjected to discrimination under any education program or activity receiving Federal financial assistance."

The thirty-seven words "that changed America" would become monumental in the struggle for women's athletics, but at the time, sports were hardly considered in its passage. The impetus for the legislation dealt with admissions, job opportunities, and professional advancement. But athletics had become an important piece of the fabric of higher education. After the bipartisan legislation passed through Congress, it was signed by President Richard Nixon on June 23, 1972.

Once the bill had become law, it was then sent to the Department of Health, Education, and Welfare (HEW) in order to provide an interpretation of the law for its successful execution. Only then did the NCAA get involved in the lobbying effort to minimize the law's impact on intercollegiate athletics. HEW faced a unique challenge: Title IX had not been passed with athletics in mind, but in true American fashion, the greatest battles regarding the law in its early years involved an interpretation of how the law applied to sport—something the law, as written, had not attempted to address.

Institutional Indifference and Avoidance: Excuses, Excuses

One irony of Title IX legislation was that its now familiar close tie to advocacy for women's athletics at schools, colleges, and universities was unexpected. Between 1970 and 1972, advocates who drafted the proposed legislation had primary focus on access and admission in academic fields where women had been historically underrepresented, such as the natural and physical sciences, engineering, mathematics, medicine, and law. Late in the deliberations the proposition surfaced that interscholastic and intercollegiate athletics that formally and legally defined themselves as "educational activities" would therefore come under the purview of the nondiscrimination features of the evolving Title IX. That proposal met with strong resistance from college athletics directors and coaches of major sports such as football and basketball, with the stern warning that if enacted, "it would end college sports as we know it."[69] The men's coaches' objections were in fact one of the precise reasons college sports were incorporated into the Title IX case—to change what colleges and their athletics officials had enjoyed as "business as usual."

As HEW developed its first draft of the guidelines for Title IX, the NCAA lobbied against applying the law to intercollegiate athletics. The president of the National Association of Collegiate Directors of Athletics, John Winkin, wrote President Nixon, urging him not to "destroy the growth of intercollegiate athletics" by allowing a liberal interpretation of Title IX and its application to college sports.[70] Then Republican John Tower, a Texas senator, lobbied to have revenue sports exempted from Title IX, arguing that undermining those sports would hurt other men's and women's teams alike. Tower's proposed exemption aligned with Walter Byers's assertion that equal sharing of all athletic revenue could lead to the demise of intercollegiate athletics.[71]

The Department of Health, Education, and Welfare rejected Tower's amendment and instead adopted an amendment by another Republican senator, New York's Jacob Javitz. The Javitz amendment made an accommodation to avoid strict equality in the distribution of funds between different programs. It stated that "reasonable provisions considering the nature of particular sports" could be made. Although the amendment provided the flexibility many Title IX opponents requested, Byers and the NCAA disliked the Javitz amendment because it acknowledged federal oversight in the implementation of Title IX.[72]

The NCAA and its supporters had issued doomsday proclamations about college sports if Title IX forced athletics departments to share revenue with women's sports. Some individual college and university officials also resisted including sports for women on the untested claim that resources for formal women's intercollegiate athletics programs would drain existing budgets and established (men's) sports. It's useful, then, to test this hypothesis in light of financial trends in intercollegiate athletics after passage of Title IX in 1972 into the 1980s.[73]

The federal government granted to colleges and universities nationwide a generous grace period during which Title IX goals were not enforced. It justified as a reasonable allowance for athletics departments and their host colleges to achieve gradual but persistent compliance with equity and equality for women's college sports programs. It was a good-faith gesture to promote "good sports." Unfortunately, many colleges and universities were laggard in honoring the letter or spirit of Title IX. Consider the allegation that providing some approximation of adequate funding for women's sports would drain the established men's sports.

The historical record is that by the 1970s, many big-time NCAA college sports programs (for men) were suffering financial strains. According to the data, many men's athletics programs ran a deficit. More surprising was that often the alleged revenue of football and men's basketball operated in the red. The first source of inflated spending was that numerous colleges added new men's teams. An additional financial strain on men's college sports programs was a move to extend athletic scholarships (grants-in-aid) to a large number of nonrevenue sports such as baseball, track and field, hockey, wrestling, gymnastics, tennis, swimming, and water polo. Conferences such as the SEC analyzed the financial situation and by 1978 rejected the strategy of reducing expenses in favor of attempting to increase revenues through television broadcasts and other media enterprises. This strategy seldom worked. Men's sports, including football, often received subsidies from the university.

What were the financial burdens that women's sports placed on the athletics budget following the passage of Title IX? A 1973 NCAA survey revealed that budgets in big-time athletics programs averaged approximately $2 million. The revenue-producing sports in these departments gave an average of $9,000 to women's athletics.[74] In 1977, within the category of NCAA Division I-A member institutions, expenditures on women's varsity sports was fourteen percent of the institutional support budget for all intercollegiate sports. A snapshot of the aggregate data is that, on average, an NCAA Division I-A athletics budget was $3 million per year, with the women's athletics budget averaging $97,000 per year. The average institutional salary for a men's basketball coach was between $60,000 to $70,000 per year. The highest salary for a woman coaching a women's intercollegiate basketball team in 1976 was $9,000 per year, earned by Pat Summit of the University of Tennessee.

The end date of 1977 is important because it precedes by four to five years the start of women's intercollegiate sports being under the purview of the NCAA and before rigorous federal enforcement of Title IX compliance. Despite these exemptions, the NCAA Division I-A men's programs already were showing persistent, growing deficits. Without any responsibility for funding or sponsoring women's sports, athletics directors opted for a strategy of "tiering," characterized by differential funding and resources depending on the prestige or priority of a sport. At some universities, notably the Universities of Colorado and Washington, athletics directors and university boards of trustees approved the elimination of such men's sports as wrestling, baseball, tennis, and swimming. Cost-cutting measures and strained men's varsity sports budgets were a fact of NCAA life long before these programs had any responsibility to offer and fund women's varsity sports.

Between 1979 and 1981 the University of Maryland's men's intercollegiate sports ran a deficit of $1 million per year, including net losses of $300,000 from football and $150,000 from men's basketball. Men's college sports by the late

1970s showed few signs of fiscal fitness. Most troubling was that the trend of deficits was going to extend over time to a growing number of big-time men's sports programs.

Even as women's sports grew after the passage of Title IX, it did not come at the expense of men's programs. For example, when the University of North Carolina at Charlotte decided to move women's sports out of the Physical Education Department and into the athletics program, Coach Judy Rose noted that the women's budget grew from $10,000 to $83,000 almost overnight. Nevertheless, the remainder of UNCC's athletic budget of $2.5 million supported men's programs. In the mid-seventies, the University of Texas rapidly expanded the women's athletic budget to $128,000, but it paled in comparison to the more than $3 million available to the entire athletics department. Texas was not alone, and the impressive gains made across the country paled in comparison to the size of men's athletic budgets.[75]

Walter Byers noticed this growth and did not plan to transfer funds from revenue sports like football to nonrevenue sports without maintaining oversight. Just before the NCAA's annual convention in January 1975, Byers announced to the NCAA council that because of the logistical, financial, and legal implications, the NCAA should begin sponsoring women's sports. Failure to do so would leave the NCAA open to lawsuits and create an inefficient duplication of programs. The "only satisfactory approach" was to govern both men's and women's sports. The NCAA council then allowed its membership to vote on bringing all women's championships under its umbrella or offer select "pilot championships." NCAA members soundly voted down both measures.[76]

All of this political maneuvering occurred before the Department of Health, Education, and Welfare delivered its 1975 regulations to Congress and the president. The guidelines affirmed the prohibited discrimination based on sex and provided ten factors that would address "equal opportunity" in athletics. The regulations remained vague and open to interpretation. Interestingly, the regulations encouraged expeditious implementation but still provided three additional years as an "adjustment period" for colleges and universities. Issuing of the new guidance also provided an opportunity for additional comments. Once again, both sides came with their complaints during the hearings. With nearly a thousand comments on the regulations, Caspar Weinberger quipped, "I had not realized . . . that the most important issue in the United States today is intercollegiate athletics."[77]

Gains in Women's Sports and the NCAA (Legal) Challenge to Title IX

The Department of Health, Education, and Welfare's three-year grace period for universities to implement compliance procedures for Title IX witnessed rapid growth in women's athletics, legal attempts by the NCAA to nullify Title IX in the sports realm, and multiple failed attempts by Walter Byers to convince the NCAA to vote for offering women's college championships. The NCAA sued HEW in 1976, arguing that Title IX regulations did not apply to athletics programs because athletics departments did not receive any direct financial aid. The case, *NCAA v. Califano* (1978), was dismissed twice (once on appeal). The courts determined that the NCAA's independent (association) status did not allow it to sue HEW. Not a single NCAA member institution joined the suit, and the case died.[78]

During the NCAA's lawsuit, Walter Byers continued pushing for the NCAA to assume control of women's athletics. In 1976 the NCAA stopped participating in its joint AIAW-NCAA Committee. In 1977, Byers pushed to have women's sports added at NCAA Division II level, but the motion was defeated in early 1978. The following year, a vote on adding women to NCAA Division III ended with the same result. Having grown into a powerful executive director over the previous quarter century, Byers rarely faced multiple defeats at all divisions of the NCAA. Having been rebuffed, Byers changed his strategy to bring women's athletics under the NCAA's control. Instead of campaigning through the NCAA council, Byers began recruiting likeminded individuals—both men and women—at the institutional level to promote his plan to offer women's sports championships.[79]

Byers's plan to recruit key Division I programs to adopt women's athletics would ultimately succeed because of a number of converging factors. An essential impetus for success stemmed from the tremendous growth of women's sports. In the late sixties, competitive intercollegiate sports were just beginning to develop, and approximately 15,000 young women participated. By 1972 and the passage of Title IX, that number had grown to 30,000. With the legal force of Title IX, the expansion of girls' sports at the high school level, and a growing interest in women's athletics, the number had swelled to nearly 60,000 by the 1976–77 academic year. This growth developed as a result of team expansion at AIAW member institutions. From 1972 to 1978 the number of women's basketball teams expanded from 251 to 883. The two most "acceptable" sports women grew as well. Tennis jumped from 231 to 773 teams, while swimming programs grew from 184 programs to 408. The population of male athletes grew from just over 150,000 participants in 1967 to 168,000 in 1977. Clearly, men's opportunities vastly outweighed those for women, but the percentages and real number of participants revealed that change was underway, despite the efforts of many in the NCAA.[80]

Closely tied with the growing number of female student-athletes, funding for women's programs expanded as well. Although the numbers remained embarrassingly distant to the money available for men, real gains had been made. The budget for women's athletics at the University of Texas jumped from $20,000 for the 1973–74 academic year to $128,000 for 1975–76.[81] Firebrand Linda Estes, the women's AD at the University of New Mexico, with a sympathetic president, watched her budget expand from $5,000 annually to $118,000 in the matter of four years. Increased funding meant increased scholarships as well. In 1974, only sixty schools offered athletic scholarships, but that had grown to more than five hundred institutions by 1978. While drastically below men's levels, by 1978 almost one-third of college athletes were female, and women's sports commanded sixteen percent of athletic budgets.[82]

While women's sports remained drastically below the men's level, the tangible gains during the 1970s, a clear result of Title IX, should not be overlooked. The Pac-10 conducted an anonymous survey among its member institutions to track the gains in women's sports since the passage of Title IX. In 1973, one institution provided $60,000, which represented the highest expenditure for women's athletics. Another school offered $50,000, while three others provided approximately $40,000. The lower half of the conference offered around $30,000, while the lowest level of funding from "Institution H" stood at $7,205. By the 1977–78 school year, the lowest level of funding reported $63,200, while the strongest funding came from an institution providing more than $500,000 in operating expenses. The majority of institutions stood well above $250,000 in funding. This did not represent "equal" support (one institution came close at forty-seven percent), but the gains represented a move in which more than twenty-five percent of sport expenditures went to women's athletics in the conference. Title IX had not brought equality, but it prompted unparalleled growth in participation.[83]

Walter Byers remained well aware that as women's opportunities expanded, most institutions merged their athletics departments into a single administrative unit. No woman was offered an athletics director post in the mergers, but many women remained ADs over women's sports—reporting to male athletics directors. At the beginning of the 1970s, most men's and women's athletics programs operated separately. As women's opportunities and budgets expanded, institutions began merging men's and women's programs. By the late 1970s, approximately eighty percent of institutional athletics departments had been combined. This fact strengthened Byers hand as he strategically moved forward with his plans to offer women's sports.[84]

Another impetus for integration of sports programs was incredible inflation during the late 1970s. This inflationary pressure led to streamlining services across university departments and programs. The NAIA provided a perfect example. With a contentious relational history with the NCAA, the NAIA remained sensitive to athletics administrators who possessed smaller budgets and remained committed to a different model of athletics. Because of this context the AIAW and the NAIA remained natural allies during the 1970s. When the final rules for Title IX were issued by HEW in 1979 and budgetary pressures forced economy, the NAIA finally caved and announced it would begin offering women's championships the following year.[85]

Consensus and Conflict within the Association for the Intercollege Athletics for Women

Not long after the passage of Title IX and the creation of the AIAW, the young organization faced its first legal challenge. Student-athlete Kathy Kemper attended Marymount College in Florida on an athletic scholarship to play tennis. The newly formed AIAW barred Kemper from its national tennis championship because her grant-in-aid violated the new association's policies. Marymount College's PE instructor and tennis coach, Fern "Peachy" Kellmeyer, proceeded to file a lawsuit against the AIAW and multiple allied educational organizations, which had supported the AIAW's scholarship ban.

A West Virginia native, Kellmeyer had played tennis in the sixties at the University of Miami. After dominating women's competition, Miami's tennis coach listed Kellmeyer on the men's roster. The move touched off a firestorm as Miami's best men's tennis player, South African Rodney Mandelstam, threatened to quit the team because of Kellmeyer's presence. As Mandelstam stated, he "had not come 10,000 miles to play on a team with a girl." He proceeded to note that he feared the psychological struggle a man from another team might face if being beaten by a "girl." Miami's coach held firm, and Kellmeyer ended up playing for both the women's and men's tennis teams.[86]

Kellmeyer was the type of competitive athlete who had challenged the philosophy of the Division of Girls and Women's Sports during the previous decades. Now armed with Title IX, Kellmeyer brought the suit to represent her scholarship players at Marymount College and Broward Community College, where she also coached the women's tennis team. Utilizing the Equal Protection Clause of the Fourteenth Amendment, the suit argued that the AIAW, along with numerous other educational organizations (which supported the AIAW), were denying women the same constitutional rights offered to men. After examining the facts, the National Education Association (NEA), which was also named in the lawsuit, refused to support the AIAW's grant-in-aid ban, so the AIAW acquiesced. Kellmeyer dropped the suit, and colleges and universities were free to provide athletic scholarships to women.

Title IX and the Fourteenth Amendment to the US Constitution dismantled a foundational piece of AIAW's "amateur" philosophy for women's athletics. The debate also revealed some of the first dissension within the organization. Kellmeyer and other women coaches and administrators felt betrayed by the very association that they believed had been established to advocate for women in competitive college sports. Linda Estes at the University of New Mexico became a chief critic of the organization. As Estes explained, she wanted to strengthen the AIAW but could not "as long as the officers of the AIAW continue to *encourage* discrimination against women by women." Estes believed that women's leadership in the AIAW still held the "anti-competition, anti-Olympics" views of the DGWS, which she sarcastically said stood for "Don't Give Women Sports."[87]

The expansion of women's athletic scholarships, the relative increase in budgets, and policy implications of an increasing level of championships created additional cracks in the solidarity of the AIAW leadership. As historian Mary Jo Festle noted, "In the mid-1970s the AIAW stood at a crossroads. One wing wanted a somewhat more competitive version of the old PE programs while the other wanted to jump wholeheartedly into big-business sports."[88] A lack of shared vision became a growing problem. In many ways, the AIAW responded in a manner that resembled the NCAA. By 1975 the AIAW began seeking out sponsors for the association. Eastman Kodak paid six thousand dollars to sponsor the AIAW all-American basketball team. The organization secured modest clothing and apparel sponsorships as well. Women's leadership sought out television contracts and changed their recruiting policies. Soon, complaints surfaced among coaches concerning prohibited inducements and paying for players. The AIAW had completed a 180-degree turn with regard to its philosophy. This led to the creation of "divisions" within the organization to separate the larger schools from the smaller institutions, just as the NCAA had done.[89]

The move into commercial athletics required an attorney, and the AIAW secured the services of Margot Polivy from the firm Renouf, McKenna, and

Polivy. After her first year as legal counsel, she became a lightning rod for controversy during the remainder of her time with the AIAW. When Laurie Mabry from Illinois State became AIAW president in 1975, she created a subcommittee to address challenges with the AIAW's legal counsel. Apparently, Polivy had not completed all of the legal work requested of her, and many believed the AIAW leadership had allowed Polivy's personal (rather than legal) opinions dictate the organization's policies.[90]

As Maybry stated, Polivy possessed "self-confidence in her ability to see the only right way in all instances." Maybry further argued that Polivy's propensity to assume control of the organization needed to be addressed, and Polivy should be informed that her legal opinions should be "advisory in nature—rather than an individual that most singly are frightened to deal with." Complaints concerning Polivy also came from the AIAW members at the regional level. By the end of her term as president, Maybry decided that Polivy, rather than the members of the AIAW board, was determining organizational policy, so she attempted to remove her as legal counsel. Polivy, however, had her supporters among the AIAW leadership. Past president Leotus Morrison, who had hired Polivy, argued that the problem was with the women who were not used to Polivy's strong leadership and blamed the AIAW leadership for not handling their own responsibilities in an efficient manner. Maybry's efforts fell short, by a single vote.[91]

As Margot Polivy remained with the AIAW, her legal fees continued to increase. During her first year, the AIAW paid twenty-six thousand dollars for her services. Three years later, the AIAW paid her firm seventy-five thousand dollars. Trying to defend herself from critics who believed the AIAW was spending too much of its budget on legal fees, Polivy asserted that the NCAA spent approximately twenty percent of its budget on legal counsel. NCAA records for that year, however, state that the NCAA spent less than four percent for legal services. Polivy and her firm continued charging even more, all while asserting that her firm was providing a discounted rate. On average, the AIAW paid Polivy and her firm approximately twenty percent of its modest revenue. During the 1981–82 year, the AIAW spent more than forty percent of its revenue on legal expenses. Yet during Polivy's time as legal counsel, the AIAW never used even ten percent of its budget to finance its own championships.[92]

Linda Estes, the outspoken women's athletics director at the University of New Mexico, disapproved of Polivy and the direction she had been taking the AIAW. Questioning both Polivy's costs and her behavior and hoping the organization's members would relieve her of service, Estes sent all AIAW members a copy of the AIAW's retainer agreement with Polivy. This action angered the AIAW's Executive Committee, which called Estes's moves unprofessional. Then, at the AIAW Annual Assembly, the committee never addressed Estes's position. Polivy was clearly in control, and her single focus remained keeping the NCAA out of women's athletics—a position that neither she nor the AIAW ultimately controlled. Title IX demanded greater opportunities for women, but it did not prohibit the NCAA from offering women's sports.[93]

Sensing the AIAW's primary purpose had shifted from offering more opportunities for collegiate athletics to protecting its own power, UCLA's Judie Holland and USC's Barbara Hedges created the Council of Collegiate Women Athletic Administrators in 1979. Nine other like-minded women's athletics directors, including Linda Estes, joined the organization. The purpose of the group was to encourage greater opportunities for women to play college sports. Frustrated with governance of the AIAW, the council determined that female college athletes would be better served if they joined the NCAA. This small but powerful group of women eventually gave Walter Byers the support he needed, at the Division I level, to turn the tide on the battle for women's college sports.[94]

As the NCAA moved slowly toward the integration of women's athletics, another organization first made the move. In the late seventies, the NAIA announced that it was exploring the option of sponsoring a women's basketball tournament for its members. The news devastated the AIAW leadership. While the NCAA and the AIAW had been political foes, the NAIA had largely supported the AIAW and its efforts. Unlike the antagonistic relationship with the NCAA, the NAIA cooperated with and encouraged expansion of the AIAW. The high inflation and stagnant economy of the 1970s forced the small colleges of the NCAA to move toward consolidation of athletics programs. With men's and women's athletics programs housed within the same department, offering a women's championship made sense. So, the NAIA made plans to offer a national basketball tournament for women at the end of the 1980–81 season.[95]

With the NAIA announcing its intentions to delve into women's championships, it appeared that the smaller schools in the NCAA would follow suit. Trying to head off the intrusion, in 1979 the AIAW called for a five-year moratorium on any changes in women's intercollegiate athletics—including a prohibition of the NCAA or NAIA providing women's championships. The AIAW request was too little, too late. The NAIA refused to rescind its plan to incorporate women's sports. All eyes turned to the NCAA.

Following the NAIA's lead, in 1980 the NCAA's Division II and III institutions voted to begin offering women's athletic championships. The next year, at the NCAA convention, members considered doing the same at the Division

I level. Unlike the relatively convincing vote for incorporating women's sports at the DII and DIII levels, the battle for control of the big-time programs was far closer and the debate more contentious. Members initially rejected the motion to sponsor DI women's championships by a razor-thin margin. After a break and a request for another vote, however, the tally ended up in favor of offering nine women's sports championships beginning during the 1981–82 academic year. The AIAW sued, requesting an injunction against the NCAA operating a women's basketball tournament, but it lost the case.[96]

During the 1981–82 academic year, both the AIAW and NCAA sponsored women's national tournaments. On March 28, 1982, two national champions were crowned. Rutgers won the AIAW championship, while Louisiana Tech claimed the NCAA tournament crown. Two teams may have won championships, but the AIAW suffered greater losses off the court. Of the top twenty teams in the country, seventeen chose to participate in the NCAA tournament. Television networks and sponsors also terminated their contracts with the AIAW.

Even though the AIAW would have retained hundreds of members for the following year, the organization chose not to renew memberships. Instead, the AIAW ended its administration of women's college sports in 1982 and filed an antitrust lawsuit against the NCAA, arguing that the men's organization offered "irresistible inducements" designed to destroy the AIAW and monopolize intercollegiate sport. US District Judge Thomas P. Jackson found that some individuals making such claims represented institutions that had actually participated in the AIAW tournament, proving that the inducements were not irresistible. The judge also found that what historians have characterized as a "hostile takeover" was the opposite. Member institutions themselves had voted for the NCAA to offer women's championships. In addition, the NCAA allowed its membership to participate in either organization's tournament, and when both organizations sponsored women's events in 1981–82, more schools participated in the AIAW events. While participation among women in college athletics had exploded during the 1970s, the idea of women's intercollegiate athletics controlled by women had died with the decision handed down in *AIAW v. NCAA* (1984).

Intercollegiate Sports for Women: A Complex Legacy

Title IX proved to be a watershed moment in women's college athletics, but the history reveals that a much richer and more complex story existed before and after the passage of the famous legislation. After World War II, women's college sport was controlled by women physical education instructors who designed it for healthy "play" and broad participation among women matriculates. In the 1950s the women's collegiate population remained largely white and upper or upper-middle class. Athletics for these students provided a last bastion of the amateur model inherited by the British upper class, and it was maintained by women professors and professional organizations such as the American Association of Health, Physical Education, and Recreation.

The debate concerning the role of athletics for collegiate women carried with it a subtext surrounding issues of gender and sexuality. These conversations remained taboo for most of the twentieth century, and they usually only gained attention when male sportswriters discussed "Amazons," "Muscle Molls," or women who seemed to break those stereotypes. The conservative ethos of the post–World War II Era only helped maintain these conventions and limit the opportunities of athletics for women.

Already marginalized, Black collegiate women athletes were the first to break the mold of the appropriate or "polite" way to engage in sports. Already outside of the elite groups that helped set cultural standards, two HBCUs experienced success by engaging in recruiting and intense training. Tuskegee and Tennessee State became the first colleges to gain notoriety for Olympic success, even as American women had relatively poor showings in international competition when compared to other nations.

The Cold War culture and a battle for control over amateur athletics between the AAU and the NCAA soon involved women's athletics. This development predated Title IX and the struggles faced by the AIAW. It also highlighted the role of women's sport in the American psyche and in Cold War diplomacy. Americans expected to be "the best" (i.e., highly specialized and intensely trained). The philosophy and governance of women's athletics by physical educators—both men and women—generally prevented this from happening. Knowing more competitive opportunities for women were on the horizon, the NCAA's executive director, Walter Byers, began making plans for the administration of women's intercollegiate athletics. Few within the male-only organization shared his vision.

When Title IX was signed by President Richard Nixon, few had even considered its ramifications for intercollegiate athletics, but it quickly became a focal point of civil rights legislation. Just as the bill was passed, the AAHPER created the Association for Intercollegiate Athletics for Women. Its mission was to develop athletics as a natural part of the higher education enterprise, as defined by faculty members. As such, the AIAW banned recruiting and athletic scholarships. Commercialized athletics, it argued, fostered myriad problems that had been on display among institutions competing in the NCAA. In short, the AIAW planned to promote a "women's model" of athletics far different than the commercialized "men's model" adopted by the NCAA.

Many historical accounts of the "hostile takeover" have left the impression that when the NCAA offered women's championships, it commercialized them. Scholar Ying Wushanley offered an alternate historical perspective. He revealed that in its failed attempts to maintain women's control of women's college sports, the AIAW had adopted the commercial model *before* the NCAA and NAIA offered opportunities for women. In 1979 the AIAW formally terminated its association with the AAHPER, the organization that anchored the educational/athletic model.

The AIAW's legal separation from the AAHPER highlighted an often overlooked event in college sports history: a faculty-led group gave up any legal authority over all of women's college athletics. Shortly thereafter, the newly independent AIAW sold its television rights to NBC and a fledgling cable company called ESPN. AIAW's president then proclaimed, "Recognition, money, and winning are not incompatible with an educational model of athletics." A half century earlier, the Carnegie-funded study *American College Athletics* had argued just the opposite when highlighting the abuses in men's athletics. In less than a decade, the mission of the AIAW had changed.[97]

The battle that ensued between the AIAW and the NCAA offered a decade of complex history that created odd alliances and cast a troubling light on the allure of power in administering "amateur" athletics. When the NCAA voted to begin offering women's championships at the DI or big-time level, the measure would likely not have passed had it not been for a small group of powerful women's athletics directors who determined that the NCAA provided a better option than the AIAW at promoting high-level college sports for women. Not all of those who voted to keep the two organizations separate were interested in promoting women's sports, however. For example, Arkansas football coach and athletics director Frank Broyles represented one of the many men's ADs who had sided with the AIAW in voting against the NCAA's move to sponsor women's events. Indifference (rather than advocacy) provided a reason some male coaches and athletics directors were willing to vote against offering women's sports. Clearly, there were more than two sides to the debate.[98]

After the NCAA voted to sponsor women's championships, the lawsuit filed by the AIAW provided additional perspectives worth noting. When Title IX became law in 1972, only six percent of athletics programs had integrated men's and women's programs. By 1983, eighty percent had merged. In the process, not a single female became the athletics director over a men's program. Instead, most women's athletics directors accepted the title of assistant AD and proceeded to administer athletics through the already developed structure of the men's athletics department. As this occurred, the AIAW provided an invaluable national network for college athletes and their female administrators.

Nevertheless, Margot Polivy and other leaders within the AIAW shifted their original focus from providing championships to preventing the NCAA from doing so. This bothered a minority of women's athletics directors. As former AIAW president and women's athletics director at UCLA, Judith Holland testified during the litigation: "The AIAW does not devote its financial resources to national championships. The lack of attention directly and adversely affects women student-athletes." Holland supported the NCAA, therefore, because she believed it offered "superior quality."[99]

Looking back at the AIAW's failed attempts to maintain control of women's college sports, in 1993, former AIAW president Christine Grant surmised that "90 percent" of the organization's efforts had been spent on fighting the NCAA, and that left "only ten percent of the energies to do the things that should have been our primary considerations." Her conclusion was correct, but the historical record suggests that it might not have mattered. The same Victorian Era British influences in American higher education that created the ethos of the amateur also created a similar myth that convinced many men and women in American higher education that competitive athletics developed virtues in men but created vices in women. This belief caused male and female administrators in colleges to clamp down on competitive intercollegiate competition among women and replace it with play days designed for healthy leisure. This general view held sway well into the 1960s and beyond.[100]

Guided by faculty members, women's sports remained almost entirely uncommercialized and unprofessionalized. Then, the feminist movement altered many opinions regarding the role of women in American culture, and the Cold War galvanized patriotic fervor for athletic champions—including women. In response, the older guard of the women's college sports administration dug in their heels. As Walter Byer's righthand man at the NCAA (but future arch nemesis) Chuck Neinas remembered, the US Olympic Committee approached the DGWS and offered to put money into women's intercollegiate athletics in order to promote competitive sports and improve America's standing in the Olympics. The DGWS rejected the USOC's offer, and as Neinas recalled, "they [the DGWS] didn't want to have too high a level of competition."[101]

Historian Mary Jo Festle supported Neinas's claims when she summarized that women physical educators were not interested in promoting athletes. Instead, they hoped to develop "sports-women." These coeds would be "casually swinging a golf club or a tennis racquet." College women could use sports to embrace their femininity and be a "healthy, vibrant, graceful woman familiar with swimming and croquet." Holding the line, women physical educators discouraged the development of a female athlete who dedicated themselves to mastery of a particular sport. Such a "strong woman" loved competition and strove to perform and win. Adding the complexity of gender, the issue sounded similar to those in men's sports during the nineteenth century.[102]

Since the DGWS, which was housed within the larger academic organization of the AAHPER, rejected the call for competitive athletics in the 1960s, Walter Byers saw an opportunity to use women's athletics as a way to wrest amateur athletic control from the AAU and place it under control of the NCAA. Byers, whose motives were not altruistic with regard to expanding opportunities for women, still managed to envision what the future held. Byers's greatest challenge became convincing the NCAA members, many of whom expressed disinterest to open hostility toward women's sports. The key concern for men's athletics directors centered on the fact that Title IX might force institutions to share money, especially from football.

A common mistake among historians has been to assume that Byers and the NCAA fought women's college sports when they lobbied against Title IX regulations. Unlike the old guard of the DGWS, most men were fine with expanding opportunities for college women to play sports. But they opposed accountability with regard to sharing their revenue. Women athletes did not bother them. Equity did. Therefore men's claims that Title IX would destroy college sports were disingenuous. As Walter Byers would eventually admit in his memoir, it was the platoon system in football, and an ever-increasing appetite to expand funding in football, not the introduction of women's sports, that threatened athletic budgets.[103]

Nevertheless, in the late 1970s and early 1980s, multiple historic events converged, dooming the AIAW's attempts to control women's athletics. First, the final Title IX regulations from HEW were distributed, and it became apparent that universities would be required to offer some move toward equality in women's athletics. Second, the 1970s economy that created stagflation affected college sports' operating budgets, and streamlining operations provided some relief from the skyrocketing costs of college athletics—especially football. Finally, the AIAW had managed to monetize its women's basketball championship.

Although the quarter of a million dollars in television revenue the AIAW would receive paled in comparison to the NCAA's budget, the women's tournament posed a threat to the NCAA's control of the television market. These various historic trends led institutions in the NCAA to finally support what Byers had wanted for years: women's athletic championships.

While women's athletic opportunities at the college level expanded, the demise of the AIAW had another, often overlooked impact. The lack of resources provided to women's athletics programs had created an egalitarian effect in that small schools often challenged and defeated the big-time programs. Immaculata College in Pennsylvania and Delta State University in Mississippi claimed more than half of the women's basketball championships during the AIAW's short history. The first ever NCAA-sponsored women's basketball championship featured Louisiana Tech versus Cheyney State College in Pennsylvania— the first HBCU established in the United States. In a few short years, big-time programs and their resources, with few exceptions, came to dominate the intercollegiate athletics landscape.

The grand irony of Title IX was that its initial impetus did not involve athletics but women working in a university setting. As American culture and the US Constitution would dictate, Title IX created vastly more opportunity for college women playing competitive sports. At the same time, nearly as soon as the legislation passed, the demise of women's control of women's athletics ensued. In a desperate attempt to retain control, the AIAW emulated the NCAA: commercializing athletics while claiming to hold to the amateur mission. As historian Joan M. Chandler noted, the AIAW was a representation of the past, not a reality for the future.[104] She also summarized well the dilemma of intercollegiate sport: "Hypocrisy is a necessary condition for survival among intercollegiate athletic empires . . . the best we can probably do is to mourn the passing of hope for an alternative."[105]

Lonely Voyagers: Exemplary Women in
Intercollegiate Sports

A focus on the larger policy battles in women's intercollegiate athletics has often overshadowed individual women and teams that had a profound impact on women's sports. Their individual (or institutional) stories reveal the courage of pioneers in women's athletics. At the same time, their combined history highlights the difference of opinion among these trailblazers. All wanted greater opportunity and equal treatment for women athletes. Some chose different ways to promote it.

A contrast of two leading figures in women's sports, Donna Lopiano and Linda Estes, highlight the challenges faced by women attempting to provide greater equality for female student-athletes. Both grew up as athletes and had been denied opportunities to play sports because of their sex. Both were vocal advocates for civil rights, especially as applied to women's athletics. Both took different approaches to athletics policy that applied to college women.

Linda Estes became the University of New Mexico women's athletics director in 1971, a position housed in the Physical Education Department. She first organized intramurals, but after Title IX, she began fighting for greater opportunities for college women to play competitive sports. Her desire for women to receive scholarships put her at odds with the AIAW from its earliest years. She challenged the AIAW's decision to continue contracting with Margot Polivy for her legal counsel, and she eventually decided the NCAA provided a far-from-perfect solution for women, but it was a better option than that proposed by the AIAW.

When the NCAA offered women's championships, Estes served as one of the first members of the NCAA's Executive Committee. Already holding a similar position in the AIAW, leadership in the women's organization decided to expel Estes from her position in the AIAW. Upon hearing the news, the UNM president sent letters to AIAW member presidents. The news upset many, and the AIAW lost the votes to remove her from its executive board. Lest one believe Estes had been a traitor to the women's cause, when UNM athletics director and former football coach John Bridgers announced his plans to retire in 1986, he told the *Albuquerque Journal*, "The most disruptive force, the most disruptive person in the seven years I've been here has been Linda Estes. . . . She has consistently and constantly discredited me and the sport of football." Estes liked football, but she believed that its hoarding of funds hindered women's athletic equality. Her no-nonsense disposition frustrated those playing political games. More than fifty years after the passage of Title IX, Linda Estes remembered her idealistic positions often left her feeling as though she was standing alone. Yet on the move to the NCAA, she claimed, "I think there's (still) a long way to go, but we're a lot better off."[106]

Donna Lopiano offers a different perspective. Graduating with a degree in physical education from Southern Connecticut State University in 1968, Lopiano excelled in several sports as a youth and was the top player picked in the Stamford, Connecticut, Little League local draft. She was forbidden to play baseball with the boys, however, because of specific language about gender restrictions in Little League's bylaws. Lopiano started playing women's softball at the age of 16. After graduating college, she was an assistant athletics director at Brooklyn College; coached basketball, volleyball, and softball; and then took on leadership roles in national women's sports associations. Eventually she was named director of women's athletics at the University of Texas and received a succession of honors and appointments in sports policies and programs. In 2019, she was named president of the Drake Group, a nonprofit organization of scholars committed to the reform of college sports. She also was one of the most honored athletes of her era. Her experiences, including being excluded from teams, shaped her dynamic leadership over several decades.

When the NCAA offered women's championships, Lopiano's Texas teams played in the AIAW-sponsored events. Once the AIAW closed its doors and then lost its lawsuit, she remained at the University of Texas into the 1990s to push for greater opportunities. Despite this, in the early 1990s, the football team still boasted more scholarships than all of the women's teams combined. So, she moved on to become the chief executive officer of the Women's Sports Foundation, where she worked to highlight inequities in women's sports and fight for compliance with Title IX. Before she left Texas, however, Lopiano connected a women's coach with an attorney who helped file a claim against UT for violating Title IX. The university settled and vastly expanded its rosters and recruiting money for collegiate women athletes.[107]

Amid the political battles surrounding Title IX and the control of women's athletics, it is easy to forget the students involved and their own part in pushing for equity. For example, in 1974, Mariah Burton accepted an offer to play for Stanford's nascent women's varsity basketball team. The offer came with no scholarship, and the team wore white t-shirts and used tape to put numbers on their shirts. A graduate assistant coached the team, and the girls paid for their own sweatshirts and basketball shoes. Stanford did not offer an athletics trainer, and the women's team played in the Roble Gym while the men played in the Maples Pavilion.[108]

Distressed at the conditions Stanford provided for the women's basketball team, Burton said, "I spent all of my free time in athletics director Dick DiBiaso's office, demanding equal treatment with the men." Stopping by uninvited, Burton would wait for meetings and continuously reminded Stanford's athletics director of the stipulations in Title IX. Friends and teammates Sonia Jarvis and Stephanie Erickson often joined her. After two years of pressure, DiBiaso hired Dotty McCrea, previously an assistant at Immaculata College in Pennsylvania. During Burton's junior year, the team moved all of their games to the Maples Pavilion, and Stanford provided uniforms as well as access to a trainer and the weight room. During Burton's senior season, Stanford finally had a scholarship player. Without her persistence, the struggle would have taken much longer.[109]

Across the country at Yale, the women's crew team implemented a more efficient way to improve their conditions. Unlike the men, the Yale women's crew had no shower or equipment facilities in Derby, Connecticut, where they practiced. After each practice, the women made the thirty-minute drive back to campus to store their boat and take showers. Repeated requests for adequate facilities were denied. The women took a different approach. On a winter day in 1976, nineteen women on the crew team undressed out of their sweats in front of Joni Barnett, Yale's director of physical education. The members had written "TITLE IX" across their chests and backs. Crew captain Chris Ernst read a written statement that began, "These are the bodies Yale is exploiting. On a day like today the ice freezes on this skin. Then we sit for a half an hour as the ice melts and soaks through to meet the sweat that is soaking us from the inside." Within days, a temporary trailer was set up, and the next year the women's crew team had a new boathouse with showers, lockers, and a place to store their boat.[110]

As Donna Lopiano had warned, even with the federal protections of Title IX and the official inclusion in the NCAA, within many colleges, opposition to women's programs was unabashedly blatant and biased. Some students did not even have a team with which to start a protest. For example, Merrily Dean Baker recalled about her first years as Princeton's associate director of athletics and director of physical education. When Baker tried to discuss starting women's crew at Princeton, the head of the Princeton crew program "looked me right in the eye and he said, 'There will be women in this boathouse over my dead body.'"[111]

For several years following 1972 passage of Title IX, both legal decisions and administrative practices showed a checkered, often confusing pattern of what compliance meant for the reformed conduct and place of women's sports programs on campus. One legal setback for proponents of women's sports came about in the case of *Grove City v. Bell*. The US Supreme Court's 1984 decision represented a strict constructionist interpretation of what institutional compliance with Title IX meant—and did not mean. Grove City College's refusal to comply with Title IX had confined the impact of regulatory penalties to pertaining only to its office of financial aid since it was the exclusive institutional recipient of federal student financial aid. No other program or unit—nor the college as a whole—fell under the Title IX regulatory penalties.

The important implication was that henceforth a college whose varsity sports program was not in compliance with Title IX carried little if any jeopardy for the institution's federal research grant projects or other offices and departments, for example. In response to the *Grove City* decision, members of Congress authored and eventually passed the Civil Rights Restoration Act over the veto of President Reagan. The new law required all divisions within a unit (such as a college or university) to comply with civil rights legislation in order to receive federal funding. In essence, the law reversed the Supreme Court's decision in the *Grove City v. Bell* decision.[112]

A sequel was that in the mid-1980s, groups of women's athletes and coaches sought relief in lawsuits when an athletics department complied only nominally in adding women's sports. An important case was Colgate University in Upstate New York and its ice hockey program. Colgate had complied with Title IX by establishing a women's hockey team. But it did so in a marginal way. The women's club had to use cast-off high school uniforms. Practices, known as "ice time," were slotted into late-night and early-morning hours. Road trips to away games relied on vans and little in the way of money for meals and lodging. In contrast, the men's team traveled first class. Financial records from the athletics department showed that Colgate spent fifty times more on men's varsity hockey than it did for the women's team. Starting in 1983, the women student-athletes made repeated requests to the athletics director for their sport to be elevated from club to varsity status. All requests were denied. Reasons for the refusal included the arguments that hockey was an expensive sport; its teams were regional, confined to fifteen states within the continental United States; and there was no base of women's ice hockey in secondary schools. The women student-athletes eventually filed a lawsuit. The 1988 court case led to the decision that Colgate was obligated to grant varsity status and commensurate funding to the women's ice hockey team, starting with the 1993–94 season. Women as pioneering college athletes and coaches had demonstrated courage and commitment on the court and in court.

Just as important as the women mentioned above were the Black women who had played at Tennessee State University, Tuskegee, and other HBCUs. Long before Title IX and women's athletics were part of the national conversation, athletes like Missouri Arledge, Alice Coleman, Mae Faggs, and Wilma Rudolph faced prejudice at the intersection of race and gender. Despite the discrimination they faced, their trailblazing efforts brought acclaim to their universities, their male athletics directors, and the nation. Yet integration and Title IX actually harmed the success of HBCUs, as Black athletes chose to attend universities with greater resources to pursue their academic and athletic careers.

Women's Athletics and American Higher Education

A common thread in the history of college sports has been the many parallels it shares with higher education itself. Some scholars have been tempted to look at intercollegiate athletics and its "sins" and determine that it is an anomaly within higher education. As previous chapters have shown, college sports remain an integral part of American higher education, and their development provides an additional insights and examples of how colleges and universities in America operate. The saga of women's intercollegiate athletics is no different.

In 1980, Harvard president Derek Bok wrote an editorial in the *Public Interest* in which he argued for limited government interference in the affairs of colleges and universities. He noted: "Government intervention may not only narrow diversity, inhibit innovation, and result in costly errors; it can also force universities to spend substantial sums complying with federal regulations." Bok then cited expenses and challenges related to complying with civil rights legislation that required accommodations for individuals with disabilities, occupational safety regulations, among other items. Harvard's president concluded that "As a result, we can be reasonably sure that many academic institutions will have to defray the cost of complying with federal regulations by reducing their budgets for teaching and research."[113]

Bok's argument also included a reference to Title IX. By this time, Harvard and the Ivy League had stepped away from big-time college sports, and yet one of the leading figures in higher education still called for restraint from the federal government in ensuring compliance with its policies. Bok's arguments—along with his assertion that complying with federal mandates would harm teaching and research—were nearly identical to the arguments made by men's athletics directors across the country. Rather than an anecdotal outlier, the NCAA's response to Title IX mirrored the complaints of other university presidents on federal regulations across the board. The NCAA's opposition to federal oversight in athletics was not an anomaly in the world of higher education. Rather, the fight for equality in women's sports provided a public spotlight on the larger academy's feelings toward federal accountability in its diverse endeavors.

If one needs additional evidence of the conservative nature of higher education that still projected liberal platitudes on the larger culture, the University of California, Berkeley, provides a case in point. The first woman anthropologist at UC Berkeley was Laura Nader, hired in 1960. Her tenure track appointment in anthropology, along with a handful of other women faculty members, exemplified the definition of "tokenism." Nader and her female colleagues were not allowed to attend faculty senate meetings at Berkeley even though they were faculty members. It turned out that the faculty meetings were held at the Faculty Club, a privately incorporated building that remained exclusive to men. Professor Nader noticed an open window leading to the men's restroom, so she had another woman faculty member hoist her through the window, and she integrated faculty meetings at Berkeley in the 1960s.[114] Nader's persistence and pioneering commitment resulted in a victory for all women. Her actions, however, stood in contrast to the AIAW's attempts to remain administratively separated and segregated from men's varsity sports programs.

Higher education scholar Welch Suggs noted this dilemma in his work *A Place on the Team: The Triumph and Tragedy of Title IX*. As Suggs stated, "no other segment of academe was required to maintain single-sex programs." In short, the AIAW fought its battle at a time when "the task of regulator and educators alike was to ensure that women did not face discrimination as programs were integrated and opened."[115] As many formerly all-male colleges and universities had opened their doors to women during the previous decades, the AIAW's call for segregated activities ran counter to the desegregation efforts for women and minorities in other areas of American life. In this way, Title IX expanded opportunities for women athletes while it also prompted the demise of the AIAW.

The NCAA's vote to offer Division I women's championships was not the first challenge to gender-segregated administration of athletics. In fact, the big-time NCAA programs remained the last holdout. As high schools offered more young women's sports, they operated under the direction of state high school athletics associations that already existed. The National Junior College Athletic Association began offering women's championships in 1975, and the NAIA announced its decision to provide women's championships in the late 1970s. Divisions II and III of the NCAA followed suit. The Division I vote to offer women's sports incited controversy because it involved more money and power.

The key issue, in the minds of many, was what type of representation women would have upon entering the NCAA. Consider Lincoln University president James Frank's letter to a fellow president in the NCAA. When discussing the minimum number of women that would hold leadership positions in the NCAA, the numbers were far too low for advocates of equality. Frank pointed out that the NCAA intended to hold a minimum of four out of twenty spots for women on the NCAA's Executive Council. In addition, two out of the ten positions on the Executive Committee would be held by women. On the DI steering committee, a minimum of six women would be appointed to the twenty-member committee. Facing criticism, Frank shared the numbers of other higher education committees or boards. The American Association of State Colleges and Universities had one woman and sixteen men. The American Association of Universities did not have a single female on its board. The American Council on Education had six of its thirty-six positions occupied by women, and the National Association of State Universities and Land-Grant Colleges had one woman and twenty men on its executive board.

As James Frank noted, the NCAA's minimum quotas provided a commitment that "exceeds that of any other organization of higher education of which we are aware." As a Black athlete, coach, and university president, Frank understood inequality and had been heralded for his advocacy of women's athletics. Born in 1930, Frank loathed segregation and was a firm believer that "'separate but equal' does not lead to equality." His informative letter revealed that, once again, college sports were not an anomaly in American higher education. Instead, sports' popularity brought a spotlight to challenges already existing in colleges and universities.[116]

Arguably the most legendary coach in women's college basketball, Pat Summitt of the University of Tennessee summed up the dilemma for many. While expressing support for the AIAW pioneers, Summitt added, "I also recognize that what really gave our sport the boost in the eyes of the country was the NCAA. That gave us some clout, and eventually brought about the TV package that otherwise we never would have gotten." Summitt also found the AIAW's governance as "restrictive" and appreciated the opportunity to engage in big-time sports.[117] Opportunities and equality were two different items, and hard-fought battles lay ahead after women joined the NCAA. In addition, the saga that created women's sports and eventually merged them within men's organizations highlighted the inequities faced by women. Many gains continued to be made, but much of the discrimination women faced would continue during the decades after joining the NCAA.

7

The Ascendance of College Sports Business, 1970 to 2000

Deliberations and Decisions in the NCAA

In the world of Walter Byers and the NCAA headquarters in Kansas City, two key threats (or potential opportunities) dominated policy and strategy during the 1960s and early 1970s. The first, a battle with the American Athletic Union for control of amateur athletics and Olympic administration, was inextricably tied to the second: Title IX and the growth of women's intercollegiate sports. The feud that had existed between the AAU and the NCAA for control of amateur athletics was finally resolved with the passage of the Amateur Sports Act of 1978. The law changed the charter of the US Olympic Committee (USOC) by giving it control to create and maintain relationships with national governing bodies for individual sports. The existing bodies, which Walter Byers helped create, had close ties with the NCAA. In effect, the AAU had finally been stripped of any control in governing the NCAA or any Olympic qualifying event. The demise of the AAU strengthened the NCAA's position immeasurably.[1]

With the AAU out of the power struggle, the NCAA had now gained the necessary momentum to remove the Association for Intercollegiate Athletics for Women (AIAW) from its governing role in women's athletics. As this issue evolved during the 1970s, the never-ending spending increases in football created rifts among member institutions in the NCAA. The power struggle that ensued in the NCAA resulted in new divisions—both literal and figurative. Central to the debate was who controlled the finances and how revenues were to be distributed. These disputes produced landmark decisions and policies that ushed in a new era of modern big-time competition.

Since the late 1940s, debates concerning televised college sports—especially football—involved athletics directors and university presidents alike. Preliminary studies revealed that expanded television coverage caused game attendance to decline in various locations around the country. From 1947 to 1950 the number of televisions in America jumped from seven thousand to nine million, and the number would inevitably increase during the next decade.[2]

Gate receipts provided the lifeblood for funding both big-time athletic teams and minor sports. This threat to an essential revenue stream led the NCAA to create a committee in 1951 to study the impact of televised football on game attendance. Chaired by World War II veteran and admiral Tom Hamilton, a standout player for Navy in the 1920s before assuming a career in coaching and athletics administration, the committee determined that televised games had "an adverse effect on attendance." Additionally, it asserted that the growth of televised games had the potential to "destroy college football."[3]

After considering the television committee's report, the NCAA members voted 161–7 to ban institutionally contracted broadcasts and allow the NCAA to develop a national television strategy that would promote the sport by offering a limited number of televised games in order to protect gate receipts. Notre Dame and the University of Pennsylvania remained the most notable holdouts, and despite the vote, both had contract offers for the 1951 season. Penn's location in Philadelphia and its games against other "Ivy League" schools (a term that would not become official for a few more years), provided lucrative TV markets. Notre Dame's status as a football powerhouse and the most prestigious Catholic university in the country afforded it a nationwide fan base.

Penn and its fiery president continued to oppose the NCAA's decision, while Father Joyce at Notre Dame remained less confrontational but equally convinced of the injustice of the NCAA's decision. Although Notre Dame backed away from its contract with the Dumont Network, Penn announced its plan to move forward. NCAA then declared Penn a member "not in good standing," and its elite peers in the Northeast announced that they would boycott their games with the Quakers. Unwilling to lose its Ivy League status, Penn relented and backed out of its contract. Although the threat to gate receipts was real, the competitive advantage television would have given the two universities over every other football team in the country played a role in the landslide vote to give the NCAA regulatory authority over televised football.[4]

With little fanfare outside of Notre Dame and Pennsylvania, the NCAA had assumed control of the relatively new medium and in so doing radically increased its authority over member institutions. Interestingly, the NCAA's regulation of televised football was eventually interpreted as a means to control unbridled commercialism in intercollegiate athletics. While true, the NCAA's initial reason for overstepping its bounds was to keep football ticket revenue from being "destroyed" by television. Commercialism already dominated the thinking of administrators at big-time programs, and in the early days of television, most believed TV threatened an already viable commercial product. This, along with a desire keep Notre Dame and Penn from a competitive advantage, led the NCAA to overwhelmingly pivot from its home rule (i.e., institutional control) policies.[5]

The television policy set in the early 1950s held sway for more than three decades. The NCAA's initial contract with NBC paid less than two million dollars a season to broadcast one game a week, providing the only college game on television. During the next three decades, Walter Byers became one of the most influential individuals in televised and commercialized sports. Byers used the commercially successful "product" of college football to demand substantially more revenue for the NCAA with each new contract negotiation. Additionally, new contracts required a surcharge of approximately five percent of the funds for the NCAA. This allowed maximum flexibility for the football revenue accrued by the organization, as its men's basketball television contract supported day-to-day operations. In addition, television funds helped subsidize the costs of national tournaments for minor sports.

The commercial appeal of televised football increased as networks improved their broadcast philosophy and developed better technology. For example, in the early 1960s, upstart network ABC outbid NBC for the 1961 and 1962 seasons by offering $6.25 million. Roone Arledge changed the cold production style of the 1950s by "humanizing" the game—showing close-ups of cheerleaders, fans, and coach's wives in agony. When CBS won the contract for two years, Tony Verna introduced the "instant replay," giving fans at home a better look of the action on close plays. As college football bounced around from network to network, Walter Byers managed to secure greater funds with each contract. In the mid-1960s, ABC agreed to a four-year contract worth more than $32 million. In each of these contracts, Byers pressured networks to televise lesser-known universities or sports programs, trying to offer some balance for the larger intercollegiate athletics landscape outside of football.[6]

As television contracts grew, so did the NCAA's funding. The NCAA used the annual windfall to subsidize the US federations—the collegiate groups aligned with Olympic sports—which provided a direct challenge to the AAU and its control over amateur Olympic sports. As Ronald Smith noted, by the late 1960s, the NCAA spent more money on the federations than on football projects. By 1970 the NCAA's cut of football revenue supported twelve NCAA initiatives, "only two of which were directly related to football or television."[7] At the same time, mid-major and small programs remained upset that the majority of the television contracts still benefitted the televised football teams, which were overwhelmingly from the power conferences or independents like Notre Dame.

Financial Challenges of the Late 1970s and Early 1980s

College sports shared with all campus programs nationwide severe budget problems in an extended period that Berkeley economist Earl Cheit described as "The New Depression in Higher Education."[8] Despite this shared fate of financial challenge, intercollegiate athletics departments stood apart from other units, especially academic departments, in how they responded and then fared between 1977 to about 1990. One glaring finding is that financial shortfalls for big-time college sports that began to surface around 1977 tended to become more acute over the next decade.[9] In this regard, intercollegiate athletics veered in a different trajectory than overall college and university practices and policies, as most deans, directors, provosts, and department chairs participated in a "managerial revolution" based on data collection and informed planning to promote both effectiveness and efficiency. By 1985, most colleges had adopted disciplined budgeting procedures to keep expenses low and at the same time implement innovations to enhance sources of revenue. To analyze this differential response pattern, it's useful to place an intercollegiate department into context of the overall campus management.

According to economists Arthur Padilla and Janice Boucher, in 1987–88, an appropriate way to think about a big-time intercollegiate athletic budget is that it was comparable to that of a large academic unit, such as a professional school of business, law, or engineering with a budget of about ten to fifteen million dollars per year in 1989–90.[10] This meant that within the ranks of big-time programs, the size of the university sports budget ranged from a low of about seven million dollars to a high of over twenty million dollars. Stanford University had the highest intercollegiate athletics budget in 1989–90, at twenty-four million dollars. Among state universities, the University of Michigan was highest, with twenty-one million dollars. An example of a medium-sized budget was that of the University of Kentucky, at fifteen million dollars.

Eventually, what became unavoidable and undeniable was that many of the premises of big-time intercollegiate athletics financial models ceased to work well, even at established and traditionally strong universities and programs. A good example of the problem was highlighted in a *Sports Illustrated* cover story in 1981 about the University of Missouri's intercollegiate athletics program, including its football team. Despite large crowds, robust ticket sales, and parking and concession revenues, the University of Missouri was running a deficit over several years. This was puzzling because it had many advantages as the state's only big-time football program along with a full slate of men's varsity sports. The problem was that even maximum revenues from traditional sources were insufficient to meet growing expenses of insurance liability, increased number of grants-in-aids (scholarships), and the addition of new varsity sports.[11]

This profile repeated and resonated throughout the major conferences and their member institutions. Financial recordkeeping heretofore had been uneven and idiosyncratic. But compilations and comparisons increasingly provided more detailed documentation, all of which bore the bad news of cost overruns. One obvious response was to trim budgets. But a task force report sponsored by the Southeastern Conference suggested that the response of athletics departments and their related fundraising units and athletics associations was to try to increase revenues rather than reduce expenses.[12]

The National Collegiate Athletic Association required all Division I intercollegiate athletics programs to be "self-supporting." Major revenue sources typically were ticket sales, media rights, advertising, and donations. Athletic contests were geared toward the external community and the public. Student-athletes at DI universities were allowed to receive grants-in-aid, based on athletic ability, irrespective of financial need.

An important distinction within NCAA Division I ranks defined the truly big-time sports programs. Division I-A, which referred to a special category of institutions, had national-caliber football programs with average home attendance of thirty-five thousand per game. By 1990, more than two hundred institutions had Division I-A football programs. About one hundred additional colleges and universities had big-time basketball programs but did not have a big-time football team. According to an American Council on Education report, these were the dominant players in "The Money Game."[13]

A corollary of these categories is that high-profile athletics directors and coaches starting in the 1970s made bold public statements that they saw college sports as a business. Variations on this self-definition included programs that were "in the entertainment business" and "in competition with professional teams for spectators and broadcasts." College sports were not merely a business, they were big business. Problematic, however, is that analysis of data over several years indicates that many programs were not operated successfully as a business. In other words, taking stock around 1989, many big-time programs were losing money. Far from being genuinely self-sustaining, many programs chronically relied on subsidies from universities' general funds to pay departmental bills. Another practice that was contrary to the genuine business model was that many big-time athletics departments received annual revenues from mandatory student fees.[14]

The business character of DI intercollegiate athletics also was suspect in that many departments relied on support from an affiliated unit—an athletics association that had tax-exempt status as a 501(c)3 nonprofit educational activity. This hybrid arrangement meant that a big-time university athletics program enjoyed the simultaneous advantages of a business and that of an educational program. But the Internal Revenue Service exempts only educational activities from taxes, not entertainment.

Attempts to Solve Financial Problems at the National Level

As small colleges and some large universities alike looked for ways to cut costs of football programs in the 1970s, the approximately seventy to eighty big-time football programs regularly found themselves outvoted by small institutions because their votes counted equally on various policy measures. For example, in the early 1970s, the NCAA repealed the "freshman rule" for men's basketball and football. Many big-time programs opposed the move, but smaller football schools hoped to play freshmen in order to get the most out of their scholarship players. It also allowed colleges to drop their junior varsity teams, which provided cost savings to programs.

Less selective universities—many of which would eventually be termed "mid-majors"—championed dismantling the NCAA's 1.6 rule for academic eligibility of its first-year students. This model considered a potential athlete's grade point average, scores on the Scholastic Aptitude Test (SAT), and the strength of their high school curriculum to determine potential success in college. It was the so-called cost-cutters that ditched the 1.6 rule for a flat high school grade point average of 2.0 to be eligible for competition.[15] These two "reforms" in the early 1970s were not the initiatives of big-time programs. As Keith Dunnavant stated, "many big-time football schools were horrified when the NCAA rescinded the so-called 1.6 predictor rule."[16]

When some university leaders, generally from smaller and less wealthy institutions, began agitating for grants-in-aid only to financially needy athletes (a policy that failed for a half century), the big-time programs had enough. Instead, power conferences pushed for divisions within the NCAA that would vote on issues in their own divisions. Tempers flared at the January 1973 conference when the Eastern College Athletic Conference proposed three divisions but wanted each of the 667 institutions to choose their divisional status. Big

Ten Commissioner Wayne Duke said, "I don't believe the E.C.A.C. They say they want reorganization, but I know they don't want any such thing. They just want to ruin the N.C.A.A." The University of Texas football coach summed up the attitude of the big-time sports university by saying, "Texas doesn't want Hofstra telling [Texas] what to do and vice versa." The NCAA decided to hold a special session that summer to devise a reorganization plan.[17]

In August the NCAA approved the creation three divisions, but reorganization proved more complex. One-hundred and twenty-six "major football institutions" would be required to play at the new Division I level in all sports. At the same time, the other members were given a month to identify their preferred division for all non-football sports. The net result was that many mid-major football programs and another 100 non-football institutions (which maintained competitive basketball teams) entered the NCAA's Division I. With 237 members, the approximately 75 big-time programs could still be outvoted.[18]

The NCAA's new television contract included provisions for the Division II and III football schools, which would eventually have their own televised championship games. The NCAA also added more championships for Division III institutions, which were subsidized with NCAA revenue. Even though leaders representing the big-time programs were not entirely pleased with these results, they still hoped to control their own destiny and stem the tide of cost-cutting measures.[19]

Despite the division of the NCAA into three distinct groups, most NCAA institutions remained overextended and continued looking for ways to cut costs and generate more revenue. Even after allowing freshman basketball and football players to participate in varsity sports and limiting the number of football scholarships to 105, there were many institutions stretched to the brink in the 1970s. Of the more than 600 NCAA members, 237 institutions had requested membership in Division I, the big-time sports division. This included more than 100 non-football-playing institutions and many other football schools hoping to beat one of the approximately 80 institutions truly engaged in big-time football. Many of the universities just outside of the big-time programs desperately wanted to keep up with their rivals, but their relatively small fan bases and limited resources made it nearly impossible to compete with big-time universities. That more than 200 institutions wanted to play at the big-time level also revealed the extent to which less powerful schools viewed college sports as a marketing tool for their institutions.

With television contracts for football growing during the previous decades, the NCAA continued to give most of the revenue to the big-time conferences while also funding national tournaments for other members schools. Hence Division II and III institutions benefited from the NCAA's subsidies for its now multiplied national championships. Big-time schools wanted to keep a larger share of the profits they generated from football, and mid-major universities wanted the television profits to help them maintain some semblance of competitive equity. Walter Byers had managed to keep both sides at bay, but that was all about to change.

Stephen Horn's "Robin Hood" Plan at the NCAA and the Creation of the College Football Association

Stephen Horn began serving as the president of California State University, Long Beach, in 1970. Two years into his presidency, the NCAA began an inquiry into Long Beach's basketball program, coached by Jerry Tarkanian. Coach Jim Stangeland's Long Beach football program faced an investigation as well. The investigations revealed multiple rules violations, and both coaches left the institution. Less than a year after joining the newly created Division I, the NCAA placed Long Beach on three years' probation, during which time its basketball and football teams could not be televised or participate in postseason games.[20]

In 1975 the NCAA held another special session aimed at minimizing the costs of athletics programs. President Horn, whose Long Beach teams could not keep up with big-time DI competition while on probation, sent a letter to all the presidents of member institutions in the NCAA. In it, he called for a redistribution of football television funds to favor the smaller divisions and conferences. Horn proposed the idea of splitting bowl game profits as well, which could not be done because contracts were negotiated with individual institutions and not with the NCAA. Even though the number of scholarships on football teams had been limited to 105 by the NCAA in 1973, Horn called for another drastic cut to 65 scholarship players.[21]

Horn's "Robin Hood" plan, as his detractors called it, made little headway in the NCAA. Viewed by many as a shortsighted pitch to help his own institution, solid majorities rejected his proposals. The threat of Horn's plans, however, galvanized the big-time football institutions into action. The major football-playing conferences met to discuss Horn's proposals and find a way to shrink the membership of Division I to universities able to play a certain brand of commercialized football. As representatives from the power conferences discussed the issues at hand, they eventually formed an organization within the NCAA to protect and promote their own interests. In 1976, Big Ten commissioner Wayne Duke made a motion, which was approved, to create the College Football Association.[22]

When the members of the CFA met in Atlanta in early 1977, the Big Ten and the Pacific-8 were absent. Despite protests from some athletics directors and coaches, the presidents of the Big Ten claimed that they feared the new organization placed too much emphasis on commercialized football. Others within the CFA argued that the Big Ten and Pac-8 viewed it as an opportunity to practice academic and athletic snobbery. Afterall, the Big Ten and the Pacific Coast Conference signed an exclusive contract with the Rose Bowl during a time when other conferences were adopting athletic grants-in-aid. When the Big Ten and the Pac-8 eventually adopted athletic grants-in-aid, they did not open the Rose Bowl to other conferences.

In addition, the Big Ten had particularly close ties with the NCAA. The NCAA had once been operated out of the Big Ten office, and Commissioner Duke had worked for Walter Byers at the NCAA. Historian John Sayle Watterson argued that it was "just as likely that the two conferences refused to join [the CFA] because of their strong position in NCAA policy-making and number of TV appearances under the Byers regime."[23] To put it more bluntly, one CFA insider recalled, Wayne Duke and Wiles Hallock (commissioner of the Pac-8) "were always in bed with Walter on all kinds of matters . . . and Byers was deathly afraid of the CFA."[24] Years later, Duke admitted, "We may have felt somewhat elitist" and added, "We looked at football differently than . . . a lot of those people."[25]

Despite these reasons, the CFA carried on without the Big Ten or the Pac-8. The association consisted of the Atlantic Coast Conference, the Southeastern Conference, the Big Eight, the Southwest Conference, the Western Athletic Conference, and key independent universities like Florida State, Notre Dame, Penn State, and Pitt. Father Edmund Joyce of Notre Dame played an important role in the formation of the group, as did Commissioner Duke, until the Big Ten backed out of the group. Eventually, the organization elected Fred Davison, president of the University of Georgia, to become chair of the new organization. Although remembered for its impact on television rights and policy, the early CFA meetings focused on gaining more influence in the NCAA, being able to return some legislative power to conferences or individual institutions, *and* the CFA's often ignored attempt to address the academic crisis in intercollegiate athletics.[26]

As Edmund Joyce would share with the rest of the association, the CFA possessed three key goals. First, the members wanted to preserve high-level competitive football. Second, these institutions desired an equitable distribution of funds for the schools playing at the highest level. Finally, Joyce highlighted the needed for "total academic integrity" among CFA members. The CFA's first attempts to develop a fourth division failed to materialize. Without the support of the Big Ten or Pac-8, the CFA remained unable to convince more than 150 other DI institutions who were not fully big time to let the power schools separate into their own division.[27]

Only when it appeared that the NCAA might be doomed did the CFA gain support for a new division. As the *Washington Post* reported in an article titled "NCAA Divided, May Be Headed for Destruction," many smaller athletic institutions, including Stephen Horn's Long Beach, wanted to further economize athletic budgets by awarding grants-in-aid based on financial need. Conventional wisdom suggested that if the measure passed, the big-time schools would form "a new NCAA" even if the Pac-8 (soon to be Pac-10) and Big Ten refused to leave the NCAA. With the threat of a CFA secession from the NCAA, the financial need-based formula failed to gain traction. As SEC commissioner Boyd McWhorter surmised, such proposals were less about economizing and "more of an attempt to level competition." McWhorter was partly correct, the only way the "mid-majors" could level the playing field and compete with the big-time schools was if the NCAA forced the power conferences to economize.[28]

With that victory at the NCAA, in 1978 the CFA also pushed for the creation of a new division composed of only football powers, which narrowly failed in an NCAA. That summer, the mid-major programs agreed to become members of Division I-AA only after negotiating a deal in which approximately 150 new DI-AA colleges would have a televised football playoff. The NCAA also secured televised playoffs for DII and DIII, along with a handful of minor sport championships. It appeared that the big-time programs were not the only ones interested in television exposure and increased profits. The new divisions, however, failed to meet the CFA's goals. The Big Ten and Pac-10 supported what became known as the Ivy Amendment. Rather than basing DI-A membership on revenues and attendance, the amendment based it on the number of varsity programs the universities offered. Passing by only three votes, the amendment allowed the Ivy League members to remain a part of Division I. It also made developing a consensus for policy at the DI-A level much more difficult, keeping the CFA at bay.[29]

Having won only a slight victory with the creation of Division I-AA, the CFA had even less success when lobbying for academic reform. CFA president Fred

Davison had written Penn State coach Joe Paterno, who chaired the CFA Committee on Academics and Research, and requested that the committee develop a proposal that would return some standards to the admissions process in the college recruiting. By 1978 the CFA offered its "Triple Option," which consisted of a high school GPA of 2.5, a 750 on the SAT, or a 17 on the ACT (formerly known as American College Testing). The NCAA membership voted down the proposal. The CFA, which historians have accused of pushing big-time football and its abuses, proposed these less stringent academic standards in front of the NCAA, and the mid-major members voted against them.[30]

The Big-Time Basketball Alternative

In the meantime, other Division I members that were not football powerhouses began to see the writing on the wall and jockeyed for their own position within the organization. A key legislative change in the NCAA came in 1978 when the NCAA approved a policy to only award "automatic bids" to conferences in which the teams played each other two times (presumably home and away). This move improved the administrative efficiency of the tournament but damaged the long-standing ECAC (a loose affiliation of 150 institutions, most of which were not football powerhouses). This group, which attempted to vote with some uniformity, could not possibly play a round robin schedule.[31]

One visionary saw a way to separate a small group of high-quality academic institutions from "lesser" schools while also breaking away from the twentieth-century football powers. His name was Dave Gavitt, head basketball coach of the Providence University Friars. Gavitt had enough experience to understand the importance of television to the NCAA's member institutions. At the same time, he recognized that some high-caliber basketball schools did not fit within the CFA formula. Looking for an alternate path, Gavitt met with a number of similar institutions and pitched the idea of a power conference based on basketball. The "Big East" would appeal to television stations from Washington, DC, up the East Coast, and it would avoid the problems that plagued the football power conferences.[32]

Gavitt invited Boston College, Georgetown, Holy Cross, Rutgers, Seton Hall, St. John's, Syracuse, and the University of Connecticut to join the new Big East Conference, focused on highly competitive men's basketball. Rutgers declined the initial invitation but would eventually join. Holy Cross, however, rejected the offer on—interestingly—educational grounds. In the first half of the twentieth century, Holy Cross was not dominant in intercollegiate sports, but it had an athletic reputation worth celebrating. The Holy Cross Crusaders won the NCAA Men's Basketball Championship in 1947 and made an appearance in the semifinals the following year. Multiple National Invitation Tournament appearances were coupled with some strong football records. The institution's academic aspirations, however, had grown during the 1950s and 1960s. By the 1970s, Holy Cross viewed itself, correctly, as one of the leading liberal arts colleges in the United States.

The decision of Holy Cross to decline an invitation to join the Big East remained curious. Its basketball team had been ranked in the Associated Press Top 20 leading up to the creation of the new league. Nevertheless, Holy Cross decided to deemphasize athletics as two of its chief rivals, Boston College and Georgetown University, signed on with the Big East. For the Big East, this did not mean that its member universities could not have football teams. It simply placed a focus on the commercialization of basketball programs. With its season-ending conference tournaments at Madison Square Garden, the Big East soon stole the basketball spotlight across the country.

At the same time, Holy Cross also chose to separate into the NCAA DI-AA for football while its historic rivals like Army, Boston College, Rutgers, and Syracuse, continued to compete at the Division I-A level. On the gridiron, Holy Cross replaced these historic foes with teams like Bucknell, Lafayette, and Lehigh. While this fit well within Holy Cross's academic profile, some alumni became upset with the trajectory of other historic rivals and their exploits on the national level—especially Boston College and Doug Flutie's masterful season leading up to his Heisman Trophy win. Instead, Holy Cross found its way into the Metro Atlantic Athletic Conference (MAAC) with members like Fairfield, Fordham, Iona, Manhattan, St. Peter's, and West Point. These institutions failed to keep up with the high-profile Big East programs, which began to dominate the basketball landscape in March during the NCAA tournament.[33]

Holy Cross eventually joined the Colonial Athletic League, which would later change its name to the Patriot League. This league's institutions were not wealthy or prestigious enough to join the Ivy League, but the Ivy League found their athletic philosophies similar enough to compete with the new conference on a regular basis. In the early 1990s, Patriot League members stopped offering grants-in-aid but still competed at the DI level, earning one automatic bid to the NCAA's basketball tournament. Falling into mediocrity, Holy Cross announced its intention to begin offering basketball scholarships in the mid-nineties. The Patriot League then followed the lead of Holy Cross, allowing scholarships in basketball only. This would eventually expand to other sports as well.[34]

The Holy Cross athletics dilemma offered a primary example that big-time sports, whether basketball or football, fit well within aspiring and established research universities. For institutions still emphasizing the residential liberal arts model, trying to keep up with larger universities proved a difficult task. At the same time, Holy Cross was the exception, not the rule. Most higher education institutions that had a chance to play big-time sports jumped at the opportunity. The discipline displayed by Holy Cross did not escape the anger of some alumni who longed for the glory days of victories over the likes of Boston College, Georgetown, and Syracuse.

The Big East, in contrast, successfully utilized their large urban centers with millions of basketball fans as well as a nascent ESPN to successfully monetize college basketball. During the 1980s, the meteoric rise of the conference on the national stage culminated with the 1985 Final Four, in which three Big East teams (Georgetown, St. John's, and Villanova) represented a conference less than a decade old. The Big East Conference Tournament in Madison Square Garden became a national commercial spectacle as well. In the decades ahead, however, the Big East would eventually struggle to find its place among the power conferences that emphasized football.

The College Football Association Turns Its Attention to Television

Despite the failure of some of its lobbying efforts, it remained clear that the NCAA had to incorporate some of the CFA's wishes. The truth remained: the hundreds of colleges with smaller athletics programs received only a fraction of the revenue generated by big-time programs in football and basketball. Nevertheless, pushing the power conferences and independents like Notre Dame and Penn State into their own association would have been devastating to small colleges that relied on television revenue from the NCAA basketball tournament to fund travel for national championship tournaments in many sports at all levels of the NCAA.

Since its inception, there was no doubt that the CFA wanted to ensure that big-time programs' financial interests would be protected. As Michigan president Robben Fleming declared when the Big Ten decided not to join, "The purpose of the CFA is money." But the CFA did not begin to study televised football until 1979, after it had first attempted to bring back academic admissions standards in recruiting. Not until the CFA hired Chuck Neinas, commissioner of the Big Eight, as its executive director did the organization begin to focus primarily on challenging the NCAA's monopoly on televised football.[35]

Chuck Neinas had worked as assistant executive director of the NCAA from 1961 to 1971. After a decade of loyal service, Byers recommended him as the next commissioner of the Big Ten. That position, however, eventually went to Wayne Duke, who had also worked for Byers at the NCAA until 1963 when he became commissioner of the Big Eight. Neinas then accepted Duke's former role for the Big Eight. As Commissioner of the Big Eight, Neinas's relationship with Byers disintegrated.[36]

Neinas played a key role in the CFA. In 1979 he recommended the creation of a CFA committee to study the NCAA's television plan. Neinas had worked with the NCAA television committee as Byers's assistant, and he then served on the same committee as the Big Eight commissioner. In short, he knew a great deal about the workings of the NCAA's monopoly. Once again, the CFA's actions influenced NCAA policy, even if Walter Byers was unwilling to admit it. With the CFA looking into the NCAA's television policies in 1979, the NCAA allowed Byers to negotiate the next television contract (which would begin in 1982).[37]

Neinas took the lead on the CFA's report examining the television practices during the previous years. From 1976 (before the formation of the CFA) through 1979, CFA members' televised football appearances decreased by more than ten percent. Those games had been replaced with a modest increase of Big Ten and Pac-10 appearances and a substantial increase in the number of televised games including universities that would not be classified as big-time programs. In the minds of universities like Georgia, Notre Dame, Oklahoma, and Texas, the report provided evidence that the NCAA had attempted to punish CFA members by decreasing their television appearances. More importantly, as CFA members were replaced by mid-major programs, the Nielsen ratings for each college football season declined. At a time when universities were facing financial pressure, declining ratings diminished the commercial value of the NCAA's most prominent product. Still, the NCAA seemed willing to spite the CFA members, even if it meant fewer people watched on TV. This justified the importance of the CFA football programs and emboldened the CFA leadership to be more aggressive in pressuring the NCAA to change its policies.[38]

Having provided a detailed report describing the NCAA's vengeful practices, the CFA leadership hired Chuck Neinas as its first executive director in the spring 1980. With Neinas in charge of the CFA, he would pressure Byers and the NCAA to increase the exposure of CFA teams though multiple networks and retain more of the profits for the big-time programs. As John Sayle Watterson highlighted, it was clear to both sides that television had not posed a threat to gate receipts as feared in the 1950s. In addition, the CFA members (along with the Big Ten and Pac-10) provided the financial "lifeblood" of the NCAA.[39]

Facing a breakup of the NCAA, the organization finally addressed some of the CFA's concerns. Byers negotiated the first contract with two networks, both of which agreed to pay $131.75 million over four years for a $263.5 million payout to the NCAA's featured schools. The agreement also drastically expanded the number of games on television, a key frustration for the CFA members. This did not stop Chuck Neinas from signing a deal for the CFA. Only weeks after the NCAA announced its contract, the CFA and NBC announced a deal worth $180 million over four years, with all proceeds going to the CFA members (or their conferences). In short, the CFA universities would keep all the proceeds, rather than the NCAA taking its share to fund itself and the many minor sports championships at the DII and DIII levels.[40]

The NCAA had warned its members that participating in a separate televised contract would lead to suspension. Then, after news of the NBC contract surfaced, the NCAA threatened CFA members with expulsion. Despite the warning, a slim majority of CFA universities voted to continue with the NBC contract (and likely destroy the NCAA). The NCAA then gave CFA members an ultimatum: let the organization know by September 10, 1981, if it intended to play its games under the NCAA contract.[41]

Just two days before the deadline, the Universities of Georgia and Oklahoma filed a lawsuit against the NCAA in Federal District Court in Oklahoma. That same day, the University of Texas sued the NCAA at the state level in Austin. Immediately after being sued, the NCAA responded. Later that same day, NCAA president James Frank (also president of HBCU Lincoln University in Missouri) announced that the NCAA would hold a special convention in early December to consider policy changes that would allow big-time programs greater autonomy over television rights. Frank added that the special convention could also vote on the following statement: "Football television is a matter to be determined by the football playing institutions only."[42]

The NCAA appeared to avoid calamity when the CFA members expressed interest in the special convention. At the same time, members of the big-time group largely remained silent on their intentions as NBC gave Chuck Neinas until December 14, 1981, to inform the network if enough teams (the exact number required remained undisclosed) remained to fulfill the contract. In the meantime, the University of Texas lawsuit had been dismissed, but not before a fascinating exchange between two university employees occurred. As Keith Dunnavant noted, University of Texas's president Peter Flawn, a supporter of the CFA, made sure that UT law professor Charles Wright, who chaired the NCAA Committee on Infractions, was served papers acknowledging the university's lawsuit, making "a point about who represented the University of Texas."[43]

During the special convention in December, the NCAA set a separate threshold to participate in DI-A football. Teams had to average a minimum of seventeen thousand fans over the past four years or they needed to have a stadium that seated a minimum of thirty thousand. Members of the special convention voted in favor of the new division, removing the Ivy League and members of other smaller conference from DI-A. This would cut the number of DI-A institutions from almost 140 down to approximately 100. The new alignment in DI-A, along with the lucrative contract Byers had negotiated with multiple networks, led most of the CFA institutions to abandon the deal Chuck Neinas and the CFA had developed with the NCAA. Neinas and NBC cancelled the contract, noting that not enough members had committed to play the games.

The Board of Regents Case and the Altering Landscape of Big-Time Football

The NCAA had averted disaster by making concessions that appeased most CFA institutions. But the lawsuit brought by CFA members Georgia and Oklahoma against the NCAA remained, and the case would determine which entities controlled the property rights of football. Filed in western Oklahoma, a district judge recused himself because he was a University of Oklahoma alum. Judge Juan Burciaga of the Federal District Court in New Mexico heard the case.[44]

Having weighed arguments from the Universities of Georgia and Oklahoma as well as the NCAA's defense for exclusive control over televised intercollegiate football, Burciaga ruled that the NCAA's policies violated the Sherman Antitrust Act. Taking aim at the NCAA's position that football remained part of the institutions' educational programs, Burciaga found it disingenuous for the NCAA to claim that "that college football, or indeed higher education itself, is not a business." The judge noted that colleges and universities were in competition for grants, students, faculty, and donations. Such competition, stated Burciaga, was part of American culture—including higher education.[45]

None of the arguments posited by the NCAA provided justification for denying Oklahoma and Georgia the rights to their own football games. The judge noted that ABC had recommended that the NCAA seek an exemption from antitrust laws. This provided evidence that the NCAA "attempted to conceal the extent of its anti-competitive activities." Burciaga wrote: "The court concludes that the NCAA controls over college football make [the] NCAA a classical cartel." He continued, "The veiled threats which came from NCAA officials and NCAA's entire course of conduct constituted classic cartel behavior."[46]

A federal appeals court upheld the district court's opinion, setting up a showdown when the Supreme Court agreed to take the case. Having heard the case, the Supreme Court, in *NCAA v. Board of Regents of the University of Oklahoma* (1984), ruled 7–2 against the NCAA. In the majority opinion, Justice Stevens noted that "There can be no doubt that the challenged practices of the NCAA constitute a 'restraint of trade' in the sense that they limit members' freedom to negotiate and enter into their own television contracts." The NCAA's television plan had an anticompetitive effect and included a price structure that was "unresponsive to viewer demand." The majority opinion noted the essential role the NCAA had in preserving amateur sports at the college level, but the "rules that restrict output are hardly consistent" with the role of administering amateur sport. Justices White and Rehnquist dissented, arguing that the NCAA had maintained competitive athletics as part of the larger higher education enterprise. A "viable system of amateur athletics," they argued, would be difficult to maintain in a "perfectly competitive market." Nevertheless, the ruling stood.[47]

Focused on freeing itself from the cartel behavior, the CFA might not have paid enough attention to one line in the Supreme Court's majority opinion: "The anticompetitive consequences of this arrangement are apparent. Individual competitors lose their freedom to compete. *Price is higher and output lower than they would otherwise be*" (italics added). With a free market for televised football, executives at television corporations knew that an abundance of televised games meant the value or cost of those games would decrease. As the executive vice president of CBS Neal Pilson noted, "Suddenly . . . you have greater supply. . . . I would guess for the most part we'll be paying, except for with the very best schools, a lot less." It would take the rest of the 1980s for the big-time football programs to determine how to proceed with their newfound freedom.[48]

Despite all these privileges and advantages, numerous NCAA Division I programs persisted as "poor cousins" within their conference—and lost money. For example, in November 1989 the University of Wisconsin in the Big Ten Conference reported a deficit of $1.9 million. At the University of Maryland in the Atlantic Coast Conference, the football program lost $300,000 to $400,000 each year between 1978 to 1981. Perhaps the most surprising news about the financing of college sports came in September 1988, when the University of Michigan announced budget deficits increasing from $2.5 million for the 1989 fiscal year and projected to increase to $5.2 million over the coming four years. A summary published in the January 8, 1990, issue of *U.S. News and World Report* showed an annual budget of $21.1 million in expenses and $18.5 million in revenues.[49] The athletics department had teams in twenty-one sports, a staff of 140 full-time employees (including a travel agent, mechanics, caterers, and engineers), and several hundred part-time employees who worked at sporting events. In 1987 its facilities consisted of twelve buildings valued at more than $200 million, including a stadium that seated over 100,000 spectators. The University of Michigan filled its stadium at home football games. In addition, its football team appeared on national television two or three times each season, regularly earned a bid to a major football bowl, sold out its basketball games, and enjoyed substantial revenues from its NCAA championship men's basketball team. If this established program projected a deficit, the financial outlook for intercollegiate programs at other universities was bleak.

Not surprisingly, the financial future that faced NCAA Division I-AA varsity sports program was especially grim. Consider in 1988–89 a Division I-AA department with an annual budget of $5 million. This was far below the Division I budgets of $10 million to $20 million, so one could argue that the I-AA programs had kept expenses relatively low. But with relatively small crowds and little television coverage, revenues remained low as well. It was not unusual for such a program to rely on $3 million in mandatory student fees to cover sixty percent of its expenses each year.

New Funding for Intercollegiate Athletics:
Corporate Sponsors, Bundled Rights, and Licensing

Even before the Supreme Court's decision, Walter Byers began contemplating new methods to make up the NCAA's impending revenue shortfall. He turned to Jim Host, chief executive officer of Host Communications Inc. (HCI), which had operated the NCAA Radio Network for the men's basketball tournament since the mid-1970s. Aware that radio was not the future of sports broadcasting, Host had unsuccessfully attempted to convince Byers to utilize his company to broker corporate sponsorships to promote the tournament.

Basketball had played a distant second to football in commercialized college athletics. Since the NCAA first sponsored a basketball championship in 1939, the event continued to grow in popularity. During the fifties and sixties, the NCAA jealously guarded its football contract but allowed conferences to negotiate their own regular-season television packages for basketball. The NCAA, then, assumed its exclusive rights only during the basketball tournament that it sponsored at the end of the season.

During the 1970s, interest in and viewership of the NCAA basketball championship grew at a rapid pace. During the 1979 finals featuring Michigan State's Earvin "Magic" Johnson and Indiana State's Larry Bird, the NCAA basketball championship drew more viewers than the highest-rated football game—which had featured Michigan and the University of Southern California in the Rose Bowl. With such exposure, the NCAA basketball tournament became worth much more money.

With the NCAA's revenue from television broadcasts in jeopardy, Byers employed Host Communications to implement a corporate sponsorship program for the NCAA. In turn, HCI began brokering lucrative deals, starting with Gillette, to become the "official" or "exclusive" sponsor of the NCAA Men's Basketball Tournament, bringing tens of millions of dollars into the NCAA's coffers during the eighties and nineties.[50]

A great deal of the success of the corporate sponsors program stemmed from the NCAA's new broadcast deal for the tournament. In 1981, CBS outbid NBC for the rights to future men's basketball tournaments. CBS ramped up its own promotion of the NCAA men's tournament. Then, after the *Regents* case, the NCAA expanded the tournament field to sixty-four teams in an effort to generate more revenue. CBS had instituted a selection show on Sunday night to reveal the tournament field. ESPN did not control the rights to the tournament but had broadcasters like Dick Vitale to offer commentary on the NCAA's tournament selections. Filling out brackets became a cultural phenomenon.

In short, the convergence of the CBS television deal, corporate sponsorships, an expanded tournament field, and ESPN's twenty-four-hour sports coverage helped turn the NCAA Men's Basketball Tournament into a commercial "spectacle," a term that had generally been reserved to describe college football. In so doing, "March Madness" filled the funding void for the NCAA, which continues nearly fifty years later.

While the NCAA found a way to continue financially after the *Regents* case, the years following the Supreme Court's decision were much more difficult for big-time programs and conferences that had supported the CFA. For example, Oklahoma and Georgia were from the Big Eight and Southeastern Conference, respectively. In the first year of television deregulation, the Big Eight's TV revenue shrank from more than $6 million to less than $4 million. The SEC's revenue fell from more than $11 million to $7.5 million. This limited the payouts conferences gave to their member institutions.[51]

In order to make up these revenue shortfalls, individual universities came to rely heavily on sports businesses like Host Communications Inc. and Learfield Communications Inc., which cultivated sponsorships for individual universities. HCI began offering "bundled rights" packages to individual athletics departments. The company would pay big-time university athletics departments millions of dollars to control its broadcast and media rights. In turn, the companies would sell sponsorship deals to companies that wanted to be known for supporting a specific university's athletics program. For example, car dealerships or insurance companies would pay to become "proud supporters" of Bulldog athletics. While HCI controlled dozens of "properties" (i.e., a university's athletics rights), its single most valuable sports client remained the NCAA. Learfield Communications and its CEO Clyde Lear then set out to expand sports media rights to college athletics programs across the country, eventually becoming the most ubiquitous name for university media rights.[52]

In the 1980s, individual universities also generated new revenue by licensing their trademarks and logos. In 1981, former college football player and coach Bill Battle created what would become the Collegiate Licensing Company (CLC). His alma mater, the University of Alabama, became his first college client, but his business rapidly expanded throughout the Southeastern and Atlantic Coast Conferences. In the ACC, Clemson University had won its first national football championship in 1981. In the ensuing months the university had been unable to enforce rules regarding its trademarked tiger paw. Clemson and other universities realized the need for CLC to offer the legal enforcement side of trademarks in order to prevent "rogue T-shirt makers" from using official school sports logos without paying a rights fee.[53] CLC took the market by storm, representing universities, conferences, bowl games, and other properties. In so doing, manufacturers who wanted to stamp a team logo on a glass, T-shirt, or cooler had to pay a fee to both the university and CLC.

Companies like HCI, Learfield Communications, and CLC helped monetize intercollegiate athletics with few fans or boosters understanding the new business revolution that had developed. Beyond the revenue, this quiet transformation altered the landscape of college athletics administration. Consider the following example: in the 1960s the University of Michigan promoted former athlete, alum, and track coach Don Canham to the position of athletics director. During Canham's eighteen years as the track coach, he had also become a wildly successful sports businessman. As AD, he used his sports marketing acumen to transform the Michigan athletics department into a successful business enterprise. Canham accomplished this through multiple entrepreneurial policies including advertising campaigns, new season ticket promotions, and the sale of merchandise. But this all occurred within the structure of the University of Michigan athletics administration.[54]

In addition to these changes, the new college sports business model that expanded rapidly during last two decades of the twentieth century operated with external partners. Universities began contracting with companies that held different governance models. These arrangements brought certain athletic practices "above board." Previously, football and basketball coaches negotiated their own side deals with shoe companies, soft drinks, and local television networks for coaches shows. For example, when Georgia Tech fired football coach Franklin "Pepper" Rogers in 1979, he sued the university's athletics association for perks it owed him as well as for benefits received by "third parties." The case set a precedent for elaborating specifics regarding third-party perks, and it ushered in a new era of buyout clauses in coaching contracts.[55]

When universities signed bundled media rights deals, it meant that coaches' exorbitant salaries came not primarily from the university itself (which paid a much smaller base salary) but from the company that held the institution's athletic rights. These businesses developed much more complex contracts for coaches. Previous coaching salaries, which had seemed exorbitant at the time, paled in comparison to the multimillion-dollar deals ushered in under this new scheme. This professionalized model provided a business subcontracting arrangement that would eventually expand in higher education to include other campus services.

These trends spread rapidly across the country as universities successfully created new revenue streams. Oregon State University's faculty athletic representative, John R. Davis, served as president of the NCAA in the mid-1980s. After noting the financial strain faced by athletics departments, he stated, "Anything that can help college athletics survive, we're all for, and corporate sponsorships can do just that."[56] Indeed, corporate sponsorships played an important role in what scholar Murray Sperber termed "College Sports, Inc." His book by the same title raised many important questions concerning the control that corporate sponsors would demand after providing millions of dollars to individual campuses. The results were evident in the eighties and nineties (and continue today) with 9:00 p.m. basketball tip-off times and the ever-expanding length of the season for both basketball and football.

Beginnings of Conference Expansion

Athletics directors and presidents at big-time programs hoped the unregulated television market would bring in vast amounts of money to solve budgetary problems. The CFA's initial success would lead to its eventual failure. As the US Supreme Court noted, each institution owned its own broadcast rights. All of the most powerful football programs, save one, understood that that they did not have a national media market, and rather than strike individual deals, big-time programs turned to their conferences to make decisions about television contracts in the new era of deregulation.

Even though Notre Dame remained the only university that could "go it alone" and generate huge profits because of its national fan base, it had remained with the CFA. Having taken a while to develop its own premium package to be broadcast, the CFA was closing in on a five-year deal with ABC and ESPN worth $320 million. Then, Notre Dame bolted the CFA and signed its own contract with NBC to broadcast all of its home games for five years with a payout in excess of $35 million. Although members of the CFA complained, the *LA Times* noted that in 1989, only three nationally televised games earned double-digit ratings and Notre Dame had played in each of those games. In addition, ABC's and CBS's top four games also involved the Irish.[57]

Part of Notre Dame's reasoning for signing its own contract might have come from the fact that in late 1989 the president of the Big Ten, who had shunned the CFA, extended an invitation for Pennsylvania State University to join the conference. Penn State was the second most powerful independent in the CFA. Its impending departure revealed cracks in the unanimity of the CFA. Penn State saw a way to expand its own television coverage while the Big Ten viewed Penn State's addition as a way to expand into television markets in the East.

In 1990, *Los Angeles Times* sports reporter Mark Maske predicted what would happen in the future. As the nation's "elite schools and conferences scurry to establish regional strangleholds in anticipation of megabucks television contracts," relations at the NCAA DI-A level would be strained. He envisioned an Atlantic Coast Conference that extended from the Northeast to Florida and a Big Ten that would expand farther east and west, taking schools like Nebraska. The SEC would expand into South Carolina and potentially move into Texas. The Pac-10 might add schools like the University of Colorado.[58]

Maske's prophetic article from 1990 stated, "The dominoes are lined up, waiting for a nudge to send them falling."[59] The moves would certainly threaten the CFA as conferences would look to negotiate their own television deals. In addition, the creation of super conferences would eventually lead to conference championship games and an eventual national playoff. Some of these developments would be decades in the making, but the first major conference realignment in the 1990s (and eventually the College Football Playoff) was a direct result of the Supreme Court's *Regents* decision and conferences asserting their own right to negotiate televised football deals.

After the Big Ten added Penn State, the SEC offered expanded from ten to twelve teams by inviting Arkansas and South Carolina into the conference. The ACC, in turn, added Florida State. With Arkansas bolting for the SEC, the Southwest Conference (which included smaller schools like Houston, Rice, Southern Methodist University, and Texas Christian University) disbanded, and its larger schools joined with the Big Eight to form the Big Twelve Conference. Even the Big East, which began as a basketball conference, determined that it needed to sponsor football if it were to keep pace with the other big-time conferences. So, the Big East added Miami, Rutgers, Temple, Virginia Tech, and West Virginia as football members. Notre Dame then joined the Big East in all sports *except* football. The Pac-10, which had added Arizona and Arizona State in the late 1970s, was the one power conference that remained unchanged, for the time being.

The conference expansion and realignment blitzkrieg of the 1990s was wrapped up in the expansion of television sets. The broader the media market, the more revenue each conference could expect from their television packages. As cable expanded to the American middle class, ESPN became pivotal in conference negotiations. The major networks could offer Saturday for football and basketball, but ESPN's twenty-four-hour sports network provided greater flexibility, even if it meant broadcasting games at nontraditional times.

The University of Louisville provided an example of an administration that understood this development and the importance of ESPN's growing market. U of L also desired to work its way into one of the "power conferences" to expand its national media presence and its athletic budget. As ESPN's Mark Shapiro remembered, "Louisville came to us and said, 'We'll play anyone, anywhere, anytime.'"[60] The result of that attitude could be seen in Louisville's conference membership. A longtime independent, U of L journeyed through the old Metro Conference to Conference USA. During the first decade of the twentieth century, they bolted for the Big East and spent one year in the American Athletic Conference before earning an invitation to join the ACC. Its athletic strategy worked.

Historian Howard Chudacoff correctly noted that during the nineties, no one event marked "the major turning point" in big-time sports, but during the late nineties, an important shift was under way. By the beginning of the twenty-first century, "media and money intertwined with college sports to create one of America's most powerful entertainment entities." Conference realignment and a deregulated television environment were important pieces of this expanding entertainment industry.[61]

Amidst conference expansion, the College Football Association closed its doors. Its demise was somewhat predictable. An organization determined to win the rights of televised football for each individual campus was unlikely to be able to create a coalition that would convince those same institutions to give up those rights. Before its death, however, the CFA had altered the landscape of intercollegiate athletics.

Growing Scandals and Presidential "Reform"

As mentioned at the beginning of the chapter, numerous efforts at cutting costs in athletics actually had a greater impact on leveling the playing field for some institutions desperate to be able to compete with the big-time schools. The first measure was to overturn the freshman rule, which banned first-year athletes from playing on varsity teams. The policy had been in place since the inception of the NCAA, but a motion to abandon the freshman rule in all sports was adopted by the membership in 1972. The move was to be a cost-savings matter, abolishing JV teams and spending money on scholarship players who could not even compete at the varsity level. In reality, it was a boon to the smaller schools looking to level the playing field.[62]

Adding to the abandonment of the freshman rule, two key policy moves passed in 1973 helped create an environment ripe for controversy. First, the NCAA Annual Convention adopted Proposition 39, a measure to remove the four-year scholarship offer and replace it with one-year offers. Arguing that many academic scholarships and graduate assistantships were renewed annually, the membership voted to adopt the one-year athletic grant-in-aid. As scholar Michael Oriard has highlighted, this policy effectively professionalized student-athletes as athletes. Coaches could now lure an athlete to campus with a scholarship and then revoke it a year later if need be.[63]

The other legislation that the NCAA membership overturned in 1973 was its 1.6 GPA policy. The 1.6 rule was an academic formula that included high school rank, high school GPA, courses taken, and standardized test score to ensure that the student-athlete would likely earn a 1.6 GPA (or better) in college. If a student could not meet the 1.6 formula, he was not eligible to enroll in college. Leaders of municipal colleges and other institutions with open enrollment policies challenged the 1.6 rule. Even though many big-time programs were opposed to ending the policy, the NCAA had enough members to abolish the requirement in favor of a straight 2.0 GPA in high school. Walter Byers called this "one of the most painful experiences" he had as the executive director of the NCAA. Byres noted later in his memoir that he knew ending the freshman rule and the four-year grant-in-aid, coupled with the abolition of the 1.6 rule, meant that teams would be forced to compete at the "lowest common denominator."[64]

By the late 1970s and early 1980s, the NCAA policy changes made unethical recruiting and academic cheating even easier. Two of the most notable cases involved Dexter Manley and Kevin Ross. Both players maintained the minimum 2.0 high school GPA but were unable to complete college-level work. Manley spent four seasons at Oklahoma State before being drafted in the NFL in 1981. Manley did not graduate, but he made it through Oklahoma State even though he remained functionally illiterate. Manley kept his illiteracy a secret while playing in the NFL and attending the Lab School of Washington, a school that helped him work through his dyslexia and illiteracy.[65]

Kevin Ross played basketball for Creighton University in the Missouri Valley Conference. An excellent athlete, Ross could perform on the court but did not have the support needed to complete his collegiate coursework. Secretaries helped him complete his papers and other assignments. He managed to keep his eligibility for four years, but his grades started to plummet during his senior season even though he was doing nothing different. Without any NBA prospects, Ross had used his four years of eligibility. Creighton then paid to have him enrolled at Westside Preparatory School, where he sat with grade school students. Under the tutelage of Marva Collins, Ross graduated a year later, finally having been prepared for college classes.[66]

At the University of Georgia, English instructor Jan Kemp shed light on practices at one of the leading CFA institutions. Kemp operated the university's remedial English program. In the fall of 1981 the administration demanded that nine football players have their failing grades changed to passing marks. The athletes needed to be available for the Sugar Bowl against Pitt on January 1, 1982. Kemp protested the unethical dictate. When she refused to relent, she was fired from her position.[67]

Kemp sued the University of Georgia in a whistleblower case in which her attorneys successfully argued that her right to free speech had been violated. Georgia, in response, argued that Kemp had been terminated for disruptive conduct and a lack of research productivity. Kemp won her case, and UGA eventually paid her a million dollars in the wrongful termination suit. A month after the case, the University of Georgia Board of Regents renewed the contracts of all its chief executive officers in the multicampus system except that of President Davison. The regents wanted to investigate the remedial programs operating on the Athens campus. Davison responded by resigning. Interestingly, Davison, as chair of the CFA in the 1970s, had requested that Joe Paterno and the Committee on Academics develop a plan to reinstitute greater academic standards among NCAA members. The CFA's proposal to the NCAA failed to garner enough votes for implementation. One could question whether the regulations would have been enforced either way.[68]

Such scandals marked the opening of the floodgates on excesses and abuses in big-time intercollegiate athletics. Fundraising, recruitment of student-athletes, hiring and firing coaches, intrusion by trustees and politicians, problems associated with race and gender among student-athletes, and derailing of institutional and national safeguards characterized the era. It was a period of reform—or at least attempts at reform—mainly because numerous scandals called for attempts to reconsider campus and conference governance for varsity sports that unfortunately overemphasized winning and moved away from educational activities. The foremost enigma in this period was the role of college and university presidents. There were few signs of consensus, consistency, clarity, or effectiveness in their leadership of athletics as part of the missions of American higher education institutions.

One sign of life for reform was collective action by some presidents to establish leadership within the NCAA. Initiated in 1984, the resultant Presidents' Commission signaled that at least a critical mass of presidents had started to assert their collective voice in an organization that had been dominated by high-profile athletics directors, coaches, and NCAA officials themselves. At the same time, external groups including US Congress, higher education associations, and private foundations showed concern about college sports as an important and problematic part of American life.

After the Jan Kemp and Kevin Ross scandals came to light, the NCAA adopted Proposition 48, which resembled the CFA's initial proposal five years earlier. This time the legislation was adopted. It required that a student-athlete earn a 2.0 GPA in eleven core courses in high school and that the student earn either a 700 on the SAT or a 15 on the ACT in order to be admitted and play as a freshman. When the rule went into effect in 1986, it included a provision for partial qualifiers. Students who had met one of the criteria (usually the high school GPA) but not the other (typically the test score) could earn a scholarship, but they were not allowed to play with the team during their freshman season.[69]

The newly created Presidents' Commission now provided an opportunity for CEOs in higher education to discuss issues, encourage policy, sponsor legislation, and call for special sessions if necessary. When the measure passed, the Presidents' Commission proposed different topics for the NCAA to address, although most issues were the same as in years past. The impact of the Presidents' Commission remained minimal. For example, its initial proposals included scaling back football scholarships from ninety-five to ninety, and basketball scholarships from fifteen to thirteen. Neither proposal would have created substantive change, and both proposals lost at the NCAA convention.[70]

In 1989, in an odd move, the NCAA added an amendment (Proposition 42) to the existing Proposition 48. The new regulation disallowed partial qualifiers to enter school on scholarship even though they were prohibited from playing with their respective teams until they met minimum academic standards. By rescinding the provisions that had been made in the original Proposition 48, university members were basically denying students on the fence an opportunity to prove that they could make it in college.

Based on numbers from the previous three years, Prop 42 would deny approximately six hundred students, most of them Black men, from attending college. The head men's basketball coach at Georgetown University, John Thompson Jr., took exception to the policy. In response, he boycotted his team's next game, walking off the court before the Hoyas took on Boston College. The protest brought enough attention to the matter that the Presidents' Commission and other NCAA officials backtracked on Proposition 42, rescinding the policy before it ever took effect.[71]

Such were the challenges faced by presidents seeking to help reform the NCAA and its image. Not only was it difficult to accomplish anything substantive, but the Presidents' Commission also created tensions among the employees under their charge. The attitude of some ADs was expressed by outgoing University of Michigan athletics director and football coach Bo Schembechler: "School presidents will completely confuse intercollegiate athletics directors then they'll dump it back to athletics directors and say, 'You straighten this out.'" He quipped, "About [year] 2000 it may be back on track."[72] The comment itself provided evidence of the feelings of athletics directors and coaches. Despite the challenges, some high-minded reformers continued to view presidential reform as the best path forward.

The Knight Foundation Commission on Intercollegiate Athletics

One notable initiative was the creation of the Knight Foundation Commission on Intercollegiate Athletics in October 1989. Its plenary sessions and background work eventually led to 1990 hearings in Washington, DC, about the character and condition of college sports.[73] A prime mover in the founding and scope of the Knight Commission was Creed Black, a longtime newspaper editor whose most recent involvement was sponsoring a prize-winning series of articles called "Above the Rim," dealing with the extreme practices of the basketball program at the University of Kentucky. The Knight Commission gained national attention and respect with the appointment of William C. Friday and Rev. Theodore Hesburgh, two icons in higher education, as the founding co-chairmen. They assembled a blue-ribbon panel and provided leadership.

The Knight Commission's 1991 seminal report, *Keeping Faith with the Student-Athlete: A New Model for Intercollegiate Athletics* provided a road map for reform and was distributed to higher education leaders. It proposed a new "one-plus-three" model for governing intercollegiate athletics: presidential control directed toward academic integrity, financial integrity, and independent certification. The Knight Commission devoted energy and effort to reforming the governance of college sports. In the 1990s, for example, the commission pushed for presidential leadership at the national, conference, and institutional levels. Its major areas of concern were as follows.

- *Academic Performance.* Data on grade point averages and graduation rates raised questions about the status of student-athletes as genuine students, especially for those participating in the major revenue sports. Disparities in retention and graduation rates were especially pronounced for student-athletes who were minorities and from modest-income families.

- *Financial Health.* College sports continued to soar in media and broadcast popularity and revenues, yet by 1989, distant early warnings indicated that even many big-time college sports programs were running deficits. One convenient strategy adopted by many athletics directors was to reduce budgetary pressures by eliminating nonrevenue Olympic sports, including women's varsity squads.

- *Practices and Policies Involving Gender and Equity.* Promisingly, Title IX had been passed in 1972, and after initial resistance, the NCAA absorbed women's intercollegiate athletics under their sponsorship. Yet by the start of the twenty-first century, that sponsorship had not yet led to approximation of equity or accommodation. To the contrary, contentious lawsuits were brought by women student-athletes such as at Colgate and Brown. Opportunities for women in educational activities, including intercollegiate athletics, remained unfinished business.

Among these troubling trends, perhaps most surprising, especially to sportswriters and media reporters who covered college sports, was the belated discovery by 1989 that most college sports programs lost money. An alarming and counterintuitive finding was that this included many of the big-time conferences and university programs. Football, once heralded as the "golden goose" that would provide abundant funding for all sports, in fact was a money loser even within many NCAA Division I programs. Big-time sports programs, which according to the NCAA guidelines were expected to be self-sufficient, frequently relied on cross-subsidies and bailouts from the university general fund. One irony was that the rate of spending on big-time college sports increased at a higher rate than university spending on educational programs—even when college sports programs were running a deficit. The dominant big-time college sports model was broken, or at very least in need of repairs and reforms. A limit of this initiative was that the Knight Commission had no formal ties with organizational or institutional decision-making with such group as the NCAA, the various athletics conferences, or individual universities. It raised good questions, hosted informative hearings, and published provocative reports. But the burden of formal change in decision-making or conduct of college sports ultimately was left to other groups.

Title IX: An Easy (and Unacceptable) Excuse

The 1980s and 1990s were a mixed bag regarding women's athletics. On the one hand, budgets dramatically increased after the NCAA assumed administrative control of women's intercollegiate championships, especially for programs housed at big-time athletic universities. Gone were the days when the University of Texas might find themselves playing UCLA in a championship contest. Bringing women's athletics under the men's umbrella meant the unleveling of a playing field across women's athletics that had previously been based in poverty across the board. Now, even as women's programs remained a distant second to men's, the television revenue generated from power conferences created a stratification that had not previously existed. Many of the teams that had been nationally competitive in the AIAW became Division II or Division III programs in the NCAA structure. In the 1980s, for example, the Olympic representation of the HBCU Tennessee State Tigerbelles had been supplanted with new Olympic stars like Florence Griffith Joyner and Jackie Joyner-Kersee—both educated at the University of California, Los Angeles.

For the women's programs that remained nationally competitive, a new tension emerged: the popularity and revenue that came along with women's championships—especially in basketball—opened new opportunities for women's athletics, but it also transformed the nature of the competition. It was, as scholar Welch Suggs described, "the triumph and tragedy of Title IX." The triumph came with new opportunities that women in previous generations were denied. The tragedy was that opportunity came with a cost. Women's sports would follow the mold of men's athletics. At the most competitive level, coaching positions were contingent upon winning. College women entered the business of intercollegiate athletics.[74]

The business of college athletics brought in revenue and exposure. Although not nearly as lucrative as the men's side of athletics, by 1990 the NCAA had found a corporate sponsor for women's sports in Sara Lee. The corporation signed a three-year sponsorship worth more than six million dollars to the NCAA. Part of the sponsorship included advertising in women's championships, which had grown to sixteen events in 1990. During the 1980s, the number of women competing in intercollegiate athletics had jumped from less than ten thousand to more than ninety thousand by the end of the decade. The triumph and tragedy were woven together.[75]

The 1980s and 1990s witnessed the ascendance of women's coaching legends such as Geno Auriemma, Muffet McGraw, Vivian Stringer, Pat Summitt, and Tara VanDerveer. At the same time, the administration of men's and women's programs merged under a single department, and women lost control of their athletics programs. As salaries climbed with commercial success, more men entered the women's coaching ranks, and women's programs still lost out on funding. A lesser-known legend, Carol Hutchins, who had an impressive softball coaching record at the University of Michigan, was matched by her continual vigilance in fighting for gender equity in women's athletics. The challenges were not easy, and women generally found themselves fighting an uphill battle with administration, often requiring litigation to be resolved.

In 1997 the US Supreme Court ruled that it would not hear an appeal from Brown University in its case of *Cohen v. Brown* (1996), thus upholding a lower-court decision to require the university to adhere to strict criteria for demonstrating gender equity in intercollegiate athletics. Media coverage described this as a "landmark victory" for women's athletics programs that would fulfill compliance with the 1972 Title IX legislation.[76] In contrast, many higher education associations objected that the court's interpretation of Title IX was unreasonable to colleges and universities in two respects. First, requisite new funding for women's varsity sports would strain athletics department budgets. Second, the court's ruling relied on compliance with statistical tests that imposed "insurmountable burdens on colleges and universities" and might "lead to the very discrimination that Title IX prohibits." Such complaints raised a troubling question about higher education as part of athletics and public policy: Were colleges behaving like "poor losers" rather than "good sports"?[77]

That the higher education community of national associations in Washington, DC's One DuPont Circle was worried by the Supreme Court's ruling came as little surprise. Brown University's intercollegiate athletics program represented a "best case scenario" to demonstrate commitment to women's athletics.[78] If Brown were found to be out of compliance with Title IX tests, then most institutions in NCAA Division I probably would be vulnerable to sanctions. Indeed, a study released by the NCAA shortly after the *Brown v. Cohen* ruling projected that it would be "at least a decade" before "most colleges would achieve equity in funding for women's sports."[79] Many college and university representatives said that they supported Title IX principles but merely disagreed with the compliance criteria. As such, they echoed Harvard President Derek Bok's 1980 claim that in athletics and other activities colleges and universities had been subjected to excessive, unreasonable regulation by the federal government.[80]

How did these general claims match with the events and actions at Brown University that undergirded the case? The court rulings marked the end of a six-year contest between student-athletes from two women's varsity teams—gymnastics and volleyball—during which a group of student-athletes and their coach, primarily from gymnastics, had taken numerous steps to urge official reconsideration of the demotion of both squads from varsity status. These protests met with little success because the university had also cut two men's varsity teams—golf and water polo. Hence the university argued that its decision had been equitable. The women student-athletes then sought assistance from a concerned Washington, DC, attorney and took on the unusual path of a lawsuit. Even more unusual was that the student group won in court at several levels, consummating with the Supreme Court denial. Beyond its particulars, the case demonstrated the nationwide character of the fits and starts, partial gains, and setbacks women as student-athletes and coaches faced within their own institutions to gain some measure of equity in varsity athletics.[81]

On close inspection, one finds that the women's varsity gymnastics team had not received resources, facilities, staffing, or travel provisions comparable to norms for most men's varsity squads. The coach, Jackie Court, had been a long-time leader and successful high school coach who received only a part-time salary at Brown.[82] In addition to these imbalances and shortfalls, the Brown athletics department was susceptible to one significant criterion used to op-erationalize Title IX compliance—namely, a continuing record of showing improvement in provisions for women's teams. Records at Brown and else-where indicated that women's varsity programs were hardly distinctive in failing to generate adequate revenue from ticket sales, donations, and media coverage to balance their annual budgets. Such was the financial performance of most men's teams in NCAA Division I, often including football and men's basketball. The residual legacy for higher education and public policy was rea-sonable doubt that the voluntary associations to which colleges and universi-ties belonged—namely, the NCAA and conferences—were yet adequately committed to timely and adequate support of intercollegiate athletes for women as student-athletes.

The 1997 *Brown v. Cohen* case ruling was soon followed by subsequent land-mark events. For example, the National Women's Law Center filed a com-plaint with the US Department of Education alleging that twenty-five colleges had violated federal law by awarding women athletes less sports-related aid than their men counterparts.[83] A year later, a group representing college women athletes filed suit in federal court to make the case that the NCAA itself as an organization, not just its member institutions, was subject to Title IX compliance.[84]

Such episodes provided an ironic context for news coverage of June 17th, when the president of the United States hailed the twenty-fifth anniversary of Title IX legislation. Even though the traditionally popular men's sports of foot-ball and basketball continued to dominate in media and money, the cases and events of 1997 indicated that women's varsity sports could no longer be ignored or treated in an arbitrary manner by athletics directors, presidents, and boards of trustees. Often overlooked, however, was the price paid by the dedicated women student-athletes and coaches who pursued justice and often forfeited their own varsity eligibility as court cases took years to decide. In addition, en-forcement by federal agencies as well as athletics conferences moved slowly even though female students showed increasing interest in playing college sports.[85] Amy Cohen, the Brown University student-athlete and star varsity gymnast whose name appeared as plaintiff in the case, made the perceptive observation that the organized efforts by women's advocates to make substantial gains inside the institution and in the courts was comparable to "winning a losing battle."[86]

The New Television Dilemma

When the NCAA first addressed television and its potential opportunities and challenges, the impact on game-day attendance remained the primary concern. By the time the Universities of Oklahoma and Georgia won their lawsuit against the NCAA in 1984, television had proven to be an asset rather than a threat with regard to building the fanbase and commercial appeal of intercollegiate athletics. Football and basketball became the "cash cows" for universities, conferences, and the NCAA.

The advent of cable television ESPN played a particularly large role in the expansion of television during the 1980s and 1990s. When ESPN began broadcasting in 1979, it was to fewer than 1.5 million American homes. By the conclusion of 1980, that number had grown to more than 7 million. By the close of the decade, it had more than 50 million subscribers in the United States and expanded into more than sixty countries around the globe. By the turn of the century, ESPN could be watched in more than 80 million American homes. While growth of ESPN had slowed during the nineties, more than 70 million homes had access to ESPN 2, with millions more able to watch ESPN Classic and ESPNews.[87]

The Supreme Court's decision in the *Regents* case meant that more "product" would be required to generate more revenue to support big-time athletics as well as the DII and DIII championships that the NCAA sponsored for both women and men. ESPN provided the medium for the content to be delivered during primetime hours in the middle of the week, with reruns and news broadcast during the night hours. The 24–7 coverage in the twentieth century only bolstered attendance at sporting events, and television contracts for conference football games and the NCAA basketball tournament grew exponentially during the 1990s.

The increased value did not come without its own cost. As Keith Dunnavant highlighted, television companies, corporate sponsors, and advertisers exacted a different kind of price. Starting with the Fiesta Bowl and its enterprising executive director, Bruce Skinner, the television landscape began to change. The Fiesta Bowl started in the early 1970s to provide a bowl game for Western Athletic Conference (WAC) football champs, who were generally snubbed by the historic Cotton, Orange, Rose, and Sugar Bowls. When Arizona and Arizona

State left the WAC to help create the Pac-10, the Fiesta Bowl seemed to be in danger without a guarantee of a big-time conference champion in the WAC (since the Arizona universities drew the largest number of fans). Its executive director, however, schemed to get the Fiesta Bowl televised on New Year's Day along with the other leading bowls. After convincing Sunkist to sponsor the upstart bowl in 1985, the Fiesta Bowl found itself in an envious position: with no contractual obligations, it was able to attract "national championship" contenders in 1987 with Penn State and Miami. Then, in 1989, the Fiesta Bowl served as the de facto national championship between Notre Dame and the University of West Virginia. Payouts to participating teams grew from $185,000 in 1973 to $3 million in 1989.[88]

In the process of bringing in megabucks for participating universities and their conferences, network executives began to realize that they could move sporting events off of their traditional times. If universities wanted the largess, they needed to adapt to the consumers' demands for content at different times. Coupled with the one-year scholarship, changing academic standards, and unregulated television, athletes and their universities faced a dilemma that it rarely (if ever) rejected: more money for more content, which required more games.

One of the greatest examples of the expansion of content was an idea hatched by SEC commissioner Harvey Schiller and executed by his successor, Roy Kramer. Having expanded to twelve teams and divisions, NCAA bylaws allowed conferences with divisions to host a conference championship game. After the SEC added Arkansas and South Carolina, the conference divided into east and west divisions. The SEC was growing into a dominant force, threatening the supremacy of Big Ten (and to a lesser extent the Pac-10), but it still lacked the revenue and resources of the Big Ten. Conference commissioner Roy Kramer viewed an SEC championship game as a way to bring in the revenue, which would be shared by all conference members. The threat, however, was that a conference championship game could knock a team out of contention for a national championship.

As has been highlighted in *SEC Storied*, the first SEC championship pitted undefeated Alabama (11–0) against a three-loss Florida team coached by an up-and-coming Steve Spurrier. An upset by the Gators would have knocked Alabama out of a chance to play for a national championship. Alabama led 21–7, but Florida gained momentum after scoring two touchdowns to tie the game. A Florida win would have likely ended future experiments with conference championships in big-time football, but an Alabama interception that was returned for a touchdown preserved the win for Alabama, and the SEC's conference championship became a model all power conferences would eventually follow.

After watching Notre Dame abandon the CFA for an exclusive contract with NBC and having success with the SEC championship, Roy Kramer helped seal the demise of the College Football Association by negotiating a separate television deal between CBS and the SEC for the 1996 season. The contract brought nearly twenty million dollars a year to the conference. The Big Ten and Pac-10 remained outside of the CFA and had already signed their own deals. The other power conferences went their own way, and the revenue the big-time programs wanted finally started rolling in, more than a decade after the *Regents* case had been decided.

By the turn of the century, college sports had become big business for the favored few. Yet the allure of those dollars and recognition kept many other mid-majors looking for an opportunity to crack the big time and benefit from the prestige it brought to a university in a Final Four or New Year's Bowl. For all but a few, however, the windfall remained illusory. In addition, universities themselves had lost some of the controls that had previously kept some semblance of amateurism part of the sport—even for football and basketball. Those hindrances were regularly discussed when a new scandal would hit the newspapers. Rather than create opportunities for change, such headlines and responses became a familiar tradition of their own.

Conclusion: Walter Byers and the Dilemma of Big-Time College Sports

In the midst of this transformation, Walter Byers retired as executive director of the NCAA in 1987. Byers had begun his work in athletics administration in 1947 as the assistant to Tug Wilson, who was both the commissioner of the Big Ten and secretary-treasurer of the NCAA. In 1951, Byers became the first executive director of the NCAA. His staff consisted of one administrative assistant, and the organization had 381 members and possessed no enforcement authority. Its administrative tasks consisted largely of supporting the eleven national championships it sponsored. By the time Byers retired, the NCAA staff had grown to more than 140 employees with a budget exceeding a hundred million dollars.[89]

During Byers's three and a half decades at the helm of the NCAA, the membership expanded to more than a thousand institutions. Unable to reconcile the competing aims of intercollegiate athletics, the NCAA first divided between university and college divisions. Still unable to satisfy its diverse membership,

Walter Byers testifying before the 1975 President's Commission on Olympic Sport.
Robert Walker, *New York Times*

the NCAA moved to three divisions in the early 1970s. During that time, the NCAA struggled to find agreement on various policies, such as academic standards and cost containment in sports. While athletics were desegregated, true integration for African Americans often remained elusive. Many universities fought to keep women outside of athletics, but when forced to incorporate women's sports, men generally took over administrative posts as well as many coaching positions previously held by women. Despite fits and starts, college sports eventually absorbed these marginalized populations, but universities generally moved slower on social justice issues than other agencies and institutions.

As college athletics evolved to both resemble and influence the larger educational culture, three divisions no longer met the needs of all the NCAA's constituencies. With the big-time programs seeking to maximize profits and share less money with smaller schools, they forced new policies and procedures to protect their interests. This bargain went both ways: many underfunded women's athletics programs and other nonrevenue sports, and virtually all competition at the DII and DIII levels, purported to operate on a different model than big-time football and basketball. Yet those programs, institutions, and divisions still needed the revenue generated from big-time athletics to subsidize the thousands of student-athletes who traveled across America to participate in national championships.

In short, the NCAA's evolution during Walter Byers's tenure in many ways modeled the growing complexity of higher education itself. Considered in this way, the NCAA looked less like an anomaly and more like an accurate representation of the competing interests and tensions across higher education in America. The "old-time" college had given way to a far more complex system. As *U.S. News and World Report* published its infamous rankings, university administrators generally denounced such simplistic classifications, all while jockeying to move up a number of points ahead of the competition or manage to jump categories from a "Regional University" to a "National University." Interestingly, the best Division III teams tended to find themselves in the "National Liberal Arts Colleges" category, while the NAIA membership came largely from a grouping of "Regional Colleges." In short, college sports very much resembled higher education and its aspirations.

As an extension of higher education rather than an aberration from colleges and universities, college sports faced many of the same challenges as their sponsoring schools. As one history of higher education has noted, the last decades of the twentieth century created a "proliferation of problems" for colleges and universities. Many institutions had become overextended in their annual operating budgets, and they were ill-equipped to deal with economic downturns or funding cuts. This "lack of fiscal fitness" led to haphazard expansion into new markets (i.e., majors and degree programs) that relied on continuous enrollment growth and funding sources. As mass higher education moved toward a universal access model, students and universities alike introduced new trends of commercialism. In short, American universities shared many of the same problems with its athletics programs.[90]

It is here where critical scholars will be able to identify a common thread between the expansion of the neoliberal university and athletics programs. Modern American universities began to focus on the primacy of markets, the emphasis on competition, and preparation of a trained workforce to supply labor to (and within) an existing political system. Hard-fought access for marginalized groups often came at a deep cost: the powerbrokers in the entrenched system maintained their control. These common themes in both the history of higher education and in athletics presented parallels that help illuminate a closer relationship between the modern university and its athletics program.

It was not surprising that after the NCAA lost the *Regents* case and Walter Byers had moved into retirement, he became disillusioned with his life's work. After retiring, Byers wrote his memoir, *Unsportsmanlike Conduct: Exploiting College Athletes*, becoming one of the first to compare college athletics to a plantation system. As he said, "The neo plantation" believed "that the enormous proceeds from college games belong to the overseers (the administrators) and supervisors (Coaches)." He continued, "The plantation workers performing in the arena may receive only those benefits authorized by the overseers." This was most noticeable at the big-time level, but these proceeds subsidized minor sports and the other divisions of the NCAA as well. The athletes in revenue-generating sports were unable to benefit from their talents beyond an athletic grant-in-aid.[91]

The Walter Byers era of intercollegiate sport should not be confused with any form of utopia or "glory days." In reality, his dictatorial approach had created problems with every new social dilemma faced in college sports. Byers's term "student-athlete" had been utilized to avoid responsibility for injuries inflicted on students. Rather than work with different groups (such as the AAU, AIAW, and NAIA), he simply hoped to diminish these organizations or incorporate them into his own NCAA model. At the same time, there remained some form of amateurism and some element of the educational enterprise—no matter how much of it had been eroded. Finally, under his leadership, violators of NCAA policy could be sure they would face punishments that the offending universities found to be draconian in nature. This approach did not stop scandals from being uncovered, however. For example, Southern Methodist earned the "death penalty" from the NCAA the year that Byers retired.

With Walter Byers's departure, big-time athletics became an unbridled business. Once again, the dilemmas in college sport resembled the same problems facing higher education itself. Intercollegiate athletics was the vanguard for the enterprise of American higher education by 1990, as it had entered a distinct transformational era of expanded commercialization. It was a model and strategy that would extend and accelerate into the twenty-first century, perceptively identified by Harvard President Derek Bok as "Universities in the marketplace."[92]

8

Keeping Up with the Joneses,

2000 to 2012

An Era of Optimism and Innovation

The last fifteen years of the twentieth century witnessed a true transformation in college athletics. Gone were the days filled with fear that the power conferences would leave the NCAA entirely. Instead, big-time programs developed a model that met their own needs. A new order had been established within the NCAA's financial framework. Power conferences had fully embraced corporatized, televised, and monetized athletics. Even smaller schools playing at non-scholarship levels relied on the big-business model to help subsize their own championships, which they lobbied to have broadcast on television—all while publicly shunning the model.

While college athletics had struggled with similar issues throughout its entire history, never had it contended with twenty-four-hour-a-day sports television networks, corporate sponsorships, and a deregulated market for football. This new model of college sports, however, was still in its earliest phase. The Bowl Championship Series (BCS), a landmark agreement among the power conferences regarding bowl rotations and selection, remained brand-new. Nationally televised access to a full slate of March Madness games did not yet exist. No conference had its own sports network on cable or satellite television. No smartphones existed yet to stream games. In short, the model or framework of college sports had been established, but many of the details remained in doubt. The next decade would answer many of these questions.

At the start of the twenty-first century, television contracts and the corporate partnership model for college sports had been such a success that billion-dollar deals were being brokered for television rights in football and basketball. Although college football income remained with conferences and individual schools, the NCAA kept most profits from its basketball tournaments. This funding model made it more difficult for conferences emphasizing basketball to compete with the power football conferences. The mid-major college sports programs struggling for revenue, along with historically Black colleges and universities, have since become increasingly dependent on student fees and general operating budget reallocations to be able to compete with power conference teams.

Even so, basketball tournament successes by small schools like Gonzaga revealed that the television attention from the Big Dance provided valuable publicity and exposure for some institutions. At big-time programs, luxury skyboxes, elaborate tutoring centers, and opulent facility upgrades became commonplace as "not-for-profit" athletics departments found ways to spend income.

These innovations literally changed the game by representing the dramatic events taking place within an elaborate network of nationwide intercollegiate athletics, the scope of which would have made college sports officials and higher education leaders incredulous three decades earlier. Before examining the growth and complexity of new commercial and collegiate practices, it is important to take stock of the structure and alignments within the college sports enterprise between 2000 and 2010.

Taking Stock: A Profile of the NCAA and the College Sports Enterprise

The vital statistics of intercollegiate athletics in number of institutions, sports, contests, spectators, and participating student-athletes depict a structural skeleton that was vast in participants and in geographic scope. Whereas intercollegiate athletics in the twentieth century had been largely decentralized and even localized to regions and conferences, this changed markedly in the first decade of the twenty-first century. For example, member institutions of the NCAA accounted for championships in twenty-four varsity sports in 2016. In addition to the obvious ones such as football and basketball, the roster includes field hockey, lacrosse, wrestling, soccer, rowing, bowling, golf, ice hockey, cross-country, track and field (both indoor and outdoor seasons), women's gymnastics, tennis, volleyball, softball, baseball, fencing, rifle, and skiing. Furthermore, several sports had their own national collegiate championships *outside* NCAA sponsorship.[1]

The number of colleges participating in the NCAA was large, with 1,092 member institutions. NCAA games were played by more than 460,000 student-athletes nationwide. In football, one of the major sports, 655 teams played 3,693 games, with a total attendance of more than forty-nine million spectators.

In men's basketball, more than thirty-two million fans attended. The total revenue for all NCAA college sports in 2013 was fourteen billion dollars.

But even these numbers tend to understate the pervasiveness of college sports. They further increase when one adds to the NCAA summaries the comparable data for institutions belonging to other associations. The National Association of Intercollegiate Athletics (NAIA) had more than 250 member institutions and championships in twenty-five sports. In addition, the National Association of Junior and Community Colleges, along with the California Community Colleges, provided representation for hundreds of additional institutions.

Each year the spotlight of media broadcasts showcased high-profile championship games, especially in football and basketball for the high-powered NCAA Division I category. Their institutional membership consisted of 345 teams, of which 250 had varsity football programs. Within this group, the top tier of the Football Bowl Subdivision consisted of 125 college teams that accounted for just under 35 million attendees in 2014, with an average game attendance of a little more than 44,000. Thirty football teams reported an average attendance of more than 57,000 per game. The highest average attendance for home games included Alabama, 101,534; Louisiana State University, 101,723; Ohio State University, 106,296; Pennsylvania State University, 101,623; Texas A&M, 105,123; and University of Michigan, 104,909.

In men's basketball, the 345 institutions playing in NCAA Division I had an average attendance of 4,754. At the highest level, forty-one colleges averaged more than 10,000 spectators per game. College teams with the highest attendance per game included Syracuse University, 23,854; the University of North Carolina at Chapel Hill, 19,582; the University of Kentucky, 23,572; the University of Louisville, 21,386; and the University of Wisconsin, 17,279.

Intercollegiate athletics were pervasive in the nation's spectator sports, thanks to broadcasts and branding. On a typical Saturday in October, a sports fan has the opportunity to watch twelve college football games broadcast on major television networks—namely, ABC, NBC, CBS, and ESPN. These viewing opportunities could be expanded to at least another ten games if one were willing to pay a modest subscription or pay-per-view charge. Saturday, of course, has long been the premier day for college football. It started with ESPN's *Game Day*, a sophisticated and successful television show that broadcasts from various college campuses, and interview shows hosted by college sports announcers and commentators who have become media celebrities.

Starting on December 20th each year, after the finish of the regular college football season, which had started in August, television networks broadcast forty postseason bowl games, culminating in January with the playoff quarter finals and then, in early February, the championship game. These latter games attract televising viewing audiences of about twenty-eight million per game. The 2015 championship game between Ohio State University and the University of Oregon attracted about thirty-four million viewers.

Football may have been the favorite college sport for the American public, but it was not the whole story of college sports broadcasts. On a typical January weekend, a slate of intercollegiate basketball games available to a television viewer were thirty-two men's games and four women's games. Whereas college football tended to be concentrated into weekend games, college basketball broadcasts regularly tallied six games per night during the week. Playing college sports—and broadcasting big-time college games—became a nearly 24/7 feature in American popular culture that was a blend of educational, commercial, and cultural activity.

This quantitative profile of spectator college sports in the early twenty-first century extended beyond attendance at the games and the media viewing audiences to include the financial impact on intercollegiate athletics programs. The forty postseason Football Bowl Subdivision (FBS) games distributed $505.9 million to the participating conferences and schools. These same participating institutions and their conferences spent $100.2 million to take part in the bowl games, leading to a net gain of more than $400 million for the college programs. This was a dramatic increase from $310 million in 2013–14 and $301 million payouts for the 2012–13 bowl seasons. One result was the emergence of five "super conferences" that acquired lucrative television contracts. For the Southeastern Conference in 2014–15, this meant distribution of more than $455 million, which broke down to $31.2 million to each of its fourteen member institutions, plus an additional $10 million from football bowl revenues.

Disaggregating Divisions within the NCAA

The composite profile of the NCAA accurately conveyed the large membership and scope of intercollegiate athletics programs. What it masked, however, was that since 1973 the NCAA has been subdivided into important categories according to the manner in which a college or university defined its athletics program as part of its overall institutional character. Outside the big-time, revenue-producing programs of Division I, for example, was NCAA Division II, which comprised approximately three hundred institutions. Most members were relatively small public universities that opted for a hybrid model of the big-time Division I programs and the scholarship-free Division III model. This DIII system is worth special analysis.

NCAA Division III: Anatomy of College Sports outside the Commercial Model

Most media coverage of college sports understandably focused on a small number of institutions and "money" sports in NCAA Division I. In contrast, small-college sports usually associated with NCAA Division III received scant attention. This was often simplistic and even patronizing as an idyllic, inexpensive, and problem-free model that contrasted the highly publicized profits, problems, and scandals associated with big-time schools. In fact, the NCAA Division III institutions had a substantial presence and distinctive set of strengths and liabilities.

Comparing and contrasting Division III with the big time of Division I also was important because over time, DIII coaches and athletics directors adopted or at least mimicked some of the characteristics of big-time sports programs. During this era, many DIII programs increased the number of coaches and support staff, extended the calendar of each sports season, and intensified recruitment of potential varsity athletes even without offering athletic grants-in-aid. These same programs encouraged student-athletes to specialize in a single sport and promoted informal year-round practices and program commitment. The result was that although Division III sports remained distinctive, their character and conduct were still shaped in part by innovations and ideas from Division I.

Division III, established in 1973, eventually became home to more than 440 institutions and 195,000 student-athletes—the most in any division of the NCAA. Many small colleges were balanced with membership by such major research universities as Carnegie-Mellon University, Case Western Reserve University, Emory University, Johns Hopkins University, the Massachusetts Institute of Technology, the University of Chicago, and Washington University. Their teams and athletes competed in twenty-eight national championships. The Division III philosophy claimed that athletics were an integral part of a well-rounded college experience. The public pronouncement was that the athletic experience allowed student-athletes to focus on their academic programs and the ultimate goal of earning a degree. This traditional commitment was accompanied by an acceleration of both academic and athletic intensity for athletes and coaches—and increased expenditures from a college's general fund.[2]

Around 2010, a median athletic budget for a Division III college ranged between $1 million and $2.5 million. A major differential was whether a college fielded a football team. No Division III program was self-supporting in terms of revenues from ticket sales or broadcasts. In contrast to NCAA Division I programs, however, Division III did not include athletic grants-in-aid, and expenses for scholarships and financial aid were separate from the athletics department. Typically, Division III programs were found at colleges with relatively small enrollment. Programs typically provided a large number of sports for both men and women, with twenty-five to thirty-three percent of undergraduates playing a varsity sport.

An important implication for this high-percentage participation was that athletic ability often came to be a factor in admissions decisions. Especially acute at selective academic colleges such as Amherst College and Williams College, high student participation in sports meant that much of the campus land was dedicated to varsity sports facilities. In some cases, as much as thirty to forty percent of a campus would be devoted to intercollegiate athletics. All these issues converged as decisive factors in institutional planning regarding admissions as well as which sports to offer.

In coeducational institutions, a nationwide trend toward an increasing percentage of women undergraduates prompted Division III colleges to reconsider the advantages and disadvantages of fielding a football team, given its high number of squad members—all men—and relatively high expenses for equipment, travel, and construction and maintenance of stadium and training facilities.

Integral to these deliberations was the priority of college sports in the governance and structure of small liberal arts colleges. The athletics director typically reported to the dean of the college or to the vice president for student affairs. This was in marked contrast to the Division I practice in which the AD reported directly to the university president or to the board of trustees. The Division III model meant that ADs and coaches usually had to participate at the budget bargaining table with directors of other extracurricular programs such as performing arts, student activities clubs, theatre, college orchestra, and community service projects. To increase cooperation and collaboration, ADs and coaches had to persuade deans of admissions regarding special provisions and reserve slots for those applicants who had been designated as potentially strong players for a particular varsity sport.[3]

NCAA Division II: A Middle Ground

The NCAA had split into three divisions in 1973 in response to the differing needs and desires within the ranks of its large, diverse institutional membership. While the NCAA's Division III remained committed to prohibiting athletic grants-in-aid, Division II allowed athletic scholarships even though their teams generated far less exposure, revenue, and public pressure. During the ensuing decades, the NAIA continued to lose membership to both NCAA DII and DIII. At the same time, many institutions in DIII also moved to DII in order to offer athletic scholarships.

DII membership remained in flux because of these individual institutional decisions and ambitions regarding athletic classification. New members would join, and then some teams with sustained success at the DII level sought to join DI. In comparison to the "up-or-out" scenario common in big-time athletics, DII offered a more benign option. Winning programs such as Butler University, North Dakota State, Texas State University, and Troy University moved up, landing in DI conferences. But other schools like Grand Valley State University, Northwest Missouri State University, and Valdosta State University decided to stay in DII and continue on their current athletic trajectories.

By the early 2020s, membership in DII hovered around three hundred member institutions, as each new season usually saw some teams leaving for a different division while new colleges were regularly joining the "middle ground" of DII athletics. The three hundred institutions were spread across the continental United States, with members in Alaska, Hawaii, Puerto Rico, as well as at Simon Fraser University in British Columbia, Canada, the only Canadian university with NCAA ties.[4]

Among the member institutions comprising NCAA Division II, approximately fifty percent remained private, with the other half drawn from the ranks of public universities. More than half had twenty-five hundred students or fewer. At the same time, a handful of institutions boasted enrollments exceeding fifteen thousand matriculants. Among DII membership, more than fourteen thousand students participated in conference sports. Median expenses for athletics departments at the DII level stood at just over six million dollars in 2022.[5]

Division II athletic championships have gradually gained greater television (and streaming) exposure beyond the era under consideration. In 2023, semifinal and final games in football as well as men's and women's basketball appeared on one of the ESPN or CBS Sports networks. Other championships moved toward streaming at NCAA.com.[6] In many ways, this arrangement mirrored many "minor" or Olympic sports in some Division I conferences. Interestingly, in 2022 the DII South Atlantic Conference signed a five-year media deal with Flo-Sports, including a seven-figure payout. Although the exact amount was undisclosed, the deal would stream more than thirteen hundred games online and televise twenty-three championships. A few months later, FloSports signed an even more lucrative deal with the Great Lakes Intercollegiate Athletic Conference.[7]

The Mix of Enterprise, Entertainment, and Education in Big-Time College Sports

American universities' increased support for big-time intercollegiate athletics between 2000 and 2010 illustrated the perils of publicity and prestige. The conventional wisdom, as told to boards of trustees and presidents, was that a powerful football and basketball team brought many good things to a university—visibility on television, affiliation for alumni and donors, half-time promotional clips to attract students, and revenues that would support numerous Olympic sports. Furthermore, ADs claimed that a winning sports program stimulated donations to the whole university, including academic programs.[8]

At best, the strategy worked in a few exceptional places. The University of Florida drew from its revenues from championship football and men's basketball teams to funnel massive funding into such sports as volleyball, swimming and diving, soccer, and track—for both men's and women's squads. Ohio State University offered thirty-six varsity sports and had an operating budget of nearly eighty million dollars per year.[9] According to the OSU athletics director, "all athletics dollars were university dollars"—a genuine commitment that included marking nine million dollars for university library improvements over a three-year period, along with other annual transfers for educational programs.

The problem was that by 2010 the University of Florida and Ohio State University were the exception, not the rule. Only seventeen athletics programs among the more than three hundred NCAA Division I institutions were truly self-supporting. Even this estimate was dubious, as Rachel Bachman reported in Portland's newspaper *The Oregonian* in 2010. Bachman described the University of Oregon's athletics department financial profile as follows:

> The Oregon football program's rise in national prominence has brought an increase in donations and ticket sales. For the better part of a decade, University of Oregon officials have touted the athletic department's economic self-sufficiency, a rarity in the world of big-time college sports. But for at least nine years, athletics has used

hundreds of thousands of dollars annually from the university's general fund to cover the cost of academic support for athletes, according to files obtained by *The Oregonian*. The general fund has paid nearly $8.5 million over the past nine years for academic support for athletes, which includes exclusive tutoring and counseling, increasing sixfold from less than $300,000 in 2002–03 to a budgeted $1.8 million this academic year. Meanwhile tuition has nearly doubled, and state support has plummeted to 7 percent of the university's overall budget.[10]

Most athletics departments, including those with high-profile programs associated with the BCS, lost money each year. Particularly surprising was that varsity football, intended to be the golden goose of intercollegiate sports revenue, often cost more to operate than it brought in from ticket sales, television contracts, product endorsements, and alumni donations. Almost all big-time football programs relied on subsidies from the educational side of the university budget. One would be hard-pressed to find a more dysfunctional, disappointing outcome for such an expensive, long-term university investment. In contrast to the enhanced funding for Olympic sports at the University of Florida, most universities looked to reduce their nonrevenue sports, while making certain that they had protected—and enhanced—funding for football and men's basketball. For example, in September 2010 the University of California, Berkeley, announced that it was cutting five of its twenty-four varsity teams.[11] This move was in part a concession to faculty discontent upon discovering that the chancellor had been authorizing annual subsidies of about thirteen million dollars per year, flowing from the campus general fund to the athletics department.

Whatever the athletics balance sheet showed, athletics directors and boards of trustees were prepared to offer yet another justification for funding the arms race in big-time sports. If a program fell short of its mandate to be self-supporting, the deficit was justified because a homecoming game boosted campus morale and brought alumni and donors back to the alma mater, and it was unfair for critics to put a price tag on such important intangibles. Meanwhile, universities also were in a legal bind that impeded cost reductions. Compliance with both Title IX guidelines and the even more stringent NCAA requirements meant that an athletics department was required to maintain a large number of sports and to approach some measure of equity between men and women student-athletes in the areas of scholarship grants-in-aid, training facilities, and coaching salaries. Selective pruning of teams or soliciting for subsidies from the university was the temporary solution. Such measures, however, begged the fundamental question of university priorities and payments.

A few fortunate conferences such as the SEC, the Big Ten, the Atlantic Coast Conference, and the Pac-10 received a reprieve of sorts by negotiating new, lucrative television contracts. Yet even with revenue-sharing within these conferences, some member institutions strained to keep pace financially. Outside these conferences, the vast majority of intercollegiate athletics programs were struggling—and evading genuine resolutions.

The trends within the big-time varsity sports associated with the NCAA's Division I gave rise to what came to be known as "College Sports, Inc.," an institutional commitment to winning teams that tended to position the athletics department as an increasingly special entity within the university structure.[12] This arrangement had consequences for the intercollegiate athletics programs of all colleges and universities. There was a trickle-down effect in which athletics directors and coaches nationwide tended to mimic the entitlement associated with the most powerful programs. It included such practices as preferential admissions for student applicants who were recruited as athletes, allocation of financial aid for athletics scholarships, construction of elaborate new training facilities, and high pay for high-profile coaches. At both Amherst College and the University of Texas, for example, the "branding" of winning teams to market the institution to prospective students and to please alumni had become a common denominator across higher education. By 2005, presidents and board members at several financially stressed small, unselective private liberal arts colleges—such as Adrian College in Michigan—relied on investment in new athletics facilities, coaches' salaries, the addition of new varsity teams, and aggressive recruitment of athletes both to bolster athletics reputation in NCAA Division III and as a strategy to rescue the entire college from its pattern of declining student enrollments and sinking tuition revenues.[13]

Challenges for the Mid-Major Conferences and Colleges

The identity crisis of the NCAA was reflected in its organizational complexity. Its laudable aim of providing an umbrella and uniform voice representing all colleges—and all college sports—suggested a clear mission. But the sheer number of member colleges and universities predictably led to conflicts and family quarrels. Given the prospect that the universities with historic, major established big-time sports programs and their affiliated conferences could always threaten to leave the NCAA, a foremost structural principle was to provide a special category for those colleges and conferences with the perennially most powerful and popular football programs. This prevailed over any other accommodation or refinement in which the aim was to provide functional and logical categories for defining and then regulating institutions and their programs.

Often overlooked by the public was that the NCAA sometimes discouraged bigness. In other words, it was wary of ambitious university presidents and ADs who wished to gain institutional prominence by quickly focusing on, for example, striving to create a national championship football program, to the neglect of other sports. Hence membership in the NCAA's top category of Division I required universities to offer a large number of varsity sports and to ascertain the threshold number of women's sports. An irony of the efforts to create coherence was that they created confusion. The categories followed logic and guidelines, but by the early twenty-first century the result was a complicated mosaic in which athletics programs were imperfectly placed.

Division I, ostensibly the home of colleges and universities with big-time programs geared to large spectator crowds and broadcasts on television, was itself subdivided into Division I-A, I-AA, and I-AAA. Yet the demarcations were not indelible. A big-time football program in Division I-A could schedule a game with a team from Division I-AA—a frequent choice for early season contests or for homecoming games. The DI-AA college and coach often welcomed such invitations as a way to gain revenues and perhaps to score a major upset victory. Complications on who competed against whom increased as one surveyed the roster of more than thirty-five varsity sports.

The foremost example of mixed responses was the split of Division I-A football into the Football Bowl Subdivision (FBS) and the Football Championship Subdivision (FCS). In functional terms, this meant that the FBS conferences and teams, although competitive and excellent, usually did not win most games against the established top powers. But each year there might be a Cinderella story exception, like the Boise State University team shocking Oklahoma in 2007. A recurrent and unavoidable tension in the NCAA categories for institutions and conferences was that a subdivision such as NCAA Division I-AA worked imperfectly in its identities and demarcations. The universities with sports programs in the big-time conferences complained, but on close inspection, they needed the NCAA Division I-AA conferences for early-season games, homecoming opponents, and in some cases geographically convenient fillers in their schedules.

The exceptions and complications increased when one considered varsity sports beyond football. Sports such as lacrosse, swimming, soccer, and field hockey—including both championships for women's teams and men's teams— were not necessarily replications of a university's football or men's basketball reputation. Placing a limit on the minimum and maximum number of athletic grants-in-aid allowed for a particular sport in a particular category to spare some institutions from running up expenses. But such measures were imperfect and often led to dysfunctions. A further complication was that in the twenty-first century, the changes in the membership of conferences altered traditional rivalries and configurations. The net result was that the NCAA categories provided a precarious truce that would require continual revisions and reconsiderations.

The Struggle of Historically Black Colleges and Universities

The challenges faced by mid-majors were only exacerbated at HBCUs playing at the DI level, which included only the Mid-Eastern Athletic Conference and the Southwestern Athletic Conference. The lack of large fan bases and historic underfunding from state legislators placed HBCUs in a precarious situation athletically. The athletic drain to primarily white institutions with vastly superior facilities and funding created an additional burden. In 2006 the median recruiting budgets for HBCUs at the DI level ranged between 278 and 292 out of a total of 308 teams. Only one institution, Delaware State University, had an athletic budget ranked among the top 200.[14]

In this context, HBCUs relied on the same patterns faced by other mid-majors: student fees and guarantee games. Guaranteed-payout games were all away games scheduled against teams from power conferences and helped fund the rest of the season's expenses. HBCUs witnessed a few triumphs over big-time programs in the NCAA Men's Basketball Tournament. In 1997, Coppin State beat the University of South Carolina. In 2001, Hampton upset Iowa State, and in 2012, Norfolk State beat Missouri. All three victories represented 15-seeds defeating 2-seeds. While the games brought press coverage, little came in the way of revenue.[15]

In all, HBCUs had to recruit and compete with its greatest strength: a smaller campus environment that provided more personal contact with professors and coaches. For those who chose that route, it generally meant giving up on the opportunity to compete for a national championship. In this current context, some scholars suggested that the two DI conferences remove themselves from DI competition and focus on DII opportunities.[16]

Billion-Dollar Basketball: The NCAA, CBS, and the Limits of March Madness

Many Division I institutions found themselves in a much different position. As power conferences had begun to capitalize on televised football with stunning financial packages negotiated by individual conferences, the NCAA proceeded to do the same with its one prized revenue generator: the NCAA Men's Basketball Tournament. Since Walter Byers had agreed to allow corporate sponsorships in the 1980s, the tournament had exploded in popularity. Along with it came the NCAA's lifeblood: revenue to fund its business operations and its many other national championships, most of which were not lucrative events.

In the wake of the *Regents* case in 1985 the NCAA tournament expanded from thirty-two to sixty-four teams to generate more revenue. In 1990 the NCAA's annual revenue from the men's basketball tournament amounted to more than $55 million. At that time, it would have been difficult to predict the eye-popping contract negotiated between CBS and the NCAA at the turn of the century. Between 1991 and 1994, CBS paid the NCAA $142 million a year for the men's tournament. A new deal in 1994 upped that amount to $215 million annually through 2002, but the NCAA retained the right to renegotiate a deal in 1999.[17]

Like most professional sports contracts, the current television network reserved a period to be the exclusive negotiator. This meant that for a few weeks in 1999, CBS had the opportunity to provide the sole bid for a new contract. But CBS and the NCAA failed to come to an agreement despite a lucrative offer from CBS Sports executives. The impasse allowed the NCAA to seek bids from other networks, which they did. Both the Fox Network as well as ABC/ESPN entered negotiations, pressuring CBS to offer more than its competitors. Adding to the stress faced by CBS, the network had lost its contract for NASCAR and the Daytona 500, an important piece of its sports portfolio.[18]

Facing the possibility of a rapidly shrinking sports programming, CBS offered the NCAA $6 billion over eleven years (starting in 2003). Averaging out to $545 million a year over the life of the contract, it represented more than a 250 percent increase over the current payout of $216 million annually. What seemed to be the most puzzling aspect of the NCAA's new windfall was the fact that even though March Madness still possessed incredible popular and cultural appeal, the tournament's Nielsen ratings had been on a downward trend during the second half of the nineties. Why was the tournament worth so much more money? Many believed it was not, and that CBS had overbid on the package.[19]

The six-billion-dollar contract made the three-week tournament one of the most lucrative deals in sports history. The increased value of the tournament stemmed from multiple developments. First, ESPN and its parent company ABC hoped to use ESPN's multiple cable networks to broadcast more games. CBS still planned on using its regional approach to the first weekend of the tournament. This meant that while multiple games would be played at the same time, all games would be broadcast exclusively on CBS. The network would determine which game to show on local television affiliates. This approach had been utilized when the NCAA held exclusive rights to football broadcasts. In the age of growing cable and satellite television, along with nascent capabilities to broadcast online, the one-channel broadcasting approach became outmoded. The contract had bundled all media rights, however, including those for cable, satellite, radio, and Internet. As those markets matured, CBS controlled the content.[20]

The other bundled portion of the deal involved corporate sponsorships, or what became known as "corporate partners." Previously, the NCAA's corporate sponsors did not necessarily involve television advertising. In the new deal, all of the NCAA's corporate partnerships would bundle rights to licensing, merchandise, all media advertising into one deal. The impact on advertising revenue proved substantial. For example, in 2001, CBS collected $310 million in advertising. When the new CBS contract began in 2003, that amount jumped to $362 million. The first CBS payout to the NCAA on the deal was $360 million—not exactly a lucrative deal for CBS. By 2007, advertising revenue exceeded $500 million for the first time.[21]

The increase in advertising came in part from commercials on new media—novel ways in which consumers could watch the product. CBS had begun streaming games online for free the previous year on its sports website. The network also partnered with DirecTV to offer all the games through the satellite provider for a sixty-nine-dollar subscription fee. While the revenue increases kept CBS in the black, the payments to the NCAA kept the deal a risky proposition for the network.[22]

The Forgotten March Madness Snub

It appeared that the NCAA Men's Basketball Tournament had been worth CBS's $6 billion gamble. As the *Wall Street Journal* opined, "One of the most bloated sports deals in television . . . isn't turning out to be quite as mad as many thought." CBS's online and satellite initiatives gave hoops fans the opportunity to watch any and all of the games they desired. The release of the iPhone in 2007 also provided a new media, and ATT signed an exclusive mobile deal to stream the tournament on smartphones. Advertisers spent approximately $640 million in 2008, and CBS was putting a wider margin between its NCAA payout and the revenue it generated from advertising. Yet many of those contracts had been signed before the near collapse of the economy and the beginnings of the Great Recession.[23]

In 2009, CBS's advertising revenue dropped (nearly ten percent) for the first time under the contract as it collected an estimated $580 million. Even though the CBS March Madness deal extended through 2013, in 2010 the NCAA would have an opportunity to seek another contract. Sports television contracts extending multiple years often included such options in case the value of the televised product had vastly increased. With the growing online broadcast market, the NCAA believed it could leverage the negotiating window to make even more money.[24]

At the 2010 Final Four in Indianapolis the NCAA held a press conference to roll out its proposed tournament platform. Greg Shaheen, senior vice president for basketball and business strategies, explained the NCAA's decision to move toward a ninety-six-team playing field. During a question-and-answer session, Shaheen struggled to explain how the expanded field would enhance the quality of the tournament. *Washington Post* reporter John Feinstein grilled Shaheen on his disingenuous responses regarding the extended amount of class time students would miss with more games.

Regarding the NCAA's plan and Shaheen's press conference that, ESPN reporter Dana O'Neil wrote:

This is what we learned from NCAA head honchos . . .
- They don't care about fans.
- They don't care about the regular season.
- They don't care about conference tournaments.
- And they sure don't care about student-athletes' being bothered by that pesky "student" portion of their hyphenated moniker by going to class.
- What do they care about? Cash.[25]

No doubt, the NCAA's plan to keep up with the college sports growth model, offered more games for more revenue. Despite the proposal's unpopularity, most reporters resigned themselves to the fact that more money meant a dramatic change to the tournament structure.

Three weeks later, the NCAA announced that they had agreed to a new fourteen-year, $10.8 billion deal that included both CBS and Turner Broadcasting.

The league heralded the fact that for the first time, every game in the tournament would be broadcast nationally (with Turner's cable channels TBS, TNT, and truTV). Interestingly, the new deal created a sixty-eight-team field instead of the NCAA's proposed ninety-six-team format. ESPN had made what they called an "aggressive bid," but it didn't match that of CBS and Turner.[26]

Behind the press releases was the clear fact that the NCAA Men's Basketball Tournament, which provided the NCAA with approximately ninety-five percent of its revenue, was at its profitability ceiling. Thinking that ninety-six teams and a bid from ESPN would boost its profits, the market corrected the NCAA's thinking. As Sean McManus, CBS's president for news and sport, stated, "It was no secret that those three years [remaining on the previous contract] would be very challenging." While NCAA officials remained tight-lipped, Ohio State AD Gene Smith alluded to the NCAA's miscalculation when he said, "It was thought that 96 teams would generate more money . . . but we were able to come to an understanding that gave us the support without adding many teams."[27]

A closer look at the numbers revealed that even with a slight increase in games and national coverage of all games on cable television, the revenue paid to the NCAA during the next three years (2011–13) mirrored the last three years of its exclusive contract with CBS. Simply put, expanding to ninety-six teams was not going to be profitable in ways NCAA executives had believed it would. In fact, CBS had tried to sell the remainder of their contract, but no other network would agree to CBS's terms. Nevertheless, a contract with $770 million annually was still big-time money that would help fund the organization and the growing list national championships it sponsored.[28]

The Bowl Championship Series: The First Step toward a College Football Playoff

While the NCAA focused on cultivating the men's basketball tournament, big-time conferences focused on their own football television deals. Beyond conference television contracts and championships, fans also wanted a football national championship. Divisions I-AA, II, and III, those apparently outside of the commercial influence of intercollegiate sports, had long managed to provide such a football championship for years. After winning the *Regents* case, Chuck Neinas hoped to topple the NCAA with his own College Football Association television contract and eventually institute a college football playoff. The roadblock for the big-time schools, suggested some, was the tradition of historic bowls. In reality, the problem was not just a century of history, but the current bowl contracts that guaranteed power conferences substantial revenue to remain committed to specific bowls, even if meant that the two best teams in the country would not be able to face each other on New Year's Day.

With the power conferences comfortable with their exclusive football contracts, television network executives began looking for ways to create a national championship bowl game. The greatest resistance came from the Big Ten and the Pac-10, which did not want to sacrifice their exclusive deal with the Rose Bowl in order to participate. Over two years' time, Roy Kramer finally convinced Big Ten commissioner Jim Delany that the move would benefit all of college football. The agreement eventually required the Big Ten and Pac-10 to abandon their exclusive claim to the Rose Bowl in favor of the Bowl Alliance, which included the Rose Bowl, the Orange Bowl, the Sugar Bowl, and the Fiesta Bowl. The national championship would be a separate game that would rotate its location among those bowls.[29]

Started in 1998, the BCS was praised for finally developing a way to match the top two ranked teams in college football. In addition, it brought in increased revenue. An appearance in any of the BCS bowl games paid between eleven and thirteen million dollars (in 1998) to the participating teams in each bowl game. Save Notre Dame, which would keep its full share, television revenue was returned to the team's respective conferences to distribute among its members. In order to get an agreement among conferences, the BCS included "automatic qualifier" bids for six conferences: the Atlantic Coast Conference, the Big East, the Big Ten, the Big Twelve, and the Pac-12. The three other spots were available to the highest-ranked teams (determined through a complex series of computer calculations).[30]

Those outside of the power conferences bemoaned the computer formulas, which took into consideration a team's strength of schedule. During the years of the BCS, Boise State, Hawaii, Texas Christian, and Utah made it to BCS bowl games, generating substantial profits for their conferences. After the conclusion of the 2009 season, however, the BCS Committee placed undefeated Boise State and Texas Christian in the Fiesta Bowl instead of providing the non–power conference schools a chance to compete against teams from the elite six conferences.[31]

By the second decade of the twentieth century, the BCS had accomplished its goals. First, it continued to generate astounding revenue from its television contracts, which had bounced from ABC to Fox and then to ESPN. In 2011 the BCS distributed $174 million among its participants. At the same time, the one-game national championship had created enough controversy that the BCS looked to another format: the College Football Playoff. Beginning in 2014, the top four teams would face off in a final four of football, adding an extra game and extra revenue. Yet the four-team playoff was a creation of the conferences, and they kept the money rather than the NCAA. Another major impact on conferences (and realignment) was the fact that with the new format, the College Football Playoff would not provide automatic qualifier status for the six most powerful conferences.[32]

Conference Realignment Puzzle and the Big East

When the Bowl Championship Series began operations in 1998, it boasted 112 (DI-A) BCS teams participating in ten conferences, along with a few independent universities. All conferences, however, were not equal. The Power Six Conferences each earned an automatic qualifier (AQ): a conference champion that was guaranteed a spot in one of the premier bowl games along with a massive payout that covered expenses and then went to each respective conference, where it would be distributed among members. The Atlantic Coast Conference (ACC), Big East, Big Ten, Big Twelve, Pac-12, and SEC comprised the power group, but the Big East, which began as a "basketball conference," held the weakest financial position among its peers. The goal for any aspiring DI BCS school was to land a spot in one of these conferences.[33]

Six AQ conferences meant that two teams from mid-major conferences might be able to land a prized spot (and substantial revenue) in a BCS bowl, even if it was not the national championship matchup. Hence conference shake-ups in the BCS era started with aspiring mid-major institutions and conferences. For example, the Western Athletic Conference (WAC) raided the Big West Conference's key football powers, including Boise State and Utah State. The newly formed Sun Belt Conference took on new members like Middle Tennessee State University and New Mexico State University. Conference USA added Texas Christian to its group of football institutions.[34]

The Power Six Conferences were not immune from realignment, as universities sought to join leagues with greater revenue to boost their programs. The first major post-BCS realignment involving a power conference came in 2004 when the University of Miami and Virginia Tech left the Big East to join the ACC. The following year, Boston College joined the ACC, while the Big East replaced these losses with Cincinnati, Louisville, and South Florida in 2006. During the same decade, some smaller programs from the Football Championship Subdivision (formerly DI-AA) moved to the FBS in an attempt to gain exposure and revenue. By 2010, 120 universities fought to claim a BCS bowl bid, even though only a handful of teams could legitimately contend for a championship.[35]

The elite BCS bowl games included the Fiesta, Orange, Rose, and Sugar Bowls. Even though schools from the power conferences dominated the bowl bids, invitations brought notoriety for schools like Boise State, TCU, and Utah, all of which managed to make it to BCS bowls. In turn, aspiring universities fought to emulate the success of these few institutions. With the support of their governing boards and presidents, these institutions jockeyed for position in stronger conferences. One can find the memberships of the mid-major conferences and see the multiple membership transitions that took place.

The greatest dilemmas occurred as the power conferences sought to expand their media footprint by adding powerful teams in new television markets. As they did, the dominoes would fall conference by conference, with each university trying to land in the best-possible league. As one athletics director noted, conference alignment "was a game we likened to musical chairs. You don't want to be the one standing when the music stops." For example, in 2009 the Big Ten announced it would study potential expansion and the following year added the University of Nebraska. With twelve members, the Big Ten created two divisions and added a conference championship game. Sensing the need to follow suit, the Pac-10 became the Pac-12 when, in 2010, it poached Colorado and Utah from the Big Twelve and WAC, respectively. The following year, Texas A&M and Missouri made plans to join the SEC. The Big Twelve then set out to find the best football programs to fill the gaps created by recent departures.[36]

At the bottom of the pecking order among power conferences stood the Big East. Its television contract with ESPN had generated (only) $37 million annually, but it was up for renewal in 2011. ESPN offered to increase its annual payments in a new contract that would pay $150 million annually with a total of $1.3 billion for the life of the contract. Despite the proposed deal, some institutions felt that the conference could command larger television profits, and the Big East rejected ESPN's offer and invited other networks to bid on their media rights. Before a new contract had been signed, Syracuse and Pitt bolted the Big East for the ACC in September 2011. TCU, which had agreed to join the Big East less than a year earlier, reversed course and accepted membership into the Big Twelve. The Universities of Louisville and West Virginia then vied for the last invitation from the Big Twelve, which ultimately went to the Mountaineers. In time, Louisville would find a big-time home in the ACC.[37]

If the above conference puzzle narrative was difficult to follow, it was only the beginning of the chaos. This particular round of realignment mayhem began when the Big Ten announced its plans to study expansion options, which resulted in the addition of Nebraska to the Big Ten. By the time the ACC had realigned, eighty-four universities in twenty-eight Division I conferences managed to change their league membership. Geographic proximity and institutional similarity had given way to television profits.[38]

Desperate to maintain its status as an elite football conference and find universities that would provide a bargaining chip for their next television deal, Big East commissioner John Marinatto announced that Central Florida, Houston, and Southern Methodist University would join in all sports, while Boise State and San Diego State would become football-only members. Marinatto heralded the new agreement that would greatly expand television markets, with the Big East becoming the first coast-to-coast conference.[39]

To understand the logic of the Big East's decision, which required support of its member university presidents, one only need listen to Commissioner Marinatto, who noted that the conference would have "the single largest media footprint in . . . football." As the first "truly national football conference," he argued, member schools would be part of a base including nearly thirty million television sets in four different time zones. Marinatto thought he had addressed the two driving factors in conference realignment, and they were both related. From a business perspective, it appeared that the conference had found a way to stay among the elite big-time conferences. Of course, adding teams on the West Coast to the *Big East* struck some as odd.[40]

Then the BCS announced that it would move to a four-team playoff model in 2014 and no conference would possess automatic qualifier status. The allure of the Big East for its new football members was gone. John Marinatto resigned his commissioner post, and the league hired former CBS Sports executive Mike Aresco to salvage a lucrative TV contract. Along with Texas Christian's departure, San Diego State and Boise State found no advantage in its Big East membership and signed with the Mountain West Conference. Notre Dame, which had competed in all Big East sports except football, left for the ACC. As the conference continued to look at creative ways to stabilize its football programs, the seven Catholic schools that participated in big-time basketball but not football announced their desire to leave the Big East. In the end, the conference sold its Big East name back to the Catholic Seven and created a new conference that would promote football: the American Athletic Conference.[41]

The Big East proved to be the power football conference casualty. The league's short history, however, provided an important glimpse into the increasing influence of football and the division of revenue in DI college sports. When Dave Gavitt Sr. organized the Big East in the late 1970s, his vision had been the creation of a power conference for basketball among universities in the

Northeast. The conference had been wildly successful in its three decades of existence. Shortly before its demise, the Big East set a record by placing eleven different institutions into the NCAA Men's Basketball Tournament.[42]

The Lesson of the Big East's Demise

As mentioned in chapter 7, the Big East was the brainchild of Dave Gavitt Sr. As he watched football create fissures among NCAA conferences, he envisioned a basketball power conference with a base of members located in the large metropolitan areas in the Northeast. During its first two decades (with the help of ESPN and its "Big Monday" basketball slate), the young conference became a dominant league, challenging other conferences for intercollegiate supremacy on the hardwood.

But the Big East established itself during an era when the NCAA still held a monopoly on televised football. The College Football Association had managed to earn concessions from the NCAA, but Walter Byers's association still controlled the purse strings—and the power. This would all change after the NCAA lost the *Regents* case in 1984. Eventually, the deregulation of televised college football would alter the entire landscape of intercollegiate athletic finances. In the 1980s, however, the initial effect of the US Supreme Court decision led to a glut of football games available for broadcast. The large supply of content led to smaller rights deals, and the power conferences in football experienced revenue shortfalls.

In this environment, the Big East found itself in a favorable position. In the early 1990s, Notre Dame would sign its own football contract, which ultimately led to the demise of the College Football Association and its attempts to piece together a national television contract with the football power conferences. As each conference went its own way and signed deals with different television networks, a new financial model developed: the NCAA would finance its operation through the men's basketball tournament, and the conferences (and their member institutions) would fund their athletic programs with funds from televised football.

This new financial model spelled trouble for the Big East in the twenty-first century. By the time the Big East realized the financial necessity of sponsoring big-time football, the conference had already missed its greatest opportunity to remain relevant in big-time athletics. Long before this landscape had emerged, Pennsylvania State University's legendary football coach Joe Paterno had hoped to build a powerful football conference in the Northeast that was just like the Southeastern Conference in the South or the Big Ten in the Midwest.[43]

Paterno believed the first step to building such a conference in the Northeast was to have Penn State join a league. At first, the Nittany Lions would play in all sports except football, but it would then lure other competitive football programs into the league. With this in mind, Penn State applied for admission into the Big East. While all schools in the Big East played big-time basketball, some members fielded far less competitive football teams while some institutions did not even field a varsity football squad in the early 1980s.[44]

The Big East's bylaws required that seventy percent of its membership approve by vote to accept any new members. With eight institutions, six needed to support Penn State's bid to join the conference. But Georgetown University, St. John's University, and Villanova voted as a block to deny Penn State's admission to the league. In doing so, it hoped to solidify the Big East as a basketball conference. When conference commissioner Dave Gavitt asked his righthand man Mike Tranghese what he thought about excluding Penn State, Tranghese said, "We will all rue the day about this decision." The Big East instead accepted the Pitt Panthers, who were willing to set aside their football ambitions (for the time being) in favor of the profitable funding that came from the Big East Conference's basketball tournament. By the end of the 1980s, Penn State became the eleventh member of the Big Ten.[45]

During the late 1990s and early 2000s, the Big East continued to attempt to boost its football profile, but it ended up being a short-term landing spot for many schools. Louisville, Miami, Virginia Tech, and West Virginia were all short-term members. The admission of members with a football focus gave the Big East enough sway to earn the conference an automatic qualifier spot in the BCS bowl games. But the division in philosophy among members created tension within the league. This was especially acute as football powers left to join more powerful football conferences.[46]

The lesson of the conference realignment puzzle was that funding a big-time conference required big-time football. Surviving as an elite athletic conference in the twenty-first century meant signing lucrative television contracts to fill the conference coffers. The fact that the Big East received eleven bids for the NCAA tournament not long before the league fell apart was the result of the conference's original mission. Yet this mission conflicted with the twenty-first-century financial reality, and the Big East could not keep up with the top one percent of the elite athletics programs in the other power conferences.

When the "old" Big East died, the basketball members retained the conference name and invited Butler, Creighton, and Xavier as members. Since that time, the Big East has remained a force in both men's and women's NCAA DI basketball. It is interesting to ponder why the Big East's continued success in basketball has not lured other conferences to pursue such a path. An answer might lie in the fact that most of its members remained small Catholic universities in urban areas that did not fit the mold of the standard American university.[47]

The Flutie Effect: Athletic Success and Academic Recruitment

In both football and basketball, expanded television not only brought in revenue for big-time programs; it also increased exposure for mid-majors and small schools that experienced athletic success on a national stage. While research indicates that sports victories do not have a clear correlation to university giving, the "Flutie effect," as it became known, was a real phenomenon. The reference stemmed from Boston College quarterback Doug Flutie, who threw a last-second Hail Mary during a nationally televised game on Thanksgiving weekend to defeat the then-powerhouse Miami Hurricanes in 1984. Applications to BC jumped thirty percent the following year.[48]

The phenomenon continued in the 2000s as well. When Boise State defeated the University of Oklahoma in the Fiesta Bowl in January 2007, applications the following year jumped by eighteen percent. Texas Christian University did not have a dramatic victory like Boise State, but its success on the gridiron during the first decade of the 2000s, coupled with institutional recruitment efforts, led to the doubling of applications between 2000 and 2008. Even an established and nationally recognized institution like Notre Dame witnessed significant jumps in applications in 2003, 2006, and 2007—the years after successful football seasons. While athletic prowess might not have convinced philanthropists to write checks to their alma maters, evidence pointed to the fact that it mattered to many college-bound high school seniors.[49]

Probably the most systematic use of football as part of an institutional revival occurred when the University of Alabama hired Nick Saban in 2007. To many, Saban's eight-year contract worth thirty-two million dollars provided evidence of everything wrong with higher education. During the ensuing years, however, Alabama's football dominance paralleled an increase in applications and matriculates. Further, as the state slashed its higher education funding during the Great Recession, the University of Alabama saw a dramatic rise in out-of-state students who paid higher tuition.[50]

Alabama surged past its in-state rival in applications and enrollment only after Saban's arrival. Five years later, the student enrollment growth in Tuscaloosa was palpable. An undergraduate student body of fewer than nineteen thousand existed when Saban signed with the Crimson Tide. By 2012, that number had exploded to more than twenty-eight thousand. During the same time, Alabama's faculty grew from thirteen hundred to seventeen hundred. The growing out-of-state students had increased tuition revenue in excess of fifty million dollars.[51]

The relationship between Alabama's football success and enrollment growth should be approached with caution. It would be unwise to assume that football—in a vacuum of all other factors—created such growth. Nor should one assume football was *the* growth strategy. When Saban was hired, for example, university president Robert Witt had already announced his strategic plan to build a national university with an enrollment of twenty-eight thousand by 2013. The initiative included an elaborate marketing campaign, and over the next decade, Alabama added dozens of full-time recruiters, most of whom worked outside of the state. Still, President Witt would eventually state in an interview that hiring Saban was "the best financial investment this university has ever made."[52]

While some might disagree with Witt's assessment of Saban as an investment, studies have confirmed that athletic success has a correlation to growth in student applications and enrollment. In a study titled *The Dynamic Advertising Effect of Collegiate Athletics,* Doug Chung, a Harvard Business Administration professor, found that gridiron success had a significant impact on both the number of applicants as well as the quality of applications. When universities had wildly successful seasons, applications rose by an average of eighteen percent. Even though athletic success had a greater impact on students with lower SAT scores, such success still had a positive influence on students with high scores as well. Another study by two brothers, Devin and Jaren Pope, found similar results. But the authors separated the results of their study from any policy suggestions that investing in athletics for recruiting was a sound policy.[53]

Not all colleges had the opportunity for the Flutie effect in football, but smaller schools witnessed similar results with successful tournament runs in March Madness. The automatic qualifier bid given to each DI conference placed many small schools in the NCAA tournament field each year. When Virginia's George Mason University made a run to the Final Four, it saw a twenty-two percent jump in applications, an eight percent jump in out-of-state matriculants, and admissions inquiries jumped over three hundred percent.[54]

George Mason was not alone in seeing a Cinderella story result in an admissions spike. Virginia Commonwealth University experienced a similar jump when it made it to the Final Four in 2011. The following year, VCU experienced a twenty-two percent increase in applications and saw the same eight percent increase in out-of-state students, driving up tuition revenue. Butler University in Indianapolis made repeat appearances in the Final Four in 2010 and 2011. During the following two years, applications bounced fifty-two percent. A study commissioned by the university estimated the media coverage from their tournament success ran in excess of a billion dollars.[55]

These short-lived spikes and additional "long-term goodwill effect on future applications and quality," as Doug Chung characterized it, certainly captured the attention of university administrators. Yet sustained basketball tournament success had its own version of Alabama, albeit at a much smaller institution. The greatest example of a sustained Flutie effect in college basketball began in the late nineties and belongs to Gonzaga University. The Jesuit university in Spokane, Washington, had fallen on hard times during the 1990s. Enrollment had shrunk from more than 4,000 in 1990 to 2,700 in 1998. That same year, the incoming freshman class numbered approximately 550 students. After one year of a run to the Elite Eight in the NCAA Men's Basketball Tournament, the next freshman class exceeded 700 students. Gonzaga's head coach capitalized on the success and accepted an offer from a big-time program at the University of Minnesota.[56]

Gonzaga then offered the head coaching position to assistant coach Mark Few. His Bulldog team managed to make a run to the Sweet Sixteen in his first season as head coach. The following year, Gonzaga matriculated more than 900 first-year students. Big-time programs sought to lure Few away from the small DI school, but the coach chose to stay in Spokane. His continued success on the basketball court made him an iconic figure in Spokane and beyond.

As Gonzaga University began its impressive postseason basketball, university supporter Jack McCann accepted an invitation to join the institution's board of trustees. He quickly realized Gonzaga was in financial trouble. The school had run a deficit for years, but that year the university decided to eliminate thirty positions and terminate employment for an additional handful of employees who were poor performers in their jobs. The cuts revealed the type of economic challenges faced by Gonzaga. In fact, many faculty members suggested Gonzaga needed to remove itself from DI athletics in order to save money.[57]

Gonzaga continued its tournament success for the next decade (and beyond). It translated into greater fundraising, stronger admissions standards, and growing status in the larger academy. For starters, individuals inside and outside of the academy learned where Gonzaga was located and the proper pronunciation of the institution: Gon-ZAG-uh rather than Gon-Za-GUH.

Fundraising efforts lead to campus expansion that included both athletic and academic projects. As former president Father Robert Spitzer noted, Gonzaga had not determined to close its doors during the late nineties, but board members were acutely aware that if the precipitous drop in enrollment had continued during the next few years, a shuttering of the university was possible. Instead of closing its doors, basketball success led Gonzaga into a new and prosperous era. As Father Spitzer stated, "Thank God for the basketball team."[58]

Numerous scholars have pointed out that admissions and enrollment are complex processes that involve more than just athletic success. This is certainly true. But the increased competition among universities for students provides a glimpse into the differing views between the academic mission espoused by faculty and the collegiate experience sought by entering college students in the twenty-first century. In addition, the very discussion and growing body of research on the topic suggests a growing understanding of both the cultural impact of athletics and the business-oriented university administrators who are keenly aware of this data. As Alabama administrator Kevin Whitaker discussed the entire recruitment process with the *New York Times*, he noted, "I hate very much to use this analogy, but it's like running a business."[59]

Changes in NCAA Leadership: New President Myles Brand in 2004

Amid the changing dynamics of college sports and the beginnings of conference realignment, a real and symbolic change in the NCAA came about in 2004 with appointment of Myles Brand as the new NCAA president, marking the first time that a university president had served as leader of the NCAA. It also marked the first time the NCAA president held a PhD and served extensively as a tenured full professor, academic dean, and provost prior to serving as a university president. Prior to joining the NCAA, Brand had been president of Indiana University, where he gained national attention for his firm dealings with the highly publicized and highly controversial basketball coach Bobby Knight. Before accepting the presidency of Indiana University in 1996, Brand had been president of the University of Oregon.[60]

Brand was committed to reconciling athletics with academics. For example, NCAA promotions emphasized that most college athletes did not go on to professional sports careers—but they did complete degrees and went on to achievement in professions. One of Brand's hallmark acts as NCAA president was to recruit faculty scholars nationwide to be charter members in the NCAA's

Research Advisory Group. They received resources and a free hand in organizing a research symposium on college sports, showcased at the start of the NCAA's annual convention. Unfortunately, Brand's leadership and academic emphasis were unexpectedly cut short in 2009 when he was diagnosed with pancreatic cancer and died shortly thereafter. After that, the NCAA resumed what might be termed "business as usual."

Futile Attempts at Faculty Control

One group conspicuously absent from big-time college sports deliberations were professors. The NCAA did have an explicit provision for each member institution to have a faculty athletic representative, or FAR. But this group had little formal or informal influence. A professor serving as a college's FAR was appointed by the college president, not the faculty senate or other representative academic body. Their role within NCAA policy councils was limited to being advisory—and could readily be ignored. Perhaps one of the few and best indications of a grassroots initiative that included a faculty voice was formation of the national body known as the Drake Group. This group's autonomy allowed it to be candid and prompt in response to major college sports issues. Autonomy also was one of its limits, as it had no formal connection with decision-making at the level of the NCAA, collegiate conferences, or at colleges and universities.

Stadium Expansion and Luxury Boxes: A Sign of Corporate College Athletics

One new development at the turn of the century revealed that, indeed, faculty were not in control of athletic policy. In the late 1990s and early 2000s the ever-increasing television contracts for the football power conferences continued to produce revenue, grow fanbases, and increase the demand for tickets. Long gone were the debates among NCAA members as to whether television would harm gate receipts. The answer for half a century was a resounding "no," at least among the big-time sports programs. This led to a massive boom in stadium expansion during the 1990s and 2000s. At the wealthiest programs, stadium expansion and renovation became practically a never-ending process.

To be sure, stadium construction and expansion for the wealthiest schools was nothing new. In 1903, Harvard's class of 1879 donated $100,000, and along with $75,000 from the Alumni Association, the Crimson built a stadium seating more than 30,000 spectators. Not to be outdone, Harvard's rival opened the Yale Bowl in 1914 with more than double the capacity at 70,000. Across the country, funds were used to build stadia honoring boosters, presidents, or students lost to one of the World Wars.[61]

What seemed stunning for "amateur" sport at the turn of the twenty-first century was the jaw-dropping amount of money big-time programs would spend to one-up the competition. The University of Tennessee's addition brought its seating capacity to over 104,000 in 2000. A year earlier, the University of Texas had added grandstands to bring its seating to more than 80,000. Not to be outdone, Texas A&M completed an addition costing more than $30 million, bringing its capacity to 2,000 more than their in-state rivals. In the Midwest, Ohio State expanded Ohio Stadium, partially enclosing the Horseshoe with capacity above the 100,000 threshold. As these trendsetters expanded in the late 1990s and early 2000s, less wealthy football programs in the same power conferences followed suit. At Stanford, for example, the administration decided to demolish its historic but deteriorating stadium in favor of a new facility.[62]

Two particularly conspicuous gifts came to athletics departments during the 2000s. The largest was a donation from T. Boone Pickens. After getting cut from the Texas A&M baseball team (in the 1940s), Pickens transferred to Oklahoma State University. After graduating, Pickens became a giant in the oil industry. Later in life, he gave substantial sums to his alma mater, including a $165 million donation to OSU athletics for an athletic village and stadium expansion, among other items. Millions more came in from Pickens for both athletics and academics, and the stadium now bears his name.[63] Although a smaller gift, Nike founder Phil Knight gave the University of Oregon Athletic Department $100 million, to be used to construct a new arena. A regular donor to both Oregon athletics and academics, Knight's philanthropy had already been solicited for expansions at Autzen Stadium.[64]

Beyond stadium (and occasionally arena) expansion and construction, a ubiquitous new element appeared in collegiate renovations: the luxury box. First introduced in the Houston Astrodome in 1965, skyboxes slowly made their way into other professional sports venues during the next decades. In 1982 the University of Oregon opened the Stadium Club at Autzen Stadium, to be used for football team meetings as well as "gatherings for UO donors."[65] The University of Tennessee added executive suites to Neyland Stadium in 1987, and the University of Texas followed suit in the 1990s. Luxury boxes remained a rarity in college football during the twentieth century, however.

During the 2000s, enough universities added executive suites that competitors had to follow suit. In the Big Ten, Penn State added three stories of luxury boxes at Beaver Stadium in 2001. That same year, Ohio State's renovations featured luxury boxes (sold at $70,000 a season) along with substantial "club seating."[66] Fellow Big Ten member Wisconsin did so in 2005. Similar growth occurred among other power conferences at the same time.

The luxury box phenomenon hit an impasse at the University of Michigan's Big House. Boasting the largest seating capacity in the country (107,501), Michigan Stadium had an iconic history. It also had major infrastructure problems that needed to be rectified. In order to pay for it, athletics director Bill Martin proposed the addition of luxury boxes, which commanded greater revenue. But Michigan alum John Pollack started an opposition movement to the renovation that included Feilding Yost's grandson and former university president James Dunderstat, who had retired and returned to faculty. Dunderstat noted that rival Notre Dame deliberately rejected the idea of luxury suites and Michigan should do the same, because they sent a message that sport viewing was for the elite rather than Michigan's working class. Despite their efforts, the project was approved.[67] In a few years, Notre Dame followed suit.

The luxury suite era of stadium expansion followed trends in big-time football. During a time of corporate sponsorships, universities wanted to reward personal and corporate donors as well as cultivate new ones. At the same time, the cost of constructing luxury boxes excluded many universities that did not have the capital to invest or the big-time donors to recruit. For many, the luxury box phenomenon pointed to everything wrong with college athletics. For athletics departments that could afford it, it provided another level of status and separation in the continued escalation in college athletics.

The Sports Spending Spiral: Findings of the 2009–2010 Knight Commission Report

In 2009 the Knight Commission on Intercollegiate Athletics convened a symposium in Miami, Florida, to bring together a mix of college and university presidents, athletics directors, conference officials, some professors, television network executives, journalists, and other influential figures involved in college sports. The focus was on the convergence of two disconcerting findings: first, that spending on college sports was spiraling upward and far outpaced spending on educational and instructional programs within colleges. Second, the summary of surveys indicated that college and university presidents acknowledged that they had little control over these imbalances.[68]

One example of the limited effectiveness of university presidents intending to implement sound practices came from William E. "Brit" Kirwan, former chancellor of the University of Maryland and former president of the Ohio

State University who had been a longtime leader in the Knight Commission panels and studies urging the reform of big-time college sports. Looking back at the 2009–10 Knight Commission projects and panels, he noted in his valedictory interview in 2015 with *Inside Higher Ed* reporters that one of his biggest regrets was that college and university leaders, including himself, had lost control of intercollegiate athletics. That year at his institution, the University of Maryland, the intercollegiate athletics department reported a $95 million debt, including $31 million owed to the Atlantic Coast Conference for leaving the conference to join the Big Ten. Despite these debts, the athletics department was planning to spend $155 million to convert its old basketball arena into a new football practice facility. Kirwan noted that college sports were "the one area of a university where presidents were not in control." He continued, "There's sort of the face that they are in control, but can you imagine a president of a big-time football power announcing that they were going to de-emphasize intercollegiate athletics and concentrate more resources on academics?" Kirwan concluded, "It's a sad state of affairs, but short of some intervention by a powerful outside source I don't see how we move off this trajectory."[69]

Conclusion: Athletics as a Window into the Academy

A key theme in college sports during the first decade of the twenty-first century clearly involved the ability to keep up with the competition. From stadium expansion and conference realignment/expansion, "keeping up with the Joneses" certainly appeared out of control. A closer look at the numbers showed impressive growth in football revenue *and* profit. The University of Arkansas, for example, had grown its revenue from $14 million in 1999 to $61 million in 2012. This growth of over three hundred percent was far below the leader of the pack. The University of Texas had increased revenue from $18 million to more than $130 million. The jaw-dropping increases among football schools in the power conferences could be directly related to the growing negotiating ability of conferences in schools who in some respects were novices at the craft heading into the twenty-first century.[70]

For the rich, the profitability of football remained intact as well. The University of Michigan had made $12 million on football at the turn of the century. That number increased to more than $60 million in 2012. Not to be outdone, the University of Texas led the profitability margin as well, jumping from $10 million to $77 million. More modest growth existed across the power conference teams, but it was clear that athletics in general (and football in particular) had found new methods to exploit untapped markets.[71]

The trendsetters in collegiate sport business created an environment in which rival teams felt pressure to keep up with the competition. This took the form of smaller stadium expansion projects, locker room renovations, weight room improvements, and other enticements to lure the best players to sign with one campus over another. Doing the most they could with substantial but limited revenue, most colleges ran a deficit in their attempts to measure up to their wealthiest peers. Maryland's situation addressed above provided a case in point. Virtually no school chose to give up the quest to keep up with the Joneses, however. Hence presidents, professors, and critics called it the growing "arms race" in college athletics.

What these critics often failed to consider were the ways in which college athletics mirrored universities themselves, albeit it in a much more public fashion. Using a sports analogy to describe a troubling economic development, in 1995, Philip Cook and Robert Frank detailed a "winner-take-all" approach that was the natural outcome of an athletic event but was being applied in areas across society, to the detriment of all. Closely related to the arms race analogy, the ability to outspend one's competition was the surest way to stay on top.[72]

A few years later, Robert Frank gave a speech titled "Higher Education: The Ultimate Winner-Take-All Market?" Frank suggested that the growing race for prestige and rankings in higher education had created similar problems. In a quest for top rankings, institutions engaged in a "positional arms race." Frank noted that universities needed to recruit the very best students to maintain elite status.

> Schools are spending more now not just to attract good students, but also to keep them happy when they arrive. For example, as the material living standards of affluent Americans have escalated in recent years, universities have felt increasing pressure to upgrade campus amenities. Yesterday's double-room occupancy standard in dormitories is giving way to apartment-like suites that house one student per bedroom. Centralized athletic complexes [for nonathletes] are giving way to in-dorm training facilities that resemble expensive private health clubs. Dining halls are being supplanted by facilities modeled after the food courts in up-market shopping malls. . . . Universities that fail to offer such facilities often fail in their efforts to attract the disproportionate share of high-achievement students who come from affluent families. But these facilities also create new financial hurdles for middle- and low-income parents.[73]

Using an example from 1997, Frank highlighted Columbia University's failed attempt to lure a leading scholar by offering a salary of three hundred thousand dollars, subsidized living arrangements, a position for his spouse, as well as a spot at an elite private school for their child. The faculty member could then also hire a half dozen additional faculty members. The examples continued: excessive spending on recruitment and marketing, career services, dining facilities, and new classroom buildings. Most critical to this problem was the tendency toward merit-based aid alone. The biggest scholarships often went to the "best" students, even if they were wealthy, leaving it more difficult for students with demonstrable financial need to gain access and scholarship aid to elite universities.[74]

As one history of higher education has noted, the quest for funding, publicity, students, and rankings deserved a name change for many universities. The historic land grant mission and its A&M model could be altered from "agriculture and mechanics" to "athletics and medicine." For land grant institutions and flagship universities that boasted a medical school, the parallels to athletics provided a glimpse into the changing philosophical nature of the modern American university in the twenty-first century.[75]

The new A&M provided two highly visible programs that many viewed as critical to institutional identity. Since both athletics and medicine brought in copious sums of money, whether through research grants or television contracts, they represented the new pillars of a powerful, prestigious university model. A challenge emerged in both new A&M areas—it cost a great deal of money to make money, placing many programs in a precarious position. Leading medical academics were often courted like coaches, being offered lucrative contracts and the promise to build their own staffs. The payoff would come in grant funding, a stronger applicant pool, and increased visibility.[76]

Such strategies did not always pan out, as some medical schools in the early twenty-first century struggled to make ends meet. Too often, finances were dependent on external forces (such as the stock market fluctuations or changes in Medicare or Medicaid policy). When medical schools fell on hard times, they were viewed as too indispensable to fail. In one case, a president proposed bailing out a medical school and its finances by taking money from other academic colleges and programs.[77]

Similar challenges and policies occurred with athletics as well. At the same time, other traditional campus units were struggling. Once considered the heart of many universities, colleges of arts and sciences (A&S) often found themselves in dilapidated buildings with shrinking finances. Across campus, university athletics programs or medical schools were seeking huge capital outlays for the latest construction project. The competition (and challenges) was as complicated as ever.[78]

Economists Howard Bowen and Charles Clotfelter applied the winner-take-all mentality to the cost of college attendance. Tuition had skyrocketed because "universities raise all the money they can, and they spend all that they have." As universities engaged in this practice, it was convenient for presidents to highlight runaway costs of athletics in one discussion, and the problems of escalating tuition in another. In this way, the relationship between the two remained unexamined. The very fact that universities themselves were examining and highlighting the market value of a Final Four run or the Flutie effect on applications suggests the prevalence of this theme. University personnel were doing what they were charged to do: figure out a way to be the best.[79]

These arguments first posited in the 1990s proved prophetic in the twenty-first century. One of the more interesting developments in the 2000s was the creation of recreation centers including resort-style lazy rivers. The University of Houston opened theirs (along with a rock-climbing wall and pool) with a waterfall in 2003. The Mizzou Rec opened in 2005 at the University of Missouri, complete with tranquil pools and an indoor lazy river. Texas Tech completed its pool and recreation center in 2009, with multiple pools and a 645-foot lazy river at a cost of $8.4 million.[80]

After lazy rivers, universities turned to private developers to build high-end, resort-style apartment complexes, often adjacent to (and occasionally on) campus. Taking Frank's prediction to extremes, universities across the country promoted such lodging, which might include designer furniture, walk-in closets, single bedrooms and bathrooms, and kitchens boasting granite countertops.[81]

In this context, university presidents, athletics administrators and coaches found themselves in a dilemma that had existed for decades but had reached unparalleled heights: how to slow down excessive university spending. The "new normal" represented what Howard Nixon called "The Athletic Trap."[82] For this, Robert Frank suggested a mutual détente. No university president could "go it alone" and survive. Yet by the time the Bowl Championship Series announced that it would be moving to a four-team "College Football Playoff," nobody had chosen to step out of the arms race. For both higher education as a whole and athletics in particular, there were concerns about an unsustainable bubble that would eventually burst.

9

Commercialism, Conflicts, Conferences, and COVID-19, 2012 to 2024

The Crises and Reconfiguration of College Sports

An Era of Unprecedented Change Begins

The year 2012 marked a new era in college sports. On the one hand, the most powerful programs and conferences solidified greater control than in preceding decades. Illustrative of this trend was that the Bowl Championship Series fell by the wayside, and a new college football playoff confined to the four top-ranked teams was announced with great fanfare. The new four-team playoff was a welcomed expansion for college football fans who found the BCS format confusing and suspect. The computer-generated rankings and bowl matchups frustrated many, eliciting responses that included a book titled *Death to the BCS: The Definitive Case against the Bowl Championship Series*. Placed in historical perspective, the BCS, which had been ushered in during the nineties under the guidance of Jim Delany (Big Ten commissioner) and Roy Kramer (Southeastern Conference commissioner), proved to be the first stepping stone to postseason expansion and greater profits for big-time football programs and conferences. Ultimately, however, it was a temporary measure, not a final resolution.[1]

Another critical development at first barely raised any eyebrows outside of a small group of scholars. During Myles Brand's era of leadership at the NCAA, the organization developed a long-overdue plan to sponsor an academic conference. Academics studying college sports would come together and present their research to inform decision-makers facing challenging dilemmas in the world of higher education and athletics. The conference got off to an inauspicious start, but within a few years it had developed into a substantive event during which pressing economic, educational, and ethical dilemmas were addressed. Brand's brainchild, the Academic Colloquium, operated for a half-dozen years. This innovative feature did not continue after Myles Brand's untimely death, however. Its last meeting was in 2012. Early in 2013 the NCAA simply announced it was discontinuing the event.

Scott Kretchmar, a professor at Pennsylvania State University who helped organize the conference, recalled that when Mark Emmert became NCAA president, it became clear that the new executive "shared neither Brand's academic interest nor his leadership vision." Kretchmar then speculated that the demise of the Academic Colloquium may have begun with Emmert's arrival at the NCAA. Emmert led the NCAA from 2010 to 2023. During this final era under consideration, the NCAA witnessed unprecedented scandal, unmatched control assumed by power conferences, and unparalleled influence from the government concerning the rights of college athletes, the last of which the NCAA vehemently opposed. These issues, about which the dissemination of research from scholars at the Academic Colloquium might have helped policymakers at the NCAA, were now cast aside and ignored by the new NCAA executive leadership.[2]

The Conference Television Network Boom

Just as the NCAA continued to negotiate a more lucrative March Madness contract with CBS, the power conferences managed to further monetize their own deals with various television networks. The evolution of televised sports at the big-time level revealed how long it took for conferences to fully leverage their "content" or "product" to the viewing public. In 1984 the US Supreme Court struck down the NCAA's right to monopolize televised college football with the *Board of Regents v. NCAA* (1984) decision. But it would be nearly three decades before the majority of power conferences fully exploited this opportunity. The development of cable and satellite television, along with streaming services, played a role in this delay as well.

Interestingly, the first conference sports network was not a product of the Power Five Conference. Instead, the aspiring Mountain West Conference held the distinction as first league to negotiate terms for its own conference television network. Headquartered at the Comcast Media Center in Denver, "The Mtn." began broadcasting the MountainWest Sports Network in September 2006. With few big-time programs, the network struggled to sign cable deals to expand viewership. Utah then left the Mountain West for the Pac-12, and the first sports channel devoted to a single conference ceased operations in 2012. The short history highlighted the difficulty for aspiring mid-major conferences and universities to compete in off-the-field commercialized athletics, even when developing competitive teams on the field or hardwood.[3]

Following closely behind the Mountain West Conference, the Big Ten announced its decision to create its own sports network in 2006 and went live before the opening of football season in 2007. Unlike The Mtn., when the Big Ten Network went live, it was available in more than thirty million homes. One of its first football broadcasts witnessed a historic upset of the University of Michigan by Appalachian State. With viewers tuning in from across the country, even when a conference member lost on the field, it won in viewership and advertising revenue. In one year, the Big Ten Network expanded to more than sixty million homes, creating a true national network, partially thanks to its network partner Fox and its distribution on satellite television giant DirecTV. While the Big Ten did not reveal its revenue agreement, the conference reported to the Internal Revenue Service that Fox paid the conference $72 million in 2009.[4]

Many sports commentators expected other power conference to quickly follow the Big Ten's lead, but that did not happen. Instead, other big-time conferences used this opportunity to leverage more lucrative deals with preexisting partnerships. With the Big Ten network's financial success, however, it was only a matter of time until the other power conferences joined the broadcast world with their own exclusive television channels. The Pac-12 Network launched before the 2012 football season, and for fiscal year 2012–13, the conference generated $334 million in revenue, edging out both the Big Ten and the SEC.[5]

The SEC soon followed suit with its own network. Even though it had inked a fifteen-year deal worth more than $2 billion in 2008, by 2013 the league opted to form a network. When the SEC Network launched in 2014, it had gained access to ninety million homes. Although projected to turn a profit in its third year, the SEC Network generated more than $100 million in its first nine months of operation (which included football and basketball season). During the summer of 2015, *Forbes* proclaimed that "The SEC is finally the most valuable conference in college sports." It estimated that the conference generated nearly $350 million in TV revenue. Of the approximately $1.3 billion that the leading ten conferences brought in during the previous year, the SEC claimed twenty-seven percent of that revenue, while the Big Ten claimed twenty-one percent of national college sports revenue.[6]

Not to be outdone, the Big Ten had recently poached the University of Maryland from the Atlantic Coast Conference and Rutgers University from the American Athletic Conference. Although neither school was perennial power in football, they added important television markets for the Big Ten. With its new members, the conference renegotiated its deals with both Fox and ESPN and once again took the lead in revenue generation.

In 2015 the ACC generated the least amount of revenue among the power five conferences. In 2013 the conference had added the University of Pittsburgh and Syracuse as members. Notre Dame also joined the ACC in all sports except football. Finally, the University of Louisville became an ACC member in 2014. The ACC lacked the large group of football powers that both the Big Ten and SEC boasted. In addition, the compact membership of universities in North Carolina (with Duke, North Carolina, North Carolina State, and Wake Forest) created an overlapping map of television markets, which networks closely monitored. Still, the basketball-heavy conference eventually announced plans with ESPN to operate the ACC Network, which launched in August 2019. After its first year, the ACC Network helped increase television revenue by $40 million for the 2019–20 fiscal year. This led to payouts of more than $32 million per member school. While impressive, it remained more than $10 million below the payouts for members of the Big Ten and SEC.[7]

The Big Twelve remained the only conference that did not develop its own conference network. For starters, it did not distribute television profits equally. The biggest challenge, however, remained the fact that the conference's most influential member chose to form its own sports channel. Launched before the beginning of the 2011 football season, the Longhorn Network provided twenty-four-hour coverage of University of Texas sports, academic programs, and cultural arts events. Operated by ESPN, the twenty-year contract served to enrich the University of Texas, which did not share profits with the rest of the Big Twelve. The deal also ensured that Texas would not leave the Big Twelve for the Pac-12 during that particular season of conference realignment. But the Longhorn Network failed to develop a truly national scope in its first years, costing ESPN nearly $50 million during the first five years of operation. It also hindered the rest of the conference from creating its own network. Nevertheless, the Big Twelve negotiated a lucrative television package with ESPN and Fox that was worth more than $2.5 billion over thirteen years.[8] Unfortunately, the major growth in revenue gains among big-time sports programs paralleled increasingly shocking scandals at such institutions.

Big Problems for Big-Time College Sports

On the evening of November 18, 2018, ESPN broadcast to a national prime-time television audience an exciting men's basketball game that pitted the University of Louisville against Michigan State University. It accompanied the live fan game attendance of 14,600. All this was part of the excitement of two perennial national powerhouse teams picked by sportswriters to be contenders for the NCAA championship. But March Madness could wait. This highly publi-cized ACC/Big Ten conference challenge was no less than a big game with a big crowd and a big upset, as the University of Louisville won in overtime, 82–78. Isn't this what big time college sports were all about?

The answer was a resounding "Yes!" But the popularity and success of the game masked other developments at the two competing institutions: scandals, resignation of presidents, firing of coaches, litigation, suspensions, and penalty fees—all associated with intercollegiate athletics. The fact that these problems and embarrassments did not disrupt the game for coaches, players, fans, alumni boosters, or networks was a testimony to the resilience of big-time college sports to prevail in American life. It also was symptomatic of the deep-rooted traditions of conflict and corruption that had accompanied the commercialism of college sports. Most troubling was that commercial success persisted despite concerns about educational ethics and calls for reform.

This episode conveyed how in the years from 2012 to 2024, newspaper cov-erage of intercollegiate athletics in the United States often went from the sports page to the front page.[9] Stanford historian David Labaree's provocative claim in 2017 was that "Nobel prizes are great, but college football is why Amer-ican universities dominate the globe." His detailed explanation was that the popular appeal of college sports placated many who were either indifferent to or critical of higher education. And on a more positive note, the color and ap-peal of big-time college sports had long provided streams of political capital and private donations to colleges and universities, not just for sports but for numer-ous academic and educational programs and services elsewhere on campus. The reasoning was that any abuses or problems associated with college sports evidently were bearable because, on balance, "football, along with other inter-collegiate sports, has been enormously helpful in building the college brand."[10]

Would these practices and policies be adequate for the future American higher education? A convergence of events in the years following Labaree's op-timistic 2017 article indicated that scandals involving college sports often went beyond a few coaches, athletics directors, boosters, and student-athletes accused of misconduct. The sports-related abuses were serious and rightfully cast into the public spotlight. Flagrant violations included sexual abuse of mi-nors (Michigan State University and Penn State), academic fraud (Auburn University and of North Carolina), and illegal payments to student-athletes (Louisville).[11]

When the media broke a story of sports scandal, presidents and boards went through what journalist David Perlmutter called a "crash course in crisis communications." It included a public litany of penance and remorse, with swift measures to demonstrate their resolve "to get to the bottom of this." Headlines invoked themes of "shame and betrayal." Soon thereafter, an interim president would announce that "the healing has begun." These immediate responses, once a story had broken, were then followed by a chorus of denial and defiance. Whatever concerns alumni and other constituents have about "changing the culture of the institution" over such transgressions, the first, strong response from presidents and boards was to rely on public relations as a source of "crisis management" and "damage control."[12] Revelations of misdeeds by prominent coaches, for example, led to dramatic pronouncements that the longtime scandals were no less than a "tragedy without a hero."[13] Later, in addition to various reform proposals, the alumni, boosters, students, and coaches resolved that the punished university must regain its athletic greatness.

The story might have ended there as an interesting but arcane side exhibit if it were merely to show the peculiar penchant for college sports to dominate American higher education. Exposés of college sports went deep into the fabric of American universities. What the athletic scandals eventually highlighted was how colleges and universities really worked. Investigative reporting about fired presidents often included unexpected details about presidential compensation packages. Above all, these scandals included the university leadership beyond the athletics department. In recent years, publicity and problems with rogue athletics department behavior led to the firing, retirement, or resignation of presidents or chancellors at Michigan State University, the Ohio State University, Pennsylvania State University, University of Louisville, and University of North Carolina at Chapel Hill. University boards of trustees with ultimate power and responsibility over these institutions were ill informed and either acquiescent or supportive of numerous abuses.[14]

Despite some cries for reform, what one usually found was an immediate rush to quick solutions. Damage control opened the floodgates on spending to counter critics. At one scandal-ridden state university in the Big Ten Conference, the board hired an attorney at $995 per hour, running up fees over $4 million. At Pennsylvania State University, expenditures on penalties soared, with estimates including $37 million spent on public relations and legal fees, followed by a fine of $60 million levied by the NCAA.[15] At Michigan State University, stopgap measures by trustees did little to regain the trust and support of student and faculty constituencies.[16]

In 2023 the added power and numbers of the Big Ten (due in part to the addition of the University of California, Los Angeles, and the University of

Southern California along with the University of Washington and the University of Oregon) were accompanied by a major internal problem of even more allegations of abuses. Most dramatic in terms of media coverage was the controversy over hazing and systemic coaching misconduct at Northwestern University, the only private university in the Big Ten, with probably the highest undergraduate academic admissions standards.[17]

From Athletics to Academics

A consequence for the entire university, beyond the athletics department, was that state legislators and even private donors wondered how state universities could plead poverty if they could afford these crisis management expenditures. *USA Today* databases indicated that the top paid state employee in more than forty states was a coach at a public university. The highest total compensation package for a college football coach was about $9 million, with $8 million for one basketball coach. In NCAA Division I athletics programs, head football coaches had an annual compensation surpassing $1 million. Some assistant coaches in high-profile sports programs received salaries ranging from $500,000 to $1 million. In 2018, seventeen athletics directors at universities nationwide had compensation of more than $1 million per year.[18]

These headline stories were sensational. They were significant because they provided a glimpse at institutional priorities. Presidents often protected high-profile college sports programs with subsidies at a time when academic programs were being reduced in funding. In 2019, Louisiana State University opened a new $28 million rest and recreation center for exclusive use by its football team even though the flood-damaged university library remained in decrepit condition.[19] The president of the University of Central Florida provided a $24 million annual subsidy for varsity football. At the University of California, Berkeley, the football program lost $10 million per year over several years and left the chancellor with a large capital improvement debt for stadium renovation.[20]

In addition to athletics program subsidies and high coaching salaries, another mystery to solve was how boards of trustees treated presidents who had resigned in the wake of college sports scandals. An article in the *Detroit Free Press* on January 25, 2018, summarized the lifetime perks the president of Michigan State University was scheduled to receive after her resignation over allegations she had failed to provide adequate oversight of Larry Nassar, a university-employed medical doctor convicted of abusing young women gymnasts who trained at the university over several years. The article set out the details of "Lifetime free tickets to MSU football games, a 12-month paid research leave if she returns to the faculty. If she chooses to return to the faculty, she gets a salary of 75% of her presidential salary of $750,000 per year for two years, office space, secretarial support, the title of 'president emeritus.' " Her faculty salary of $562,000 was more than double that of any faculty member in the College of Education. In fact, her salary was substantially more than the highest-paid faculty member at MSU, a renowned physicist who earned $433,441. Perks included numerous athletics-related perks, such as free tickets and parking for games. A few weeks later, the board of trustees named her a John Hannah University Professor, the institution's highest scholarly honor.[21] The real and symbolic awards and rewards led a reporter for *Inside Higher Ed* in 2023 to ask, "Should colleges honor disgraced ex-presidents?"[22]

The expenses for these scandals continued to mount when universities were found liable for wrongdoing. On May 16, 2018, MSU trustees announced that they had agreed to a $500 million settlement with the 332 women and girls who had been abused by Nassar. Where the money was coming from remained unclear and unannounced. This was an unprecedented amount paid in a settlement by a university, far more than Penn State paid to settle abuse allegations a few years earlier, estimated at $109 million. The MSU amount was a large proportion of the university's annual operating budget. According to an article in the *New York Times*, "The $500 million settlement would amount to almost 37 percent of the annual general fund budget of $1.36 billion for 2017–18, according to university documents. Of that, almost three-quarters, or $983 million, came from tuition and fees, while state appropriations accounted for a fifth, or $281 million."[23] The university's $2.7 billion endowment could not be used to pay settlement costs.

Mounting Athletic Expenses across All NCAA Categories

One historical finding from 2012 through 2024 was that presidents at all levels faced problems with college sports that were high profile and high priority. Problems of inequities in college sports across institutional categories played out in budget decisions. A flagship state university with an annual operating budget of $3 billion and an intercollegiate athletics budget of $150 million had advantages over a comprehensive regional university whose total budget was $350 million, with $30 million dedicated to college sports. The former could afford to pay a high-profile head coach a compensation package of $3 million, whereas the latter could afford to pay only $200,000.

Yet these macro figures masked other significant differences that had wide-ranging consequences. These gaps became more evident at the micro level.

A major research finding between 2012 and 2024 was the link between contact sports such as football and long-term health effects from concussions. A partial solution arising from that research included carefully redesigned football helmets that reduced head and brain injuries. But one of these custom-designed helmets cost $1,600. Since it was molded to the shape of an individual player's head, it could not be worn by another player. For a well-funded program such as the University of Oregon, there was no hesitation in purchasing new helmets for their student-athletes. They could even afford to purchase four different-colored helmets for each player, to match multiple uniform combinations throughout the season, for a total expense of $6,400. In contrast, at a financially lean college football program, budgetary constraints meant that the athletics director could afford at most a single special helmet per player. More likely, the coach and staff out of financial necessity would opt to buy only standard helmets at $150 each, items that could be used by multiple players over several seasons because the helmets were not custom fitted.[24]

The handful of big-time programs pulled ahead in terms of safety and style. These small decisions were marbled throughout all levels of preparation and play, with the cumulative effect of widening the gap between affluent and impoverished programs. At historically Black colleges and universities, such as Grambling in Louisiana, football locker rooms were infested with mold, putting student-athletes' health at great risk. The university simply did not have the budget to tend to these fundamental matters of maintenance and facilities. Institutional differences in health plans and liability insurance for student-athletes accelerated the spending gap. All these items compounded to dramatize differences within the ranks of colleges as to what they could afford to provide their students.[25]

The upshot was that at any and all NCAA levels, an intercollegiate athletics program was deceptively expensive, whether at a large state university or a Division III liberal arts college. It could not be quarantined and dismissed as a minor auxiliary service or extracurricular activity because the expenses were a substantial percentage of many institutional budgets. Among the hundreds of colleges offering big-time sports programs, only about fifteen were financially self-supporting year after year. Football, which indulged in its spending because it was intended to be the golden goose whose profits subsidized other sports, often lost money, even at big-time programs. A good example was UCLA, whose home games played at the historic Rose Bowl in Pasadena had sparse crowds. Fans could obtain free tickets at local supermarkets. UCLA's football financial problems spread to weaken the overall Pac-12 Conference, which lagged the other members of the Power Five Conference in landing lucrative television contracts.[26] Even at highly successful football programs in the Midwest and South—such as the University of Alabama, the University of Georgia, and the University of Michigan—student seating for some home games often went unfilled. Across all institutions, there were increased situations where awarding subsidies to maintain equipment, salaries, and scholarships for intercollegiate athletics drained scarce dollars from a college's general education budget.[27]

Excellence in the Nonrevenue Sports: Profile
of a Championship Tennis Team

One recurrent source of tension in discussions of intercollegiate athletics funding pitted the high-profile revenue sports such as NCAA Division I football and men's basketball against a cluster of varsity teams often labeled as "nonrevenue sports," with subgroups such as "Olympic sports," "minor sports," and "country club sports." One combative complaint by proponents of big-time football and basketball was that the so-called country club sports did not generate revenue, and that often they were considered less arduous than football and basketball Furthermore, they were depicted as havens for student-athletes disproportionately from upper-income families and graduates of prep schools.[28]

The problem with this myopia was its ignorance of the excellence and demands fostered by these so-called minor sports. For example, water polo was among the most demanding of all scholastic or collegiate sports. Crew was grueling and excruciating. Lacrosse was rough and fast. Ironically, Jim Brown—the all-time, all-pro running back for the Cleveland Browns—considered his lacrosse seasons in high school on Long Island and later at Syracuse University to be his strongest memory of sports. So, for genuine athletes, the skills and demands of these sports were formidable. Competition to make the team along with competition to gain admission based in part on athletic talent was keen. And the intensity ratcheted up at academically strong universities playing NCAA Division I sports, especially at the schools and conferences allowing full athletic grants-in-aid, such as Boston College, Duke, Northwestern, Stanford, Syracuse, the University of Southern California, the University of Denver, and Vanderbilt.[29]

A college that wanted to have winning teams in Olympic sports and country club sports tended to give an admissions advantage to applicants with high-level athletic skills who were also women, international, or affluent. By extension, this advantage favored students at private and suburban public high schools (which often offered a wider array of Olympic sports). There was nothing sinister about this trend, as it was clinical and "data driven," akin to the decision-making of "Billy Ball" and the Oakland Athletics Major League Baseball team, whose analyst held a PhD in economics from Yale. Whereas preferential admissions consideration for "legacies" (daughters and sons of alumni parents) were not based on achievement or talent, consideration of athletes was rigorous and competitive.[30]

To understand the gravity of an academically selective university's decision to be serious about a varsity sport outside the obvious "money sports" of big-time football and basketball, it was useful to consider the case of the Wake Forest University men's tennis team.[31] They were defending NCAA Division I champions who appeared to have a good chance of repeating as national champions. The 2018–19 roster of fourteen varsity players showed that six players graduated from high school in the United States. Eight players were from other nations—Croatia, two from Cyprus, the Czech Republic, India, Israel, Montenegro, and Uzbekistan. Furthermore, Wake Forest University awarded full grants-in-aid of about sixty-five thousand per year for each student-athlete, with no consideration of financial need. On balance, the admissions office and coaching staff helped Wake Forest University increase the diversity of its student body, competed effectively to recruit students with special (athletic talent), and gained favorable institutional publicity for its NCAA championship. It was an excellent example of what economist Charles C. Clotfelter described about a small number of private, prestigious colleges who were "buying the best," whether in intercollegiate athletics, physics, or student financial aid packages.[32]

If a university offered country club sports for men, most likely it inherited an obligation to offer a large number of women's sports that were well funded. Compliance with Title IX along with NCAA and conference requirements on gender equity tended to increase substantially the number of admissions slots and athletic grants-in-aid for women. Since football can consume eighty-five grants-in-aid and admissions slots, an athletics director and provost must ensure that this large number is followed by a cumulative number of women admits and scholarships to assure gender parity. Hence a relatively small undergraduate student body would dedicate a disproportionate number of slots to women with strong, specialized athletic skills. Soccer, lacrosse, field hockey, crew, ice hockey, track and field, golf, and softball readily come to mind but hardly exhaust the roster of women's varsity sports. Since many of these sports have a strong correlation with private secondary schools and affluent families, a university increased its opportunities for women while tending to admit and reward a relatively affluent and athletic constituency.[33]

Often overlooked in grumbling about admissions priorities and preferences were the complaints by what some considered a privileged group: the parents of stellar, high-achieving high school students who do not play varsity sports. Or, rather, applicants who do not play varsity sports at a sufficiently high level to excel as a member of the college team gain no edge with the admissions evaluations and rankings. Another variation on the controversies associated with prestigious colleges and elite intercollegiate athletics was the "Varsity Blues" scandal, circa 2018 through 2023. Evidently, children of wealthy celebrities and donors who did not have strong academic records received preference as "athletic admits" for such sports as sailing, rowing, water polo, and fencing. An irony of these abuses, some of which led to criminal charges against parents and their paid admissions agents, was that the athletics teams were being used to give admission to applicants who were neither strong students nor outstanding athletes.[34] In contrast to the usual syndrome of admission favoritism for recruited athletes with relatively low academic grades, in these cases, athletics teams were being used and abused for admissions purposes.

Many of these controversies and crises involved institutions that were academically selective and relatively small in size of enrollment. At a large state university with an enrollment of thirty thousand, it is not especially consequential if eight hundred admissions slots go to recruited athletes. Such is not the case at Ivy League universities and prestigious small liberal arts colleges. The situation is exacerbated by the fact that the prestigious private colleges tend to offer many varsity sports. Harvard University offered the most varsity sports (forty-two) in NCAA Division I, surpassing even the Ohio State University. The Ivy League sponsored thirty-five varsity sports. Approximately one out of seven Harvard undergraduates played on a varsity team. This was not done casually, as most players had been recruited. At an Amherst College or a Williams College, varsity athletes constituted between thirty and forty percent of the student body. Seldom were these walk-ons, as most were carefully scouted and recruited by the college's coaching staff.

Why shouldn't Harvard emphasize crew? Rowing was after all the original, historic intercollegiate sport whose rowers picked crimson as the distinctive Harvard color (after having rejected magenta). Also underappreciated was that competitive crew had an elaborate network of international clubs and participants from Australia, New Zealand, and eastern European nations such as

Croatia and Serbia as sources of recruits for US intercollegiate teams. Elsewhere, other historic and academically prestigious colleges have made athletics a priority as part of their educational offerings. For example, over several years, Williams College had won the Directors' Cup, the prize for having the top overall intercollegiate sports program in NCAA Division III. This did not happen by accident. Each college and university makes deliberate, conscious choices about which sports to emphasize. Such decisions are not inherently good or bad, but a matter of heritage, priority, and choice. In the case of compliance with gender equity, expanding the number of teams and roster slots is a matter of legal and ethical obligation.

In 2023 the Supreme Court of the United States handed down a decision in *Students for Fair Admissions v. President and Fellows of Harvard College,* finding that using race as a factor in college admissions violates the Equal Protection Clause of the US Constitution. The suit, brought against Harvard and UNC Chapel Hill, dealt a blow to the decades-long policy of affirmative action to promote diversity in student enrollment. In contrast to the conventional and disproportionate news coverage of big-time conferences and revenue sports such as football and men's basketball, the SCOTUS decision shifted attention to high-stakes empirical studies in which economists and sociologists documented the substantial advantage that recruited athletes, men and women, in country club sports had in being admitted to selective academic colleges such as Harvard and other Ivy League schools.[35] These findings were not lost on the parents and counselors of high school students who excelled in such niche sports as lacrosse, field hockey, crew, tennis, and golf. Student-athletes in these sports were increasingly active in emphasizing their achievements in presenting their admissions portfolios to college officials and coaches.

If country club sports conferred an advantage to students from affluent backgrounds and private secondary schools, what were some antidotes other than eliminating the affluent sports? A partial solution would be to extend country club sports to underserved groups. Trinity College in Hartford, Connecticut, was a perennial national power in intercollegiate squash. And for years it funded and supported a squash instructional program and competitive league for children in neighborhoods adjacent to campus. In New York City, donors created a promising lacrosse program that is accessible at no charge to students, many of whom were from modest-income families.[36] In both cases, participants in those developmental programs earned athletic scholarships.

But intervention to transform class differences across scholastic and collegiate sports is difficult, perhaps impossible. A half century ago, baseball was a favorite and accessible sport among African American children and young adults. This was no longer the case. Numerous other sports faced a class divide—such as ice hockey, squash, field hockey, water polo, and sailing—therefore accessibility and affordability to a broad constituency remained limited at best.

The Character and Condition of NCAA Division III Sports in 2023–2024

Academically selective colleges that did not grant athletic scholarships had their own headaches. For example, at an institution like Amherst or Williams in Division III—or at an Ivy League institution in NCAA Division I—the high-stakes tension came in deciding which among many academically strong applicants to admit. Varsity sports were crucial, since between twenty-five and thirty-three percent of an entering freshman class were recruited athletes. Furthermore, the teams were in the public spotlight, both favorably and otherwise. In 2016 the men's varsity soccer team at Harvard, Princeton's swimming team, the cross-country team at Amherst College, and the wrestling team at Columbia University faced penalties ranging from reprimand to canceling their season over allegations of harassment and misconduct, including charges of vulgar social media messages and sexual harassment.[37]

Colleges in NCAA Division III faced decisions that were hard and divisive. In the Los Angeles area, for example, two historic private liberal arts colleges—Occidental College and Whittier College—dropped their varsity football programs. Both had rich football traditions, having played for more than 120 years and being charter members of the Southern California Intercollegiate Athletic Conference. Yet at Occidental College in 2017 and at Whittier College in 2023, the respective presidents and trustees voted to discontinue their varsity football programs in part because of concerns about student-athlete injuries, mounting expenses, and doubts about being able to field competitive teams.[38]

There were, however, unexpected success stories and favorable publicity for NCAA Division III teams that did fulfill the ideal of the serious student who played and sacrificed for the love of amateur sports. A front-page story in the *New York Times* on January 26, 2023, provided a lengthy profile of New York City's Baruch College men's volleyball team. The unlikely publicity for this conference-winning squad was that newly elected US Congressional Representative George Santos claimed to have been a member of this varsity team that had defeated such opponents as Harvard and Yale. Reporters found no evidence to support Santos's claims, but what they did find was that the Baruch Bear

Cats were a winning team, including conference championships. The team's players were outstanding students who received no athletic scholarships at the school's commuter campus. The men's volleyball team "had a 3.42 grade point average and included thirteen players majoring in finance, two studying accounting and others pursuing degrees tied to a career path. In the off-season, many of the student-athletes interned at financial firms or real estate companies. They practiced in a gymnasium located in a basement three-stories below ground." Baruch College's skilled student-athletes received well-deserved applause and recognition in the publicity windfall, even if it all started from a politician's dubious claims.[39]

The news coverage of the Baruch College Division III volleyball team had implications beyond its particular novelty. The important consideration for small-college presidents, boards, provosts, and faculty was that investment in a comprehensive varsity sports program for women and men showed potential as an effective recruiting tool and in enhancing overall institutional reputation for a comprehensive, well-rounded campus experience. For example, in September 2023 the director of enrollment management of the University of Lynchburg in Virginia made the compelling argument that college sports programs in Division III could enhance admissions and enrollments. No one expected such varsity sports programs to generate revenue, and hence they awarded no athletic scholarships. The programs received funding from the general budget, as was the case with all of the college's educational programs and services. It was an important, intriguing theory worthy of consideration and analysis.[40]

COVID-19 and the Stress Test on Funding College Sports

In March 2020, most colleges and universities, along with the NCAA and conferences, curtailed athletic events, including league and national championships, due to the COVID-19 pandemic. In addition to these concerns for public health and campus safety and protection of student-athletes and spectators from illness, COVID and pandemic sequestering provided a stress test on the finances of intercollegiate athletics.

Most dramatic was the announcement on July 8, 2020, by Stanford University that it was going to cut eleven varsity sports.[41] The sports were men's volleyball, wrestling, field hockey, men's and women's fencing, lightweight rowing, men's rowing, coed and women's sailing, squash, and synchronized swimming. Stanford had won the Directors' Cup, given to the top athletics department in Division I, for twenty-five straight years. The following year, facing criticism and even threats of lawsuits, on May 21, 2021, Stanford reinstated several sports.[42]

The announcement and then the reversal illustrated the fragility of college sports spending and the longtime pattern of overspending. Coaches for the big-time revenue sports of football and men's basketball lobbied persistently to have conference commissioners restore their games during the pandemic, at least for television broadcast audiences if not for in-person, ticket-purchasing fans. These initiatives indicated that intercollegiate athletics in Division I were dependent on ticket sales and broadcast revenues—and that for even formidable programs with major donors and large endowments, cancellation of regular season games and postseason championship events would be financially disastrous.[43]

An official decision by a college to approve playing during at a time when most campuses had suspended traditional class meetings, closed dormitories, and sent students home may have calmed the financial fears of athletics directors, but doing so raised the important question of the health and safety of student-athletes. The dilemma was illustrative of growing concern about numerous questions about the well-being and rights of intercollegiate student-athletes that came to a head in this decade.

Cost Escalation from Contracts for Coaches, Consultants, and Construction

The consequences of the COVID-19 pandemic included changes in athletic game schedules, including postponed and cancelled contests, and reductions in staff. These austerity measures stripped bare some of the cover that athletics directors typically used to deflect questions about budgetary shortfalls. What became increasingly evident was that most college sports programs experienced spending spirals whereby the customary funding model became "unsustainable." The relatively small number of affluent, big-time programs could cover these expenses for a while. But if one looked beyond the Power Five Conferences and into the football subdivision conferences and institutions, what one found was that the second-tier programs tended to mimic the strongest programs in their voracious appetite to spend. In other words, even during good times expenses outstripped revenues. This became more evident in the years 2020 through 2024.

The habit of overspending that diffused from the powerful programs throughout NCAA Division I was intoxicating and disastrous. The practice of "buying out" a fired coach's salary was one foremost example. Also, the practice of relying on highly paid external consultants on a wide range of internal decisions had little accountability for cost-benefit. The University of Louisville spent more than two million dollars on legal and consulting fees in 2019–20. Its institutional and athletics budgets were both much larger than those for East Carolina University.

East Carolina University was a case study that captured and conveyed the syndromes of imitation and excess in its intercollegiate athletics program. It regularly ran a deficit of about $4 million. Its football attendance at home games never topped twenty thousand and consistently declined year by year to about twelve thousand. Its financial model was unsustainable. The athletics department had spent $60 million on a new office tower. At the same time, the department spent substantially on administrative matters. A director of athletics who was fired received a buyout of over $1.26 million over five years—indicating an annual salary of approximately $250,000 per year.

While paying the previous AD's buyout, the university spent more than $31,000 a month to hire a special advisor to the chancellor for athletics. Even after hiring a new AD (who had previously worked with the consultant) in late 2018, the consultant remained in his role through 2019, earning nearly $700,000 in less than two years. So, ECU was paying three senior-level sport administrators in 2019. When COVID-19 altered the sporting landscape, ECU become one of the first institutions to announce that it would be making cuts to its athletics teams and to some rosters. Their case study illustrated how consulting became a lucrative cottage industry within higher education, especially with athletics departments. It also represented a college sports budget model that was unsustainable for all but the wealthiest institutions.[44]

The College Student-Athlete Reconsidered

Even before the COVID-19 events and institutional policies brought attention to student-athletes, several groups had been asking questions and then analyzing the policies and practices encountered by students who played varsity sports. The NCAA relied on the image of the amateur student-athlete, but it then devoted voluminous pages to operationalizing codes of conduct and statements of regulations and penalties student-athletes faced if they did not comply with the layers of college, conference, and NCAA regulations. What the regulations—and cases of offenses—indicated was that the image and reality of the college athlete as a genuine student, without pay for play, were both embellished and tarnished.

A good example of systematic research contributing to this reconsideration of the student-athlete was edited by Eddie Comeaux, a professor at the University of California, Riverside, who as an undergraduate at the UC Berkeley was a star player on the baseball team that qualified for the College World Series. Comeaux's anthology, published in 2017, *College Athletes' Rights and Well-Being*, drew from multiple academic disciplines to provide a comprehensive and up-to-date critical perspective on policy and practice in varsity sports programs and conferences nationwide. Its approach was first to describe the principles, structures, and conditions that influence how athletes experience campus life, as well as the increasingly commercialized business enterprise of college sports. Told from the perspective of athletes and written by leading scholars on athletics, the book addressed topics from concussion protocols and collective bargaining to amateurism, Title IX's gender-separate allowance, and conference realignment.

The scholarly research was precipitated by a growing number of incidents in which college student-athletes and their families pushed back against regulations and restrictions on their activities, with the prohibitions being justified on the grounds that students were jeopardizing genuine student-athlete philosophies and practices. It included, for example, objections to official restrictions on a student-athlete paying an agent or an attorney for representation in negotiations over athletic grants-in-aid and explorations of endorsements, as well as restrictions on employment during the summer and during the regular academic year. In disparate incidents, also, college students began discussing prospects for being classified as institutional employees or as eligible for protections under the National Labor Relations Act. Student-athletes at numerous colleges were restricted in their right to talk to newspaper reporters and other media reps. Athletics departments began monitoring student-athletes' social media communications. Student-athletes also objected to restrictions on their ability to transfer from one college to another without loss of intercollegiate varsity sport eligibility.

These frustrations came to a head at Northwestern University when its football team attempted to unionize. Spearheaded by former Northwestern quarterback Kain Colter, the Wildcats' vote to unionize was eventually turned down by the National Labor Relations Board. In the process, however, the effort resulted in changes to NCAA policy. It allowed power conferences (those with the resources) to provide slightly more tuition money and educational expenses to players. The four-year scholarship rule was also reintroduced. Improved long-term health care benefits were also instituted. Although the Northwestern unionization effort failed, it brought about key reforms and raised awareness of the growing debate regarding the denial of pay and benefits to college athletes.[45]

The cumulative individual intercollegiate incidents eventually led to some grievances in which present and former student-athletes took their concerns to the courts. A key turning point in this debate came when former UCLA basketball star Ed O'Bannon organized and filed a class action lawsuit against the NCAA. It started when O'Bannon visited a friend, who then told the former UCLA start that his son was playing "him" in an Electronic Arts (EA) Sports video game. The two watched as the young boy chose someone who had O'Bannon's skin tone, shared his number, played his position, and shot left-handed, even though his name was not on the back of the jersey. The former college star's image was clearly being utilized.[46]

O'Bannon sued the NCAA, arguing that the use of his name, image, and likeness—without compensation—was a violation of antitrust legislation. More former student-athletes decided to join the lawsuit, and O'Bannon eventually won his case. The court ruled that paying athletes expenses up to the full cost of attendance could be used as a possible remedy to the situation. Both the NCAA and O'Bannon unsuccessfully appealed the case to the US Supreme Court. Even though the case did not bring sufficient revenue to former athletes, *O'Bannon v. NCAA* (2015) opened the door for more litigation, and EA Sports offered a forty-million-dollar settlement.

Shortly thereafter, a class action suit brought by Jason Marshall and a group of fellow former college football players against such media corporations as ESPN and CBS argued that players were unjustly being excluded from contracts and endorsements that could bring them income—all at a time when universities and some of their coaches and athletics officials were reaping substantial revenues from a variety of commercial products, endorsements, and events. The college players did not prevail in the federal court decision, but the presiding judge did give pause, noting that college sports had become a "big business."[47]

Whether student-athletes won or lost in these court cases, the important development was that public and legal opinion was moving away from its customary deference to the NCAA in its alleged protection of amateurism in college athletics. In some states, such as California, legislatures drafted bills that provided markedly different treatment and compensation of college student-athletes.

The capstone to these accumulated concerns came about in the 2021 case of the *NCAA v. Alston,* in which the US Supreme Court ruled by a unanimous 9-0 vote to reject the NCAA's historic model for regulating student-athlete regulations over endorsements and earnings, leaving future arrangements to states and other agencies.[48] In its opinion, the court highlighted the NCAA's changing definition of amateurism over multiple decades. In a more scathing rebuke, Justice Kavanaugh's concurring argument noted, "Nowhere else in America can businesses get away with agreeing not to pay their workers a fair market rate on the theory that their product is defined by not paying their workers a fair market rate. . . . The NCAA is not above the law."[49]

An interesting sequel to the efforts by an NCAA Division I and Big Ten entity such as Northwestern University's football team to form a union was the diffusion of collective action outside the power conferences to the Ivy League. For example, in March 2023 a group of former athletes at Brown University sued the Ivy League over the conference's no-scholarship policy, alleging that the conference and its institutional members "illegally conspired to limit financial aid by banning athletic scholarships."[50] To continue this trend of student-athlete activism in the Ivy League, on September 16, 2023, the *New York Times* reported that the entire Dartmouth men's basketball team filed a petition to the National Labor Relations Board for formal approval of a union.[51] The indication was that such collective student actions would become increasingly prevalent across a span of sports and institutions.

Among the most enduring legacies of the "student-athlete rights" movement between 2012 and 2024 was the recognition that prospective college athletes and their parents took seriously the commitment associated with playing a varsity sport after high school. Such commitment included the tradition of high-stakes recruitment of star players in big-time football and basketball. Some case studies of big-time football programs, such as the University of Alabama, indicated that many of the grant-in-aid recipients were first-generation college students from modest-income families. A widespread practice was that these student-athletes regularly sent a large portion of their monthly financial award home to their parents to assist with family living expenses and care of their younger siblings.

Also important was that this attention to opportunities and risks extended to women as well as to men. It included NCAA Divisions II and III as well as Division I. It pertained to all sports, not just the high-profile revenue-generating variations. One estimate was that a family paid as much as forty thousand dollars per year for a child who pursued serious ice hockey while in elementary and high school. Sports such as volleyball, basketball, and soccer—for both young women and young men—included conferences, teams, and competitions that supplemented the traditional schedules and games sponsored by the high school athletics department. Promising athletes in such sports as gymnastics, tennis, cheerleading, and swimming often moved to live close to special academies and professional staff. In other words, playing a college sport had ceased to be an informal or casual activity. Specializing in one sport at an early age, buoyed by private coaching, was the new norm. The age of a college student-athlete playing more than one sport had passed, with only a few exceptions. Participation and competition in high-level athletics for children and adolescents predictably included health and liability insurance coverage expenses along with purchase of expensive equipment and uniforms, all of which fueled the professionalization and commercialization of youth sports, long before these children ever entered college.

An added element of professionalism and commitment that flourished in college sports was the appeal that American intercollegiate teams offered to aspiring Olympic athletes not only from the United States but also from numerous countries worldwide. A young woman who swam for the Stanford varsity team might also represent her home nation of Greece in the summer Olympics. This changing tenor then was carried over into the serious business of negotiating athletics grants-in-aid, meeting with college recruiters and coaches and myriad other details that changed the landscape for student-athletes and their families—and for academic and athletic officials.

This interest spread to popular women's Olympic sports as certain university teams became dominant. In September 2023 the University of Nebraska's perennial national championship women's volleyball team played before a crowd of ninety-two thousand in the university's football stadium—a feat that showed the public appeal of women's college sports and set a record for the largest attendance at a women's sporting event, amateur or professional. Yet at the same time, it was not evident that the exception set the rule. Most women's intercollegiate programs had not drawn large crowds or generated substantial revenues—and the prospect that they would enjoy publicity and prosperity in the future was not likely. Reconciling the extremes of ticket sales and attendance persists as unfinished business.[52]

The growing popularity of women's sports, along with various court rulings, opened the door to name, image, and likeness (NIL) profitability for women as well as men. A few high-profile and lucrative NIL deals for women hinted at some signs of gender equity. Illustrative of the untested terrain that created complications for both Title IX and NIL was Louisiana State University's gymnast Olivia Dunne from New Jersey. In 2023, Dunne signed a multimillion-dollar contract for television advertisements on sports and recreational wear while an undergraduate student-athlete.[53] Beyond the headlines and television advertisements of such spectacular deals for a select number of women student-athletes, the overriding policy question remained: whether program and institutional funding for the range of women's varsity sports would keep pace with institutional and external resources for high-profile men's varsity sports.[54]

Another corollary to the high-profile Supreme Court cases was that some advocacy nonprofit organizations such as the Drake Group were considering filing lawsuits for Title IX violations because, not unexpectedly, women student-athletes were receiving far less monies than the teams and men student-athletes.[55] As these contrasting examples suggested, recent developments in NIL and Title IX had only made the trajectories of various intercollegiate student-athletes and teams more complex and challenging to navigate.

Universities Partner with Sports Gambling Casinos, 2018–2023

When intercollegiate athletics went from the sports page to the front page, it was big news, but not always *good* news. Nowhere was this more evident than in a *New York Times* article about "how college and sports betting companies 'Caesarized' campus life." It chronicled how some universities had signed lucrative contracts with sports betting companies to promote online gambling to their students and campus communities.[56]

The most conspicuous evidence of this new practice was the signage along the rim of the Michigan State University football stadium proclaiming, "CAESARS SPORTSBOOK & CASINO—OFFICIAL SPORTS BETTING PARTNER OF SPARTAN ATHLETICS." In addition to Michigan State University's $8.4 million, five-year contract with Caesars Sportsbook, seven other major universities nationwide—including Louisiana State University and the University of Colorado Boulder—signed Internet sports betting contracts and "at least a dozen athletic departments and booster clubs have signed agreements with brick-and-mortar casinos," according to the *Times*. The agreements raised questions "about whether promoting gambling on campus—especially to people who are at an age when they are vulnerable to developing gambling disorders—fits the mission of higher education."[57]

The gold rush for online college sports betting contracts started in 2018 following the US Supreme Court's decision allowing states to legalize sports betting. Over the past four years, some higher education officials and politicians have pushed back. In 2020, for example, a group of university presidents and athletics directors in Massachusetts testified before the state legislature with the strong recommendation not to legalize college sports betting in Massachusetts. (Massachusetts ultimately did legalize sports betting—sportsbooks opened there on January 31, 2023, though the legislation does not allow betting on in-state college teams unless they are participating in a tournament.)[58]

In late November 2022, shortly after publication of the *New York Times* investigation, US Senator Richard Blumenthal from Connecticut wrote a letter to Caesars Entertainment CEO Tom Reeg registering his "grave concerns" about sports betting promotions on college campuses, and calling on Caesars to "discontinue any existing partnerships with schools" and "abide by industry standards that prohibit marketing to college students."[59]

Senator Blumenthal's letter put pressure on the gambling industry to cease and desist in campus contracts. But there is little evidence in the public record that higher education leaders have policed their own ranks. They did not, for example, call for fellow university presidents and boards to discuss or explain their actions in entering into sports gambling contracts. Most perplexing was that university presidents had shown little public inclination to consider rescinding their existing contracts and promotions with sports betting corporations.[60]

Why was college endorsement of campus sports betting activities a big deal? Historically speaking, universities' sponsorship of and revenues gained from college sports gambling are surprising because back in 1951, the NCAA gained its regulatory power from its college and university membership in the wake of point-shaving scandals at college tournaments played at Madison Square Gardens. The aim was for the NCAA and its member institutions to root out and punish college student-athletes who engaged in cheating. The corollary was that university officials also were held responsible for having allowed such student misconduct, leading in some cases to the NCAA and its conferences levying strong penalties.[61]

In 2022, NCAA regulations made plain that any university involvement with gambling should be prohibited and punished. In particular, the NCAA's 2022–23 "Ethical Conduct" guidelines in Article 10 of their bylaws prohibit athletics department staff members—or any college official (e.g., a president) who has responsibility "within or over" an athletics department—and student-athletes from knowingly participating in gambling on intercollegiate contests. Louisiana State University, Michigan State University, and the University of Colorado, among others, appeared to be in violation of this prohibition, their contracts raising a number of ethical and policy flags. Their procedures seemed disconnected from shared governance and protocols set by regional accreditation agencies. Their contracts seemed at odds with sound ethics and education principles and policies.[62]

The articles by the *New York Times* reporters combined with the letter of concern by Senator Blumenthal showed some signs of influence about four months after the casino-campus contracts were publicized. On March 30, 2023, for example, one press release announced that "PointsBet and the University of Colorado have decided it is mutually beneficial to end their partnership at this time."[63] On April 27 the Drake Group—a coalition of concerned faculty, scholars, former legislators, and student-athletes—announced nationwide that they would be sponsoring on May 18, 2023, a free webinar on "Sports Betting: What Are the Risks for Intercollegiate Athletics?" But these discussions made no mention of participation by university presidents and their traditional professional associations.

Shortly thereafter, in May 2023, a succession of incidents involving college sports and gambling signaled that the problems and lack of clear standards were going to escalate controversies for intercollegiate athletics policies and programs. The University of Alabama quickly fired its head baseball coach when sports betting syndicates flagged unusually high bets on the Alabama baseball team that were traced to the head coach.[64] Two weeks later, media headlines included stories about fifteen student-athletes at the University of Iowa and Iowa State University who had been charged by their university athletic officials for placing college sports bets that violated university and NCAA rules. The official announcement was that for such acts, "ignorance of the law was no excuse."[65]

These swift administrative responses suggested that athletics departments and universities had low tolerance for employees and athletes engaging in college sports gambling. A problem with such actions was their potential inconsistency with the fact that since 2018 and state legalization of sports betting (including college sports), universities themselves had entered into high-profile, lucrative contracts with sports casinos that encouraged fans—and students—to wager on their colleges' games. An added unresolved question was whether it was appropriate for a college athletics department to prohibit student-athletes from engaging in college sports gambling, an activity that was allowable for the general student body. Once again, a common thread in these episodes was the public silence and avoidance by college and university presidents about the appropriate mission and programs sponsored by a university. Meanwhile, various external groups including state governments and regulatory commissions publicly announced that they intended to impose added controls on college sports gambling.[66]

The Continuing Commercialization of Conferences

In 2012, college sports had come to be dominated by what was known as the Power Five Conferences: the ACC, the Big Ten, the Big Twelve, the Pac-12, and the SEC. Within that elite club, power became more concentrated over the next decade. By 2024, two conferences—the Big Ten and the SEC—had each completed television broadcast contracts and added new universities to their conference memberships, resulting in further concentration of power. For example, the University of Southern California and UCLA announced their decisions to leave the Pac-12 to join the Big Ten in a new configuration that ended historic geographic identities and memberships of the conferences. In 2023, SEC officials announced that the future addition of the University of Texas and the University of Oklahoma expanded the number, financial strength, and national presence of the SEC. It marked the rise of the conference commissioners of the SEC and Big Ten as the most powerful intercollegiate sports leaders.[67]

Some higher education commentators (particularly in the South) strongly suggested that growing athletics prominence had some correlation with higher academic prestige. When looking at SEC members in the mid-1990s, for example, all but one had earned a Carnegie classification as a research university. This was an improvement from the 1980s when three schools did not have research university status (the Universities of Arkansas and Mississippi joined Alabama in the doctoral category). Even in the early 2000s, a number of research universities remained at the R2 level, a category quantitatively below the R1 measures for research and development funding. Then, as the SEC came to dominate national championships in football, academic distinctions improved as well. By 2019 the SEC proudly announced that it was only the fourth conference to have all members reach R1 status. The others were the Ivy League, the Big Ten, and the Pac-12.

The SEC's claims about the influence of national football championships on academic prominence were not wholly convincing. First, there is the logical fallacy of *post hoc ergo propter hoc*—"after this, therefore because of this." What the SEC suggested was that what appeared to be cause and effect may have been coincidence. Consider, for example, another interpretation of the research rise of universities in the South: the creation of the Southeastern University Research Association (SURA) in 1980. This 501(c)3 nonprofit educational corporation was the result of collaboration between US governors, senators, university presidents, scientists, and researchers in fourteen southern states. Quite apart from athletics, SURA organized the various institutions and elected officials so that the corporation competed successfully in nationwide competition for major federal research grants, especially in nuclear physics. SURA has continued this collaboration in research and development and now includes fifty-four universities in the South—a consortium that includes SEC member institutions and many other southern colleges and universities. It remains difficult to parse out the specific role and timing of the SEC in these research and academic gains. Meanwhile, public announcements and claims about the hand-in-glove partnership of athletics and academics continued.

The brand appeal of the elite conferences informally and officially fused academic and athletic reputations of institutional members. A graphic example of the ascendancy of a handful of major athletic conferences was the full-page color ad by the Southeastern Conference published as a special supplement in the *Chronicle of Higher Education* in 2023:

IT JUST MEANS MORE

Not a marketing slogan. Not a catchphrase. For 14 Proud Universities committed to

TEACHING, RESEARCH, AND SERVICE

IT'S A PROMISE

In 2022, the Promise Meant:

$80 BILLION

Pumped Into Our State Economies

$6 Billion invested in research and development

$5.2 Billion Awarded in Academic Scholarship and Aid

THERE IS SO MUCH MORE TO THIS PROMISE

AND MORE IS YET TO COME

SEC

IT JUST MEANS MORE

What did this self-congratulation mean? What did its statistics on dollars measure? It did conjure the image of the modern university as a "knowledge factory," pumping billions of dollars into state economies. But the isolated dollar data, albeit seemingly large, meant little in terms of any substantive analysis of economic effectiveness or efficiency of a university and its community or state. It is well known that universities and colleges often are the largest employers and landowners in their respective communities. But such data lack context or explanation. Is the implication that a strong commercialized athletics program is integral to this economic impact?

Above all, for the SEC as an institutional consortium, precisely how did academics and athletics integrate in this cumulative conference profile? The halo effect of an athletic conference as a symbol of educational or academic prestige was not clear or completely convincing. "More" did not necessarily mean "better" or "outstanding," especially in education. One way to clarify the connotations was to consider the overlap of the SEC summary celebration of itself with institutional membership in the consortium of leading research universities, the American Association of Universities. The AAU had sixty-two members from the United States and two from Canada. It was the apex of research university prestige. In 2021 within the SEC, only four universities out of fourteen (less than thirty percent)—Texas A&M University, the University of Florida, the University of Missouri, and Vanderbilt—were members of the AAU. Furthermore, two of those four—Texas A&M University and the University of Missouri—were longtime members of the AAU but relative newcomers to the SEC, having joined in 2012.

In contrast, the Big Ten Conference could claim that in 2021 thirteen of its fourteen members also belonged to the AAU. That same year, the Pac-12 membership included eight AAU members—Berkeley, Colorado, Oregon, Stanford, UCLA, the University of Utah, USC, and Washington. All eight members of the Ivy League conference had athletics programs that were in NCAA Division I, and all institutions were members of the AAU consortium of leading research universities. Some of these configurations would change around 2024, with departures and arrivals within the Power Five Conferences. The 2021 compilations showed that there was not necessarily a tight overlap of academic excellence with athletic excellence among the large research universities nationwide.

In many ways, the SEC was experiencing in the academic prestige race that other conferences or institutions faced in the athletic arms race. Rice University, for example, has long maintained its world-class academic reputation but has not been in a power conference since the dissolution of the Southwest Conference. Still, Rice remained determined to move "up" from Conference USA to the American Athletic Conference. It had some remarkable peaks in high-stakes competition, such as in baseball, with numerous conference championships and in 2003 winning the College World Series (including defeating the University of Texas team twice) to claim the NCAA crown. In 2022, Rice was halfway through a hundred-million-dollar fundraising campaign for its athletics program, which would help fund a major renovation to its historic football stadium. Rice athletics director Joe Karlgaard stated, "I absolutely believe that football will pull everything else along with it." Rice's president, Reginald DesRoches, formerly served as the faculty athletics representative at Georgia Tech and expressed his public support for athletics. Despite this newfound emphasis,

Rice remained outpaced by other in-state private universities like Baylor and Texas Christian University.[68]

Rutgers University provided another interesting case study. Joining the Big Ten in 2014, it hosted a "Discover Rutgers" webpage on which it heralded "The Big Ten Experience." The same page stated that Rutgers was "proud to be a member" of the group of leading research universities "that together conduct $10.5 billion in funded research annually." Despite this fact, Rutgers struggled to compete against conference foes and continued to run multimillion-dollar deficits in athletics.[69]

In both academics and athletics, gains in prestige among aspiring institutions proved to be a difficult task, as leading institutions had only grown stronger in both realms in recent years. Trying to break into a more powerful peer group of institutions or a stronger conference was often a frustrating task. Nevertheless, comparisons between big-time athletics and big-time research continued to be tied together, even if the relationships were not entirely clear or confirmed.

A corollary to the success story and large television contracts associated with the Power Five Conferences was that the gap between "have" and "have not" conferences in NCAA Division I widened. The ability of, for example, the Middle Atlantic Conference or American Athletic Conference to compete for student-athlete recruits, coaches, broadcasts, and donors experienced a substantial relative decline. Balances within the NCAA, even among its big-time programs, remained unsettling and uncertain.

To compound these discussions, the higher education community faced increasing financial problems when in August 2023 an article in the *Wall Street Journal* reported that several major flagship state universities, including the University of Arizona, Penn State and West Virginia University, faced severe budget shortfalls. At West Virginia University, for example, revelation of a forty-five-million-dollar deficit led to substantial cuts in academic programs and faculty positions. At the same time, massive construction expenses, including expansion of athletic facilities, evidently were exempted from such cuts, rekindling questions about institutional priorities and problems.[70]

The NCAA in Disarray

The dramatic rise of the Big Ten and the SEC as the prime movers nationwide in college sports coincided with the decline of the leadership and influence of the NCAA, which seized defeat from the jaws of victory. The powerful national organization lost court cases and, more important, lost the confidence of member institutions and their conferences. Its customary response to a proposal for reform was to take a public stance of opposition or resistance. But when critics or reformers persisted in their demands, the NCAA eventually made belated compromises and concessions.

The NCAA gained substantial publicity and self-promotion for its announcements about its contributions to women as student-athletes and coaches, including NCAA sponsorship of championship events such as the women's March Madness basketball tournament. Yet these claims tended to deflate in March 2021 when women as coaches and student-athletes put out on social media a video showing the subpar training facilities and weight room available to women at the NCAA tournament. The video showed to a large media audience a stark contrast with the accommodations and provisions for the men's NCAA tournament.[71] This was the tipping point to bring into the public arena the allegation that the NCAA reform record was uneven or laggard for issues involving gender equity, and led to inquiries and investigations that extended over the next six months.[72]

The NCAA also faced growing concerns about its uneven enforcement of regulations. Between 2012 and 2023 the NCAA showed a disappointing record of leadership and effectiveness. It belatedly attempted measures to limit the public relations damage. In September 2021, Robert Gates, former president of Texas A&M University who also had served as US secretary of defense and as the head of the Central Intelligence Agency, accepted an invitation to serve as chair of a twenty-eight-member committee whose charge was to rewrite the NCAA constitution. He told a reporter that "running the NCAA was harder than trying to run the Pentagon."[73] He found the assignment to be difficult owing to the unnecessary details of the organization's governance and regulations. Also evident at the time was that the commissioners of the major conferences along with legal counsel had become increasingly skeptical of the NCAA to provide leadership for all college sports.

The development of name, image, and likeness also provided an example of a vacuum of leadership and direction. Many claimed the Supreme Court's decision in the *Alston* case weakened the NCAA and its governing structure. While this is certainly correct, it is an incomplete observation. In many ways, NCAA leadership marginalized itself in the years prior to the landmark NIL lawsuit. First, the NCAA refused to acknowledge that the revenue explosions among big-time programs (especially in football and basketball) had altered the "value" of a small but group of athletes. Two years before the *O'Bannon* decision, for example, *Time* magazine placed Texas A&M star quarterback Johnny Manziel on the cover with an accompanying story by Sean Gregory titled, "IT'S TIME TO PAY COLLEGE ATHLETES." Beyond athletics directors and university administrators, the piece was not even considered controversial. The article cited multiple academics. Stanford sports economist Roger Noll stated, "The rising dollar value of the exploitation of athletes . . . is obscene, is out of control." Scholar Charles Clotfelter remained more understated but summarized it well: "Here is a situation where we're not living up to our best selves."[74] Nevertheless, the NCAA remained unmoved.

The NCAA—an association of colleges and universities—also failed to consider the nonmonetary yet often life-changing value of higher education. Would an organization governed by higher education administrators not want to develop policies that helped keep students in college? These issues extended beyond football and basketball. Take, for example, the story of Sydney McLaughlin. The track star participated in the 2016 Olympics as a 16-year-old. Attending the University of Kentucky, McLaughlin broke collegiate and junior world records during her freshman year. Nevertheless, McLaughlin signed a contract with New Balance worth an estimated $1.5 million, thus forfeiting her NCAA eligibility. What if McLaughlin and other college student-athletes had been afforded the opportunity to appear on a television commercial and remain in college? It was simply a reality the NCAA was unwilling to lead on, instead waiting for a lawsuit and fighting it all the way to the Supreme Court.[75]

Rather than develop a plan, the NCAA asked Congress for legislation to help guide policy for intercollegiate athletics. In the vacuum of any strategic leadership, the NCAA allowed the unabashed consumerism it had for decades apparently abhorred. Shortly after the Supreme Court made its unanimous decision on June 21, 2021, Darren Heitner and Eddie Rojas created the Gator Collective, which raided money from boosters "to provide opportunities for student-athletes." One year later, 120 collectives were in development or full-blown operation. Collectives operate independently of a university and have become increasingly complex. Although some work to connect players with businesses, many simply exist to find ways to pay players.[76]

A March 11, 2022, story in *The Athletic* provided an example of a collective's operations while maintaining the anonymity of the college athlete as well as the collective. Because the NCAA prohibits deals that are considered an inducement to play for a specific school, the contract stipulates that the recruit enroll and play football at an NCAA school. By not naming the institution (which the collective supports), the collective manages to engage in pay for play without breaking any rules. Many other NIL deals include "a deep financial inducement to stay at that university." Not surprisingly, in 2022 the NCAA became concerned that NIL deals violated NCAA recruiting regulations and "may be impacting the student-athlete experience negatively in some ways."[77]

In short, rather than create a regulated structure that served to protect student-athletes as they found endorsement deals from companies for their name, image, or likeness, the NCAA left the NIL world largely unregulated. Further, since collectives were not officially part of any institution, one wondered how the NCAA would penalize a collective or the university its boosters support when they violated NCAA regulations or government-established laws. As the NCAA struggled with NIL collectives, it also opened the door for more manipulation of students when they approved (just months before the *Alston* decision) rescinding the rule that an athlete transferring from one university to another had to sit out a season before playing. While there were merits on both sides of this issue, it stood to reason that it put teenagers more at risk of being manipulated or illegally recruited even after they signed to play with a specific college.

These organizational syndromes persisted. Mark Emmert, who had been appointed NCAA president in 2010, announced in April 2022 his plans to resign. In February 2023 a *New York Times* article reconstructed how over several years the NCAA's "daunting problems" were of its own making, as it had ignored signals and issues over the preceding decade. Its public statements by the president were not persuasive to external groups. In several cases, court judges dismissed and rejected arguments by NCAA legal counsel.[78] The prospect was that many policy decisions would now be addressed at the state level or in the various athletics conferences. By 2023 the NCAA faced a serious crisis of credibility at a time when intercollegiate athletics at all levels nationwide was undergoing serious reconfiguration and reconsiderations in court and off the court. The participation and achievements of student-athletes in all categories of institutions and sports was outstanding, yet the intercollegiate athletics enterprise as a whole nationwide appeared to be rudderless.

The Rich Grow Richer: College Football Playoff Expansion and Conference Realignment

While the larger philosophy and direction of the NCAA remained unclear and in flux, the power conferences' vision for the future of intercollegiate sport remained far more focused, even if relationships among the big-time leagues faced tension at certain points. With NIL deals available to college athletes, the most powerful programs faced the potential of losing future revenue to corporations who might choose to sponsor athletes rather than specific programs.

While this did not affect any existing television contracts or university media rights, the prospect of diminished funding increased momentum for a larger postseason football playoff. Even after the very first four-team playoff in January 2015, a popular sporting website ran an article titled, "7 Reasons College Football Playoff Needs to Expand." One of the seven arguments, all of which were related, was "Money, Money, Money." Of course, the myriad challenges kept expansion from happening. Then, in June 2021 (the same month the Supreme Court ruled in favor of NIL rights for college players), a subcommittee of the College Football Playoff Board of Mangers recommended expanding to twelve teams.[79]

All seemed to be moving forward with the expansion when, on July 21, 2021, the *Houston Chronicle* broke a story claiming that Texas and Oklahoma had initiated talks with the SEC about joining the conference. In less than a week, Texas and Oklahoma formally applied to join the SEC, and two days later, the SEC presidents voted unanimously to invite them into the conference. Before the end of the month, both schools accepted the invitation.[80]

The conference shake-up rocked the Big Twelve and the other three power conferences. In response to the news, the Big Ten, ACC, and Pac-12 created an official alliance. The three leagues emphasized that they wanted to keep education at the forefront of college sports as they addressed key issues such as social justice and gender equity. As Big Ten commissioner Kevin Warren stated, "Today, through this alliance, we furthered our commitment to our student-athletes by prioritizing our academic and athletics values systems."[81]

Concerned about the growing strength (and wealth) of football in the Southeastern Conference, the alliance decided to stop the College Football Playoff expansion. When the ten major conferences (and Notre Dame) voted on the twelve-team model, eight voted for expansion, but the alliance conferences all voted against it. All of the other conferences viewed the twelve-team playoff (which would have given automatic spots to the six highest-ranked conference champions and then the next six highest-ranked teams) as the best opportunity to compete for a national championship. The move seemed to support what Commissioner Warren had said regarding the purpose of the alliance, which he claimed was a move to "steady and stabilize college athletics" after the announcement that Texas and Oklahoma would join the SEC.[82]

But Warren's stabilization argument for the alliance seemed rather disingenuous in 2022 when news broke that UCLA and USC would leave the Pac-12 for the Big Ten. Such a move created the first coast-to-coast conference (although not in contiguous states). It expanded the Big Ten's negotiating power, television markets, and profitability. It also solidified the reality that tradition, conferences with long histories, geographical proximity, and rivalries all paled in comparison to money.

Unsurprisingly, the Big Ten's move destroyed the much-discussed alliance with the ACC and the Pac-12. The Big Ten also renegotiated television contracts, once again making it the most profitable conference on TV. With the Big Ten's expansion, the ACC and Pac-12 (along with the Big Twelve) understood that the best opportunity for their members to compete on the national stage was to support the twelve-team playoff. Even so, a few conference commissioners and university presidents wanted to stall on the expansion. At that point, Mississippi State University president Mark Keenum, who also chaired the College Football Playoff Board, forced the issue with his fellow presidents. In a series of secret meetings, Keenum "insisted" that the presidents vote rather than continue the discussion on details of the playoff format. Aided by West Virginia president Gordon Gee, who reminded board members of the money being left on the table ($450 million annually), the College Football Playoff Board finally voted unanimously to move forward with playoff expansion.[83]

The twelve-team College Football Playoff was designed to provide six automatic bids to the highest-ranked conference champions, with the top four conference champions receiving a bye. Teams seeded 5–8 would host on-campus games against seeds 9–12. The plan guaranteed at least one team outside of the Power Five Conferences would earn a playoff spot, with the opportunity for other "Group of Five" teams to make the playoff. In sum, it expanded the exposure for universities while also creating a windfall of revenue for the conferences and teams that will participate. At the same time, it incorporated six historic bowls in the process: the Cotton, Fiesta, Orange, Peach, Rose, and Sugar Bowls would rotate in the quarterfinal and semifinal rounds.

These best-made plans then were abruptly complicated by more conference realignment announcements in August and September of 2023 that members of the Pac-12 conference were leaving for new affiliations. With the Pac-12 Conference's future in doubt, Arizona, Arizona State, Colorado, and Utah left for the Big Twelve. At nearly the same time, Oregon and Washington joined the Big Ten. With only four teams left in the Pac-12, West Coast teams Stanford and Cal Berkeley joined the Atlantic Coast Conference (along with Southern Methodist in Texas). The Power Five became the Power Four. Traditional conference rivalries and alignments were reconfigured or terminated, leaving scheduling and coherent planning in disarray. As many noted, the new associations seemed less like long-term solutions and increased the odds that two super conferences would come to dominate college football.[84]

In the final weeks of 2023 the American public and higher education officials saw some signs of the potential organizational reconfiguration of intercollegiate athletics in the wake of a decade of disputes, including court cases and resignations. Acrimony and uncertainty had characterized relations among several constituencies. Florida State University highlighted this tension, announcing that it would sue its own conference, the ACC, regarding the grant of rights that FSU and other member institutions had signed over to the ACC through 2036 in order to keep the league intact.[85] Continued criticism had also been directed at the NCAA for its failure to provide strategic leadership amid a changing collegiate athletic landscape.

The emerging proposed structural innovations in governance and control took place against a backdrop of business as usual. The NCAA announced a full slate of forty-one televised college football bowl games that would start on December 16th and culminate with a Division I championship game six weeks later. And this overlapped with national television coverage of hundreds of college basketball games.

Off the playing field and courts, however, news coverage focused on controversial developments. Texas A&M University, for example, announced that fired football coach Jimbo Fischer would receive a salary contract buyout of more than seventy-five million dollars—during a year when media such as the *Wall Street Journal* and *Forbes* published stories about the severe budgetary shortfalls of many major flagship state universities such as West Virginia University and Pennsylvania State University.[86]

Many college student-athletes were participating in new opportunities made possible by Supreme Court cases and other litigation against the NCAA. This included expanded rights for income from NIL contracts along with the implementation of the "transfer portal," which allowed a college athlete to change school enrollment without any waiting period to play a varsity sport at their new home campus.[87]

The capstone of these activities occurred in December 2023. After participating in congressional hearings regarding NIL in October, the new president of the NCAA, former Massachusetts governor Charles Baker, released a comprehensive plan in which the NCAA maintained leadership in college sports. Once again, the NCAA's new administrative proposal embraced many of the practices that the NCAA had historically opposed during its 120 years of existence. Foremost was the new advocacy of unlimited earning opportunities for college student-athletes.[88]

The NCAA proposal included creation of a new supergroup of a small number of powerful conferences and their member institutions. Having previously ceded its authority to the court system, the NCAA's new president finally provided a proposal that might, in the long run, prevent the dissolution of the NCAA. The outlook for 2024 was for an era of continued success and excess in big time college sports in these disparate initiatives, which demonstrated the problems in fusing activities and programs at academic institutions with corporate commercialism.

More than ninety years earlier, in the 1920s, the Carnegie Foundation's *American College Athletics* naively argued that college presidents were the individuals best suited to remove overemphasis and commercialism. In the 2020s, it took a group of presidents to increase the emphasis on college football and expand its commercial appeal. The big change, however, is that students as athletes gained formal status on May 25, 2024, when the NCAA agreed to a "landmark settlement" of $2.8 billion to pay college players. If approved by a US district judge in California, in the case of *House v. NCAA*, this settlement of a class action antitrust lawsuit "would allow for the creation of the first revenue-sharing plan for college athletics."[89] On the one hand, the settlement replaces the historic ideal of the amateur college student-athlete. And, at the same time, with compensatory provisions going back to 2016 and full implementation in 2025, it provides a means to end the exploitation of high-profile college athletes as "unpaid professionals."

The settlement remains controversial because of its potential to put severe financial strains on women's sports and programs lacking major television contracts. It also marks a new era in NCAA Division I athletics.[90] College sports in 2024 have been cast into a new organizational and financial model.

Conclusion

Why History Matters for College Sports

To make sense out of more than 150 years of college sports as a part of the history of American higher education is neither easy nor obvious. One attractive organizing theme is the character of the college student-athlete. No doubt coaches, athletics directors, alumni boosters, cheerleaders, and numerous others have added to the pageantry of American college sports.[1] And famous coaches probably dominate press coverage, media interviews, and biographies. But without college students as athletes, there simply are no games or matches. The supporting cast is important, but on balance the student-athlete is essential to the history of college sports.

The *ideal* of the college student-athlete is historically useful because it allows for tracking over time the continuity and changes in how—and how well—our colleges have come to meshing realities with the ideal. We can measure the ideal by looking at vacillations and variations and asking such questions as whether participation in college sports help or hinder a student's academic performance.[2] This also brings attention to the recurring question as to whether there is a substantial "academic-athletic divide" in many, perhaps most, of our colleges and universities. Whether in 1924 or 2024, have colleges and their coaches helped students as athletes—or have they exploited them as little more than "meat on the hoof?"[3] A key clue leading to the answer to this question may be found in the creation of the term "student-athlete," which Walter Byers and the NCAA employed in order to ensure that athletes would not be considered employees and open up workers' compensation issues for injuries.

Student-Athletes Began Intercollegiate Sport

College sports began as an intramural enterprise, organized and played by students for their own pleasure and entertainment. During the nineteenth century, largely white, male, and privileged college students participated in numerous games, sports, and organizations that they had created. Football games in the 1800s, for example, provided an opportunity for bragging rights as battles between class cohorts ensued before or during the fall semester. What little oversight was offered by the administration came in the form of regulations or the banning of such violent intramural activities. The key was that college games were part of the extracurriculum led by students on individual campuses across the country. It should not be overlooked that this tradition remains today: millions of American students continue to play intramural athletics within an organized system on their various campuses.

The first *inter*collegiate contest—a boat race between Harvard and Yale in August 1852—also put students front and center. But the first regatta between the two also involved outside commercial influence, as the race was sponsored by the new Boston, Concord, and Montreal Railroad. The company agreed to subsidize the event in order to promote the business venture. Still a student-dominated activity, the boat race required cooperation between students and a business (without any faculty or administrators involved). With throngs of people along the shore, the first intercollegiate sporting event in the United States fell within the "big-time" definition that would be used to characterize certain sports and athletics programs during the twentieth century.

Regattas between and among various institutions grew in popularity among students, alumni, and promoters. Sponsorships continued from various businesses, and up-and-coming institutions viewed victory in a crew race as an opportunity to claim status among America's elite institutions. Some multiteam regattas developed into a carnival-like atmosphere, with other sports like baseball being played the same weekend. Interestingly, as less prestigious schools began dominating competitions, Harvard and Yale students pulled out of the races, indicating that prestige was involved to some extent. If they could not maintain their elite status, they would not participate against others.

Like other sports, the first football game played in the United States had been organized by students when Rutgers and Princeton agreed to a game in November 1869. Even without thousands of spectators or a commercial sponsor, the press took time to report on the Rutgers victory. During the last three decades of the nineteenth century, newspapers dramatically increased its coverage as leading football games grew to draw crowds in the tens of thousands. Colleges and universities recruited academically marginal students, and some schools played "ringers" or "tramp athletes" who moved from roster to roster, playing football even if they were not enrolled at the institutions. From the earliest days of intercollegiate athletics, commercial interests, press coverage, and big-time sports existed—as did scandal and controversy. At the same time, administrators and faculty members began various attempts to regulate the activities student-athletes had created.

The Changing Relationship between Student-Athletes and Their Respective Institutions

Interestingly, the growth of big-time intercollegiate athletics occurred alongside the transformation of many American colleges into universities. The importance of scientific discovery as a key area of study to advance knowledge made the modern research university an integral part of American higher education. Perhaps unintentionally, the modern American university ushered in an era that created a new type of relationship with its undergraduate students, including its student-athletes.

It is important to contrast universities with institutions that remained smaller liberal arts colleges. These colleges also developed multiple sports teams to compete in intercollegiate sports during the nineteenth century. For example, Amherst and Williams played a baseball game for the first time in 1859, with an accompanying chess match held the same weekend. The same two began their football rivalry during the 1880s. At these two schools (and many other small colleges), multiple sports were adopted into the larger curriculum. Yet such institutions continued to employ the more traditional college role, which was rooted in the classics and maintained a version of in loco parentis. This close contact between faculty and undergraduates as a community of learners created an environment that was not conducive for the development of big-time sports. To this day, Amherst, Wesleyan, and Williams call themselves the "Little Three" in contrast to the "Big Three" that at one time consisted of Harvard, Princeton, and Yale.

Unlike the traditional liberal arts college, the development of modern research universities in America provided the conditions for big-time athletics to flourish. The emphasis on enrollment growth, research and publication, subject specialization, and encouragement of professional fields of study all helped define the modern university. In addition to this transformation, universities employed a new kind of chief administrator who no longer focused on eternal truths, denominational doctrine, and student discipline. Instead, new managerial presidents emphasized growth, the financial bottom line, fundraising, positive press coverage, academic productivity, and a systematic division of labor (through colleges and departments). This "scientific" governance of the modern American university created a new separation of students from both faculty and administration in a way that had not previously existed.

As discussed at the beginning of this book, Laurence Veysey's seminal 1964 book, *The Emergence of the American University*, provided a detailed historic narrative on this transformation. Among many insightful conclusions, Veysey highlighted that the new university structure provided greater autonomy for professors within their discipline, but it also limited faculty authority across the various silos that comprised a modern university in America. For this reason, athletics programs had an insulated space in which they could grow free of the control from faculty dictates—which in earlier years had regulated athletics among students on their own specific campuses.

At the same time, students willingly gave up some of their own authority by hiring professional coaches. Engaged coaches, focused on scientific study of a game (scouting) in order to prevail through new knowledge and innovation, found their place within the modern American university. While helping teams win, they also gained authority over student-athletes. This quiet development radically altered the ways in which athletic policy would occur during the twentieth century.

The modern game of American football provides an excellent example of this development. In the early twentieth century, coaches, professors, and presidents came together and created a national association to discuss challenges in athletics. The National Collegiate Athletic Association utilized "scientific" methods to modernize the game of football to make it safer (relatively speaking) for players while keeping it a commercially viable enterprise. The unruly and dangerous scrummage was replaced by a line of scrimmage, forward passes helped to spread out players across the field, and the gridiron marked off the field. All such reforms protected the commercial viability of the game. To a lesser extent, baseball and basketball also witnessed similar evolutions with regard to the official rules of the game. In all cases, however, the student-athletes lost their voice in the governance of intercollegiate sport.

Student-Athletes and Social Justice

The same approach can be then applied to numerous historical questions about social justice. For example, have college sports promoted exclusion or inclusion of historically underrepresented groups, of children from immigrant groups or from modest-income families?[4] What have been patterns of changing accommodation or exclusion according to race, ethnicity, gender, and religion?

Colleges, of course, celebrate and salute legendary figures. It could be the admirable achievements of a Byron "Whizzer" White, an honors student and an all-American football player at the University of Colorado in the 1930s and later a justice of the Supreme Court of the United States. Or, from the early 1960s, the Hall of Fame might include Bill Bradley of Princeton, an all-American basketball player, Rhodes Scholar, all-NBA player, and then a US senator. These iconic figures are a start. A sequel is to ask questions about changing demographics. How, for example, have the demographics of race, gender, ethnicity, religion, and family income shaped the collective profile of those playing college sports over time?

Focusing on the criterion of race, a pertinent question might be, When and how did such pioneering African American college athletes from 1910 to 1940—such as Fritz Pollard of Brown, Jerome Holland of Cornell, or Paul Robeson of Rutgers—acquire a rightful place in the changing images and ideals of the student-athlete? Later, in the late 1960s, how did conflicts and disappointments lead to what was called the "revolt of the Black athlete?"[5] And how did this lead in the latter part of the twentieth century to a syndrome of racial exploitation that was called "the shame of college sports"?[6]

An equally challenging issue remained the fate of historically Black colleges and universities after predominantly white institutions had integrated their teams. During the Jim Crow Era, certain coaches had accomplished a great deal with little in the way of resources. Coach Ed Temple's Tigerbelles at Tennessee State provided an example of unparalleled success amid systemic racial oppression. He was not the only one to create a legacy. Legendary basketball coach John B. McClendon coached at Tennessee State along with other colleges and in the pros, using his position to fight for civil rights. In football, Jake Gaither's dominant career at Florida A&M included sending more than forty of his players into professional football. Although Hall of Fame coach Eddie Robinson carried the torch for HBCUs after integration, schools still witnessed a precipitous decline in resources and influence. As scholar Derrick E. White concluded, "Integration was necessary, but it came at a cost. The sporting congregation crumbled, especially for Black coaches."[7]

Questions remained after integration as well. The increasingly lucrative television contracts in the football and basketball occurred as larger numbers of Black athletes filled the rosters of PWIs. Yet student-athletes did not share in the wealth. In 2014, for example, the University of Connecticut's Shabazz Napier helped his team win a national championship, but he also informed reporters that he would go to bed hungry many nights. Only after Napier's revelation did the NCAA grant schools the right to offer unlimited meals and snacks to its student-athletes.[8]

In the same analytic spirit, what are the stories we record and then share about women like Chris von Saltza of Stanford or a Donna Lopiano of Southern Connecticut? They were heroes in the gradual, slow, and contentious extension of college sports to include women as players and coaches. A common thread in the various cases and trends is that college sports revealed a tension, suggesting a schizoid identity that was both a source of social inclusion and upward mobility as well as an obstacle and opponent of social justice, as when a prominent college football coach refused to play against an opposing team with African American players.

Closely tied to the character of the intercollegiate student-athlete is the image and principle of the amateur player. Amateur status distinguishes the college athlete from professional athletes of the National Football League, the National Basketball Association, and Major League Baseball. Or does it? Had college and university officials and coaches allowed student-athletes in the high-profile sports to become what economist Andrew Zimbalist has called "unpaid professionals"?[9] The "reasonable doubt" triggered by a slate of federal court decisions in recent years prompted all constituencies to rethink the connotations of the college student-athlete. To start the critical reexamination, it is useful to set forth some historical strands.

The Supreme Court and a New Deal for Students as Athletes: *NCAA v. Alston*, 2021

As discussed in chapter 9, by 2012, the NCAA faced a growing number of complaints and then lawsuits from college student-athletes who felt exploited and neglected owing to limits on their athletic grants-in-aid and other potential sources of compensation. A capstone to this litigation surfaced in a case before the US Supreme Court in 2021. This coincidental timing overlapped with March Madness, ensuring a highly publicized matchup both on the court and in court. College sports fans could watch games leading to the Final Four in basketball—good news after the cancellation of the 2020 season championship tournament. The other main event was a case being argued before the Supreme Court pitting the NCAA against former West Virginia University football player Shawne Alston and other student-athletes about its eligibility rules regarding compensation.[10]

Deliberations over the next three months involved legal precedents associated with the Sherman Antitrust Act. In addition to law and economics, however, this case was special because the opening arguments showed that in reforming college sports, history matters. Seth Waxman, the attorney for the NCAA, built his presentation on a historical foundation drawn from a 1984 case in which Justice John Paul Stephens wrote, "The N.C.A.A. plays a critical role in the maintenance of a revered tradition of amateurism in college sports."[11]

No one disagreed with that claim. Yet its meaning was unclear. What exactly is the character and content of the NCAA's "revered tradition of amateurism in college sports"? The NCAA and its lawyers argued that it has been to make certain, for more than a century, that college athletes were students foremost and should not be paid for playing college sports—a distinction that ostensibly separated them from professional athletes. The implication was that if the NCAA were to lose this case, amateur athletics at our colleges and universities would lose their guardian and customary privileges.

But a team of six historians led by Ronald Smith, professor emeritus of Pennsylvania State University, filed an amicus brief that documented a markedly different record of NCAA actions and advocacy on amateurism.[12] Smith, joined by historians Taylor Branch, Richard Crepeau, Sarah Fields, Jay Smith, and John Thelin (coauthor of this book) presented in that brief a detailed chronology showing that the NCAA had, in fact, frequently accommodated financial compensation for student-athletes when convenient and beneficial for the NCAA. An apt metaphor for NCAA participation has been the "electric slide," in which "amateurism" had been conveniently redefined several times over the years to allow and even encourage some compensation. The terms usually were to the benefit the NCAA and college athletics departments in their quest to compete for talent and to attract spectators. These concessions by the NCAA often were reluctant, with only incidental concern for the rights of student-athletes.[13]

The National Collegiate Athletic Association liked to invoke an embellished past that celebrated its creation in 1906 during a series of meetings of college leaders with President Theodore Roosevelt. In fact, the organization was founded as the Intercollegiate Athletics Association of the United States, or IAAUS, and only later became the NCAA. More substantive is that some of the oldest universities—such as Harvard, Princeton, and Yale, which in that era also had the most powerful sports programs in the nation—did not attend those formative meetings. The main agenda dealt with violence and injuries on the football field, not a code of amateurism.[14]

Moreover, one finds little evidence since then that the NCAA was effective in establishing or enforcing standards of amateurism in college sports nationwide. The NCAA had no significant role in policies or regulation of college student-athlete definitions or requirements until after World War II. Starting in 1951, the NCAA gave primary attention to policies involving television and revenues and dealing with concerns about how to halt declining spectator attendance at college football games nationwide.[15]

Indeed, it was difficult to identify a golden age of amateurism in college sports, whether in 1852, 1922, or 1962. Over time, the NCAA endorsed colleges offering full athletic grants-in-aid, a significant shift from their prior objection to such practices. The NCAA's operational definition of amateurism for college athletes at one point in the 1970s was even stretched to allow a student to be a college amateur athlete in one sport while being a paid professional athlete in another. The amicus brief by the historians was concise and disciplined in its fusion of documents to its main argument and interpretation. It showed that history matters—and that historical research has a place in policy discussions and court cases. The brief was hailed by *Forbes* magazine and received an award as the "outstanding Supreme Court amicus brief of the year" for cases dealing with education.[16]

It relied substantially on lead author Ronald Smith's timely book, *The Myth of the Amateur* (University of Texas Press, 2021).[17] The resultant brief understated its strong case and avoided exaggeration, focusing on the big-time spectator sports such as football and men's basketball in the major intercollegiate conferences. The big-time episodes did not exhaust the historical record. Indeed, fulfillment of the college student-athlete ideal was more likely to have taken place in the conferences, colleges, sports, and constituencies that were less likely to have received high-profile media coverage, television broadcasts, and marketing contracts customarily dominated by powerful programs and conferences. To the contrary, the NCAA's characterization of the tradition of the student-athlete glossed over significant incidents that would have brought its imagery into question.

One significant historical example not covered in the brief was that of the Pacific Coast Conference between 1946 and 1959, when discovery of "slush funds" organized by alumni boosters to pay recruited athletes led to suspension and severe penalties for four member institutions: the University of California, Berkeley; the University of California, Los Angeles; the University of Southern

California; and the University of Washington. Players on those teams were limited to the number of games they could play in a season, and the football teams from the four culprit universities were declared ineligible for the Rose Bowl. Tensions and conflicts among member institutions were so strong that the conference was dissolved by 1959. One legacy of the scandal was that it revealed that conferences and their member institutions—not the NCAA— were the real sources of reforms and policies to enforce student amateurism.[18]

A corollary was that in reviewing the history of the NCAA, it was difficult to discern any adherence to a coherent definition or ideal of a student-athlete over time. The problem has gotten worse, not better, in the twenty-first century. A new generation of serious student-athletes and their families have devoted a lot of time and money to training and preparation for playing on a college varsity squad and perhaps to receive a grant-in-aid. Tacit compliance and encouragement of "one-and-done" strategies highlight the professional connection and aspiration of college and professional sports for some athletes, especially big-time men's college basketball.[19]

Adding to the combustible discussion was that the proliferation of social media provided young athletes opportunities for endorsements, publicity, and income that were not available to an earlier generation. A good example of conflicts with the NCAA's definitions of athletic amateurism was the case of double-amputee Hunter Woodhall, an outstanding sprinter who gained national fame as a member of the University of Arkansas's championship track and field team. According to a *New York Times* article on March 29, 2021, Woodhall's success story as a student and athlete had gained him more than three million social media followers and an estimated income potential of eight hundred thousand dollars. Woodhall left college competition after waiting to hear from the NCAA on a release from its compensation restrictions for student-athletes.[20]

Other important cases provide insight into the transitioning landscape for outstanding student-athletes. Olympic gold medalist swimmer Katie Ledecky of Stanford University illustrated the changing landscape of commitment and reward for students who are outstanding athletes. She was a high-achieving student who had been selected as an undergraduate research assistant for the Stanford Psychology Department. She also won numerous NCAA individual swimming championships and led her Stanford team to the NCAA title. In foregoing intercollegiate competition her senior year, she continued Olympic training and competition—and signed a ten-million-dollar contract for endorsements with Speedo sports apparel company. Here was the new acme of the college student-athlete.

Another candidate for recognition in the twenty-first century was Myron Rolle, a 2010 graduate of Florida State University who won all-conference honors as a defensive back and was a Rhodes Scholar at Oxford University. Upon return to the United States, he attended the Florida State University College of Medicine and was a neurosurgery resident at Harvard Medical School/Massachusetts General Hospital. These two stellar examples were joined by numerous remarkable student-athletes from numerous colleges and sports, from NCAA Divisions I, II, and III. The amicus brief by historians looked to the past and the present to provide a guide to creating an appropriate, realistic "New Deal" for student-athletes.

Commercialism and College Sports on Trial: Where Were the Presidents?

The historical finding that resonated from *NCAA v. Alston* was that college sports faced a whole new ball game. The court ruled unanimously in June 2021 that "the district court's injunction pertaining to certain National Collegiate Athletic Association (NCAA) rules limiting the education-related benefits that schools may make available to student-athletes is consistent with established antitrust principles." Since then, news-media coverage has included statements from athletics directors, coaches, conference commissioners, governors, student-athletes, marketing agents, and lawyers about plans for compliance with the landmark case. Negotiations about the new rights and responsibilities of student-athletes would be crucial to the financial condition of athletics departments.[21]

Yet, for the most part, higher education leaders were conspicuously silent. An exception was a letter to the *New York Times* by the president of Endicott College in Massachusetts, who emphasized that NCAA Division III programs were different than those in NCAA Division I. The general lack of public commentary by presidents at universities with big-time sports programs was puzzling, given that *NCAA v. Alston*—combined with name, image, and likeness (NIL) legislation in several states—signaled that commercialism and college sports were on trial. Adding to the uncertain financial outlook has been the fact that even with post-pandemic resumption of NCAA championship tournaments, ticket sales at many sporting events have continued to decline in a trend that began before 2020.[22]

In the absence of public commentary by most college and university presidents about the future of intercollegiate athletics, it was useful to review what these higher education leaders had been saying when the case went to court.

A good approximation comes from the amicus brief filed by the American Council on Education (ACE) and ten other national higher education associations as part of the opening arguments for the *NCAA v. Alston*. The ACE brief argued that the case should represent and reflect all colleges and universities offering varsity sports programs. Its other main points included:

- Colleges and universities do not operate for-profit sports franchises;
- Colleges and universities' mission is education, not sports;
- The educational character of intercollegiate athletics depends on rules that keep student-athletes and institutions focused on education, not profit; and
- Colleges and universities, not antitrust courts, should set the requirements for intercollegiate athletics.

The ACE brief was not convincing. Most disconcerting was its claim, "Nor does it matter that a tiny fraction of sports teams at a tiny fraction of institutions generate significant revenue."[23]

It did matter. Seemingly overlooked is an important legacy from ACE's own 1980 book, *The Money Game: Financing Collegiate Athletics*, written by Robert Atwell, Donna Lopiano, and Bruce Grimes. Atwell served as president of ACE from 1984 to 1996. One of its major findings was that even though there were relatively few big-time programs and conferences, policies were skewed toward their desires. The commercialization in the conferences and university programs identified by the ACE team forty years ago endured into the twenty-first century.[24]

Whereas in 1980 the American Council on Education was a leader in critically analyzing and reforming college sports, by 2020 it had become much more of a follower. The 2021 ACE brief was correct in stating that no college sports program was a "for-profit" activity. But according to NCAA regulations, all colleges and universities programs belonging to Division I were required to be self-supporting. In contrast, colleges in Divisions II and III had no such obligation or expectation. That meant that serious concerns about commercialization and the business model for the present and future of college sports should look critically at financial differences *within* NCAA Division I. The ACE brief noted the expense colleges and universities face in sponsoring such nonrevenue sports as tennis, swimming, lacrosse, gymnastics, and soccer. That included women's sports. A historical question was, then, Were the nonrevenue women's sports to blame for the budget shortfalls at Division I programs?[25]

In probing that question, college and university officials should consider both legal and financial responsibilities. First, the nonrevenue or Olympic sports were relatively inexpensive. Second, institutions and their athletics departments are required to fund athletic scholarships and teams for women in compliance with NCAA and conference guidelines. At some colleges and universities, such as the University of California, Berkeley, the athletics department and chancellor signed a binding agreement with the federal government that if Cal ever did eliminate any of its thirty athletics teams, it would *not* be women's varsity squads.[26]

Using women's sports as a convenient place to cut expenses probably would put the athletics department out of compliance with Title IX. This then would put the entire university's federal funding in jeopardy, including National Institutes of Health and National Science Foundation research grants to academic programs and the medical center. It also would risk the university's eligibility to receive Pell Grants and other federal student financial aid payments. Paying for women's athletic scholarships is not merely a nice thing to do: it's the right and legal thing to do. An overlooked complication for higher education leaders was that nonrevenue sports were not the major source of budget shortfalls for Division I programs.[27]

A weakness in the Division I business model was that those supposed "golden goose" sports often laid goose eggs. Only a small minority of football programs in NCAA Division I showed a surplus. Big-time college football may be good at generating revenues, but it is even better at generating expenses. The net result is that in many NCAA Division I conferences, such as the Mid-American Conference (MAC), mandatory student fees provided more than half of the annual operating budget for athletics departments. At the same time, some of these same universities were cutting tenured professors to address budget shortfalls.[28]

The financial problems of 2021 extended even into the elite Football Bowl Series conferences, such as the Big Ten and the Pac-12. Rutgers University, a relatively new member of the Big Ten, reported a shortfall of $45.2 million for its intercollegiate athletics budget for 2018–19. It relied on $14.5 million in university funds, $12.1 million in student fees, $15.4 million in internal loans, and $3.2 million in direct state funding to balance its budget. According to an article in *Inside Higher Ed*, Rutgers athletics was "losing to win," with $121.5 million in internal debts. In the Pac-12, Cal Berkeley's financial reports for the intercollegiate athletics program represented a recipe for disaster, including a $16 million deficit in 2018. The football stadium renovation debt is $238 million. This means that its annual debt-service payment in 2025 will be $18 million, of which $9.5 million was subsidized by the university's central campus.[29]

What about colleges' other major money sport, NCAA Division I basketball? In 2013–14, a third of the sixty-eight men's basketball teams in the NCAA tournament reported that they did not show an annual surplus. They either broke even or lost money for their seasonal operating revenues and expenses. These sixty-eight teams represent the most successful programs, so as one goes down the complete list of NCAA Division I men's basketball teams, the sobering finding was that many teams lost money or broke even at best.[30]

If university presidents were torn over emphasis on big-time college sports, many trustees did not seem to have hesitation or reservation about the growth and power of college sports. On balance, these cumulative developments lead to the reality that at many institutions, intercollegiate athletics have become central to their mission and character. Unfortunately, this reality has not been formally recognized in the ACE brief or in university organizational charts, mission statements, or reports to regional accrediting associations. To update and acknowledge this change in institutional mission would require increased transparency, not to mention institutional integrity to numerous constituencies inside and outside a campus. It would also benefit the majority of colleges and athletics programs that are *not* engaged in truly big-time athletics.[31]

One sign that structural reform of college sports was imminent was a comment to ESPN in 2021 by NCAA president Mark Emmert, who said, "This is the right time to consider decentralized, deregulated college sports." He also announced that the NCAA planned to organize a specially called constitutional convention in fall 2021 to discuss possible major changes in its governance of athletics programs.[32]

Reform efforts were slow and complicated. At the same time Emmert was calling for decentralization and deregulation within the NCAA, other parts of athletics reform were pulling in toward centralization. Higher education legal scholar Michael A. Olivas, who had recently retired from the University of Houston Law Center, had been tracking these developments and noted that "for too long, the NCAA was the sole outlet for determining college athletic benefits, and it showed, as the billions earned by the athletes' sweat was not invested in their welfare. Now, it has (too) quickly swung to the best-organized and most entrepreneurial athletes and their newly installed representatives." He cited, for example, the University of Alabama sophomore-to-be starting quarterback Bryce Young, "who in his first month, signed up for almost a million dollars of sponsorships."[33]

Olivas continued:

It is clear that this train is quickly leaving the station, and the crazy quilt of state laws and institutional opportunities make it impossible to govern the Name/Image/ Likeness (NIL) rules that will have to be sorted out. I still believe the only way to organize this frenzy is for Congress to hold hearings, to draft responsible legislation, and to remind fans that they are still *student*-athletes, yearning to breathe free. . . . Also, I urge the Knight Foundation to help bring thoughtful deliberations to the table, instead of the rush to mine the Yukon gold that appears to be out there for the select few.[34]

The *NCAA v. Alston* case reinforced the need for reforms. The chaos of the commercial model for NCAA Division I sports increased between 2021 and 2024. Most likely, those programs that were struggling financially would face increased problems of reconciling intercollegiate athletics with institutional mission and finances with new definitions of the amateur student-athlete. This was a time for college and university presidents to have joined the public forum.[35]

Both the problems and prospects extended back in our historical record. For example, in 1991 the Knight Foundation's Commission on Intercollegiate Athletics released its report *Keeping Faith with the Student-Athletes*, which set forth a new model for intercollegiate athletics. Ironically, many of the excesses it criticized have become accepted practices. For example, even conferences and the NCAA noted without outrage that a college student-athlete typically devoted about forty hours per week to her or his varsity sport in some form or another. A critical response to these time demands was that, as suggested in preceding passages in this chapter, college student-athletes now were mentioned in terms of such descriptors as "indentured," "plantations," "exploitation," and "unpaid professionals." Whether the promises and pledges of the Knight Commission's 1991 "new model" were fulfilled remained unclear in light of these more recent characterizations of widespread practices that are not in the best interests of student-athletes. But it is at very least a work in progress.[36]

One could look back even further into the historical narrative (even in this book) and be reminded of the struggles presidents have faced in either holding the line or making substantive change in college sports. In 1929 a group of higher education leaders took seriously the Carnegie Foundation's study *American College Athletics* when it declared that presidents were the ones most likely to solve the abuses in college sports. These presidents formed the Southeastern

Conference. After only a few short years of trying to eradicate the recruiting and subsidizing of athletes, the SEC became the first league to openly offer athletic grants-in-aid. When Frank P. Graham, the popular president of the University of North Carolina, attempted curb scholarships in Chapel Hill and the Southern Conference, he was roundly criticized, and his plans were scrapped almost immediately after being adopted. Perhaps presidents in the 1930s as well as in the twenty-first century could have headed the words of Harvard's battle-tested President Charles Eliot in 1905. When asked to join a group of presidents in reforming football, Eliot responded that presidents "Certainly cannot reform football, and I doubt if by themselves they can abolish it."[37]

These historical lessons provide a reminder of key themes in this work. First, that the modern American university's aims and organizational structure have created an environment in which big-time athletics flourishes. These dilemmas do not seem to plague the many Division III institutions. It would be wise to remember Vanderbilt University's decision to drop the liberal arts institution Sewanee from its Thanksgiving Day game in 1930. Vanderbilt's student publication *The Hustler* offered a justification for the decision: "Tradition must give way to materialism." That same logic had been applied to the fullest with the 2022–23 conference realignment.[38]

Unregulated, unrelenting, and unapologetic materialism created an entirely new set of challenges, especially with the NCAA refusing to take the lead on policies in the new NIL era that would both help students and the higher education enterprise. Instead, as noted, NCAA president Mark Emmert pondered decentralization and deregulation before announcing his retirement. The result of this has been the rise of the "collective" in big-time sports. To date, the NCAA has refused to either exercise enforcement or offer a proposal for Congress to consider. In this environment, *Sports Illustrated* characterized the environment at an annual Southeastern Conference meeting in the following way: "There are disagreements. Frustrated administrators. Ticked off presidents." As one anonymous athletics director stated, "Let's be honest. We are all money laundering."[39]

For these reasons, Olivas's calls on the Knight Foundation and Congress are all the more crucial. At this moment, the historically monolithic views within and among the most powerful conferences have begun to unravel. With disagreement among the most powerful, the time for true reform might be at hand. As this history suggests, it will be essential that reform actually look forward rather than offer worn-out platitudes that have proven unsuccessful for more than a century.

Continued (and Future) Challenges of (and for)
the Student-Athlete

One does find numerous examples where university athletics departments invest substantial resources, facilities, and professional personnel to provide student-athletes who are receiving grants-in-aid with a variety of educational, psychological, and career services. At one university in the Southeastern Conference, athletic officials distributed posters and flyers from their office of the "student-athlete experience" in which they stated, "our mission is to develop leaders of character, competence, and consequence for play and for life." Its "core values" were character, integrity, knowledge, stewardship, and competitive greatness.

Furthermore, the program's belief system and guiding principles were that "better people make better university athletes," that "direction determines destination," and that "who you're becoming drives what you're doing." These were joined by principles that "development is a deliberate process and a mutual responsibility" and that "leaders develop leaders."

These principles then were parlayed into strategies of "engage, equip, examine, and experience" as keys to "whole person development." The operationalized outcomes were for student-athletes to graduate by earning a degree to think critically and creatively, to "pursue excellence and life-long learning" to "communicate and interact with others," and to achieve "winning" by demonstrating "resilience and possess a winner's ethos." All these concluded with the aim of becoming a "citizen" whereby a student-athlete "lives honorably and embraces one's citizenship in BBN (Building Bridges Network)."[40]

How the effectiveness of these well-intentioned elaborate services and strategies are ultimately measured remains problematic. A distinct, concrete goal is to have all student-athletes graduate in a timely manner. A standard measure is to compare student-athlete retention and graduation rates with those of all college students nationwide. But that can be problematic because it is simplistic. A student-athlete receiving a grant-in-aid must be enrolled full-time and is prohibited from holding down a job during the academic year. In contrast, looking at sources such as the US Department of Education's comprehensive statistical data bases, the population of "all college students" is a complex mosaic that includes part-time students, those who work at a job, and students who do not receive substantial financial aid. So, the comparison is dubious.

An added wrinkle in recent years is that athletics department graduation rates were skewed because data categories and comparisons may gloss over complications such as student-athletes who transfer to another institution or who leave college without completing a degree in order to sign a professional contract. The residual message is that the model of the full-time undergraduate student who graduates in four years often does not match the realities or plans of a growing number of students in American higher education today. Also worth noting is that in 2023 the NCAA, without much fanfare, eliminated its requirement that student-athletes take the SAT or ACT as a condition of athletic eligibility.[41] Although standardized tests as a sole indicator of academic success are problematic, it seems a desire for equity would require scores help determine how to best meet the needs of student-athletes.

For student-athletes in big-time sports, sound policies and valid statistical analyses of conduct as students and as aspiring professionals will be difficult to assess and monitor. As the NIL era of intercollegiate athletics commences, history has suggested the NCAA probably will require federal intervention through legislation to assist in establishing standard guidelines to follow. As stated above, some have suggested that allowing an unapologetically professional model for the limited number of big-time programs might allow the vast majority of colleges and universities to pursue an amateur model. That might be plausible in its acknowledgment and formal confirmation of the actual character of the big-time sports.

The current landscape of American higher education and American culture in general suggests this may be more difficult than some imagine. As mentioned in the introduction, the same institutions that offer intercollegiate sports boast more than three hundred degree programs in sports management. Such programs prepare students to engage in the business of sports—including college athletics. In addition, American culture is struggling with the "professionalization" of youth sports, which have become their own billion-dollar industry.[42] It has also spawned the creation of consulting businesses and speaking services like the Changing the Game Project, which hopes to "return youth sports to our children, and put the 'play' back in 'play ball.' "[43] With an overemphasis on youth sports and the allure of truly professional sports beyond college, universities find themselves in difficult predicament. One concern is that many American families enthusiastically embrace new opportunities for investing in highly competitive youth sports programs for their daughters and sons. Such extended investment and participation often include the long-term goal of these young athletes receiving offers of college scholarships and professional sports contracts.

The Health of College Student-Athletes

Cutting across all categories of institutions and levels of college sports competition, regardless of high or low commercial involvement, has been the perennial question of responsibility for the health of student-athletes. The issue has strong historical grounding in the early 1900s with concerns over illegal and dangerous tactics on the playing field and then questions of liability for serious injuries to student-athletes. In 2023 the issue resurfaced owing to a convergence of quantitative and qualitative data. One impetus has been increasingly systematic statistics on injury occurrence. And such data collection has taken place while units such as Boston University's medical institute have devoted increasing attention to analyzing sports injuries associated with chronic traumatic encephalopathy (CTE), a degenerative brain disease. Sophisticated analyses in recent years have included a focus on CTE occurring in relatively young athletes, including those in high school and college.

Such statistical and clinical tracking was punctuated in 2023 with high-profile media coverage of particularly tragic incidents. Most conspicuous was the August 29, 2023, front-page article in the *New York Times* titled "After Loss of Son, Coach Faces a Terrible Truth." The reference was to how "a deadly brain disease upends a life built around football." Such was the fate of the head football coach at the University of Maryland, Michael Locksley, and his son, Meiko. Meiko had been a longtime dedicated high school and college player who suffered severe injuries that evidently were not given adequate attention.[44] The result was the player's physical and social deterioration and errant behavior. One syndrome resulting from the high-profile case was that college coaches and student-athletes who have been long devoted to and even dependent on high-profile sports participation as part of their education and identities were hard-pressed to give up or step away from competitive sports that were high risk in terms of severe, life-changing injuries. Such were the hard questions and uneasy choices emerging from the intensity and longevity of sports competition. Injuries such as CTE and concussions were not the only concerns, as the record of serious injuries to knees, backs, and assorted joints were regarded as systemic and problematic—not isolated—for those competing in intercollegiate athletics.

It is a fool's errand for historians to masquerade as futurists. It is hard to imagine someone standing inside a packed Yale Bowl in 1919 with seventy thousand rabid fans predicting that a century later the Bulldogs would average twelve thousand fans per game while more than a hundred thousand spectators would regularly descend on Tuscaloosa, Alabama, on any given Saturday in the fall.[45] Nevertheless, honest history can inform—and lead—good policy. To expand and complicate consideration and projections, one needs to include the present and future of women's intercollegiate athletics as part of the potential growth of commercialization and spectator appeal.

The incredible growth in scholarship addressing such issues continues to provide hope for policies that acknowledge the business aspects of college sports and work within that structure for the benefit of all student-athletes. For example, only in recent years has "reform" meant something different than attempting to return athletes to a mythical amateurism that Ronald Smith has clearly established never truly existed in intercollegiate sports. Regardless, the history of college sports in America provides valuable context for future debates and decisions regarding the place of intercollegiate athletics in the context of higher education. The need to be aware of the past, present, and future of student-athletes is timely and important in the twenty-first century as American higher education encounters what may be termed a "New Deal" for college sports.

Notes

Preface

1. Frederick Rudolph, "The Rise of Football," in *The American College and University: A History* (New York: A. Knopf, 1962), 373–74.

2. Jordan Acker, "The Only Way College Sports Can Begin to Make Sense Again," *New York Times*, September 23, 2023, A22.

3. George Lynn Cross, *Presidents Can't Punt: The OU Football Tradition* (Norman: University of Oklahoma Press, 1977).

4. "Sports Records Move West," *Life*, June 7, 1937, 72–73.

5. Jairus K. Hammond, *The History of Collegiate Wrestling: A Century of Wrestling Excellence* (Stillwater, OK: National Wrestling Hall of Fame and Museum, 2006).

6. Daniel James Brown, *The Boys in the Boat: Nine Americans and Their Epic Quest for Olympic Gold in the 1936 Olympics* (New York: Penguin, 2013).

7. Murray Sperber, *Shake Down the Thunder: The Creation of Notre Dame Football* (New York: Henry Holt, 1993).

Introduction. Higher Education and Athletics

1. Alan Blinder, "Senators Express Frustration, and So Does the N.C.A.A.," *New York Times*, February 12, 2020, B10.

2. John Sayle Watterson, *College Football: History, Spectacle, Controversy* (Baltimore: Johns Hopkins University Press, 2000), 72–79.

3. Watterson, *College Football*, 72–79.

4. Charles T. Clotfelter, *Big-Time Sports in American Universities*, 2nd ed. (New York: Cambridge University Press, 2019), 40–41.

5. The North American Society for Sport History has played an important role in this growth.

6. John Jay Chapman, *Causes and Consequences* (New York: Charles Scribner's Sons, 1898), 60–61.

7. There are numerous books on what is wrong with the university and the education it provides students. How much attention do scholars of college athletics or other disciplines give to the polemical books detailing all that is allegedly wrong with higher education? We assume it is about the same amount of attention that athletics directors and presidents pay to stories of scandal in college athletics.

8. It seems essential to answer these key questions before addressing all that is allegedly wrong in college athletics.

9. From 1836 to 1872, Mark Hopkins was a Congregationalist theologian and president of Williams College in Massachusetts, a quintessential American liberal arts college.

10. John R. Thelin, *A History of American Higher Education* (Baltimore: Johns Hopkins University Press, 2004), 90. Thelin notes that historian James Axtell's research published

in the 1970s revealed that as late as 1880, only twenty-six American institutions had more than two hundred students enrolled.

11. James Turner and Paul Bernard, "The German Model and the Graduate School: The University of Michigan and the Origin Myth of the American University," in *The American College in the Nineteenth Century*, ed. Roger L. Geiger (Nashville: Vanderbilt University Press, 2000), 240.

12. Laurence R. Veysey, *The Emergence of the American University* (Chicago: University of Chicago Press, 1965), 338. Veysey asserted that at this point an "architect" was no longer needed to create a blueprint for the modern American university. The system needed only "contractors" (university presidents) to replicate the model across the country.

13. Frederick Rudolph, *The American College and University: A History*, 2nd ed. (Athens: University of Georgia Press, 1990), 340–41.

14. Thelin, *A History*, 111–12; Veysey, *Emergence*, 331.

15. Helen Lefkowitz Horowitz, *Campus Life: Undergraduate Cultures from the End of the Eighteenth Century to the Present* (Chicago: University of Chicago Press, 1987), 4–14; Veysey, *Emergence*, 439.

16. Roger L. Geiger, *The History of American Higher Education: Learning and Culture from the Founding to World War II* (Princeton, NJ: Princeton University Press, 2015), 365–423. Horowitz, *Campus Life*, 12 (Canby quote); Veysey, *Emergence*, 269–72.

17. Veysey, *Emergence*, 330–31.

18. The dismissal of sociologist Edwin Ross at Stanford University in 1900 because of his political opinions, along with other academic freedom cases, led to the founding of the American Association of University Professors in 1915.

19. Veysey, *Emergence*, 331, 338, 441.

20. Veysey, *Emergence*, 441–42.

21. Veysey, *Emergence*, 265.

22. Ronald A. Smith, *Sports and Freedom: The Rise of Big-Time College Athletics* (New York: Oxford University Press, 1988), 88.

23. This was, of course, not the case for millions of African Americans who had been coerced during the slave trade.

24. Worth noting, e.g., is that in Frederick Rudolph's history of American colleges and universities, the chapter titled "The Rise of Football" followed the chapters "Flowering of the University Movement" and "Progressivism and the Universities." Only in this new context of higher education could athletics have boomed in such a fashion.

25. John R. Thelin, *Games Colleges Play: Scandal and Reform in Intercollegiate Athletics* (Baltimore: Johns Hopkins University Press, 1996), 11. In addition, Thelin stated, "An intriguing hypothesis is that the excesses of commercialized intercollegiate athletic programs may well be the norm, not the exception, for the character and operation of the twentieth-century American university." A quarter of a century later, this certainly appears to be the case for many twentieth- and twenty-first-century universities.

26. Ronald A. Smith, *Pay for Play: A History of Big-Time College Athletic Reform* (Chicago: University of Illinois Press, 2010), 51.

27. Woodrow Wilson, "What Is a College For?," *Scribner's Magazine* (July–December 1909): 576.

28. Murray Sperber, *Beer and Circus: How Big-Time College Sports Is Crippling Undergraduate Education* (New York: Henry Holt, 2000).

29. Smith, *Sports and Freedom*, 214.

30. Edwin E. Slosson, *Great American Universities* (New York: McMillan, 1910), 374–75.

31. This is the reason the book is titled *College Sports*.

32. The NCAA definition: "An amateur sportsman is one who engages in sports for the physical, mental, or social benefits he derives therefrom, and to whom the sport is an avocation. Any college athlete who takes pay for participation in athletics does not meet this definition of amateurism."

33. This definition has come under increasing scrutiny from both sides of the political spectrum. On campus, more critical scholars are highlighting the use of such vocabulary as a way to keep the most talented athletes marginalized—without power or money. On the other side, those with political leanings toward free markets and liberty also find college's reform efforts to maintain amateurism problematic.

34. After the California State Legislature passed SB 206, the NCAA issued a statement of opposition to the legislation.

35. Clotfelter, *Big-Time Sports*, 316–18.

Chapter 1. The Creation of Sports in American Higher Education

1. "The Battle of the Delta," *Harvard Register* 8 (October 1827): 251–54, https://babel.hathitrust.org/cgi/pt?id=nyp.33433076009913&seq=269.

2. Stephen R. Fox, *Big Leagues: Professional Baseball, Football, and Basketball in National Memory* (Lincoln: University of Nebraska Press, 1998), 216; Kathleen D. Valenzi, *Champion of Sport: The Life of Walter Camp, 1859–1926* (Charlottesville, VA: Howell Press, 1990), 40.

3. Benjamin Homer Hall, *A Collection of College Words and Customs* (Cambridge, MA: John Bartlett, 1856), 214–15.

4. Ronald A. Smith, *Sports and Freedom: The Rise of Big-Time College Athletics* (Oxford: Oxford University Press, 1988), 8–10.

5. Mark F. Bernstein, *Football: The Ivy League Origins of an American Obsession* (Philadelphia: University of Pennsylvania Press, 2001), 4.

6. John A. Blanchard, ed., *The H Book of Harvard Athletics 1852–1922* (Cambridge, MA: Harvard University Press, 1923), 318–20; Brian Bunk, "The First Football Funeral and the Origins of College Sport," We're History, November 13, 2014, http://werehistory.org/first-football-funeral/.

7. John Langdon Sibley, "Sibley's Private Journal, 1846–1882," Harvard University Archives, Cambridge, MA, https://wayback.archive-it.org/5488/20170330145830/http://hul.harvard.edu/lib/archives/refshelf/Sibley.htm; Blanchard, *H Book*, 318–20.

8. Richard Goldstein, *Ivy League Autumns: An illustrated History of College Football's Grand Old Rivalries* (New York: St. Martin's Press, 1996), 3.

9. Blanchard, *H Book*, 318.

10. Smith, *Sports and Freedom*, 26; Gerald R. Gems, Linda J. Borish, and Gertrud Pfister, *Sports in American History: From Colonization to Globalization*, 2nd ed. (Champaign, IL: Human Kinetics, 2017), 120.

11. Daniella K. Garran, *A History of Collegiate Rowing in America* (Atglen, PA: Schiffer Publishing, 2012), 41.

12. Smith, *Sports and Freedom*, 28.

13. Smith, *Sports and Freedom*, 42.

14. Smith, *Sports and Freedom*, 27.

15. Thomas C. Mendenhall, *The Harvard-Yale Boat Race, 1852–1924: And the Coming of Sport to the American College* (Mystic Seaport, CT: Mystic Seaport Museum, 1993), 25–27.

16. Smith, *Sports and Freedom*, 32–33.

17. Mendenhall, *Harvard-Yale Boat Race*, 59.

18. William Blaikie, "Reminiscence of One of Harvard's Great Athletes," *Harvard Crimson*, January 16, 1885, https://www.thecrimson.com/article/1885/1/16/william-blaikie-when-i-attempted-to/.

19. *Harvard Advocate*, June 25, 1969.

20. *Harvard Advocate*, October 14, 1870.

21. Mendenhall, *Harvard-Yale Boat Race*, 77.

22. Mendenhall, *Harvard-Yale Boat Race*, 86–87

23. Smith, *Sports and Freedom*, 46–48.

24. Smith, *Sports and Freedom*, 246.

25. "Scottish Athletic Sports," *New York Times*, September 8, 1876, 8.

26. Smith, *Sports and Freedom*, 104.

27. Smith, *Sports and Freedom*, 106–8.

28. Michael Llewellyn Smith, "The 1896 Olympic Games at Athens and the Princeton Connection," *Princeton University Library Chronicle* 64, no. 3 (Spring 2003): 445–65.

29. Jim Overmyer, "July 1, 1859: Baseball Goes to College," Society for American Baseball Research, accessed February 1, 2024, https://sabr.org/gamesproj/game/july-1-1859-baseball-goes-to-college/.

30. Bernstein, *Football*, 6–7.

31. Bernstein, *Football*, 9.

32. Smith, *Sports and Freedom*, 75.

33. Goldstein, *Ivy League Autumns*, 8; Bernstein, *Football*, 11.

34. Goldstein, *Ivy League Autumns*, 11; Smith, *Sports and Freedom*, 86.

35. John Sayle Watterson, *College Football: History, Spectacle, Controversy* (Baltimore: Johns Hopkins University Press, 2002), 19; Dave Revsine, *The Opening Kickoff: The Tumultuous Birth of a Football Nation* (Guilford, CT: Lyons Press, 2014), 27.

36. Watterson, *College Football*, 13 and 20.

37. David Nelson, *The Anatomy of a Game: Football, the Rules, and the Men Who Made the Game* (Newark: University of Delaware Press, 1994), 62–64.

38. Peggy M. Baker, "Thanksgiving Touchdown," Pilgrim Hall Museum Online Thanksgiving Exhibition, 2006, https://www.pilgrimhall.org/pdf/Thanksgiving_Touchdown.pdf.

39. Michael Oriard, *Reading Football: How the Popular Press Created an American Spectacle* (Chapel Hill: University of North Carolina Press, 1993), 59.

40. Oriard, *Reading Football*, 57.

41. *The Chronicle*, October 26, 1878, 18, https://babel.hathitrust.org/cgi/pt?id=mdp.39015071371879&seq=30.

42. Winton U. Solberg, *Creating the Big Ten: Courage, Corruption, and Commercialization* (Urbana: University of Illinois Press, 2018), 27.

43. Brian M. Ingrassia, *The Rise of Gridiron University: Higher Education's Uneasy Alliance with Big-Time Football* (Lawrence: University Press of Kansas, 2015), 2–3; Watterson, *College Football*, 39–40.

44. Dean Albion Small, quoted in Laurence Veysey, *The Emergence of the American University* (Chicago: University of Chicago Press, 1964), 325–27.

45. Jean Block, "Prologue: The Gray City and the White City," in *The Uses of Gothic: Planning and Building the Campus of the University of Chicago, 1892–1932* (Chicago: University of Chicago Library, 1983), 2–7.

46. Watterson, *College Football*, 41.

47. Robin Lester, *Stagg's University: The Rise, Decline, and Fall of Big-Time Football at Chicago* (Urbana: University of Illinois Press, 1995).

48. J. Hardin Hobson, "Football Culture at New South Universities: Lost Cause and Old South Memory, Modernity, and Martial Manhood," in *The History of American College Football: Institutional Policy, Culture, and Reform*, ed. Christian Anderson and Amber Fallucca (New York: Routledge, 2021), 40–52.

49. Ronald A. Smith, "Preludes to the NCAA: Early Failures of Faculty Intercollegiate Athletic Control," *Research Quarterly for Exercise and Sport* 24, no. 44 (1983): 372–82.

50. Smith, *Sports and Freedom*, 136–37.

51. Bernstein, *Football*, 34–35.

52. Bernstein, *Football*, 51.

53. Fuzzy Woodruff, *A History of Southern Football, 1890–1928*, vol. 1. (Atlanta: Georgia Southern Publishing, 1928), 12; Watterson, *College Football*, 46–47.

54. "Yale Again Triumphant," *New York Times*, November 25, 1894, 1–2.

55. Watterson, *College Football*, 36.

56. "Faculty Control in Athletics," *Michigan Alumnus* 3 (1896–97): 84–85, https://babel.hathitrust.org/cgi/pt?id=mdp.39015071121266&seq=134; Watterson, *College Football*, 46.

57. Solberg, *Creating the Big Ten*, 13–31; Watterson, *College Football*, 49–50.

58. Nathan W. Dougherty, *Educators and Athletes: The Southeastern Conference, 1894–1972* (Knoxville: Department of Athletics, University of Tennessee, 1976), 33. The original members included Alabama, Alabama Polytechnic Institute (Auburn), Georgia, Georgia School of Technology, South Carolina, the University of the South, and Vanderbilt. The following year, twelve members were added: Central University (Centre), Clemson Agricultural College, Cumberland University, Kentucky State College (later the University of Kentucky), Louisiana State College, Mercer University, Mississippi A&M College, Nashville University (Peabody College), Southern Presbyterian University (Rhodes College), Tennessee, Texas, and Tulane.

59. Christopher C. Meyers, "'Unrelenting War on Football': The Death of Richard Von Gammon and the Attempt to Ban Football in Georgia," *Georgia Historical Quarterly* 93, no. 4 (Winter 2009): 394–404.

60. Meyers, "'Unrelenting War on Football,'" 403–4; "The Tragedy of Von Gammon," UGA Special Collections Library Online Exhibitions, accessed February 1, 2024, https://digilab.libs.uga.edu/scl/exhibits/show/covered_with_glory/von_gammon.

61. Watterson, *College Football*, 52–54.

62. Ray Glier, "Alabama Isn't the First to Rule the South," *New York Times*, January 4, 2019, B,7.

63. John R. Thelin, *A History of American Higher Education* (Baltimore: Johns Hopkins University Press, 2004), 111–12; Veysey, *Emergence*, 331.

64. Helen Lefkowitz Horowitz, *Campus Life: Undergraduate Cultures from the End of the Eighteenth Century to the Present* (Chicago: University of Chicago Press, 1987), 4–14; Veysey, *Emergence*, 439.

65. Roger L. Geiger, *The History of American Higher Education: Learning and Culture from the Founding to World War II* (Princeton, NJ: Princeton University Press, 2015), 365–423; Horowitz, *Campus Life*, Canby quote, 12; Veysey, *Emergence*, 269–72.

66. The dismissal of sociologist Edwin Ross at Stanford University in 1900 because of his political opinions, along with other academic freedom cases, led to the founding of the American Association of University Professors in 1915.

67. Veysey, *Emergence*, 331, 338, 441–42.

68. Smith, *Sports and Freedom*, 141.

69. Smith, *Sports and Freedom*, 142.

70. George Santayana, "Philosophy on the Bleachers," *Harvard Monthly* 18 (July 1894): 94.

71. Santayana, "Philosophy on the Bleachers," 183.

72. Walter Camp, *Football Facts and Figures: A Symposium of Expert Opinions on the Game's Place in American Athletics* (New York: Harper & Brothers, 1894), 4.

73. Camp, *Football Facts and Figures*, 5

74. Camp, *Football Facts and Figures*, 188.

75. Henry Seidel Canby, *Alma Mater: The Gothic Age of the American College* (New York: Holt and Rinehart, 1936), xi.

Chapter 2. Building Local, Regional, and National Programs

1. Mike Lessiter, *The College Names of the Games: The Stories behind the Nicknames of 293 College Sports Teams* (New York: Contemporary Books, 1989).

2. Daniel J. Boorstin, *The Image: A Guide to Pseudo-Events in America* (New York: Harper Colophon, 1962).

3. Michael Oriard, *Reading Football: How the Popular Press Created an American Spectacle* (Chapel Hill: University of North Carolina Press, 1993).

4. James Michener, "The Media," in *Sports in America* (New York: Random House, 1976), chap. 10, 285–336.

5. "Rose Parade History," Pasadena Tournament of Roses, accessed February 3, 2024, https://tournamentofroses.com/about/rose-parade-history/.

6. Bill Loomis, "Fielding Yost, Godfather of UM Sports," *Detroit News*, October 28, 2017, https://www.detroitnews.com/story/news/local/michigan-history/2017/10/28/fielding-yost-godfather-michigan-sports/107078302/.

7. Jay Barry and Martha Mitchell, *A Tale of Two Centuries: A Warm and Richly Pictorial History of Brown University, 1764–1985* (Providence, RI: Brown Alumni Monthly, 1985), 95.

8. "Yale Sports Cost $107,397," *New York Times*, July 16, 1909, 7, https://timesmachine.nytimes.com/timesmachine/1909/07/16/101818072.html?pageNumber=7.

9. "Football Is a Fight, Says President Eliot," *New York Times*, February 2, 1905, 6.

10. Henry Beach Needham, "The College Athlete: How Commercialism Is Making Him a Professional. Part I—Recruiting and Subsidizing," *McClure's Magazine* 25, no. 2 (June 1905): 115–28.

11. Henry Beach Needham, "The College Athlete: How Commercialism Is Making Him a Professional. Part II—Summer Ball, the Gate-Money Evil, and Unnecessary Roughness in Football," *McClure's Magazine* 25, no. 2 (June 1905): 272.

12. Needham, "The College Athlete Part II," 261–62.

13. Needham, "The College Athlete Part I,"117.

14. Needham, "The College Athlete Part II," 271–72.

15. John Sayle Watterson, *College Football: History, Spectacle, Controversy* (Baltimore: Johns Hopkins University Press, 2002), 68–70; John J. Miller, *The Big Scrum: How Teddy Roosevelt Saved Football* (New York: Harper, 2011), 187–90.

16. Miller, *The Big Scrum*, 196–97.

17. Miller, *The Big Scrum*, 196–97.

18. Miller, *The Big Scrum*, 197.

19. "Football Player Killed," *New York Times*, November 26, 1905, 1.

20. Watterson, *College Football*, 72.

21. Ronald A. Smith, *Sports and Freedom: The Rise of Big-Time College Athletics* (New York: Oxford University Press, 1988),199.

22. Those voting to abolish football were Columbia, New York University, Rochester, Stevens Institute, and Union College. Those voting for reform rather than abolition were Army Fordham, Haverford, Rutgers, Swarthmore, Syracuse, and Wesleyan.

23. "Football Committee Suggests New Rules," *New York Times*, December 10, 1905, 2.

24. Ronald A. Smith, *Pay for Play: A History of Big-Time College Athletic Reform* (Champaign: University of Illinois Press, 2010), 49.

25. "December 21, 1891: First Game of Basketball Played in Springfield," Mass Moments, accessed February 3, 2024, https://www.massmoments.org/moment-details/first -game-of-basketball-played-in-springfield.html.

26. Chad Carlson, *Making March Madness: The Early Years of the NCAA, NIT, and College Basketball Championships, 1922–1951* (Fayetteville: University of Arkansas Press, 2017), 1.

27. Neil D. Isaacs, *All the Moves: A History of College Basketball* (Philadelphia: J. B. Lippincott, 1975), 22–23.

28. Carlson, *Making March Madness*, 2.

29. Carlson, *Making March Madness*, 25.

30. Maresi Nerad, *The Academic Kitchen: A Social History of Gender Stratification at the University of California, Berkeley* (Albany: State University of New York Press, 1999); Helen Lefkowitz Horowitz, *Campus Life: Undergraduate Cultures from the End of the Eighteenth Century to the Present* (New York: Knopf, 1987).

31. Betty Spears, "Senda Berenson Abbott—New Woman: New Sport," in *A Century of Women's Basketball: From Frailty to Final Four,* ed. Joan S. Hult and Marianna Trekell (Reston, VA: National Association for Girls and Women in Sport, 1991), 44.

32. "Clara Gregory Baer," Howard-Tilton Memorial Library, accessed February 3, 2024, https://exhibits.tulane.edu/exhibit/tulanewomen/athleticwomen/clara-gregory-baer/; Joan Paul, "Clara Gregory Baer: Catalyst for Women's Basketball," in Hult and Trekell, *Century of Women's Basketball*, 37.

33. "The First Game," 125 Stanford Stories, accessed February 3, 2024, https://125 .stanford.edu/the-first-game/.

34. Marc Horger, "Basketball and Athletic Control at Oberlin College, 1865–1915," *Journal of Sport History* 23, no. 3 (Fall 1996): 269.

35. Horger, "Basketball and Athletic Control," 271 and 278.

36. Gregory Kent Stanley, *Before Big Blue: Sports at the University of Kentucky, 1880–1940* (Lexington: University Press of Kentucky, 1996), 98; Peggy Stanaland,

"The Early Year of Basketball in Kentucky," in Hult and Trekell, *Century of Women's Basketball*, 170–71.

37. Stanley, *Before Big Blue*, 102–11.

38. Stanley, *Before Big Blue*, 105.

39. Stanley, *Before Big Blue*, 107–8.

40. Joan S. Hult, "The Governance of Athletics for Girls and Women: Leadership by Women Physical Educators, 1899–1949," in Hult and Trekell, *Century of Women's Basketball*, 58.

41. Welch Suggs, *A Place on the Team: The Triumph and Tragedy of Title IX* (Princeton, NJ: Princeton University Press, 2006), 23.

42. John S. Watterson, "The Gridiron Crsis of 1905: Was It Really a Crisis?," *Journal of Sport History* 27, no. 2 (Summer 2000): 291–98.

43. Jim Morrison, "The Early History of Football's Forward Pass," *Smithsonian Magazine*, December 28, 2010, https://www.smithsonianmag.com/history/the-early-history-of -footballs-forward-pass-78015237/.

44. Frederick Rudolph, "The Rise of Football," in *The American College and University: A History* (New York: Alfred Knopf, 1962).

45. Nathan W. Dougherty, *Educators and Athletes: The Southeastern Conference, 1874–1972* (Knoxville: Department of Athletics, University of Tennessee, 1976), 60–62.

46. Ronald A. Smith, "The Early Failure of Inter-Institutional Faculty Control," in *Sports and Freedom*, 134–46.

47. Arnold William Flath, *A History of Relations between the National Collegiate Athletic Association and the Amateur Athletic Union of the United States (1905–1963)* (Champaign, IL: Stipes Publishing, 1964), 38.

48. Flath, *History of Relations*, 33.

49. Flath, *History of Relations*, 67–68.

50. Flath, *History of Relations*, 68–73.

51. Flath, *History of Relations*, 84–85.

52. "Griffith Attacks A.A.U. on Olympics," *New York Times*, April 17, 1928, 22.

53. Flath, *History of Relations*, 90.

54. "Colleges and A.A.U. Agree upon Peace," *New York Times*, April 16, 1929, 37.

55. Evan J. Albright, "Blazing the Trail," *Amherst Magazine* (Winter 2007): https:// www.amherst.edu/news/magazine/issues/2007_winter/blazing.

56. Rachel Reed and Greg Kinney, "Celebrating George Jewett: A Look at the Achieve- ments of Michigan's First African American Football Letterman," Bently Historical Library, University of Michigan, accessed February 3, 2024, https://bentley.umich.edu /features/celebrating-george-jewett/.

57. Ocania Chalk, *Black College Sport* (New York: Dodd, Mead, 1976).

58. Gerald Horne, *Paul Robeson: The Artist as Revolutionary* (London: Pluto Press, 2016), 14–15; Rich Shea, "Paul Robeson Football Star," Rutgers Today, March 13, 2019, https://www.rutgers.edu/news/paul-robeson-football-star.

59. Sam Farmer, "True Pioneer Gets His Due," *Lost Angeles Times*, August 7, 2005, https://www.latimes.com/archives/la-xpm-2005-aug-07-sp-pollard7-story.html.

60. John Rosengren, "A Football Martyr," *SB Nation*, November 25, 2014, https:// www.sbnation.com/longform/2014/11/25/7275681/jack-trice-iowa-state-football-profile.

61. "A Stadium Says His Name: Jack Trice," *New York Times*, July 20, 2020, D1; Rosengren, "A Football Martyr." See also Jamie Schultz, *Moments of Impact: Injury, Racialized Memory, and Reconciliation in College Football* (Lincoln: University of Nebraska Press, 2016).

62. Patrick B. Miller, "To 'Bring the Race along Rapidly': Sport, Student Culture, and Educational Mission at Historically Black Colleges during the Interwar Years," *History of Education Quarterly* 35, no. 2 (Summer 1995): 117–18.

63. David K. Wiggins, "The Biggest 'Classic' of Them All: The Howard University and Lincoln University Thanksgiving Day Football Games, 1919–1929," in *Rooting for the Home Team: Sport, Community, and Identity*, ed. Daniel A. Nathan (Urbana: University of Illinois, 2013), 37.

64. David Wiggins and Chris Elzey, "Creating Order in Black College Sport: The Lasting Legacy of the Colored Intercollegiate Athletic Association," in *Separate Games: African American Sport behind the Walls of Segregation*, ed. David K. Wiggins and Ryan A. Swanson (Fayetteville: University of Arkansas Press, 2016), 147–52.

65. Wiggins, "Biggest 'Classic' of Them All," 37.

66. Wiggins and Elzey, "Creating Order in Black College Sport," 147–48.

67. J. Kenyatta Cavil, "Early Athletic Experiences at HBCU's," in *The Athletic Experience at Historically Black Colleges and Universities: Past, Present, and Persistence*, ed. Billy Hawkins, Joseph Cooper, Akilah Carter-Francique, and J. Kenyatta Cavil (Lanham, MD: Rowman & Littlefield. 2015), 29.

68. Cavil, "Early Athletic Experiences at HBCU's," 29.

69. Grantland Rice, "The Four Horsemen," *New York Herald Tribune*, October 18, 1924, https://archives.nd.edu/research/texts/rice.htm.

70. Oriard. *Reading Football*, 278.

71. "October 8, 1921: WVU vs. Pitt Marks First Live Football Radio Broadcast," WV Public Broadcasting, October 8, 2019, https://www.wvpublic.org/radio/2019-10-08/october-8-1921-wvu-vs-pitt-marks-first-live-football-radio-broadcast.

72. "1924 with the Irish," Forever Irish, accessed February 3, 2024, http://ndfootball history.com/1924-with-the-irish-2. See also Jim Lefebvre, *Loyal Sons: The Story of the Four Horsemen and Notre Dame Football's 1924 Champions* (Great Day Press, 2008).

73. "CFB150 Stories: The Granddaddy of Them All and Media Firsts," Pasadena Tournament of Roses, accessed February 3, 2024, https://tournamentofroses.com/cfb150-stories-the-granddaddy-of-them-all-and-media-firsts/.

74. Robert S. Gallagher, "The Galloping Ghost: An Interview with Red Grange," *American Heritage* 26, no. 1 (December 1974): https://web.archive.org/web/2009020 2114014/http://www.americanheritage.com/articles/magazine/ah/1974/1/1974_1_20 _print.shtml.

75. "Red Grange, the Galloping Ghost," *New York Times*, October 18, 1924, https://archive.nytimes.com/www.nytimes.com/packages/html/sports/year_in_sports/10.18a .html.

76. "Grange and His Team to Play in Florida," *New York Times*, November 22, 1925, 5.

77. John R. Thelin, *Games Colleges Play: Scandal and Reform in Intercollegiate Athletics* (Baltimore: Johns Hopkins University Press, 1996), 6; Smith, *Pay for Play*, 67.

78. Smith, *Pay for Play*, 68.

79. Thelin, *Games Colleges Play*.

80. Chris Dufresne, "When They Were Riding High," *Los Angeles Times*, October 2, 2007, https://www.latimes.com/archives/la-xpm-2007-oct-02-sp-rosebowl2-story.html; Michael Oriard, *King Football: Sport and Spectacle in the Golden Age of Radio and Newsreels, Movies and Magazines, the Weekly and Daily Press* (Chapel Hill: University of North Carolina Press, 2004), 128–29; Ronald Smith, *Play by Play*, 44.

81. Thelin, *Games Colleges Play*, 93–96; Smith, *Pay for Play*, 65.

82. George P. Morris, "The Harvard Stadium," *Overland Monthly* (May 1903).

83. Brian M. Ingrassia, "Stadiums: Between Campus and Culture," in *The Rise of Gridiron University: Higher Education's Uneasy Alliance with Big-Time Football* (Lawrence: University Press of Kansas, 2012), chap. 6, 139–70.

84. John R. Thelin, "Picture Perfect: Postcards and the Image of the American Campus," in *"Having a Great Time . . .": The John B. Hawley Higher Education Postcard Collection*, ed. John B. Hawley and Craig Kridel (Columbia: University of South Carolina Museum of Education, 2001).

85. Abraham Flexner, *Universities: American, German, English* (New York: Oxford University Press, 1930), 66.

86. US Military Academy, *The Howitzer* (West Point, NY: Corps of the Cadets of the US Military Academy, 1925), 219–73.

87. Edwin Slosson, *Great American Universities* (New York: Macmillan, 1910), 383.

88. M. Knoll, "Dewey as Administrator: The Inglorious End of the Laboratory School in Chicago," *Journal of Curriculum Studies* 47, no. 2 (2014): 203–52.

89. "The Sterling Professors of Yale: Evolution of a Species," *Yale Daily News*, January 21, 2011, https://yaledailynews.com/blog/2011/01/21/the-sterling-professors-of-yale-evolution-of-a-species/.

90. "Several Distinguished Professors Added to 1920 Teaching Staff," *Harvard Crimson*, September 25, 1920, https://www.thecrimson.com/article/1920/9/25/several-distinguished-professors-added-to-1920/.

91. Slosson, *Great American Universities*, 508–9.

92. Ingrassia, *Rise of Gridiron University*.

93. David O. Levine, *The American College and the Culture of Aspiration, 1915–1940* (Ithaca, NY: Cornell University Press, 1988), 15.

94. Slosson's fourteen great American universities were: California, Chicago, Columbia, Cornell, Harvard, Illinois, Johns Hopkins, Michigan, Minnesota, Penn, Princeton, Stanford, Wisconsin, and Yale. Edwin Slosson, *Great American Universities* (New York: Macmillan, 1910).

95. Slosson, *Great American Universities*, 502.

96. Slosson, *Great American Universities*, 502–4.

Chapter 3. Big-Time Football and Backlash

1. Ellen Condliffe Lagemann, *Private Power for the Public Good: A History of the Carnegie Foundation for the Advancement of Teaching* (Middletown, CT: Wesleyan University Press, 1983).

2. Howard J. Savage et al., *American College Athletics, with a Preface by Henry S. Pritchett*, Bulletin No. 23 (New York: Carnegie Foundation for the Advancement of Teaching, 1929).

3. "College Sports Tainted by Bounties, Carnegie Study Finds in Wide Study," *New York Times*, October 24, 1929, 1; "Carnegie Report Hits Big Ten Athletics: Three Year Probe

Indicts American College System," *Chicago Daily Tribune,* October 21, 1929, 1; "U. of M. Accused," *Detroit Daily,* October 24, 1929, 1.

4. Savage et al., *American College Athletics,* 237.

5. Savage et al., *American College Athletics,* 224–65.

6. "U. of M. Accused," 1.

7. John R. Thelin, *Games Colleges Play: Scandal and Reform in Intercollegiate Athletics* (Baltimore: Johns Hopkins University Press, 1994), 28–29.

8. "College Sports Tainted by Bounties," 23.

9. Raymond Schmidt, "The 1929 Iowa Football Scandal: Paying Tribute to the Carnegie Report?," *Journal of Sport History* 34, no. 3 (Fall 2007): 343–51.

10. Ronald A. Smith, *Play-by-Play: Radio, Television and Big-Time College Sport* (Baltimore: Johns Hopkins University Press, 2001), 70.

11. Schmidt. "1929 Iowa Football Scandal," 348.

12. Raymond Schmidt, *Shaping College Football: The Transformation of an American Sport, 1919–1930* (Syracuse, NY: Syracuse University Press, 2007), 178.

13. Schmidt, *Shaping College Football,* 174–98.

14. Savage et al., *American College Athletics,* 307.

15. Savage et al., *American College Athletics,* 145.

16. Savage et al., *American College Athletics,* 307.

17. Savage et al., *American College Athletics,* 310.

18. Savage et al., *American College Athletics,* xxi.

19. Savage et al., *American College Athletics,* 265.

20. Allan W. Rowe, review of *American College Athletics,* by Howard J. Savage et al., *Bulletin of the American Association of University Professors* 15, no. 8 (December 1929): 592.

21. Rowe, review, 595.

22. Rowe, review, 594.

23. Savage et al., *American College Athletics,* 265.

24. Andrew Doyle, "Turning the Tide: College Football and Southern Progressivism," *Southern Cultures: Sports in the South* 3, no. 3 (Fall 1997): 28–51; J. Hardin Hobson, "Football Culture at New South Universities: Lost Cause and Old South Memory, Modernity, and Martial Manhood," in Christian K. Anderson and Amber C. Fallucca, eds., *The History of American College Football: Institutional Policy, Culture, and Reform* (New York: Routledge, 2021), 37–58.

25. Eric A. Moyen, "Redefining Reform: Presidents, Football, and Athletic Policy in the Southeastern Conference, 1929–1936," in Anderson and Fallucca, *History of American College Football,* 93.

26. Moyen, "Redefining Reform," 95–96.

27. Eric A. Moyen, *Frank McVey and the University of Kentucky: A Progressive President and the Modernization of a Southern University* (Lexington: University Press of Kentucky, 2011), 212–15.

28. Moyen, "Redefining Reform," 99.

29. "Southeastern Conference Constitution and By-Laws," Drawer 34, Folder 432, "Athletic Board of Control (Aug. 3–Sept. 30, 1933)," Hugh Critz Presidential Files, Mississippi State University Archives and Special Collections; emphasis added.

30. Moyen, "Redefining Reform," 98–100.

31. Moyen, "Redefining Reform," 100.

32. Moyen, "Redefining Reform," 102.

33. Richard Stone, "The Graham Plan of 1935: An Aborted Crusade to De-emphasize College Athletics," *North Carolina Historical Review* 64, no. 3 (July 1987): 281–82.

34. John Sayle Watterson, *College Football: History, Spectacle, Controversy* (Baltimore: Johns Hopkins University Press, 2002), 186.

35. Stone, "Graham Plan of 1935," 286.

36. Moyen, "Redefining Reform," 100–102.

37. Stone, "Graham Plan of 1935," 280.

38. "On Influences Inimical to the Best Interests of Intercollegiate Sport," in *Proceedings of the Thirty-First Annual Convention of the National Collegiate Athletic Association* (Indianapolis: NCAA, December 27–29, 1936), 72–75.

39. Moyen, "Redefining Reform," 104–5.

40. Winton U. Solberg, *Creating the Big Ten: Courage, Corruption, and Commercialization* (Urbana: University of Illinois Press, 2018), 224–26.

41. Watterson, *College Football*, 186.

42. Solberg, *Creating the Big Ten*, 198–213.

43. Bureau of Internal Revenue, US Treasury Department, *Statistics of Income for 1930: Compiled from Income Tax Return and Including Statistics from Estate Tax Returns* (Washington, DC: US Government Printing Office Washington, 1932), 67, https://www.irs.gov/pub/irs-soi/30soirepar.pdf.

44. "Still Making History," University of Georgia timeline, accessed February 5, 2024, https://president.uga.edu/_resources/uploads/documents/UGA225_Timeline.pdf.

45. "Faults of P.C.C. Are Listed," *San Jose News*, January 5, 1940, 1.

46. "Faults of P.C.C."

47. Stone, "Graham Plan of 1935," 190–92.

48. For the earliest attempts to create an athletic association, see Germaine M. Reed, "Charles Holmes Herty and the Establishment of Organized Athletics at the University of Georgia," *Georgia Historical Quarterly* 77, no. 3 (Fall 1993): 525–40.

49. Thelin, *Games Colleges Play*, 68–97.

50. Smith, *Play-By-Play*, 31–33.

51. Smith, *Play-By-Play*, 35–37.

52. "Epic Connection: Family, Religious and Immigrant History Bind Subway Alumni to Notre Dame," University of Notre Dame Stories, accessed February 5, 2024, https://www.nd.edu/stories/epic-connection/.

53. Chad Seifried, Matthew Katz, and Adam Pfleeger, "Megalomaniac or Narcissist? Re-examining the Leadership Style of Huey P. Long through Sport," *Journal of Sport Studies* 42, no. 1 (Spring 2015): 47.

54. Seifried et al., "Megalomaniac or Narcissist?," 48–29.

55. Peter Finney, *The Fighting Tigers II: LSU Football, 1893–1980*, rev. Ed. (Baton Rouge: Louisiana State University Press, 1980), 118–22; Robert Mann, *Kingfish U: Huey Long and LSU* (Baton Rouge: Louisiana State University Press, 2023).

56. Ray Glier, "Long before Alabama, the South Had Sewanee," *New York Times*, January 4, 2019, https://www.nytimes.com/2019/01/04/sports/sewanee-tigers-alabama-oklahoma.html.

57. For a detailed description of Sewanee's departure from the SEC, see Jim Watkins, "The Fall of Sewanee from 'Big-Time' College Football," *Journal of Issues in Intercollegiate Athletics* 12 (2019): 114–32.

58. Hal A. Lawson and Alan G. Ingham, "Conflicting Ideologies Concerning the University and Intercollegiate Athletics: Harper and Hutchins at Chicago, 1892–1940," *Journal of Sport History* 7, no. 3 (Winter 1980): 37–67.

59. Robin Lester, *Stagg's University: The Rise, Decline and Fall of Big-Time Football at Chicago* (Urbana: University of Illinois Press, 1995).

60. Robin Lester, *Stagg's University*, 179–83.

61. Robert Maynard Hutchins, "Gate Receipts and Glory," *Saturday Evening Post,* December 3, 1938.

62. Pittsburg and Penn implemented deemphasis policies but failed to do away with football. In both instances, successors eventually returned to a big-time model for football.

63. Lawson and Ingham, "Conflicting Ideologies," 37–67.

64. Savage et al., *American College Athletics,* ix–x.

65. Savage et al, *American College Athletics,* xi–xvii.

66. Savage et al, *American College Athletics,* xii and xviii.

67. W. H. Cowley, "Editorial Comments," *Journal of Higher Education* 1, no. 6 (June 1930): 356.

68. John L. Griffith, "The Carnegie Reports," *Journal of Higher Education* 1, no. 6 (June 1930): 325–26.

69. David O. Levine, *The American College and the Culture of Aspiration, 1915–1940* (Ithaca, NY: Cornell University Press, 1986).

70. "The End to Big Time Football, 1930–1942" (Sewanee academic paper 4), *Vanderbilt Hustler,* December 6, 1929.

71. "Historical Enrollment," University Registrar, University of Chicago, accessed February 5, 2024, https://registrar.uchicago.edu/data-reporting/historical-enrollment/.

72. Lawson and Ingham, "Conflicting Ideologies," 59–60.

73. Savage et al., *American College Athletics,* x.

74. Savage et al., *American College Athletics,* x and xvi.

75. William D. Snider, *Light on the Hill: A History of the University of North Carolina at Chapel Hill* (Chapel Hill: University of North Carolina Press, 2004), 221; Stone, "Graham Plan of 1935," 281.

76. Stone, "Graham Plan of 1935," 281.

77. American Council on Education, *The Student Personnel Point of View* (Washington, DC: American Council on Education, 1937), 1.

78. Solberg, *Creating the Big Ten,* 206.

79. Delbert Oberteuffer, "The Athlete and His College: The Southern Athlete Situation and Its Implications," *Journal of Higher Education* 7, no. 8 (November 1936):439.

80. Ronald A. Smith, *Sports and Freedom: The Rise of Big-Time College Athletics* (Oxford: Oxford University Press, 1988), 88.

81. Edwin E. Slosson, *Great American Universities* (New York: McMillan, 1910), 374–75.

82. *Proceedings of the Thirty-First Annual Convention,* 76.

Chapter 4. The Consolidation of Control in College Sports

1. John R. Thelin, *Games Colleges Play: Scandal and Reform in Intercollegiate Athletics* (Baltimore: Johns Hopkins University Press, 1996), 99–100.

2. Murray Sperber, *Onward to Victory: The Crisis that Shaped College Sports* (New York: Henry Holt and Company, 1998), xx.

3. "College 'Purity Code' in Athletics Certain to Fail, Experts Believe," *New York Times*, December 19, 1947.

4. "N.C.A.A. To Vote on 'Purity Code,'" *New York Times*, December 28, 1947; "Colleges Adopt the 'Sanity Code' to Govern Sports," *New York Times*, January 11, 1948.

5. "Nathan Dougherty to SEC Members," undated (1948 only), Box 5, "Department of Athletics," Herman Lee Donovan Papers, University of Kentucky Archives and Special Collections, Lexington.

6. "Nathan Dougherty to SEC Members."

7. Mickey Dover, "A Look into NCAA 'Sanity Code' Reveals Violators Still Unchecked," *Kent Stater*, January 16, 1948.

8. "H. L. Donvan to Bernie Shively (Confidential)," March 9, 1949, Box 5, "Department of Athletics," Herman Lee Donovan Papers, University of Kentucky Archives and Special Collections, Lexington.

9. "A Joint Meeting of the Southern, Southeastern, and Southwest Conference, May 28, 1949," Box 19, Early Presidents Collection, Georgia Tech Archives, Atlanta.

10. John J. Cavanaugh, "Reformers Protest Too Much," *Notre Dame Alumnus* 25, no. 1 (February 1947): 8, https://archives.nd.edu/Alumnus/VOL_0025/VOL_0025_ISSUE _0001.pdf; "Cavanaugh Calls for Sensible Code: Pledges Notre Dame to Join Any Honest, Serious Move for Better Athletics," *New York Times*, January 14, 1947.

11. "Virginia Ready to Fight Expulsion From N.C.A.A. for Violating Code," *New York Times*, December 25, 1949.

12. "Virginia Ready to Fight Expulsion"; Lincoln A. Werden, "Motion to Expel 7 in N.C.A.A. Beaten by Vote of 93–111," *New York Times*, January 15, 1950.

13. Werden, "Motion to Expel."

14. Kurt E. Kemper, *Before March Madness: The Wars for the Soul of College Basketball* (Champaign: University of Illinois Press, 2020), 93.

15. Chad Carlson, "'Doing Just What the Others Were Doing': The University of Kentucky Wildcats and the Debate over Commercialized Athletics, 1946–1954," in "New Directions in Kentucky Sport History," ed. Andrew Doyle, special issue, *Register of the Kentucky Historical Society* 115, no. 4 (Autumn 2017): 550.

16. Chad Millman, "The Mavericks Who Remade Sports, Part I: Charles McNeil, Father of the Point Spread," *Baltimore Sun*, June 1, 2020, https://www.baltimoresun.com /gambling/sns-actnet-mavericks-who-remade-sports-part-i-point-spread-20200601 -rzikvzhnzjefbdrinxij3fwrzu-story.html.

17. Richard O. Davies and Richard G. Abram, *Betting the Line: Sports Wagering in American Life* (Columbus: Ohio State University Press, 2001), 52.

18. Ronald A. Smith, "The William and Mary Athletic Scandal of 1951: Governance and the Battle for Academic and Athletic Integrity," *Journal of Sport History* 34, no. 3 (Fall 2007): 58.

19. Smith, "William and Mary Athletic Scandal," 361–63.

20. Smith, "William and Mary Athletic Scandal," 53 and 365.

21. Richard P. Hansen, "The Crisis of the West Point Honor Code," *Military Affairs* 49 (April 1985): 57–62.

22. Hansen, "Crisis of the West Point Honor Code," 57–62; "The West Point Affair," *New York Times*, September 7, 1951.

23. Carlson, "'Doing Just What the Others Were Doing,'" 551–53.

24. Charley Rosen, *The Scandals of '51: How the Gamblers Almost Killed College Basketball* (New York: Seven Stories Press, 1999), 202.

25. "Excerpts from Judge Streit's Comments on College Basketball Fixing Scandal," *New York Times*, November 20, 1951.

26. "Excerpts from Judge Streit's Comments."

27. Walter Byers and Charles Hammer, *Unsportsmanlike Conduct: Exploiting College Athletes* (Ann Arbor: University of Michigan Press, 1995), 59.

28. Thelin, *Games Colleges Play*, 107–9.

29. "College Presidents Ready to Hurl Flying Block at Football Scandals," *New York Times*, November 14, 1951; David J. Young, *Arrogance and Scheming in the Big Ten: Michigan State's Quest for Membership and Michigan's Powerful Opposition* (Lansing, MI: DJY Publishing, 2012); Beth J. Shapiro, "John Hannah and the Growth of Big-Time Intercollegiate Athletics at Michigan State University," *Journal of Sports History* 10, no. 3 (Winter 1983): 30–31.

30. Kemper, *Before March Madness*, 113.

31. Kemper, *Before March Madness*.

32. Chad Carlson, *Making March Madness: The Early Years of the NCAA, NIT, and College Basketball Championships, 1922–1951* (Fayetteville: University of Arkansas Press, 2017), 232–33.

33. Kemper, *Before March Madness*, 166–88.

34. Kemper, *Before March Madness*, 166–68 and 184–87.

35. Carlson, *Making March Madness*, 300–301; Kemper, *Before March Madness*, 186–87; Milton S. Katz, *Breaking Through: John B. McLendon, Basketball Legend and Civil Rights Leader* (Fayetteville: University of Arkansas Press, 2007), 76.

36. Kemper, *Before March Madness*, 121.

37. Kemper, *Before March Madness*, 209 and 212.

38. Kemper, *Before March Madness*, 215–17.

39. Mark F. Bernstein, *Football: The Ivy League Origins of an American Obsession* (Philadelphia: University of Pennsylvania Press, 2001), 175.

40. Richard Goldstein, *Ivy League Autumns: An Illustrated History of College Football's Grand Old Rivalries* (New York: St. Martin's Press, 1996), 112.

41. Bernstein, *Football*, 175.

42. Thelin, *Games Colleges Play*, 56–57.

43. David L. Goldberg, "What Price Victory? What Price Honor? Pennsylvania and the Formation of the Ivy League, 1950–1952," *Pennsylvania Magazine of History and Biography* 112, no. 2 (April 1988): 230.

44. Thelin, *Games Colleges Play*, 56–57; Bernstein, *Football*, 178.

45. Mark F. Bernstein, "Harold Stassen and the Ivy League," *Pennsylvania Gazette*, November 1, 2001, https://thepenngazette.com/harold-stassen-and-the-ivy-league/.

46. Bernstein, "Harold Stassen and the Ivy League."

47. Thelin, *Games Colleges Play*, 124–25; Richard Goldstein, "Franny Murray, 82, Major Figure in Penn Sports, Dies," *New York Times*, July 1, 1998, https://www.nytimes.com/1998 /07/01/sports/franny-murray-82-major-figure-in-penn-s-sports-dies.html; David L. Goldberg, "Something for the Boys," *Newsweek*, August 21, 1959, 82.

48. Goldberg, "What Price Victory?," 239–44; Bernstein, *Football*, 198.

49. Bernstein, "Harold Stassen and the Ivy League."

50. Ronald A. Smith, *Pay for Play: A History of Big-Time College Athletic Reform* (Chicago: University of Illinois Press, 2010), 105–7.

51. Keith Dunnavant, *The Fifty-Year Seduction: How Television Manipulated College Football* (New York: Dunne Books, 2004), 8.

52. "Universities Split on Football Video," *New York Times*, June 8, 1951.

53. "Universities Split on Football Video."

54. Bernstein, *Football*, 202.

55. Bernstein, "Harold Stassen and the Ivy League."

56. Chares Grutzner, "8-College Pure-Sports Pact Formalizes the 'Ivy Group,'" *New York Times*, July 10, 1952.

57. Bernstein, *Football*.

58. Thelin, *Games Colleges Play*, 127.

59. Thelin, *Games Colleges Play*, 132.

60. Harvey Knox, "Why Ronnie Knox Quit California," *Sports Illustrated*, September 6, 1954, https://vault.si.com/vault/1954/09/06/why-ronnie-knox-quit-california.

61. "Sport: The Coach Speaks Out," *Time*, February 13, 1956, https://content.time.com /time/subscriber/article/0,33009,893400,00.html.

62. Dan Raley, "'Cowboy Johnny' and the Outlaws of Montlake," *Seattle Post-Intelligencer*, December 25, 2005, https://www.seattlepi.com/sports/article/Cowboy -Johnny-and-the-outlaws-of-Montlake-119091.php.

63. Byers and Hammer, *Unsportsmanlike Conduct*, 114–15; John Sayle Watterson, *College Football: History, Spectacle, Controversy* (Baltimore: Johns Hopkins University Press, 2000), 282; "'Under Table' Pay Is Laid to U.C.L.A.," *New York Times*, March 2, 1956, 26.

64. "Southern California and U. of California Fined," *New York Times*, July 9, 1956.

65. "Coast Conference Bars Washington from Post-Season Title Events," *New York Times*, May 7, 1956; "Southern California and U. of California Fined," *New York Times*, July 9, 1956; "U.C.L.A. Probation to Cost It $95,000," *New York Times*, May 20, 1956.

66. "Knox Criticizes Coast Football," *New York Times*, September 25, 1956, 36.

67. "Hollis Opposes Lifting Penalties against Seniors," *Ellensburg Daily Record*, July 27, 1956; Herman Hickman, "Pacific Coast Conference," *Sports Illustrated*, September 24, 1956, https://vault.si.com/vault/1956/09/24/pacific-coast-conference.

68. Byers and Hammer, *Unsportsmanlike Conduct*, 115.

69. Thelin, *Games Colleges Play*, 139–41.

70. Watterson, *College Football*, 283; Byers and Hammer, *Unsportsmanlike Conduct*, 115.

71. Thelin, *Games Colleges Play*, 141.

72. Thelin, *Games Colleges Play*, 148–49.

73. Byers and Hammer, *Unsportsmanlike Conduct*, 116.

74. Thelin, *Games Colleges Play*, 141.

75. "Pact Continues Rose Bowl Game," *New York Times*, March 31, 1959; "Hamilton Quits Pitt to Head New Coast Conference," *New York Times*, June 30, 1959.

76. "Olympians," Friends of Cal Crew, University of California, Berkeley, accessed February 7, 2024, https://calcrew.com/olympians.

77. John R. Thelin, "College Sports: Big Games, Big Problems," in *Going to College in the Sixties* (Baltimore: Johns Hopkins University Press, 2018), 146.

78. "NIRSA History," NIRSA: Leaders in Collegiate Recreation, accessed February 7, 2024, https://nirsa.net/nirsa/about/history/.

79. "NIRSA History."

80. "Yale Elects First Negro Captain as Jackson Heads Football Team," *New York Times*, November 23, 1948, 1; "Jackson, Yale Football Star, Tapped by 3 Social Societies," *New York Times*, May 13, 1949, 1; "Levi Jackson, a Pioneer at Yale, Is Dead at 74," *New York Times*, December 29, 2000, C10; Judith Ann Schiff, "Levi Jackson: Hometown Hero," *Yale Alumni Magazine* (October 1999): http://archives.yalealumnimagazine.com/issues/99_10/old_yale.html.

81. "The Great George Taliaferro," *Pride and Tradition*, February 2, 2021, https://www.myiu.org/stories/pride-and-tradition/the-great-george-taliaferro/.

82. Lane Demas, *Integrating the Gridiron: Black Civil Rights and American College Football* (New Brunswick, NJ: Rutgers University Press, 2010), 62–69. See also John R. Thelin, "College Sports since World War II," *History of Education Quarterly* 51, no. 3 (August 2011): 389–96.

83. Kristine Setting Clark, *Undefeated, Untied and Uninvited: A Documentary of 1951 University of San Francisco Dons Football Team* (Seattle: CreateSpace, 2014), 4–8

84. Charles H. Martin, *Benching Jim Crow: The Rise and Fall of the Color Line in Southern College Sports, 1890–1980* (Urbana: University of Illinois Press, 2010), 55–57.

85. Scott Ellsworth, *The Secret Game: A Wartime Story of Courage, Change, and Basketball's Lost Triumph* (New York: Little, Brown, 2015).

86. Larry Keech, "Southern/ACC Split Surprised Some," *Greensboro News and Record*, February 25, 1996, https://greensboro.com/southern-acc-split-surprised-some/article_f016955d-d036-5309-89c4-638ce1689b8b.html.

87. J. Samuel Walker, *ACC Basketball: The Story of the Rivalries, Traditions, and Scandals of the First Two Decades of the Atlantic Coast Conference* (Chapel Hill: University of North Carolina Press, 2011), 51–53; Keech, "Southern/ACC Split Surprised Some."

88. Thelin, *History of American Higher Education*, 260–61.

89. Thelin, "College Sports since World War II," 389–96.

90. Robert M. Hutchins, "Report of the President's Commission on Higher Education," *Educational Record* 29 (April 1948): 107–22.

91. Clyde Barrow, "The Theory of Capitalist Regulation and the Development of American Higher Education," paper presented at the Annual Meeting of the American Educational Research Association, Chicago, Illinois, April 3–7, 1991, 19–23, https://files.eric.ed.gov/fulltext/ED332607.pdf; Henry Rosovsky: *The University: An Owner's Manual* (New York: Norton, 1990).

92. Clark Kerr, *The Gold and the Blue: A Personal Memoir of the University of California*, vol. 1, *Academic Triumphs* (Berkeley: University of California Press, 2001), 153.

93. Kerr, *The Gold and the Blue*, 172 and 403.

94. Kerr, *The Gold and the Blue*, 404.

95. Clark Kerr, *The Uses of the University*, 4th ed. (Cambridge, MA: Harvard University Press, 1995), 7.

96. Kerr, *The Gold and the Blue*, 71.

97. Page Smith, *Killing the Spirit: Higher Education in America* (New York: Viking Penguin, 1990), 13.

98. "Historical Enrollment and Term End Reports," Office of the Registrar, Michigan State University, accessed February 7, 2024, https://reg.msu.edu/ROInfo /EnrollmentTermEnd.aspx.

99. Byers and Hammer, *Unsportsmanlike Conduct*, 44.

100. Ronald A. Smith, *Play-by-Play: Radio, Television, and Big-Time College Sport* (Baltimore: Johns Hopkins University Press, 2001), 73.

Chapter 5. Civil Rights, Racial Desegregation, and Regulations

1. Ronald Smith, *Play by Play: Radio, Television, and Big-Time College Sports* (Baltimore: Johns Hopkins University Press, 2001), 106–8.

2. Arthur A. Fleisher III, Brian L. Goff, and Robert D. Tollison, *The National Collegiate Athletic Association: A Study in Cartel Behavior* (Chicago: University of Chicago Press, 1992). See also Paul R. Lawrence, *Unsportsmanlike Conduct: The National Collegiate Athletic Association and the Business of College Football* (New York: Praeger, 1987).

3. John M. Heisman and Mark Schlabach, *Heisman: The Man behind the Trophy* (New York: Howard Books, 2012), 185–86.

4. John Sayle Watterson, *College Football: History, Spectacle, Controversy* (Baltimore: Johns Hopkins University Press, 2002), 316.

5. Charles H. Martin, *Benching Jim Crow: The Rise and Fall of the Color Line in Southern College Sports, 1890–1980* (Urbana: University of Illinois Press, 2010), 81.

6. Lane Demas, *Integrating the Gridiron: Black Civil Rights and American College Football* (New Brunswick, NJ: Rutgers University Press, 2002), 72–73 and 87.

7. Demas, *Integrating the Gridiron*, 88.

8. Demas, *Integrating the Gridiron*, 100.

9. J. Michael Kennedy, "A Return Engagement for Compton Players of '55," *Los Angeles Times*, October 16, 1994, https://www.latimes.com/archives/la-xmp-1994-10-16-me-51042 -story.html; Kirby Lee, "Members of 1955 Compton Team That Broke Color Barrier Honored," *Los Angeles Times*, October 27, 1994, https://www.latimes.com/archives/la-xpm -1994-10-27-hl-55169-story.html.

10. James W. Silver, "Mississippi: The Closed Society," *Journal of Southern History* 30, no. 1 (February 1964): 3–34.

11. Russell J. Henderson, "The 1963 Mississippi State University Basketball Controversy and the Repeal of the Unwritten Law: 'Something More Than the Game Will Be Lost,'" *Journal of Southern History* 63, no. 4 (November 1997): 830.

12. Jason A. Peterson, *Full Court Press: Mississippi State University, the Press, and the Battle to Integrate College Basketball* (Jackson: University Press of Mississippi, 2016), 25.

13. Henderson, "1963 Mississippi State University Basketball Controversy," 830; Peterson, *Full Court Press*, 25.

14. Henderson, "1963 Mississippi State University Basketball Controversy," 832.

15. Henderson, "1963 Mississippi State University Basketball Controversy," 836–37.

16. Henderson, "1963 Mississippi State University Basketball Controversy," 848.

17. Charles H. Martin, "The Rise and Fall of Jim Crow in Southern College Sports: The Case of the Atlantic Coast Conference," *North Carolina Historical Review* 76, no. 3 (July 1999): 265.

18. Charles H. Martin, "Jim Crow in the Gymnasium: The Integration of College Basketball in the American South," *International Journal of the History of Sport* 10, no. 1 (April 1993): 77.

19. Martin, "Jim Crow in the Gymnasium," 106–7.

20. Martin, "Jim Crow in the Gymnasium," 104–5.

21. Ronald E. Marcello, "The Integration of Intercollegiate Athletics in Texas: North Texas State College as a Test Case, 1956," *Journal of Sport History* 14, no. 3 (Winter 1987): 287 and 315.

22. "First Black Player in ACC Paved Way for Equality," *ESPN News*, December 13, 2008, http://www.espn.com/espn/wire/_/section/ncf/id/3767096.

23. J. Samuel Walker, *ACC Basketball: The Story of the Rivalries, Traditions, and Scandals of the First Two Decades of the Atlantic Coast Conference* (Chapel Hill: University of North Carolina Press, 2011), 224.

24. Martin, "Rise and Fall of Jim Crow," 271.

25. Walker, *ACC Basketball*, 241–48.

26. Martin, *Benching Jim Crow*, 141–45.

27. Martin, *Benching Jim Crow*, 186–89.

28. Asher Price, "Memo by Secret Memo, the University of Texas Kept Segregation Alive into the 1960s," *Mother Jones*, January 12, 2020, https://www.motherjones.com/politics/2020/01/memo-by-secret-memo-the-university-of-texas-kept-segregation-alive-into-the-1960s/.

29. Asher Price, *Earl Campbell: Yards after Contact* (Austin: University of Texas Press, 2019), 77–83.

30. Martin, "Jim Crow in the Gymnasium," 81–82.

31. Jerry Hill, "John Westbrook Blazed a Trail for Others to Follow," Baylor Football News, February 8, 2018, https://baylorbears.com/news/2018/2/8/John_Westbrook_Blazed_A_Trail_For_Others_To_Dream_And_Follow.aspx.

32. Hayden Fry with George Wine, *Hayden Fry: A High Porch Picnic* (Champaign, IL: Sports Publishing, 2001), 67–70.

33. Xander Peters, "The Lone Star of Texas," Think Progress, December 28, 2016, https://archive.thinkprogress.org/jerry-levias-mark-on-college-football-and-the-civil-rights-movement-eac43a60d735/.

34. S. Zebulon Baker, "'On the Opposite Side of the Fence': The University of Kentucky and the Racial Desegregation of the Southeastern Conference," in "New Directions in Kentucky Sport History," ed. Andrew Doyle, special issue, *Register of the Kentucky Historical Society* 115, no. 4 (Autumn 2017): 580–81.

35. Baker, "'On the Opposite Side of the Fence," 585–88.

36. Baker, "'On the Opposite Side of the Fence,'" 588; Robert Thomas Epling, "Seasons of Change: Football Desegregation and the University of Tennessee and the Transformation of the Southeastern Conference, 1963–67" (PhD diss., University of Tennessee, 1994), 125.

37. "A Rough Day for the Bear," *Sports Illustrated*, November 26, 1962, https://vault.si.com/vault/1962/11/26/a-rough-day-for-the-bear; Ken Sugiura, "The Odd History between

Tech, Mississippi State, Ole Miss," *Atlanta Journal Constitution*, December 22, 2014, https://www.ajc.com/sports/college-football/the-odd-history-between-tech-mississippi -state-ole-miss/zUwORXYzjdL2W1z4HmSsPJ/.

38. Baker, "'On the Opposite Side of the Fence,'" 592.

39. Mark Bradley, "Fifty Years Ago, Georgia Tech Left the SEC," *Atlanta Journal-Constitution*, January 24, 2014, https://www.ajc.com/sports/fifty-years-ago-georgia-tech -left-the-sec/o7w1mrefY4QgzlmzzSXr9O/.

40. Bradley, "Fifty Years Ago."

41. Baker, "'On the Opposite Side of the Fence,'" 561–610.

42. Baker, "'On the Opposite Side of the Fence,'" 592.

43. Baker, "'On the Opposite Side of the Fence,'" 595.

44. Baker, "'On the Opposite Side of the Fence,'" 601.

45. Tammy Nunez, "Tulane's Stephen Martin, an African American Pioneer in College Sports, Was an Inspiration to Those around Him," NOLA.com, May 17, 2013, https://www .nola.com/sports/tulane/article_971cdbbb-cbf9-5acc-99fa-cb5342b25540.html; "Tulane's Stephen Martin Made History 50 Years Ago as the First African-American SEC Player," *Times-Picayune*, updated July 18, 2019, https://www.nola.com/sports/tulane /article_e676abb8-c4c5-5dfb-93e1-1632a95b9d6f.html.

46. Martin, *Benching Jim Crow*, 259.

47. "The New Rage to Win: A Grim Commando Mood Has Hit Football. It Is Especially Evident at Kentucky, Where the Coach Is Demanding Total Dedication to Victory," *Sports Illustrated*, October 8, 1962, https://vault.si.com/vault/1962/10/08/the-new-rage-to-win; Shannon P. Ragland, *The Thin Thirty: The Untold Story of Brutality, Scandal and Redemption for Charlie Bradshaw's 1962 Kentucky Football Team* (Louisville, KY: Set Shot Press, 2007).

48. Bill Traughber, "Wallace Was the First Black Player in the SEC," Commodore History Corner Archive, February 7, 2013, https://vucommodores.com/wallace-was-first -black-player-in-sec/.

49. Epling, "Seasons of Change," 129–30.

50. Mark McCarter, "Holloway Appreciated Bryant's Honesty that Alabama 'Wasn't Ready' for a Black Quarterback," AL.com, February 20, 2011, https://www.al.com/sports /2011/02/holloway_always_appreciated_be.html.

51. Xander Peters, "The Lone Star," Think Progress, December 28, 2016, https:// archive.thinkprogress.org/jerry-levias-mark-on-college-football-and-the-civil-rights -movement-eac43a60d735/.

52. James Duane Bolin, *Adolph Rupp and the Rise of Kentucky Basketball* (Lexington: University Press of Kentucky, 2019), 274–85.

53. John Greenya, "Black Man on a White Field," *Washington Post Magazine*, February 1, 2004, https://www.washingtonpost.com/archive/lifestyle/magazine/2004/02/01 /black-man-on-a-white-field/55688ca2-fd64-4d93-9936-00445967b78f/; Don Markus, "Maryland Football's First Face of Social Justice," *Maryland Today*, February 5, 2021, https://today.umd.edu/maryland-footballs-first-face-social-justice-b17e465f-6702-4aa6 -9921-806f67c82a69.

54. Greenya, "Black Man on a White Field."

55. Greenya, "Black Man on a White Field"; Markus, "Maryland Football's First Face of Social Justice."

56. Markus, "Maryland Football's First Face of Social Justice."

57. Melissa Pepko, "SMU Alumni Remember a Visit by the Rev. Martin Luther King Jr.," Southern Methodist University website, January 18, 2014, https://www.smu.edu /AboutSMU/MLK.

58. Pepko, "SMU Alumni Remember."

59. Peters, "Lone Star of Texas."

60. "Former SMU Football Player Recounts Trials of Integration," TCU 360, September 21, 2007, https://tcu360.com/2007/09/21/former-smu-football-player-recounts -trials-of-integration-12289341/.

61. Steve Campbell, "LeVias Now Making a Difference off the Playing Field," *Houston Chronicle*, December 22, 2008, https://www.chron.com/sports/college/article/LeVias-now -making-a-difference-off-playing-field-1782142.php.

62. Baker, "'On the Opposite Side of the Fence,'" 606.

63. Nathaniel Northington, *Still Running: The Autobiography of Kentucky's Nate Northington, the First African American Football Player in the Southeastern Conference* (Bloomington, IN: iUniverse, 2013).

64. David Steele, "'If They Could Do It, I Could Do It': The integration of Ole Miss Football," Andscape, February 18, 1921, https://andscape.com/features/if-they-could-do-it -i-could-do-it-the-integration-of-ole-miss-football/; College Football Hall of Fame, "Not Your Average Hero Ep 2 Featuring James Reed (Ole Miss)," YouTube video, February 8, 2021, https://www.youtube.com/watch?v=omlBYqUBz70.

65. Rick Cleveland, "There's a Story behind This 44-Year-Old Photo of 'Colonel Reb' and Miss Ole Miss," Mississippi Today, May 21, 2020, https://mississippitoday.org/2020/05/21 /theres-a-story-behind-this-44-year-old-photo-of-colonel-reb-and-miss-ole-miss/.

66. Derrick E. White, "From Desegregation to Integration: Race, Football, and 'Dixie' at the University of Florida," *Florida Historical Quarterly* 88, no. 4 (Spring 2010): 473.

67. White, "From Desegregation to Integration," 474.

68. Harry Edwards, *The Revolt of the Black Athlete* (New York: Free Press, 1969).

69. Michael Oriard, "College Football's Season of Discontent," Slate, September 3, 2009. See also Michael Oriard, *Bowled Over: Big-Time College Football from the Sixties to the BCS Era* (Chapel Hill: University of North Carolina Press, 2009).

70. Ronald A. Smith, *Pay for Play: A History of Big-Time College Athletic Reform Sport and Society* (Champaign: University of Illinois Press, 2011), timeline on p. 223.

71. Smith, *Pay for Play*, 224.

72. Smith, *Pay for Play*, 224.

73. John R. Thelin, "Black Male Student Athletes," in chapter 6, "College Sports: Big Games and Big Problems," in *Going to College in the Sixties* (Baltimore: Johns Hopkins University Press, 2018), 150–52.

74. Oriard, "College Football's Season of Discontent." See also Oriard, *Bowled Over*.

75. "The Black Athlete: An Editorial," *Sports Illustrated*, August 5, 1968, https://vault .si.com/vault/1968/08/05/the-black-athlete-an-editorial.

76. Smith, *Pay for Play*, esp. "Intercollegiate Athletic Reform Timeline," 213–23. And for 1960–72, see 223–25.

77. Smith, *Pay for Play*, 223.

78. Smith, *Pay for Play*, 224.

79. Ike Balbus, "Politics as Sports: The Political Ascendency of the Sports Metaphor in America," *Monthly Review* 26, no. 10 (March 1975): 27–39.

Chapter 6. Women's College Sports during the Cold War Era

1. Mary Jo Festle, *Playing Nice: Politics and Apologies in Women's Sports* (New York: Columbia University Press, 1996), 11.

2. Ying Wushanley, *Playing Nice and Losing: The Struggle for Control of Women's Intercollegiate Athletics, 1960–2000* (Syracuse, NY: Syracuse University Press, 2004), 12.

3. Ellen Gerber, "The Controlled Development of Collegiate Sport for Women, 1923–1936," *Journal of Sport History* 2, no. 1 (Spring 1975): 23.

4. Festle, *Playing Nice*, 17; Nancy R. Goodloe, *Before Brittney: A Legacy of Champions* (Vancouver, BC: Friesen Press, 2014), 9–10; "Blanche Trilling and the Evils of Competition," University of Wisconsin-Madison Archives and Record Management, accessed February 13, 2024, https://www.library.wisc.edu/archives/exhibits/campus-history -projects/health-and-fun-shall-walk-hand-in-hand-the-first-100-years-of-womens -athletics-at-uw-madison/blanche-trilling-and-the-evils-of-competition/.

5. Allen Guttmann, *Women's Sports: A History* (New York: Columbia University Press, 1985).

6. "How Women's Sports Teams Got Their Start," *New York Times*, April 28, 2022, https://www.nytimes.com/2022/04/28/sports/title-ix-anniversary-womens-sports.html.

7. Pamela Grundy and Susan Shackelford, *Shattering the Glass: The Remarkable History of Women's Basketball* (New York: New Press, 2005), 54–57; Paul J. Christopher and Alicia Marie Smith, *Greatest Sports Heroes of all Times,* North American ed. (Chicago: Encouragement Press, 2007), 2007, 59.

8. Grundy and Shackelford, *Shattering the Glass*, 57.

9. Pal Gallico, "The Texas Babe," *Vanity Fair*, 1932, quoted in Grundy and Shackelford, *Shattering the Glass*, 58.

10. Quoted in "Babe Part 2," *Sports Illustrated,* October 13, 1975, https://vault.si.com /vault/1975/10/13/babe-part-2.

11. "Babe Didrikson Barred by A.A.U.," *New York Times*, December 6, 1932, 29; "Miss Didrikson Resigns," *New York Times*, December 21, 1932, 27; "Miss Didrikson Joins Pro Ranks," *New York Times*, December 22, 1932, 23; "A.A.U. Reinstates Miss Didrikson," *New York Times*, December 23, 1932, 24; "Miss Didrikson Adhere to Plans," *New York Times*, December 24, 1932.

12. Tommy Slotcavage and Mark Dyreson, "Anomaly or Harbinger? Penn State's 1935 Female 'Letter "Man"' and New Frontiers in the History of Women's Intercollegiate Sport in the United States," *International Journal of the History of Sport* 36, nos. 17–18 (2019): 1574–611.

13. Slotcavage and Mark Dyreson, "Anomaly or Harbinger?"

14. Slotcavage and Mark Dyreson, "Anomaly or Harbinger?," 1588–89.

15. Slotcavage and Mark Dyreson, "Anomaly or Harbinger?," 1595–97.

16. Susan K. Cahn, *Coming on Strong: Gender and Sexuality in Women's Sport*, 2nd ed. (Urbana: University of Illinois Press, 2015), 4.

17. Ying Wushanley, *Playing Nice and Losing: The Struggle for Control of Women's Intercollegiate Athletics, 1960–2000* (Syracuse, NY: Syracuse University Press, 2004), 14.

18. Ina E. Gittings, "Why Cramp Competition?," *Journal of Health and Physical Education* 2 (1931): 10. See also Sarah Jane Eikleberry, "More Than Milk and Cookies: Reconsidering the College Play Day," *Journal of Sport History* 41, no. 3 (Fall 2014): 474.

19. Brad Austin, *Democratic Sports: Men's and Women's College Athletics during the Great Depression* (Fayetteville: University of Arkansas Press, 2015), 150–72.

20. Wushanley, *Playing Nice and Losing*, 15.

21. Robert A. Mechikoff, "The Olympic Games: Sport as International Politics," *Journal of Physical Education, Recreation and Dance* 55, no. 3 (1984): 23–30, doi:10.1080/0730 3084.1984.10629689.

22. Cecile Houry, "American Women and the Modern Summer Olympic Games: A Story of Obstacles and Struggles for Participation and Equality" (PhD diss., University of Miami, 2011), 140; Festle, *Playing Nice*, 9.

23. Festle, *Playing Nice*, 10–11 and 19.

24. *Standards in Sports for Girls and Women: Guiding Principles in the Organization and Administration of Sports Programs: A Project of the Nation Section for Girls' and Women's Sports of the American Association for Health, Physical Education, and Recreation* (Washington: DC, American Association for Health, Physical Education, and Recreation, 1958), 10. Also cited in Festle, *Playing Nice*, 23.

25. Festle, *Playing Nice*, 14 and 23.

26. Festle, *Playing Nice*, 11 and 22–24.

27. Quoted in Grundy and Shackelford, *Shattering the Glass*, 115; Roxy Andersen, "Battle of the Sexes," *Amateur Athlete* (July 1954).

28. "Division for Girls and Women's Sports," *Journal of Health, Physical Education, and Recreation* 114, no. 7, pt. II (October 1958): 81.

29. Welch Suggs, *A Place on the Team: The Triumph and Tragedy of Title IX* (Princeton, NJ: Princeton University Press, 2006), 30.

30. Suggs, *A Place on the Team*, 30.

31. Grundy and Shackelford, *Shattering the Glass*, 94–95.

32. Grundy and Shackelford, *Shattering the Glass*, 95–96; Ronald A. Smith, *The Myth of the Amateur: A History of College Athletic Scholarships* (Austin: University of Texas Press, 2021), 163–64.

33. Gundy and Shackelford, *Shattering the Glass*, 95–101; Smith, *Myth of the Amateur*, 163–65.

34. Gundy and Shackelford, *Shattering the Glass*, 167.

35. Susan K. Cahn, *Coming on Strong: Gender and Sexuality in Women's Sport*, 2nd ed. (Urbana: University of Illinois Press, 2015), 111 and 118.

36. Carroll Van West, "The Tennessee State Tigerbelles: Cold Warriors of the Track," in *Separate Games: African American Sport behind the Walls of Segregation*, ed. David K. Wiggins and Ryan Swanson (Fayetteville: University of Arkansas Press, 2016), 62.

37. Fletcher F. Moon, "An 'Extra-Ordinary' Man: Tennessee State University and U.S. Olympic Women's Track and Field Coach Edward S. 'Ed' Temple (1927–2016)," *Library Faculty and Staff Publications and Presentations* 16 (2016): 3–5.

38. David K. Wiggins, ed., *African-Americans in Sports*, 2nd ed. (New York: Routledge, 2015), 401–2; Van West, "Tennessee State Tigerbelles," 64–65.

39. Joseph M. Turrini, " 'It Was Communism versus the Free World': The USA-USSR Dual Track Meet Series and the Development of Track and Field in the United States, 1958–1985," *Journal of Sport History* 28, no. 3 (Fall 2001): 432–33.

40. Van West, "Tennessee State Tigerbelles," 65.

41. Van West, "Tennessee State Tigerbelles," 66–67.

42. Rita Liberti and Maureen M. Smith, *(Re)Presenting Wilma Rudolph* (Syracuse, NY: Syracuse University Press, 2015), 73.

43. Both quotes in Van West, "Tennessee State Tigerbelles," 67.

44. Van West, "Tennessee State Tigerbelles," 63. See a much more detailed and nuanced discussion in Liberti and Smith's *(Re)Presenting Wilma Rudolph*.

45. Van West, "Tennessee State Tigerbelles," 62.

46. Jennifer H. Lansbury, *A Spectacular Leap: Black Women Athletes in Twentieth-Century America* (Fayetteville: University of Arkansas Press, 2014), 134.

47. John R. Thelin, "College Sports: Big Games, Big Problems," in *Going to College in the Sixties* (Baltimore: Johns Hopkins University Press, 2018), 137–38.

48. Paula D. Welch, *Silver Era, Golden Moments: A Celebration of Ivy League Women's Athletics* (New York: Lanham, 1999), 18.

49. Smith, *Myth of the Amateur*, 162.

50. Turrini, "'It Was Communism versus the Free World,'" 436.

51. Turrini, "'It Was Communism versus the Free World,'" 436.

52. Howard P. Chudacoff, "AAU v. NCAA: The Bitter Feud That Altered the Structure of American Amateur Sports," *Journal of Sport History* 48, no. 1 (Spring 2021): 50–65.

53. Turrini, "'It Was Communism versus the Free World,'" 436.

54. Chudacoff, "AAU v. NCAA," 54; Wushanley, *Playing Nice and Losing*, 25.

55. Wushanley, *Playing Nice and Losing*, 26.

56. Turrini, "'It Was Communism versus the Free World,'" 437.

57. Chudacoff, "AAU v. NCAA," 54–55.

58. "NCAA-AAU Dispute: Hearings before the Committee on Commerce United States Senate, Eighty-Ninth Congress, First Session on The Controversy in Administration of Track and Field Events in the United States," August 16–27, 1965, Serial N. 89–40, 142 and 520.

59. "NCAA-AAU Dispute," 468.

60. Wushanley, *Playing Nice and Losing*, 37.

61. Wushanly, *Playing Nice and Losing*, 40–44.

62. Smith, *Myth of the Amateur*, 166.

63. Sandra Stutzman et al., "Did the DGWS Fail? Two Points of View," *Journal of Health, Physical Education, and Recreation* 45, no. 1 (1974): 6.

64. Wushanley, *Playing Nice and Losing*, 44.

65. Wushanley, *Playing Nice and Losing*, 44 and 49.

66. Wushanley, *Playing Nice and Losing*, 50.

67. Susan Ware, *Title IX: A Brief History with Documents*, 2nd ed. (Long Grove, IL: Waveland Press, 2014), 35.

68. Ware, *Title IX*, 40.

69. John R. Thelin and Lawrence L. Wiseman, "Fiscal Fitness? The Peculiar Economics of Intercollegiate Athletics," *Capital Ideas* 4, no. 7 (February 1990).

70. Wushanley, *Playing Nice and Losing*, 83–84.

71. Suggs, *A Place on the Team*, 67–68.

72. Suggs, *A Place on the Team*, 69.

73. John R. Thelin, "Good Sports? Historical Perspectives on the Political Economy of Intercollegiate Athletics in the Era of Title IX, 1972 to 1997," *Journal of Higher Education* 7, no. 4 (July-August 2000): 391–410.

74. Thelin, "Good Sports?," 396.

75. Thelin, "Good Sports?," 396.

76. Festle, *Playing Nice*, 168–69.

77. Festle, *Playing Nice*, 172; Department of Health, Education, and Welfare, "Regulations on Nondiscrimination on the Basis of Sex, June 4, 1975," in Ware, *Title IX*, 50–53.

78. Corye Perez Beene, "Deep in the Sports of Texas: TIAWA, Title IX and Women's Intercollegiate Athletics in the 1970s" (PhD diss., Texas Tech University, August 2013), 68–70.

79. Walter Byers and Charles Hammer, *Unsportsmanlike Conduct: Exploiting College Athletes* (Ann Arbor: University of Michigan Press, 1995), 244–45.

80. Suggs, *A Place on the Team*, 59; Beene, "Deep in the Sports of Texas," 87.

81. Beene, "Deep in the Sports of Texas," 87.

82. Festle, *Playing Nice*, 179–81; Rick Wright, "Estes Was Linchpin in UNM's Reach for Sports Equality," *Albuquerque Journal*, June 23, 2022, https://www.abqjournal.com/2510873/estes-was-linchpin-in-unms-reach-for-sports-equality.html.

83. "Pacific-10 Conference Survey: Women's Intercollegiate Athletics," Box 263, Folder 22, "Student Services and Activities (1977–1979)," Administrative Files of Charles E. Young Office of the Chancellor, UCLA Special Collections, June 24, 12:34 p.m.

84. Wushanley, *Playing Nice and Losing*, 107.

85. Smith, *Myth of the Amateur*, 168–69.

86. "A Tennis Revolt Brews at Miami," *New York Times*, March 8, 1964, 251.

87. Wushanley, *Playing Nice and Losing*, 79–80.

88. Festle, *Playing Nice*, 182.

89. Festle, *Playing Nice*, 182.

90. Wushanley, *Playing Nice and Losing*, 112.

91. Wushanley, *Playing Nice and Losing*, 112.

92. Wushanley, *Playing Nice and Losing*, 118 and 123.

93. Wushanley, *Playing Nice and Losing*, 119–24.

94. "1979—Council of Collegiate Women Athletic Administrators—Our Bold Beginning," https://40th.womenleadersinsports.org/40th-anniversary/wlcs-1979/; John Murphy, "Title IX at 50: How a Law Became a Reality," *Columbia Missourian*, June 23, 2002, https://www.columbiamissourian.com/sports/mizzou_sports/title-ix-at-50-how-a-law-became-a-reality/article_e92ca8a2-e5e8-11ec-9ab5-87e00d518f3c.html.

95. Smith, *Myth of the Amateur*, 168–69.

96. Festle, *Playing Nice*, 206–7; Murphy, "Title IX at 50."

97. Wushanley, *Playing Nice and Losing*, 135.

98. Mark Bechtel, "AIAW vs. NCAA: When Women's College Basketball Had to Choose," *Sports Illustrated*, June 14, 2022, https://www.si.com/college/2022/06/14/aiaw-ncaa-womens-college-basketball-league-title-ix-daily-cover.

99. Wushanley, *Playing Nice and Losing*, 137; Association for Intercollegiate Athletics for Women v. National Collegiate Athletic Association, 735 F.2d 577 (U.S. App. D.C, 1984).

100. Wushanley, *Playing Nice and Losing*, 136.

101. Suggs, *A Place on the Team*, 57.

102. Festle, *Playing Nice*, 12.

103. Byers and Hammer, *Unsportsmanlike Conduct*, 247.

104. Smith, *Myth of the Amateur*, 175.

105. Joan M. Chandler, "The Association for Intercollegiate Athletics for Women: The End of Amateurism in U.S. Intercollegiate Sport," in *Women in Sport: Sociological and Historical Perspectives,* ed. Amy L. Reeder and John R. Fuller (Atlanta: Darby, 1985), 15.

106. "Linda Estes, Women's Athletic Director at the University of New Mexico," UPI Archives, March 5, 1981, https://www.upi.com/Archives/1981/03/05/Linda-Estes-womens -athletic-director-at-the-University-of/2320352616400/; Rick Wright, "Estes Was Linchpin in UNM's Reach for Sports Equality," *Albuquerque Journal,* June 23, 2022, https://www .abqjournal.com/2510873/estes-was-linchpin-in-unms-reach-for-sports-equality.html# foogallery-0/p:3.

107. Amy Shipley, "Playing Field Levels at Texas," *Washington Post,* July 6, 1997, https://www.washingtonpost.com/archive/politics/1997/07/06/playing-field-levels-at -texas/f571d66e-e905-4034-8751-722c7aa6c76d/.

108. Mariah Burton Nelson, "Escaping from Roble: Stanford Women's Basketball Then and Now," Stanford Fast Break Club, accessed February 13, 2024, https://www.stanfordfbc .org/FBCFiles/EscapingFromRoble.htm.

109. Nelson, "Escaping from Roble."

110. "Yale Women Strip to Protest a Lack of Crew's Showers," *New York Times,* March 4, 1976, 47.

111. Paula D. Welch et al., *Silver Era, Golden Moments: A Celebration of Ivy League Women's Athletics* (Lanham, MD: Madison Books, 1999), 21.

112. Howard P. Chudacoff, *Changing the Playbook: How Power, Profit, and Politics Transformed College Sports* (Urbana: University of Illinois Press, 2015).

113. Thelin, "Good Sports?," 391–410.

114. Russell Schoch, "A Conversation with Laura Nader," *California Monthly* (November 2000): 28–32. Reprinted with permission in John R. Thelin, ed., "Document 9.3: Faculty Memoir: A Conversation with Professor Laura Nader," in *Essential Documents in the History of American Higher Education,* 2nd ed. (Baltimore: Johns Hopkins University Press, 2021), 334–43.

115. Suggs, *A Place on the Team*, 66.

116. James Franks to Mr. Rodney H. Brady, October 2, 1980, University of California, Los Angeles Archives, https://swac.org/news/2019/1/26/general-swac-mourns-loss-of -former-commissioner-dr-james-frank.aspx.

117. Goodloe, *Before Brittany*, 31.

Chapter 7. The Ascendance of College Sports Business

1. Howard P. Chudacoff, "AAU v. NCAA: The Bitter Feud That Altered the Structure of American Amateur Sports," *Journal of Sport History* 48, no. 1 (Spring 2021): 61–63.

2. Keith Dunnavant, *The Fifty-Year Seduction: How Television Manipulated College Football, from the Birth of the Modern NCAA to the Creation of the BCS* (New York: Thomas Dunne Books, 2004), 4.

3. Dunnavant, *Fifty-Year Seduction*, 7.

4. John Sayle Watterson, *College Football: History, Spectacle, Controversy* (Baltimore: Johns Hopkins University Press, 2002).

5. Dunnavant, *Fifty-Year Seduction*, 7–8.

6. Dunnavant, *Fifty-Year Seduction*, 84–87.

7. Ronald A. Smith, *Play-by-Play: Radio, Television, and Big-Time College Sport* (Baltimore: Johns Hopkins University Press, 2001), 146.

8. Earl F. Cheit, *The New Depression in Higher Education* (New York: McGraw Hill, 1971).

9. J. Weiner, "The High Cost of Big-Time Football," *College and University Business* 55 (1973): 35–42; John R. Thelin and Lawrence L. Wiseman, *The Old College Try: Balancing Academics and Athletics in Higher Education* (Washington, DC: Association for the Study of Higher Education and George Washington University, 1989).

10. Arthur Padilla and Janice Boucher, "On the Economics of Intercollegiate Athletic Programs," *Journal of Sport and Social Issues* 11, nos. 1 and 2 (1987 and 1988): 61 and 73.

11. Gil Gilbert, "Hold That Tiger: Big Game at Mizzou," *Sports Illustrated,* September 24, 1980, 70–86.

12. Samuel J. Nader, "Financing Intercollegiate Athletics in the Southeastern Conference, 1970–1979" (PhD diss., Louisiana State University, 1988).

13. Robert H. Atwell, Bruce Grimes, and Donna Lopiano, *The Money Game: Financing Collegiate Athletics* (Washington, DC: American Council on Education, 1980).

14. Mark Asher, "Play and Not Pay? Maryland's Kehoe Blasts Title IX, Says Women Can't Produce Income," *Louisville Courier-Journal,* June 10, 1975.

15. Watterson, *College Football,* 333.

16. Dunnavant, *Fifty-Year Seduction,* 148.

17. Gordon S. White Jr., "Officials' Mistrust Is Evident in Wake of N.C.A.A. Parley," *New York Times,* January 16, 1973, 47.

18. Gordon S. White Jr., "N.C.A.A. Reorganizes into 3 Groups," *New York Times,* August 7, 1973, 41; Watterson, *College Football,* 333.

19. Gordon S. White Jr., "N.C.A.A. Reorganizes into 3 Groups," *New York Times,* August 7, 1973, 41; Watterson, *College Football,* 337.

20. Ray Kennedy, "427: Case in Point," *Sports Illustrated*, June 10, 1974, https://vault.si.com/vault/1974/06/10/427-a-case-in-point.

21. Smith, *Play-by-Play,* 147–48.

22. Dunnavant, *Fifty-Year Seduction,* 121.

23. Watterson, *College Football,* 337.

24. Dunnavant, *Fifty-Year Seduction,* 122.

25. Dunnavant, *Fifty-Year Seduction,* 112.

26. Watterson, *College Football,* 338–39.

27. Watterson, *College Football,* 339.

28. Paul Attner, "NCAA Divided, May Be Headed for Destruction," *Washington Post,* January 14, 1977, https://www.washingtonpost.com/archive/sports/1977/01/14/ncaa-divided-may-be-headed-for-destruction/9ba3921f-5829-4e6c-8aee-f33220794354/.

29. Dunnavant, *Fifty-Year Seduction,* 130–34.

30. Ronald A. Smith, *Pay for Play: A History of Big-Time College Athletic Reform* (Urbana: University of Illinois Press, 2010), 138–39.

31. Anthony Weaver, "Declining the Big East: A Case Study of the College of the Holy Cross" *Journal of Amateur Sport* 5, no. 2 (2019): 95.

32. Weaver, "Declining the Big East," 94–98.

33. Weaver, "Declining the Big East," 100–101.

34. Weaver, "Declining the Big East," 103.

35. Smith, *Play-by-Play,* 142.

36. Walter Byers and Charles Hammer, *Unsportsmanlike Conduct: Exploiting College Athletes* (Ann Arbor: University of Michigan Press, 1995), 255–57.

37. Smith, *Play-by-Play*, 142.

38. Smith, *Play-by-Play*, 156.

39. Watterson, *College Football*, 342

40. Gordon S. White Jr., "Big Colleges Defy NCAA over TV," *New York Times*, August 9, 1981, Section 5, 3, https://timesmachine.nytimes.com/timesmachine/1981/08/09/225522 .html?pageNumber=283.

41. Gordon S. White Jr., "TV Issue Dividing Football Colleges," *New York Times*, August 23, 1981, Section 5, 6.

42. "N.C.A.A. Call Convention on TV Policy," *New York Times*, September 9, 1981, B8.

43. Dunnavant, *Fifty-Year Seduction*, 147.

44. Linda Greenhouse, "High Court Ends N.C.A.A. Control of TV Football," *New York Times*, June 28, 1984, A1.

45. Robert L. Kerr, "Last Stand for a Less Commercialized Game: Contesting Football's Place in Higher Education in *NCAA v. Board of Regents*, 1984," in *The History of American College Football: Institutional Policy, Culture, and Reform*, ed. Christian Anderson and Amber Fallucca (New York: Routledge, 2021), 175.

46. David Zizzo, "NCAA Officials Used 'Veiled' Threats to Enforce Their Policies," UPI Archives, September 16, 1982, https://www.upi.com/Archives/1982/09/16/NCAA -officials-used-veiled-threats-to-enforce-their-policies/5552400996800.

47. "Excerpts from Supreme Court Opinions in N.C.A.A. Case," *New York Times*, June 28, 1984, B8.

48. "Excerpts from Supreme Court Opinions"; Peter W. Kaplan, "Rush Likely to Sign Up More Games," *New York Times*, June 28, 1984, B7.

49. John R. Thelin and Lawrence L. Wiseman, "Fiscal Fitness? The Peculiar Economics of Intercollegiate Athletics," *Capital Ideas* 4, no. 4 (February 1990): 1–12.

50. Jim Host and Eric Moyen, *Changing the Game: My CAREER in Collegiate Sports Marketing* (Lexington: University Press of Kentucky, 2020), 116–20.

51. Dunnavant, *Fifty-Year Seduction*, 174.

52. John McGuire, *Clyde Lear and the Learfield Sports Empire* (New York: Routledge, 2020).

53. Michael Smith, "Champions: Bill Battle, Licensing Icon," *Sports Business Journal*, March 26, 2012, https://www.sportsbusinessjournal.com/Journal/Issues/2012/03/26 /Champions/Battle.aspx.

54. "Don Canham," Go Blue, accessed February 13, 2024, http://michiganintheworld .history.lsa.umich.edu/michiganathletics/exhibits/show/key-players/don-canham; Frank Deford, "No Death for a Salesman," *Sports Illustrated*, July 28, 1975, https://vault.si.com /vault/1975/07/28/no-death-for-a-salesman.

55. Martin J. Greenberg, "College Coaching Contracts: A Practical Perspective, 1," *Marquette Sports Law Journal* 207 (1991): http//scholarship.law.marquette.edu/sportslaw /vol1/iss2/5; Ken Sugiura, "Larger Than Life, Pepper Rodgers Led Inimitable Tenure at Georgia Tech," *Atlanta Journal-Constitution*, May 23, 2020, https://www.ajc.com/sports /college/larger-than-life-pepper-rodgers-led-inimitable-tenure-georgia-tech/1hSFyEGkgn ETaek6ZZMxfN.

56. Murray Sperber, *College Sports, Inc.* (New York: Henry Holt, 1990), 62.

57. Ed Sherman, "Notre Dame Deal with NBC Stirs Furor," *Chicago Tribune*, February 6, 1990, https://www.chicagotribune.com/news/ct-xpm-1990-02-06-9001110465 -story.html; Gene Wojciechowski, "Analysis: Notre Dame's Deal Shouldn't Be a Shock," *Los Angeles Times*, February 8, 1990, https://www.latimes.com/archives/la-xpm-1990-02-08 -sp-571-story.html.

58. Mark Maske, "Conference Realignment Could Reshape College Athletics," *Los Angeles Times*, July 8, 1990, https://www.latimes.com/archives/la-xpm-1990-07-08-sp-135 -story.html.

59. Maske, "Conference Realignment."

60. Howard P. Chudacoff, *Changing the Playbook: How Power, Profit, and Politics Transformed College Sports* (Urbana: University of Illinois Press, 2015), 126.

61. Chudacoff, *Changing the Playbook*, 127.

62. Gordon S. White Jr., "Freshmen Given Varsity Sport Status in Major Sport," *New York Times*, January 9, 1972, S1.

63. Michael Oriard, *Bowled Over: Big-Time College Football from the Sixties to the BCS Era* (Chapel Hill: University of North Carolina Press, 2009), 132.

64. Byers and Hammer, *Unsportsmanlike Conduct*, 164–65.

65. Smith, *Pay for Play*, 134–38.

66. Smith, *Pay for Play*, 134–38.

67. Smith, *Pay for Play*, 134–38.

68. Watterson, *College Football*, 352.

69. Byers and Hammer, *Unsportsmanlike Conduct*, 297–98.

70. Michael Goodwin, "Presidents Fumble Athletic Reform Bid," *New York Times*, July 2, 1987, B7.

71. Byers and Hammer, *Unsportsmanlike Conduct*, 314–15.

72. Laurence M. Rose, "College Presidents and the NCAA Presidents' Commission: All Bark and No Bite," 67 *North Dakota Law Review* 243 (1991): 252.

73. John R. Thelin, "Presidential Involvement and the Knight Foundation Commission," in *Games Colleges Play: Scandal and Reform in Intercollegiate Athletics* (Baltimore: Johns Hopkins University Press, 1994), 189–92.

74. Welch H. Suggs, *A Place on the Team: The Triumph and Tragedy of Title IX* (Princeton, NJ: Princeton University Press, 2005), 175.

75. "Sara Lee, NCAA Sign $6 Million Agreement," UPI, September 18, 1990, https://www.upi.com/Archives/1990/09/18/Sara-Lee-NCAA-sign-6-million-agreement /5761653630400/.

76. J. Farrell, "High Court Reinforces Sex 'Parity' in Athletics: Rejects Brown University Appeal on Funds for Sports Teams," *Boston Globe*, April 22, 1997, A1, A5; T. Mauro, "Sex Equity in Sports Backed: Court Supports Title IX," *USA Today*, April 22, 1997, 1A, 3C; J. Naughton, "Supreme Court Rejects Brown's Appeal on Women in Sports: Advocates for Female Athletes See Outcome as a Major Victory," *Chronicle of Higher Education*, May 2, 1997, A45–A46.

77. John R. Thelin, "Good Sports? Historical Perspective on the Political Economy of Intercollegiate Athletics in the Era of Title IX, 1972–1997," *Journal of Higher Education* 71, no. 4 (July/August 2000): 391–410.

78. Norman Boucher, "Title IX: The Supreme Court Bow Out," *Brown Alumni Monthly* 97, no. 8 (May 1997): 13.

79. "Title IX Still Debated while Impact Grows," *Lexington Herald-Leader,* June 24, 1997, C1, C3.

80. Derek Bok, "The Federal Government and the University," *Public Interest* 57, no. 2 (Winter 1980): 80–101.

81. Paula D. Welch, "Title IX: Cohen et al. v. Brown," in *Silver Era, Golden Moments: A Celebration of Ivy League Women's Athletics* (Lanham, MD: Madison Books, 1999), 110–11.

82. Katie Mulvaney, "'A Woman Who Overcame Everything': Paying Tribute to College Sports Pioneer Jackie Court," *Providence Journal,* April 23, 2020.

83. J. Arace, "Scholarship Bias in Women's Sports Charged," *USA Today,* June 3, 1997, 1A, 1C, 8C.

84. Katherine Haworth, "Federal Appeals Court Clears Way for Title IX to Apply to the NCAA," *Chronicle of Higher Education,* March 28, 1998, A51.

85. Welch Suggs, "More Women Participate in Intercollegiate Athletics: But Survey of Division I Colleges Shows Disparities in Financing for Men's and Women's Teams," *Chronicle of Higher Education,* May 21, 1999, A44.

86. Amy Cohen, Brown University '92, quoted in Welch, "Title IX," 110–11.

87. Dave Nagle, "ESPN, Inc.: 1980 in Review," ESPN, January 2, 1981, https://espnpressroom.com/us/press-releases/1981/01/expanded-programming-household -growth-highlight-espns-first-full-year/; Dave Nagle, "ESPN, Inc.: 1990 in Review," ESPN, January 2, 1991, https://espnpressroom.com/us/press-releases/1991/01/espn-1990-in -review/; Dave Nagle, "ESPN, Inc.: 2000 in Review," ESPN, January 2, 2001, https:// espnpressroom.com/us/press-releases/2001/01/espn-inc-2000-in-review/.

88. Dunnavant, *Fifty-Year Seduction,* 193–94; "Skinner Leaves Fiesta Bowl," UPI, January 3, 1990, https://www.upi.com/Archives/1990/01/03/Skinner-Leaves-Fiesta-Bowl /5700631342800/.

89. Jack McCallum, "In the Kingdom of the Solitary Man," *Sports Illustrated,* October 6, 1986, https://vault.si.com/vault/1986/10/06/in-the-kingdom-of-the-solitary-man -reticent-reclusive-walter-byers-the-executive-director-of-the-national-collegiate -athletic-association-will-retire-in-1988-but-as-byers-begins-to-relinquish-his-35-year -long-grip-on-the-ncaa-h; "Walter Byers, Ex-NCAA Leader Who Rued Corruption, Dies at 93," *New York Times,* May 27, 2015, A23.

90. John R. Thelin, *A History of American Higher Education,* 3rd ed. (Baltimore: Johns Hopkins University Press, 2009), 317–23.

91. Byers and Hammer, *Unsportsmanlike Conduct,* 2–3.

92. Derek Bok, *Universities in the Marketplace: The Commercialization of Higher Education* (Princeton, NJ: Princeton University Press, 2003).

Chapter 8. Keeping Up with the Joneses

1. John R. Thelin, "Intercollegiate Athletics: Higher Education's Peculiar Institution," in *American Higher Education: Issues and Institutions,* 2nd ed. (New York: Routledge 2023), see esp. 197–99.

2. "15-Year Trends in Division III Athletics Finances," NCAA Research, accessed February 14, 2024, https://ncaaorg.s3.amazonaws.com/research/Finances/2020RES_D3 -RevExp_Report.pdf.

3. John R. Thelin and Lawrence W. Wiseman, *The Old College Try: Balancing Academics and Athletics in Higher Education,* Higher Education Report No. 4 (Washington, DC:

Association of Higher Education–Education Resources Information Center, 1989), 66–69, 82, 86.

4. "2022–23 Division II Facts and Figures," NCAA, https://ncaaorg.s3.amazonaws .com/about/d2/D2_FactsFigures.pdf.

5. "2022–23 Division II Facts and Figures."

6. NCAA Television Rights Overview," NCAA, October 5, 2022, https://www.ncaa.com/ _flysystem/public-s3/files/Television%20Rights%20Overview_0.pdf.

7. Amanda Christovich, "Division II Conference Inks a 7-figure Broadcast Deal," July 15, 2022, Front Office Sports, https://frontofficesports.com/division-ii-conference-7 -figure-deal/; Amanda Christovich, "Flow Sports Breaks Its Own Record Deal with Largest DII Media Deal," August 8, 2022, Front Office Sports, https://frontofficesports.com /flosports-largest-d-ii-media-deal/.

8. John R. Thelin, "Big-Time Intercollegiate Sports: Education's Entertainment," in *A History of American Higher Education*, 3rd ed. (Baltimore: Johns Hopkins University Press, 2019), 374–77.

9. Welch Suggs, "How Gears Turn at a Sports Factory: Running Ohio State University's $79 Million Program Is a Major Endeavor, with Huge Payoffs and Costs," *Chronicle of Higher Education*, November 29, 2003, https://www.chronicle.com/article/how-gears-turn-at-a -sports-factory/.

10. Rachel Bachman, "Oregon Athletic Department Uses State Money for Academic Needs Despite Claims of Self-Sufficiency," *The Oregonian*, October 7, 2010.

11. Joe Drape, "Cal-Berkeley Cuts 5 Athletics Programs," *New York Times*, September 28, 2010.

12. Murray Sperber, *College Sports, Inc.: The Athletic Department vs. The University* (New York: Henry Holt, 1990).

13. Libby Sander, "Athletics Raises a College from the Ground Up," *Chronicle of Higher Education*, September 19, 2008.

14. Bomani Jones, "Progress, Yes; but HBCUs Paid a Price for It," ESPN, February 26, 2007, https://www.espn.com/espn/blackhistory2007/news/story?id=2780876.

15. Jones, "Progress, Yes."

16. Joseph N. Cooper, J. Kenyatta Cavil, and Geremy Cheeks, "The State of Intercollegiate Athletics at Historically Black Colleges and Universities (HBCUs): Past, Present, and Persistence," *Journal of Issues in Intercollegiate Athletics* 7 (2014): 307–32.

17. Leonard Shapiro and Mark Asher, "CBS Retains NCAA," *Washington Post*, November 19, 1999, https://www.washingtonpost.com/archive/sports/1999/11/19/cbs-retains -ncaa/a032c7eb-ccb6-4f32-9403-50685d889c42.

18. Richard Sandomir, "College Basketball: CBS Will Pay $6 Billion for Men's N.C.A.A. Tournament," November 19, 1999, https://www.nytimes.com/1999/11/19/sports/college -basketball-cbs-will-pay-6-billion-for-men-s-ncaa-tournament.html.

19. Sandomir, "College Basketball."

20. Emily Steel, "CBS $6 Billion NCAA Wager Isn't Dead Yet," *Wall Street Journal*, March 9, 2009, https://www.wsj.com/articles/SB123655728118166231.

21. Paul R. La Mónica, "CBS Prepares for March Madne$$," CNNMoney, March 6, 2007, https://money.cnn.com/2007/03/06/news/companies/cbs_ncaa/index.htm.

22. Steel, "CBS $6 Billion NCAA Wager."

23. Steel, "CBS $6 Billion NCAA Wager."

24. Richard Sandomir, "N.C.A.A. Can Opt Out of Deal with CBS after 2010," *New York Times*, March 16, 2009, https://www.nytimes.com/2009/03/17/sports/ncaabasketball/17sandomir.html.

25. Dana O'Neil, "Regrettably, Expansion Seems Inevitable," ESPN, April 1, 2010, https://www.espn.com/mens-college-basketball/tournament/2010/columns/story?columnist=oneil_dana&id=5048513.

26. Dana O'Neal, "CBS, Turner Win TV Rights to Tourney," ESPN, April 22, 2010, https://www.espn.com/mens-college-basketball/news/story?id=5125307.

27. O'Neal, "CBS, Turner Win TV Rights."

28. Richard Sandomir, "CBS Considered Paying ESPN to Take Tourney," *New York Times*, May 4, 2010, https://www.nytimes.com/2010/05/05/sports/ncaabasketball/05cbs.html.

29. Larry Steward, "With Playoff Off the table, It Took Major Networking," *Los Angeles Times*, November 26, 2006, https://www.latimes.com/archives/la-xpm-2006-nov-26-sp-petitti26-story.html.

30. Michael Smith, "TV Fee Boosts BCS Payout 22 Percent," *Sports Business Journal*, January 24, 2011, https://www.sportsbusinessjournal.com/en/Journal/Issues/2011/01/24/Colleges/BCS-payout.

31. Paul Myerberg, "Fiesta Bowl: No. 6 Boise State (13–0) vs. No. 4 Texas Christian (12–0)," *New York Times*, January 4, 2010, https://archive.nytimes.com/thequad.blogs.nytimes.com/2010/01/04/fiesta-bowl-no-6-boise-state-13-0-vs-no-4-tcu-12-0/.

32. Smith, "TV Fee Boosts BCS Payout"; Andrea Adelson, "Bye, Bye, AQ Status," ESPN, April 26, 2012, https://www.espn.com/blog/ncfnation/post/_/id/60956/bye-bye-aq-status.

33. Shayna Fawcett, "How Does the BCS Even Work?," NBCDFW, November 2, 2010, https://www.nbcdfw.com/news/sports/how-does-the-bcs-even-work/1905223/.

34. Amy Daughters, "A Timeline of College Football Conference Realignment over the BCS Era," Bleacher Report, July 2, 2014, https://bleacherreport.com/articles/2115606-a-timeline-of-college-football-conference-realignment-over-the-bcs-era.

35. Daughters, "Timeline of College Football."

36. Andrea Adelson, "Realignment Revisited: Beginning of the End for Big East football," ESPN, July 20, 2021, https://www.espn.com/college-football/story/_/id/31838915/realignment-revisited-beginning-end-big-east-football.

37. Pete Thamel, "On TV, if Not on Field, Big East Is Still a Big Deal," *New York Times*, August 2, 2011, https://www.nytimes.com/2011/08/03/sports/ncaafootball/big-east-is-still-big-deal-on-tv-if-not-on-field.html.

38. Brett McMurphy, "Louisville Propels ACC Forward," ESPN, June 30, 2014, https://www.espn.com/college-football/story/_/id/11161888/louisville-cardinals-officialmoveacc-big-step-conference.

39. Andy Katz, "Big East Introduces 5 New Schools," ESPN, December 7, 2011, https://www.espn.com/college-sports/story/_/id/7327683/big-east-conference-introduces-boise-state-broncos-san-diego-state-aztecs-houston-cougars-smu-mustangs-ucf-knights.

40. Katz, "Big East Introduces 5 New Schools."

41. Adelson, "Realignment Revisited."

42. William C. Rhoden, "The Big East Is Still Paying for a Fumble," *New York Times*, March 4, 2012, https://www.nytimes.com/2012/03/05/sports/ncaabasketball/big-east-pays-the-price-for-not-embracing-football.html?pagewanted=all.

43. Rhoden, "Big East Is Still Paying for a Fumble."

44. Luke Swanson, "Big East Week: The Day the Big East Really Died," *Daily Campus*, April 17, 2018, http://dailycampus.squarespace.com/stories/2018/4/17/big-east-week-the-day-the-big-east-really-died.

45. Rhoden, "Big East Is Still Paying for a Fumble."

46. Rhoden, "Big East Is Still Paying for a Fumble."

47. Adelson, "Realignment Revisited."

48. Austin F. Eggers, Peter A. Groothuis, and Parker T. Redding, "The Flutie Effect: The Influence of College Football Upsets and National Championships on the Quantity and Quality of Students at a University" (working paper, Department of Economics, Appalachian State University, Boone, NC, 2019), https://econ.appstate.edu/RePEc/pdf/wp1905.pdf; Dana O'Neil, "How the Basketball Program Helped Gonzaga University Flourish," ESPN, March 29, 2017, https://www.espn.com/blog/collegebasketballnation/post/_/id/119205/how-the-basketball-program-helped-gonzaga-university-flourish.

49. Doug J. Chung, "The Dynamic Advertising Effect of Collegiate Athletics," *Marketing Science* 32, no. 5 (2013): 679–98.

50. "Alabama's Bet on Saban a Lesson in Football Economics 101," *Augusta Chronicle*, January 15, 2007, https://www.augustachronicle.com/story/sports/college/2007/01/15/col-112550-shtml/14730159007/; Monte Burke, "Why Nick Saban Is the Best Bargain in College Football," *Forbes*, August 10, 2015, https://www.forbes.com/sites/monteburke/2015/08/10/why-nick-saban-is-the-best-bargain-in-college-football/?sh=51fd440d72bc.

51. Chung, "Dynamic Advertising Effect of Collegiate Athletics"; Jerry Hinnen, "Is Nick Saban Underpaid? Forbes Thinks So," CBS Sports, May 14, 2013, https://www.cbssports.com/college-football/news/is-nick-saban-underpaid-forbes-thinks-so/.

52. Laura Pappano, "How the University of Alabama Became a National Player," *New York Times*, November 3, 2016, https://www.nytimes.com/2016/11/06/education/edlife/survival-strategies-for-public-universities.html; Hinnen, "Is Nick Saban Underpaid?"

53. Devin G. Pope and Jaren C. Pope, "The Impact of College Sports Success on the Quantity and Quality of Student Applications," *Southern Economic Journal* 75, no. 3 (2009): 750–81; Devin G. Pope and Jaren C. Pope, "Understanding College Application Decisions: Why College Sports Success Matters," *Journal of Sports Economics* 15, no. 2 (2014): 120–31.

54. Dena Potter, "Schools' Sports Success Spills Over," *Lexington Herald-Tribune*, March 24, 2008, https://www.heraldtribune.com/story/news/2008/03/24/schools-sports-success-spills-over/28617276007/.

55. Alex Nowicki, "How Much March Madness Success Boosted Admissions for 5 Universities," Higher Ed Dive, March 6, 2014, https://www.highereddive.com/news/how-march-madness-success-boosted-admissions-for-5-universities/234331/.

56. O'Neil, "How the Basketball Program Helped Gonzaga."

57. O'Neil, "How the Basketball Program Helped Gonzaga."

58. O'Neil, "How the Basketball Program Helped Gonzaga."

59. Pappano, "How the University of Alabama Became a National Player."

60. John R. Thelin, "From Chaos to Coherence: Myles Brand and the Balancing of Academics and Athletics," *Journal of Intercollegiate Sport* 14, no. 3 (2021): 8–15.

61. Mairead B. Baker, "Harvard's Colosseum: A History of Harvard Stadium," *Harvard Crimson*, November 18, 2022, https://www.thecrimson.com/article/2022/11/18/fb-2022-harvard-yale-stadium/.

62. Sam Scott, "A Short History of Stanford Stadium," *Stanford Magazine* (September 2021): https://stanfordmag.org/contents/a-short-history-of-stanford-stadium.

63. "T. Boone Pickens: The Legacy That Transformed OSU," OSU Headlines: News and Media, September 11, 2019, https://news.okstate.edu/articles/communications/2019/t-boone-pickens-the-legacy-that-transformed-osu.html.

64. "Phil Knight Donates $100 Million to Oregon Athletics," *Daily Emerald*, August 30, 2007, https://www.dailyemerald.com/archives/phil-knight-donates-100-million-to-oregon-athletics/article_4f53efd4-d014-56cc-a381-6ef756e36e06.html.

65. "Stadium Club Dedicated Today," *Eugene Register-Guard*, September 4, 1982, 2B.

66. Laura Newpoff, "Ohio Stadium Suites Put Corporate Fans in Luxury," *Business Journals*, November 12, 2001, https://www.bizjournals.com/columbus/stories/2001/11/12/focus2.html.

67. Joe Lapointe, "College Football: For the People or the Powerful? Skybox Plan Divides Michigan," *New York Times*, April 9, 2006.

68. Knight Commission on Intercollegiate Athletics, *Restoring the Balance: Dollars, Values, and the Future of College Sports* (Washington, DC: Knight Commission on Intercollegiate Athletics, 2009).

69. John R. Thelin, "Where Are the Presidents?," *Inside Higher Ed,* August 20, 2021, https://www.insidehighered.com/views/2021/08/20/presidents-have-been-largely-silent-about-issues-college-sports-and-commercialism.

70. Gilbert M. Gaul, *Billion-Dollar Ball: A Journey through the Big-Money Culture of College Football* (New York: Penguin Books, 2015), 26.

71. Gaul, *Billion-Dollar Ball.*

72. Robert H. Frank and Philip J. Cook. *The Winner-Take-All Society: Why the Few at the Top Get So Much More Than the Rest of Us* (New York: Free Press, 1995).

73. Robert H. Frank, "Higher Education: The Ultimate Winner-Take-All Market?," presented at the Forum for the Future of Higher Education, Aspen, CO, September 27, 1999.

74. Frank, "Higher Education."

75. John R. Thelin, *A History of American Higher Education,* 3rd ed. (Baltimore: Johns Hopkins University Press, 2019), 381.

76. Thelin, *History of American Higher Education,* 383.

77. Thelin, *History of American Higher Education,* 382–85.

78. Thelin, *History of American Higher Education,* 385.

79. Charles T. Clotfelter, *Big-Time Sports in American Universities*, 2nd ed. (Cambridge: Cambridge University Press, 2019), 161.

80. K'Leigh Sims, "Leisure Pool Ranked as One of the Nation's Best," *Texas Tech Today*, June 11, 2015, https://today.ttu.edu/posts/2015/06/leisure-pool-ranked-one-of-nations-best; University of Missouri, "History," MizzouRec.com, https://mizzourec.com/about/history/; University of Houston, "History: Campus Recreation and Wellness Center," https://uh.edu/recreation/about/story/history/.

81. Dawn Wotapka, "Resort Living Comes to Campus," *Wall Street Journal,* December 6, 2012, https://www.wsj.com/articles/SB10001424127887323830404578145591134362564.

82. Howard L. Nixon II, *The Athletic Trap: How College Sports Corrupted the Academy* (Baltimore: Johns Hopkins University Press, 2014).

Chapter 9. Commercialism, Conflicts, Conferences, and COVID-19

1. Dan Wetzel, Josh Peter, and Jeff Passan, *Death to the BCS: The Definitive Case against the Bowl Championship Series* (New York: Penguin, 2010).

2. Scott Kretchmar, "President Brand's Gambit: Inviting Scholars Inside the Tent," *Journal of Intercollegiate Sport* 14, no. 3 (2021): 51.

3. Natalie Meisler, "OLN Joining TV Team for MWC distribution," *Denver Post*, July 19, 2006, https://www.denverpost.com/2006/07/19/oln-joining-tv-team-for-mwc-distribution/; "Mountain West Chronology," https://themw.com/mountain-west-chronology/; Mark Anderson, "The Mtn. Sports Network Pulling the Plug in June," *Las Vegas Review-Journal*, April 5, 2012, https://www.reviewjournal.com/sports/unlv/the-mtn-sports-network-pulling-the-plug-in-june/.

4. Karen Weaver, "The Big Ten Network Was Created by and for Its Fans—And Turned a Profit in Less Than Two Years," *Forbes*, January 4, 2020, https://www.forbes.com/sites/karenweaver/2020/01/04/the-big-ten-network-was-created-by-and-for-its-fans---and-turned-a-profit-in-less-than-two-years/?sh=567d9c307212; Joe Drape, "Big Ten Network Alters Picture of College Sports," *New York Times*, October 1, 2010, https://www.nytimes.com/2010/10/02/sports/02bigten.html.

5. Chip Patterson, "Report: Pac-12 Records More Revenue Than SEC, Big Ten in 2012–13," CBS Sports, May 24, 2014, https://www.cbssports.com/college-football/news/report-pac-12-records-more-revenue-than-sec-big-ten-in-2012-13/.

6. Chris Smith, "The SEC Is Finally the Most Valuable Conference in College Sports," *Forbes*, July 20, 2015, https://www.forbes.com/sites/chrissmith/2015/07/20/the-sec-is-finally-the-most-valuable-conference-in-college-sports/?sh=533995105f55.

7. Andrea Adelson, "ACC Distributed a Record $497.2 Million during 2019–20 Financial Year, an Increase of $42 Million," ESPN, May 21, 2021, https://www.espn.com/college-sports/story/_/id/31484061/acc-distributed-record-4972-million-2019-20-financial-year-increase-42-million.

8. "Longhorn Network Has Reportedly Lost $48 Million after Five Years with ESPN," *Sports Business Journal*, December 29, 2015, https://www.sportsbusinessjournal.com/Daily/Issues/2015/12/29/Media/Longhorn-Net.

9. John R. Thelin, "Intercollegiate Athletics from the Sports Page to the Front Page," in *A History of American Higher Education* (Baltimore: Johns Hopkins University Press, 2019), 404–6.

10. David Labaree, "Nobel Prizes Are Great, but College Football Is Why American Universities Dominate the Globe," *Quartz*, October 7, 2017.

11. Jack Stripling, "Unrivaled Power: Inside Auburn's Secret Effort to Advance an Athlete-Friendly Curriculum," *Chronicle of Higher Education*, February 16, 2018, https://www.chronicle.com/article/inside-auburns-secret-effort-to-advance-an-athlete-friendly-curriculum/.

12. David L. Perlmutter, "A Crash Course in Crisis Communications," *Chronicle of Higher Education*, February 23, 2018, A25.

13. Mike Hale, "At Penn State, a Tragedy without a Hero," *New York Times*, April 7, 2018, C1.

14. Recent events highlighted in this section confirm previous research and writing in Thelin, "Intercollegiate Athletics," 404–9.

15. Hale, "At Penn State," C1, C2. See also John R. Thelin, "Big-Time Intercollegiate Sports: Education's Entertainment," in *History of American Higher Education*, 374–77.

16. Sarah Brown, "At Michigan State, a Shaken Campus Struggles through Its Shame," *Chronicle of Higher Education*, February 9, 2018, A21. In the same issue, see Fernanda Zamudo-Suarez, "Faculty Panel Is Upset with Michigan State's Choice of Interim Leader," A21, and Eric Kelderman, "Michigan State Trustee Calls for University's Top Lawyer to Resign," A21. See also Sarah Brown, "Michigan State's Faculty Senate: No Confidence in Trustees," *Chronicle of Higher Education*, February 23, 2018, A23; Adam Harris, "Michigan State Moves to Fire Medical Dean in Wake of Nassar Scandal," *Chronicle of Higher Education*, February 23, 2018, A23; Marc Tracy, "For Nassar Accusers at Michigan State, Feelings of a Trust Betrayed," *New York Times*, February 6, 2018, B9–B10.

17. Eduardo Medina, "Northwestern Fires Coach after Allegations of Widespread Hazing Among Players," *New York Times*, July 11, 2023, Section B, 11.

18. Jennifer Smith, "Kentucky Gives AD Barnhart a Raise," *Lexington Herald-Leader*, June 30, 2018, 1B, 4B; Thelin, *History of American Higher Education*, 406.

19. Will Jarvis, "LSU Just Unveiled a $28 Million Dollar Football Facility: The Flood-Damaged Library Is Still Decrepit," *Chronicle of Higher Education*, July 22, 2019.

20. John R. Thelin, "To Save College Sports, Don't Look to UC Berkeley for Ideas," *Lexington Herald-Leader*, March 12, 2018, 7A.

21. David Jesse, "Lou Anna Simon's Resignation from MSU Comes with Lifetime of Perks," *Detroit Free Press*, January 25, 2018.

22. Josh Moody, "Should Colleges Honor Disgraced Ex-Presidents?," *Inside Higher Ed*, January 31, 2023. Thelin, *History of American Higher Education*, 407.

23. Mitch Smith and Anemona Hartocollis, "Michigan State's $500 Million for Nassar Victims Dwarfs Other Settlements," *New York Times*, May 16, 2018, https://www.nytimes.com/2018/05/16/us/larry-nassar-michigan-state-settlement.html.

24. Thelin, *History of American Higher Education*, 409.

25. Thelin, *History of American Higher Education*, 409.

26. Billy Witz, "In Pac-12, Football Empty Seats, TV Woes, and Recruiting Gaps," *New York Times*, September 20, 2019.

27. Thelin, *History of American Higher Education*, 409.

28. John R. Thelin, "Admissions, Athletics and the Academic Index," *Inside Higher Ed*, April 3, 2019. See also "An Embarrassment of Riches: Admissions and Ambition in American Higher Education," *Society* 56 (2019): 329–34. The excerpts from this article, coupled with the US Supreme Court's decision to overturn decades of affirmative action policies, have created new challenges for administrators that have yet to be fully addressed.

29. Thelin, "Embarrassment of Riches," 329–34.

30. Thelin, "Embarrassment of Riches," 329–34.

31. Thelin, "Embarrassment of Riches," 329–34.

32. Charles C. Clotfelter, *Buying the Best: Cost Escalation in Elite Higher Education* (Princeton, NJ: Princeton University Press, 1996).

33. Thelin, "Embarrassment of Riches," 331.

34. Anemona Hartocollis, "Ringleader in College Admissions Cheating Is Sentenced to Over 3 Years in Prison," *New York Times*, January 5, 2023, A17.

35. Douglas Belkin, "Why Some Seats at Elite Colleges Only Go to Prep School Students," *Wall Street Journal*, September 1, 2023. See also David Leonhardt, "Behind the Scenes

of College Admissions," *New York Times*, July 24, 2023. An excellent, important study by group of economists at Harvard Graduate School of Education is *Diversifying Society's Leaders?* (Cambridge, MA: Harvard Graduate School of Education, July 2023), https://opportunityinsights.org/wp-content/uploads/2023/07/CollegeAdmissions_Nontech.pdf.

36. Matthew Gutierrez, "Harlem Develops into a Hotbed for a Sport Rooted in the Suburbs," *New York Times*, May 18, 2019, B13.

37. Valerie Strauss, "Harvard and Columbia Did It in November, Now Princeton Suspends Team over Vulgar Messages," *Washington Post*, December 16, 2016.

38. Josh Moody, "What Is the State of Whittier College?," *Inside Higher Ed*, February 15, 2023.

39. Billy Witz and Corey Kilgannon, "The (Real) Team at the Center of a Santos Tale: Baruch College 'Bearcats' Volleyball Team," *New York Times*, January 26, 2023, A1, A12.

40. Aaron Basko, "Can College Sports Save Small Colleges?," *Chronicle of Higher Education*, September 5, 2023.

41. Basko, "Can College Sports Save Small Colleges?"; Billy Witz and Gillian R. Brassil, "Stanford Permanently Cuts 11 Sports amidst Coronavirus Pandemic," *New York Times*, July 8, 2020. See also "Stanford Athletics Varsity Sport Reductions: FAQ," *Stanford News*, July 8, 2020, https://news.stanford.edu/2020/07/08/athletics-faq/.

42. Juliet Macur and Billy Witz, "Stanford Reverses Plan to Eliminate 11 Sports," *New York Times*, May 19, 2021, B8; Glynn A. Hill and Molly Hensley-Clancy, "Stanford Says It Won't Cut Sports after Lawsuits and Pressure from Athletes," *Washington Post*, May 18, 2021, https://www.washingtonpost.com/sports/2021/05/18/stanford-reverses-sports-cuts-lawsuits/.

43. Kevin Draper and Alan Blinder, "The Virus Is Derailing Bowl Games. Will There Be a Playoff?," *New York Times*, December 29, 2021, B7.

44. Daniel Libit and Luke Cyphers, "Covid and the College Sports Consultant," *The Intercollegiate*, July 15, 2020; Stephen Igoe, "As ECU Prepares for Cuts, Jeff Compher is Still Getting Paid," 247sports.com, May 19, 2020, https://247sports.com/college/east-carolina/article/jeff-compher-buyout-ecu-financial-crisis-covid-19-147315734/.

45. Ben Strauss, "N.L.R.B. Rejects Northwestern Football Players' Union Bid," *New York Times*, August 15, 2015, https://www.nytimes.com/2015/08/18/sports/ncaafootball/nlrb-says-northwestern-football-players-cannot-unionize.html. For a more detailed account, see Joe Nocera and Ben Strauss, *Indentured: The Inside Story of the Rebellion Against the NCAA* (New York: Penguin, 2016).

46. Ed O'Bannon with Michael McCann, *Court Justice: The Inside Story of My Battle Against the NCAA* (New York: Diversion Books, 2018). See especially the prologue.

47. See John R. Thelin, *Essential Documents in the History of American Higher Education*, 2nd ed. (Baltimore: Johns Hopkins University Press, 2021), 379–85.

48. Joe Nocera, "The Difference between Unpaid and Paid Student-Athletes? Not Much, It Turns Out," *New York Times*, October 25, 2021.

49. National Collegiate Athletic Association v. Alston, 594 U.S. ___ (2021), Justice Kavanaugh, concurring, p. 5.

50. Susan Greenberg, "Brown University Athletes Sue Ivy League over No-Scholarship Policy," *Inside Higher Ed*, March 8, 2023.

51. Santul Nerkar, "Dartmouth Players File Petition for Union," *New York Times*, September 16, 2023, B9.

52. Santul Nerkar, "Nebraska Fans Finally Leave the Football Stadium Happy," *New York Times,* September 1, 2023, B8.

53. Kurt Streeter, "Big Payday for College Women in Sports," *New York Times,* November 8, 2022, A1.

54. Streeter, "Big Payday," A1.

55. Illustrative of the Drake Group's formal concern about the unfinished business about inequities and gender in various revenue sources was its 2023 symposium; see "NILs and Title IX: Educational Institutions Must Fix Their Promotion, Publicity, and Recruiting Inequities Critical to the NIL Monetization Success of College Female Athletes and Must Not Use Third Parties to Evade Their Title IX Obligations," Drake Group, accessed February 16, 2024, https://www.thedrakegroup.org/2021/10/12/nils-and-title-ix-educational-institutions -must-fix-their-promotion-publicity-and-recruiting-inequities-critical-to-the-nil-mone tization-success-of-college-female-athletes-and-must-not-use-third/.

56. Anna Betts, Andrew Little, Elizabeth Sander, Alexandra Tremayne-Pengelly, and Walt Bogdanich, "Universities Help Sportsbooks Sign Up Young and Vulnerable," *New York Times,* November 23, 2022, A1, A12–A13.

57. Anna Betts, Andrew Little, Elizabeth Sander, Alexandra Tremayne-Pengelly, and Walt Bogdanich, "How Colleges and Sports-Betting Companies 'Caesarized' Campus Life," *New York Times,* November 20, 2022, https://www.nytimes.com/2022/11/20/business /caesars-sports-betting-universities-colleges.html. See also John R. Thelin and Eric Weber, "Raising a Flag on College Sports Gambling Play," *Inside Higher Ed,* February 14, 2023. The excerpts from that article below highlight the predominance of profits above all else.

58. Thelin and Weber, "Raising a Flag."

59. Thelin and Weber, "Raising a Flag."

60. Thelin and Weber, "Raising a Flag."

61. Thelin and Weber, "Raising a Flag."

62. Thelin and Weber, "Raising a Flag."

63. Kevin Draper, "University and Gambling Firm End Their Deal," *New York Times,* March 30, 2023, B10.

64. Victor Mather, "Coach Fired after Bets Are Flagged," *New York Times,* May 5, 2023, B12.

65. Rick Maese and Danny Funt, "Iowa and Alabama Betting Scandals Raise Red Flags for College Sports," *Washington Post,* May 12, 2023.

66. Eric Lipton and Kevin Draper, "After the Boom in Sports Bets Come Controls," *New York Times,* May 13, 2023, A1, A18.

67. Alan Blinder and Kevin Draper, "With $7 Billion Television Deal, Big Ten Follows N.F.L. Playbook," *New York Times,* August 19, 2022, A1, A14.

68. Brian T. Smith, "The Ultimate Modern-Day Underdog, Rice Isn't Backing Away amid Upheaval in College Athletics," *Houston Chronicle,* September 1, 2022, https://www .houstonchronicle.com/texas-sports-nation/brian-t-smith/article/Rice-an-underdog -amid-upheaval-in-college-sports-17410221.php.

69. "It's More Than Sports," Rutgers University website, accessed February 16, 2024, https://newbrunswick.rutgers.edu/discover-rutgers/big-ten-experience. For details on the deficits incurred by the Rutgers University athletics department, see John R. Thelin, "Where Are the Presidents?," *Inside Higher Ed,* August 19, 2021.

70. Melissa Korn, Andrea Fuller, and Jennifer S. Forsyth, "Colleges Spend Like There's No Tomorrow. 'These Places Are Just Devouring Money,'" *Wall Street Journal*, August 10, 2023. See also Anemona Harocollis, "Slashing Its Budget, West Virginia University Asks, 'What Is Essential?,'" *New York Times*, August 18, 2023, A14.

71. Amelia Neurenberg, "The Video That Changed the N.C.A.A.," *New York Times*, March 16, 2021.

72. Juliet Macur and Alan Blinder, "Anger Erupts over Disparities at N.C.A.A. Tournaments," *New York Times*, updated August 3, 2021.

73. Alan Blinder, "Running the Pentagon Was Hard? Try Overhauling the N.C.A.A.," *New York Times*, September 19, 2021, 31.

74. Sean Gregory, "It's Time to Pay College Athletes," *Time*, September 16, 2013.

75. Erin Strout, "Sydney McLaughlin on Taking Her Career into Her Own Hands," *Women's Running*, January 6, 2020, https://www.womensrunning.com/culture/people/sydney-mclaughlin-owning-her-career/.

76. Pete Nakos, "What Are NIL Collectives and How Do They Operate?," On3.com, July 2, 2022, https://www.on3.com/nil/news/what-are-nil-collectives-and-how-do-they-operate/.

77. Stewart Mandel, "Five-Star Recruit in Class of 2023 Signs Agreement with Collective That Could Pay Him More Than $8 Million," *The Athletic*, March 11, 2022, https://theathletic.com/3178558/2022/03/11/five-star-recruit-in-class-of-2023-signs-agreement-with-collective-that-could-pay-him-more-than-8-million/.

78. Billy Witz, "The N.C.A.A. Faces Daunting Problems of Its Own Making," *New York Times*, February 19, 2023, 30.

79. Greg Wallace, "7 Reasons College Football Playoff Needs to Expand," Bleacher Report, January 28, 2015, https://bleacherreport.com/articles/2344972-7-reasons-college-football-playoff-needs-to-expand.

80. Brent Zwerneman, "Exclusive: Texas, Oklahoma Reach Out to SEC about Joining Conference," *Houston Chronicle*, July 21, 2021, https://www.houstonchronicle.com/texas-sports-nation/college/article/Texas-Oklahoma-reach-out-to-SEC-about-joining-16330080.php.

81. "Pac-12, ACC and Big Ten Announce Historic Alliance," Pac-12 Conference, August 24, 2021, https://pac-12.com/article/2021/08/24/pac-12-acc-and-big-ten-announce-historic-alliance-0.

82. Brendan Gulick, "Kevin Warren Gives Update on 'The Alliance' from Big Ten Media Day," *Sports Illustrated*, October 7, 2021, https://www.si.com/college/ohiostate/basketball/big-ten-commissioner-kevin-warren-gives-update-on-the-alliance-between-big-ten-acc-pac12.

83. Ross Dellenger, "Behind the Scenes, and Closed Doors, That Led to College Football Playoff Expansion," *Sports Illustrated*, October 20, 2022, https://www.si.com/college/2022/10/20/college-football-playoff-expansion-cfp-how-we-got-here-daily-cover.

84. Billy Witz, "New College Sports Geography Puts California on the Atlantic," *New York Times*, September 2, 2023, A1, A19.

85. Andrea Adelson, "Florida State Suing ACC over Grant of Rights, Withdrawal Fee," ESPN, December 22, 2023, https://www.espn.com/college-football/story/_/id/39167937/florida-state-sue-acc-grant-rights-withdrawal-fee.

86. Melissa Korn, "West Virginia University Slashes Majors and Cuts Staff Despite Protests," *Wall Street Journal,* September 15, 2023, https://www.wsj.com/us-news/education/west-virginia-university-slashes-majors-and-cuts-staff-despite-protests-4d237966; Michael T. Nietzel, "Budget Woes Hit Several Big Ten Universities," *Forbes,* March 18, 2023, https://www.forbes.com/sites/michaeltnietzel/2023/03/18/budget-woes-hit-several-big-ten-universities/?sh=f1a7e005f72d.

87. David Ubben, "Transfer Portal Chaos Is Overwhelming the College Football Calendar—And It's Going to Get Worse," *The Athletic,* December 5, 2023, https://theathletic.com/5112687/2023/12/05/transfer-portal-college-football-calendar-chaos/.

88. Billy Witz, "An NCAA Plan Proposes Uncapped Compensation for Athletes," *New York Times,* December 6, 2023, B11, https://www.nytimes.com/2023/12/05/us/ncaa-athlete-compensation-cap-proposal.html#:~:text=N.C.A.A.-,Proposes%20Uncapping%20Compensation%20for%20Athletes,comply%20with%20Title%20IX%20laws.

89. Billy Witz, "A Landmark Settlement Forces N.C.A.A. Schools to Pay Players," *New York Times,* May 25, 2024, A1, A12.

90. David W. Chen, Jacey Fortin, and Anna Betts, "Settlement on Athlete Pay Sends Shockwaves Across the N.C.A.A.," *New York Times,* May 26, 2024, 29.

Conclusion. Why History Matters for College Sports

1. James Michener, *Sports in America* (New York: Random House, 1976).

2. James L. Shulman and William G. Bowen, *The Game of Life: College Sports and Educational Values* (Princeton, NJ: Princeton University Press, 2001). See also William G. Bowen and Sarah A. Levin, *Reclaiming the Game: College Sports and Educational Values* (Princeton, NJ: Princeton University Press, 2003).

3. Gary Shaw, *Meat on the Hoof* (New York: St. Martin's Press, 1972). See also, for basketball, W. Leitch, "March to Madness: How the N.C.A.A. Went from Protecting Student-Athletes to Exploiting Them," *New York Times,* February 23, 2016, 17.

4. James Thurber, "University Days," in *My Life and Hard Times* (New York: Harper and Brothers, 1933), 64–74.

5. Harry Edwards, *The Revolt of the Black Athlete* (New York: Free Press, 1969).

6. Taylor Branch, "The Shame of College Sports," *The Atlantic* (October 2011).

7. Derrick E. White, *Blood, Sweat, and Tears: Jake Gaither, Florida A&M, and the History of Black College Football* (Chapel Hill: University of North Carolina Press, 2019).

8. Alicia Jessop, "The NCAA Approves Unlimited Meals for Division I Athletes after Shabazz Napier Complains of Going Hungry: The Lesson for Other College Athletes," *Forbes,* April 15, 2014, https://www.forbes.com/sites/aliciajessop/2014/04/15/the-ncaa-approves-unlimited-meals-for-division-i-athletes-after-shabazz-napier-complains-of-going-hungry-the-lesson-for-other-college-athletes/?sh=2c74b1ed15bd.

9. Andrew Zimbalist, *Unpaid Professionals: Commercialism and Conflict in Big-Time College Sports* (Princeton, NJ: Princeton University Press, 2001).

10. John R. Thelin, "A New Deal for Students as Athletes," *Inside Higher Ed,* April 5, 2021, https://www.insidehighered.com/views/2021/04/06/why-history-matters-us-supreme-court-case-about-student-athletes-opinion.

11. NCAA v. Board of Regents of the University of Oklahoma, 468 U.S. 85 (1984).

12. Ronald A. Smith, "How Historians Convinced SCOTUS That the NCAA's Idea of Amateurism Is a Myth," History News Network, July 11, 2021, http://www.history newsnetwork.org/article/180685.

13. Thelin, "New Deal."

14. Thelin, "New Deal."

15. Thelin, "New Deal."

16. Michael Nietzel, "Six Scholars Honored for Writing Best SCOTUS Brief of the Year," *Forbes,* October 4, 2021.

17. Ronald Smith, *The Myth of the Amateur: A History of College Athletic Scholarships* (Austin: University of Texas Press, 2021).

18. John R. Thelin, "Faculty Control and the Irony of Reform: The Pacific Coast Conference, 1946 to 1959," in *Games Colleges Play: Scandal and Reform in Intercollegiate Athletics* (Baltimore: Johns Hopkins University Press, 1994), 128–54.

19. Joe Nocera and B. Strauss, *Indentured: The Inside Story of the Rebellion against the NCAA* (New York: Penguin, 2016).

20. Kurt Streeter, "He's the Ideal College Athlete. So Why Did He Quit?," *New York Times* March 29, 2021, https://www.nytimes.com/2021/03/29/sports/ncaabasketball/ncaa -supreme-court-endorsements.html.

21. John R. Thelin, "Where Are the Presidents?," *Inside Higher Ed,* August 20, 2021. The narrative from this opinion piece, recaptured here, provides evidence of a key historical theme: collectively, for more than a century, university presidents have been unwilling to deny profits and publicity, even at the expense of the educational enterprise. This has been the case since the emergence of the modern American university.

22. Steven R. DiSalvo, "To the Editor," *New York Times,* June 26, 2021, https://www .nytimes.com/2021/06/26/opinion/letters/supreme-court-ncaa-speech-gay.html.

23. Thelin, "Where Are the Presidents?"

24. Robert H. Atwell, Bruce Grimes, and Donna A. Lopiano, *The Money Game: Financing Collegiate Athletics* (Washington, DC: American Council on Education, 1980).

25. Thelin, "Where Are the Presidents?"

26. Thelin, "Where Are the Presidents?"

27. Thelin, "Where Are the Presidents?"

28. Thelin, "Where Are the Presidents?"

29. Greta Anderson, "Losing to Win," *Inside Higher Ed,* November 30, 2020, https:// www.insidehighered.com/news/2020/12/01/rutgers-faculty-leaders-challenge-financial -secrecy-athletics-department; John R. Thelin, "To Save College Sports, Don't Look to UC Berkeley for Ideas," *Lexington Herald-Leader,* March 12, 2018, https://www.kentucky.com /opinion/op-ed/article204432189.html.

30. Darren Rovell, "Many Tourney Teams Don't Turn Profit," ESPN, March 16, 2015, https://www.espn.com/mens-college-basketball/tournament/2015/story/_/id/12495302 /many-ncaa-tournament-teams-did-not-turn-profit.

31. Thelin, "Where Are the Presidents?"

32. Associated Press, "NCAA's Mark Emmert Says 'This Is the Right Time' to Consider Decentralized, Deregulated College Sports," ESPN, July 15, 2021, https://www.espn.com /college-sports/story/_/id/31824357/ncaa-president-mark-emmert-says-right-consider -decentralized-deregulated-college-sports.

33. Thelin, "Where Are the Presidents?"

34. Thelin, "Where Are the Presidents?"

35. Thelin, "Where Are the Presidents?".

36. John R. Thelin, "A Whole New Ball Game for College Athletics," in *College Athletes' Rights and Well-Being: Critical Perspectives on Policy and Practice,* ed. Eddie Comeaux (Baltimore: Johns Hopkins University Press, 2017), 6.

37. Ronald A. Smith, *Sports and Freedom: The Rise of Big-Time College Athletics* (Oxford: Oxford University Press, 1990), 199.

38. *Vanderbilt Hustler,* December 6, 1929, https://www.jstor.org/stable/community .34448523.

39. Ross Dellenger, "Inside the NIL Battle That Is Splintering the SEC: 'We're All Money Laundering,'" *Sports Illustrated,* May 30, 2023, https://www.si.com/college/2023/05 /30/sec-meetings-nil-athlete-employment-collectives-hot-topics.

40. Illustrative categories, strategies, and services are paraphrased from the 2023 materials published by the University of Kentucky Department of Intercollegiate Athletics and its Kentucky Road Program for student-athletes.

41. Jeremy Bauer-Wolf, "NCAA Permanently Ends SAT, ACT Eligibility Requirements for Division I, II Student-Athletes," Higher Ed Dive, February 7, 2023, https://www .highereddive.com/news/ncaa-permanently-ends-sat-act-eligibility-requirement-division ii/642117/#:~:text=The%20NCAA%20last%20month%20permanently,eligibility%20 requirements%20like%20admissions%20testing.

42. Randi Mazzella, "Overzealous Parents Are Ruining Youth Sports. It's Past Time to Sit Quiet and Let the Kids Play," *Washington Post,* March 2, 2020, https://www .washingtonpost.com/lifestyle/2020/03/02/overzealous-parents-are-ruining-youth -sports-heres-how-do-better/.

43. "Who We Are," Changing the Game Project, accessed February 17, 2024, http:// changingthegameproject.com/about/.

44. John Branch, "After Loss of Son, Coach Faces a Terrible Truth: A Deadly Brain Disease Upends a Life Built around Football," *New York Times,* August 29, 2023, A1, A16.

45. NCAA, *2019 Football Attendance* (Indianapolis: NCAA, n.d.), http://fs.ncaa.org/Docs /stats/football_records/Attendance/2019.pdf.

Essay on Sources

The history of college sports as a significant topic in the study of American institutions and society has moved to center stage of good writing and research. We coauthors of this book are indebted to scholars, researchers, editors, foundations, and publishers who have been involved in this remarkable trend. It started about a half century ago and gained an added measure of energy and insights starting around 1990. To reinforce and supplement our end notes and references in the text, we bring special attention to selected works and writers upon whom we have relied—and about whom we have discussed and argued—as we wrote our own interpretation of college sports, past and present.

By the 1960s, spectator sports, including both intercollegiate and professional conferences and teams, were showcased as a sparkling, distinctive part of American popular culture. What is hard to believe is that university scholars tended to ignore these same teams, conferences, and competitions in the life and operation of universities, as they were underplayed as peripheral sideshows to the main events of higher education as a "knowledge industry" and the American economy grounded in applied sciences, technology, and production. But that was then. A quiet, persistent transformation was taking root in all American institutions, ranging from schools, colleges, and universities to municipalities, state governments, and business corporations. And this growing presence of intercollegiate athletics as an activity eventually commanded greater attention it from serious writers.

One pioneer in this scholarly trend was Frederick Rudolph, distinguished professor of history at Williams College. His book *The American College and University: A History* (Random House, 1962) staked out new ground on the importance of college sports in two memorable chapters. First, his chapter on the "extracurriculum" brought students and their campus clubs, societies, and organizations into the mainstream of institutional life quite apart from the organizational charts and official meetings put into place by presidents, deans, and boards of trustees. Second, within that overarching rubric of "campus life," Rudolph documented from numerous institutions nationwide the "Rise of Football" as a central feature of student life and of college and university activities and external relations.

Among the first to identify this cultural and institutional transformation was James Michener, long famous as a novelist and increasingly acknowledged for his perceptive nonfiction analyses of American society. A capstone work was his book *Sports in America* (Random House, 1976). Chapters included "Colleges and Universities," "Sports and Upward Escalation," "The Athlete," and "Women in Sports."

The scholar whose works established a coherent path of critical analysis is Ronald A. Smith, historian of sports and professor at Pennsylvania State University. Starting with *Sports and Freedom* (Oxford University Press, 1988), his reconstruction of the early decades of intercollegiate athletes provides new accounts and at the same time casts doubt on some of the myths and lore of amateurism in American college varsity programs. Illustrative of insights following from his original archival research is that in early competitions between American collegians and their counterparts at Oxford and Cambridge, the Americans in crew and in track and field followed the letter of the law while skirting the spirit of the law. Conversely, the student-athletes at British universities placed more emphasis on the spirit of sportsmanship rather than the technicalities of the rules.

Smith has built from this foundation a series of distinct yet related works over three decades: *Play-by-Play* (Johns Hopkins University Press, 2001), a history of radio, television, and big-time college sports; *Pay for Play,* a history of reform in big-time college athletics (University of Illinois Press, 2010), and most recently *The Myth of the Amateur,* a history of college athletics scholarships (University of Texas Press, 2021).

Serious inquiry about college sports received an abrupt wakeup call between 1969 and 1971 with a flurry of articles and books presenting radical interpretations from authors loosely gathered in Berkeley, California. Foremost in this genre were Jack Scott's *The Athletic Revolution* (Free Press, 1971), David Meggyesy's *Out of Their League* (Ramparts, 1970), and Harry Edwards's *the Revolt of the Black Athlete* (Free Press, 1970). The collective works were provocative and often polemical. At very least, they fostered discussion from a variety of perspectives and disciplines and were integral to some of the first academic courses offered at major universities on the character and condition of intercollegiate athletics programs.

Since that time, numerous scholars have addressed racial inequity in college sports from a historical perspective. David K. Wiggins and Patrick B. Miller in *The Unlevel Playing Field: A Documentary History of the African American Experience in Sport* (University of Illinois Press, 2003) extended their examination beyond intercollegiate athletics but offered valuable context regarding higher education and sport. Charles Martin's *Benching Jim Crow: The Rise and Fall of the Color Line in Southern College Sports, 1890–1980* (University of Illinois Press, 2010) provides a systematic account that addressed integration among the three major southern conferences: the Southwest Conference, Atlantic Coast Conference, and the Southeastern Conference. Martin's work also provides an excellent history of the "gentleman's agreement" between northern and southern universities during the early years of intercollegiate competition. Lane Demas looked at desegregation both within in and outside of the South in *Integrating the Gridiron: Black Civil Rights and American College Football* (Rutgers University Press, 2011).

In addition to broad-based works, scholarly biographies of leading Black coaches have highlighted the challenges faced by historically Black colleges and universities during the Jim Crow Era. Milton Katz's *Breaking Through: John B. McLendon, Basketball Legend and Civil Rights* (University of Arkansas Press, 2007) provided such a perspective. Derrick E. White's *Blood, Sweat, and Tears: Jake Gaither, Florida A&M, and the History of Black College Football* (University of North Carolina Press, 2019) offered a more critical perspective that incorporates the larger picture of football at HBCUs. Highlighting the challenges of racism, White also addressed the loss that came as integration lured players away from traditional HBCU powers like Florida A&M and Grambling State to institutions that had previously denied admission to Black athletes.

Literature from journalists has also made an important contribution to the history of college athletics. Keith Dunnavant's *The Fifty-Year Seduction: How Television Manipulated College Football, from the Birth of the Modern NCAA to the Creation of the BCS* (Thomas Dunne Books, 2004) provides an excellent foundation to examine the modern era of media and big-time football. Other excellent works include Joe Nocera's *Indentured: The Inside Story of the Rebellion against the NCAA* (Portfolio, 2016) and Gilbert Gaul's *Billion-Dollar Ball: A Journey Through the Big-Money Culture of College Football* (Viking, 2015). In addition, Jeff Benedict and Armen Keteyian's *The System: The Glory and Scandal of Big-Time College Football* (Doubleday, 2013) provides a provocative examination of big-time football in the twenty-first century. These works and others certainly played a role in changing opinions of many regarding name, image, and likeness (NIL) and player compensation.

Although college students originally controlled virtually all aspects of intercollegiate athletics, ranging from schedules and ticket sales to coaching and conditioning, the crucial finding was that by 1900 their influence already had started to dwindle, with college officials and other "adult" groups recognizing that college sports were not a transient fad. The pragmatic response was to take control of conferences, commissioners, coaches, and reporting to athletics directors and boards of trustees. In some cases, such groups led searches for new college and university presidents. An excellent historical case study that linked the biographies of an institution and an individual is Robin Lester's *Stagg's University* (University of Illinois Press, 1995), about coach and athletics director Amos Alonzo Stagg and the "rise, decline, and fall of big-time football" at the University of Chicago. Often forgotten today is that a century ago, Stagg created the modern structure and governance of the athletics department, including special treatment on budgets, salaries, use of facilities, and other privileges. These developments enabled Stagg to turn the University of Chicago Maroons into the "Monsters of the Midway," a powerhouse within the Big Ten Conference. Such large projects as building a state-of-the-art stadium in the center of campus were followed by an array of other profitable schemes. No detail escaped his scrutiny or control, as he even charged faculty and staff fees for the "privilege" of using university tennis courts.

The abundance of timely books about college sports has been an embarrassment of riches that has led to clogging, collisions, and confusions for readers. Illustrative of the concentration of books about college sports was Paul Lawrence's 1987 work *Unsportsmanlike Conduct* (Praeger, 1987), a highly original, well-researched reconstruction of the NCAA and its interactions with colleges, coaches, and conferences. The research documented the shift away from a student-centered activity that over time escaped control of universities and their presidents and boards. It was no less than the story of the organizational evolution of the NCAA as an American cartel.

Ironically, less than a decade after retiring as president of the NCAA, Walter Byers published his memoir with the same title (University of Michigan Press, 1995). His tone and emphases are fascinating and puzzling, as he derides presidents, coaches, athletics directors, and others—except himself and the NCAA—for the exploitation of the student-athlete. The result is that those who read about the history of college sports will have a variety of often conflicting interpretations through which to sort and sift credible stories.

National concern by some perceptive higher education leaders gained a following in the 1980s when the American Council on Education sponsored a report by Robert Atwell, former president of ACE and of Pitzer College, along with Todd Grimes and Donna Lopiano, *The Money Game: Financing Collegiate Athletics* (American Council on Education, 1980). It was one of the few examples of critical examination of nationwide data covering a large, diverse group of institutions. It provided a contrast to most media coverage that focused only on the high-powered, lucrative NCAA Division I program. The ACE report was different in that it disaggregated data by institutional category and conferences to document and guide a tour through the budgets. Its findings were sobering.

A growing body of scholarly research followed the ACE report with analysis of the structures and concentration of power within the governance of college sports. Two works addressing these issues were Jay Oliva's *What Trustees Should Know about Intercollegiate Athletics* (Association of Governing Boards, 1989) and *The National Collegiate Athletic Association: A Study in Cartel Behavior* (University of Chicago Press, 1992), by Arthur Fleischer III, Brian L. Goff, and Robert D. Tolleson.

Commercialization, a recurrent but elusive theme in the literature on intercollegiate athletics, was conveyed and critically analyzed by Murray Sperber, professor of English, in his 1990 book *College Sports, Inc.* (Holt, 1990). Sperber cast the organizational drama as "the athletics department versus the rest of the university," a bold depiction whose proclivity toward overstatement was still accompanied by detailed structural analysis of governance, funding patterns, compensation, and special allowances seldom found within academic units. On balance, Sperber captured a timely phrase in conceptualizing the inordinate presence of intercollegiate athletics within the American university of the late twentieth century. Sperber's works also include *Onward to Victory* (Holt, 1998) and *Beer and Circus* (Holt, 2000).

One consequence of the historical and autobiographical accounts of conferences, policies, and interinstitutional negotiations was to encourage studies from a variety of disciplines such as economics, sociology, psychology, and political science. John Thelin's *Games Colleges Play* (Johns Hopkins University Press, 1994) drew from a large body of scholarly literature combined with original research in documents at several university archives and major reform reports from higher education associations to analyze college scandals and resultant reform reports between 1910 and 1990. Although the NCAA receives primary attention on collective organizations, it is in fact the intercollegiate conference that has been crucial to defining the cooperation and competition across universities and their athletics programs. Here, the exemplary work is historian Winton Solberg's *Creating the Big Ten: Courage, Corruption and Commercialization* (University of Illinois Press, 2018), a critical historical analysis of "how an athletic conference turned college football into a big business" from its start in the 1890s and extending into the twenty-first century.

In a similar vein and spirit, Duke University's Charles T. Clotfelter, an economist who had long studied public policies in American society, brought these perspectives to provide an overarching analysis of powerful college sports programs in his book *Big-Time Sports in American Universities* (Cambridge University Press, 2011). An invaluable scholar in this genre has been Michael Oriard, professor of English literature at Oregon State University and a former star football player at Notre Dame and in the National Football League, who made an enduring and indelible contribution to the history of college athletics. In *Reading Football* (University of North Carolina, 1993), Oriard chronicled the critical role the print press played in promoting college football before the advent of television. His *King Football* (University of North Carolina Press, 2001) offered a comprehensive historical reconstruction of "sport and spectacle in the golden age of radio and newsreels, movies and magazines, the Weekly and the daily press." His perceptive research continued the chronological story into the contemporary era with *Bowled Over: Big-Time College Football from the Sixties to the BCS Era* (University of North Carolina Press, 2009).

Howard P. Chudacoff, long distinguished as an American social historian, also served for many years as Brown University's faculty athletic representative to the National Collegiate Athletic Association. He combined his historical scholarship in the NCAA archives with his role as participant-observer in NCAA policy deliberations in his perceptive overview, *Changing the Playbook* (University of Illinois Press, 2015), to analyze "how power, profit, and politics transformed American college sports."

Research on student-athletes tended to emphasize concerns about reducing abuses and ensuring the well-being of student-athletes—their rights, their situations. A good example of this focus was the interdisciplinary anthology edited by Eddie Comeaux, *College Athletes' Rights and Well-Being: Critical Perspectives on Policy and Practice* (Johns Hopkins University Press, 2017). Contributors and chapters within this exemplary anthology provide a good source of critical research on race and college sports, with particular attention to the use and abuse and even the exploitation of Black student-athletes, especially in the "money sports" of NCAA Division I football and basketball.

This theme of abuse has been part of a perennial debate within the field of college sports with regard to subsidization and compensation for college athletes. Economist Andrew Zimbalist, professor at Smith College, literally "wrote the book" on the topic with his work *Unpaid Professionals* (Princeton University Press, 2001) to provide empirical analysis combined with remarkable stories about "commercialism and conflict in big-time sports," ranging from cheating to exploitation. And although Zimbalist focused primarily on practices and policies for student-athletes, by extension he juxtaposed the embellished logic athletics directors and university officials invoke to pay inflated salaries to coaches whose actual records have little to do with rewarding success or punishing failure in team performance.

Economists have also contributed to the comprehensive and historical profile of student-athletes with longitudinal studies of academic performance in the context of institutions' entire student body. A major source of concern even among advocates for college student-athletes has been (and will be) the distinction between rights and well-being versus compensation. Institutions might provide support services for academics, health insurance, medical treatment, career planning, nutrition, time management, and other dimensions of a balanced life while remaining silent on the matter of salary and compensation beyond the customary scholarships and grants-in-aid. A further complication is that some student-athletes and their representatives essentially want things "both ways": to be treated as a "normal student" but perhaps at the same time wanting special treatment and perks as a valuable "athlete." Such logical binds are going to usher in long discussions.

The answers and reforms will become less obvious when one incorporates the findings of such systematic studies as William G. Bowen's coauthored books, *The Game of Life: College Sports and Educational Values* (Princeton University Press, 2001) with James Shulman and *Reclaiming the Game: College Sports and Educational Values* (Princeton University Press, 2003) with Sarah Levine. One provocative finding in these studies is that college student-athletes are not the only ones who devote a great deal of time to extracurricular activities. Campus newspaper editors and performing artists such as musicians, dancers, and actors also balance a demanding schedule of excellence in their activities as well as their studies—often with far less institutional support than student-athletes.

Furthermore, studies of college students indicate widespread stress of having to work long hours at low-paying jobs while also going deep into debt with student loans and other expenses. Is the plight of college student-athletes any more difficult than these? If the concern is with student-athletes as part of the category of rights as *students*, these larger spheres of campus life warrant consideration. Otherwise, the risk is a partial gain and a Pyrrhic victory for genuine reform of college life and activities.

One surprisingly weak link in the various perspectives on college sports has been that of college and university presidents, many of whom have been missing in action or guilty of inaction. A syndrome has been that university presidents who do not speak up about problems and conflicts while in office belatedly offer insightful commentary only after retiring. By the time these presidents offer their criticism, they are largely outside the circles of administrative influence and leadership. One example is James Duderstadt's *Intercollegiate Athletics and the American University: A University President's Perspective* (University of Michigan Press, 2003). The paradox is that Duderstadt, former president of the University of Michigan, provides an abundance of great information and insights on how college sports became a "show business," but the revelations are "too much, too late." As such the genre of presidential writings about intercollegiate athletics represents an opportunity lost.

There are, fortunately, some exceptions. Derek Bok, president emeritus of Harvard University, wrote *Universities in the Marketplace: The Commercialization of Higher Education* (Princeton University Press, 2013) to bring attention to the breadth and depth of commercialization, including scientific research, marketing, admissions—and athletics. Indeed, Bok's chapter "Athletics" is intense but not exhaustive. He returns to the topic later in the book with the chapter "Reforming Athletics," all within the orbit of "preserving educational values."

Women in college sports as coaches, administrators, and student-athletes had long been overlooked, both as a reality and later as a topic of critical analysis. This has changed gradually yet persistently since passage of Title IX in 1972. Two texts from the 1990s provide a solid starting point for scholarship on Title IX and women's athletics. Susan K. Cahn's *Coming on Strong: Gender and Sexuality in Women's Sport* (Harvard University Press, 1994) highlighted the discrimination faced by women athletes who challenged the stereotypes so prevalent in higher education and the larger American culture. Cahn's work was updated with a paperback edition (University of Illinois Press, 2015). *Playing Nice: Politics and Apologies in Women's Sports* (Columbia University Press, 1996), by Mary Jo Festile, offered a more detailed struggle between the National Collegiate Athletic Association and the Association for Intercollegiate Athletics for Women. Ying Wushanley's *Playing Nice and Losing: The Struggle for Control of Women's Intercollegiate Athletics, 1960–2000* (Syracuse University Press, 2004), in contrast, highlighted some critical errors made by the AIAW in their fight against the NCAA.

One enduring substantive study has been Welch Suggs's *A Place on the Team: The Triumph and Tragedy of Title IX* (Princeton University Press, 2009). Paula D. Welch as editor provided a model of analyzing how a conference and its member institutions fared. *Silver Era, Golden Moments: A Celebration of Ivy League*

Women's Athletics (Madison Books, 1999) documents the quarter century of events since the 1972 passage of Title IX. Ostensibly a celebration of remarkable achievements, the chronicle also provides offhanded testimony to the limited gains and partial progress for nationally acclaimed academic institutions to gain genuine parity and equity for women in college sports.

When examining the history of men's college basketball, University of Maryland English professor Neil D. Isaacs's *All the Moves: A History of College Basketball* (Lippincott, 1975) provides a valuable (but uncritical) overview of the evolution of the sport at the collegiate level. A more scholarly and detailed approach can be found in Chad Carlson's *Making March Madness: The Early Years of the NCAA, NIT, and College Basketball Championships, 1922–1951* (University of Arkansas Press, 2017). Kurt Edward Kemper's *Before March Madness: The Wars for the Soul of College Basketball* (University of Illinois Press, 2020) extended beyond 1951 and chronicled the NCAA's successful battle against the NAIA for "control" of the sport. J. Samuel Walker's *ACC Basketball: The Story of the Rivalries, Traditions, and Scandals of the First Two Decades of the Atlantic Coast Conference* (University of North Carolina Press, 2011) provides an excellent account of the rise of the ACC from the 1950s into the 1970s.

To capture succinctly the continuity and changes in books about college sports over the past sixty years, a useful starting point and book end is Allison Danzig's *The History of American Football: Its Great Teams, Players, and Coaches* (1956). Over 565 pages, sportswriter Danzig compiled detailed year-by-year profiles of college football's outstanding teams, coaches, and players. The book is illustrated with publicity photographs. An interesting sequel is John Sayle Watterson's *College Football: History-Spectacle-Controversy* (Johns Hopkins University Press, 2000). Comparable in length at 466 pages, Watterson continues Danzig's genre of celebrating the glory and glamour of intercollegiate football, especially with its big-time winning programs and coaches. A difference is that Watterson as a longtime fan and faculty member adds to the sportswriter approach represented by Danzig with thoughtful commentary and context.

Recent writings continue celebration with an ability to present even more interesting complexities and crises. An exciting contribution published within the past two years is by editors Christian Anderson and Amber Fallucca, *The History of American College Football Institutional Policy, Culture, and Reform* (Routledge, 2021). In this anthology, Anderson and Fallucca—both accomplished historians of higher education—assembled original contributions from outstanding scholars who look to the edges to flesh out the story of American college football. It includes issues such as whether conferences acknowledged students with disabilities as full-fledged participants. The pivotal case study dealt with deaf students and their teams from the early twentieth-century Gallaudet College in Washington, DC.

Other themes beyond the specifics of great coaches and teams extended to regional differences, including the colleges in the South as latecomers to the "national" collegiate football sweepstakes, are surprising and provocative. An irony of reform was that starting in the early 1930s, the new Southeastern Conference took a stand for trying to strengthen academic standards by placing presidents, not athletics directors and coaches, into leadership. In addition to regional differences, diversity in matters of race, religion, and gender shape these original essays. While recognizing the primacy of the familiar big-time programs, the anthology includes good attention to such overlooked conferences as the California State Colleges and the overlap of their varsity programs with civil rights protests and educational reform in the 1960s.

To draw from the prefatory materials, on balance, this book provides unique insight into how American colleges and universities have been significantly influenced and shaped by college football. It also considers how US sports culture more generally has intersected with broader institutional and educational issues. A legacy of this and other recent books on the history of college sports is that the work is excellent—and, most promising, the best books are yet to come!

Index

About the Authors

ERIC A. MOYEN is a professor of higher education leadership and assistant vice president for student success at Mississippi State University. After graduating from Taylor University, he earned an MA in US history from the University of Alabama and a PhD in educational policy studies from the University of Kentucky. He is the author of *Frank L. McVey and the University of Kentucky: A Progressive President and the Modernization of a Southern University* and the coauthor of Jim Host's autobiography *Changing the Game: My Career in Collegiate Sports Marketing*. He has previously served as a member of Mississippi State University's Athletic Council.

JOHN R. THELIN is University Research Professor Emeritus at the University of Kentucky. He received his MA and PhD at the University of California, Berkeley. As an undergraduate at Brown University, he concentrated in history, was elected to Phi Beta Kappa, and was a varsity letterman in wrestling. In 2006 he was selected for the Ivy League's fiftieth anniversary gallery of outstanding student-athlete alumni. He is the author of *Games Colleges Play: Scandal and Reform in Intercollegiate Athletics* and *A History of American Higher Education*, both published by Johns Hopkins University Press. He was a charter member and cochair of the NCAA Research Advisory Committee from 2008 through 2010. In 2021 he was a member of a group of six historians who wrote an award-winning amicus brief for the Supreme Court case *NCAA v. Alston* (2021). In 2023 he received the University of Kentucky Libraries Medallion for Intellectual Achievement.

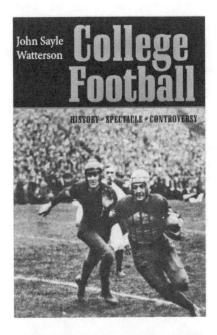